London Railway Atlas
Sixth Edition

London Railway Atlas
Sixth Edition

JOE BROWN

crecy.co.uk

First published in 2006
Second edition 2009
Third edition 2012
Fourth edition 2015
Fifth edition 2018
This sixth edition first published in 2023 by Crécy Publishing
Reprinted 2025

© Joe Brown 2023

ISBN 978 1 80035 263 6

All rights reserved. No part of this book may be reproduced or transmitted in any form or by any means, electronic or mechanical, including photocopying, recording or by any information storage without permission from the Publisher in writing. All enquiries should be directed to the Publisher.

Publisher's note: Every effort has been made to identify and correctly attribute photographic credits. Any error that may have occurred is entirely unintentional.

Printed in Lithuania by BALTO Print

Crécy Publishing Limited
1a Ringway Trading Estate
Shadowmoss Road
Manchester M22 5LH

www.crecy.co.uk

Front cover top
A Thameslink Class 700 speeds south while a southbound London Overground Class 378 calls at Brockley station in the distance on 7 April 2023.

Front cover bottom
A Shenfield-bound Elizabeth Line Class 345 approaches Liverpool Street eastbound platform on 15 March 2023.

Back cover
Under the shadow of The Shard, at Metropolitan Junctions a pair of Thameslink Class 700s pass each other working between Blackfriars and London Bridge stations, with a Class 465 'Networker' in the distance.

Preface to the Sixth Edition

London, more than possibly any other city on Earth, owes its growth and continuing success to its intricate network of railways, which have been a part of the landscape for over 200 years and show no sign of losing their relevance or importance. Unlike much of the United Kingdom, London had lost relatively little of its passenger infrastructure during the 20th Century and it could indeed be argued that with the more recent additions of the Docklands Light Railway and London Trams to the scene along with 'Heavy Rail' developments such as the Elizabeth Line, Channel Tunnel Rail Link and East London Line Extensions, London's passenger rail network is today at its zenith. Despite this, there are many long-forgotten branch lines and abandoned stations dotted around London; casualties of war, route duplication, trams, buses and the car. London's freight and industrial facilities did not fare anywhere near as well as the passenger facilities during the late 20th century; changes to the way that freight was carried and the abandonment of domestic coal in favour of central heating, combined with industrial decline, decimated the hundreds of goods and coal yards and rail-served industrial sites in London.

I commenced this project almost twenty years ago in 2004 after searching for a publication like this one to no avail: one that provided a diagrammatic representation of London's railway history. What began as a light-hearted hobby has since become a serious project, which has taken up hundreds of hours' work through map-drawing, indexing and research. Following on from publication of the first edition seventeen years ago, I have continually striven to improve the cartography and to add ever more detail with each new edition, while of course keeping abreast of developments to London's railways. At first glance the Sixth edition may look very similar to the Fifth (numerous revisions and updates aside), but this belies a mammoth task I undertook of a complete re-drawing. I have switched software to one which has a CMYK colour output which ensures crisper printing, this is in keeping with my Birmingham & West Midlands and Liverpool & Manchester titles. On the topic of these books, you may wonder why these both include historic tram systems in addition to the current ones, while in this work I have continued to only depict the current London Trams system. Quite simply, in London the majority of subsurface railways follow major roads, as did the historic tramways – to try to overlay the trams at this scale would have been nothing short of chaotic, so please forgive this apparent inconsistency between titles.

It has been almost five years since the Fifth edition was published, and a lot has happened in that time. The COVID-19 pandemic caused significant damage to the railways through both loss of demand and the operational impact of staff non-availability, the former still remaining an issue with consequent knock-on financial challenges. Projects I was able to depict in the Fifth edition as being in the pipeline like the Bakerloo Line Extension are now sadly 'on hold', but on the plus side we have witnessed the opening of the magnificent Elizabeth Line, the Northern Line extension, Bank station upgrade, and the Barking Riverside extension amongst many other improvements. HS2 is very much under construction and despite the unfortunate pause to activity at Euston, the amount of work ongoing at Old Oak Common and elsewhere reassures that another significant addition to London's railway infrastructure is imminent.

A map of this scale can never be pin-point accurate, but I have attempted to achieve as close as possible to this goal while maintaining clarity which involves sometimes manipulating the routes of lines, in particular 'tubes' which are often bored below other railways and one another. As part of the aforementioned re-drawing endeavour, I have revised the courses of some of these 'deep level' lines where I had originally simply inferred them from station locations. In some areas the railway infrastructure has changed repeatedly over time to the point that it is impossible to depict every historical permutation, so for some areas I have provided larger-scale maps giving the current layout alongside an historical snap-shot when pre-Beeching infrastructure was at its peak. Despite many hours of research, I am the first to acknowledge that there are quite probably some omissions (and dare I say it errors!), particularly regarding freight facilities on which available information is often scant. I have endeavoured to provide a hopefully near-complete history of London's passenger railways, and I have included temporary, excursion and unadvertised stations and staff halts wherever possible. Where dates were unobtainable, as a last resort I have used historical Ordnance survey maps to somewhat crudely infer an approximate date with the rationale in the index; I feel this is preferable to no date at all. I very much regard this as a work in progress, and I would be delighted to hear from anyone who can provide me with further information. There are question marks against some dates in the index, and I would be very happy to receive locations and relevant dates for other freight and industrial facilities that have been omitted, although I have had to be mindful in more complex areas not to overload the map with detail to the extent that it becomes a distraction.

Please contact me with any feedback or further information, or follow me for news of forthcoming titles at:

Email: atlasupdate@blueyonder.co.uk
Facebook: Urban Railway Atlases of the UK
Twitter: @joebrownlondon

About the author

I am a railway professional and near-lifelong London resident who since childhood had a keen interest in cartography as well as railways. I joined London Underground as a Northern Line Guard in 1997 shortly after leaving school, and progressed to a 'Guard-Motorman' on that line in 1998 before transferring to be a District Line Train Operator at Parson's Green the following year. In 2001 I was promoted to Duty Manager Trains at Earl's Court, where I remained for six years before again being promoted to Train Operations Manager at Elephant & Castle (Bakerloo Line) in 2007. Since then, I have gained experience managing station operations on the Marylebone Group of six Bakerloo Line stations, before returning to 'Trains' management in 2011 as Train Operations Manager at Wembley Park Depot on the Jubilee Line. For 18 months from early 2020 I moved to the role of Executive Officer for Line Operations, which through its timing was primarily concerned with our operational recovery from the COVID-19 pandemic. As of October 2021, I have now moved to the role of Strategic Delivery & Change Manager, combined with holding the chair of OUTbound, Transport for London's LGBTQ+ group.

I have produced the six editions of the London Railway Atlas, the two editions of the Birmingham Railway Atlas, and in 2021 the Liverpool and Manchester Railway Atlas around a busy work schedule on a home computer, self-taught on fairly basic software without any formal design training. My next project will be to recreate the late great Stuart Baker's UK & Ireland atlas for its sixteenth edition, and then after that tackle another area of the UK – likely Yorkshire – which will be several years' work I expect.

Thanks & dedications

I would firstly like to thank my husband Gary James for his never-ending patience and support during near-twenty years that it has taken for this sixth edition to be realised, also special mention to our beloved Staffordshire Bull Terrier Gypsy who has been curled up on my lap for significant periods while I have been working on my books.

Secondly a huge thank you to a multitude of people who offered feedback and information by email and post following publication of the first five editions:

Bob Allaway, Mark Armstrong, Greg Beecroft, David Bleicher, Geoff Brockett, David Burnell, Geoff Burton, Alan Collis, Andy Cope, John Cousins, John Craig, Tom Doran, John Edser, Robert Farmer, Martin Fisher, John Fletcher, Andrew Ford, Anthony Frewin, Paul Godwin, John Groves, Brian Hardy, Chris Harry, Claude Hart, Richard Hill, Colin Hills, Phil Hingley, Geoff Hutton, Ian Hutton, Martin James, Chris Jones, Norman Jones, Phil Jones, Tony Josling, Peter Kazmierczak, Joel Kosminsky, John Krol, Raj Kukadia, Chris Ladyman, Michael Leon, Malc McDonald, Peter McGow (Wandle Industrial Museum), Mike Mellor, Simon Moore, Bill Munro, Stephen Murray, Jerry Pett, Brian Polley, A Porter, Dr Sunil Prasannan, Andrew Rixon, D Roberts, Tony Roeder, Douglas Rose, Simon Sadler, Steve Sedgwick, John Sketcher, Stewart Smith, Peter Snook, Frank Taylor, James Thomson, James Tinkler, Mike Townsend, Jim Veal, Michael Vince, Christopher Walker, Alan Walters, Keith Ward, Ken Weston, Gordon Wickham and David Winter.

Finally, I'd like to reserve particular thanks for Paul Bowman, Jim Fergusson, William Graveson and Steven Taylor who have each provided an incredible wealth of information, and Paul Stewart from the Branch Line Society who had kindly provided access to the entire back catalogue of their priceless publication 'Branch Line News' as well as frequent valuable updates and corrections.

For my nephews and godsons Max & Felix Brown and nephew and niece Oscar & Jemima Thiagaraj.

In loving memory of Alice Thiagaraj 1969-2021 and Ruth Brown 1945-1989.

Joe Brown, London, May 2023

Abbreviations

AC	Alternating Current	
BAA	British Airports Authority	Renamed Heathrow Airport Holdings 2012
BAK	Bakerloo Line	Abbreviated form of BSWR
BHR	Bexley Heath Railway	Absorbed by SECR 10.07.1900
BLN	Branch Line News	
BR	British Rail(ways)	Formed 01.01.1948 (Nationalisation)
BSWR	Baker Street & Waterloo Railway	Absorbed by UERL before opening, became Bakerloo Line
c.	circa	
CCEHR	Charing Cross, Euston & Hampstead Railway	Absorbed by UERL before opening, merged with CSLR to form Northern Line 13.09.1926
CCR	Croydon Canal Railway	Short branch off the SIR serving the Croydon Canal basin adjacent to present-day West Croydon
CE	Civil Engineers	
CEN	Central Line	Originally Central London Railway
Co.	Company	
CLR	Central London Railway	Absorbed by UERL 01.01.1913
CMGR	Croydon, Merstham & Godstone Railway	Extension of SIR (see below). Opened 24.07.1805, closed 28.09.1838 (last use 27.09.1838)
CR	Caterham Railway	Absorbed by SER 1859
CSLR	City & South London Railway	Absorbed by UERL 01.01.1913, merged with CCEHR to form Northern Line 13.09.1926
CTL	Croydon Tramlink	Bought by TfL 28.06.2008, renamed 'London Tramlink Croydon' 01.01.2009 (later 'London Trams')
CVR	Chipstead Valley Railway	Absorbed by SECR 13.07.1899
C.W.	Carriage Wash	
DBC	Deutsche Bahn Cargo	
DBS	Deutsche Bahn Schenker	Formerly EWS, acquired 28.06.2007 and renamed 01.01.2009
DC	Direct Current	
DfT	Department for Transport	
DIS	District Line	Originally Metropolitan District Railway, absorbed by UERL 09.04.1902
DLR	Docklands Light Railway	Controlled by TfL since 03.07.2000
DMU	Diesel Multiple Unit	
DOO	Driver only operation	
E	East	
EB	Eastbound	
ECML	East Coast Main Line	Former GNR main line from King's Cross
ECR	Eastern Counties Railway	Absorbed by GER 01.07.1862
ECTJR	Eastern Counties & Thames Junction Railway	Absorbed by ECR 1847
EHLR	Edgware, Highgate & London Railway	Absorbed by GNR before opening, 07.1867
EL	Elizabeth Line	Westbourne Park to Abbey Wood / Stratford owned by TfL (the remainder NR)
ELL	East London Line	Originally 'Metropolitan Line East London section', name came into use during 1980's
ELR	East London Railway	GER, LBSCR, SER, LCDR, MET & MDR joint (LNER / MET 01.01.1923), absorbed by SR 1925
EMU	Electric Multiple Unit	
EOR	Epping Ongar Railway	Preserved railway, commenced operation 10.10.2004
ES	Eurostar	
E.S.	Engine Shed	
EWIDBJR	East & West India Docks & Birmingham Junction Railway	Renamed NLR 01.01.1853
EWS	English, Welsh & Scottish Railway	Acquired by DBS 28.06.2007, renamed 01.01.2009
GCC	Gaslight & Coke Company	Leased to GER after 18.03.1874
GCR	Great Central Railway	Absorbed by LNER 01.01.1923
GER	Great Eastern Railway	Formed from ECR 01.07.1862, absorbed by LNER 01.01.1923
GLA	Greater London Authority	
GNCR	Great Northern & City Railway	Absorbed by Metropolitan Railway 01.07.1913
GNPBR	Great Northern, Piccadilly & Brompton Railway	Absorbed by UERL before opening 09.04.1902, became Piccadilly Line
GNR	Great Northern Railway	Absorbed by LNER 01.01.1923
GRR	Gravesend & Rochester Railway	Absorbed by SER late 1845
GWR	Great Western Railway	Absorbed by BR 01.01.1948
HAH	Heathrow Airport Holdings	Formerly BAA, renamed 2012
HCL	Hammersmith & City Line	Formerly part of Metropolitan Line, given own name 30.07.1990
HCR	Hammersmith & City Railway	GWR & MET joint
HEX	Heathrow Express	Owned by Heathrow Airport Holdings (formerly named BAA / British Airports Authority)
HHR	Hundred of Hoo Railway	Absorbed by SER August 1880
HJR	Hampstead Junction Railway	Managed by NLR after 1864, absorbed by LNWR 1867
HS1	High Speed One	High speed route between Channel Tunnel and St Pancras
HS2	High Speed Two	Under construction high speed route between London and Birmingham / Crewe / Manchester
HST	High Speed Train	
IEP	Intercity Express Programme	Programme to replace Class 43 (Intercity 125) fleet with Class 800
Jcn.	Junction	
JUB	Jubilee Line	Formed 01.05.1979, partially from Bakerloo Line
km	Kilometres	
LBIR	London & Birmingham Railway	Absorbed by LNWR 16.07.1846
LBLR	London & Blackwall Railway	Leased to GER 18.03.1874, absorbed by LNER 01.01.1923
LBRR	London & Brighton Railway	Merged with LCRR to form LBSCR 27.07.1846
LBSCR	London, Brighton & South Coast Railway	Formed 27.07.1846 from LBRR and LCRR
L.C.	Level crossing	
LCC	London County Council	
LCDR	London, Chatham & Dover Railway	Merged with SER to form SECR 01.01.1899
LCOR	London & Continental Railway	Consortium that built Channel Tunnel Rail Link, rebranded HS1 14.11.2006, managed by NR
LCRR	London & Croydon Railway	Merged with LBRR to form LBSCR 27.07.1846
LGR	London & Greenwich Railway	Leased to SER 01.01.1845, absorbed by SR 01.01.1923
LMD	Light Maintenance Depot	
LMS	London, Midland & Scottish Railway	Formed 01.01.1923 from MID, LNWR & NLR
LNER	London & North Eastern Railway	Formed 01.01.1923 from GNR, GCR & GER
LNWR	London & North Western Railway	Formed 16.07.1846 from LBIR
LO	London Overground	Concession operated on behalf of TfL (London Overground Rail Operations Ltd / LOROL 11.11.2007 – 13.11.2016, Arriva Rail London / ARL thereafter)
LPTB	London Passenger Transport Board	Formed 01.01.1933, became LTE (1st) 01.01.1948
LRT	London Regional Transport	Formed 19.06.1984, became LUL 01.04.1985
LSKD	London St Katherine's Dock Company	Later became part of PLA, operated by GER after 01.07.1896
LSWR	London & South Western Railway	Absorbed by SR 01.01.1923, 'London & Southampton Railway' until opening day
LTB	London Transport Board	Formed 01.01.1963, became LTE (2nd) 01.01.1970
LT	London Trams	Formerly Croydon Tramlink
LTE (1st)	London Transport Executive (1st incarnation)	Formed 01.01.1948, became LTB 01.01.1963
LTE (2nd)	London Transport Executive (2nd incarnation)	Formed 01.01.1970, became LRT 19.06.1984
LTSR	London, Tilbury & Southend Railway	ECR / LBLR joint, leased to its builders 03.07.1854, absorbed by MID 07.08.1912
LUL	London Underground Ltd	Formed 01.04.1985, transferred to TfL 15.07.2003 as a subsidiary service operator
m	metres	
MDR	Metropolitan District Railway	Absorbed by UERL 09.04.1902
MER	Millwall Extension Railway	LBLR, East & West India Dock Co. and Millwall Dock Co. joint
MET	Metropolitan Railway	Absorbed by LPTB 01.07.1933
MHPR	Muswell Hill & Palace Railway	Operated by GNR from outset, absorbed 09.1911

MID	Midland Railway	Absorbed by LMS 01.01.1923
MKR	Mid Kent Railway	Absorbed by SER 29.07.1864
MoD	Ministry of Defence	
MPD	Motive Power Depot	
MPV	Multi-purpose Vehicle	Purpose built vehicles used on Network Rail for activities such as water-jetting and de-icing
MSJWR	Metropolitan & St John's Wood Railway	Worked by MET from outset, formally absorbed by MET 01.01.1883
N	North	
NB	Northbound	
NCL	Northern City Line	Abbreviated form of GNCR, transferred to BR 16.08.1976
NER	Northern & Eastern Railway	Leased to ECR 01.01.1844, absorbed by GER 1902
NLR	North London Railway	Operated by LNWR after 01.02.1909, absorbed by LMS 01.01.1923
NOR	Northern Line	Formed from CCEHR & CSLR 13.09.1926, 'Northern Line' name not used until 08.1937
NR	Network Rail	Formed 03.10.2002 when Railtrack renationalised
NSWJR	North & South Western Junction Railway	LNWR & LSWR joint (LNWR, NLR & MID joint after 1871, LMS after 01.01.1923)
OHLE	Overhead Line Equipment	
OS	Ordnance Survey	
PIC	Piccadilly Line	Abbreviated form of GNPBR
PLA	Port of London Authority	
POR	Post Office Railway	Commenced operation 03.12.1927, mothballed 31.05.2003. Renamed 'Mail Rail' 1987
PRIV	Private	
RT	Railtrack	Formed from BR 01.04.1994 (privatisation)
Rwy.	Railway	
S	South	
S&T	Signal & Telegraph	
SB	Southbound	
Sdg.	Siding	
SECR	South Eastern & Chatham Railway	Formed from SER & LCDR 01.01.1899, absorbed by SR 01.01.1923
SER	South Eastern Railway	Absorbed by SECR 01.01.1899
SIR	Surrey Iron Railway	4ft 2in gauge plateway carrying goods, using horse traction. Opened 26.07.1803, closed 31.08.1846
SOR	Sevenoaks Railway	Later became Sevenoaks, Maidstone & Tunbridge Railway. Absorbed by LCDR 21.07.1879
Sq	Square	
SR	Southern Railway	Formed from LBSCR, LSWR & SECR 01.01.1923, absorbed by BR 01.01.1948
St	Saint or Street	
TFGR	Tottenham & Forest Gate Railway	MID & LTSR joint, LMS after 01.01.1923
TfL	Transport for London	Formed 03.07.2000, took control of LUL 15.07.2003, LO 11.11.2007
THJR	Tottenham & Hampstead Junction Railway	MID & GER joint, LMS & LNER joint after 01.01.1923
TMD	Traction maintenance depot	
TVR	Thames Valley Railway	Absorbed by LSWR 11.01.1867
U/C	Under construction	
UERL	Underground Electric Railways of London	Formed by merger of MDR, BSWR, GNPBR & CCEHR 1901-1902
VIC	Victoria Line	
VSPR	Victoria Station & Pimlico Railway	LBSCR, LCDR, GWR & LNWR joint
W	West	
WB	Westbound	
WBR	Whitechapel & Bow Railway	LTSR & MDR joint
WCIR	Waterloo & City Railway	Operated by LSWR from outset, Absorbed by 1906. Transferred to LUL 01.04.1994
WCL	Waterloo & City Line	
WCML	West Coast Main Line	Former LBIR (later LNWR) main line from Euston
WCRR	Wimbledon & Croydon Railway	Absorbed by LBSCR 01.01.1866
WELCPR	West End of London & Crystal Palace Railway	Absorbed by LBSCR 1860
WLER	West London Extension Railway	LNWR, GWR, LBSCR & LSWR joint, LMS & SR joint after 01.01.1923
WLR	West London Railway	Leased to LBIR & GWR 1846, absorbed by LNWR & GWR 31.07.1854
WRR	Watford & Rickmansworth Railway	Absorbed by LNWR 1881
WW1	World War One	
WW2	World War Two	

Glossary

Aggregate	Stone, gravel, sand etc used for construction
Bay platform	Dedicated platform for terminating trains at an otherwise through station
Bi-directional	Single track signalled for train movements in both directions; Single-line working
Bradshaw	George Bradshaw's 'Monthly Railway Guide'; the industry standard of timetables published from December 1841 onwards
Chain	Unit of measurement still used on NR routes, approximately 20 metres
Chord	Short section of line connecting two joining or crossing routes
Clipped	Method of securing a set of points rendering one route out of use
Covered way	Section of line artificially covered over, usually for development above (in essence a tunnel not necessitated by topography)
Cripple siding	Siding provided for storage of defective wagons
Curve	See 'chord'
Down	Direction of travel, generally away from London ('Up to London, down to the country')
End-on junction	The line of demarcation between two railway companies on plain track (e.g. Barrington Road Junction)
Flat junction	Junction without diveunders / flyovers
Flying junction	Junction arranged with diveunders / flyovers to minimise conflicting train movements (also 'Grade separated junction')
Halt	Unstaffed platform where trains stop by request only
Head shunt	Dead-end siding provided for trains to reverse and shunt back into a depot or goods yard
Hump	Hump marshalling yards used gravity to sort wagons after being propelled over a hump (e.g. Feltham, Temple Mills)
Interlaced track	Two separate tramway tracks overlapping without merging into a single track, due to constrained width
Level crossing	Two railway lines or a railway line and road intersecting on the same level
Logistics	The management of the flow of goods
Loop	See 'chord'. Also a simple siding connected to a main line at both ends, typically to allow fast trains to overtake slow, or can refer to a much longer section of railway connected to a main line at both ends (e.g. Hertford Loop)
Mothballed	Disused infrastructure maintained for possible future use
Passing loop	Loop provided on single-track railway to allow 'up' and 'down' trains to pass each other
Plain-lined	Replacement of points with plain track, permanently rendering diverging route unavailable
Plateway	Tramway formed of flanged cast iron plates to guide wheels (as opposed to conventional railway with flanged wheels on rails)
Run-around	Loop provided (usually at a terminus) to allow a locomotive to 'run around' its rake of coaches for the return journey
Single lead junction	Junction between two double track routes where one route merges to a single track before joining the other (e.g. Old Kew Junction)
Single-line working	See bi-directional
Stabling	'Parking' of rolling stock when not in use, e.g. overnight or between peak hours
Staggered	Where platforms on adjacent tracks are not parallel, usually either side of a level crossing (e.g. Mitcham Eastfields)
Terminal loop	A loop of track allowing trains to terminate without the need to reverse (e.g. Kennington, Heathrow Terminal 4)
Ticket platform	Platform, usually on approach to a terminus, where ticket inspectors would board to check tickets
Tramway	Railway line running along roadway or an industrial railway usually disconnected from the railway system e.g. associated with mining
Turnback siding	Siding provided, usually between running lines, to allow terminating trains to reverse (e.g. Tooting Broadway, Archway)
Up	Direction of travel, generally towards London ('Up to London, down to the country')

References

It would be impossible to list every single reference source here, as they run into over a hundred in several formats. I have selected those upon which I have relied the most heavily and those in which accuracy I have the most confidence. Firstly, special mention to the **Branch Line Society** and in particular the Editor of their indispensable publication **Branch Line News**, Paul Stewart for his kind assistance. I implore anyone with an interest in the railways of the British Isles to subscribe for the most comprehensive and regular updates regarding changes to the system, as well as access to a back catalogue stretching back 65 years. Similarly, BLS member Dr Angus McDougall has been working on a closure guide for over 40 years, which has been invaluable to my research. Finally, membership of the **Railway & Canal Historical Society** is highly recommended for their peerless research in the field of British railway and canal history (website: https://rchs.org.uk/).

Chronology of London Railways
H.V. Borley
Railway & Canal Historical Society 1982
ISBN 0-901461-33-4

London's Local Railways
Alan A. Jackson
Capital Transport 1999
ISBN 1-85414-209-7

Clinker's Register of Closed Passenger Stations and Goods Depots in England, Scotland and Wales 1830 – 1977
C.R. Clinker
Avon Anglia 1978
ISBN 0 905466 19 5

Passenger Railway Stations in Great Britain – A Chronology
Fifth Edition version 5.04 (online only) – Michael Quick
Railway & Canal Historical Society 2022
https://rchs.org.uk/railway-passenger-stations-in-great-britain-a-chronology

The Railways of Great Britain – A Historical Atlas (Second Edition)
Colonel Michael H. Cobb
Ian Allan 2006
ISBN 07110-3236X

Private and Untimetabled Railway Stations, Halts, and Stopping Places
Godfrey Croughton, R.W. Kidner, Alan Young
The Oakwood Press 1982
ISBN 0 85361 281 1 1

Branch Line News – Available by subscription via the Branch Line Society website: https://www.branchline.uk/home.php

The value of this publication to any railway enthusiast or historian cannot be overstated, Paul Stewart has granted me access to more than sixty years of back issues.

Railway Track Diagrams – Quail Track Diagrams

2 – Eastern	Fifth Edition	TRACKmaps 2020	ISBN 978-1-9996271-3-3
3 – Western & Wales	Sixth Edition	TRACKmaps 2018	ISBN 978-1-9996271-0-2
4 – Midlands & North West	Fifth Edition	TRACKmaps 2022	ISBN 978-1-9996271-5-7
5 – Southern & TfL	Fourth Edition	TRACKmaps 2019	ISBN 978-1-9996271-2-6

Rail Atlas of Great Britain and Ireland – S.K. Baker   Various editions   Crecy, formerly OPC (Ian Allan)

Capital Transport Illustrated Histories

The Jubilee Line – Mike Horne 2000   ISBN 1-85414-220-8
The Bakerloo Line – Mike Horne 2001   ISBN 1-85414-248-8
The Metropolitan Line – Mike Horne 2003   ISBN 1-85414-275-5
The First Tube: The Story of the Northern Line – Mike Horne & Bob Bayman 1990   ISBN 1-85414-128-7
The Circle Line – Desmond F. Croome 2003   ISBN 1-85414-267-4
The Piccadilly Line – Desmond F. Croome 1998   ISBN 1-85414-192-9
The Central Line – J Graeme Bruce & Desmond F. Croome 2006   ISBN 1-85414-297-6
Going Green: The Story of the District Line – Piers Connor 1994   ISBN 1-85414-162-7

Middleton Press Albums (unfortunately too many of these invaluable titles to list individual publication years and ISBN numbers)

Vic Mitchell and Keith Smith
Harrow to Watford, Marylebone to Rickmansworth, Paddington to Princes Risborough, Paddington to Ealing, Ealing to Slough, Willesden Junction to Richmond, Charing Cross to Dartford, Branch Lines of West London, West London Line, Victoria to Bromley South, East London Line, North London Line, South London Line, London Bridge to East Croydon, Waterloo to Windsor, Clapham Junction to Beckenham Junction, Lines around Wimbledon, Kingston and Hounslow Loops, London Bridge to Addiscombe, Mitcham Junction Lines, West Croydon to Epsom, Victoria to East Croydon, Surrey Narrow Gauge, Holborn Viaduct to Lewisham (in association with Leslie & Philip Davis), Crystal Palace (High level) and Catford Loop (in association with Leslie & Philip Davis)

J.E. Connor
Branch Lines around North Woolwich, Finsbury Park to Alexandra Palace, Branch Line to Ongar, Fenchurch Street to Barking, Branch Lines of East London, Liverpool Street to Ilford, St Pancras to Barking, Liverpool Street to Chingford

Dr Edwin Course	Barking to Southend, Tilbury Loop	**Dave Brennand**	Ilford to Shenfield
Charlie and Jim Connor	King's Cross to Potters Bar	**Keith Scholey**	Euston to Harrow & Wealdstone
Chalk Pits Museum	Industrial Railways of the South-East	**Geoff Goslin and J.E. Connor**	St Pancras to St Albans

The London Railway Record (Multiple editions) – Connor & Butler Ltd

Websites

NLS maps	https://maps.nls.uk/os	**London Reconnections**	http://www.londonreconnections.com/
Shed Bash UK	http://shedbashuk.blogspot.com/	**Disused Stations**	http://www.disused-stations.org.uk/sites.shtml
Google Maps	http://maps.google.co.uk	**The Signal Box**	https://signalbox.org/
Kentrail.org.uk	http://www.kentrail.org.uk/index.htm	**Clive's Underground Line Guides**	https://www.davros.org/rail/culg/
Ian Visits	https://www.ianvisits.co.uk/	**National Electronic Sectional Appendix**	– use search, url is too long!

Property Asset Register Public Web Map (TfL / Arcgis) – use search, url is too long!

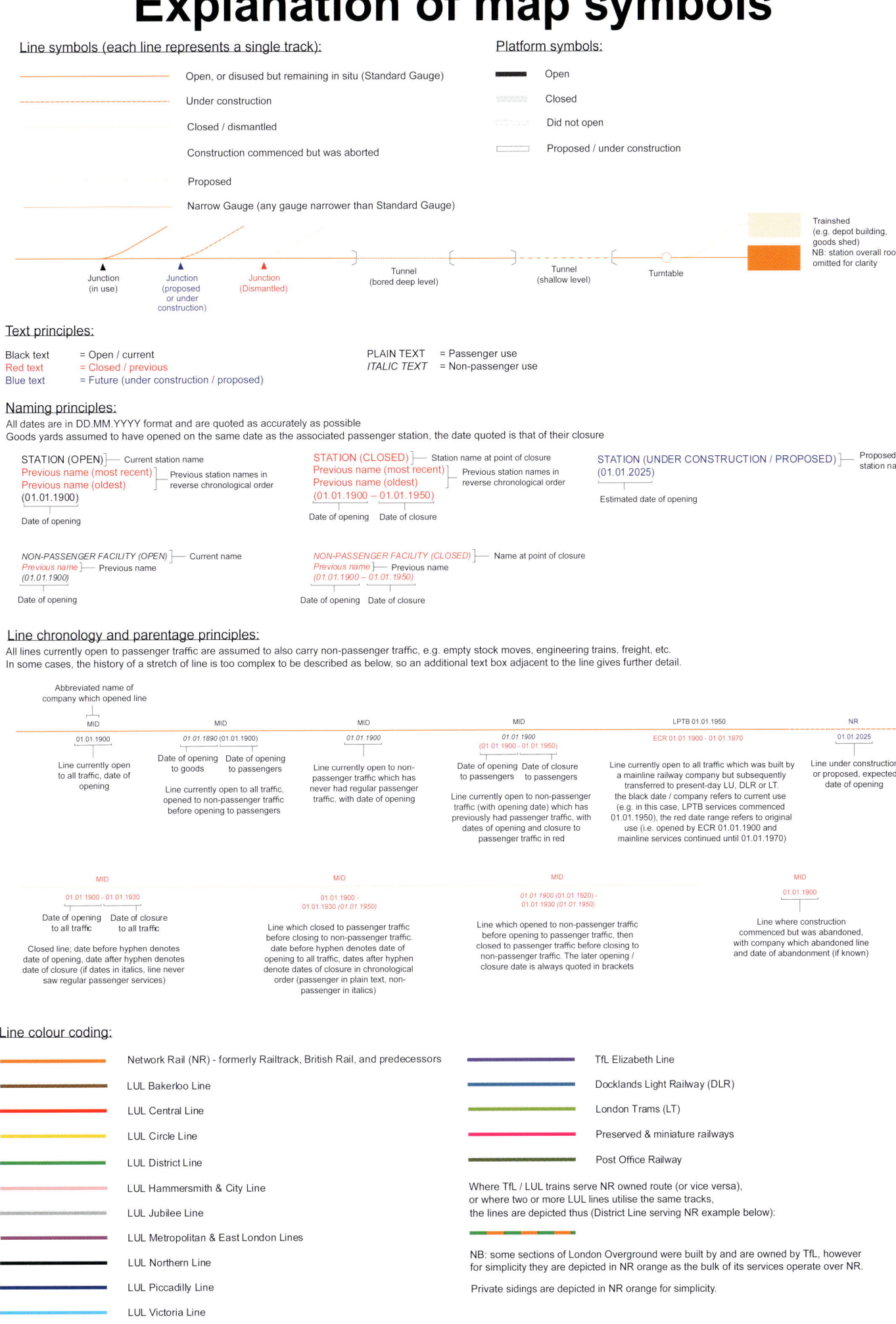

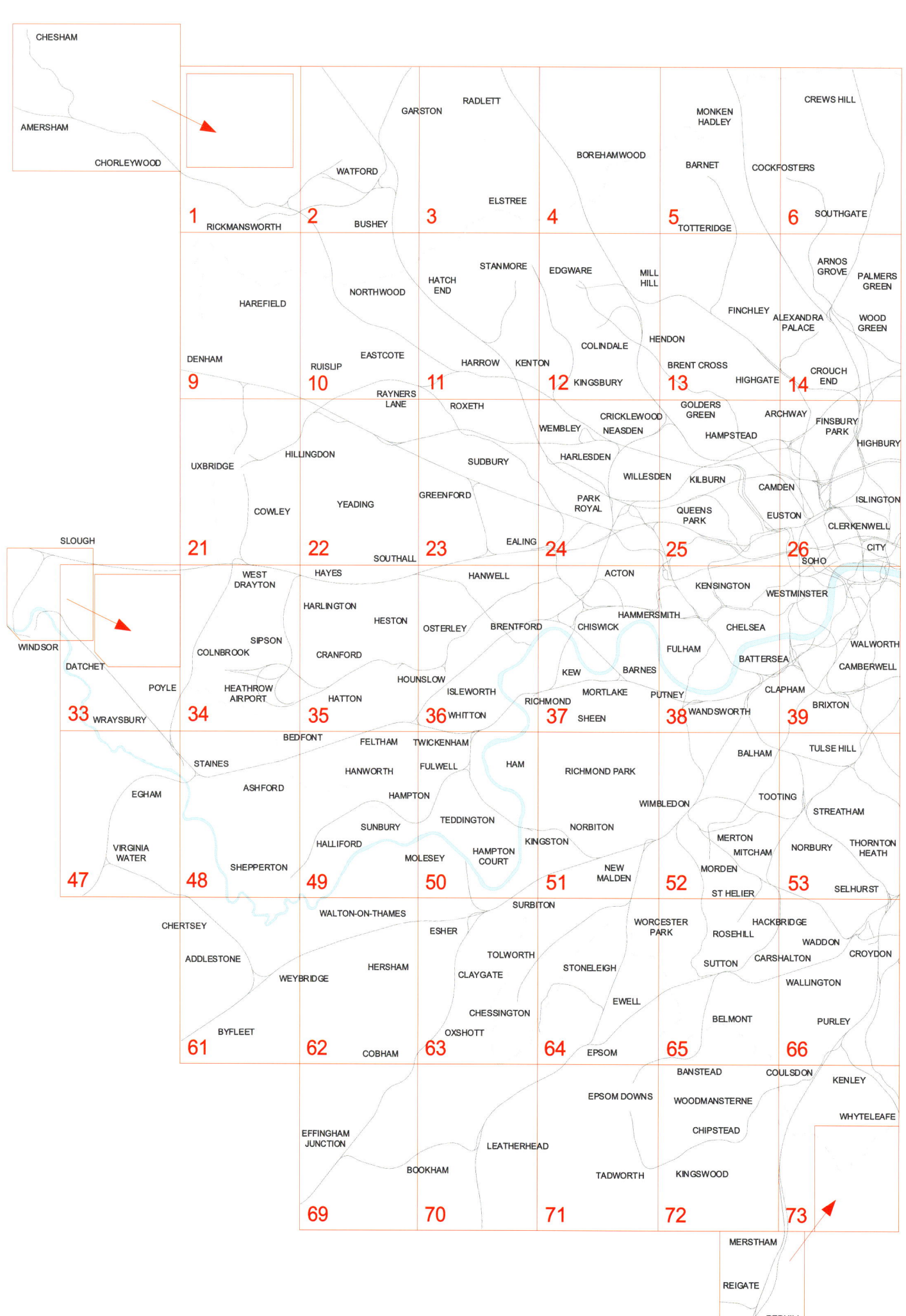

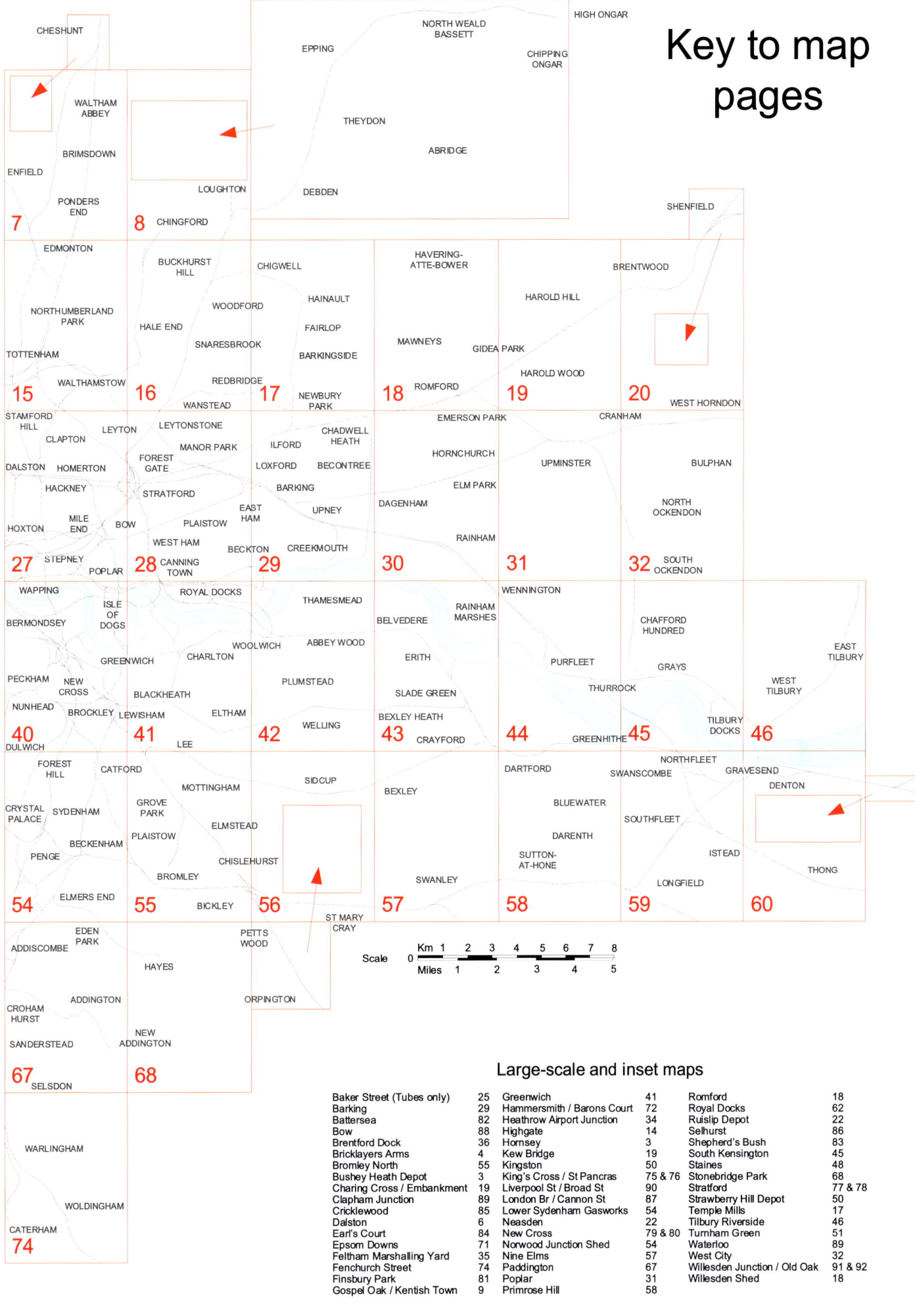

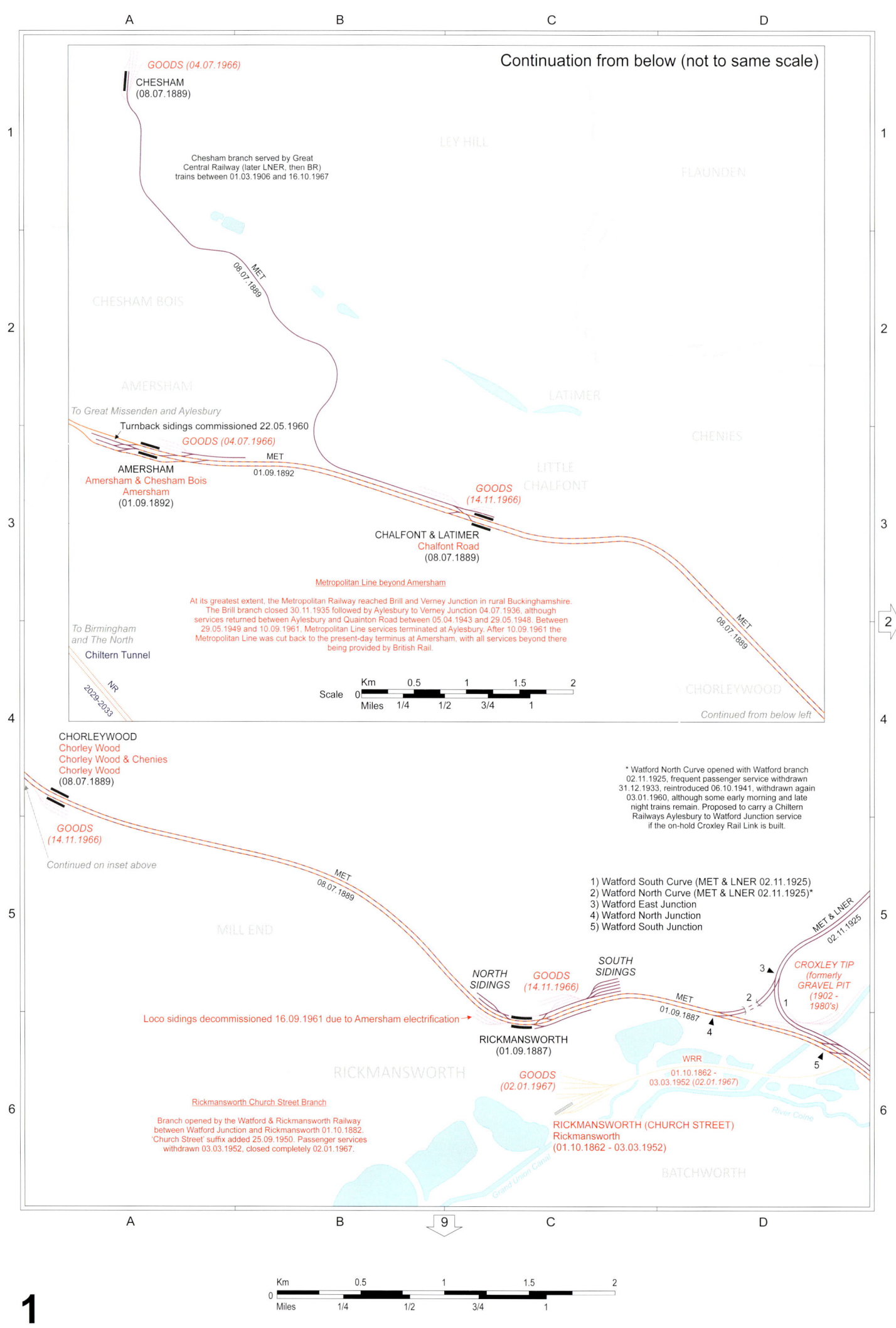

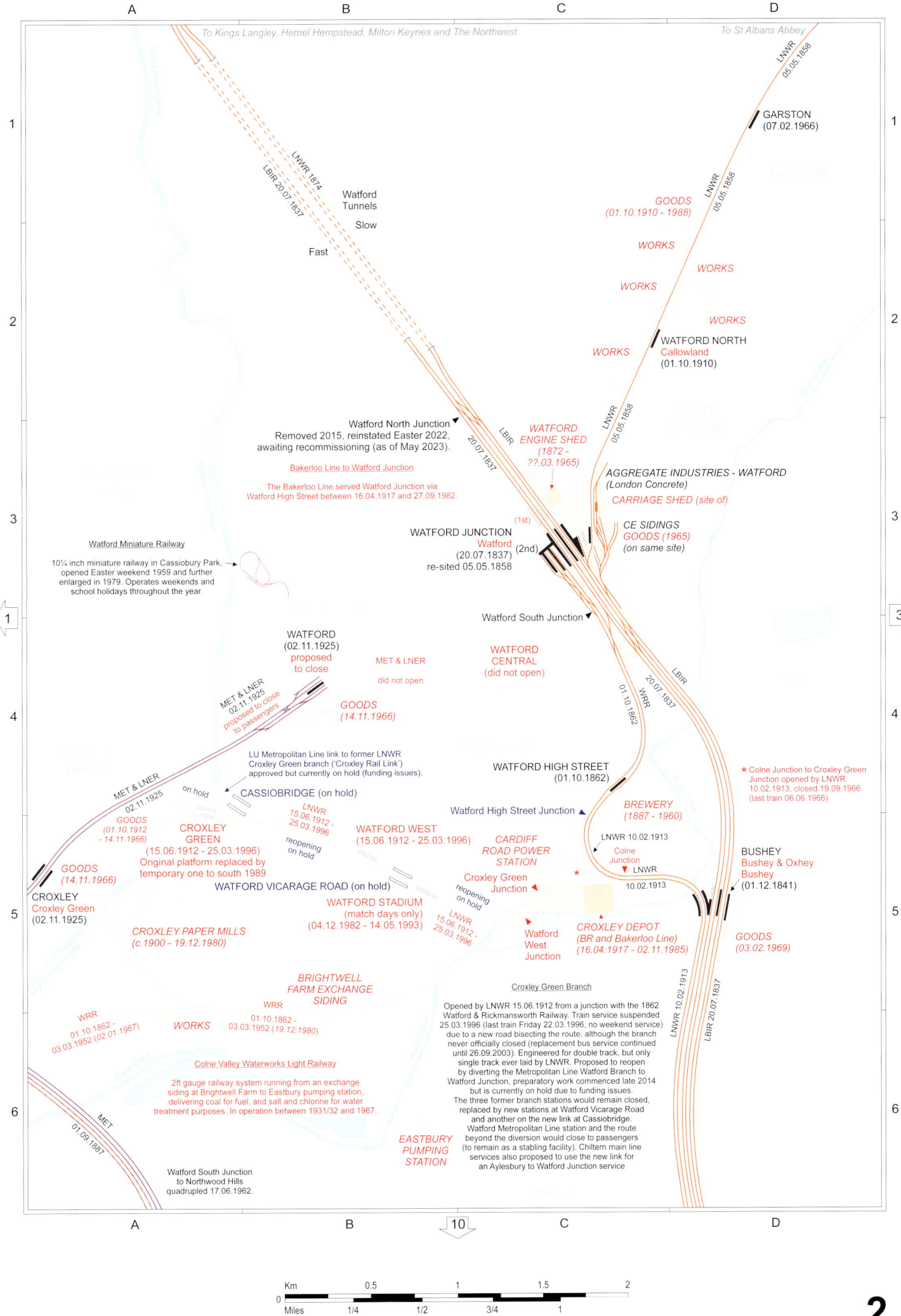

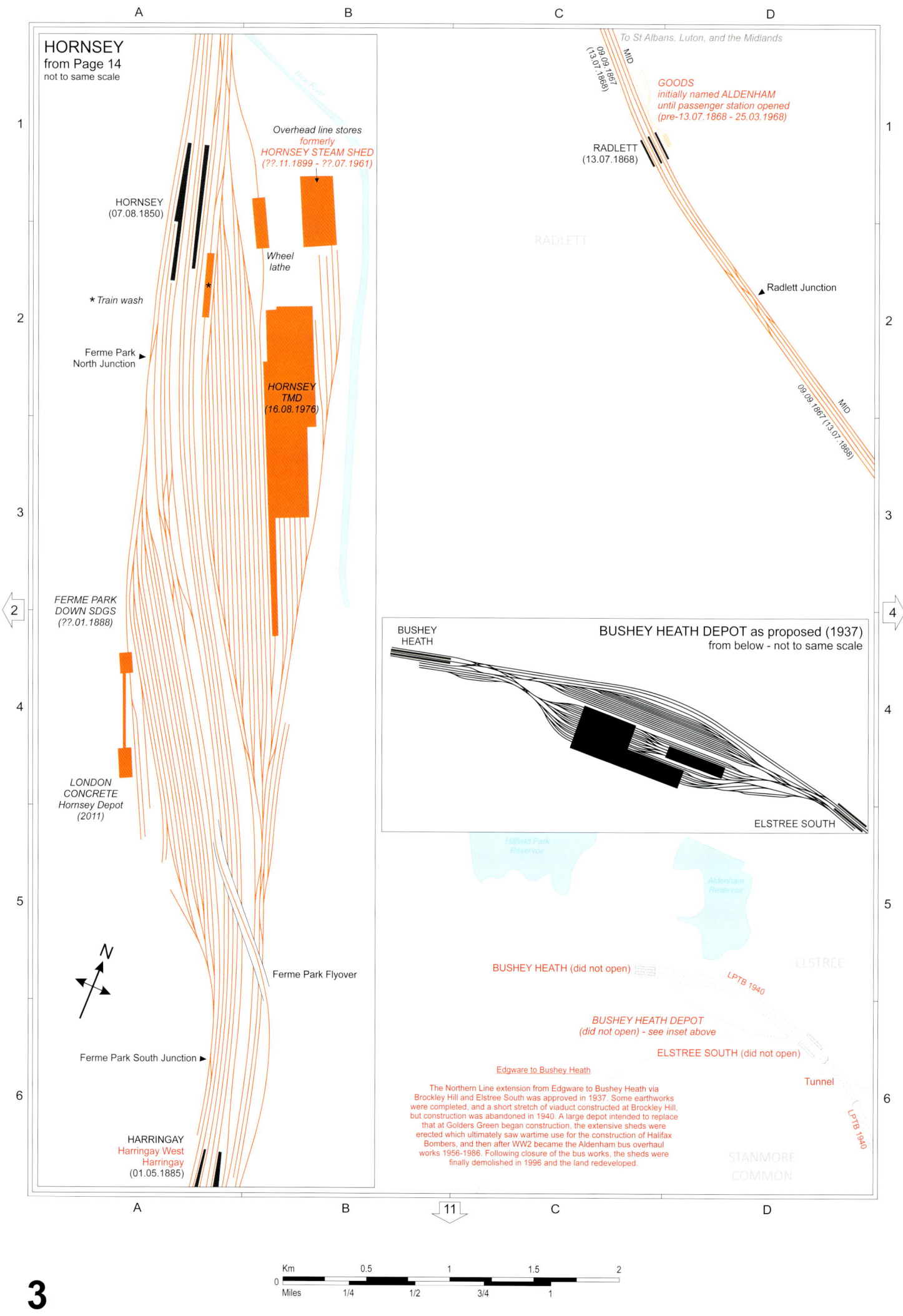

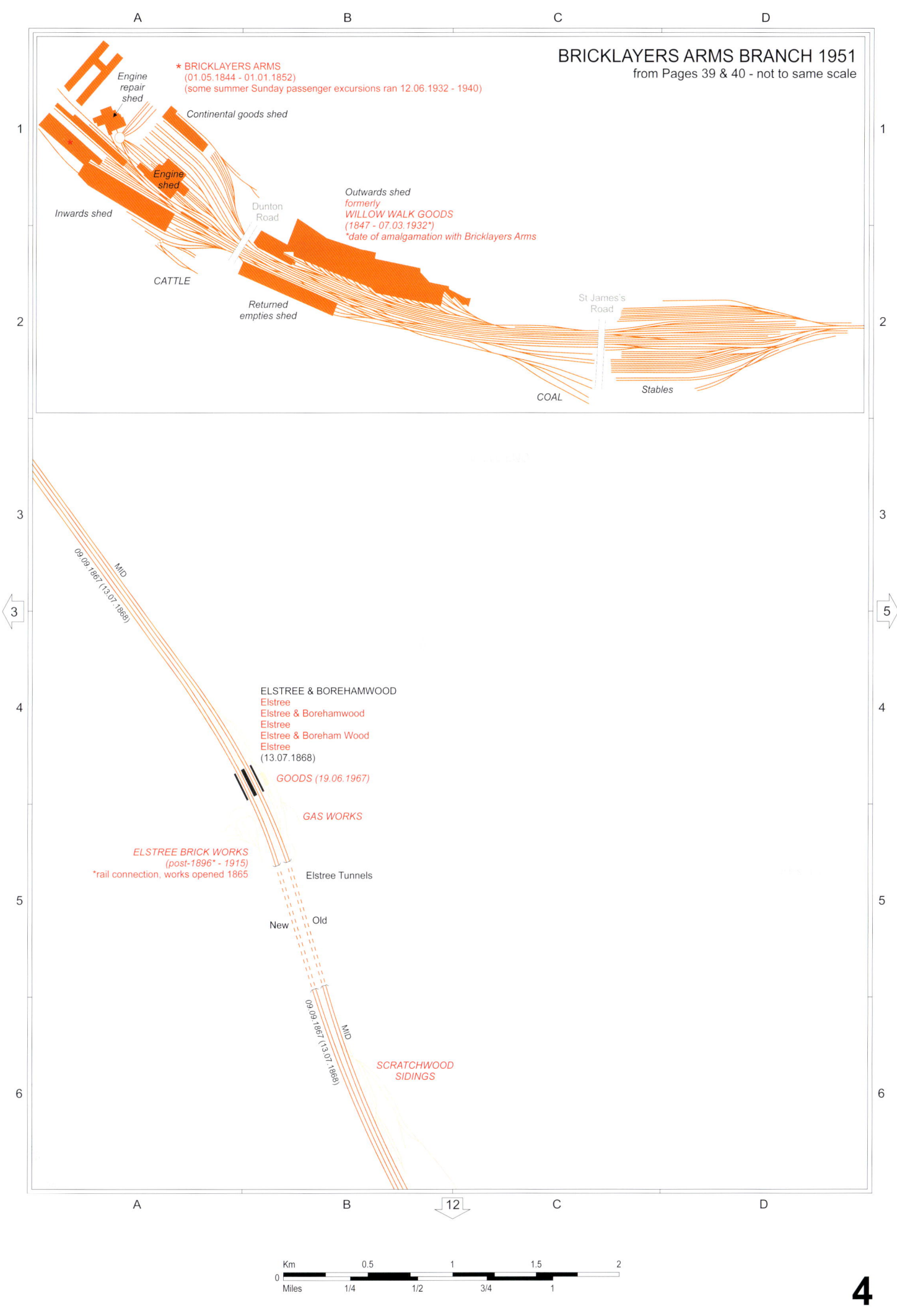

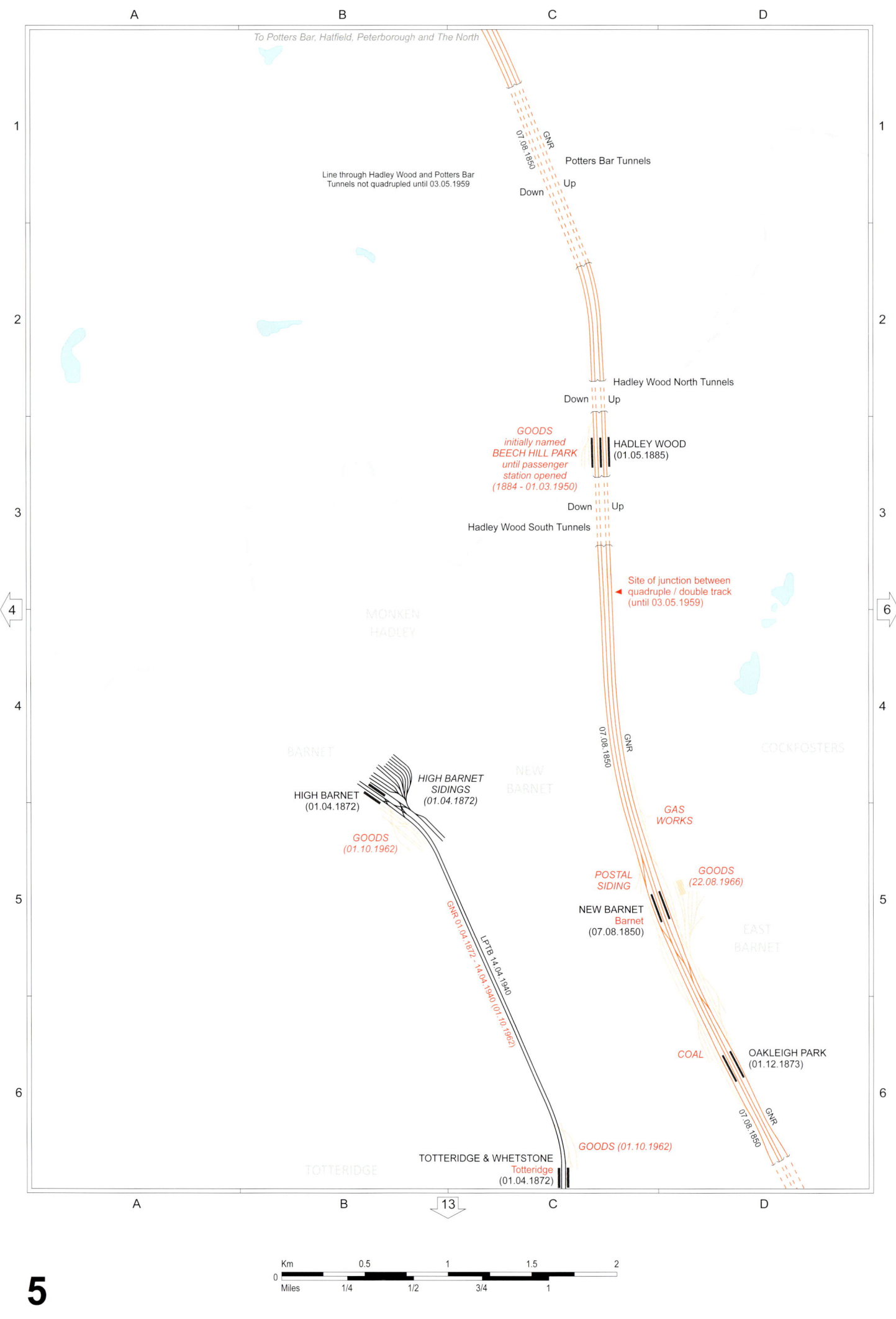

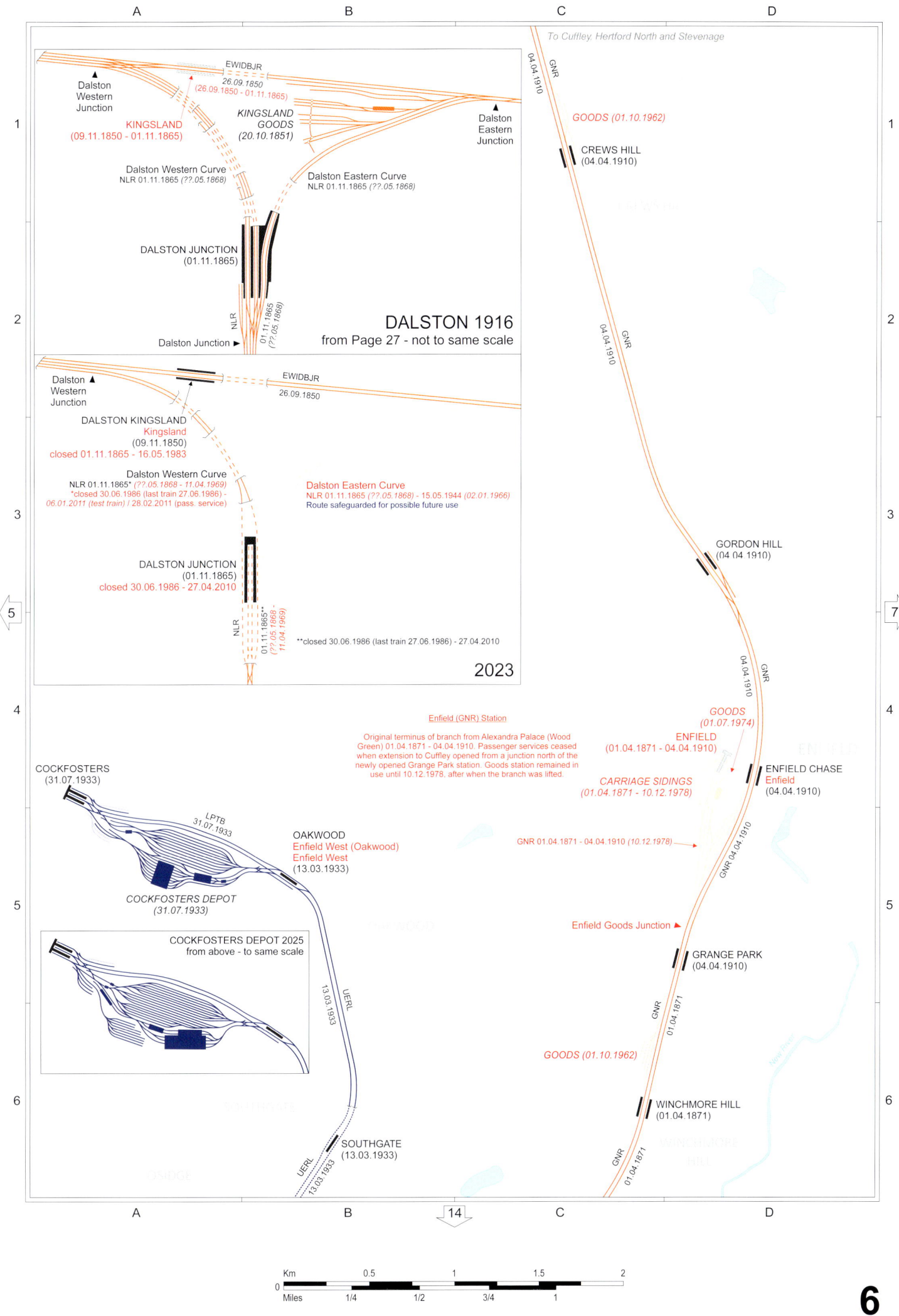

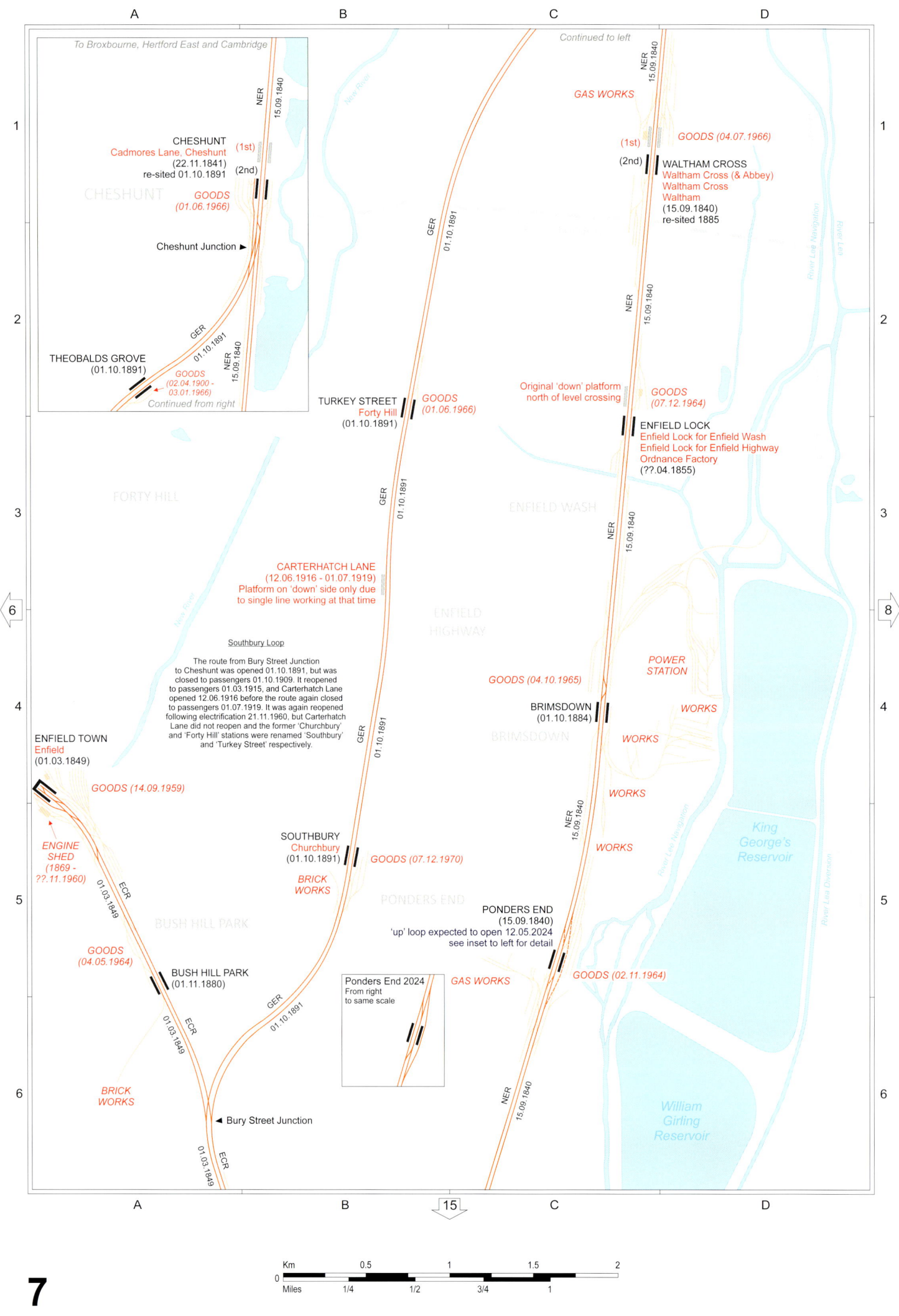

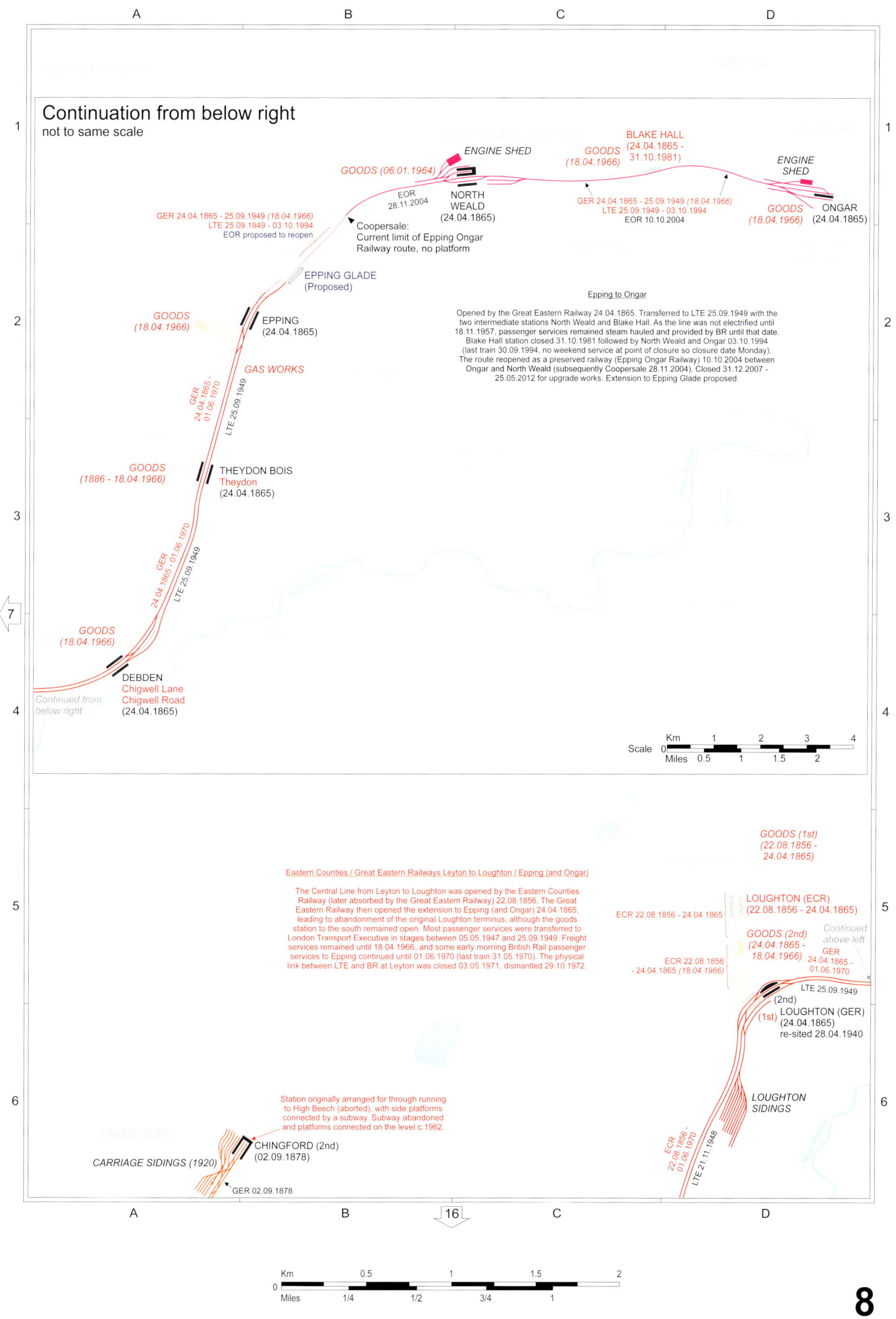

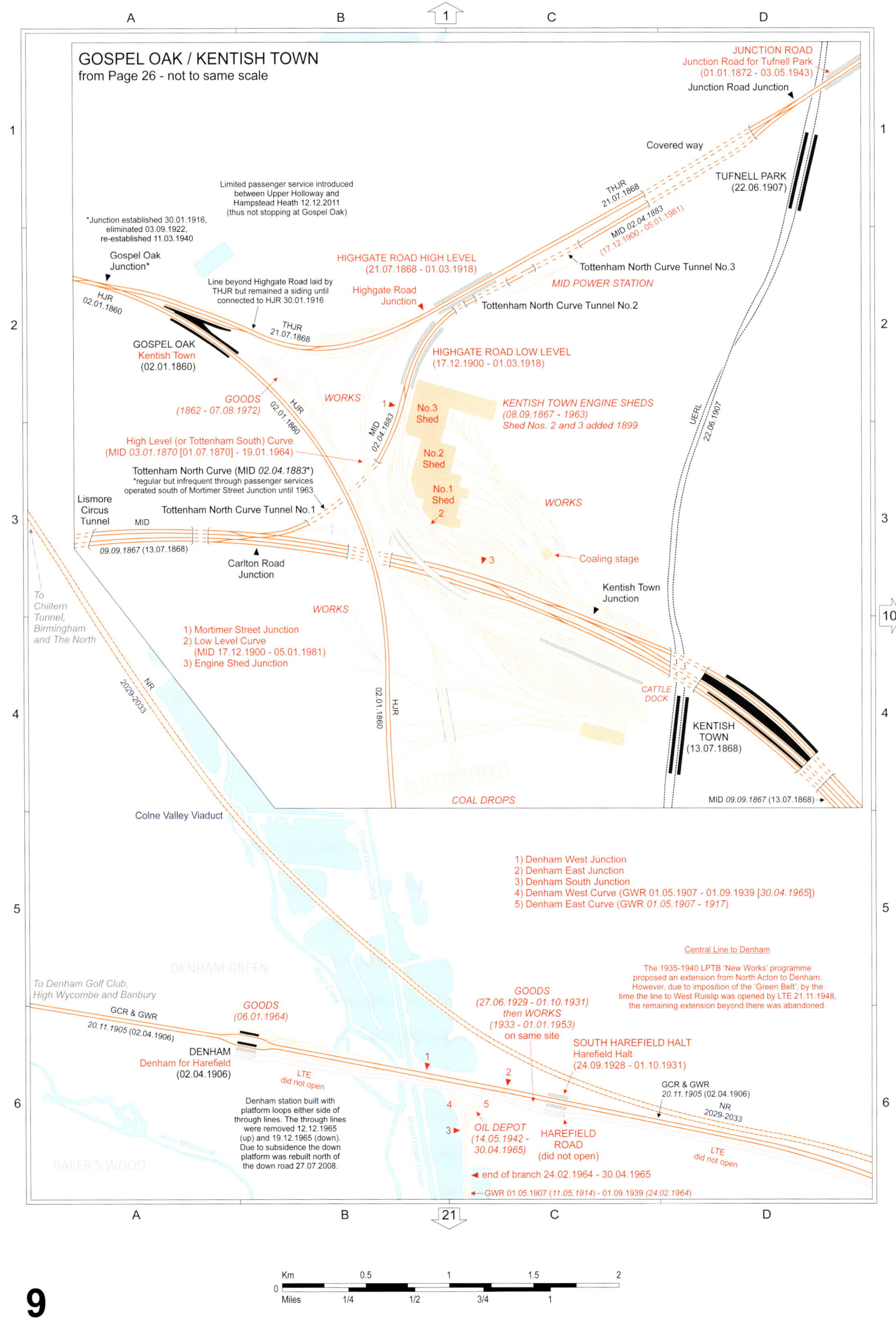

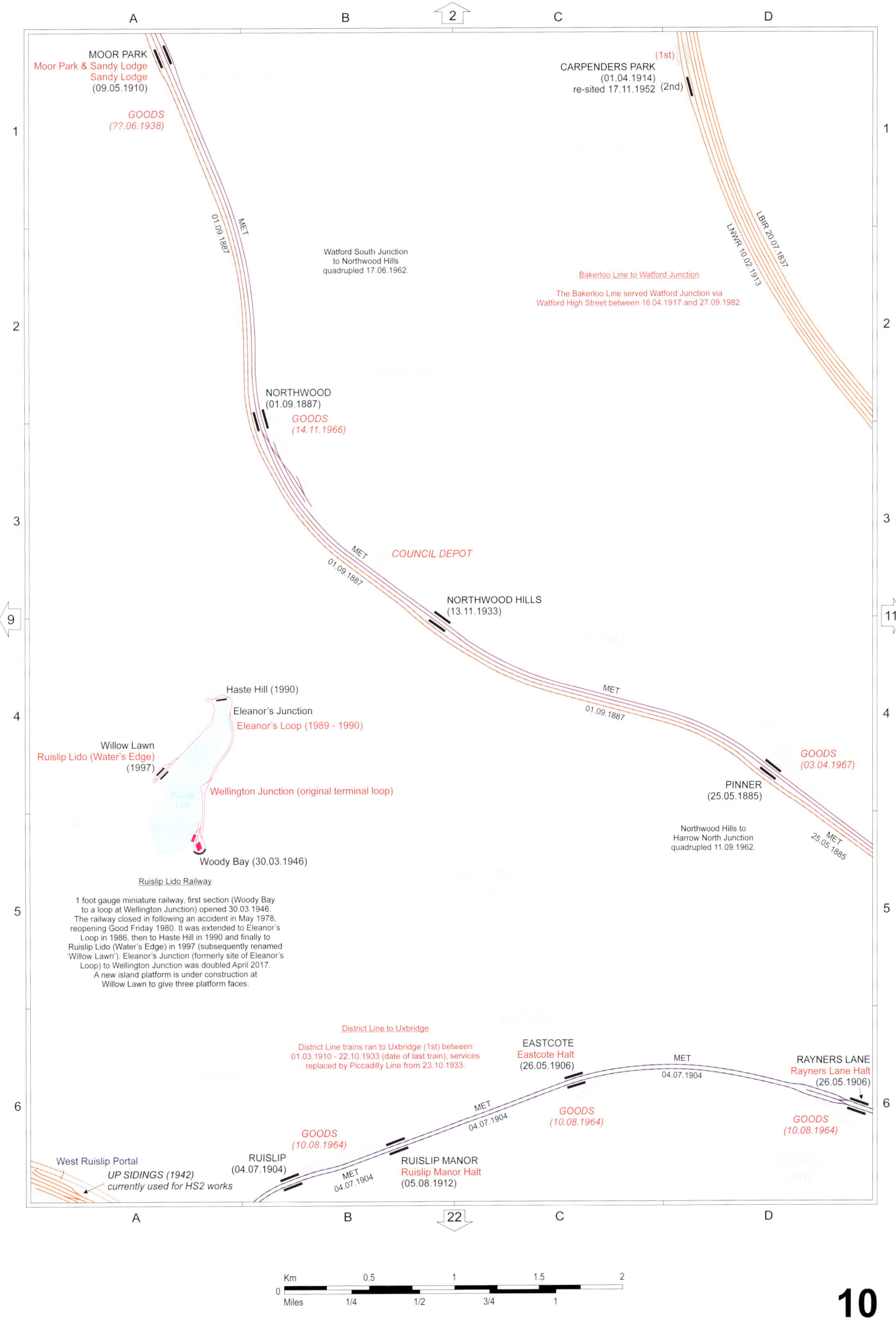

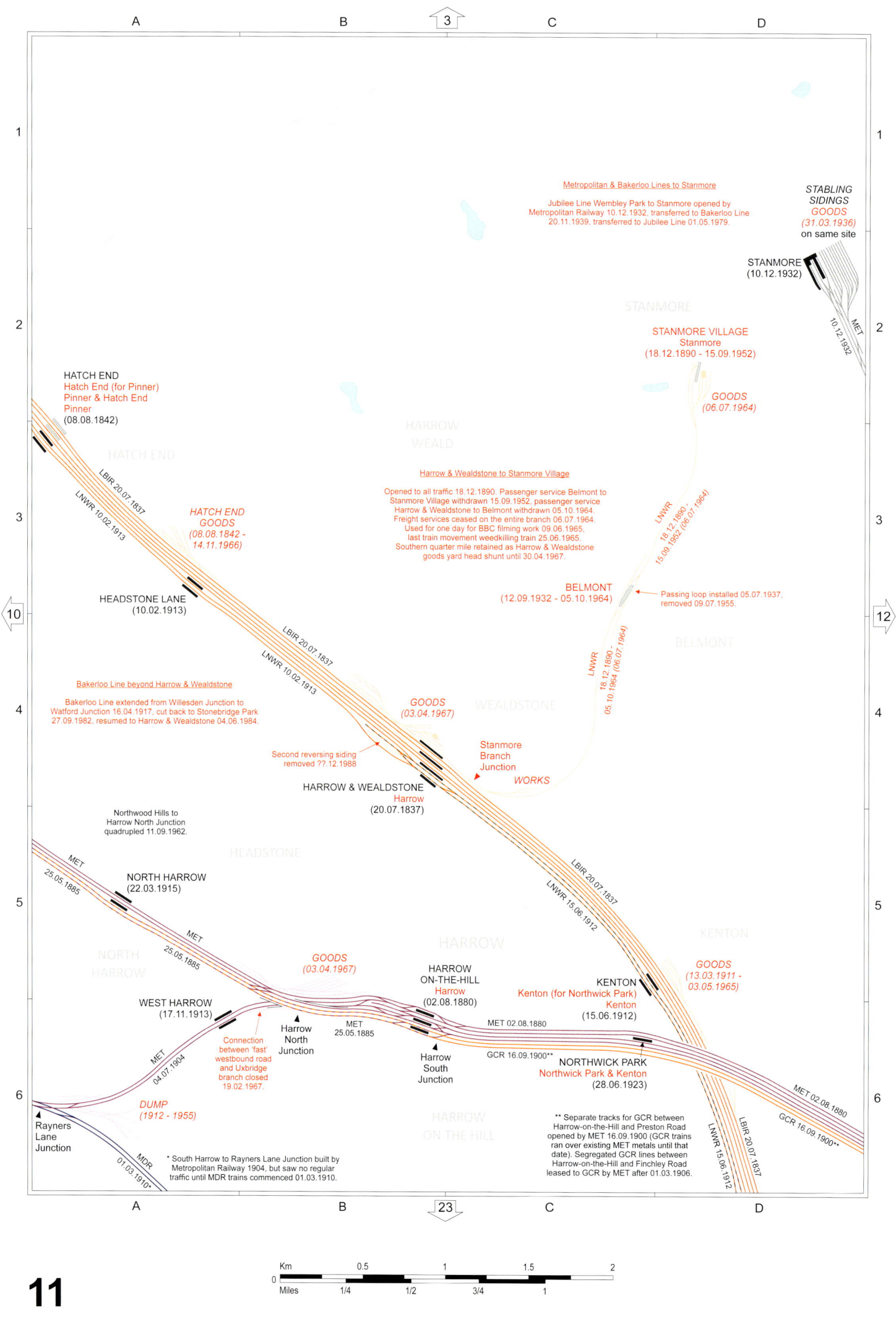

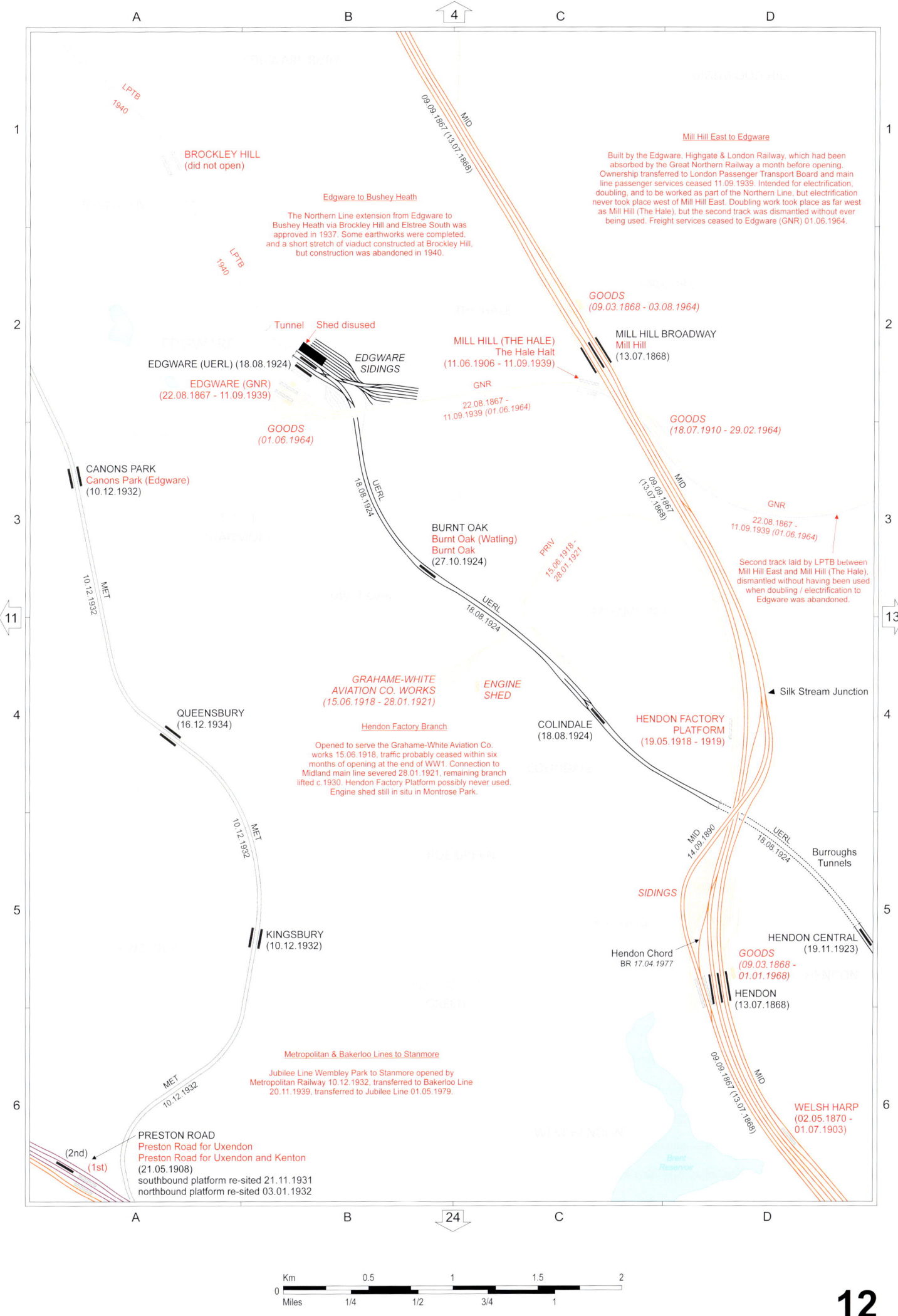

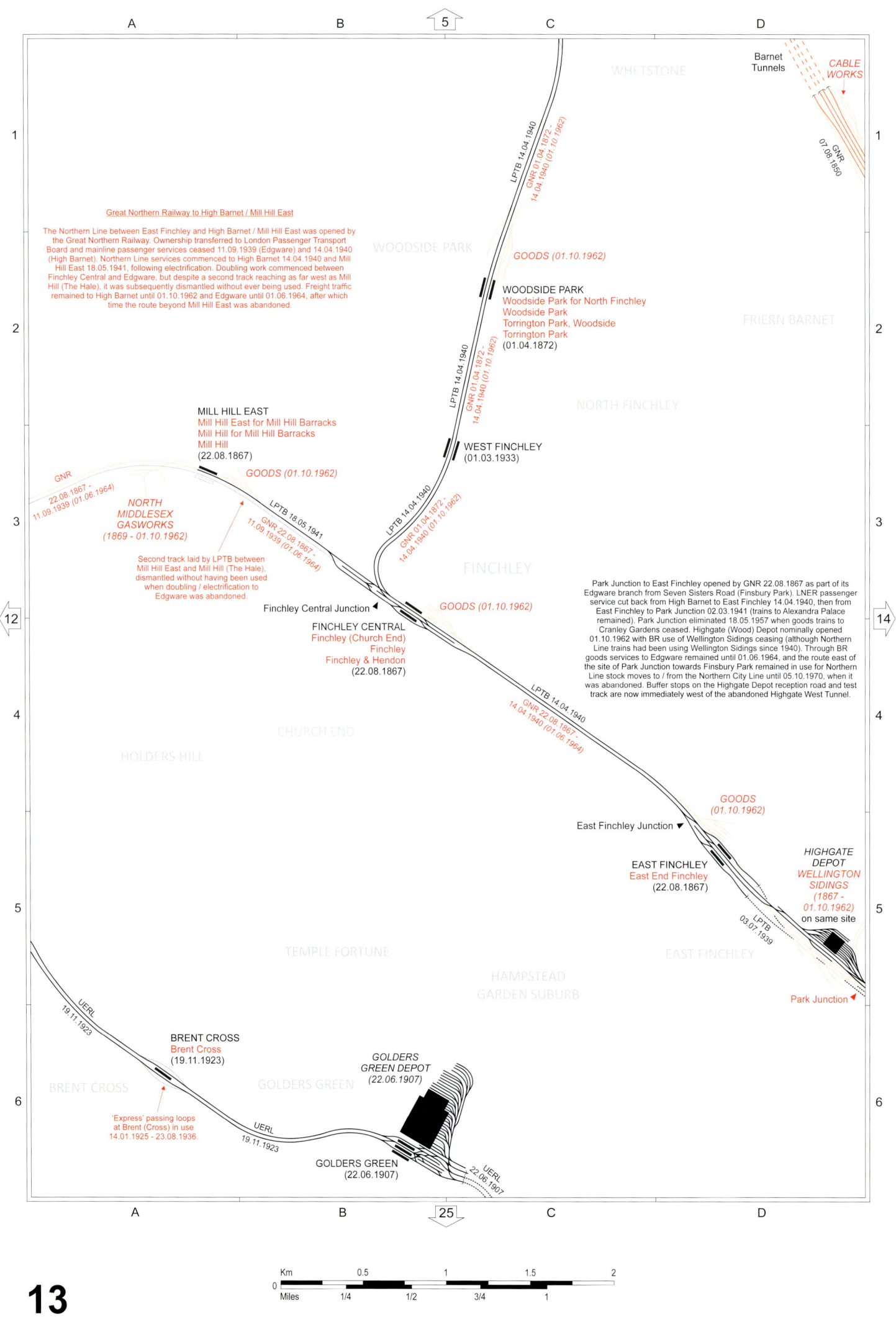

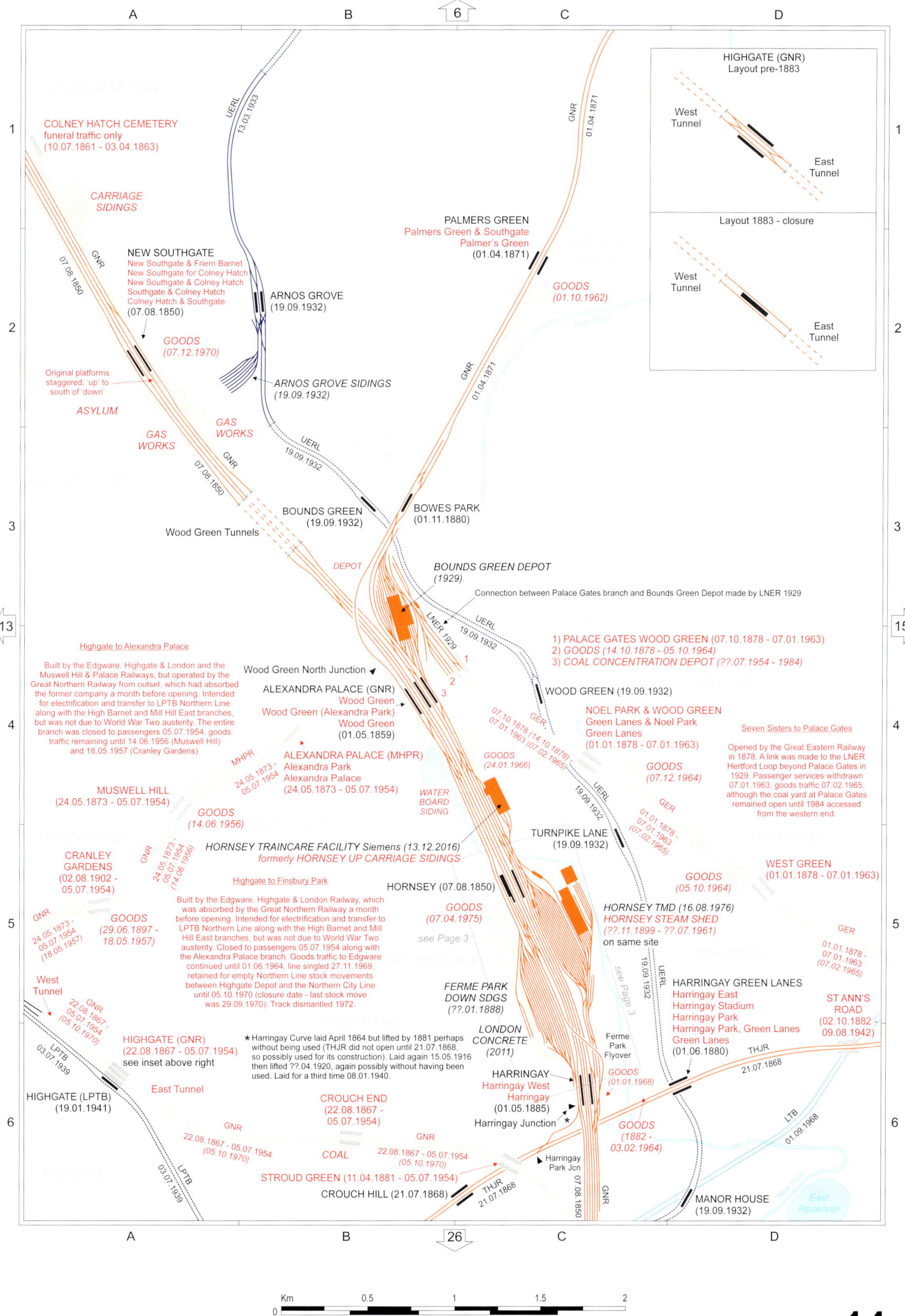

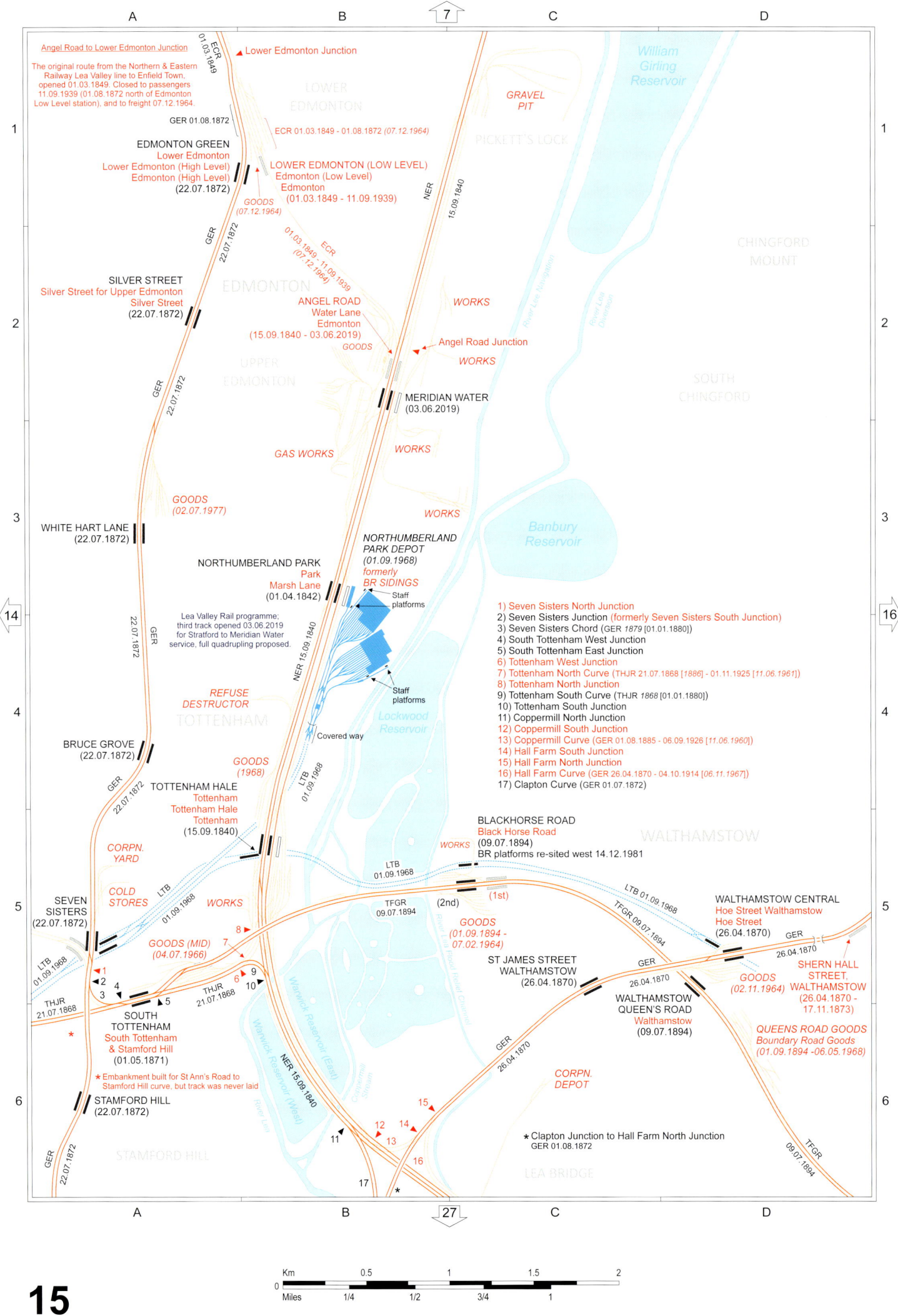

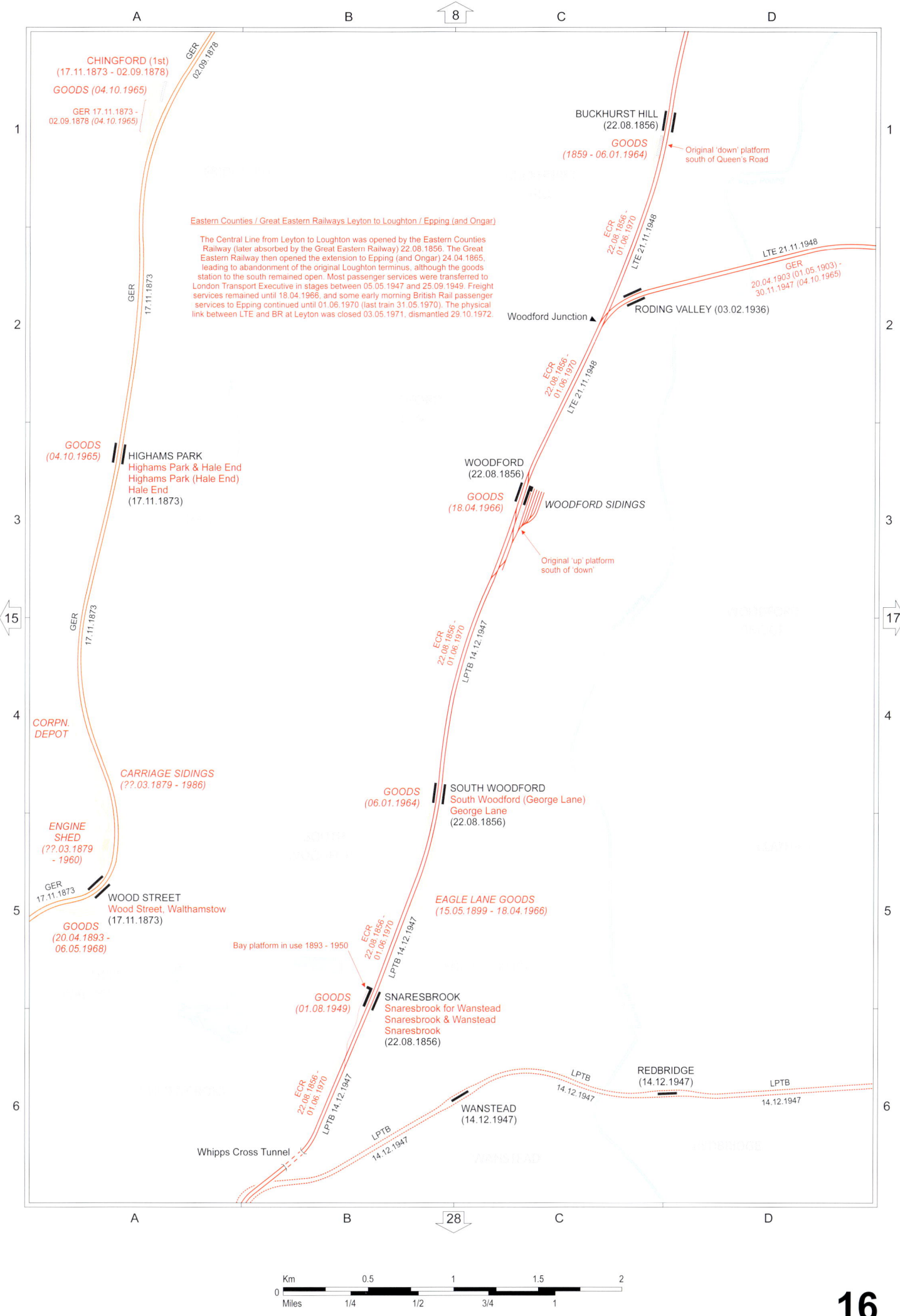

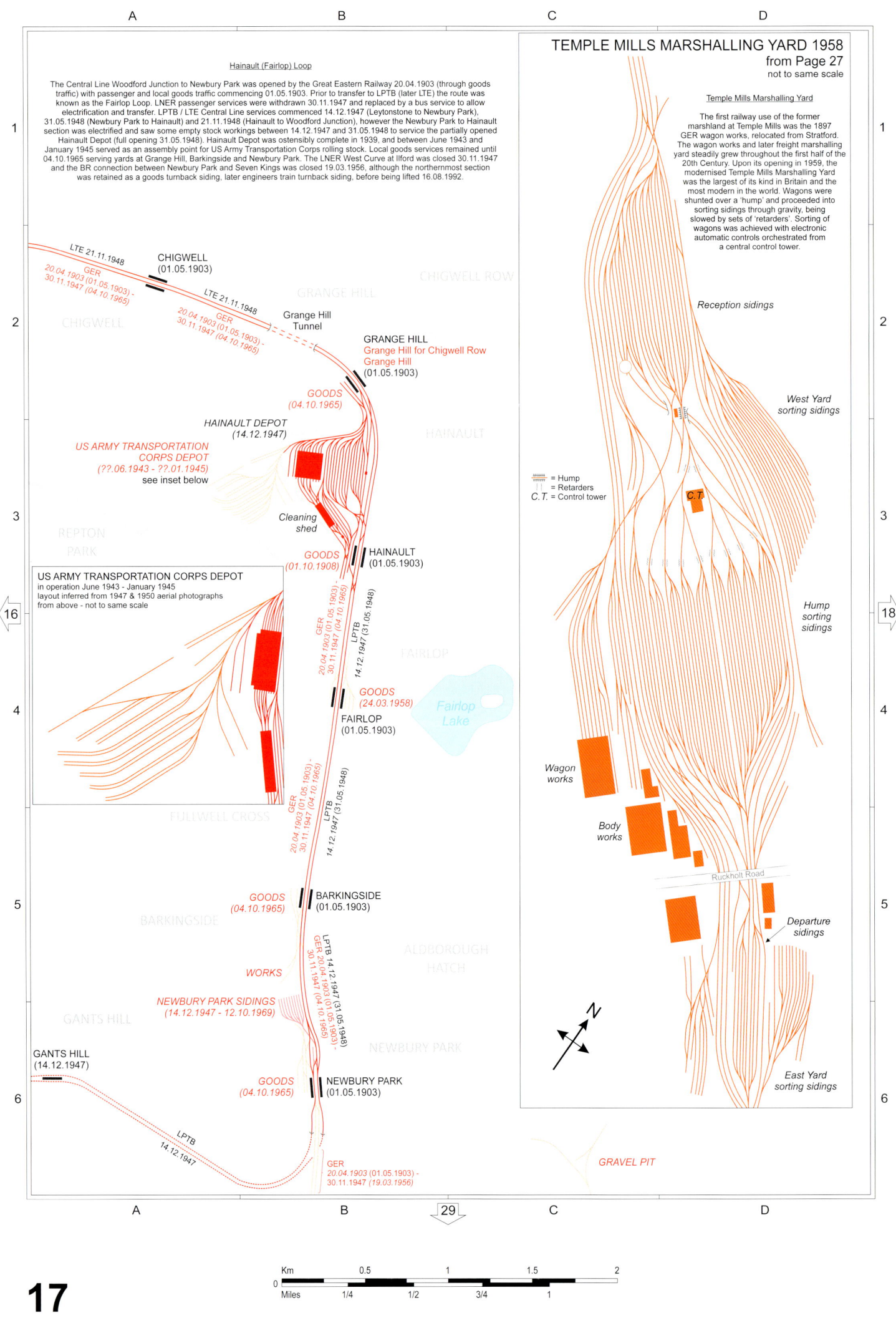

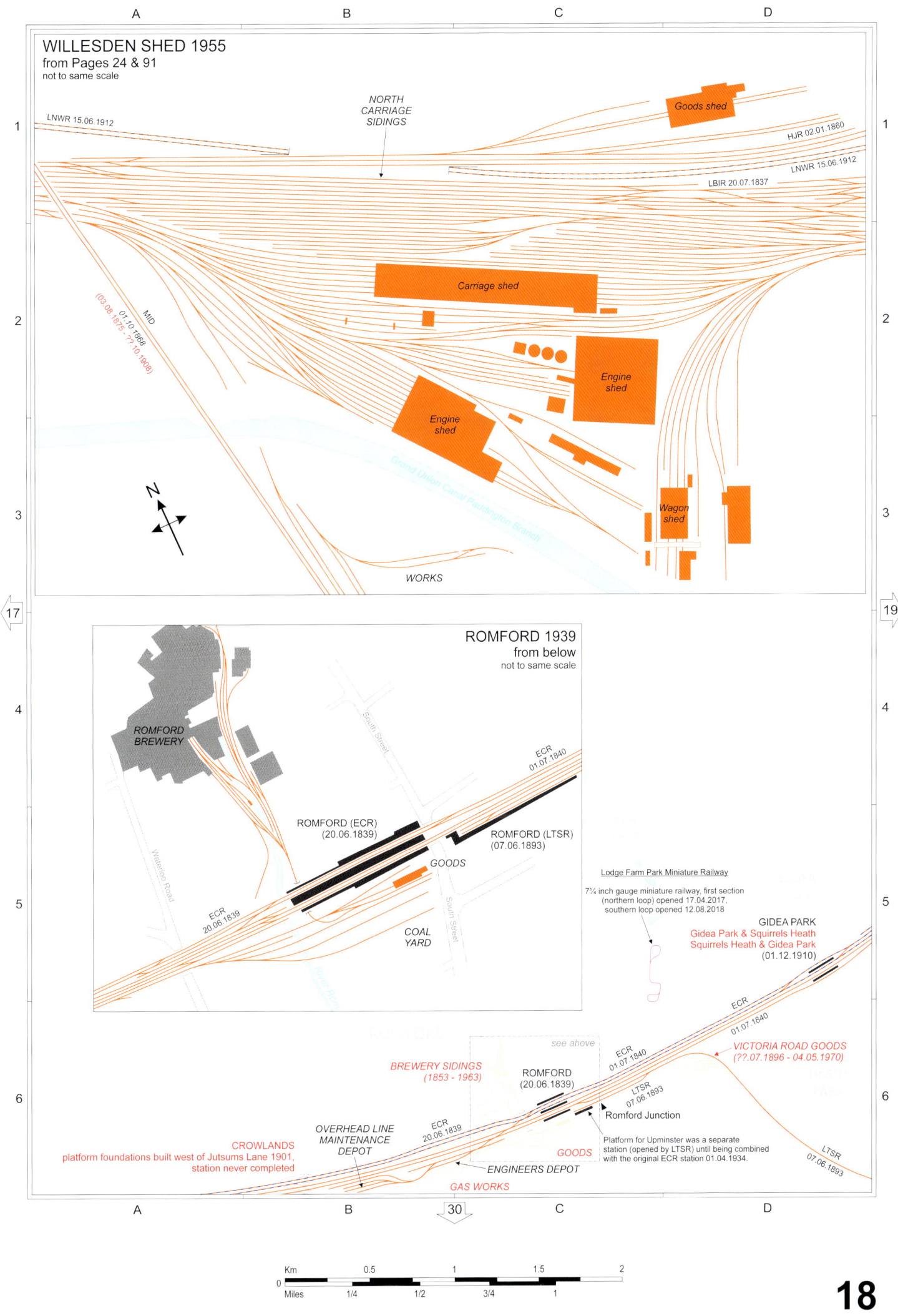

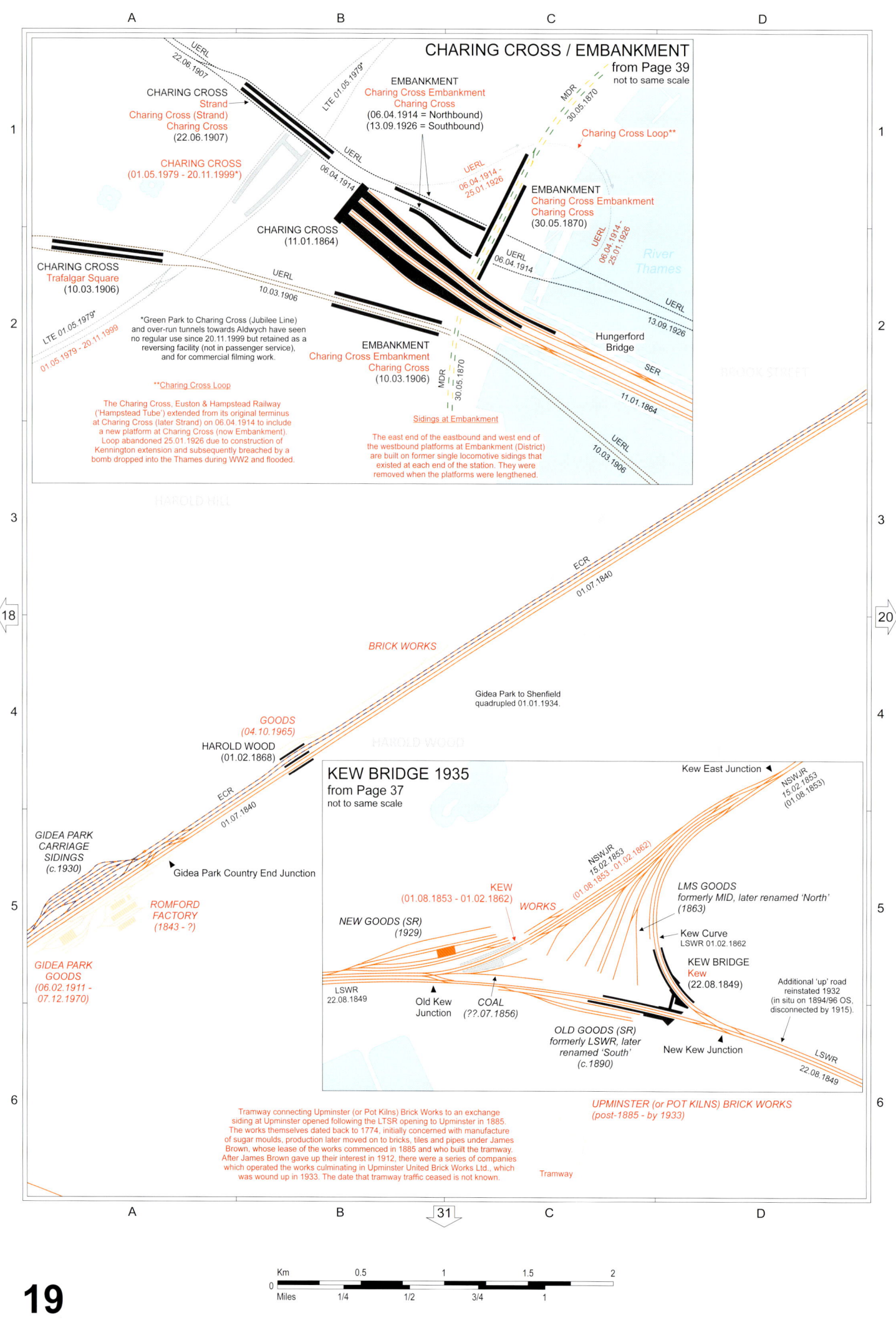

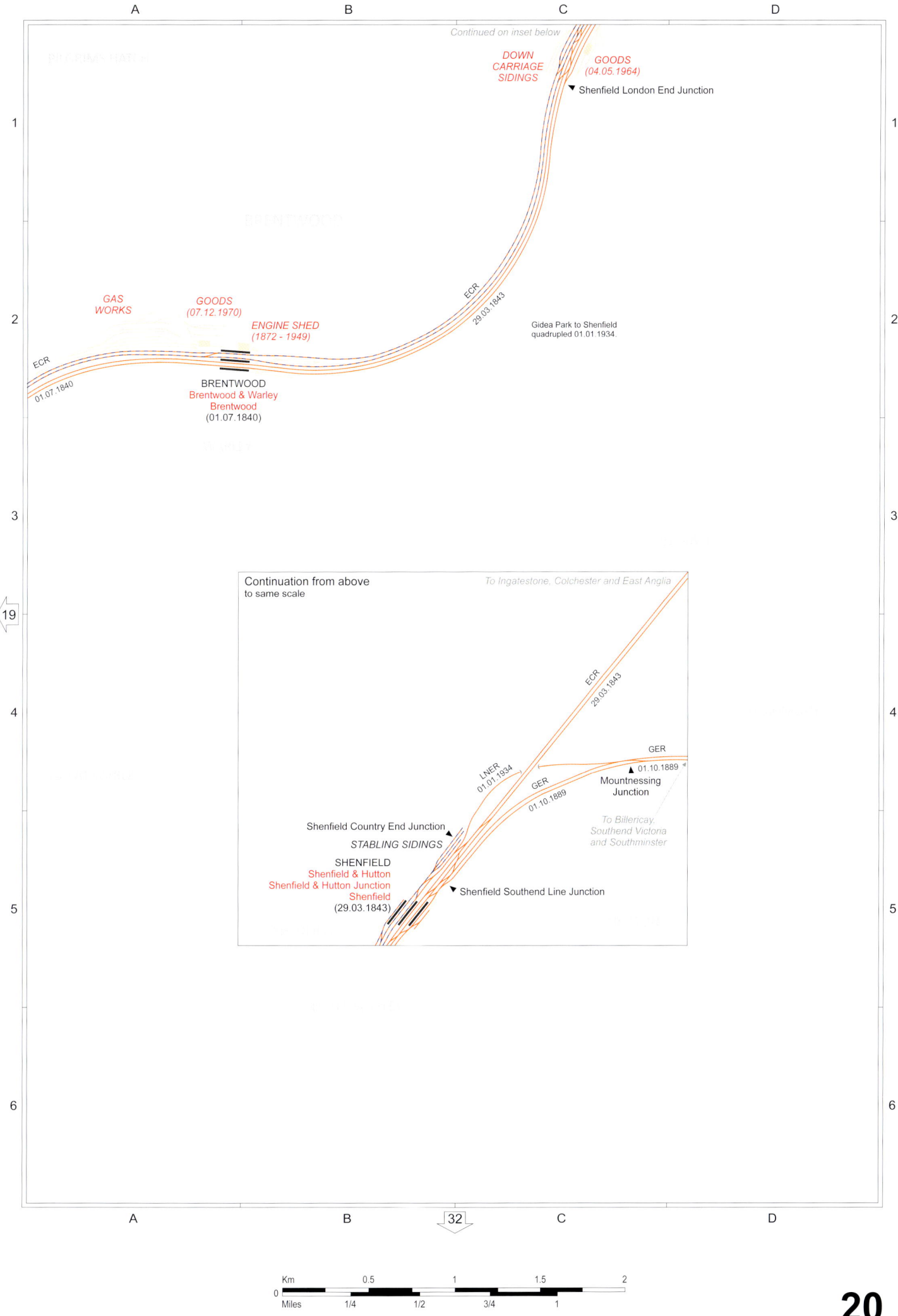

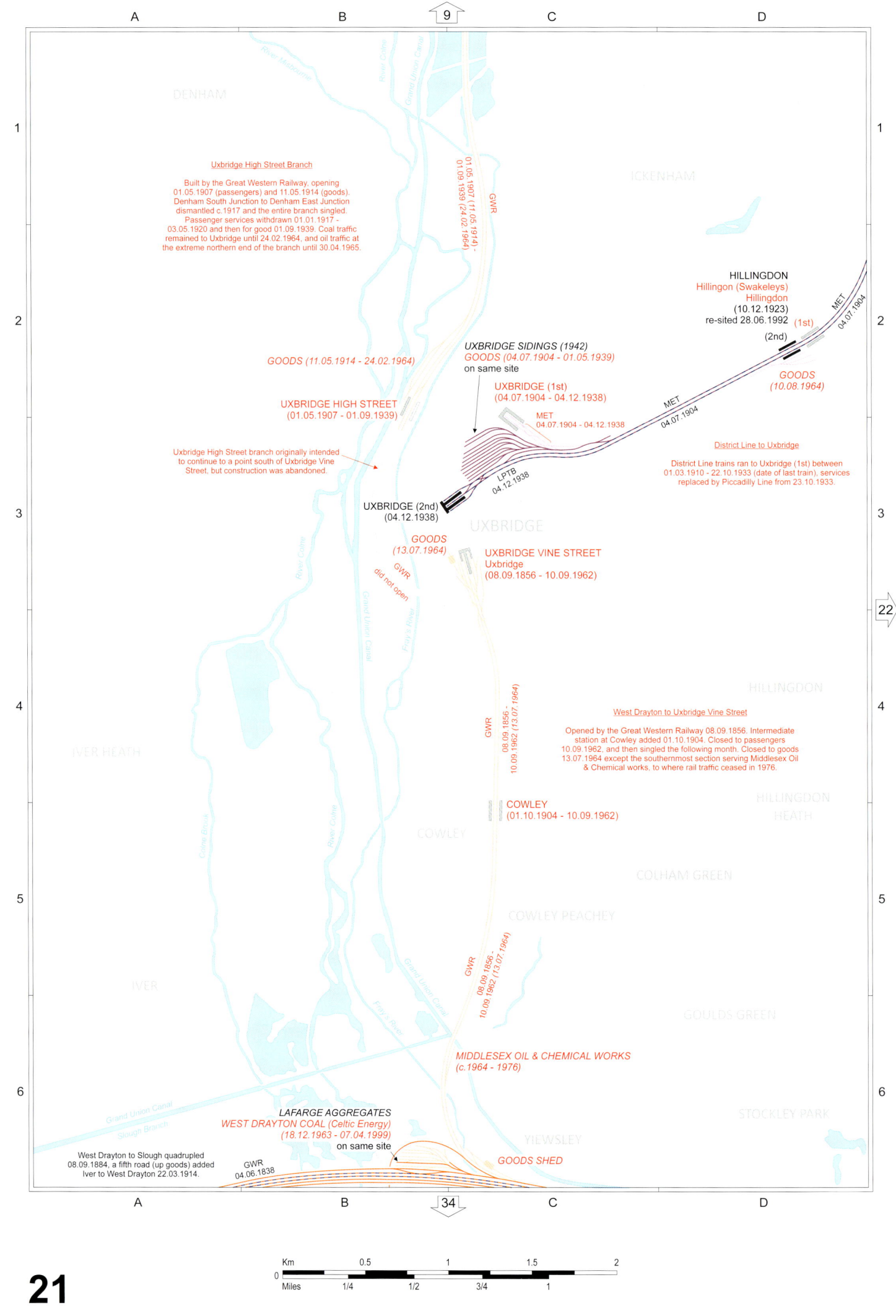

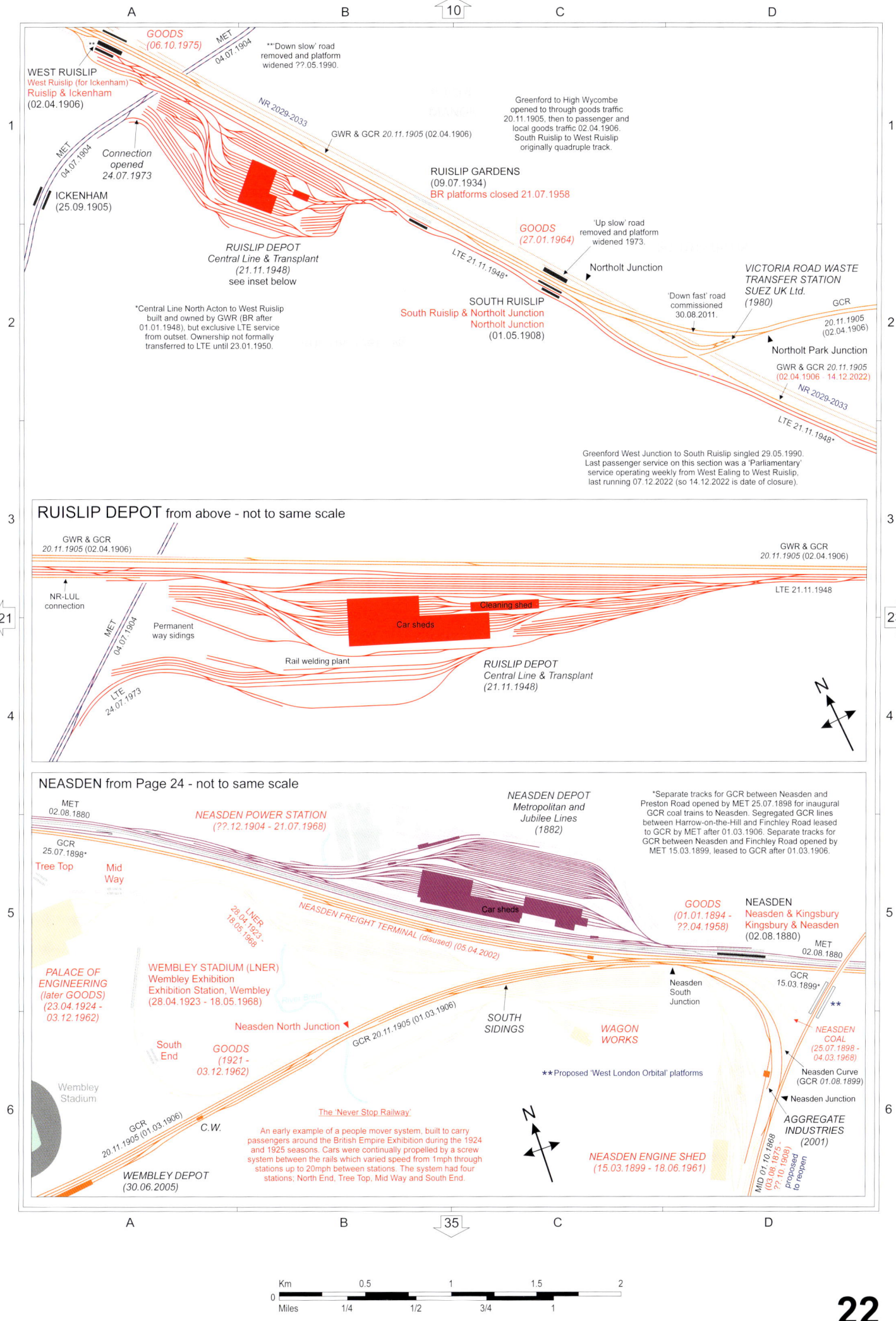

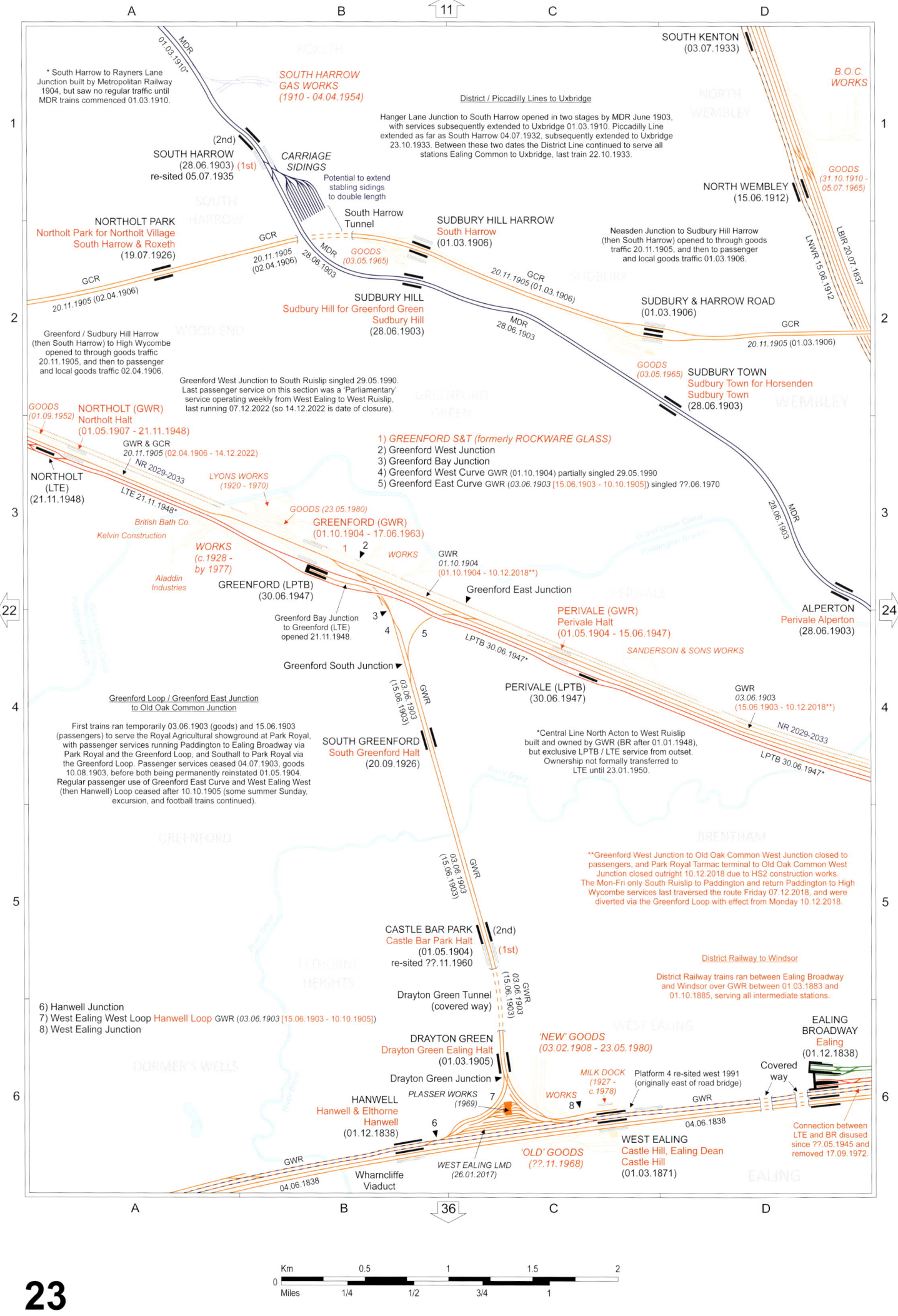

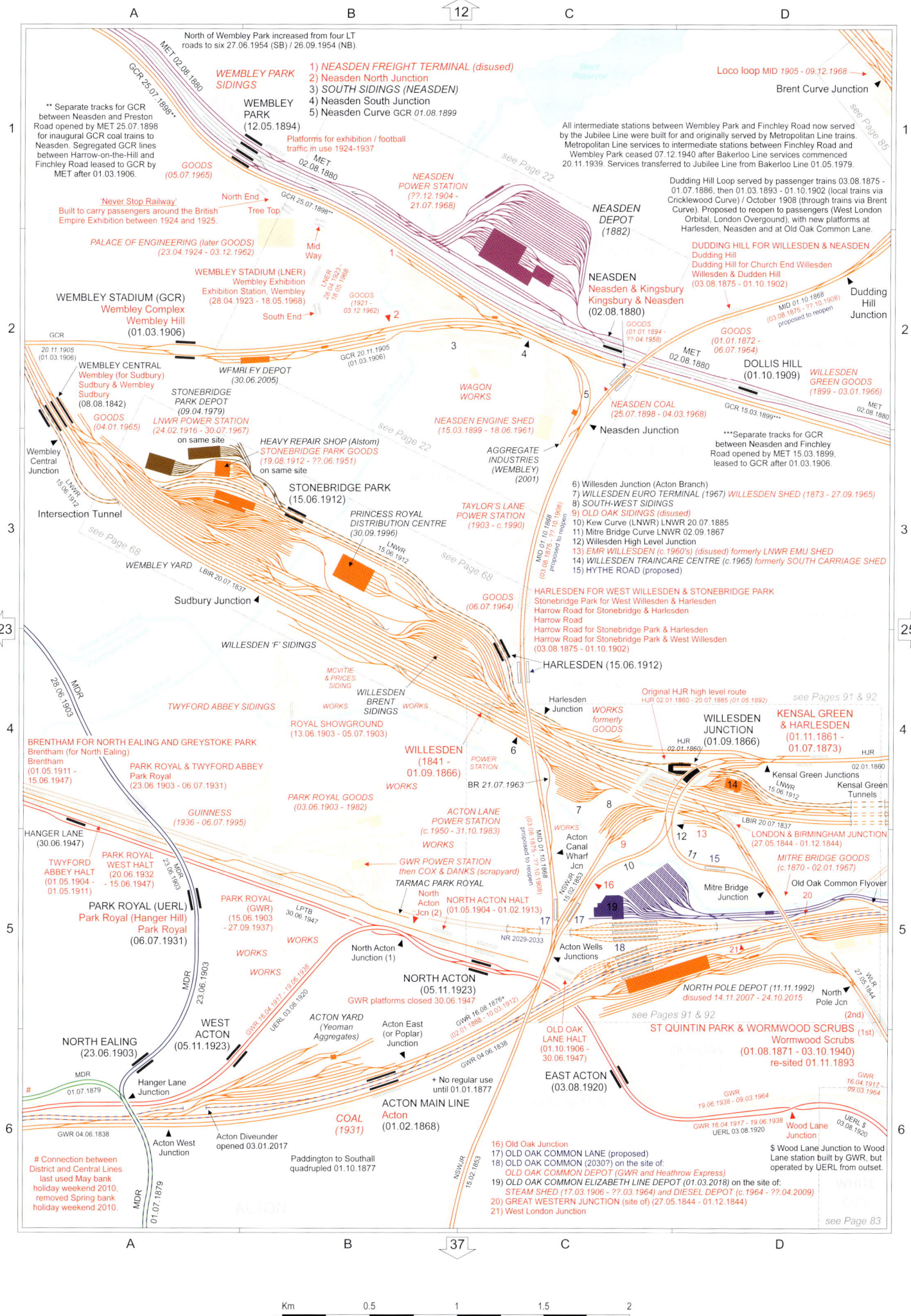

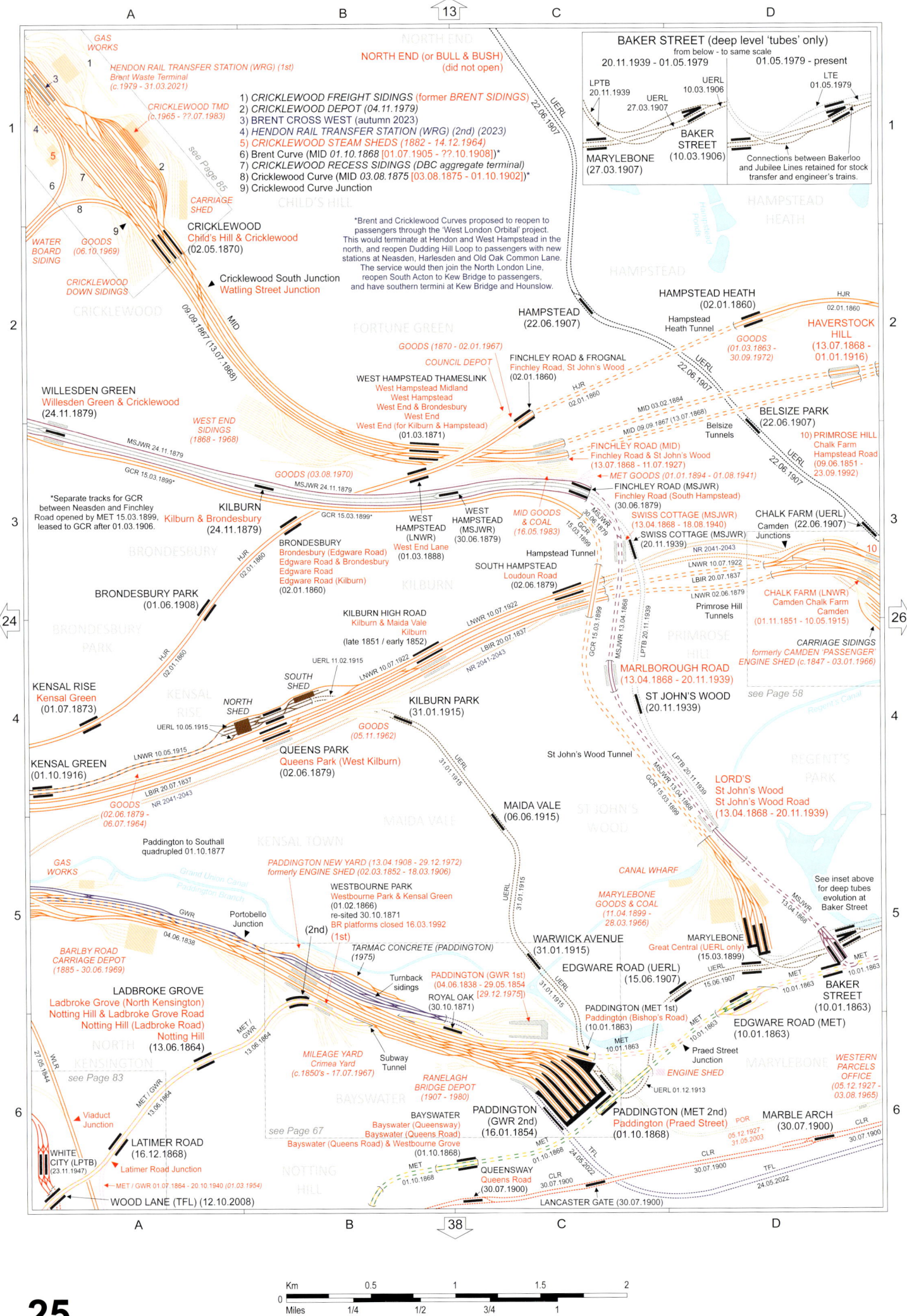

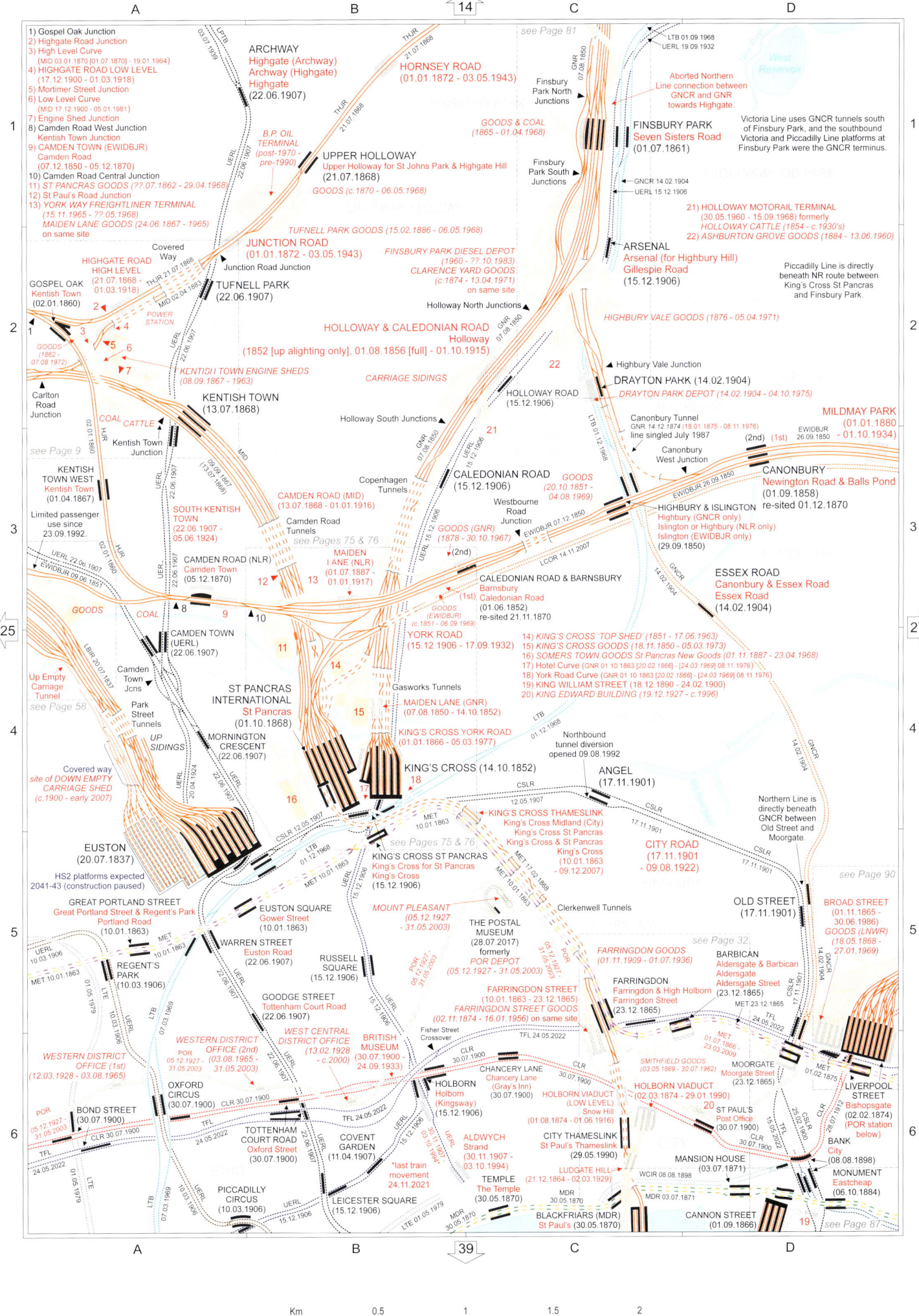

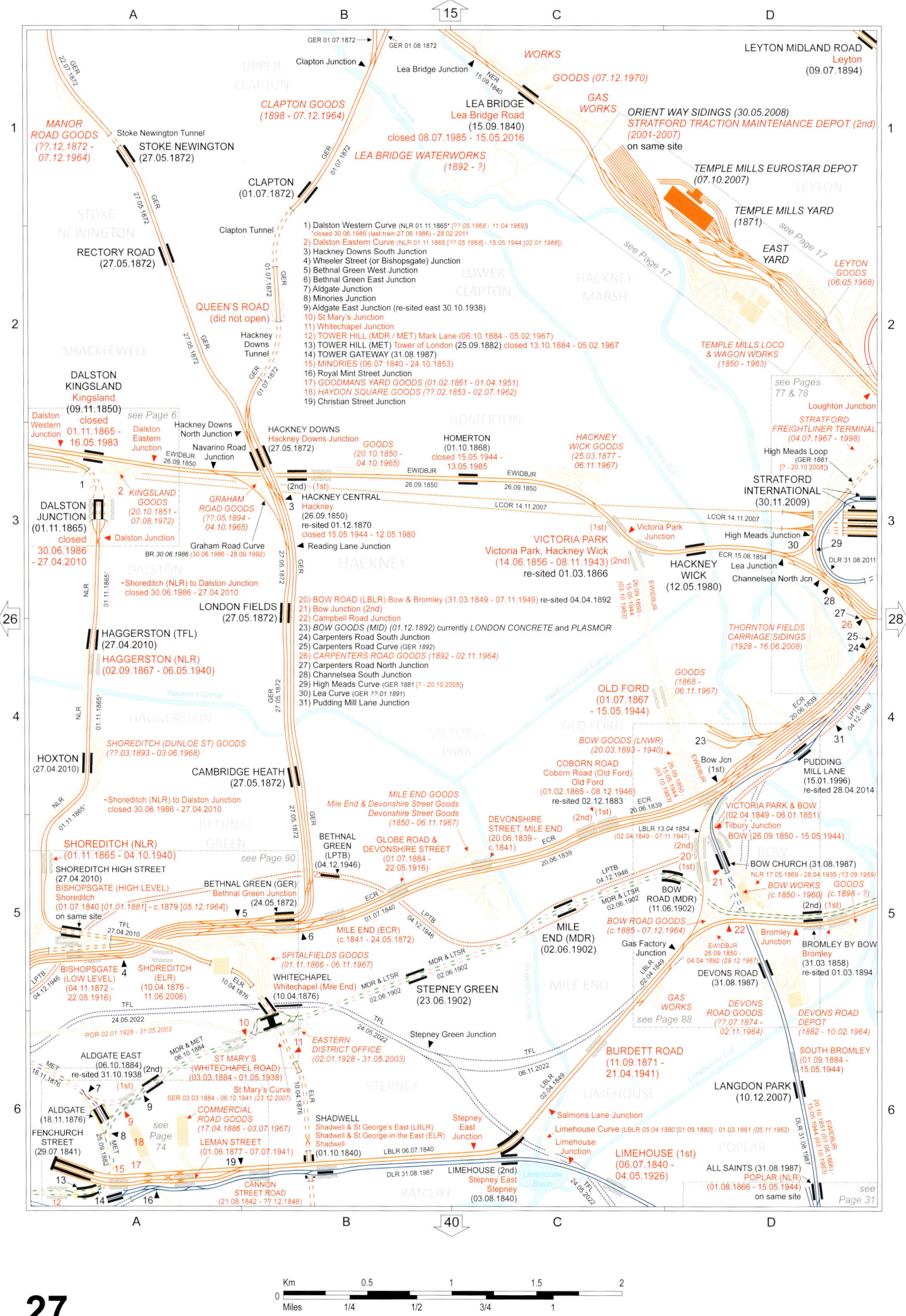

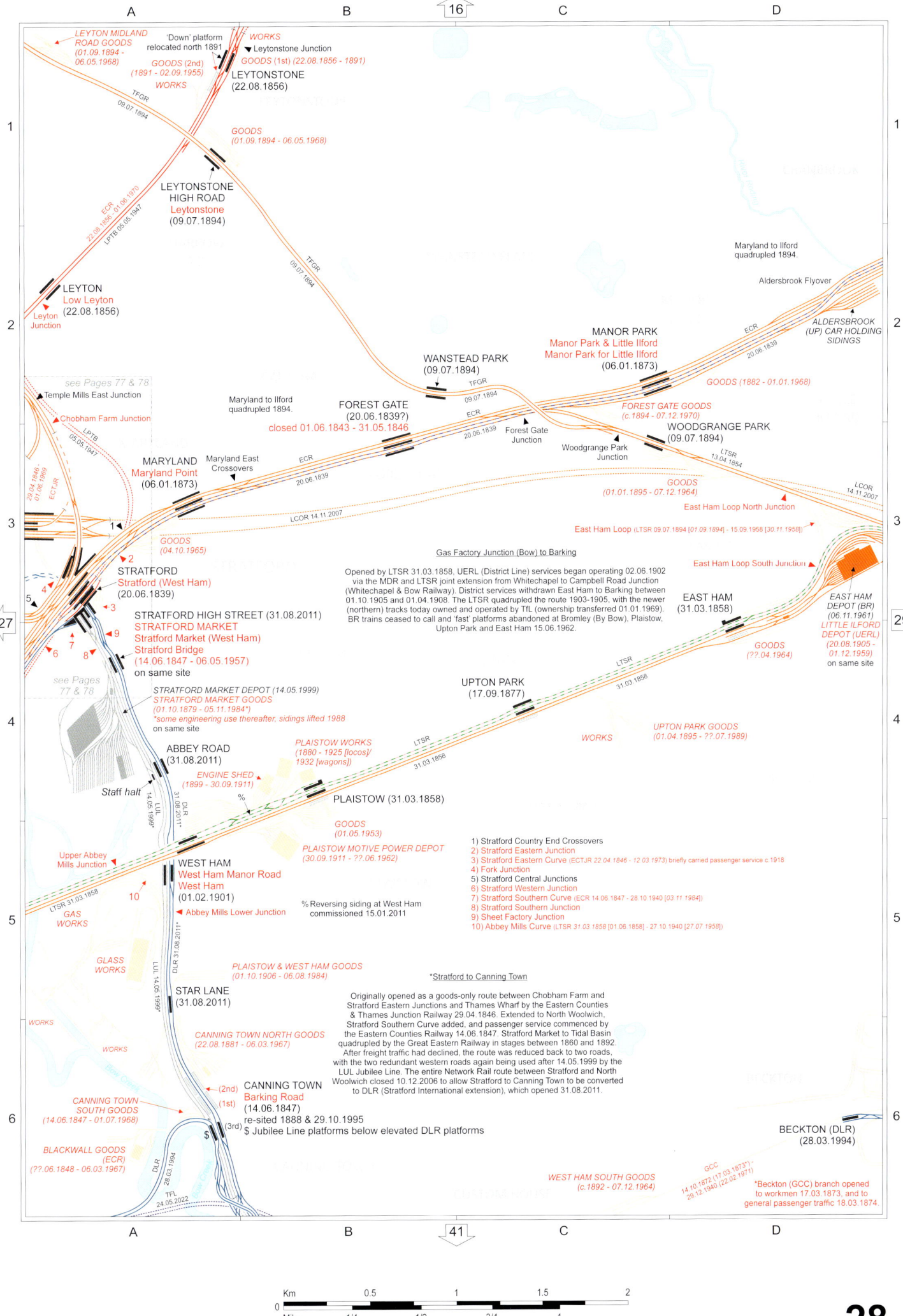

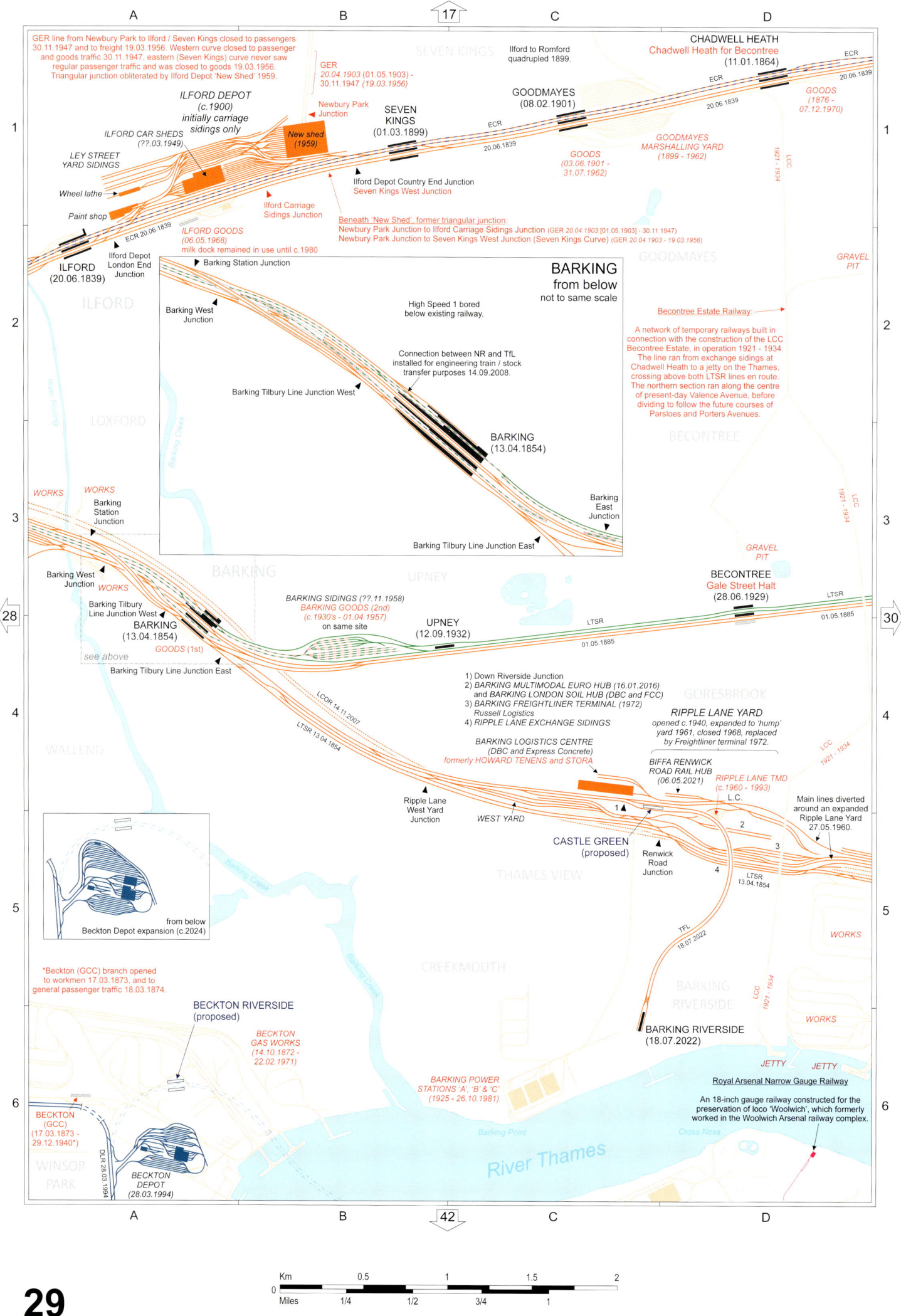

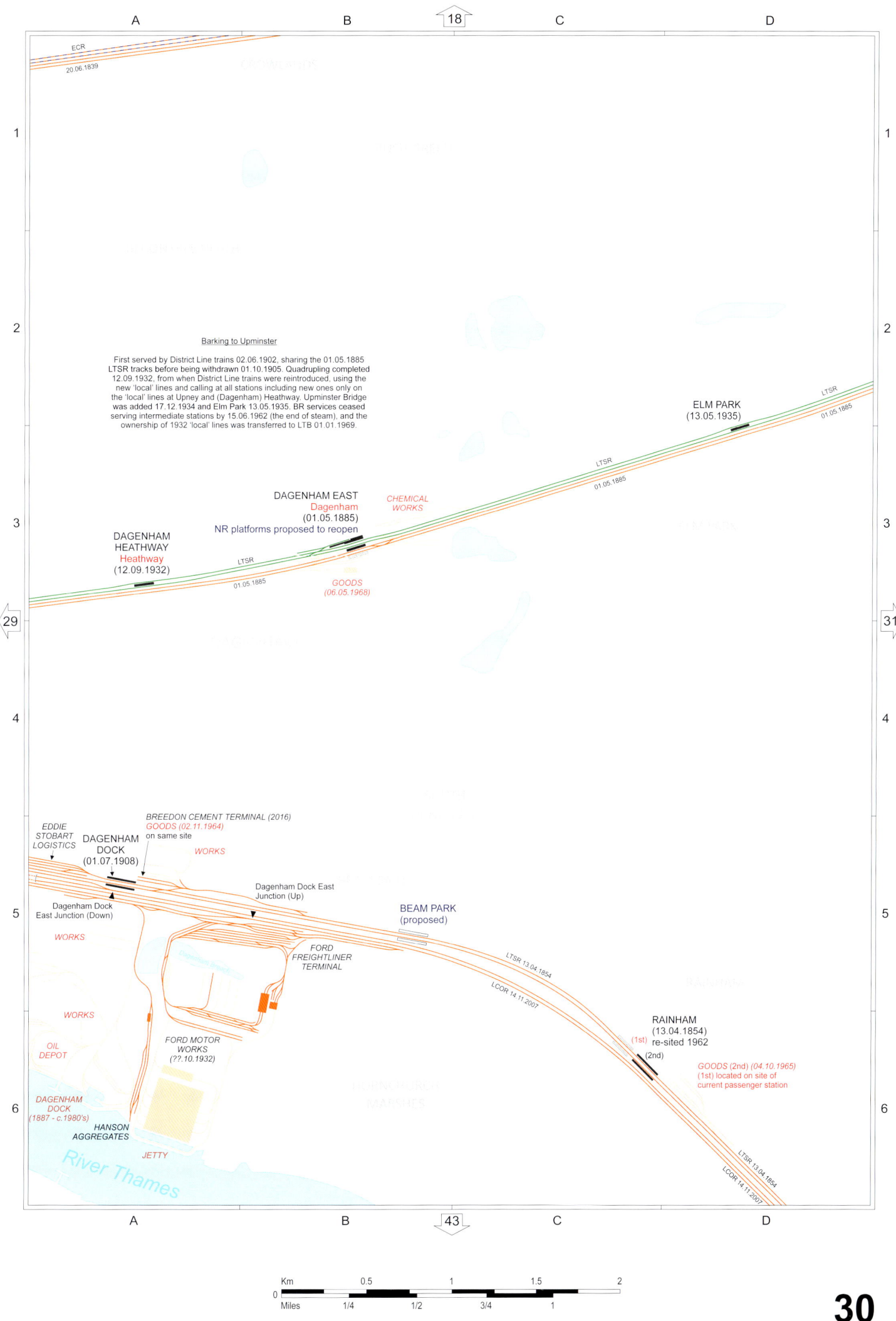

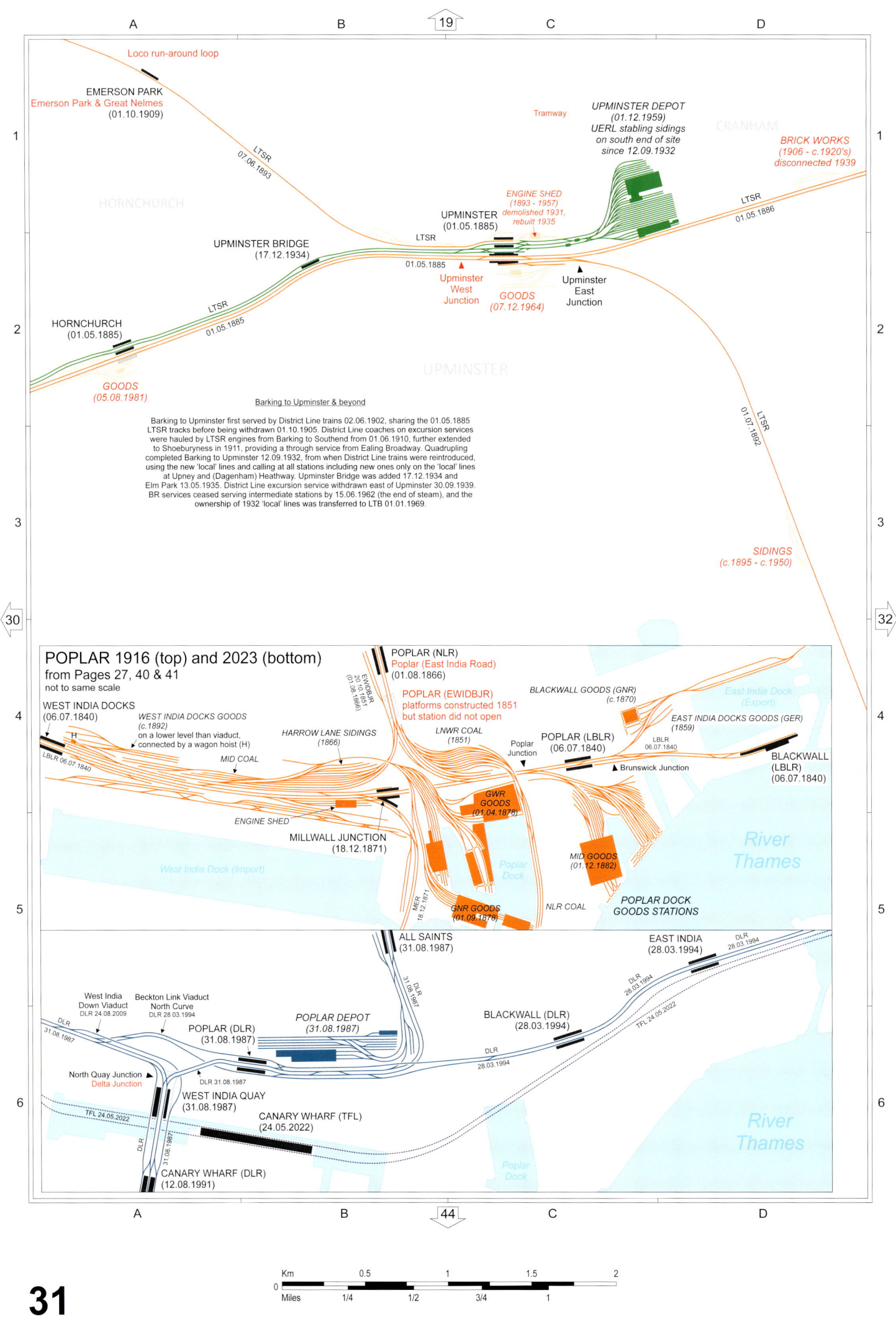

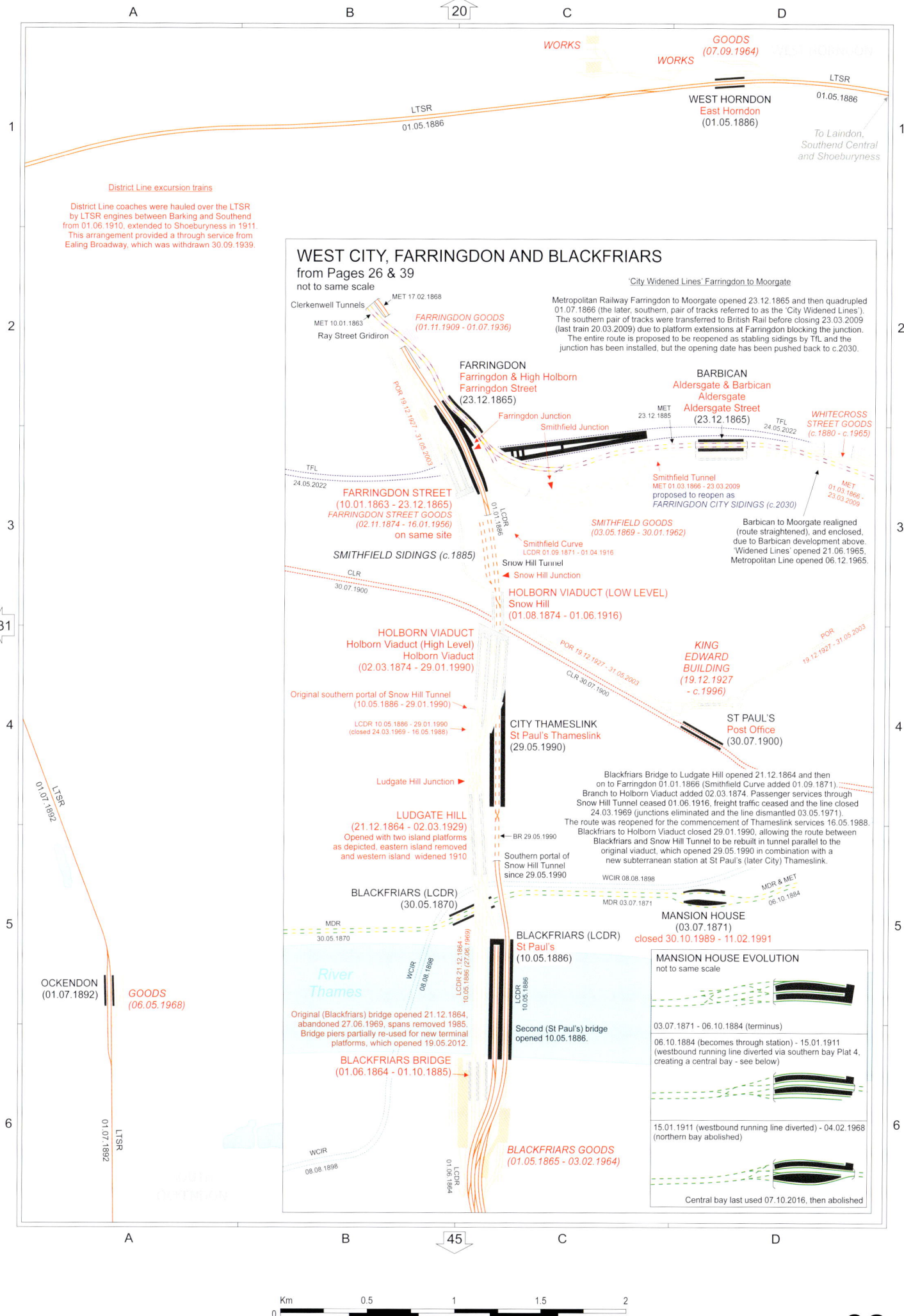

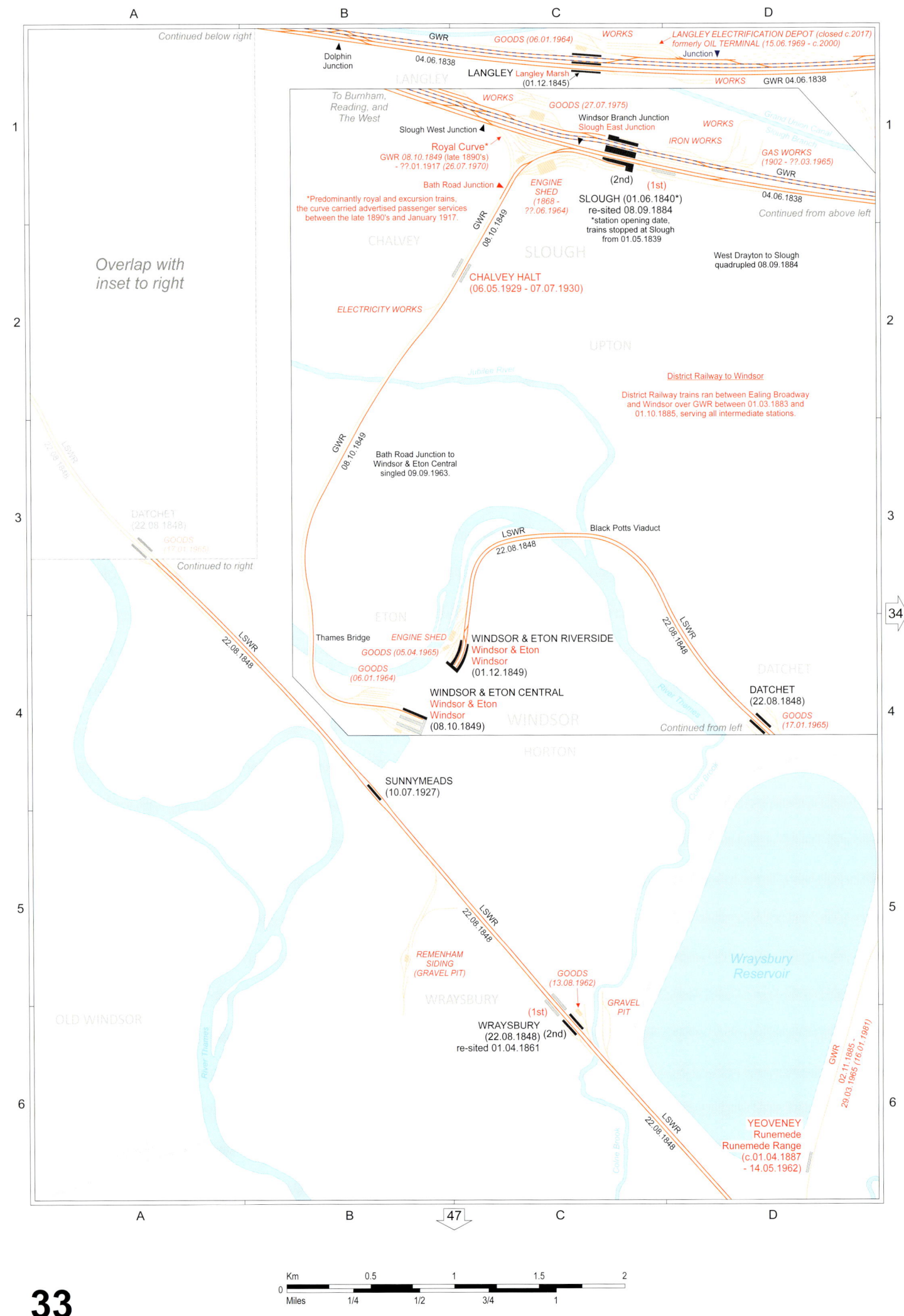

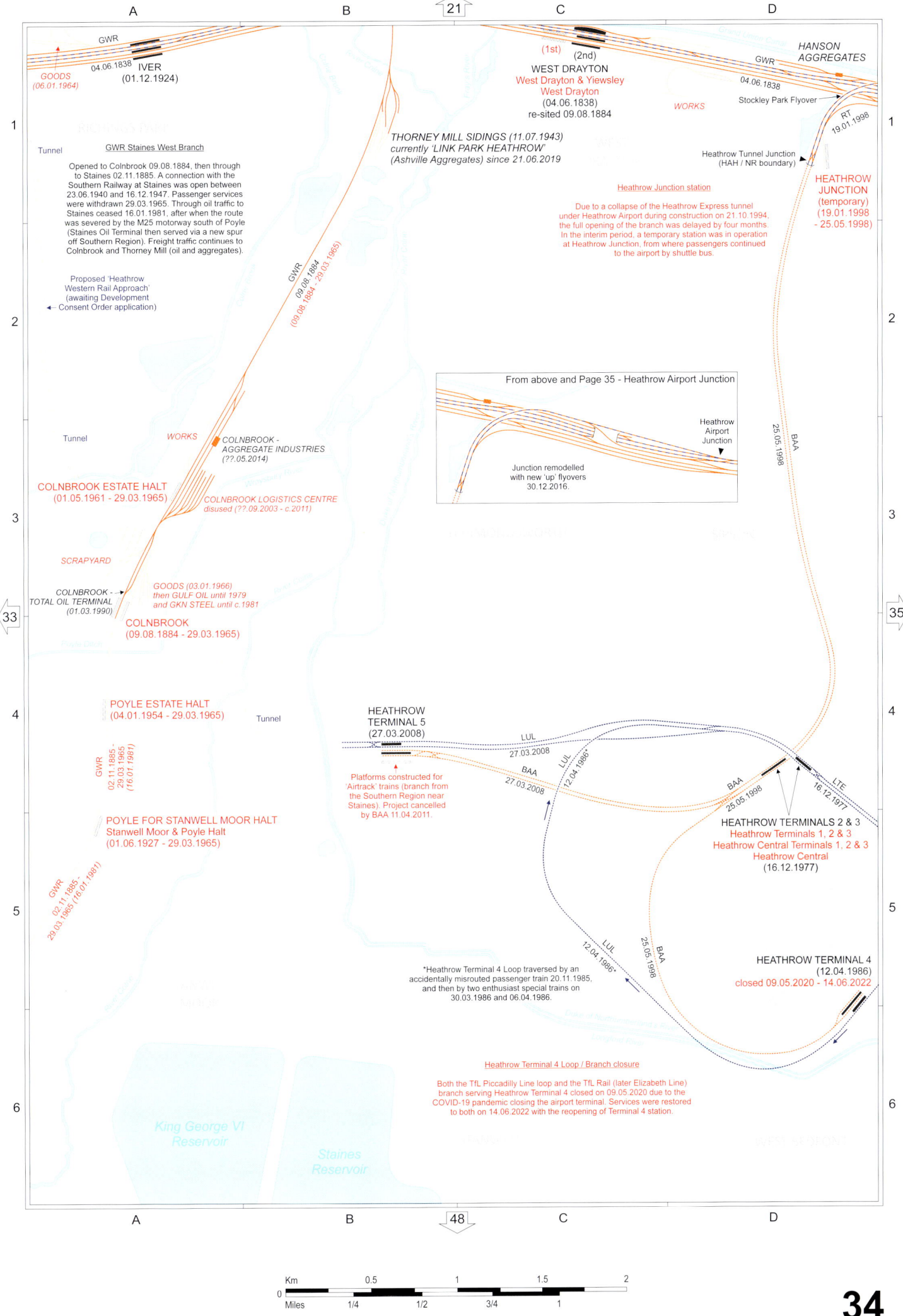

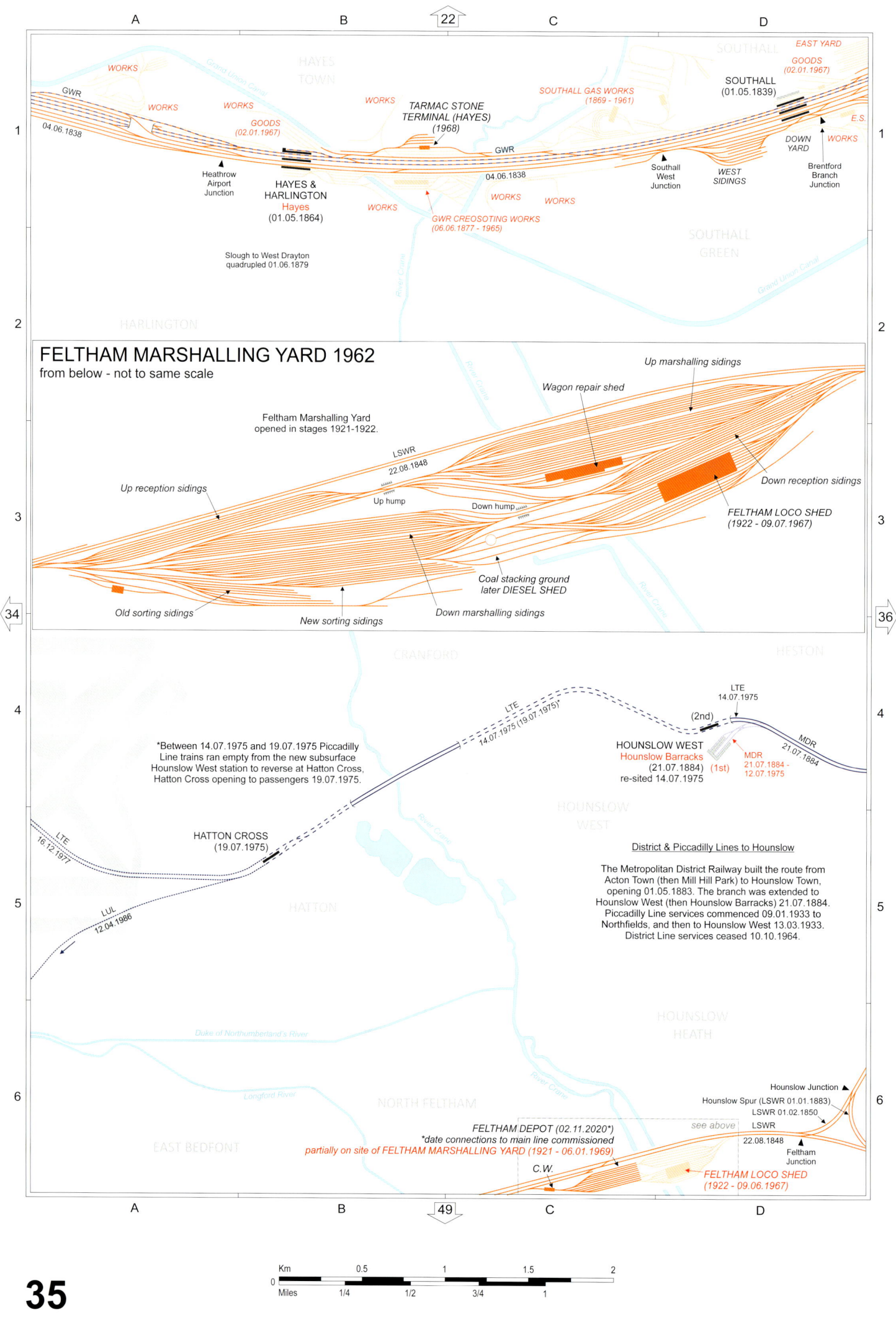

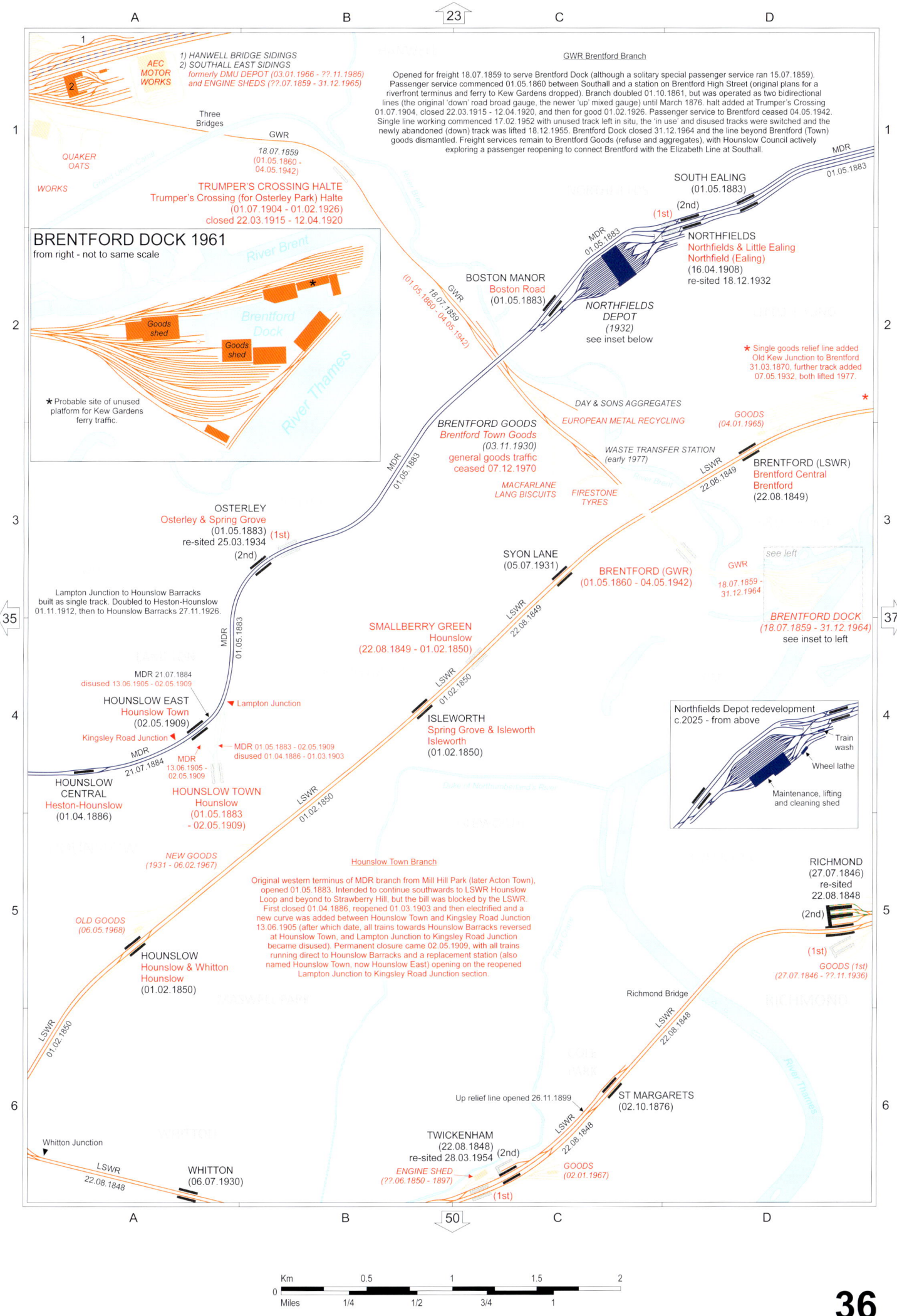

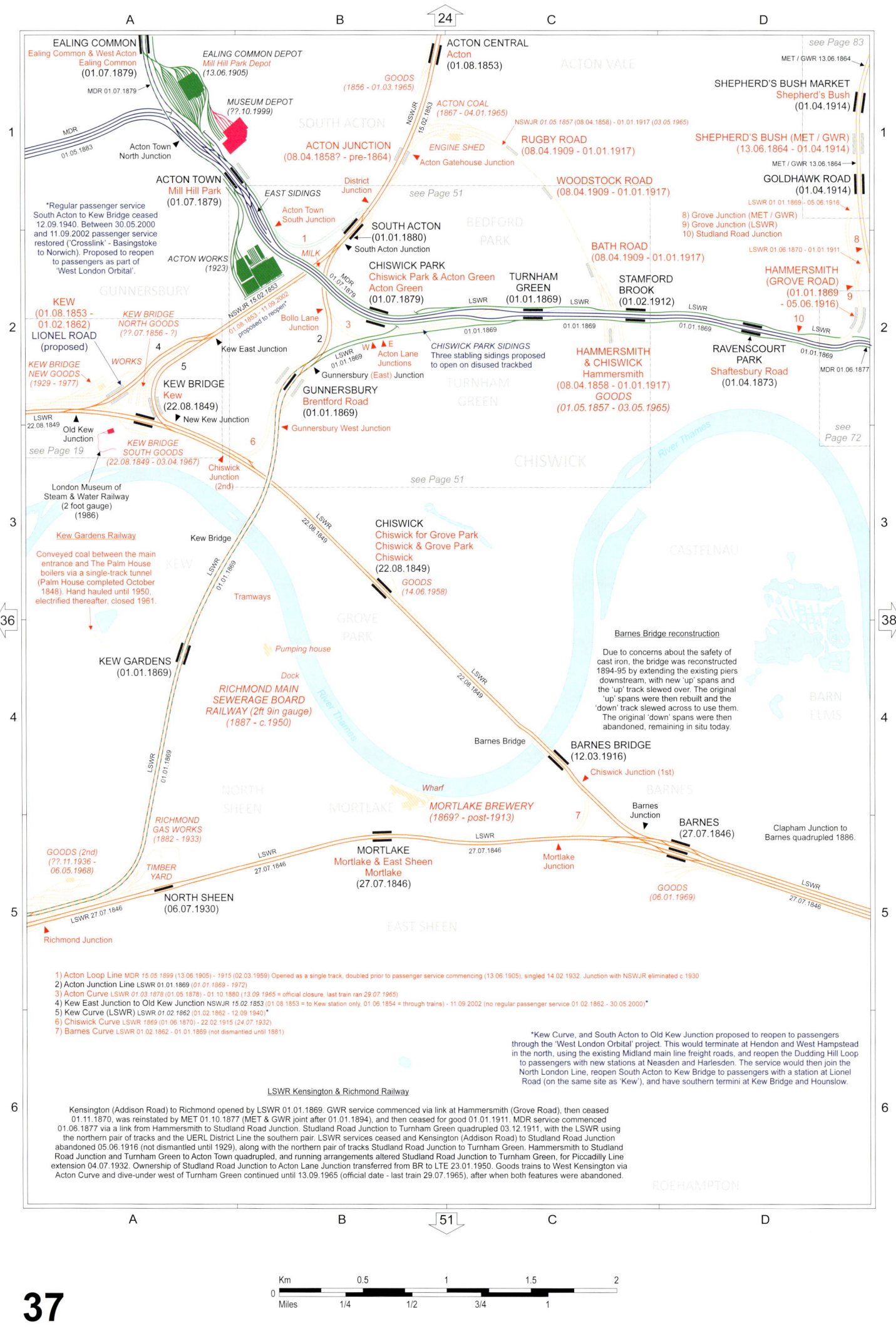

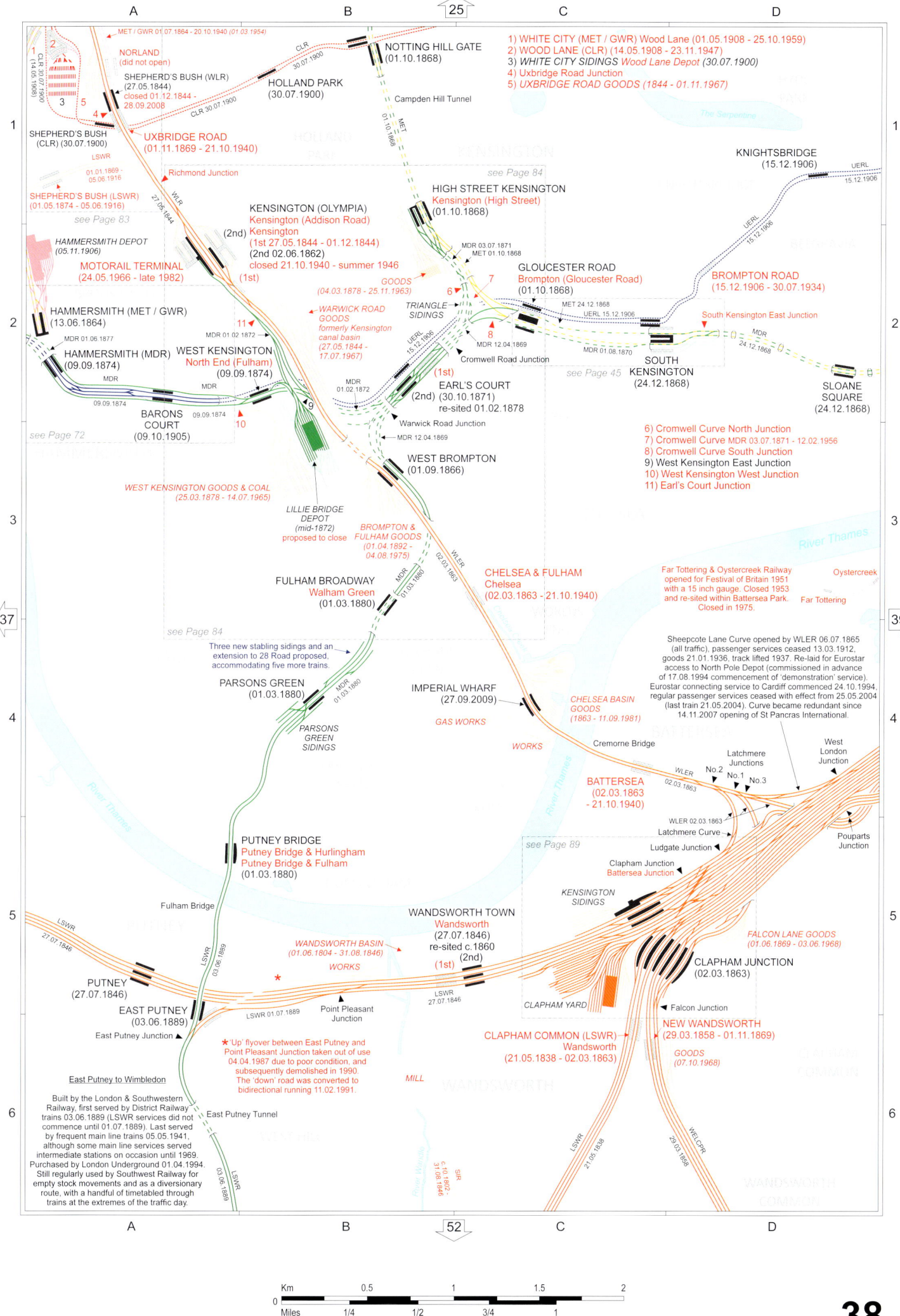

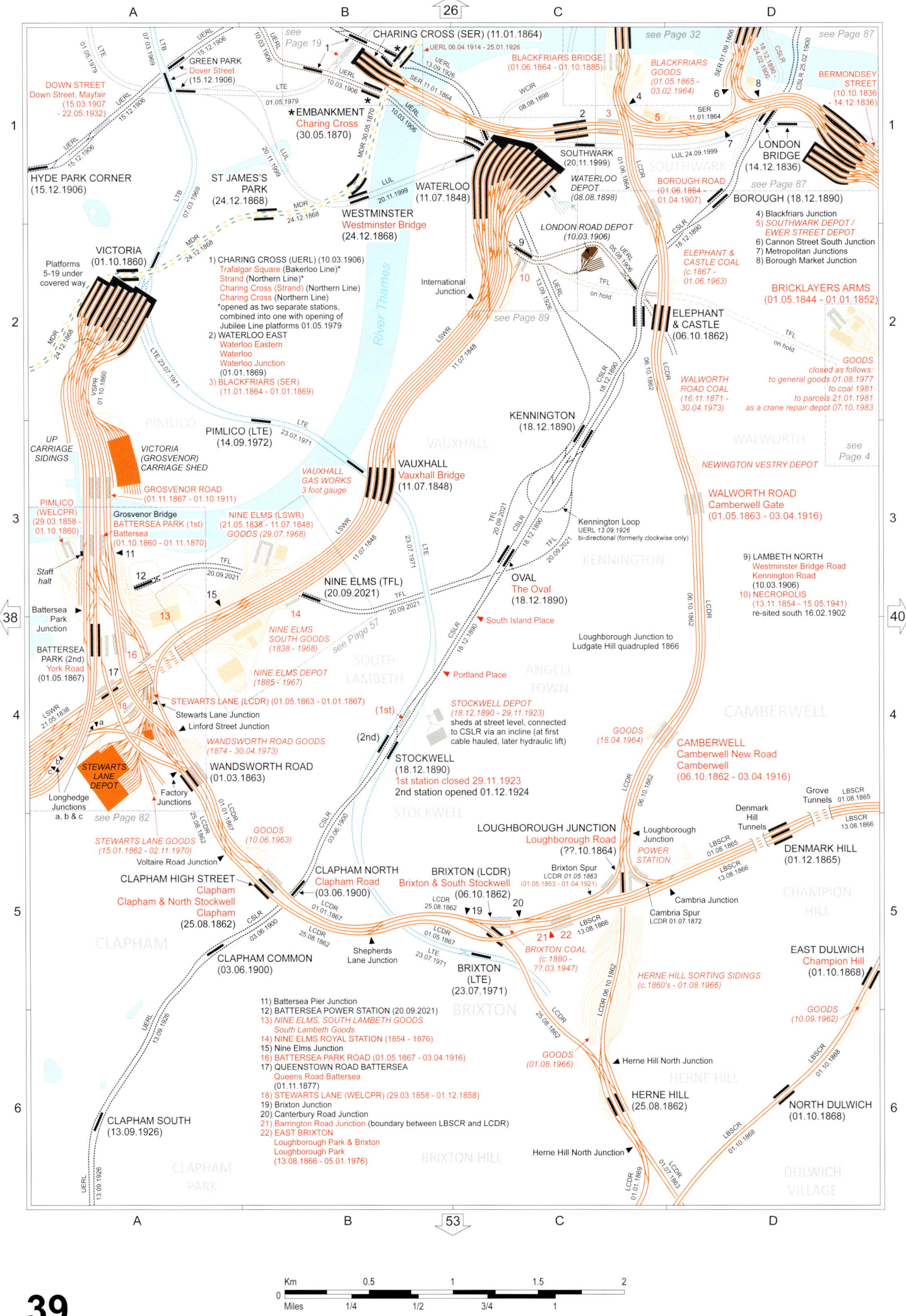

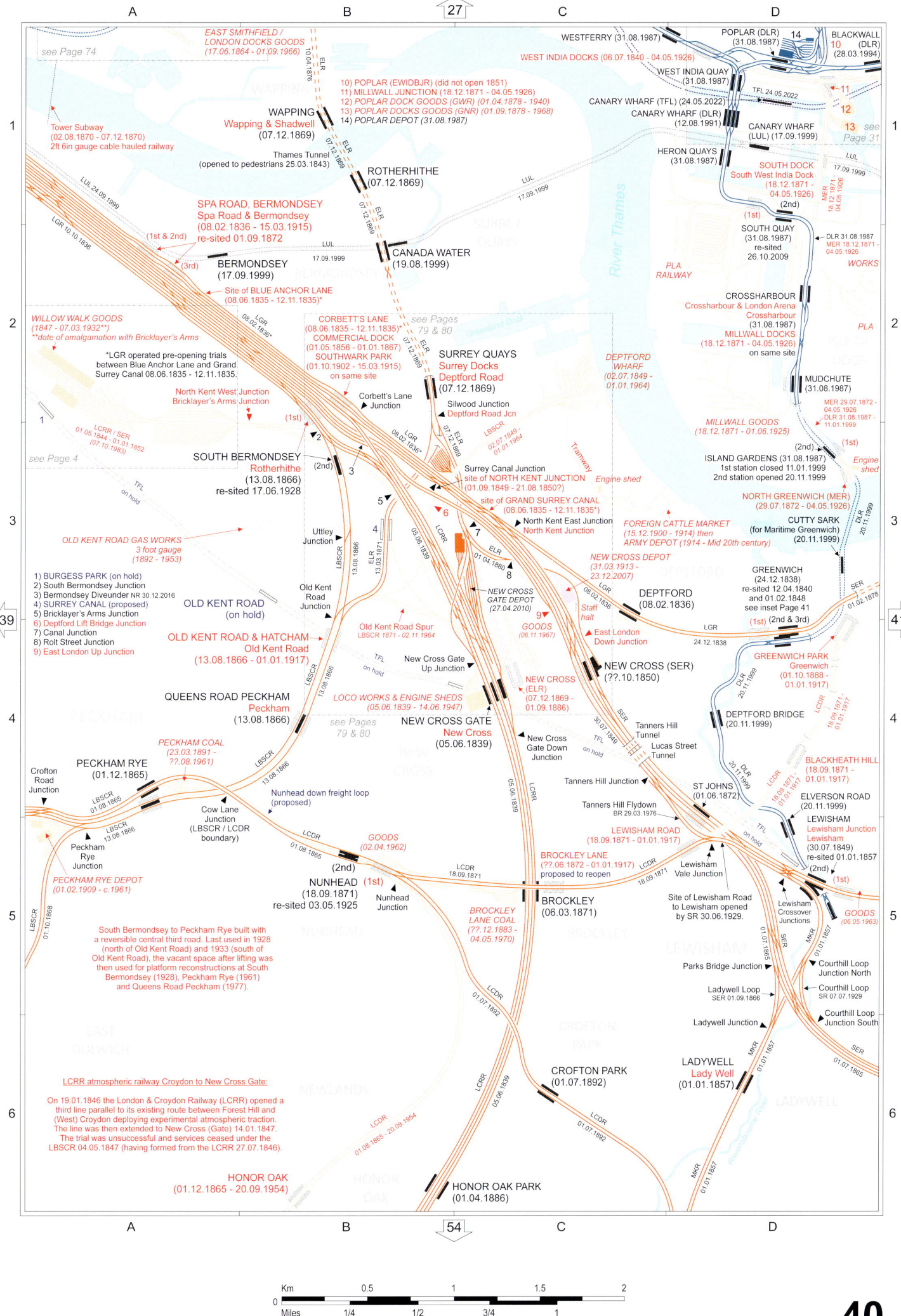

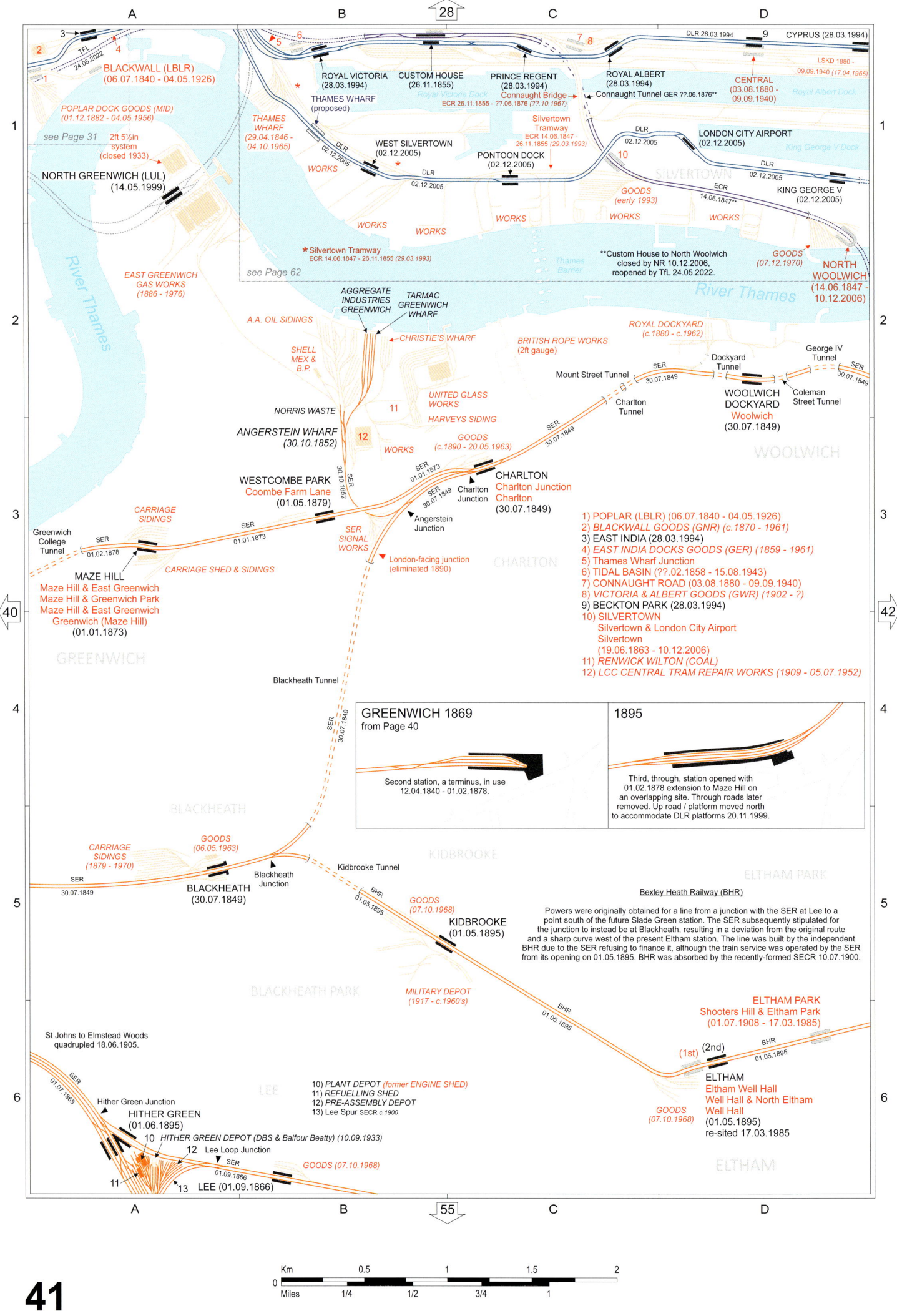

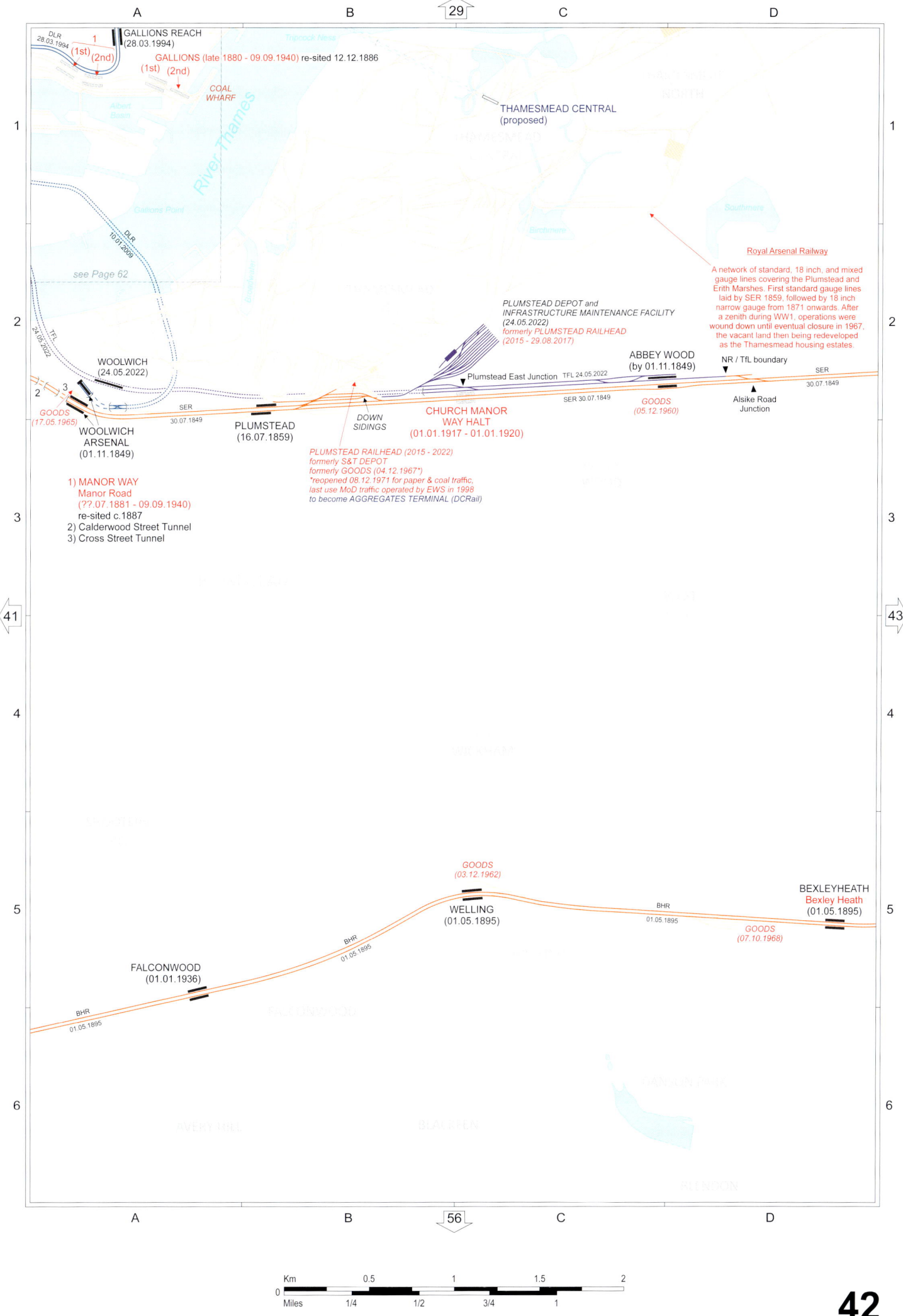

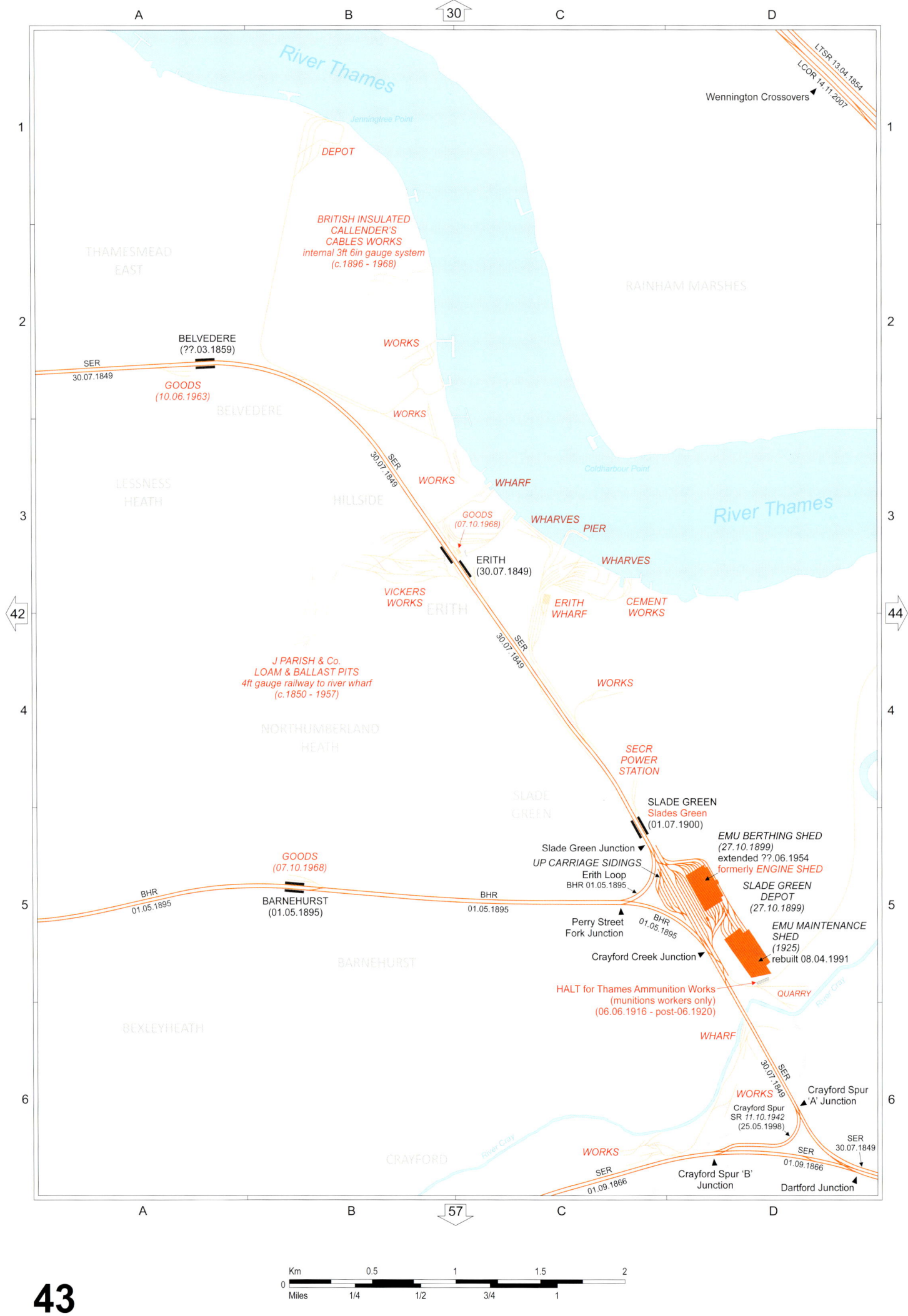

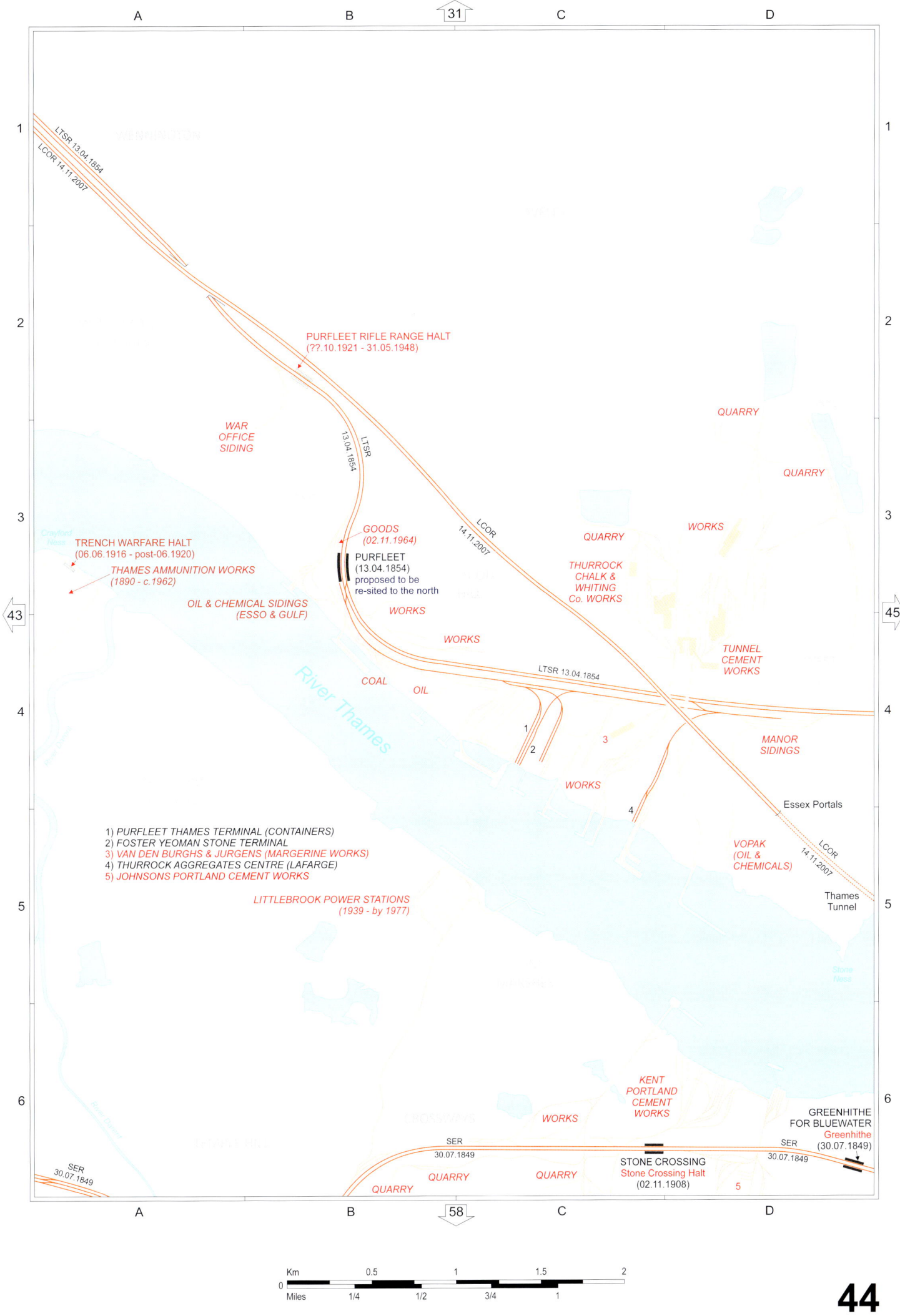

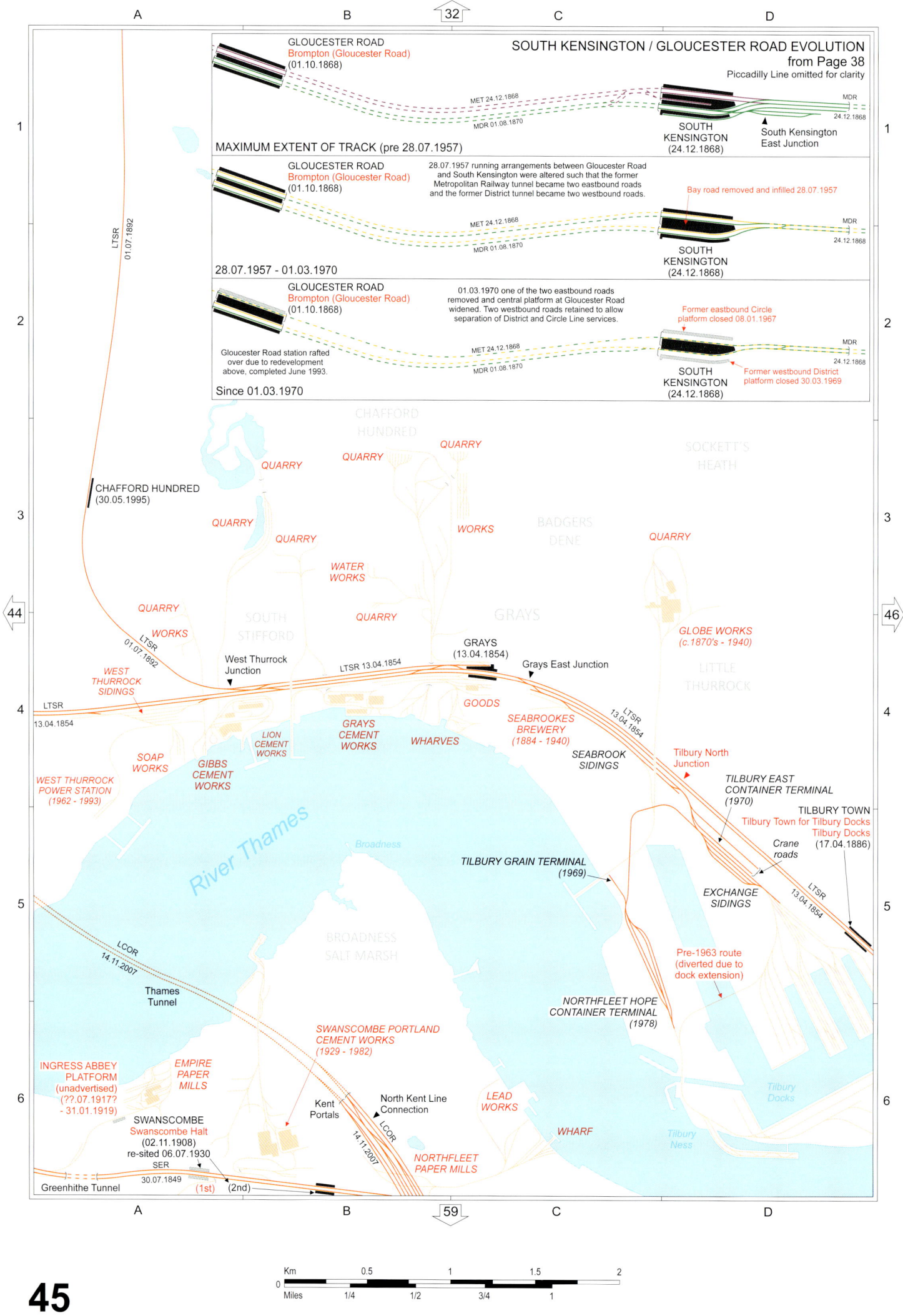

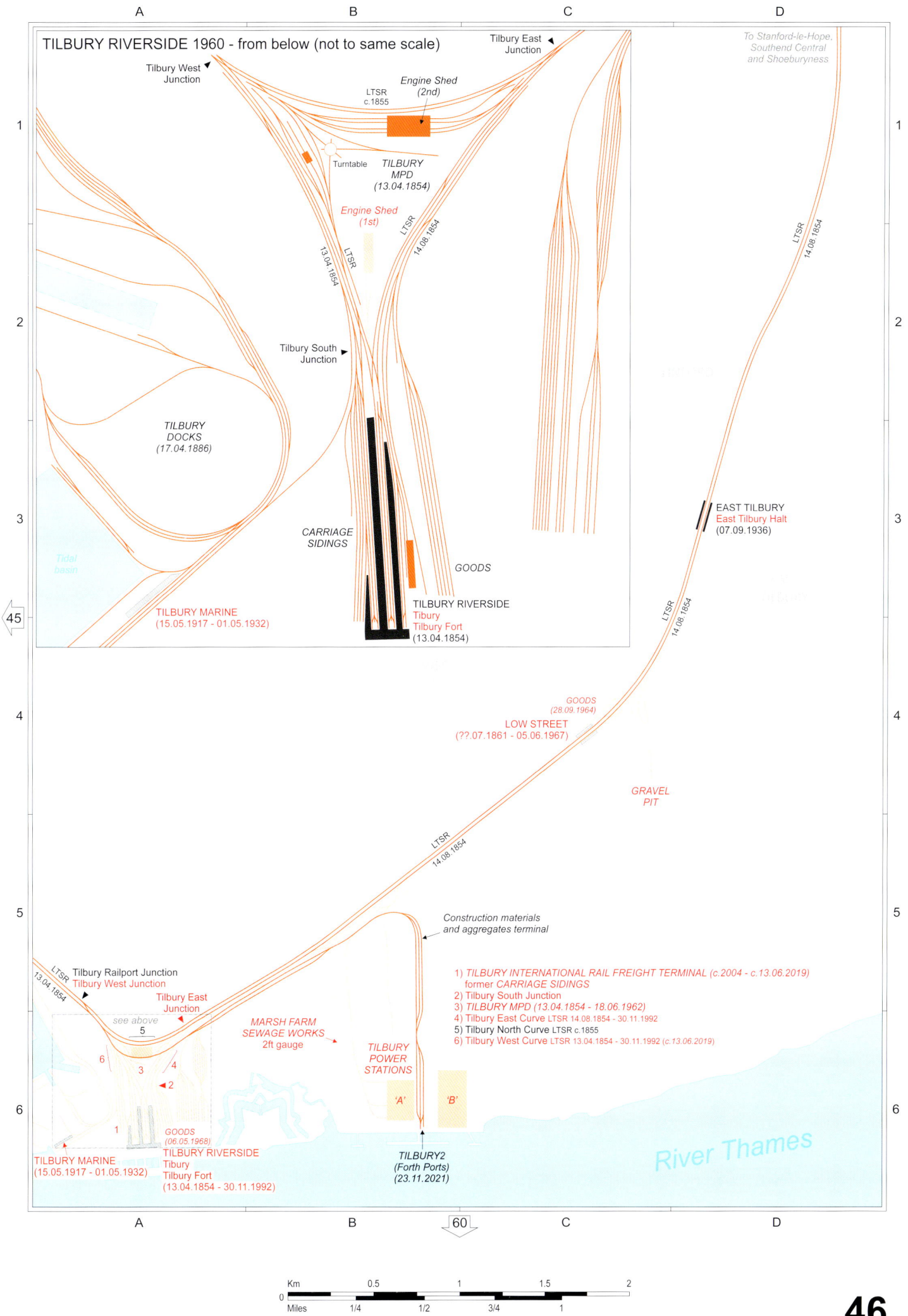

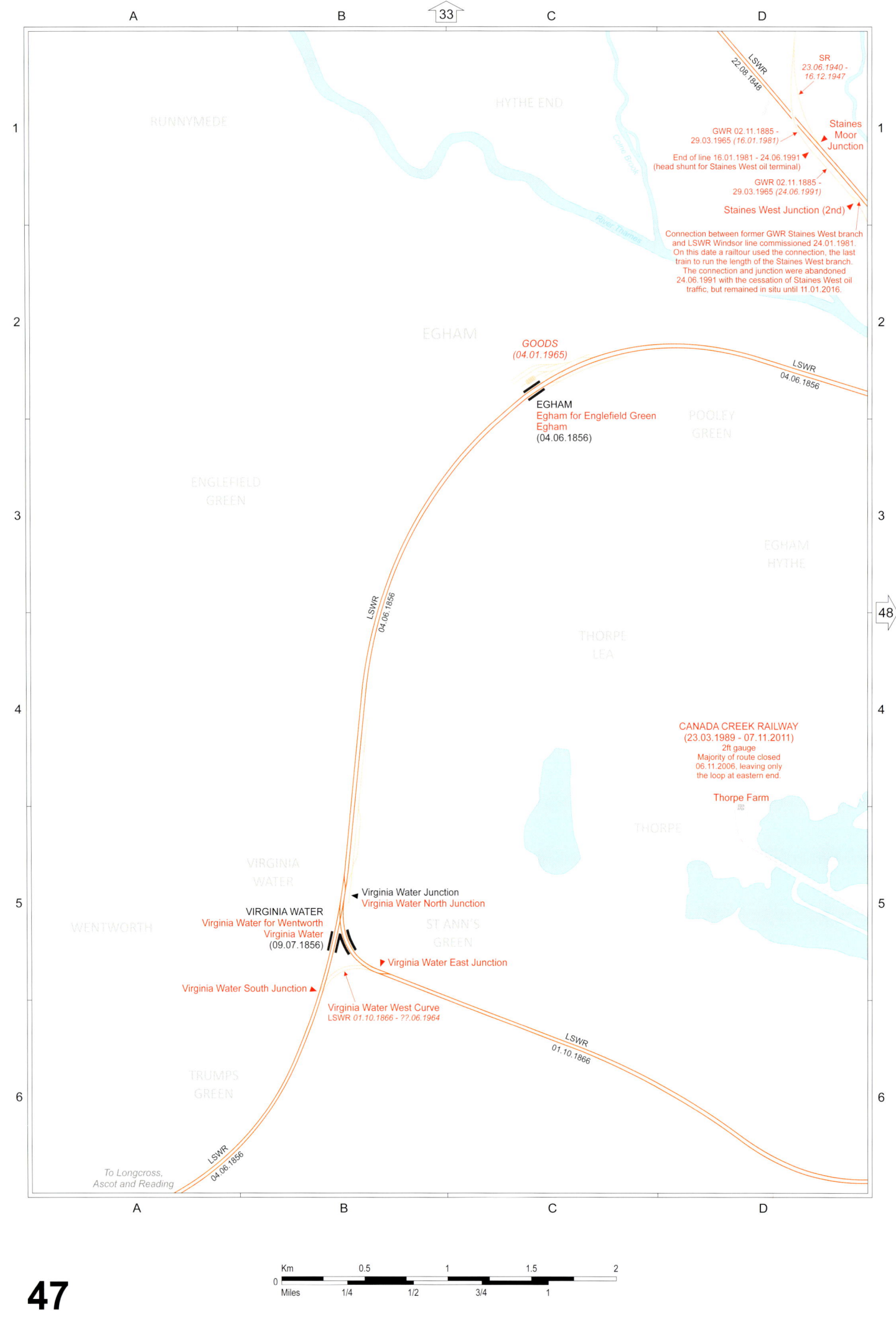

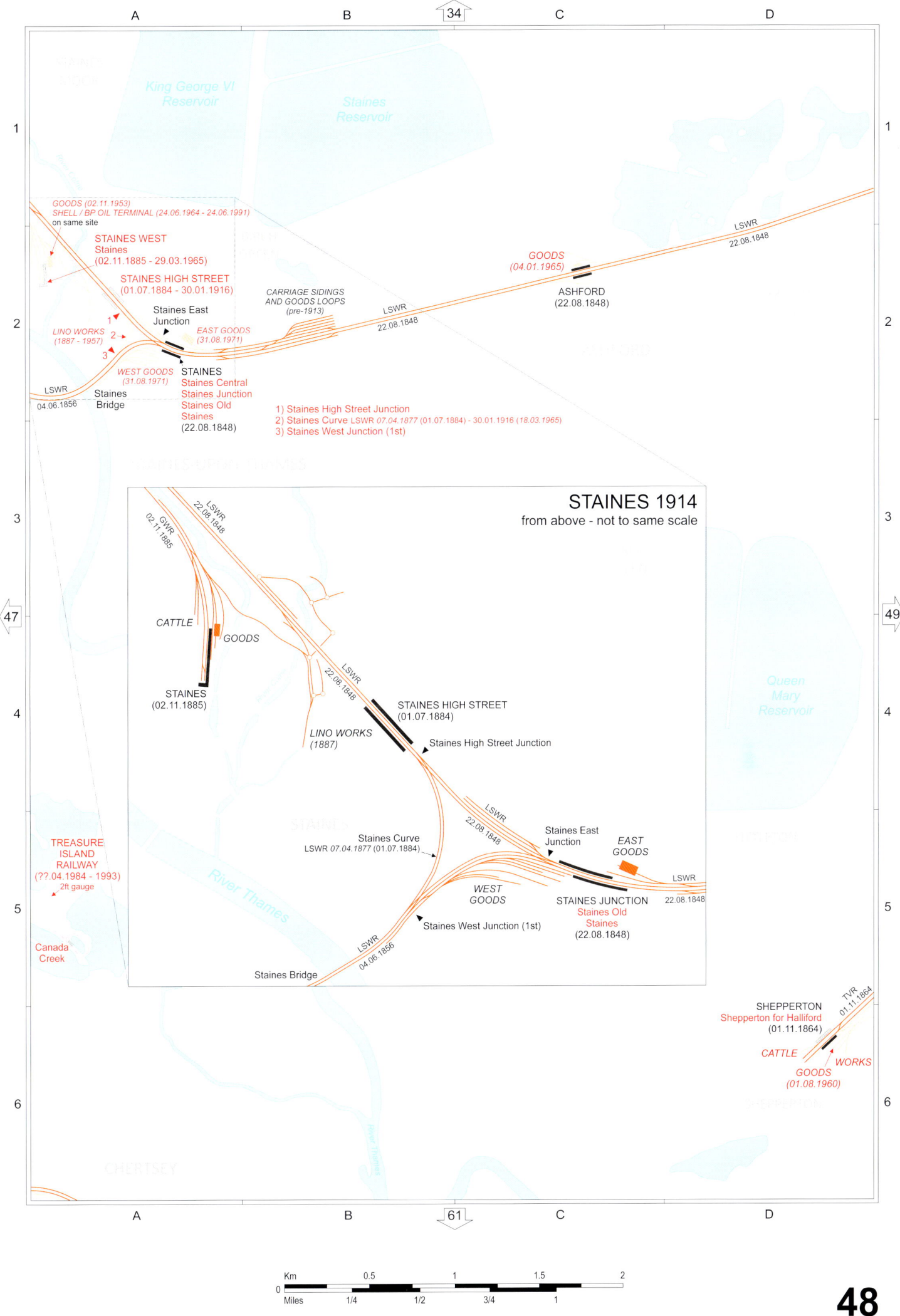

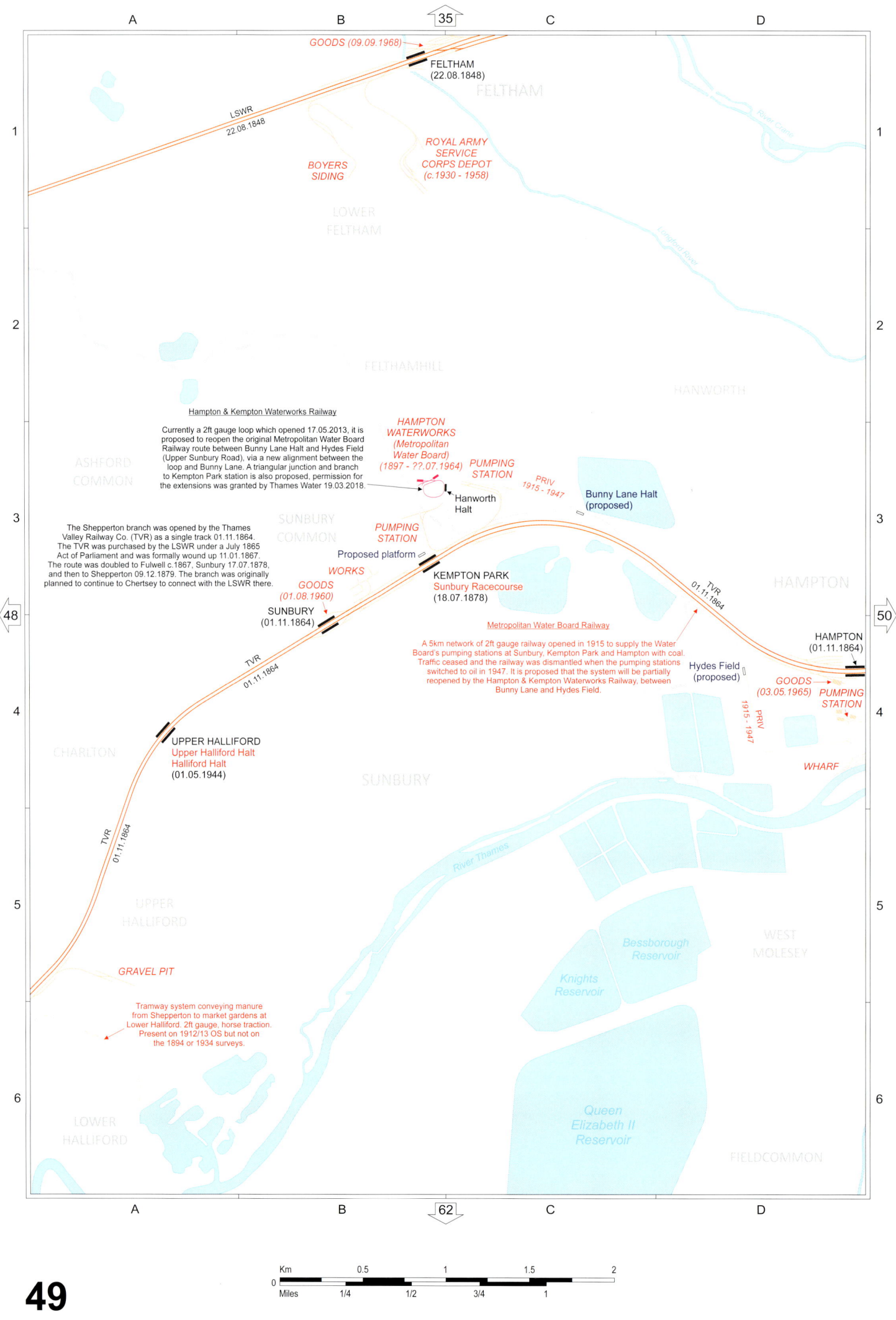

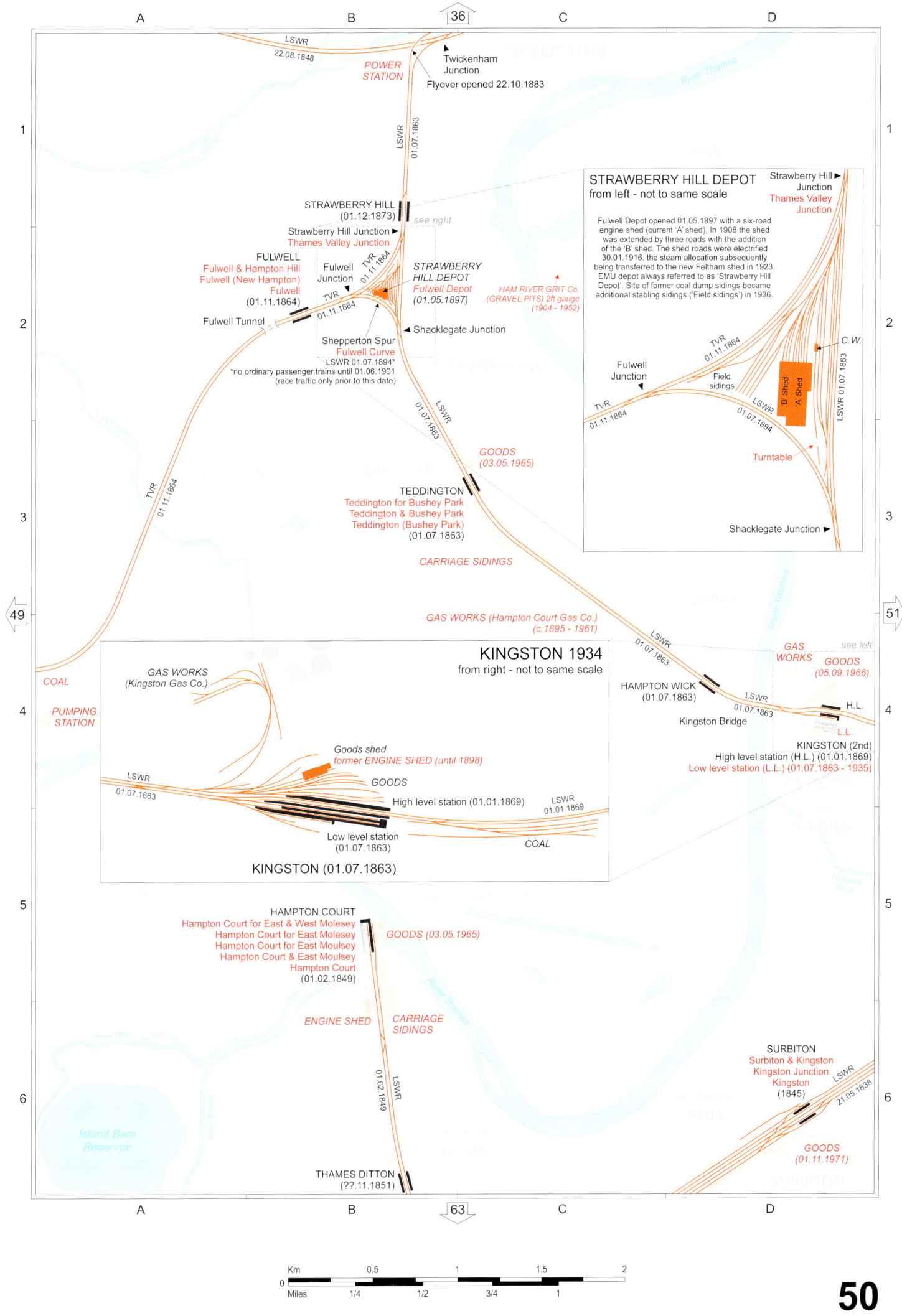

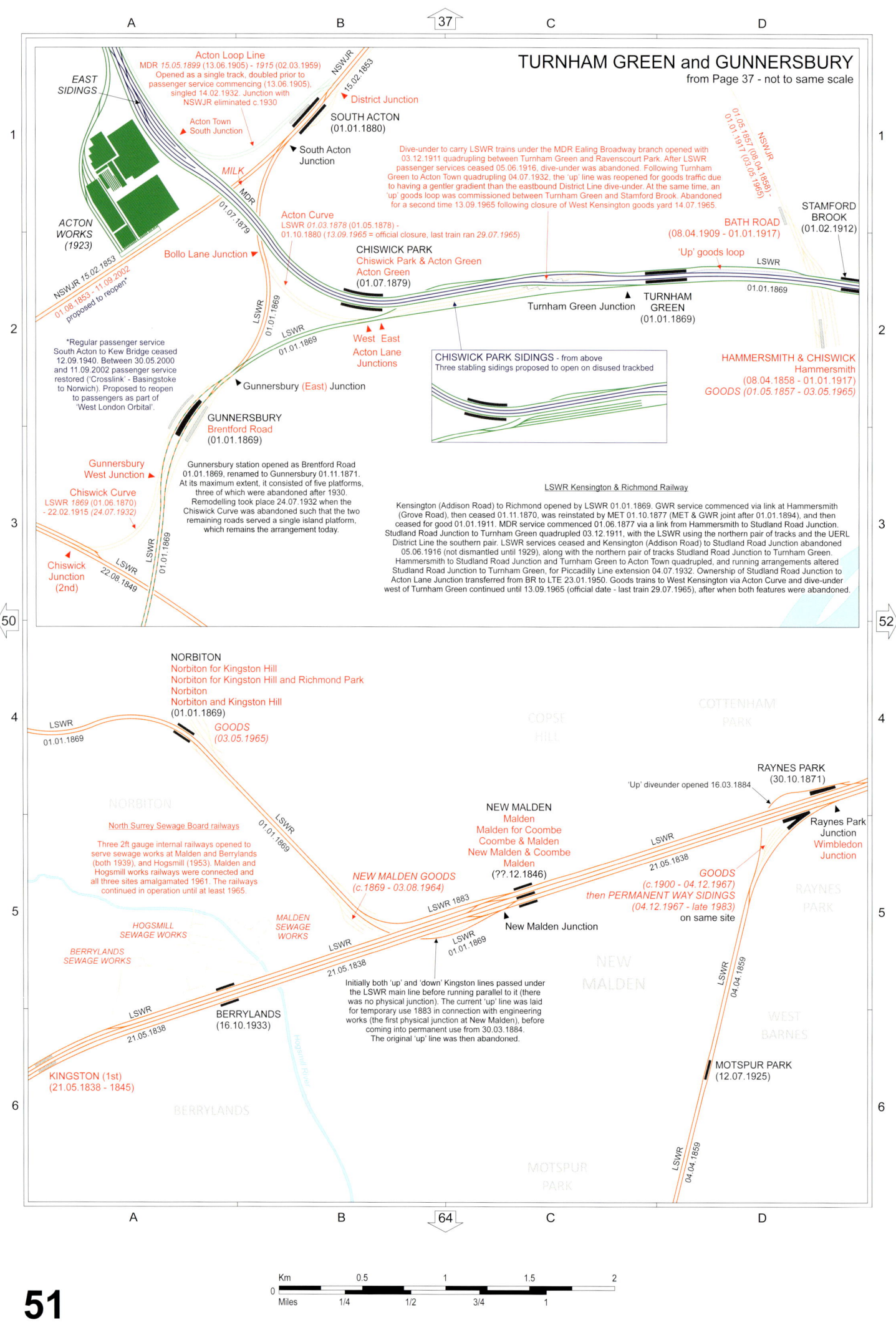

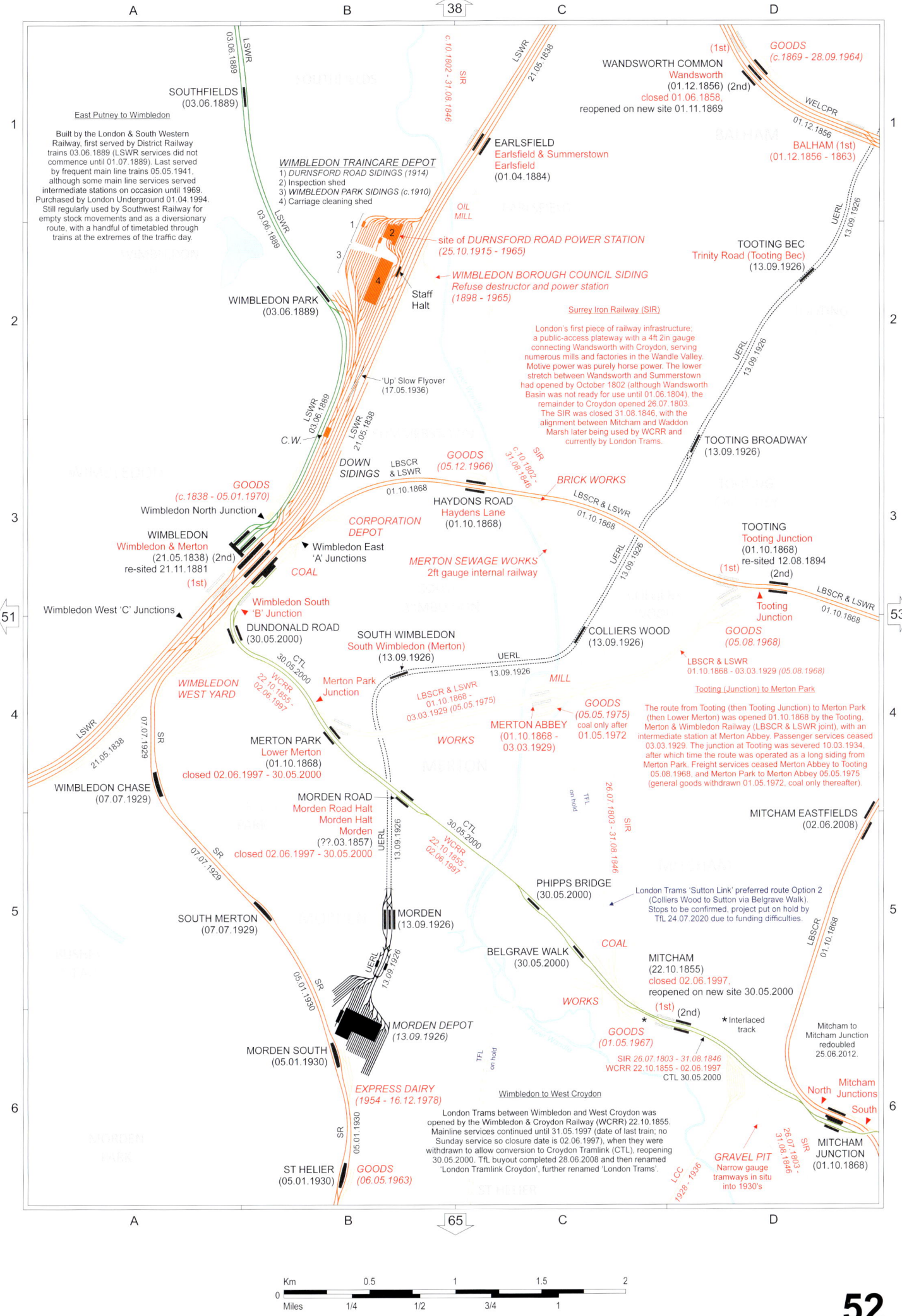

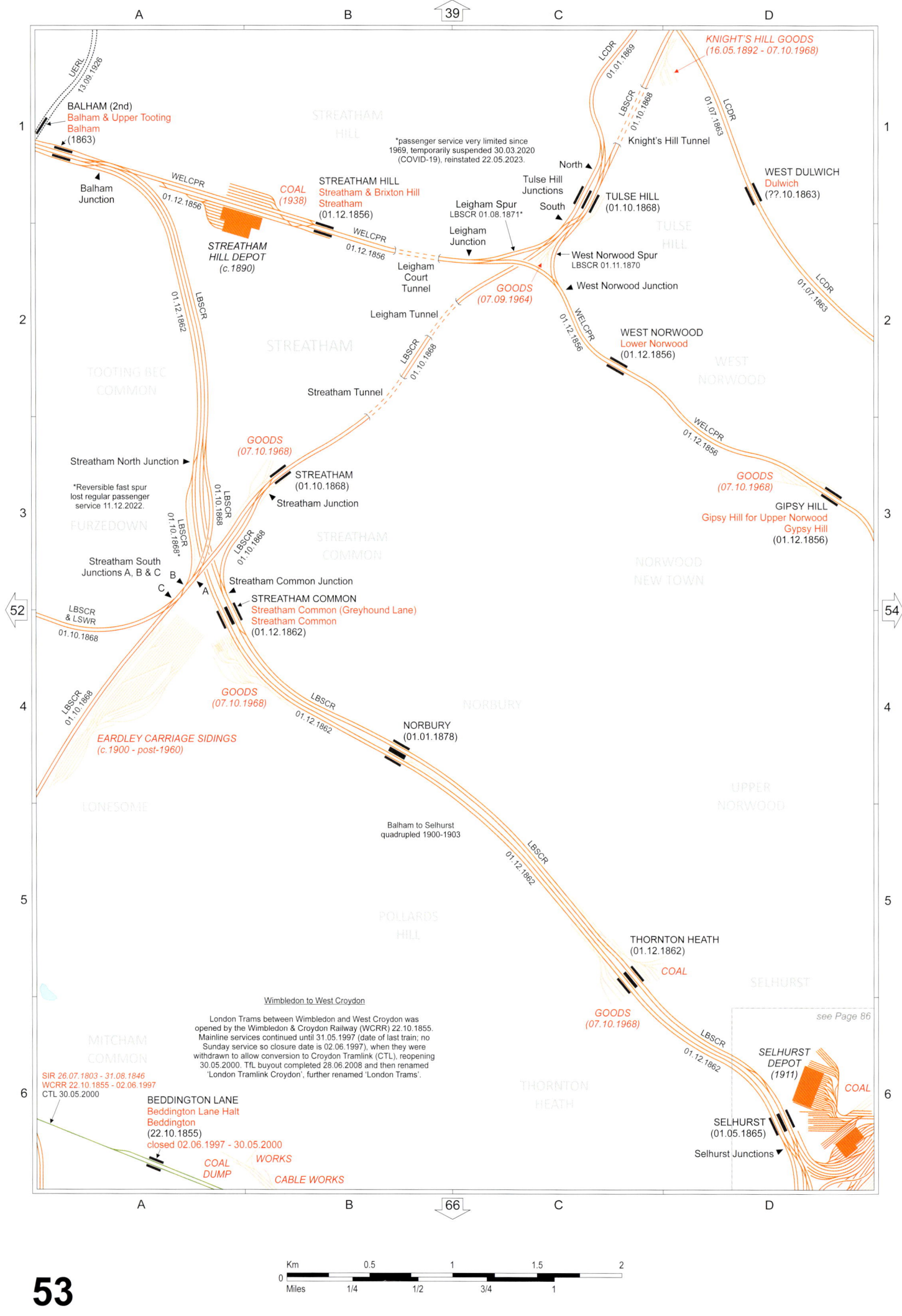

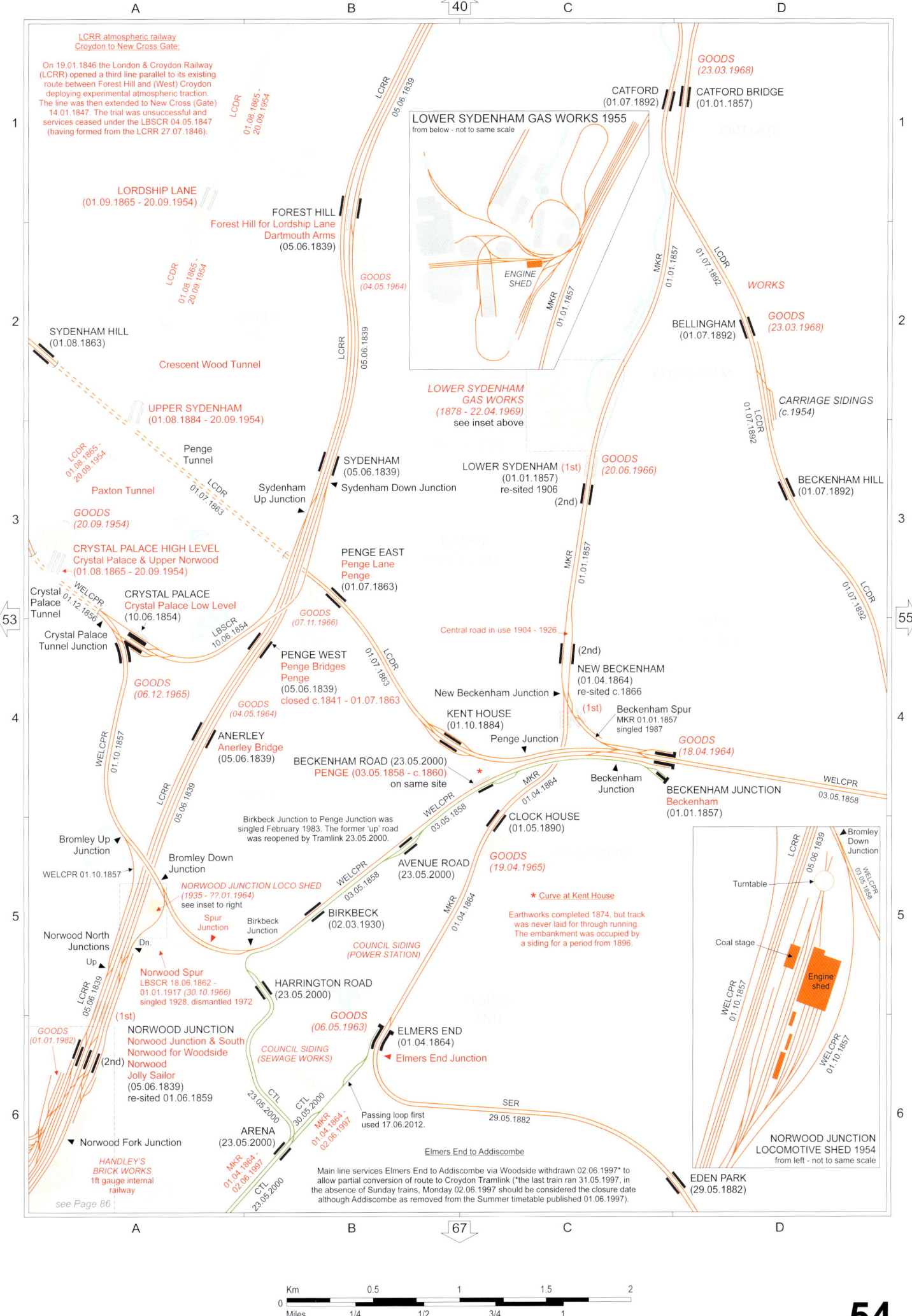

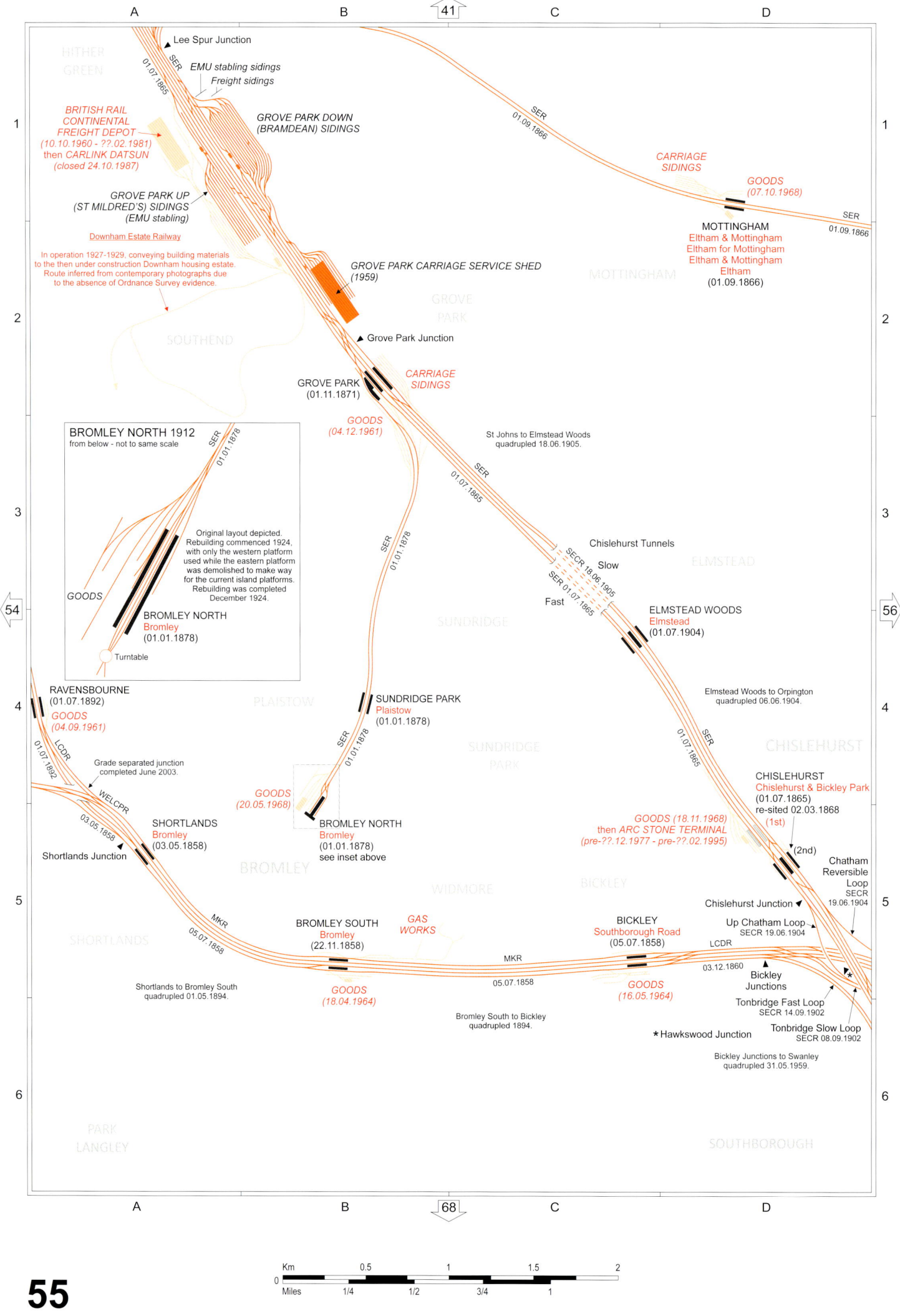

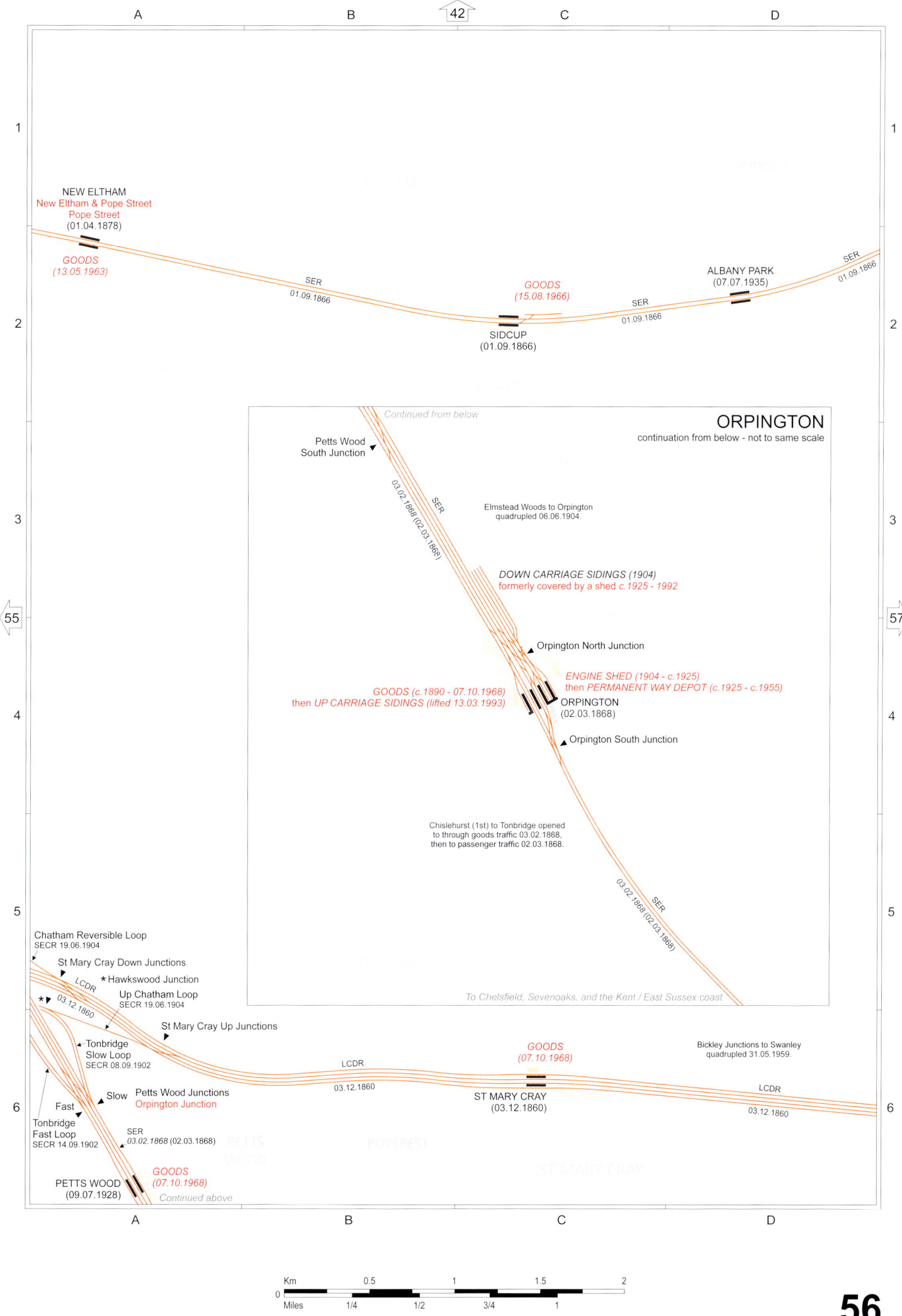

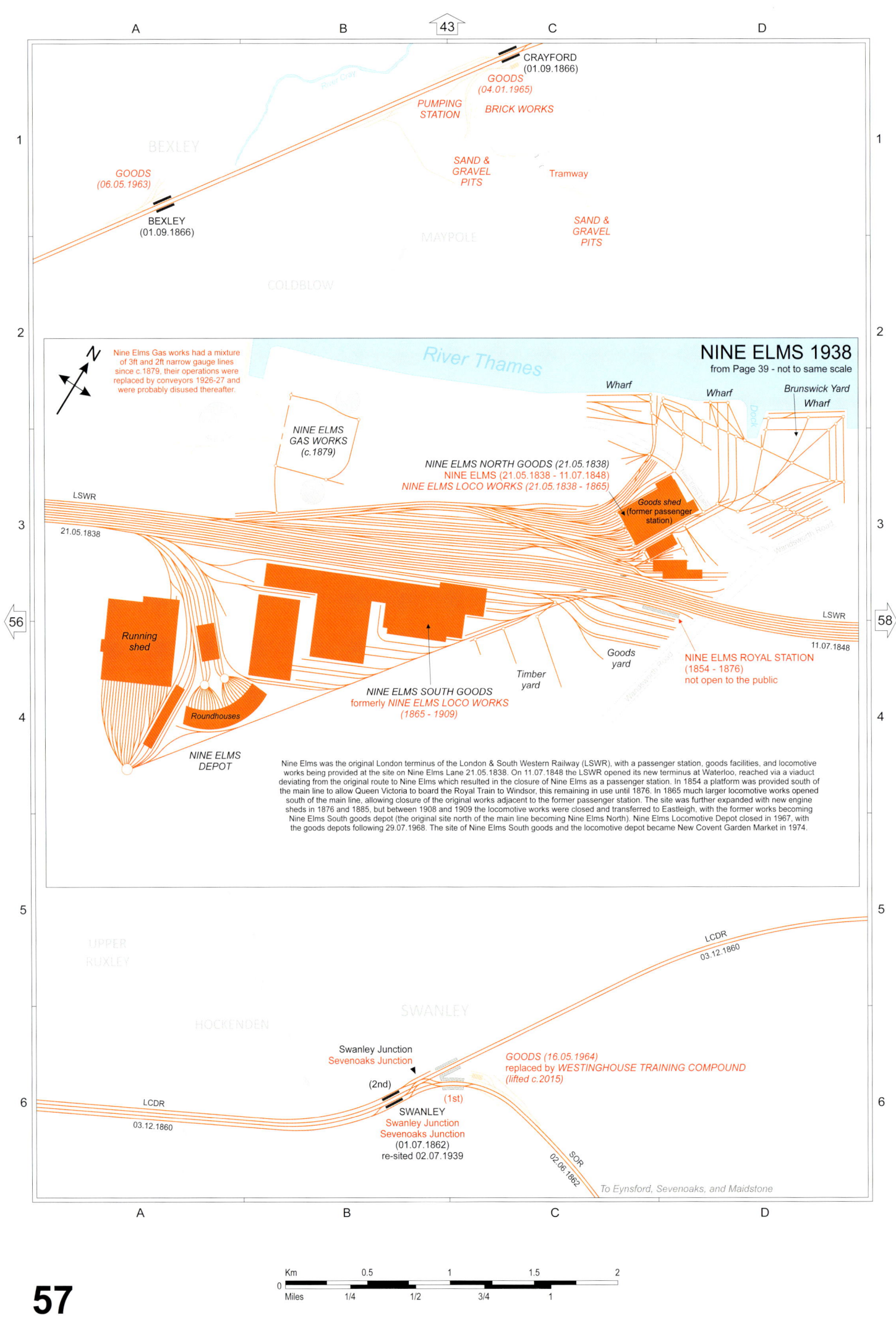

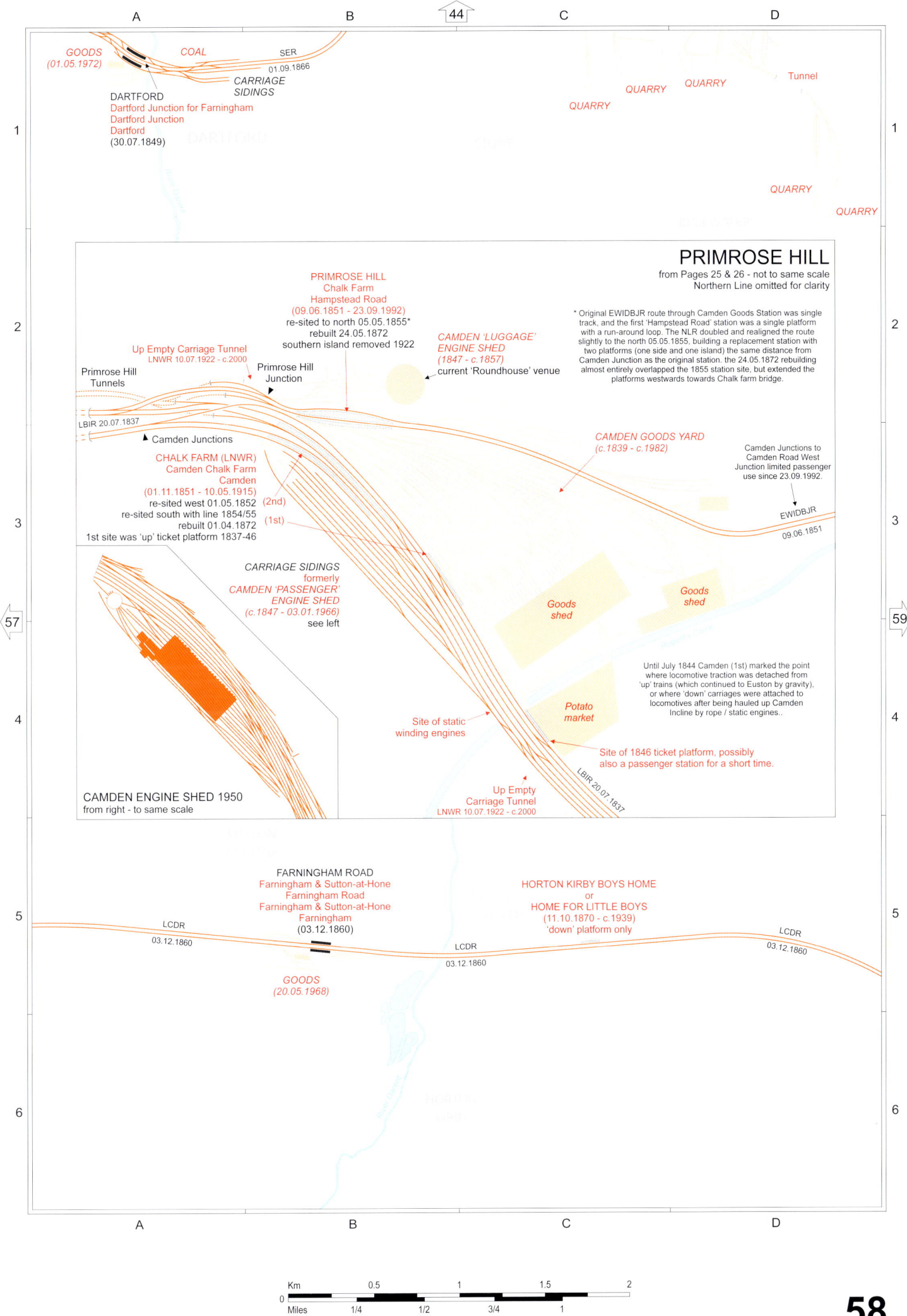

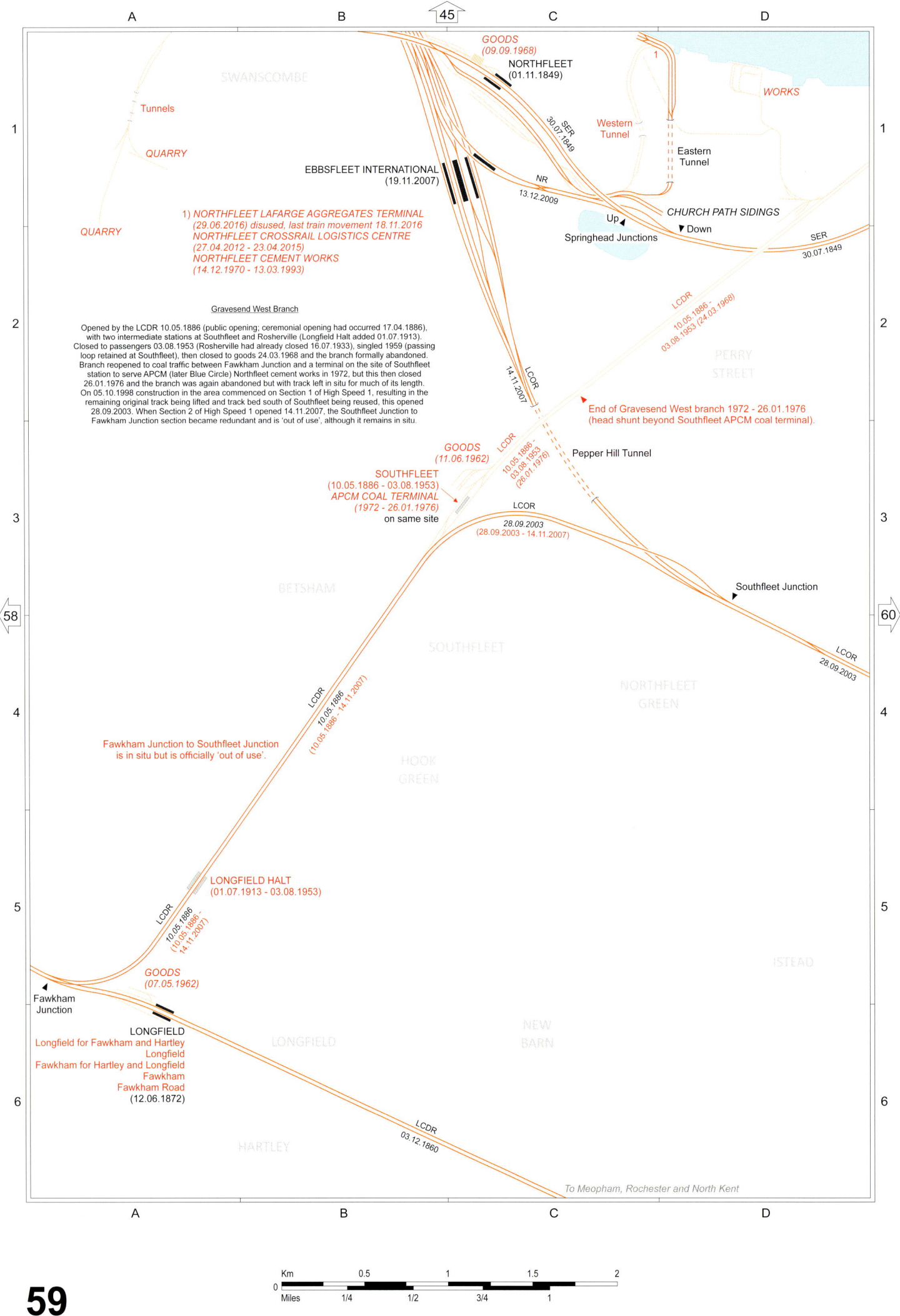

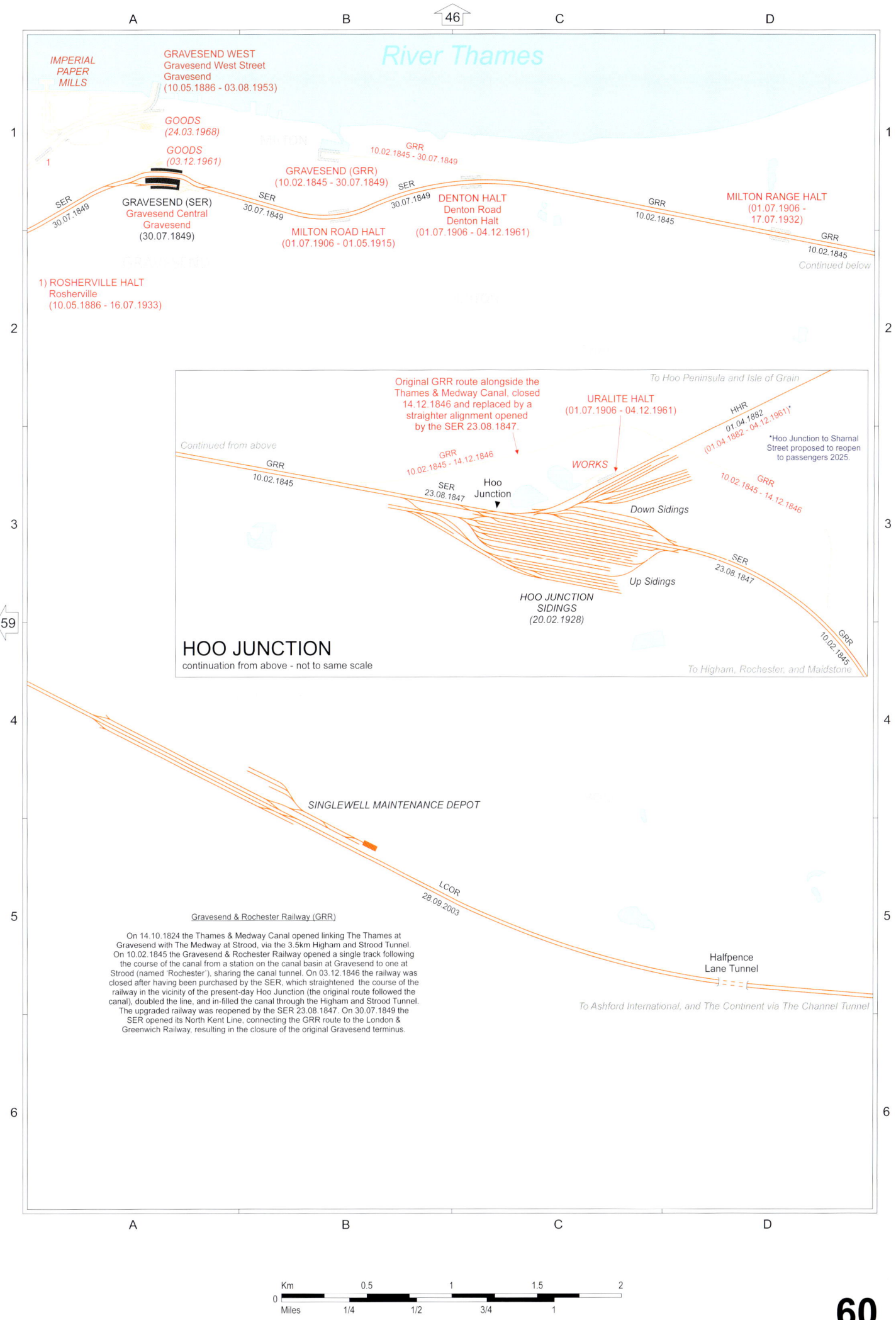

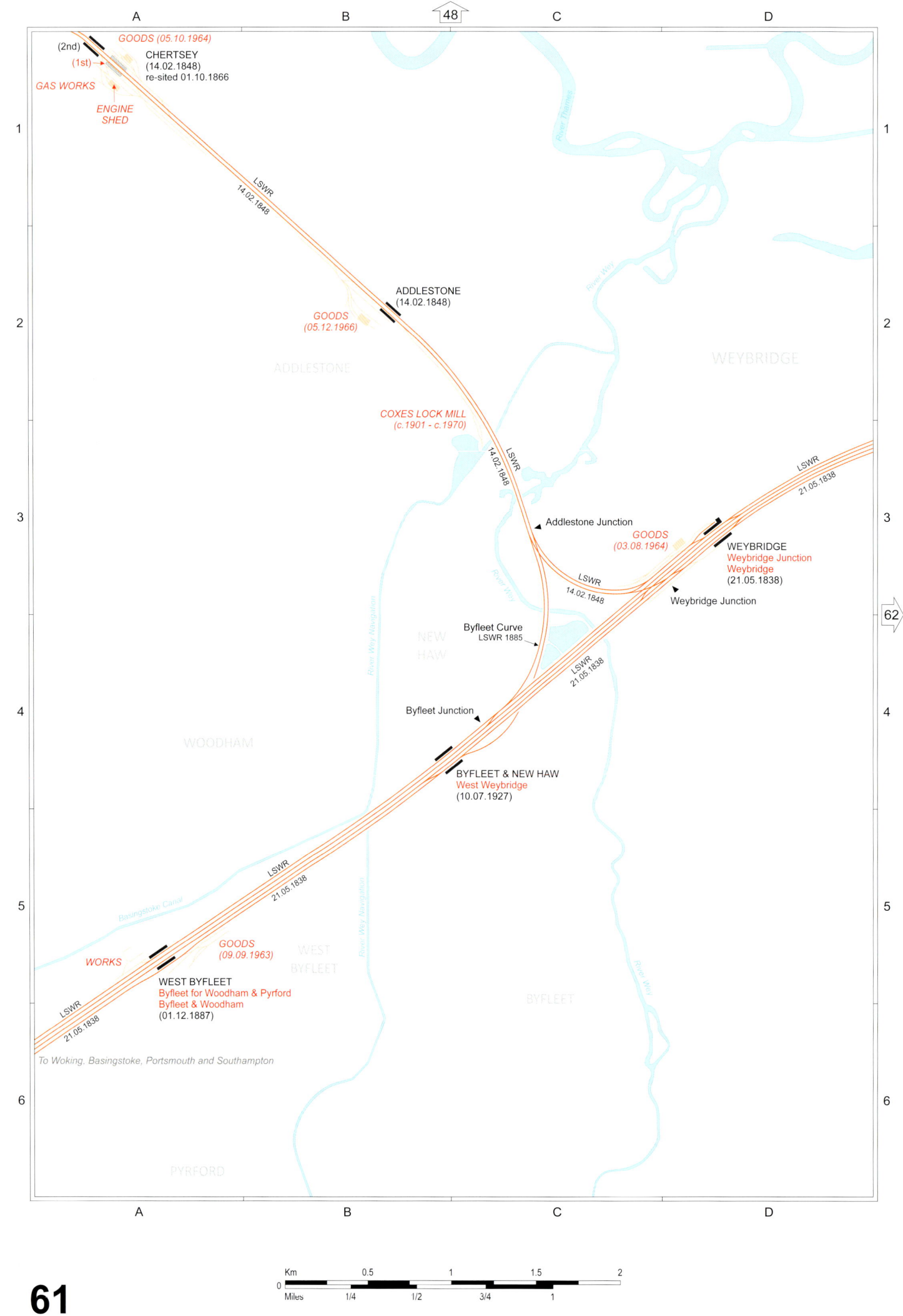

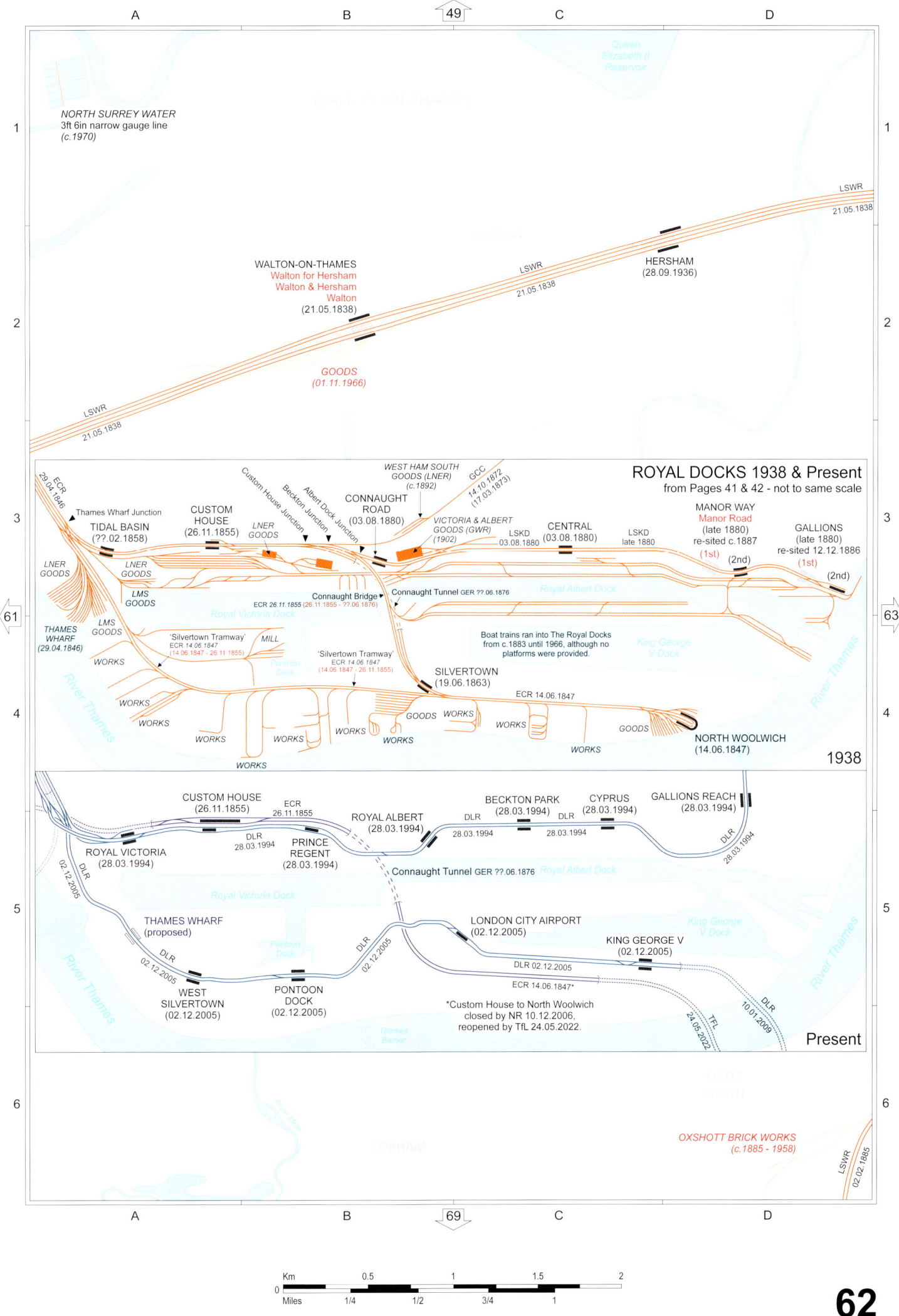

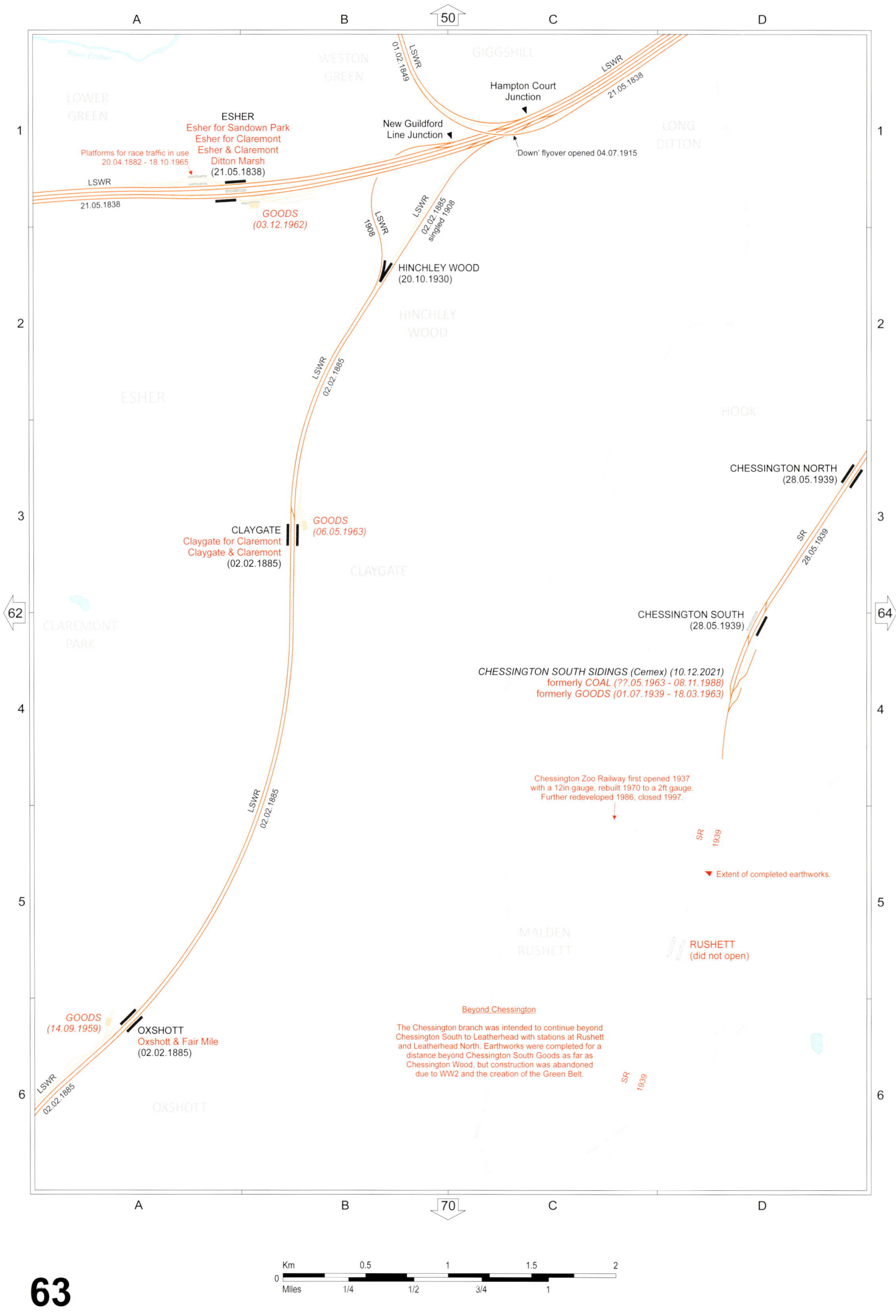

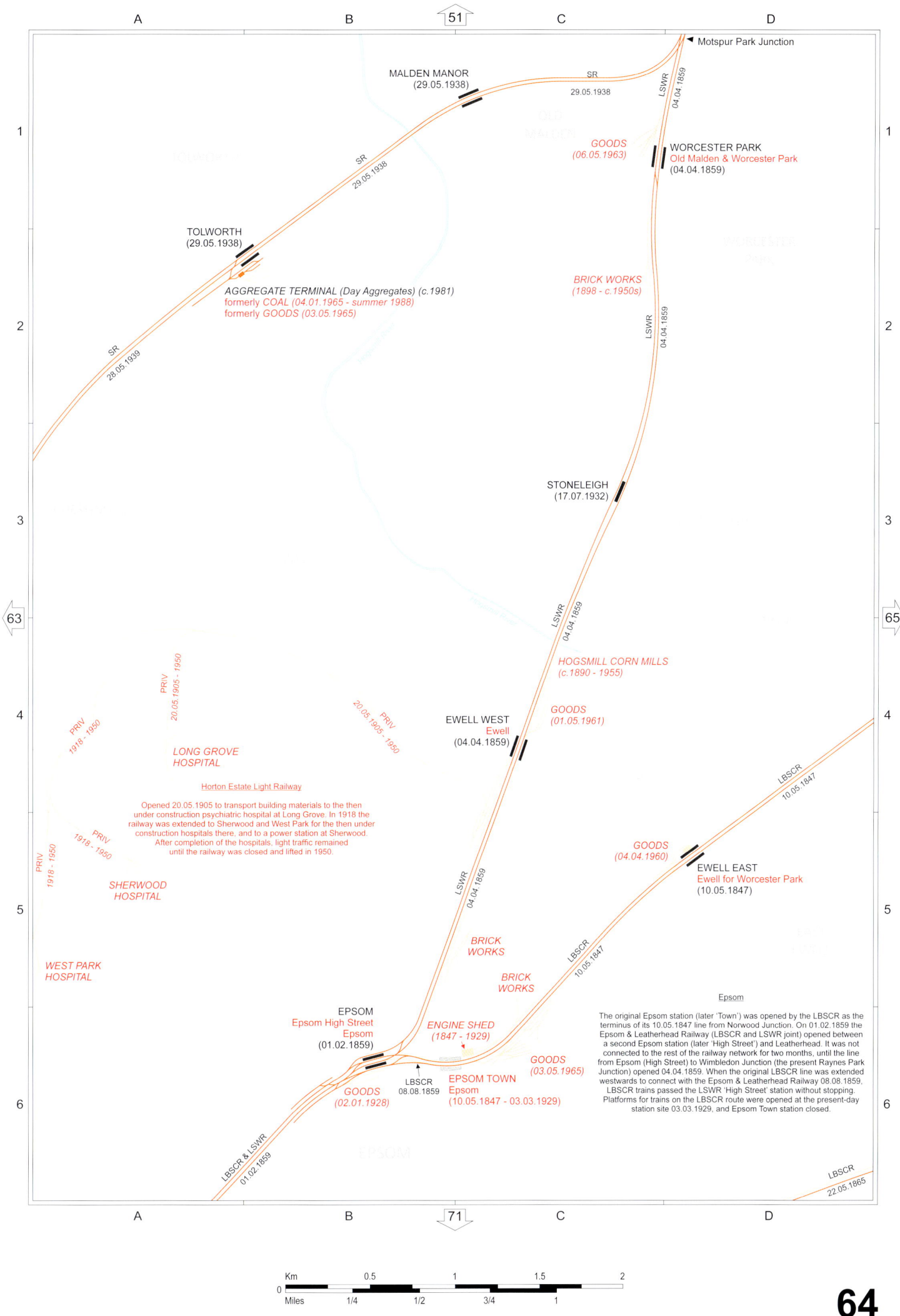

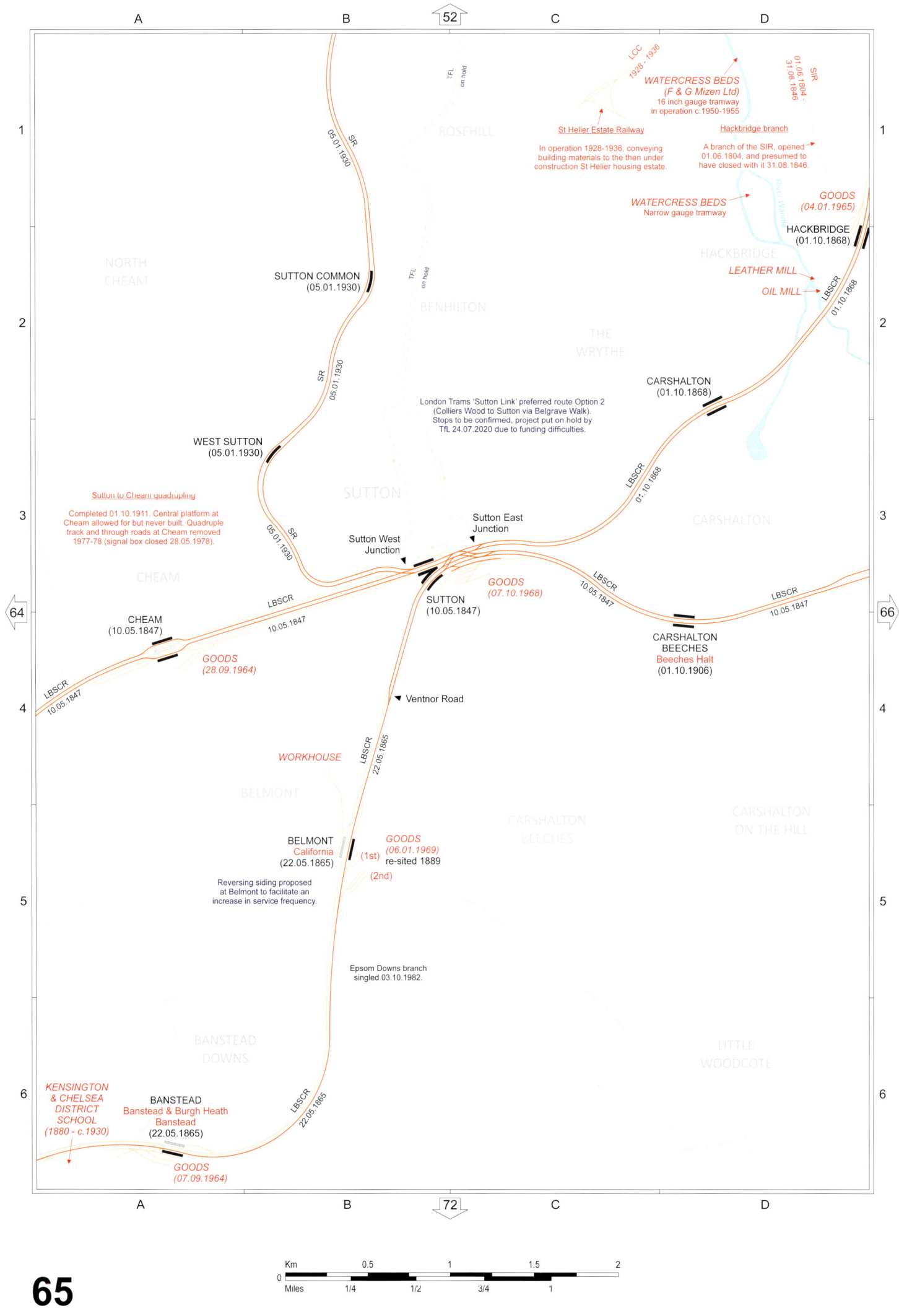

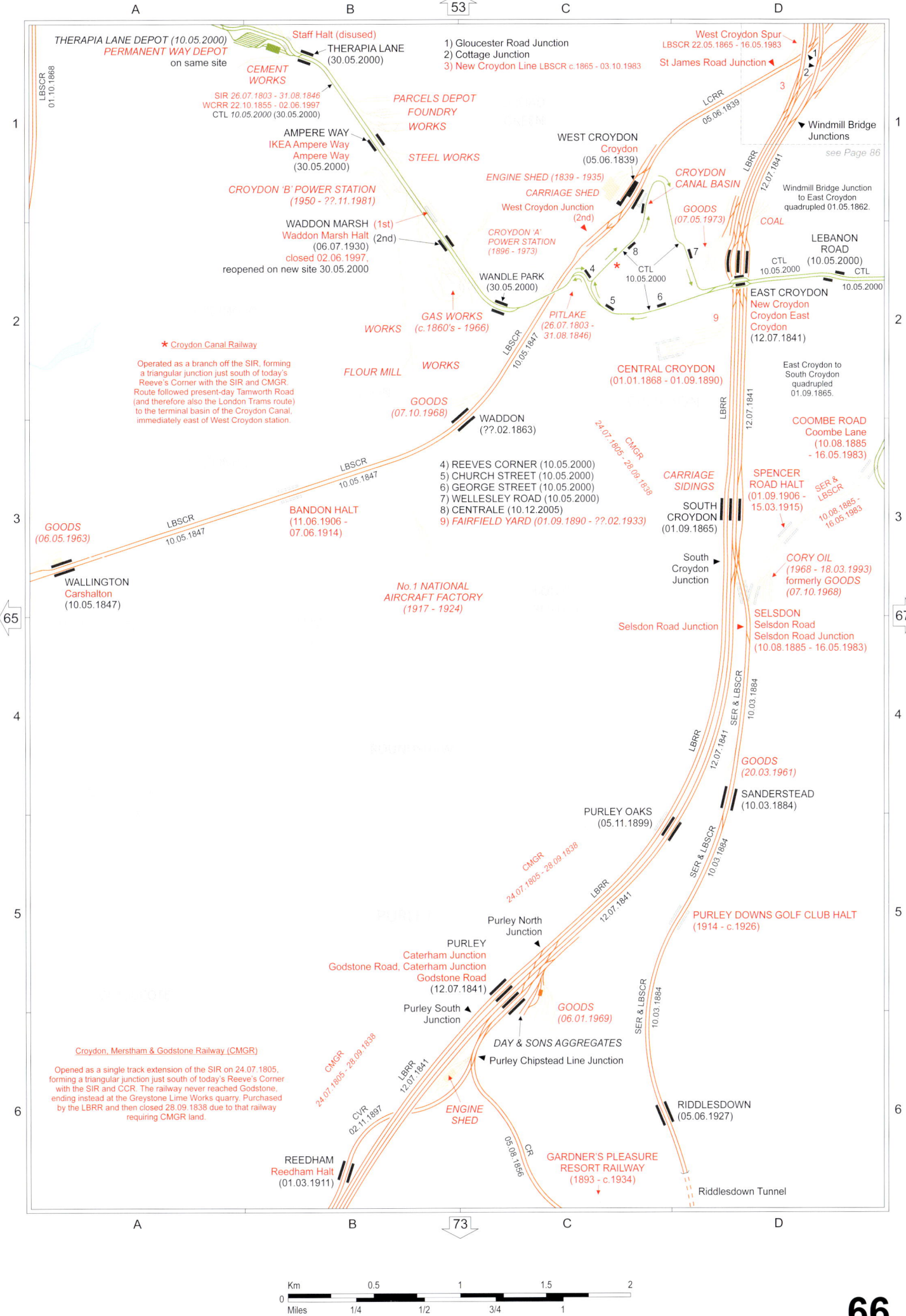

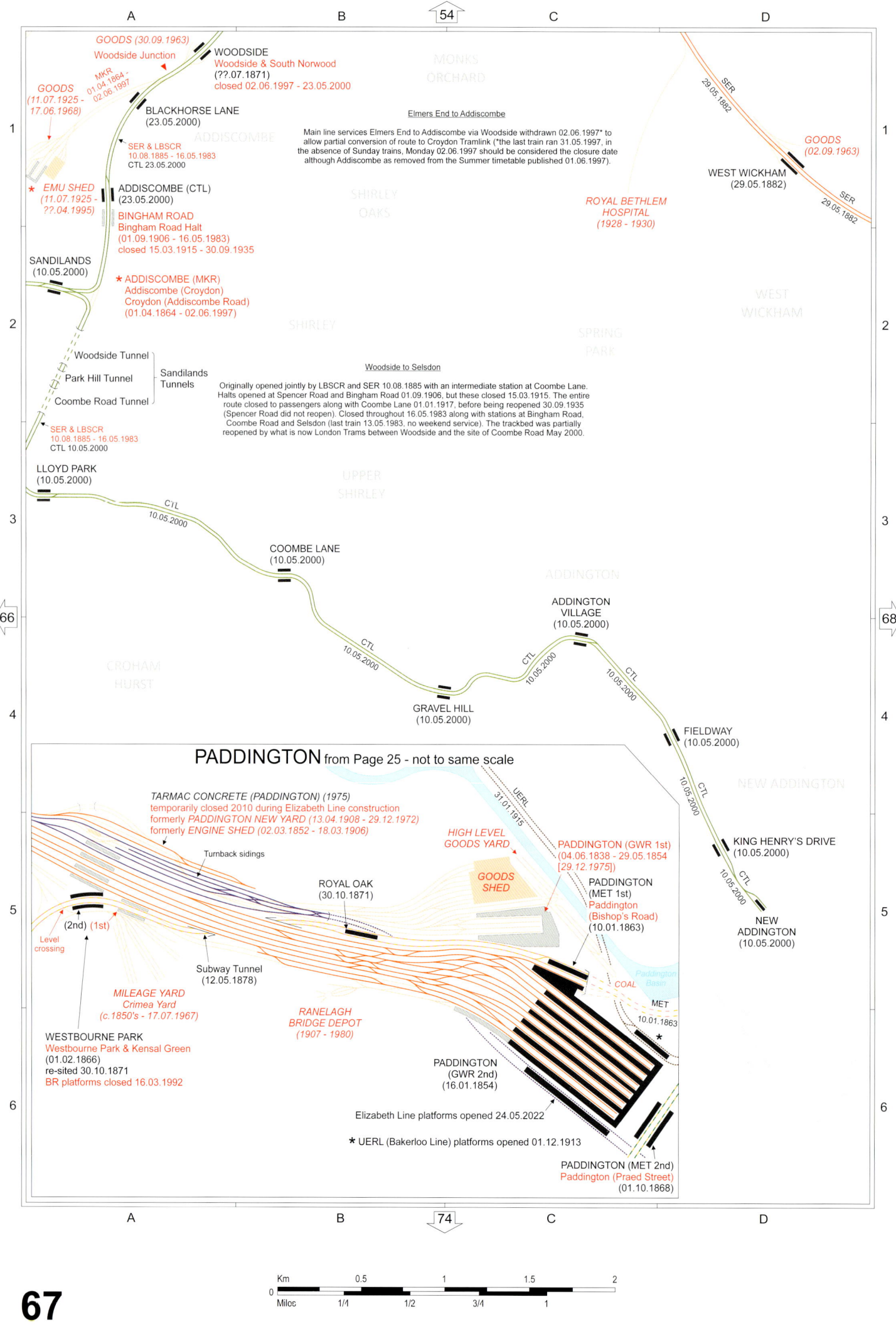

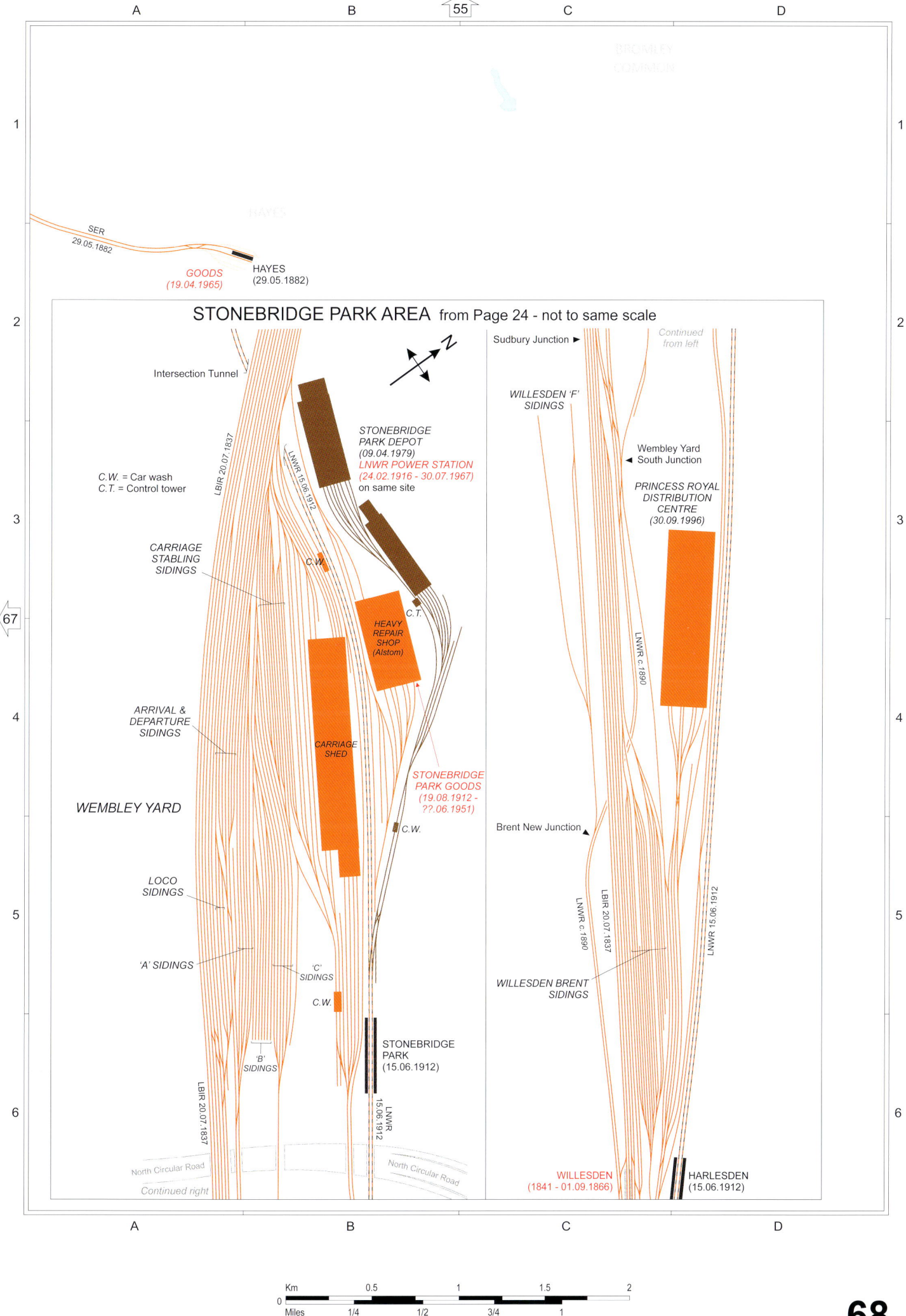

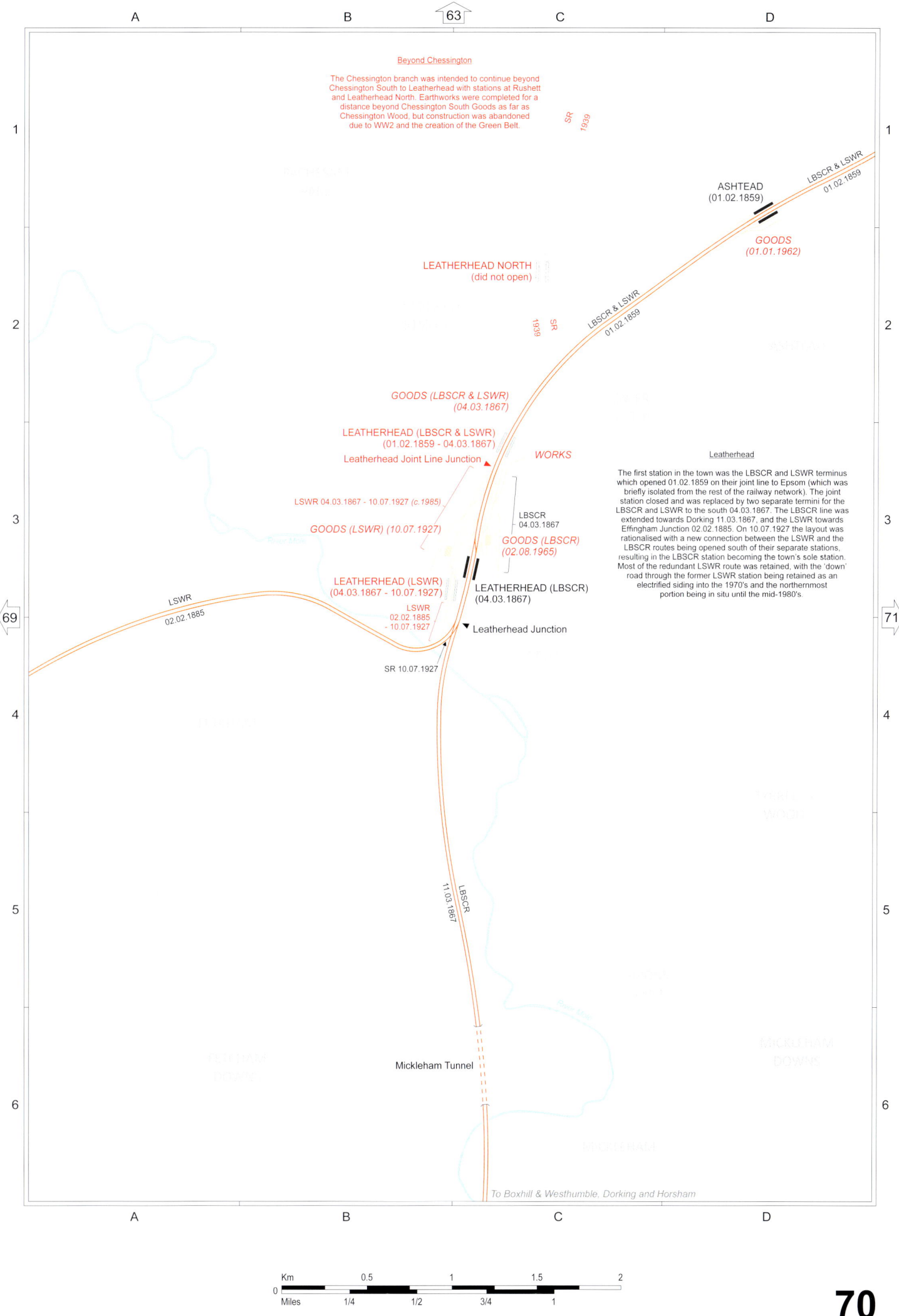

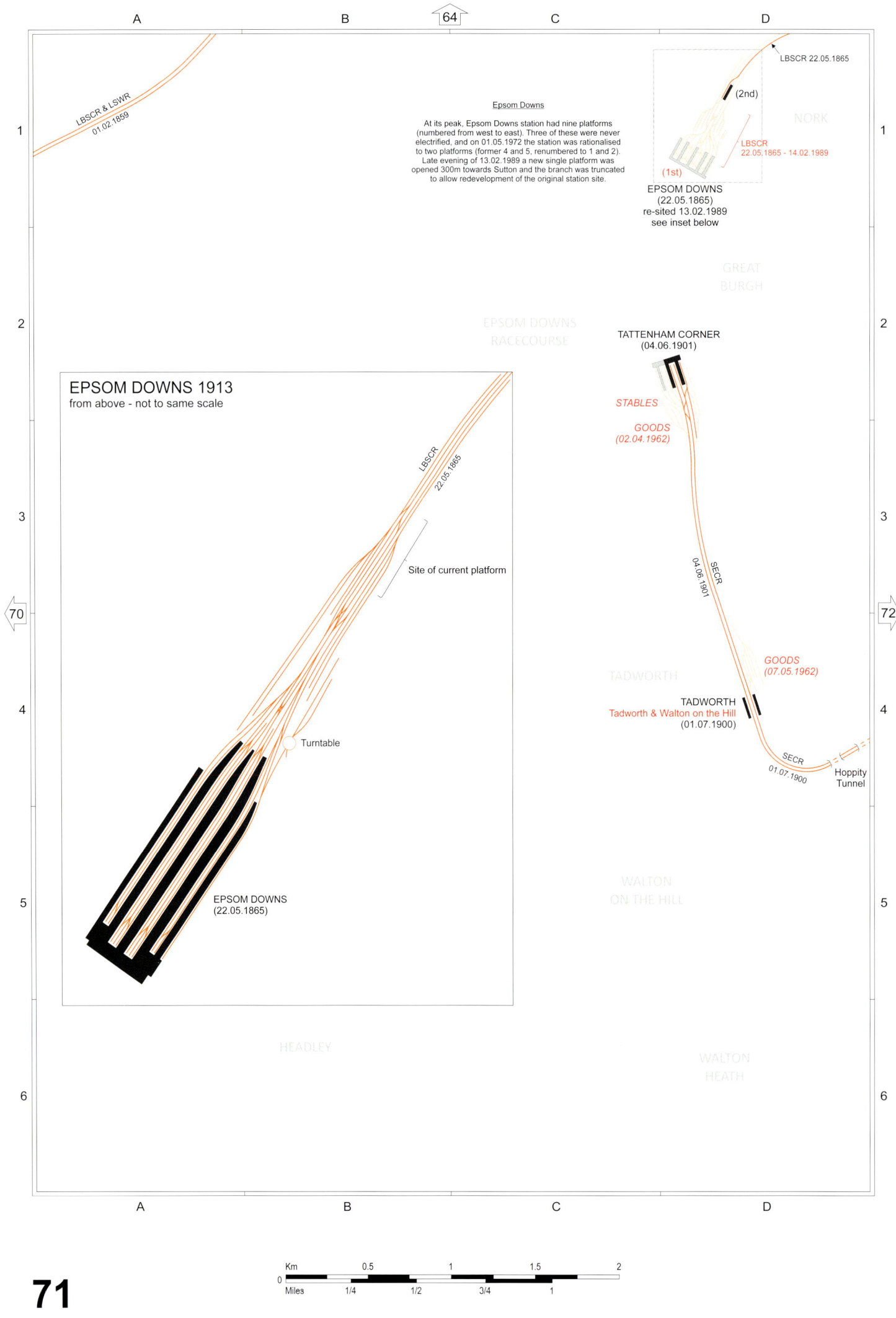

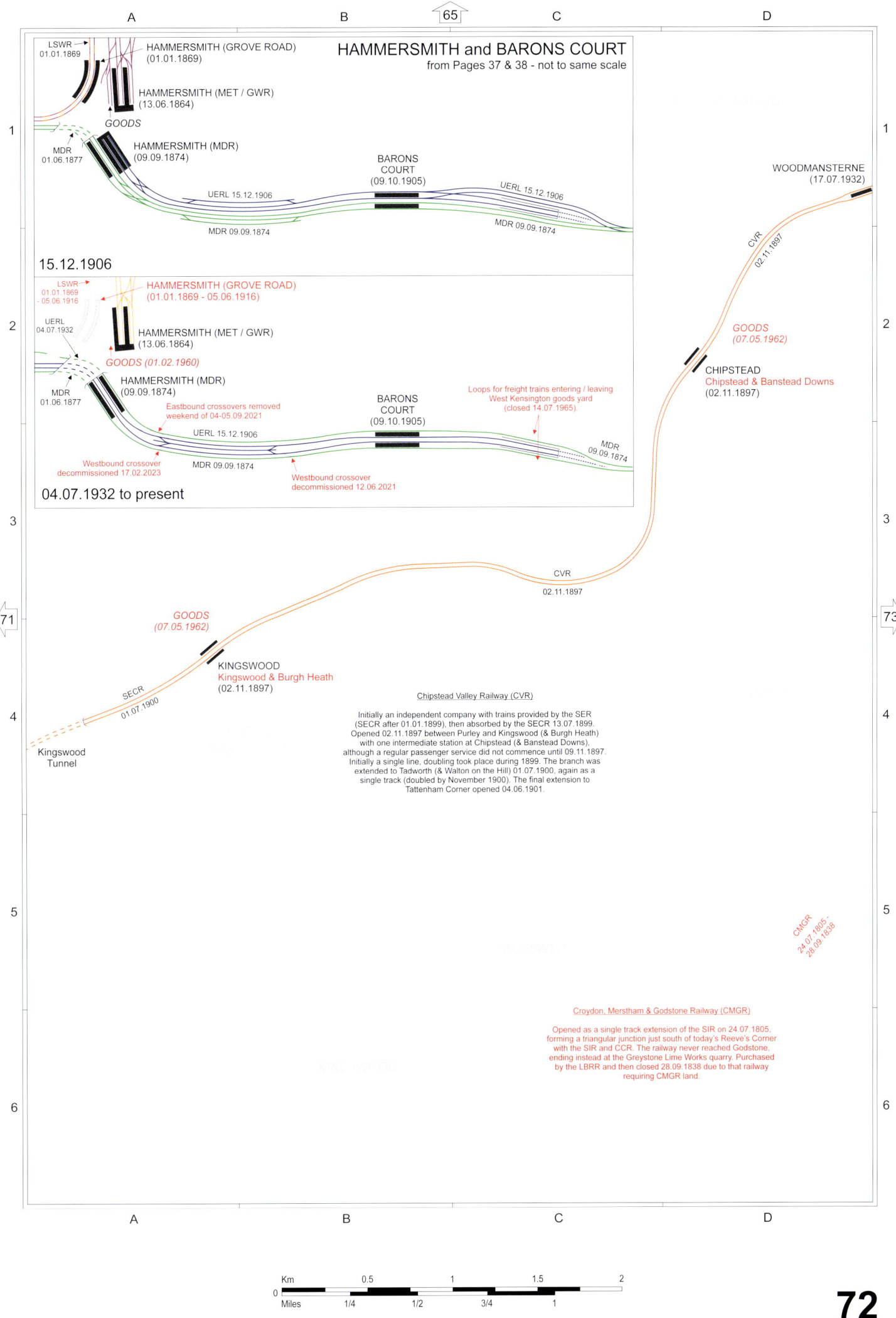

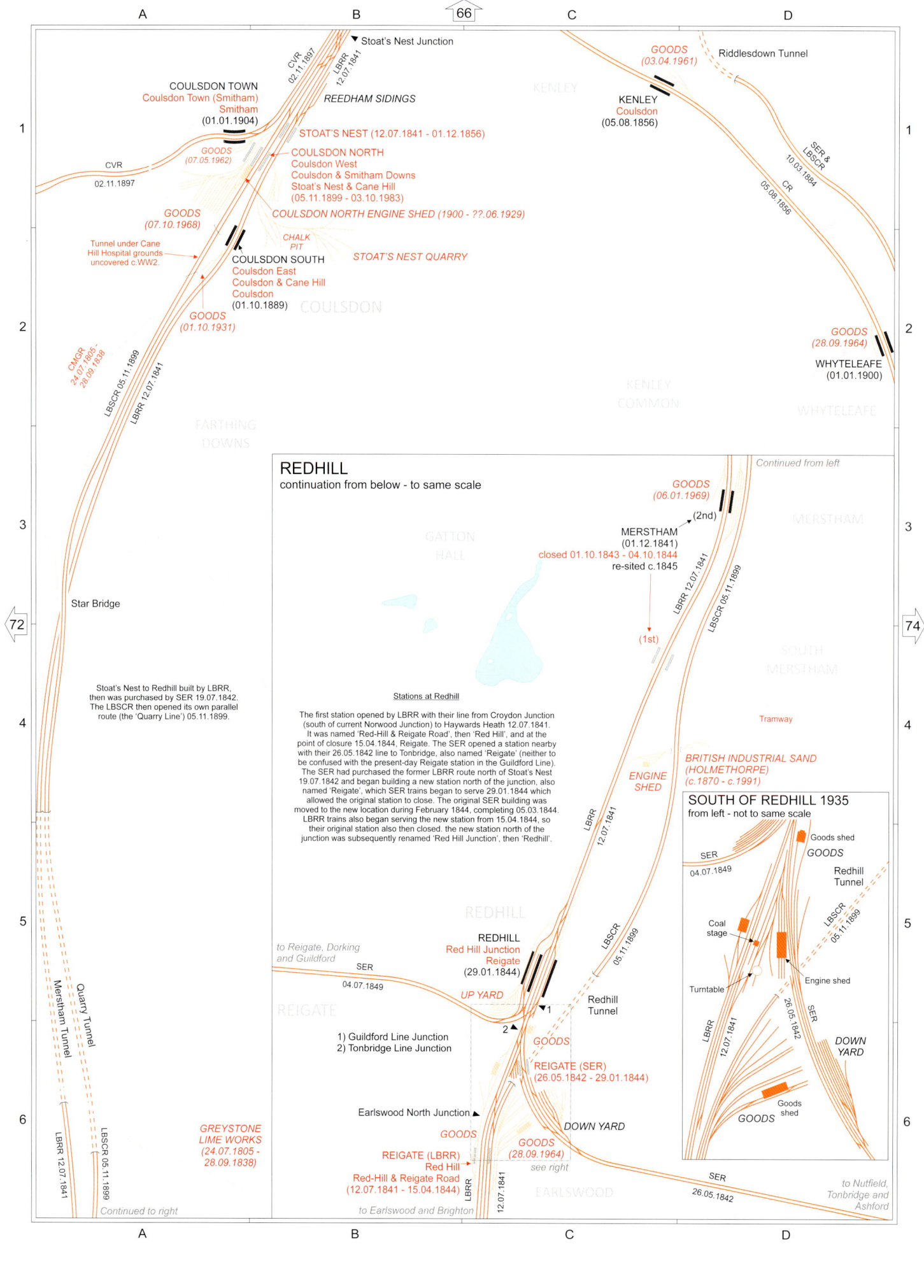

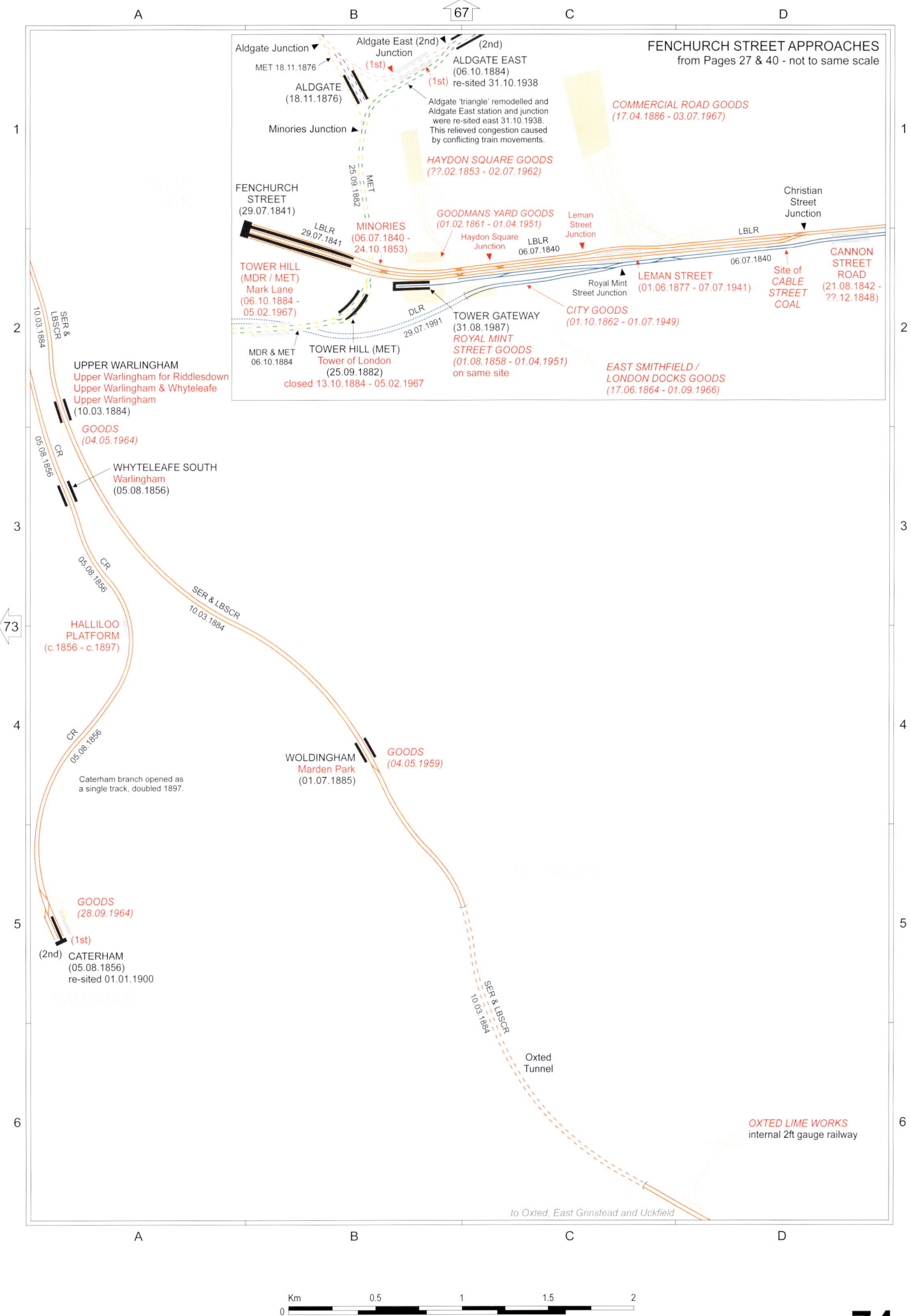

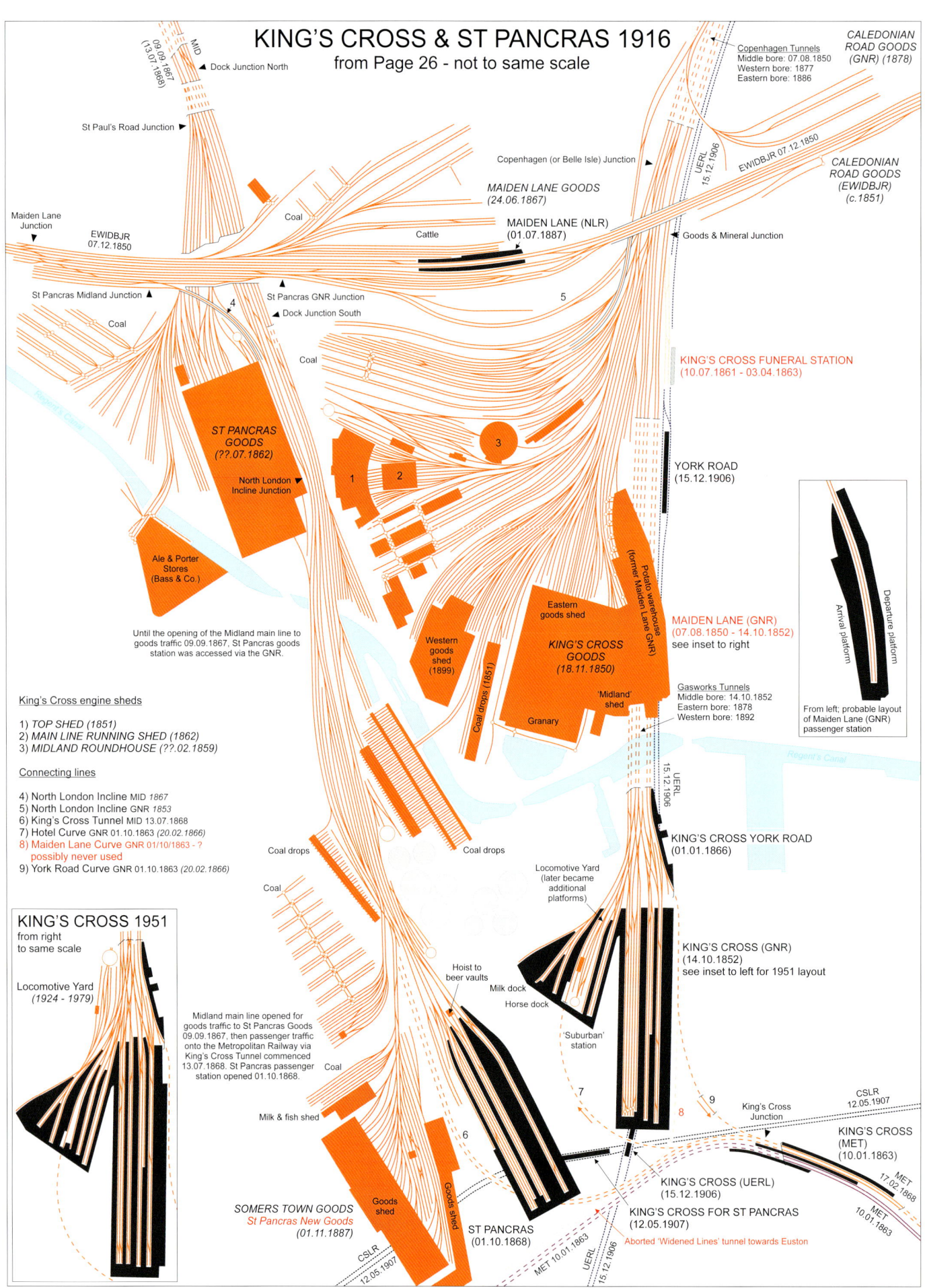

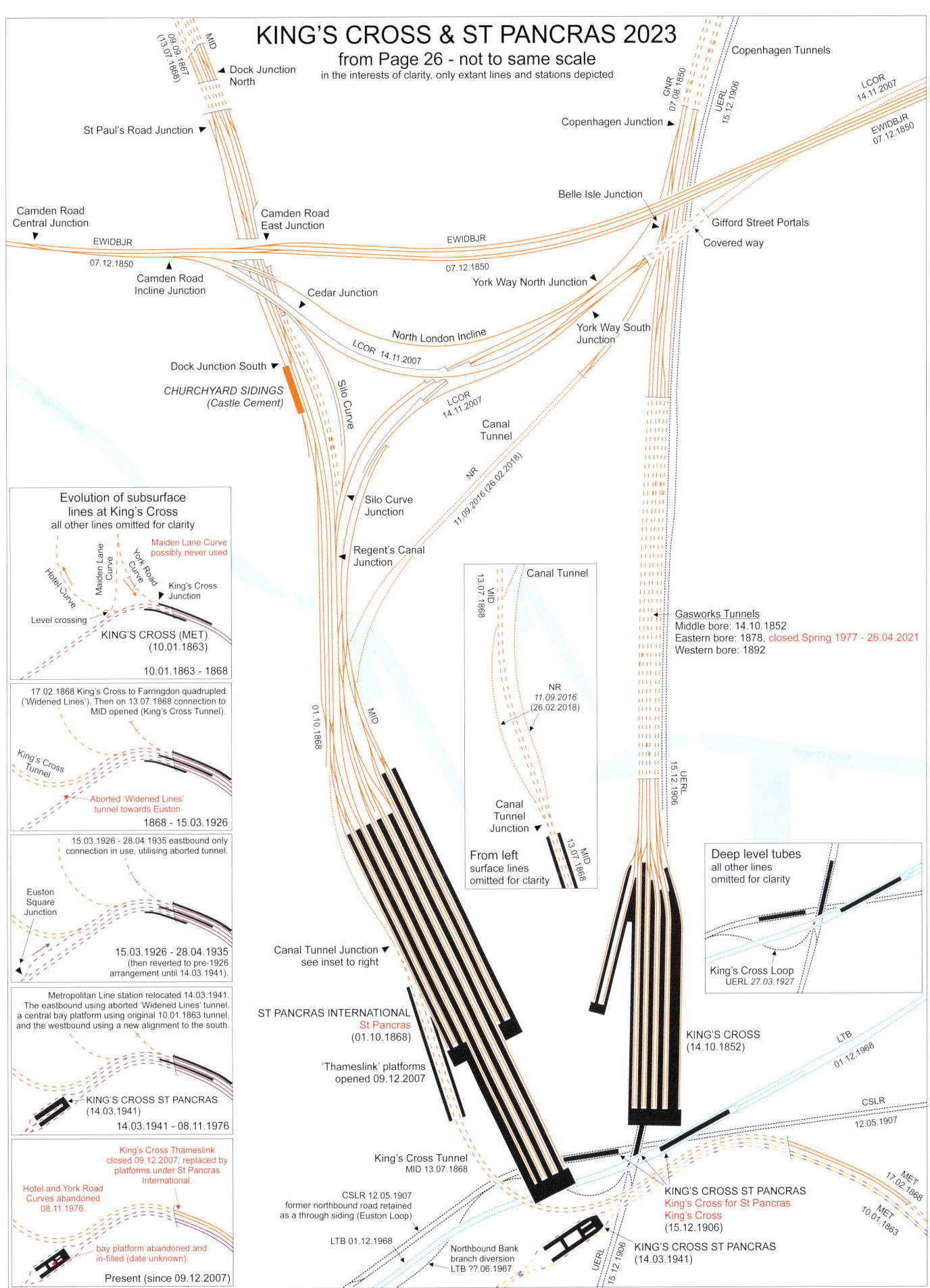

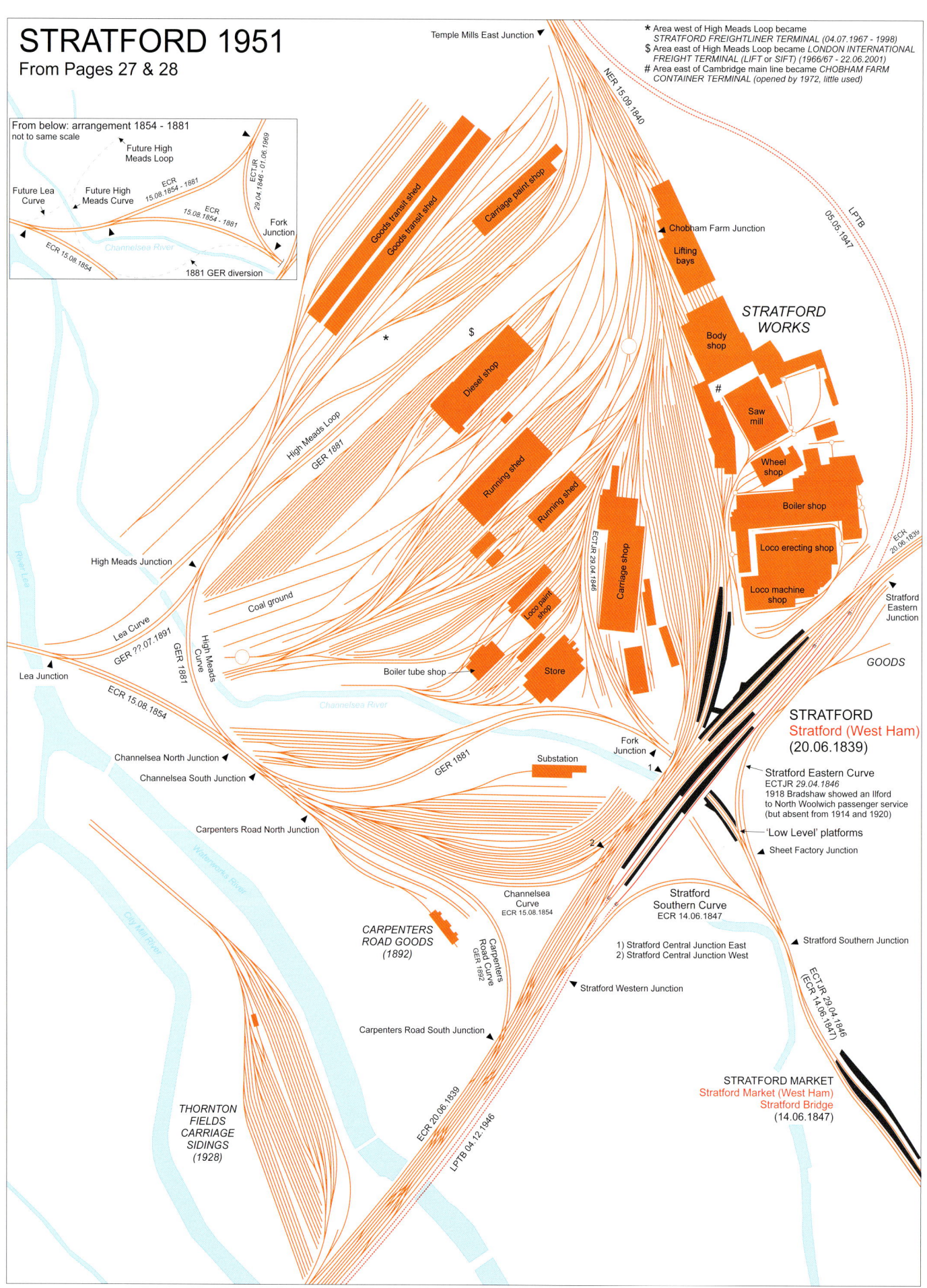

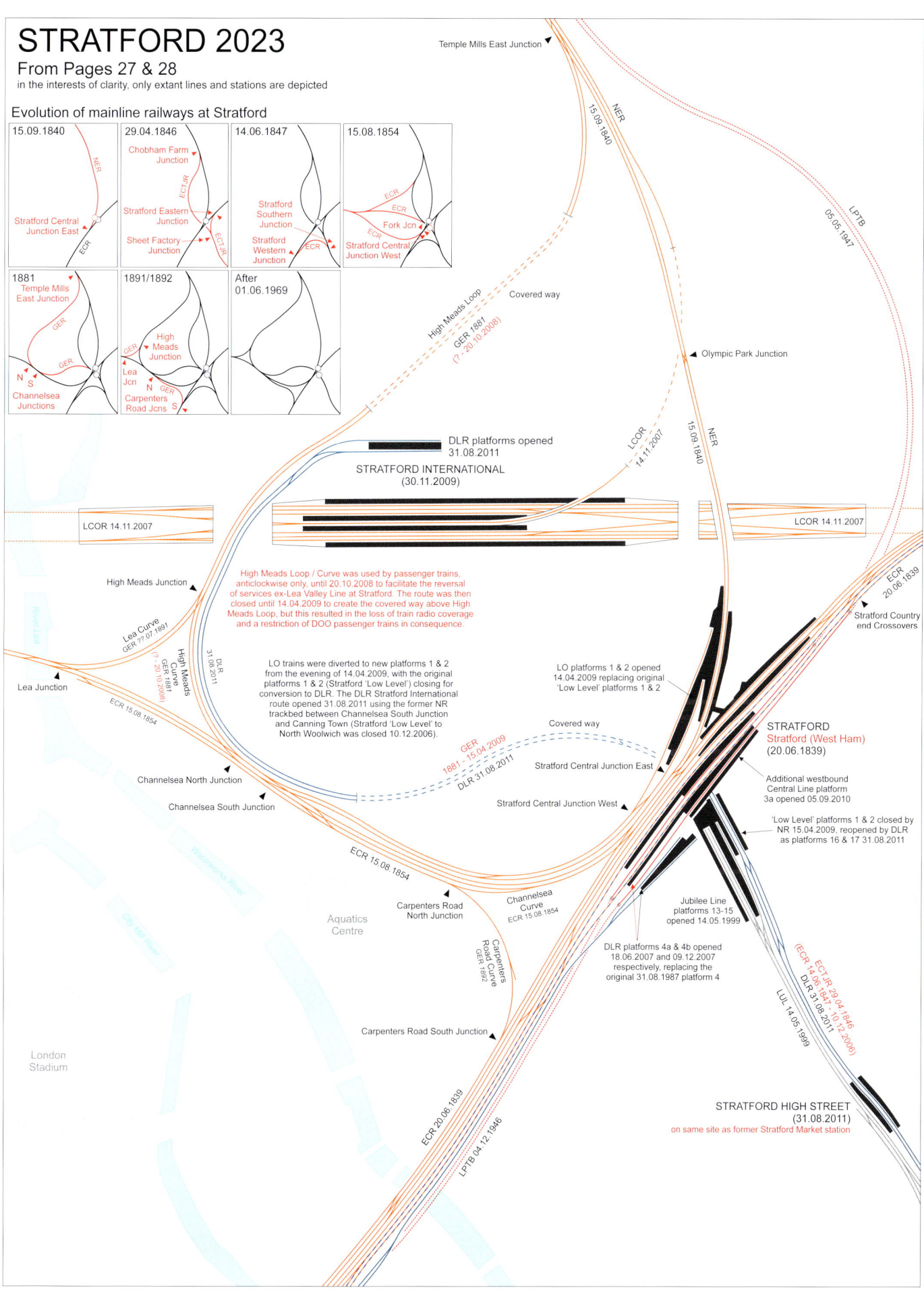

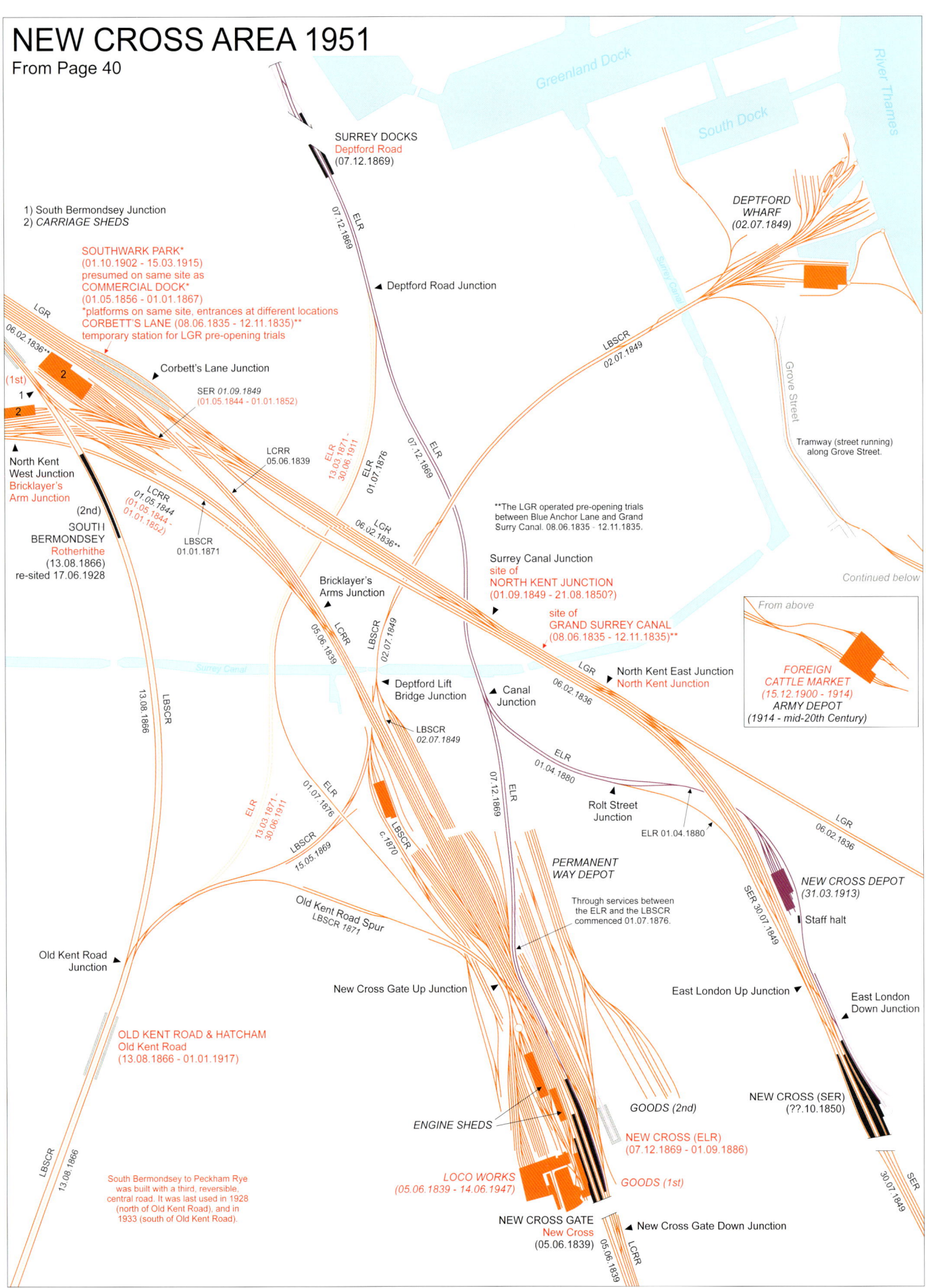

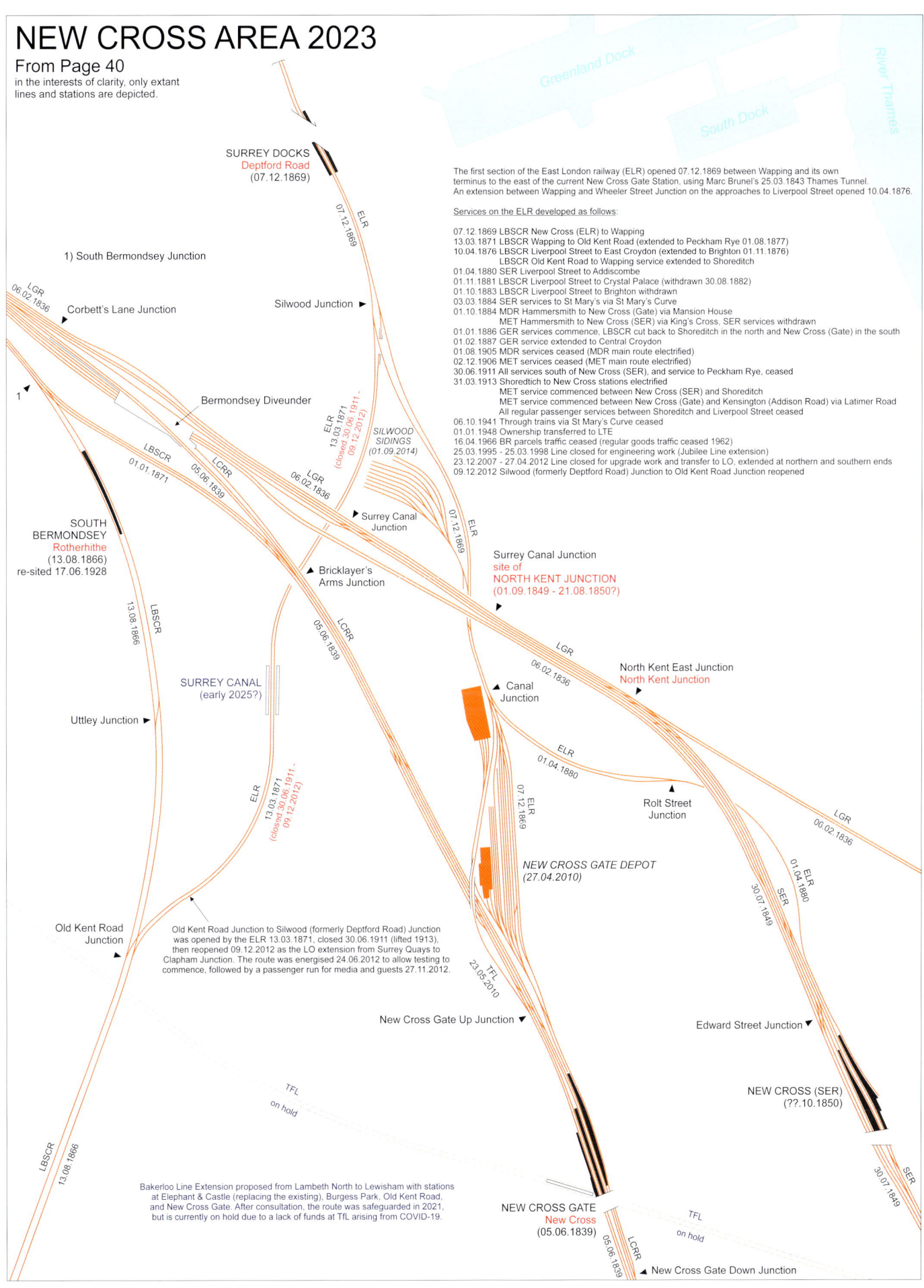

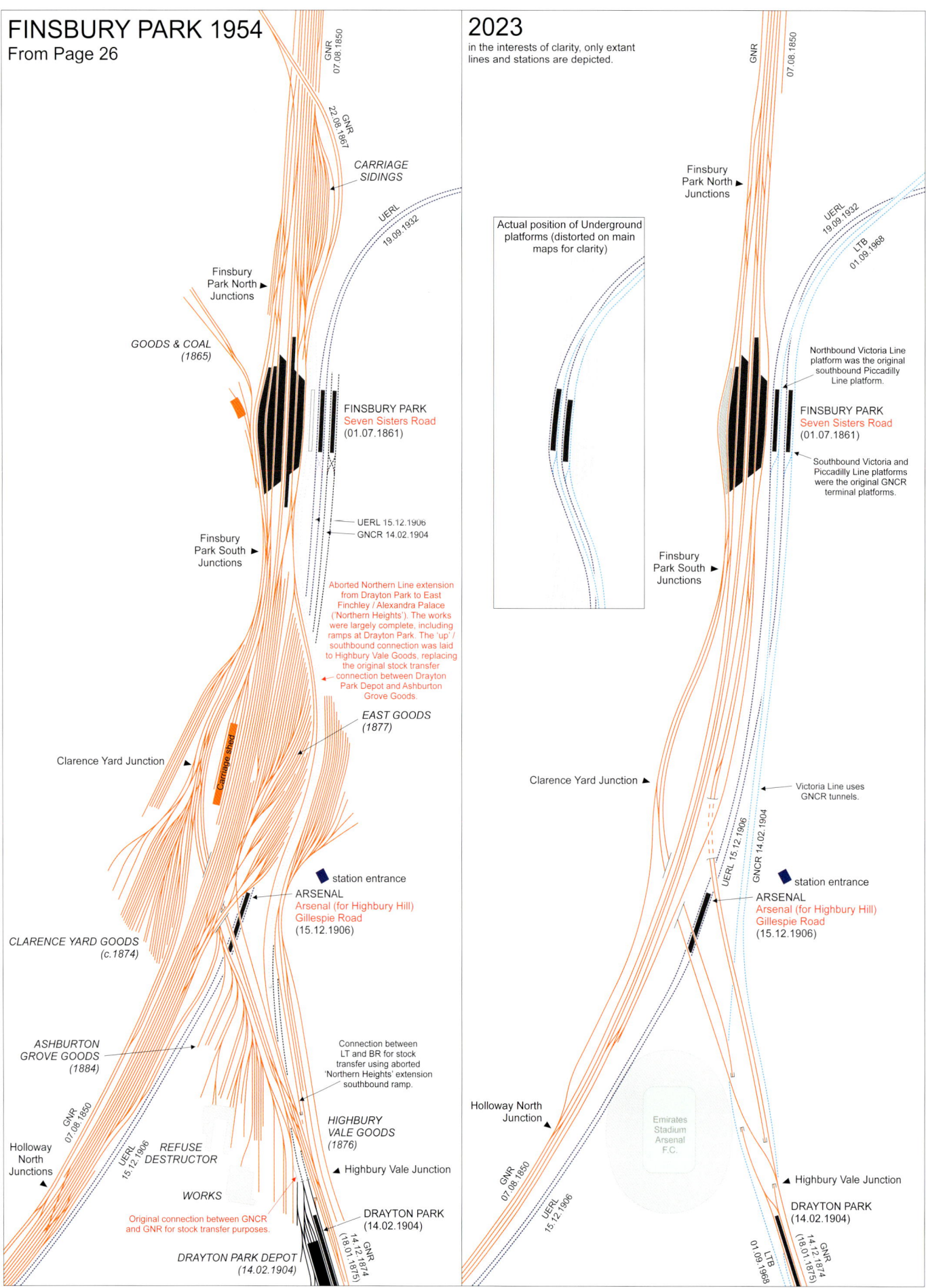

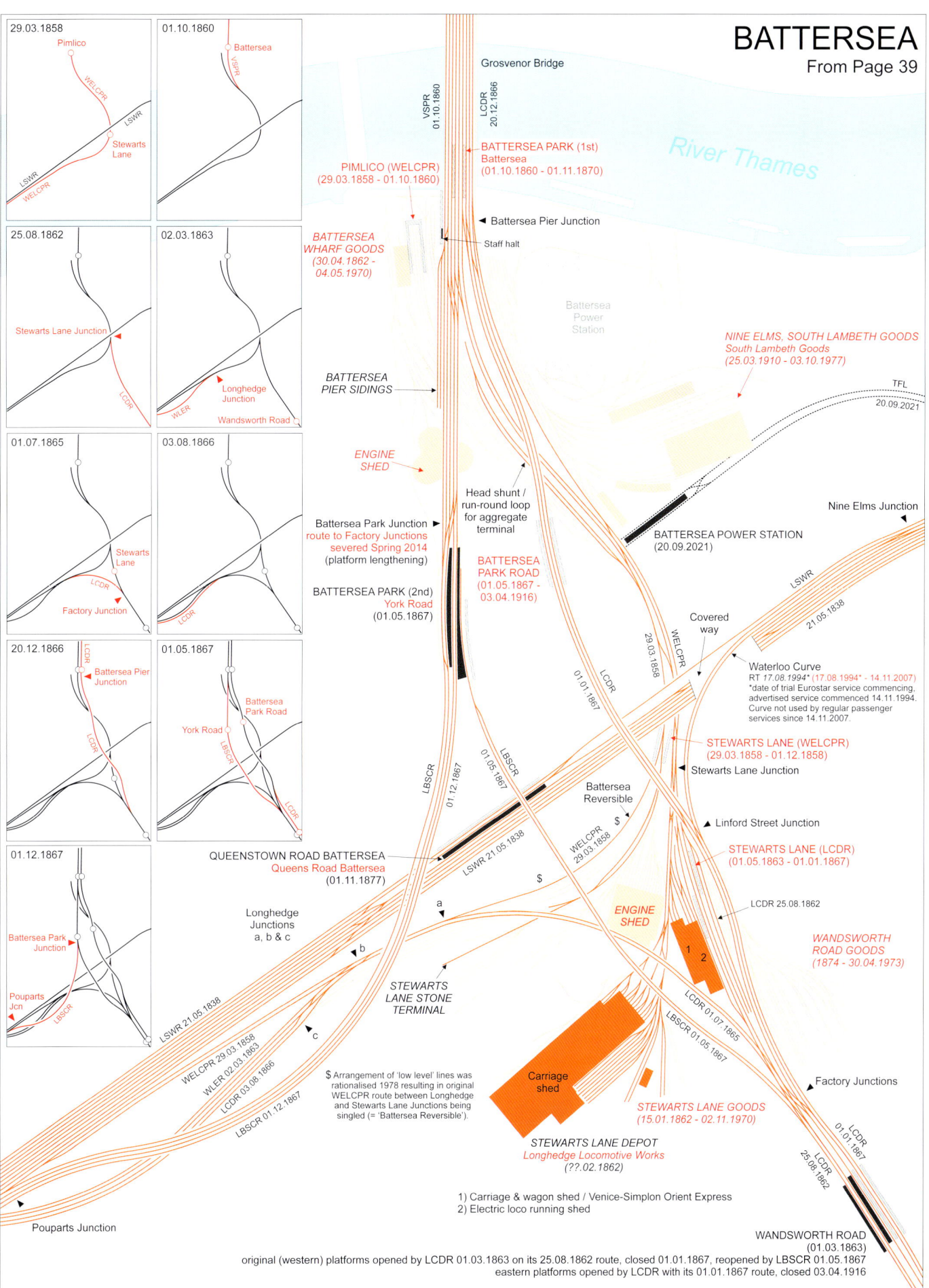

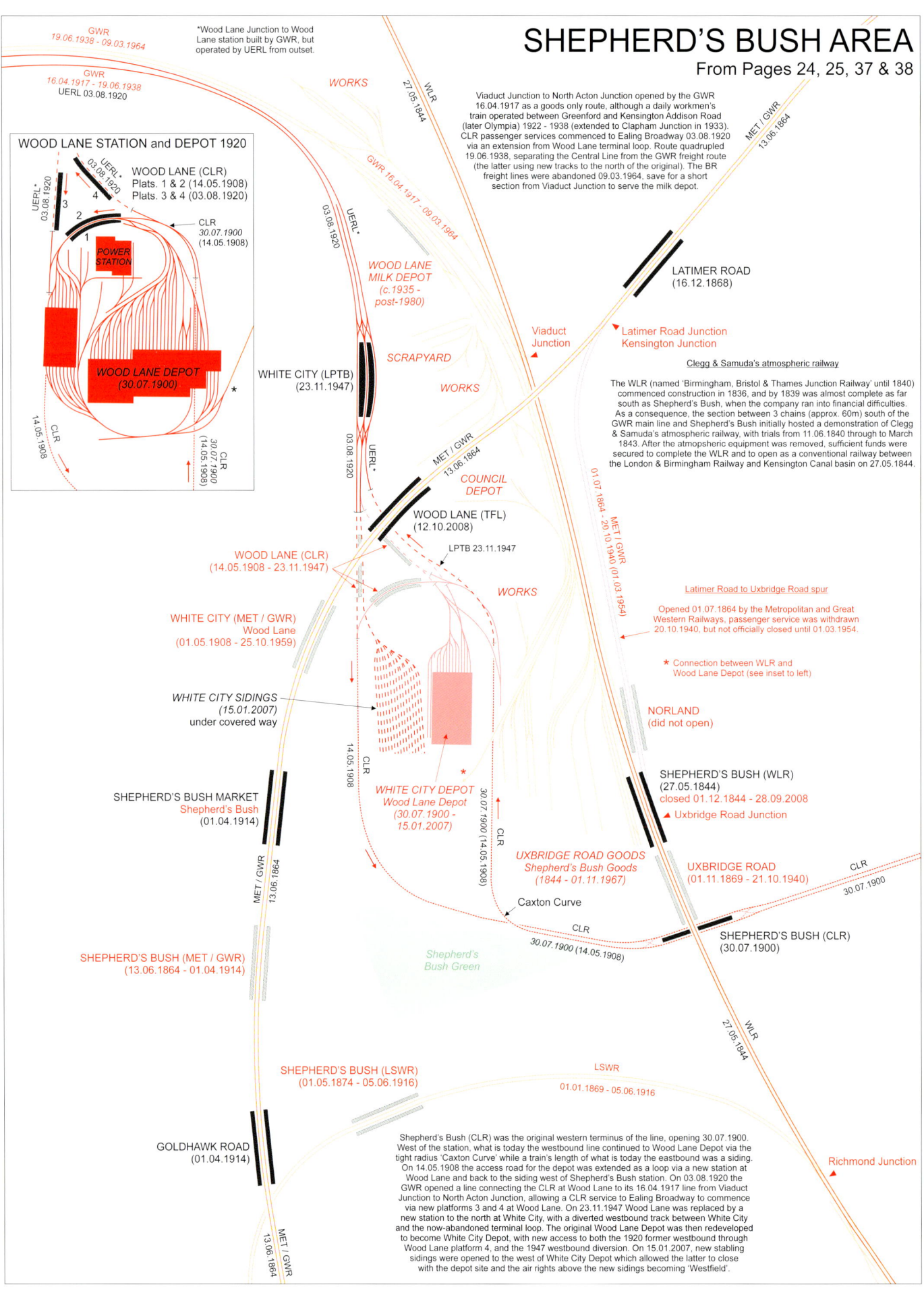

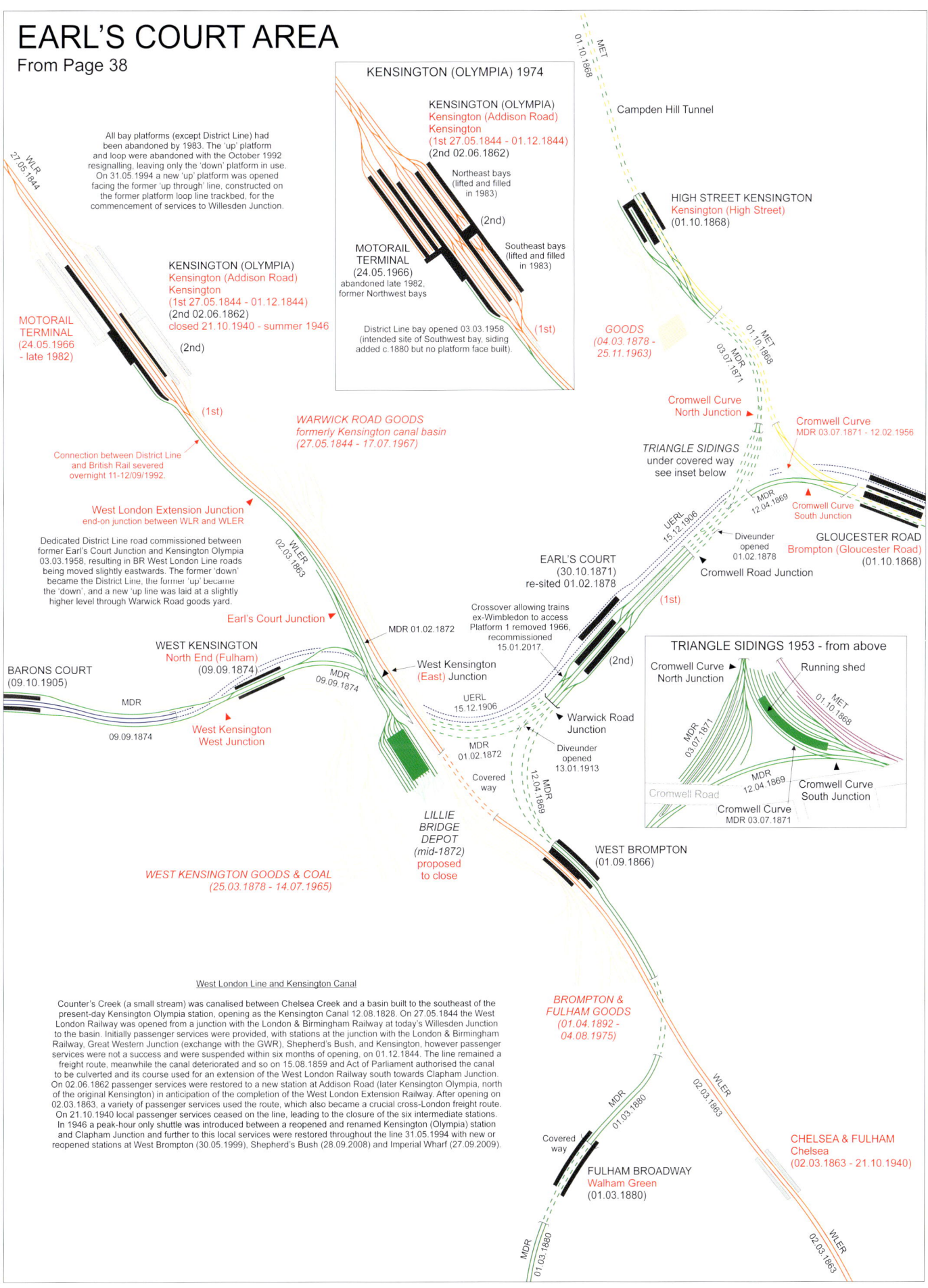

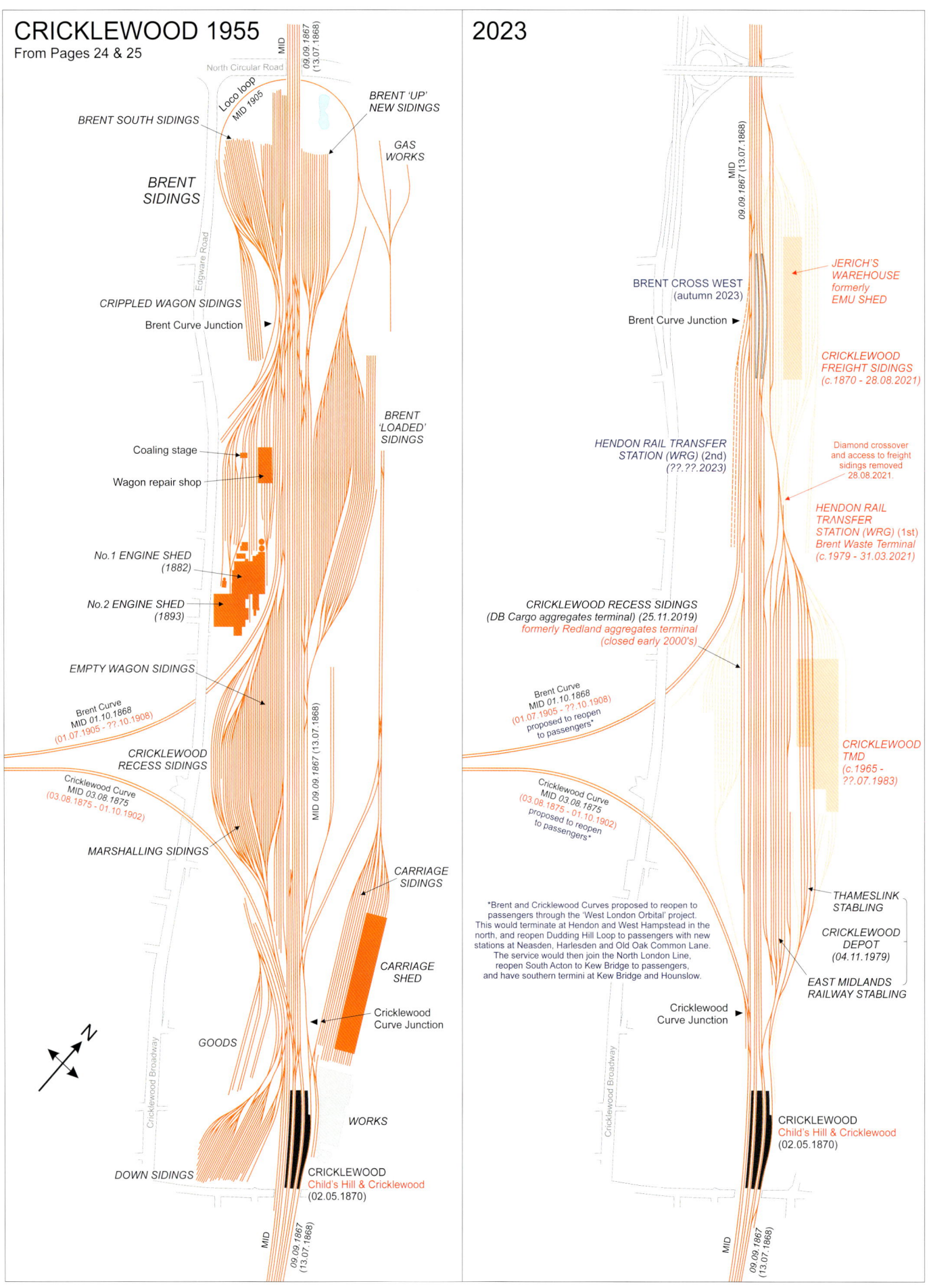

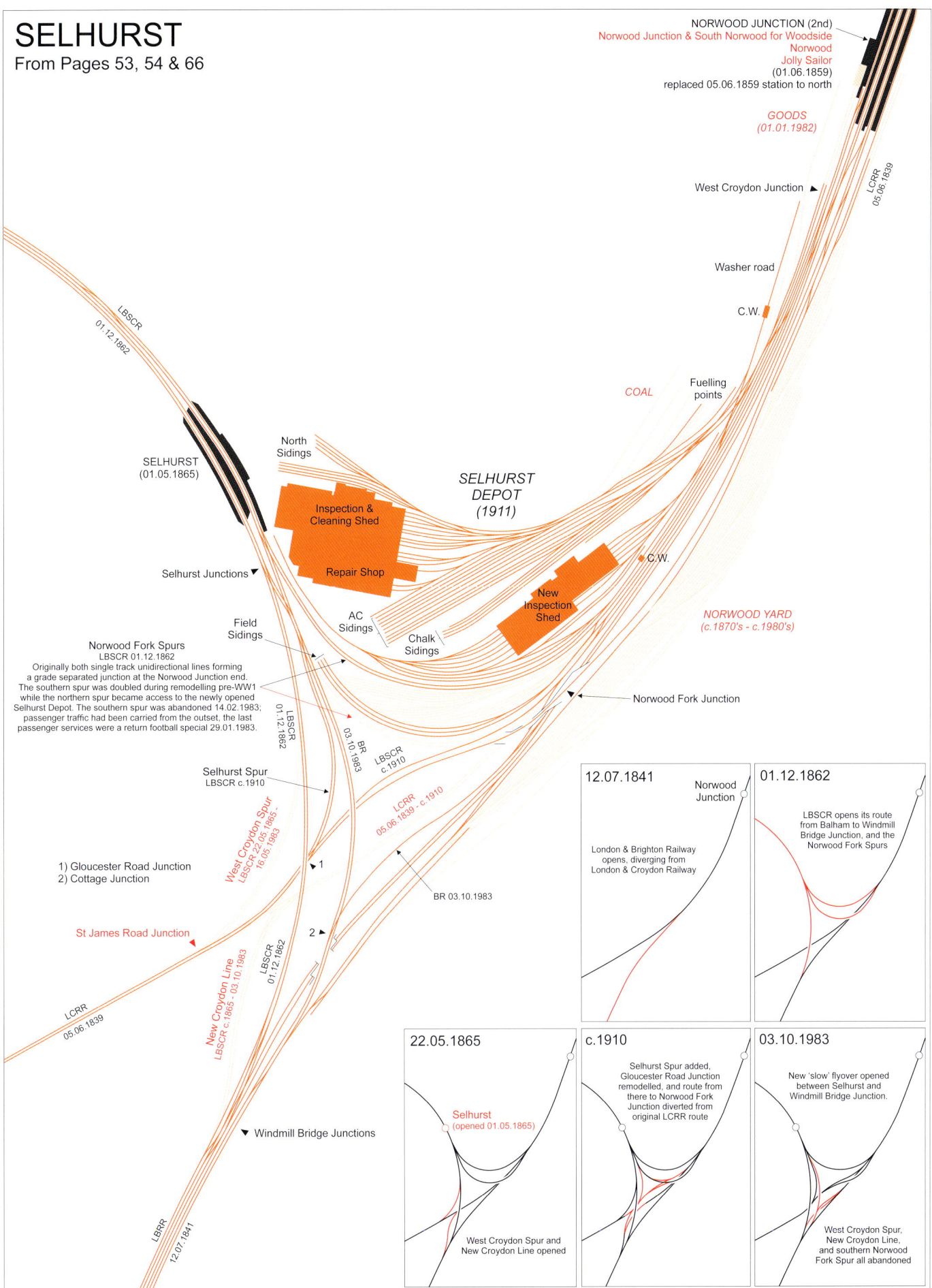

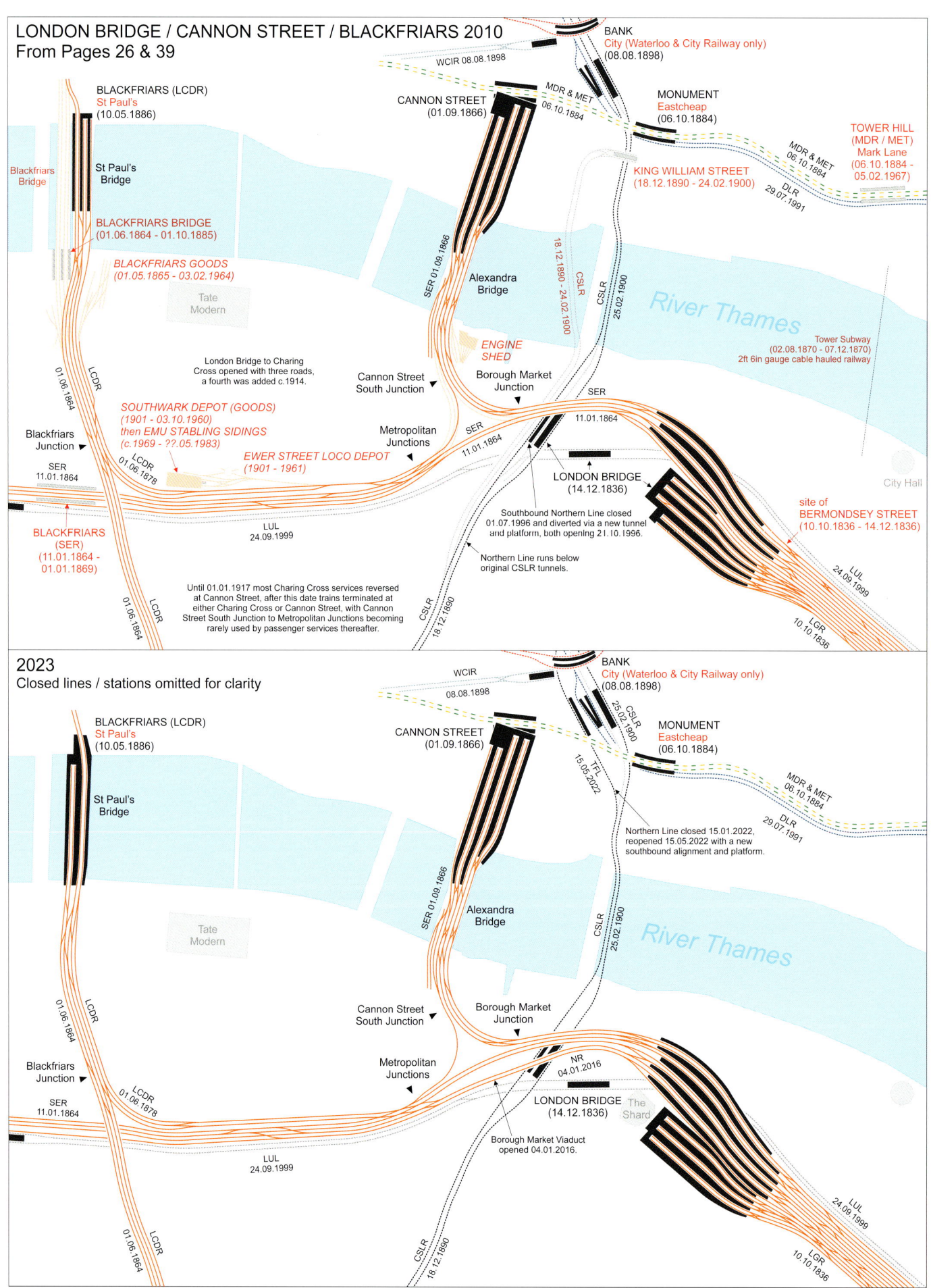

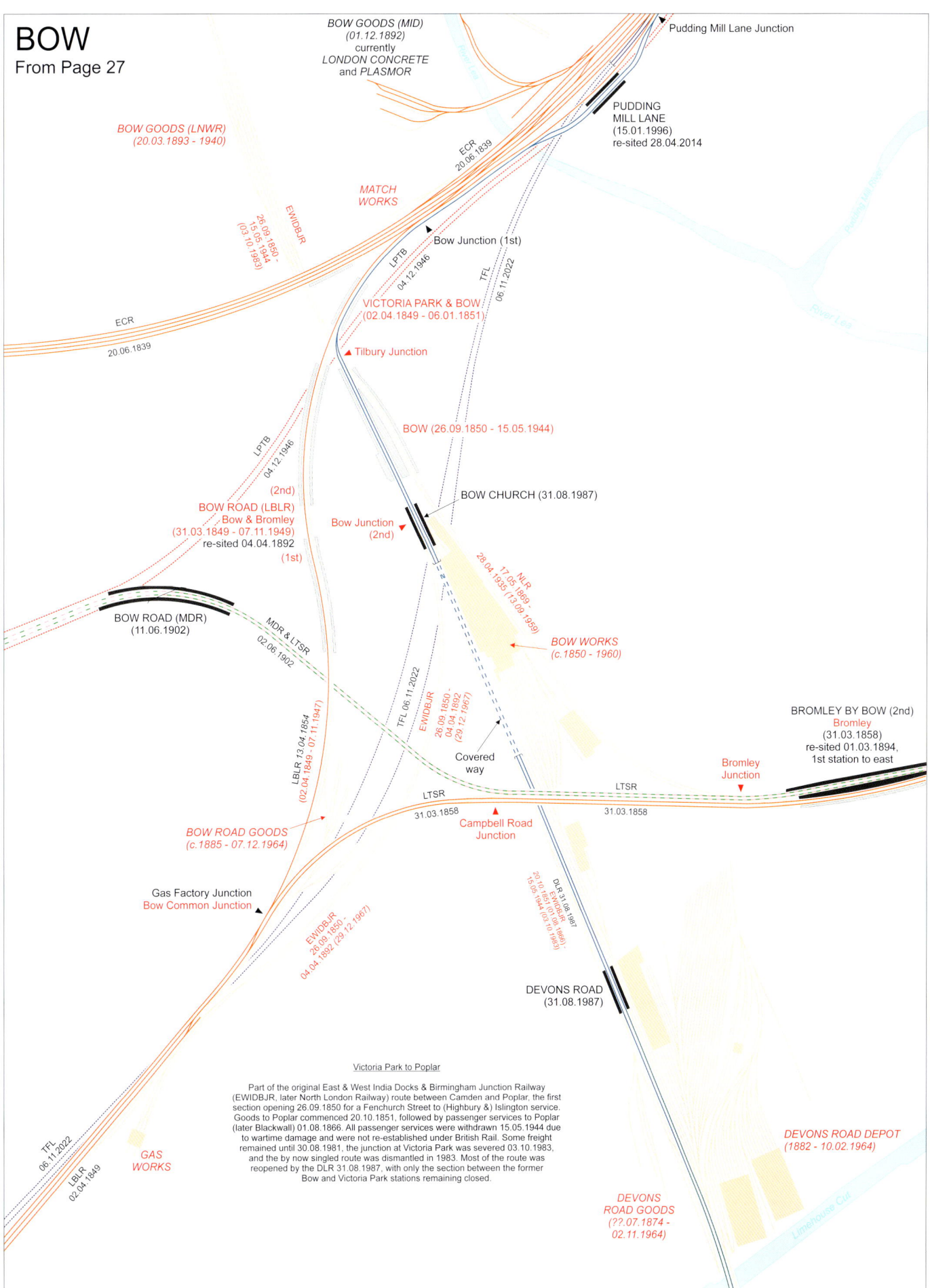

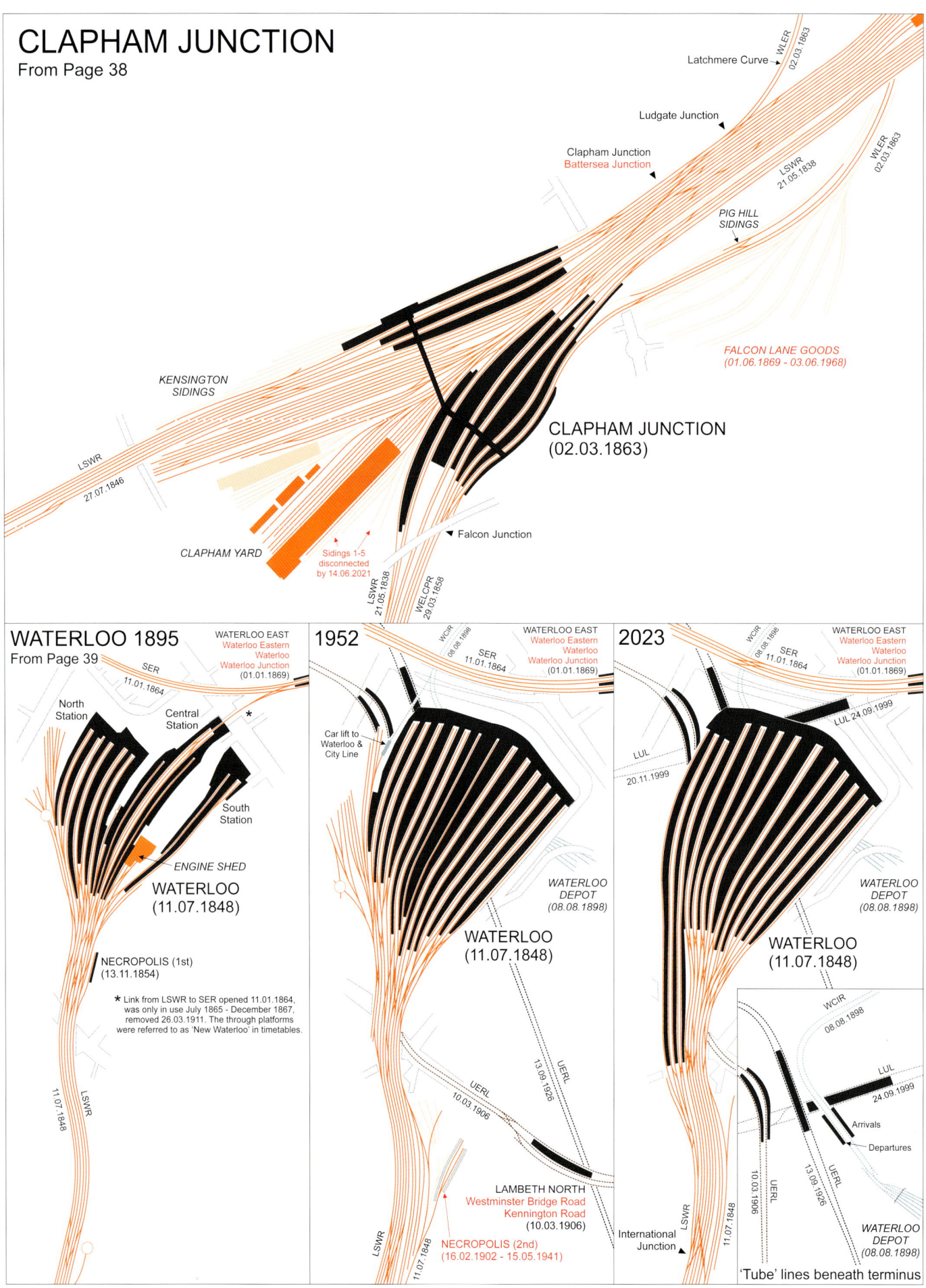

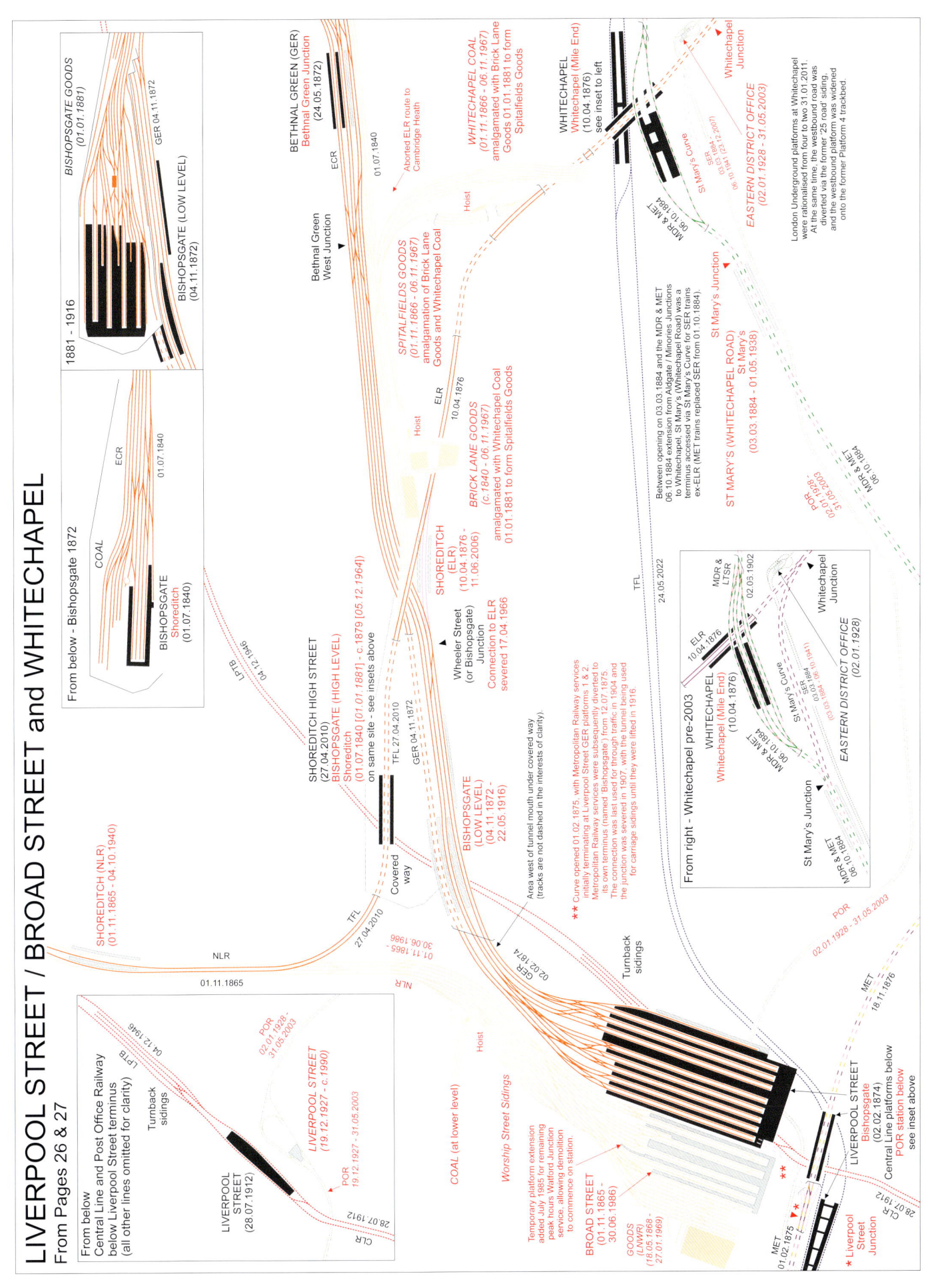

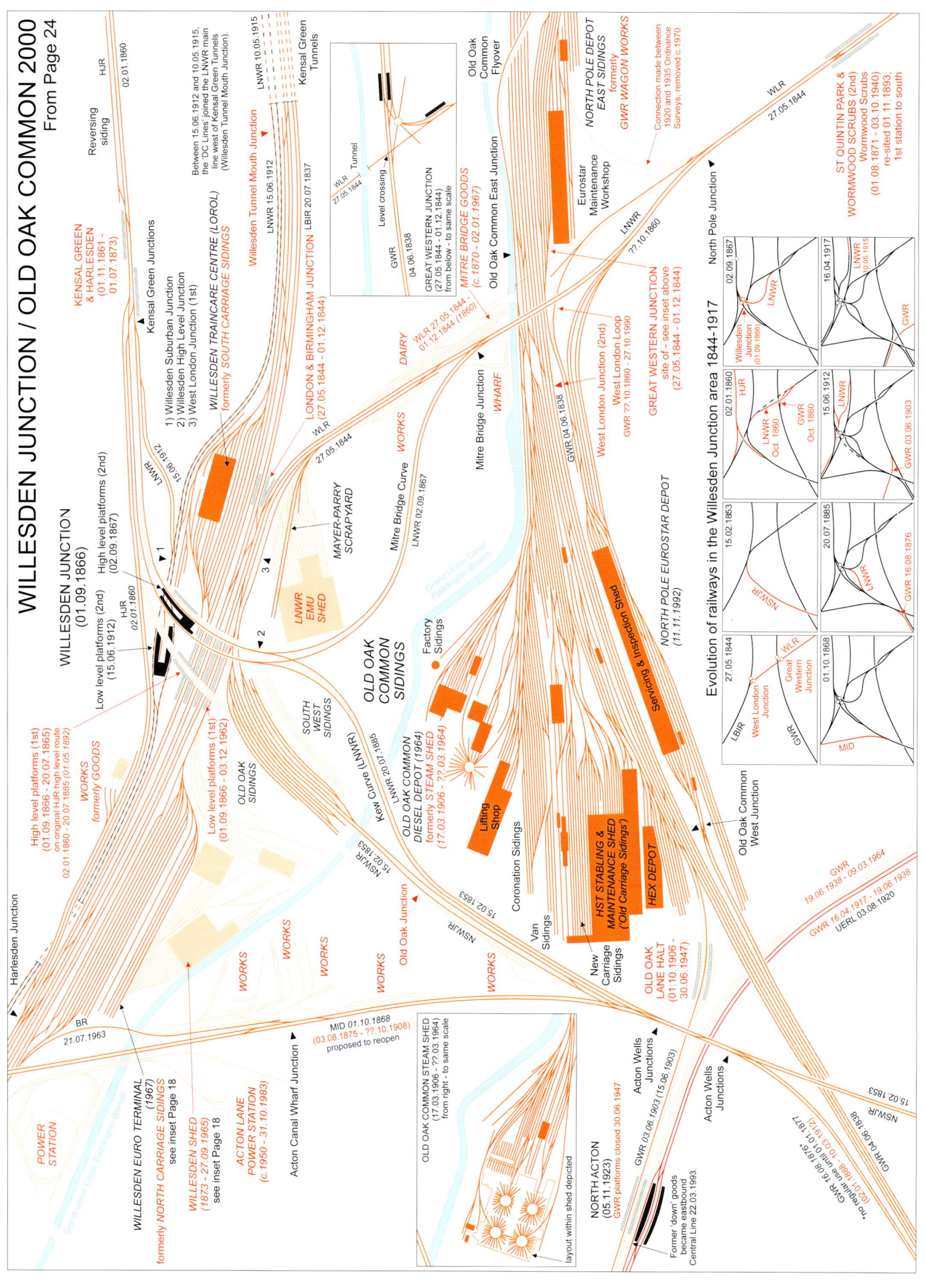

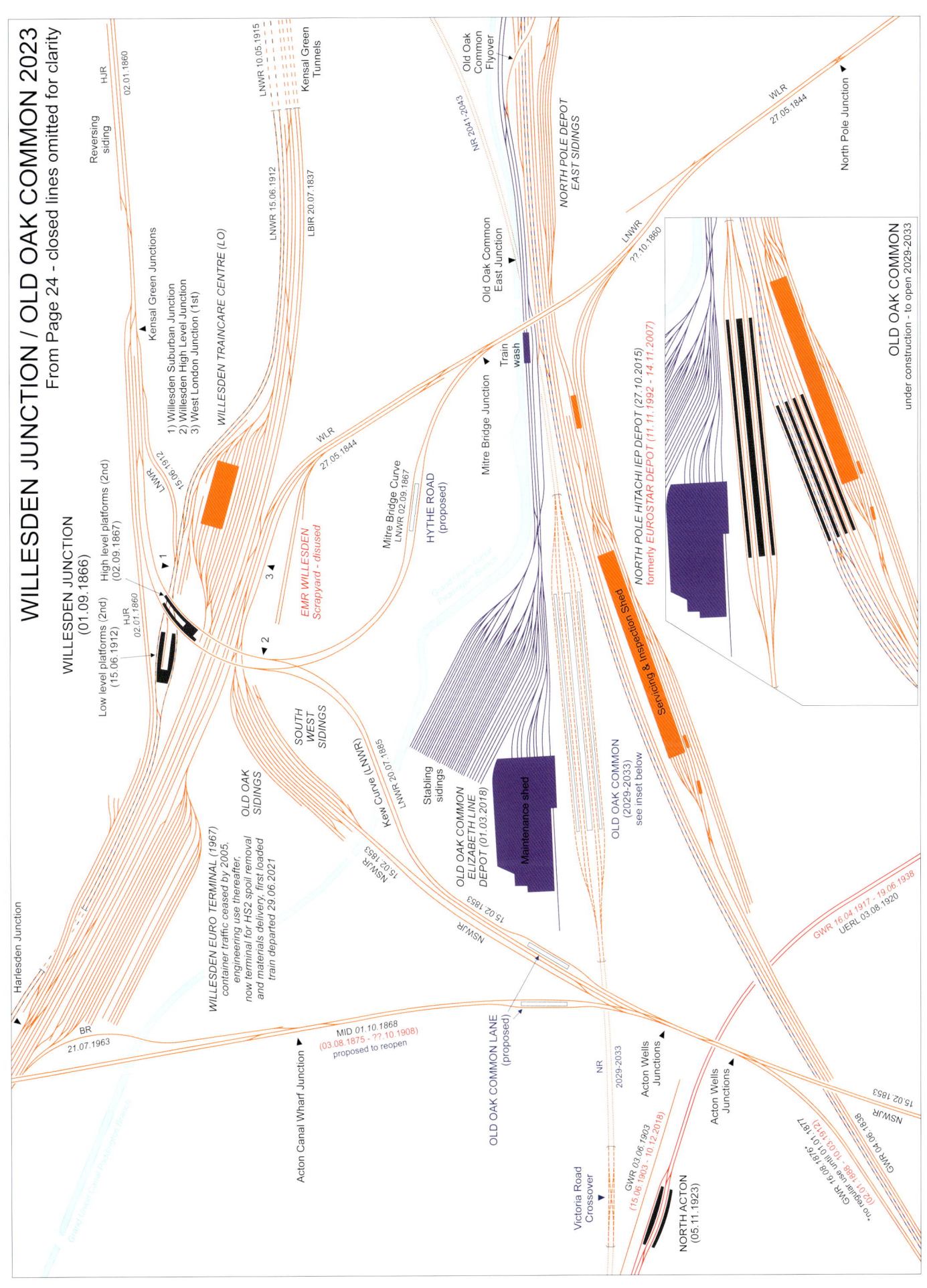

Index

Names quoted are the current names or the name at the point of closure. As many alternative names are quoted as possible with dates of name changes noted, but please note that at any given time names could vary between different timetables and station name boards, even between name boards on different platforms of the same station.
If two stations shared the same name, they are differentiated through the addition of the abbreviated name of the railway company that opened it in brackets. Where more than one station shared the same name and were built by the same railway company, they are differentiated chronologically through the suffix (1st), (2nd), etc. Entries in black plain capital text denote open passenger stations, red closed, blue under construction or proposed (May 2023). Previous names are listed in reverse chronological order in red lower-case indented text below. Entries in black italic capital text denote open non-passenger facilities, red closed, blue under construction or proposed. Entries in black lower-case text denote in-use railway features, e.g., junctions, tunnels, etc., red disused, blue under construction or proposed.

Dates are given as accurately as possible. Italic dates refer to non-passenger usage. Goods yards are listed with the associated passenger station if applicable, unless the location of the goods yard was significantly remote from the passenger station. Where a station had a goods yard associated with it, dates of opening and closing are stated for both passenger and goods facilities, differentiated by 'P' and 'G'. The same principle applies to connecting curves / loops, although in this case 'G' relates to any non-passenger usage. Unless there is evidence to the contrary, goods yards are assumed to have opened with the associated passenger station, although I recognise this may not always necessarily be the case. In some cases, approximate dates are quoted where no reliable source can be found; these are generally inferred from Ordnance Survey maps with the rationale stated in the notes. In some cases, research established conflicting information. Where sufficient doubt remains about which information is correct, all is stated with its respective sources noted.

Opening dates are the first full day of normal service unless otherwise indicated, closure dates are the first full traffic day without trains unless otherwise indicated. For example, if a station was only open Monday-Friday at the point of closure and was last served on a Friday, the following Monday's date is quoted as the closure date. Please note that a 'traffic day' can often extend into the following calendar day if the last train is after Midnight. For the purposes of a closure date, I regard such late-night trains in terms of their traffic day date, not calendar day. For example, if a station was last served at 00:05 on 01/01/1900, 01/01/1900 and not 02/01/1900 is the closure date. Dates dependent on Bradshaw (published monthly) or monthly timetables are approximated thus; if a station first appeared in January 1850, then the opening date is given as c.01/01/1850 on the assumption the station was open by 01/01/1850 in order to appear. Conversely, if a station last appeared in January 1850, then the closing date is given as c.01/02/1850 on the assumption the station was open for some or all of January.

Minor periods of closure of two weeks or less (e.g., due to engineering works, enemy action, industrial action, etc.) are generally omitted, although some shorter closures of historical interest are recorded. While two weeks is somewhat arbitrary, it excludes the vast majority of engineering closures which would have significantly added to the number of short-term closures listed in this index. Some stations were closed for long periods of their existence and demolished (e.g. Dalston Junction, Homerton, Shepherds Bush [WLR]), but as they were ultimately rebuilt on the same site with the original name, the original opening date is given with the period of closure recorded in the notes. Minor re-siting of stations is recorded in the notes under a single index entry. Often industrial sites were in operation before and/or after they were connected to the railway system. In these cases, the dates that rail traffic was in operation (including any internal system), where known, are quoted.

A

Name	Page / grid		Date opened	Date closed	Opened by	Notes
Abbey Mills Curve	28 / 5A	P	01/06/1858	27/10/1940	LTSR	Abbey Mills Curve open to passengers 01/06/1858 – 27/10/1940.
		G	*31/03/1858*	*27/07/1958*		
Abbey Mills Lower Junction	28 / 5A		31/03/1858	27/07/1958	LTSR	Junction at south end of Abbey Mills Curve.
ABBEY ROAD	28 / 4A		31/08/2011	N/A	DLR	
ABBEY WOOD	42 / 2C	P	??/??/1849	N/A	SER	Opening date unknown, either on or by 01/11/1849, does not appear to have opened with rest of line (30/07/1849). Goods yard closed 05/12/1960. New island platform opened 22/08/2016 on existing tracks to accommodate Elizabeth Line platforms to north, which opened 24/05/2022.
		G	*??/??/1849*	*05/12/1960*		
Acton Canal Wharf Junction	24 / 5C 91 & 92		21/07/1963	N/A	BR	Date is that of opening of curve to WCML, access to various works alongside canal existed before this date.
ACTON CENTRAL	37 / 1B	P	01/08/1853	N/A	NSWJR	Bay platform formerly on 'up' side. 'Central' suffix added 01/11/1925. Goods yard opened 1856, closed 01/03/1965.
Acton		G	*1856*	*01/03/1965*		
ACTON COAL	37 / 1C		*1867*	*04/01/1965*	NSWJR	
Acton Curve	37 / 2B 51 / 2B	P	01/05/1878	01/10/1880	LSWR	Briefly carried passenger traffic 01/05/1878 - 01/10/1880. Last used for access to West Kensington Goods & coal, last train 29/07/1965; 13/09/1965 is official closure date.
		G	*01/03/1878*	*13/09/1965*		
Acton Diveunder	24 / 6A		03/01/2017	N/A	NR	Diveunder carrying 'up slow' beneath Acton Yard access roads. Closed 24/01/2018 to 20/05/2018 due to partial collapse of retaining wall.
Acton East (or Poplar) Junction	24 / 6B		16/08/1876	N/A	GWR	Curve to NSWJR opened 16/08/1876, but saw no regular use until 01/01/1877.
Acton Gatehouse Junction	37 / 1B		01/05/1857	03/05/1965	NSWJR	Junction between NSWJR main line and their Hammersmith & Chiswick Branch.
ACTON JUNCTION	37 / 1B		08/04/1858?	Pre 1864	NSWJR	1858 Bradshaw recorded a station between Acton (Central) and Kew, presumably provided for exchange with the Hammersmith & Chiswick branch so an 08/04/1858 opening date is assumed. Per Jackson, initially the passenger coach for the branch was 'slipped' (detached from a moving train) in the down direction before being collected by the branch's loco, and in the up direction would be attached to the rear of trains ex-Kew. Derailments resulting from this unofficial practice led to it ceasing from 01/11/1865, with the branch train instead reversing at the junction and working to Acton (Central), where the coach would be attached or removed. The station was not recorded in the 1864 Bradshaw so is assumed to have closed before then. 1882 OS appears to show an up platform and potential station building on the north side of Acton Lane, but no down platform – however also per Jackson originally the branch joined the NSWJR main line directly, but by 1882 there was a third track parallel to the down, which could have necessitated demolition of the down platform. By the 1895 OS Acton Lane had been diverted to the north, with the current bridge crossing the road corresponding with the site of the potential platform(s).
Acton Lane East Junction	37 / 2B 51 / 2B		03/12/1911	13/09/1965	LSWR	LSWR dive-under opened due to quadrupling works Ravenscourt Park to Turnham Green, later goods use only.
ACTON LANE POWER STATION	24 / 5C 91		*c.1950*	*31/10/1983*	PRIV	
Acton Lane West Junction	37 / 2B 51 / 2B		01/03/1878	13/09/1965	LSWR	Junction at east end of Acton Curve. Remains as the NR / TfL boundary.

Name	Page / grid		Date opened	Date closed	Opened by	Notes
Acton Loop Line	37 / 2B 51 / 1A	P	13/06/1905	02/03/1959	MDR	First used for construction traffic for MDR extension to South Harrow. Doubled shortly before passenger services commenced 13/06/1905. Goods traffic ceased 22/02/1915 and connection at north end 'clipped' out of use (not physically removed until c.1930). Branch singled 14/02/1932. Service withdrawn and branch dismantled 02/03/1959.
		G	15/05/1899	22/02/1915		
ACTON MAIN LINE	24 / 6B	P	01/02/1868	N/A	GWR	Coal yard closed 1931. 'Main Line' suffix added 01/11/1949.
Acton		G	01/02/1868	1931		
ACTON TOWN Mill Hill Park	37 / 1B		01/07/1879	N/A	MDR	Rebuilt and renamed 01/03/1910, further rebuilt 1933. First served by Piccadilly Line 04/07/1932. South Acton Shuttle served bay platform 5 until 28/02/1959.
Acton Town North Junction	37 / 1A		01/05/1883	N/A	MDR	Extensively remodelled 1932 during Turnham Green to Northfields quadrupling.
Acton Town South Junction	37 / 2B 51 / 1A		15/05/1899	01/03/1959	MDR	First passenger use 13/06/1905, last freight use 1915.
Acton Wells Junctions	24 / 5C 91 & 92		01/10/1868	N/A	MID / NSWJR	Junction between MID Dudding Hill Loop and NSWJR. Junction with GWR curve to Acton added 01/01/1877.
Acton West Junction	24 / 6A		c.1931	N/A	GWR	Seemingly established during Acton Yard's 1931 expansion. Reconstructed with a grad separation 03/01/2017 (see Acton Diveunder).
ACTON WORKS (REW)	37 / 2A 51 / 1A		1923	N/A	UERL	Works for heavy overhaul of London Underground rolling stock. REW = Railway Engineering Works.
ACTON YARD (YEOMAN AGGREGATES)	24 / 6B		??/01/1877	N/A	GWR	Yard established by GWR January 1877. Expanded 03/06/1901 and again 1931. Closed as a marshalling yard 24/05/1984, remaining in use for stone traffic (Yeoman Aggregates).
ADDINGTON VILLAGE	67 / 4C		10/05/2000	N/A	CTL	
ADDISCOMBE (MKR) Addiscombe (Croydon) Croydon (Addiscombe) Croydon (Addiscombe Road)	67 / 1A	P	01/04/1864	02/06/1997	MKR	Opened as 'Croydon (Addiscombe Road)', renamed 'Croydon (Addiscombe)' 01/04/1925, 'Addiscombe (Croydon)' ??/03/1926, 'Croydon' suffix dropped 13/06/1955. Goods yard did not open until 11/07/1925, closed 17/06/1968. Reduced to one operational platform (platform 2) March 1996 due to signal box being destroyed by arson. Elmers End to Addiscombe last train 31/05/1997, but as no Sunday service timetabled, Monday 02/06/1997 is given as closure date (station removed from 1997 Summer timetable published 01/06/1997).
		G	11/07/1925	17/06/1968		
ADDISCOMBE (CTL)	67 / 1A		23/05/2000	N/A	CTL	
ADDISCOMBE EMU SHED	67 / 1A		11/07/1925	??/04/1995	SR	Shed commissioned on 11/07/1925 according to kentrail.org.uk, electrification of branch planned for 01/12/1925 but was delayed until 28/02/1926, so presumably no regular use for EMU stabling before this date. Closed as a traincrew depot 12/04/1993, although stabling of 4EPB units continued until withdrawal April 1995 (shed was never cleared for stabling of 'Networkers').
ADDLESTONE	61 / 2B	P	14/02/1848	N/A	LSWR	Goods yard closed 05/12/1966
		G	14/02/1848	05/12/1966		
Addlestone Junction	61 / 3C		1885	N/A	LSWR	Junction at north end of Byfleet Curve.
AEC MOTOR WORKS	36 / 1A		?	?	PRIV	
AGGREGATE INDUSTRIES LTD (WATFORD)	2 / 3C		c.2014	N/A	PRIV	
AGGREGATE INDUSTRIES LTD (WEMBLEY)	24 / 3C 22		2001	N/A	PRIV	
ALBANY PARK	56 / 2D		07/07/1935	N/A	SR	
Albert Dock Junction	62 / 3B		03/08/1880	08/09/1940	LSKD / GER	Junction of Gallions branch.
Aldersbrook Flyover	28 / 2D		06/10/1947	N/A	LNER	
ALDERSBROOK (UP) CAR HOLDING SIDINGS	28 / 2D		c.1894	N/A	GER	Appear on OS maps after 1895, may have been opened at same time as GER quadrupling work (c.1894).
ALDGATE	27 / 6A 74 / 1B		18/11/1876	N/A	MET	
Aldgate Junction	27 / 6A 74 / 1B		01/10/1884	N/A	MET	
ALDGATE EAST	27 / 6A 74 / 1B		06/10/1884	N/A	MDR / MET	Relocated East 30/10/1938 (Junction remodelling to ease congestion around Aldgate Triangle). Crossover east of station removed over weekend of 08-09/02/2020.
Aldgate East Junction	27 / 6A 74 / 1B		06/10/1884	N/A	MDR / MET	Relocated East 30/10/1938 (Junction remodelling to ease congestion around Aldgate Triangle).
ALDWYCH Strand	26 / 6B		30/11/1907	03/10/1994	UERL (GNPBR)	Opened as 'Strand', renamed 'Aldwych' 09/05/1915. Through trains to Finsbury Park withdrawn 04/10/1908. Closed 22/09/1940 - 01/07/1946 (WW2). Aldwych Branch closed to passengers 03/10/1994 (last train 30/09/1994, no weekend service at point of closure), but a 1972 Mk1 Stock train was retained for filming work until its removal 24/11/2021, the last known train movement on the branch. It is planned to disconnect the branch from the Piccadilly Line representing full abandonment.
Alexandra Bridge	87		01/09/1866	N/A	SER	
ALEXANDRA PALACE (GNR) Wood Green Wood Green (Alexandra Park) Wood Green	14 / 4B	P	01/05/1859	N/A	GNR	Opened as 'Wood Green', suffix '(Alexandra Park)' added 01/08/1864, dropped 18/03/1971. Renamed 'Alexandra Palace' 17/05/1982. Goods yard closed 24/01/1966.
		G	01/05/1859	24/01/1966		
ALEXANDRA PALACE (MHPR) Alexandra Park (1891-1892 only) Alexandra Palace	14 / 4B		24/05/1873	05/07/1954	MHPR	Nominally opened by Muswell Hill & Palace Railway, but operated by GNR from opening. Closed and reopened several times; closed 01/08/1873 - 01/05/1875 plus on several other occasions thereafter (mostly during Winter), known as Alexandra Park 1891-1892. Open without interruption 01/04/1898 to 29/10/1951, when closed again until 07/01/1952. Permanently closed 05/07/1954. Had been intended for electrification and transfer to LPTB, but works abandoned by LTE post-WW2.
ALL SAINTS	27 / 6D		31/08/1987	N/A	DLR	On Site of former NLR Poplar Station. Name boards carry suffix 'for Chrisp Street Market', also added to on-train digital announcements, although the suffix does not appear on the TfL map.
ALPERTON Perivale Alperton	23 / 3D		28/06/1903	N/A	MDR	Renamed 'Alperton' 07/10/1910. First served Piccadilly Line 04/07/1932, last served District Line 23/10/1933.
Alsike Road Junction	42 / 2D		02/10/2021	N/A	NR	Junction between Abbey Wood Transfer Line (Elizabeth Line) and North Kent Line (no passenger traffic permitted). Date given is that of commissioning.
AMERSHAM Amersham & Chesham Bois Amersham	1 / 3A	P	01/09/1892	N/A	MET	Suffix '& Chesham Bois' 12/03/1922 - ??/??/1934. Metropolitan Line services beyond Amersham ceased 10/09/1961. Goods yard closed 04/07/1966.
		G	01/09/1892	04/07/1966		
AMPERE WAY IKEA Ampere Way Ampere Way	66 / 1B		10/05/2000	N/A	CTL	'IKEA' Prefix 18/10/2006 - ??/03/2008 (Sponsorship deal).
ANERLEY Anerley Bridge	54 / 4A		05/06/1839	N/A	LCRR	Suffix 'Bridge' dropped c.1840. According to Mitchell & Smith, initially spelt 'Annerley'. Rebuilt 1853-4 (quadrupling).

Name	Page / grid		Date opened	Date closed	Opened by	Notes
ANGEL	26 / 4C		17/11/1901	N/A	CSLR	Terminus from opening until 12/05/1907. Closed 09/08/1922 - 20/04/1924 (tunnel widening), closed 16/10/1940 – 08/11/1940 (unexploded bomb). Northbound road routed via new tunnel 09/08/1992, with new northbound platform opening the following day. The southbound platform then closed 10/08/1992 – 19/10/1992 for rebuilding. Closed 31/08/2001 – 17/09/2001 (defective escalators).
ANGEL ROAD 　Water Lane 　Edmonton	15 / 2B	P G	15/09/1840 *15/09/1840*	03/06/2019 *?*	NER	Opened as 'Edmonton', renamed 'Water Lane' 01/03/1849, 'Angel Road' 01/01/1864. Goods yard opened with passenger station, but closure date unknown. Closed 03/06/2019 (replaced by Meridian Water station to south, opened same date). NB: last trains called Friday 31/05/2019; due to no service weekends at point of closure, Monday 03/06/2019 is the closure date.
Angel Road Junction 　Edmonton Junction	15 / 2B		01/03/1849	07/12/1964	ECR	Originally 'Edmonton Junction'; junction of ECR Enfield (Town) branch with NER Lea Valley line. Angel Road Junction to Lower Edmonton Junction closed 07/12/1964.
Angerstein Junction	41 / 3B		30/10/1852	N/A	SER / PRIV	Junction between Angerstein Wharf branch and SER North Kent Line. London-facing junction eliminated 1890.
ANGERSTEIN WHARF	41 / 2B		*30/10/1852*	N/A	PRIV	Angerstein Wharf Branch privately built by John Angerstein, but leased to SER from outset. Purchased by SER 1898. Several industrial sidings were present for various purposes: A.A. Oil Co. and B.P. / Shell Mex (oil), Christie's (sleeper & telegraph pole works), United Glass works, Renwick Wilton (coal), as well as giving access to East Greenwich gasworks and the LCC Central Tram repair works. Today the wharf handles aggregates traffic (Aggregate Industries and Tarmac) and waste (Norris Waste).
APCM COAL TERMINAL (SOUTHFLEET)	59 / 3C		*1972*	1976	PRIV	Established on site of former Southfleet station at end of branch from Fawkham Junction (former LCDR Gravesend West branch, closed 24/03/1968). Supplied coal to nearby Northfleet Cement works (APCM, later Blue Circle).
ARCHWAY 　Highgate (Archway) 　Archway (Highgate) 　Highgate	26 / 1A		22/06/1907	N/A	UERL (CCEHR)	Terminus 22/06/1907 - 03/07/1939, opened as 'Highgate'. 'Archway' prefix added 11/06/1939, reversed 19/01/1941, 'Highgate' prefix dropped ??/12/1947. Closed 19/03/2000 – 08/04/2000 (escalator repairs).
ARENA	54 / 6B		23/05/2000	N/A	CTL	Became a junction a week after opening (30/05/2000) with addition of branch to Elmers End.
ARNOS GROVE	14 / 2B		19/09/1932	N/A	UERL (GNPBR)	Terminus of extension from Finsbury Park 19/09/1932 - 13/03/1933.
ARNOS GROVE SIDINGS	14 / 2A		19/09/1932	N/A	UERL (GNPBR)	Stabling Sidings for Piccadilly Line.
ARSENAL 　Arsenal (for Highbury Hill) 　Gillespie Road	26 / 2C 81		15/12/1906	N/A	UERL (GNPBR)	Opened as 'Gillespie Road', renamed 'Arsenal (for Highbury Hill)' 31/10/1932, suffix gradually dropped. Closed 01/09/1939 – 01/12/1939, 23/07/2006 – 07/08/2006, 18/02/2006 – 03/03/2006 and 19/03/2020 – 13/07/2020 (latter closure COVID-19).
ASHBURTON GROVE GOODS	26 / 2C 81		1884	13/06/1960	GNR	
ASHFORD	48 / 2C	P G	22/08/1848 *22/08/1848*	N/A 04/01/1965	LSWR	Goods yard closed 04/01/1965.
ASHTEAD	70 / 1D	P G	01/02/1859 *01/02/1859*	N/A 01/01/1962	LBSCR / LSWR	Goods yard closed 01/01/1962.
AVENUE ROAD	54 / 5B		23/05/2000	N/A	CTL	

B

Name	Page / grid		Date opened	Date closed	Opened by	Notes
BAKER STREET	25 / 5D		10/01/1863	N/A	MET	MSJWR platforms to Swiss Cottage opened 13/04/1868 (Now Metropolitan Line Platforms), BSWR platforms opened 10/03/1906. Additional southbound Bakerloo Line platform from Stanmore opened 20/11/1939, Jubilee Line opened 01/05/1979 using existing southbound Bakerloo platform ex-Stanmore and a new northbound platform. Bakerloo and Jubilee Lines non-stopped 13/02/2000 – 03/03/2000 (escalator repairs). Northbound Bakerloo and Jubilee Lines non-stopped weekdays only from 02/09/2002. From 13/01/2003 trains stopped after 20:00, then from 03/02/2003 also between 10:00 and 15:30. Northbound Bakerloo and Jubilee services stopped as normal from 02/05/2003 (escalator repairs).
BALHAM 　Balham & Upper Tooting 　Balham	52 / 1D 53 / 1A		01/12/1856	N/A	WELCPR	Original WELCPR station west of road, re-sited east 1863. '& Upper Tooting' suffix added ??/03/1927, dropped 06/10/1969 (applied to main line only). UERL (later Northern Line) station opened 06/12/1926. Closed 01/09/1939 – 15/12/1939 (flood protection). Closed 15/10/1940 – 19/01/1941 following bomb and resulting flooding (line was closed Clapham South to Tooting Bec until 08/01/1941).
Balham Junction	53 / 1A		01/12/1862	N/A	LBSCR	
BANDON HALT	66 / 3B		11/06/1906	07/06/1914	LBSCR	
BANK 　City (WCIR only)	26 / 6D 87		08/08/1898	N/A	WCIR	Opened by WCIR as 'City' 08/08/1898. CSLR and CLR platforms opened 25/02/1900 and 30/07/1900 respectively as 'Bank'. Closed 01/09/1939 – 22/12/1939 (installation of flood protection). Waterloo & City platforms renamed from 'City' to 'Bank' 1940. Closed 12/01/1941 – 17/03/1941 (bomb damage). DLR platforms opened 29/07/1991. Southbound Northern Line closed Moorgate to Kennington 01/07/1996 – 21/10/1996 (tunnel realignment at London Bridge). Northern Line closed 15/01/2022 to allow completion of works to re-align southbound tunnel to serve a new platform, reopened 15/05/2022.
BANSTEAD 　Banstead & Burgh Heath 　Banstead	65 / 6A	P G	22/05/1865 *22/05/1865*	N/A 07/09/1964	LBSCR	Suffix '& Burgh Heath' 01/06/1898 - ??/08/1928. Goods yard closed 07/09/1964 (note: Jackson refers to goods not being into use until 'about 1880', but Borley gives goods opening on same date as passenger, and goods yard is visible on 1871 OS). Former 'up' platform closed and branch singled 03/10/1982.
BARBICAN 　Aldersgate & Barbican 　Aldersgate 　Aldersgate Street	26 / 6D 32 / 3D		23/12/1865	N/A	MET	Opened as 'Aldersgate Street', City Widened Lines platforms (later Network Rail) added 01/03/1866, 'Street' suffix dropped 01/11/1910. '& Barbican' suffix added ??/??/1923, 'Aldersgate' prefix dropped 01/12/1968. NR platforms closed 12/09/2004 – 16/05/2005 (building work at St Pancras), and then closed for good 23/03/2009 (last train 20/03/2009), although westbound NR services had ceased stopping at Barbican prior to this date. Closed 19/03/2020 – 08/06/2020 (COVID-19).

Name	Page / grid		Date opened	Date closed	Opened by	Notes
BARKING	29 / 4A	P	13/04/1854	N/A	LTSR	Served by District Railway since 02/06/1902 (no service 30/09/1905 - 01/04/1908), Served by Metropolitan Railway since 04/05/1936 ('Hammersmith & City Line' since 30/07/1990). Goods yard originally on 'up' side of station, relocated to east c.1930 to present site of Barking Sidings, closed 01/04/1957. Station rebuilt 1959-1961. Gospel Oak service suspended 04/06/2016 to 27/02/2017 due to electrification work. Regular use of bay platform 1 ceased with opening of Barking Riverside extension 18/07/2022.
		G	13/04/1854	01/04/1957		
Barking East Junction	29 / 4B		11/05/1959	N/A	LTSR	All junctions in Barking area extensively remodelled 1959.
BARKING FREIGHTLINER TERMINAL	29 / 5D		1972	N/A	BR	Partially on site of Ripple Lane 'hump' marshalling yard (closed 1968).
BARKING MULTIMODAL EURO HUB and BARKING LONDON SOIL HUB (DBC and FCC)	29 / 5D		16/01/2016	N/A	PRIV	
BARKING LOGISTICS CENTRE (DBC and Express Concrete)	29 / 4C		?	N/A	PRIV	Formerly 'Howard Tenens' and 'Stora'.
BARKING POWER STATIONS 'A', 'B' & 'C'	29 / 6C		1925	26/10/1981	PRIV	Station 'A' opened 1925, extended via Station 'B', both closed 15/03/1976. Station 'C' built 1954, closed 26/10/1981.
BARKING RIVERSIDE	29 / 5D		18/07/2022	N/A	TFL (LO)	Passive provision for future extension to Thamesmead.
BARKING SIDINGS	29 / 4B		??/11/1958	N/A	LTE (DIS)	Stabling sidings for District and Hammersmith & City Line trains, opened on site of Barking Goods (2nd).
Barking Station Junction	29 / 3A		11/05/1959	N/A	BR	All junctions in Barking area extensively remodelled and new flyovers commissioned 11/05/1959.
Barking Tilbury Line Junction East	29 / 4A		01/06/1888	N/A	BR	All junctions in Barking area extensively remodelled 1959.
Barking Tilbury Line Junction West	29 / 3A		11/05/1959	N/A	BR	All junctions in Barking area extensively remodelled and new flyovers commissioned 11/05/1959.
Barking West Junction	29 / 3A		11/05/1959	N/A	BR	All junctions in Barking area extensively remodelled and new flyovers commissioned 11/05/1959.
BARKINGSIDE	17 / 5B	P	01/05/1903	N/A	GER	Closed 22/05/1916 - 01/07/1919. LNER passenger trains ceased on Fairlop Loop 30/11/1947 to allow electrification & transfer to LTE. First served by LTE Central Line 31/05/1948. Goods yard closed 04/10/1965.
		G	01/05/1903	04/10/1965		
BARLBY ROAD CARRIAGE DEPOT	25 / 5A		1885	30/06/1969	GWR	Site partially re-used for North Pole Depot (then disused again; Hitachi IEP Depot did not re-use the eastern portion of the Eurostar depot).
BARNEHURST	43 / 5B	P	01/05/1895	N/A	BHR	Goods yard closed 07/10/1968.
		G	01/05/1895	07/10/1968		
BARNES	37 / 5D	P	27/07/1846	N/A	LSWR	Expanded to 4 platforms during quadrupling 1886. Goods yard closed 06/01/1969.
		G	27/07/1846	06/01/1969		
BARNES BRIDGE	37 / 4C		12/03/1916	N/A	LSWR	Opening coincided with electrification of Hounslow Loop.
Barnes Bridge	37 / 4C		22/08/1849	N/A	LSWR	Rebuilt 1894 - 1895 slightly downstream by extending the original piers (strengthening due to concerns about safety of the original cast iron structure). The original 'down' span was retained without track.
Barnes Junction	37 / 5C		22/08/1849	N/A	LSWR	
Barnet Tunnels	13 / 1D		07/08/1850	N/A	GNR	
BARONS COURT	38 / 2A 84 & 87		09/10/1905	N/A	UERL (MDR)	UERL (GNPBR) platforms opened 15/12/1906 to north of District platforms, reconfigured with Piccadilly Line between District Line platforms 04/07/1932.
Barrington Road Junction	39 / 5C		01/08/1865	01/01/1923	LBSCR / LCDR	'End on' junction between LBSCR and LCDR west of East Brixton station, demarcation eliminated at Grouping.
BATH ROAD	37 / 2C 51 / 1D		08/04/1909	01/01/1917	NSWJR	
Bath Road Junction	33 / 1C		08/10/1849	26/07/1970	GWR	Junction at southern end of Royal Curve (closed 26/07/1970).
BATTERSEA	38 / 4C		02/03/1863	21/10/1940	WLER	Passenger service withdrawn Willesden Junction to Clapham Junction 21/10/1940.
BATTERSEA PARK (1st) Battersea	39 / 3A 82		01/10/1860	01/11/1870	LBSCR	Renamed 01/07/1862. Also referred to as 'Battersea Park & Steamboat Pier'. Provided for connections with steamboats, local traffic to Victoria was not carried. Staff halt for Battersea Pier Sidings on site.
BATTERSEA PARK (2nd) Battersea Park & York Road York Road & Battersea Park York Road	39 / 4A 82		01/05/1867	N/A	LBSCR	Opened as 'York Road', renamed 'York Road & Battersea Park' 01/11/1870, 'Battersea Park & York Road' 01/01/1877, suffix dropped 01/06/1885. Platform 1 abandoned and track lifted Spring 2014, platform 2 became a terminal platform served by two LO services per day.
Battersea Park Junction	39 / 3A 82		01/12/1867	N/A	LBSCR	Junction with route towards Factory Junctions severed Spring 2014 to allow platform 3 to be lengthened.
BATTERSEA PARK ROAD Battersea Park (York Road)	39 / 4A 82		01/05/1867	03/04/1916	LCDR	Renamed 01/11/1877.
Battersea Pier Junction	39 / 3A 82		01/12/1860	N/A	LCDR / VSPR	
BATTERSEA PIER SIDINGS	82		?	N/A	LBSCR	Served by a Staff Halt on the adjacent Brighton Reversible.
BATTERSEA POWER STATION	39 / 3A 82		20/09/2021	N/A	TFL (NOR)	Terminus of Northern Line extension from Kennington.
BATTERSEA WHARF GOODS	82		30/04/1862	04/05/1970	LBSCR	
BAYSWATER Bayswater (Queensway) Bayswater (Queens Road) Bayswater (Queens Road) & Westbourne Grove Bayswater	25 / 6C		01/10/1868	N/A	MET	Opened as 'Bayswater', renamed 'Bayswater (Queens Road) & Westbourne Grove' 1923, suffix '& Westbourne Grove' dropped 1933, renamed 'Bayswater (Queensway)' 01/09/1946, suffix gradually dropped. First served by District Line to Edgware Road 01/11/1926, 'Circle Line' service provided by a combination of Metropolitan and District Line trains and did not receive its own identity as a line until c.1949. Closed 23/01/1996 – 18/03/1996 (reconstruction). Eastbound platform closed 30/01/2005 – 13/02/2005, westbound platform closed 13/02/2005 – 28/02/2005 (station refurbishment). Closed 23/07/2011 - 23/08/2011 (engineering work). Closed 20/03/2020 – 18/05/2020 (COVID-19).
BEAM PARK	30 / 5B		N/A	N/A	NR	Proposed station in connection with housing development. Currently delayed by a dispute between the DfT and GLA.
BECKENHAM HILL	54 / 3D		01/07/1892	N/A	LCDR	
BECKENHAM JUNCTION Beckenham	54 / 4D	P	01/01/1857	N/A	MKR	Initially terminus of MKR from Lewisham, WELCPR from Bromley Junction to Shortlands added 03/05/1858. Suffix 'Junction' added 01/04/1864. Originally two goods yards, north and south of passenger station, south yard closed c.1928 (now Tramlink platforms). North yard closed 18/04/1964, but remained in use as a coal concentration depot until 1982. Croydon Tramlink terminus platforms opened 23/05/2000 on former south goods yard site.
		G	01/01/1857	18/04/1964		
Beckenham Junction	54 / 4C		03/05/1858	N/A	WELCPR / MKR	
BECKENHAM ROAD	54 / 4C		23/05/2000	N/A	CTL	On site of former Penge station (WELCPR), closed c.1860.
Beckenham Spur	54 / 4C	P	01/01/1857	N/A	MKR	Regular passenger traffic ceased after 15/10/1939, although unadvertised railway staff trains were introduced from c.1960's onwards. Singled 1987. Passenger services re-introduced 29/05/1995.
		G	01/01/1857	N/A		
BECKTON (GCC)	29 / 6A		17/03/1873	29/12/1940	GCC	Opened 17/03/1873 (workmen only), public traffic commenced 18/03/1874. Passenger services withdrawn from Beckton and Gallions 29/12/1940.

Name	Page / grid		Date opened	Date closed	Opened by	Notes
BECKTON (DLR)	28 / 6D		28/03/1994	N/A	DLR	
BECKTON DEPOT	29 / 6A		28/03/1994	N/A	DLR	DLR Depot, to be expanded (works completed c.2024).
BECKTON GAS WORKS	29 / 6B		14/10/1872	22/02/1971	GCC	In addition to freight traffic, workmen's trains are believed to have operated into the works. Last train from works departed 01/06/1970, 22/02/1971 is official date of closure. Track lifted by 1973.
Beckton Junction	62 / 3B		03/08/1880	07/09/1940	LSKD	Divergence of Beckton and Gallions Branches.
Beckton Link Viaduct North Curve	31 / 6A		28/03/1994	N/A	DLR	
BECKTON PARK	41 / 1D 62 / 5C		28/03/1994	N/A	DLR	
BECKTON RIVERSIDE	29 / 6A		N/A	N/A	TFL (DLR)	Proposed intermediate station on DLR extension to Thamesmead Central.
BECONTREE Gale Street Halt	29 / 3D		28/06/1926	N/A	LMS	Opened on existing LTSR Main Line (now 'fast' tracks). Renamed 18/07/1932. First served by regular District Line trains after quadrupling and addition of platforms on new 'local' tracks 12/09/1932, although through excursion trains to Shoeburyness had called from opening until 30/09/1939. Last served British Rail 15/06/1962 and 'fast' platforms abandoned. Transferred to LTB 01/01/1969.
BECONTREE ESTATE RAILWAY	29 / 2D		1921	1934	LCC	Transported building materials during construction of Becontree Estate. Extended to a wharf on The Thames with branches to gravel pits in modern-day Parsloes Park and Valence Park.
BEDDINGTON LANE Beddington Lane Halt Beddington	53 / 6A		22/10/1855	N/A	WCRR	Opened as 'Beddington', 'Lane' suffix added January 1887. 'Halt' suffix added 1919, dropped 06/05/1969. Wimbledon to West Croydon closed by Railtrack 31/05/1997 (date of last train; official date of closure 02/06/1997). Reopened as Tramlink stop also named 'Beddington Lane' towards the west of original site, opening 30/05/2000.
BELGRAVE WALK	52 / 5C		30/05/2000	N/A	CTL	
Belle Isle Junction	76		11/09/2016	N/A	NR	See 'Canal Tunnel'
BELLINGHAM	54 / 2D	P	01/07/1892	N/A	LCDR	Goods yard stated as opening with passenger station in Borley, but no evidence on 1897 OS (present by 1916). Closed 25/03/1968, also accessed Robertson's jam factory. Carriage sidings south of station laid out c.1954 to replace stabling facilities closed at Crystal Palace (High Level).
		G	c.1900	25/03/1968	SECR ?	
BELMONT (LMS)	11 / 3C		12/09/1932	05/10/1964	LMS	Passing loop in use 05/07/1937 - 09/07/1955. Became passenger terminus 15/09/1952. Belmont to Harrow & Wealdstone service withdrawn 05/10/1964, branch previously closed to goods 06/07/1964.
BELMONT (LBSCR) California	65 / 5B	P	22/05/1865	N/A	LBSCR	Renamed 01/10/1875. Goods yard relocated south 1889, closed 06/01/1969 (note: Jackson refers to goods not being into use until 'about 1880', but Borley gives goods opening on same date as passenger, and goods yard is visible on 1866 OS). Former 'up' platform closed and branch singled 03/10/1982. A reversing siding is proposed to be installed (to allow service increase).
		G	22/05/1865	06/01/1969		
BELSIZE PARK	25 / 3D		22/06/1907	N/A	UERL (CCEHR)	
Belsize Tunnels	25 / 3D		07/09/1867	N/A	MID	Midland Main line first goods train ran 07/09/1867, first passenger 13/07/1868 (to King's Cross MET). Second tunnel added 03/02/1884 (today's 'slow' tunnel, with original tunnel now 'fast').
BELVEDERE	43 / 2A	P	c.01/03/1859	N/A	SER	Exact opening date unknown: first appeared in timetables March 1859. Goods yard closed 10/06/1963.
		G	c.01/03/1859	10/06/1963		
BERMONDSEY	40 / 2A		17/09/1999	N/A	LUL (JUB)	Terminus of services from Stratford 17/07/1999 - 24/09/1999. Closed 21/03/2020 – 15/06/2020 (COVID-19).
Bermondsey Dive-under	40 / 3B 80		30/12/2016	N/A	NR	Commissioned 30/12/2016.
BERMONDSEY STREET	39 / 1D 87		10/10/1836	14/12/1836	LGR	Temporary London terminus of London & Greenwich Railway.
BERRYLANDS	51 / 5B		16/10/1933	N/A	SR	
BETHNAL GREEN (GER) Bethnal Green Junction	27 / 5B 90		24/05/1872	N/A	GER	Referred to as '-Junction' at times until 1895. Platforms on Stratford lines closed 08/12/1946.
BETHNAL GREEN (LPTB)	27 / 5B		04/12/1946	N/A	LPTB (CEN)	
Bethnal Green East Junction	27 / 5B		27/05/1872	N/A	GER	
Bethnal Green West Junction	27 / 5B 90		04/11/1872	N/A	GER	Divergence of GER extension to Bishopsgate Low Level (later Liverpool Street) from original ECR route to Bishopsgate High Level (later abandoned 05/12/1964). Junction remains as set of crossovers.
BEXLEY	57 / 1A	P	01/09/1866	N/A	SER	Goods yard closed 06/05/1963.
		G	01/09/1866	06/05/1963		
BEXLEYHEATH Bexley Heath	42 / 5D	P	01/05/1895	N/A	BHR	Initially referred to as either 'Bexleyheath' or 'Bexley Heath'. Goods yard situated 400m West of passenger station, closed 07/10/1968.
		G	01/05/1895	07/10/1968		
BICKLEY Southborough Road	55 / 5C	P	05/07/1858	N/A	MKR	Terminus of MKR extension from Shortlands. Renamed 01/10/1860. Line extended to Rochester Bridge by LCDR 03/12/1860. Rebuilt 1893-4 (quadrupling). Goods yard closed 16/05/1964.
		G	05/07/1858	16/05/1964		
Bickley Junctions	55 / 5D		08/09/1902	N/A	SECR	Junctions at north end of Tonbridge Loops, 'slow' junction opened 08/09/1902, 'fast' 14/09/1902.
BIFFA RENWICK ROAD RAIL HUB	29 / 4C		06/05/2021	N/A	PRIV	First train from Doncaster Down Decoy Yard arrived 01:00 on 06/05/2021 and after loading left at 04:20 for Scunthorpe Roxby Gullet
BINGHAM ROAD	67 / 1A		01/09/1906	16/05/1983	LBSCR / SER	Closed 15/03/1915 - 30/09/1935, permanently closed 16/05/1983, later replaced by CTL 'Addiscombe' station to north.
BIRKBECK	54 / 5B		02/03/1930	N/A	SR	'Up' platform closed and route singled ??/02/1983. Croydon Tramlink opened 23/05/2000 using 'Up' alignment, with the former BR 'up' platform consequently rebuilt and reopened.
Birkbeck Junction	54 / 5B		10/01/1983	N/A	BR	Commencement of single NR track to Penge Junction (originally double track throughout, singled over weekend of 08-09/01/1983).
BISHOPSGATE (HIGH LEVEL) Bishopsgate Shoreditch	27 / 5A 90	P	01/07/1840	c.1879	ECR	Passenger terminus for ECR 01/07/1840 - 01/11/1875, occasional passenger services remained until c.1879. Renamed 'Bishopsgate' 27/07/1846 (although Bradshaw continued to refer to 'Shoreditch' until March 1850). 'High Level' suffix 04/11/1872. Goods traffic commenced 01/01/1881, ceased 05/12/1964. LO station 'Shoreditch High Street' opened on same site 27/04/2010.
		G	01/01/1881	05/12/1964		
BISHOPSGATE (LOW LEVEL)	27 / 5A 90		04/11/1872	22/05/1916	GER	Functioned as an additional GER terminus to the 'High Level' station until Liverpool Street opened 02/02/1874.
Black Potts Viaduct	33 / 3C		01/12/1849	N/A	LSWR	
BLACKFRIARS (MDR) St Paul's (LCDR only)	26 / 6C 32 / 5B 87		30/05/1870	N/A	MDR	Main line station opened by LCDR 10/05/1886 as 'St Paul's', renamed 'Blackfriars' 01/02/1937. District & Circle Line platforms closed 28/02/2009 - 20/02/2012 due to redevelopment works, NR platforms extensively rebuilt during same period and consequently closed 20/11/2010 - 16/01/2011. New entrance on South bank of The Thames opened 06/12/2011, new bay platforms opened 19/05/2012.

Name	Page / grid		Date opened	Date closed	Opened by	Notes
BLACKFRIARS (SER) 　Great Surrey Street	39 / 1C 87		11/01/1864	01/01/1869	SER	Former name of 'Great Surrey Street' referred to in Dewick, but no mention in Borley or Quick. Replaced by Waterloo Junction (= East) to west.
BLACKFRIARS BRIDGE	39 / 1C 32 / 6C 87		01/06/1864	01/10/1885	LCDR	Terminus until 21/12/1864. Replaced by St Paul's (= Blackfriars) on north bank of Thames (opened 10/05/1886).
Blackfriars Bridge	32 / 6C 87		21/12/1864	27/06/1969	LCDR	Spans removed 1985, piers remain. Easternmost piers re-used for Blackfriars station redevelopment.
BLACKFRIARS GOODS	39 / 1C 32 / 6C 87		01/05/1865	03/02/1964	LCDR	
Blackfriars Junction	39 / 1C 87		01/06/1878	N/A	LCDR	Western end of curve between LCDR and SER.
BLACKHEATH	41 / 5A	P	30/07/1849	N/A	SER	Opened with west-facing bay platforms on both 'up' and 'down' sides. Extensive carriage sidings laid out to west 1879, but were not electrified with main line 06/06/1926. Goods yard closed 06/05/1963, bays and sidings all decommissioned with rationalisation 15/03/1970 and signal boxes closed.
		G	30/07/1849	06/05/1963		
BLACKHEATH HILL	40 / 4D		18/09/1871	01/01/1917	LCDR	Terminus 18/09/1871 - 01/10/1888. Passenger service withdrawn Nunhead to Greenwich Park 01/01/1917.
Blackheath Junction	41 / 5B		01/05/1895	N/A	SER / BHR	Junction between SER North Kent Line and Bexleyheath Railway.
Blackheath Tunnel	41 / 4B		30/07/1849	N/A	SER	
BLACKHORSE LANE	67 / 1A		23/05/2000	N/A	CTL	
BLACKHORSE ROAD 　Black Horse Road	15 / 5C	P	09/07/1894	N/A	TFGR	Goods yard open 01/09/1894 - 07/12/1964. Victoria Line opened 01/09/1968. BR platforms re-sited west 14/12/1981 to improve interchange. Main line platforms originally referred to as either 'Black Horse Road' or 'Blackhorse Road', usually the former, until the 14/12/1981 re-siting when they became 'Blackhorse Road' permanently. NR platforms closed 04/06/2016 to 27/02/2017 due to electrification works on Gospel Oak to Barking Line. Closed 22/03/2020 – 18/05/2020 (COVID-19).
		G	01/09/1894	07/12/1964		
BLACKWALL (DLR)	40 / 1D 31 / 6C		28/03/1994	N/A	DLR	
BLACKWALL (LBLR)	41 / 1A 31 / 4D		06/07/1840	04/05/1926	LBLR	Served by NLR 01/09/1870 - 01/07/1890. Passenger service Stepney East to Blackwall withdrawn 04/05/1926.
BLACKWALL GOODS (ECR) 　Blackwall Pepper Warehouses	28 / 6A		??/06/1848	06/03/1967	ECR	Accessed by a branch off the ECR North Woolwich Branch and bridge across The River Lea. Also referred to as 'Blackwall Pepper Warehouses'.
BLACKWALL GOODS (GNR)	41 / 1A 31 / 4C		c.1870	c.1961	GNR	Borley gives c.1870 (shipping traffic only) and 1900 (general goods) for opening, and c.1961 for closure. Jackson gives years of opening / closing as 1860 / 1961.
BLAKE HALL	8 / 1C	P	24/04/1865	31/10/1981	GER	Epping to Ongar transferred to LTE 25/09/1949, Electrified 18/11/1957. Goods yard closed 18/04/1966. Was not reopened by the Epping-Ongar Railway on account of now being a private residence.
		G	24/04/1865	18/04/1966		
BLUE ANCHOR LANE	40 / 2A		08/06/1835	12/11/1835	LGR	Temporary London terminus of LGR during preopening trials between here and Grand Surrey Canal.
B.O.C. (British Oxygen Co.) WEMBLEY	23 / 1D		Early 1943	Early 1990's	PRIV	Planning permission granted December 1942; production had commenced early 1943. Present in 1992 Baker, absent from 1996
Bollo Lane Junction	37 / 2B 51 / 2B		01/03/1878	13/09/1965	LSWR	Junction at West end of Acton Curve.
BOND STREET	26 / 6A		24/09/1900	N/A	CLR	'Davies Street' until opening, did not open with line due to lift problems. Closed 01/09/1939 – 06/12/1939 (installation of flood protection). Jubilee Line platforms opened 01/05/1979. Central Line platforms closed 23/04/2014 – 18/06/2014, Jubilee Line platforms closed 30/06/2014 (last train 27/06/2014 – weekend engineering line closure) – 30/11/2014 (station upgrade works). Elizabeth Line platforms opened 24/10/2022.
BOOKHAM	69 / 4D	P	02/02/1885	N/A	LSWR	Referred to as 'Bookham Common' in opening notice, but had always been 'Bookham' in Bradshaw. Goods yard closed 03/05/1965.
		G	02/02/1885	03/05/1965		
BOROUGH	39 / 1D		18/12/1890	N/A	CSLR	Named 'Great Dover Street' until opening. Closed 17/07/1922 - 23/02/1925 (tunnel widening). Southbound Northern Line closed Moorgate to Kennington 01/07/1996 – 21/10/1996 (tunnel realignment at London Bridge). Closed again 02/07/1999 - 05/09/1999 (tunnel works), 19/03/2020 – 23/08/2020 (COVID-19), and 15/01/2022 – 15/05/2022 (realignment of southbound tunnel through Bank).
Borough Market Junction	39 / 1D 87		01/09/1866	N/A	SER	Junction for Cannon Street.
BOROUGH ROAD	39 / 1C 87		01/06/1864	01/04/1907	LCDR	
BOSTON MANOR 　Boston Road	36 / 2C		01/05/1883	N/A	MDR	Renamed 11/12/1911. First served by Piccadilly Line 13/03/1933. District Line service ceased 10/10/1964.
BOUNDS GREEN	14 / 3B		19/09/1932	N/A	UERL (GNPBR)	Closed 19/03/2020 – 18/05/2020 (COVID-19).
BOUNDS GREEN DEPOT	14 / 3B		1929	N/A	LNER	
BOW	27 / 5D 88		26/09/1850	15/05/1944	EWIDBJR	Platforms on line to Bromley (LTSR) added 17/05/1869, closed to regular traffic 01/01/1915 (Plaistow to Bow shuttle). Passenger service Dalston Junction to Poplar withdrawn 15/05/1944 (enemy action), official closure 23/04/1945.
BOW CHURCH	27 / 5D 88		31/08/1987	N/A	DLR	
BOW GOODS (MID)	27 / 4D 88		01/12/1892	N/A	MID	Opened by MID, transferred to BR Eastern c.1956. Currently serves London Concrete (Aggregate Industries) and Plasmor.
BOW GOODS (LNWR)	27 / 4D 88		20/03/1893	1940	LNWR	
Bow Junction (1st)	27 / 4D 88		02/04/1849	N/A	LBLR / ECR	Junction between ECR and LBLR (Blackwall Extension Railway).
Bow Junction (2nd)	27 / 5D 88		20/10/1851	29/12/1967	EWIDBJR	Junction of EWIDBJR (later NLR) routes to Poplar and Fenchurch Street (via Gas Factory Junction).
BOW ROAD (LBLR) 　Bow & Bromley	27 / 5D 88		02/04/1849	07/11/1949	LBLR	Opened with Blackwall Extension Railway (LBLR) 02/04/1849 as 'Bow & Bromley', closed 29/09/1850. Reopened 10/10/1876 on same site as 'Bow Road', re-sited north of Bow Road 04/04/1892. Closed 21/04/1941 - 09/12/1946 & 06/01/1947 - 06/10/1947. The shuttle service Fenchurch Street to Stratford which served this station was withdrawn 07/11/1949.
BOW ROAD (MDR)	27 / 5D 88		11/06/1902	N/A	MDR / LTSR	Served by Metropolitan Line since 30/03/1936 ('Hammersmith & City Line' since 30/07/1990). Closed 19/03/2020 – 18/05/2020 (COVID-19).
BOW ROAD GOODS	27 / 5D 88		1885	07/12/1964	GER	
BOW WORKS	27 / 5D 88		c.1850	1960	NLR	North London Railway Loco Works, enlarged 1863 & 1882.

Name	Page / grid		Date opened	Date closed	Opened by	Notes
BOYERS SIDING (FELTHAM)	49 / 1B		c.1900	c.1935	PRIV	Market garden. Sidings not present on 1895 OS, but had appeared by 1914. Housing built on site by WW2.
BOWES PARK	14 / 3B		01/11/1880	N/A	GNR	Terminating siding added 1911, removed 1950, re-laid 1974.
B.P. OIL UPPER HOLLOWAY	26 / 1B		Post-1970	Pre-1990	PRIV	Two-siding oil terminal accessed from Upper Holloway end on site of Tufnell Park Goods down sidings (closed 06/05/1968). Absent from 1970 OS, present on 1975/6 OS, first BLN mention 1976. Mentioned in May 1985 BLN, absent from 1990 Baker.
BREEDON CEMENT TERMINAL (Dagenham)	30 / 5A		Early 2016	N/A	PRIV	Opened early 2016. Site formerly 'East London Waste Terminal' (Shanks & McEwan), on site of former Dagenham Dock goods yard (closed 02/11/1964).
BRENT CROSS Brent	13 / 6A		19/11/1923	N/A	UERL (CCEHR)	Express passing loops commissioned 04/01/1925, abolished 23/08/1936, used by a handful of timetabled trains daily. Renamed 20/07/1976.
BRENT CROSS WEST	12 / 6D 85		Autumn 2023	N/A	NR	Opening date expected to be announced Summer 2023 for an Autumn 2023 opening (originally planned to open with 21/05/2023 timetable change).
Brent Curve	25 / 1A 85	P	01/07/1905	??/10/1908	MID	Opened to goods, along with rest of Dudding Hill Loop, 01/10/1868. Some through passenger services operated between 01/07/1905 - October 1908. Passenger traffic proposed for re-introduction (West London Orbital).
		G	01/10/1868	N/A		
Brent Curve Junction	24 / 1D 85		01/10/1868	N/A	MID	Junction between Midland Main Line and Dudding Hill Loop.
Brent New Junction	68 / 5C		c.1940	N/A	LMS	Junction with Willesden 'F' sidings.
BRENTFORD (GWR)	36 / 3D		01/05/1860	04/05/1942	GWR	Closed 22/03/1915 - 12/04/1920. Passenger service on GWR Brentford Branch withdrawn 04/05/1942.
BRENTFORD (LSWR) Brentford Central Brentford	36 / 3D	P	22/08/1849	N/A	LSWR	'Brentford Central' 05/06/1950 - 12/05/1980. Goods yard closed 04/01/1965, parcels traffic ceased 07/09/1980.
		G	22/08/1849	04/01/1965		
Brentford Branch Junction	35 / 1D		18/07/1859	N/A	GWR	
BRENTFORD DOCK	36 / 3D		18/07/1859	31/12/1964	GWR	Originally intended to have a passenger station to serve ferries to Kew Gardens; platform may have been constructed for this purpose on north side of dock. Special passenger service ran on branch 15/07/1859, regular goods traffic commenced three days later.
BRENTFORD GOODS Brentford Town Goods	36 / 3C		03/11/1930	N/A	GWR	Opened as 'Brentford Town' goods as distinct from LSWR goods station, today known as 'Brentford Goods'. Closed to general goods traffic 07/12/1970, but stone (Day & sons) and domestic waste traffic remain. The domestic waste terminal opened in early 1977.
BRENTHAM FOR NORTH EALING AND GREYSTOKE PARK Brentham (for North Ealing) Brentham	24 / 4A		01/05/1911	15/06/1947	GWR	Replaced Twyford Abbey Halt. Closed 01/02/1915 - 29/03/1920. Suffix 'for North Ealing' added 1932, with further suffix 'and Greystoke Park' subsequently added, until closure.
BRENTWOOD Brentwood & Warley Brentwood	20 / 2A	P	01/07/1840	N/A	ECR	Country terminus of ECR from opening until 29/03/1843. Name carried suffix '& Warley' 01/11/1882 - 20/02/1969. Engine shed opened 1872, closed 1949. Rebuilt through quadrupling work 01/01/1934. Goods yard closed 07/12/1970.
		G	01/07/1840	07/12/1970		
BREWERY SIDINGS (ROMFORD)	18 / 6C		1853	1963	PRIV	Originally accessed via a wagon hoist and turntable, tunnel under and incline up to main line added in 1860's.
BRICKLAYERS ARMS	39 / 2D 4	P	01/05/1844	01/01/1852	SER / LCRR	Closed to passengers 01/01/1852, although some Summer Sunday excursion trains operated 12/06/1932-1940. Amalgamated with Willow Walk Goods 07/03/1932. Parcels Concentration Depot established 05/05/1969. Remained in use for general goods until 01/08/1977, some coal traffic remained until 1981, Parcels Concentration Depot closed 21/06/1981 (last train 20/06/1981), then part of site continued in use as the Southern Region Crane Repair Depot until 07/10/1983 (last train 06/10/1983).
		G	01/05/1844	07/10/1983		
Bricklayers Arms Junction	40 / 3B 79 & 80		01/05/1844	N/A	LCRR	Originally junction between LCRR and LCRR / SER Bricklayers Arms branch (traffic ceased 07/10/1983). Today junction where spur leaves former LCRR to join South London Line (opened 01/01/1871).
BRIMSDOWN	7 / 4C	P	01/10/1884	N/A	GER	Goods yard closed 04/10/1965.
		G	01/10/1884	04/10/1965		
BRITISH INDUSTRIAL SAND (Holmethorpe)	73 / 4D		c.1870	c.1991	PRIV	Rail-served brickworks had existed on site since at least 1871 (OS). Later became Standard Brick Co., then British Industrial Sand. Complex included exchange sidings with three shunters and engine shed, closure date unknown, extant in 1990 edition of Baker, disused in 1992 edition. 2 foot gauge internal system also present until c.1965.
BRITISH INSULATED CALLENDER'S CABLES	43 / 2B		c.1896	1968	PRIV	3ft 6in narrow gauge internal system within cable works. Works and railway absent from 1895 OS but present on 1897, so opening date for railway of c.1896 presumed. System closed 1968.
BRITISH MUSEUM	26 / 6B		30/07/1900	24/09/1933	CLR	Replaced by Central Line platforms at Holborn (Kingsway) (opened 25/09/1933).
BRITISH RAIL CONTINENTAL FREIGHT DEPOT (Hither Green)	55 / 1A		10/10/1960	24/10/1987	BR	Replaced Southwark Goods Depot, handled imported perishable goods from continental Europe. Imported goods traffic ceased February 1981 and site sold to Nissan, became a Speedlink-served private terminal (Carlink Datsun), closed 24/10/1987.
BRITISH ROPES WORKS	41 / 2C		c.1930	c.1970	PRIV	2ft gauge internal system. Not present on 1920 OS, but had opened by 1939. Still operational 1965 but not on 1971 OS.
BRIXTON (LCDR) Brixton & South Stockwell Brixton	39 / 5C		06/10/1862	N/A	LCDR	Suffix '& South Stockwell' 01/05/1863 - 09/07/1934. Platforms on route to Denmark Hill closed 1929, demolished during 1930.
BRIXTON (LTE)	39 / 5C		23/07/1971	N/A	LTE (VIC)	Southern terminus of Victoria Line.
BRIXTON COAL	39 / 5C		c.1880	??/03/1947	MID	
Brixton Junction	39 / 5C		01/05/1863	N/A	LCDR	Junction between 1862 LCDR route from Herne Hill to Stewarts Lane and 01/05/1863 line to Loughborough Junction.
Brixton Spur	39 / 5C	P	01/05/1863	01/04/1921	LCDR	Previously closed to passengers 02/04/1916 - 04/10/1920, remains in use primarily for stock transfer. Also referred to as 'West Curve'.
		G	01/05/1863	N/A		
BROAD STREET	26 / 6D 90	P	01/11/1865	30/06/1986	NLR	Ex-Richmond trains diverted to North Woolwich 13/05/1985, remaining ex-Watford Junction services diverted to temporary platform north of original station July 1985, allowing demolition to commence. Temporary platform closed due to diversion of remaining trains to Liverpool Street via Graham Road Curve 30/06/1986 (last train 27/06/1986).
		G	18/05/1868	27/01/1969	LNWR	
BROCKLEY	40 / 5C		06/03/1871	N/A	LBSCR	
BROCKLEY HILL	12 / 1A		N/A	N/A	LPTB (NOR)	On Northern Line extension to Bushey Heath from Edgware. Construction abandoned 1940.
BROCKLEY LANE	40 / 5C		??/06/1872	01/01/1917	LCDR	Exact opening date unknown (June 1872). Passenger service withdrawn Nunhead to Greenwich Park 01/01/1917. Proposed to reopen for interchange with Brockley station.
BROCKLEY LANE COAL	40 / 5C		??/12/1883	04/05/1970	GNR	'Martins Siding' on down side became LNWR Coal Yard 1885.

Name	Page / grid		Date opened	Date closed	Opened by	Notes
BROMLEY-BY-BOW Bromley	27 / 5D 88	P	31/03/1858	N/A	LTSR	Opened by LTSR as 'Bromley', damaged by fire 1892, rebuilt to West 01/03/1894. Goods yard opened c.1898. First served by District Railway 02/06/1902, line quadrupled 1905, District trains then using 'Slow' lines. Served by Metropolitan Line since 30/03/1936 ('Hammersmith & City Line' since 30/07/1990). 'Fast' platforms abandoned 15/06/1962. Renamed 18/05/1967. Ownership transferred to LTB 01/01/1969. Goods yard closure date unknown. Crossover west of station removed over weekend of 10-11/10/2015.
		G	c.1898	?		
Bromley Down Junction	54 / 5A		03/05/1858	N/A	WELCPR	
Bromley Junction	27 / 5D 88		17/05/1869	13/09/1959	NLR / LTSR	Re-sited to the West with Bromley Station 01/03/1894.
BROMLEY NORTH Bromley	55 / 5B	P	01/01/1878	N/A	SER	Renamed 01/06/1899. Originally two side platforms astride three roads terminating at a turntable. In 1924 rebuilding commenced, with the western platform remaining in use while the eastern was demolished, replaced by current island platforms. Completed December 1925, remaining original platform abandoned. Goods yard closed 20/05/1968.
		G	01/01/1878	20/05/1968		
BROMLEY SOUTH Bromley	55 / 5B	P	22/11/1858	N/A	MKR	Opening date given as 22/11/1858 in Borley but 05/07/1858 in Quick (latter is date line through station opened). Alternative original name of 'Bromley Common' given in Dewick, but not mentioned in any other publication. Renamed 'Bromley South' 01/06/1899. Rebuilt 1893-1894 (quadrupling). Goods yard closed 18/04/1964.
		G	22/11/1858	18/04/1964		
Bromley Up Junction	54 / 5A		03/05/1858	N/A	WELCPR	
BROMPTON & FULHAM GOODS	38 / 3B 84		*01/04/1892*	*04/08/1975*	LNWR	
BROMPTON ROAD	38 / 2D		15/12/1906	30/07/1934	UERL (GNPBR)	
BRONDESBURY Brondesbury (Edgware Road) Edgware Road & Brondesbury Edgware Road Edgeware Road (Kilburn)	25 / 3A		02/01/1860	N/A	HJR	Opened as 'Edgeware Road (Kilburn)', '& Brondesbury' suffix added 01/01/1872, renamed 'Brondesbury (Edgware Road)' 01/01/1873, renamed 'Brondesbury' 01/01/1883. Closed 29/10/1995 - 29/09/1996.
BRONDESBURY PARK	25 / 3A		01/06/1908	N/A	LNWR	Closed 29/10/1995 - 29/09/1996 (engineering works).
BRUCE GROVE	15 / 4A		22/07/1872	N/A	GER	
Brunswick Junction	31 / 4C		1859	Post 04/05/1926	LBLR	Services to Blackwall (LBLR) ceased 04/05/1926, date signal box closed unknown (had closed by 26/07/1958).
BUCKHURST HILL	16 / 1D	P	22/08/1856	N/A	ECR	'Down' platform originally south of Queen's Road. Majority of Passenger services transferred to LTE 21/11/1948. First Trains in the morning remained British Rail services until 01/06/1970. Goods yard open 1859 - 06/01/1964.
		G	1859	06/01/1964		
BURDETT ROAD	27 / 6C		11/09/1871	21/04/1941	LBLR	Closed 29/12/1940 - 05/01/1941 (enemy action), damaged again 10/04/1941 (enemy action) and did not reopen. 21/04/1941 is the 'official' closure date.
BURGESS PARK	40 / 3A		N/A	N/A	TFL	Proposed station on Bakerloo Line extension, safeguarded but on hold.
BURNT OAK Burnt Oak (Watling) Burnt Oak	12 / 3B		27/10/1924	N/A	UERL (CCEHR)	Was to be called 'Sheves Hill', with this name appearing on a 1924 Tube map produced prior to opening. 'Watling' suffix introduced c.1928, gradually dropped by c.1950.
Burroughs Tunnels	12 / 5D		18/08/1924	N/A	UERL (CCEHR)	
Bury Street Junction	7 / 6A		01/10/1891	N/A	GER	No passenger service Bury Street Junction to Cheshunt Junction 01/10/1909 - 01/03/1915 & 01/07/1919 - 21/11/1960.
BUSHEY Bushey & Oxhey Bushey	2 / 5D	P	01/12/1841	N/A	LBIR	Served by London Underground Bakerloo Line Trains 16/04/1917 - 24/09/1982. '& Oxhey' dropped 06/05/1974. Goods yard closed 03/02/1969.
		G	*01/12/1841*	*03/02/1969*		
BUSHEY HEATH	3 / 5C		N/A	N/A	LPTB (NOR)	Intended terminus of Northern Line extension from Edgware. Construction abandoned 1940.
BUSHEY HEATH DEPOT	3 / 6D		N/A	N/A	LPTB (NOR)	Was to replace Golders Green Depot. Sheds constructed but track never laid, sheds used for construction of Halifax Bombers during WW2, and then later became Aldenham bus overhaul works 1956-1986.
BUSH HILL PARK	7 / 5A	P	01/11/1880	N/A	GER	Goods yard closed 04/05/1964.
		G	*01/11/1880*	*04/05/1964*		
BYFLEET & NEW HAW West Weybridge	61 / 4C		01/07/1927	N/A	SR	Opened as 'West Weybridge', renamed 12/06/1961.
Byfleet Curve	61 / 4C	P	1885	N/A	LSWR	Lightly used by passenger services.
		G	*1885*	N/A		
Byfleet Junction	61 / 4C		1885	N/A	LSWR	Junction at south end of Byfleet Curve.

C

Name	Page / grid		Date opened	Date closed	Opened by	Notes
CABLE STREET COAL	74 / 2D		*c.1893*	*post-1954*	PRIV	On south side of LBLR viaduct between Grove St and Cannon St Rd. Not noted in Borley, but illustrated in Connor 'Fenchurch St to Barking', which notes wagon traversers supplied in 1893 and shows yard open in 1954.
Calderwood Street Tunnel	42 / 2A		30/07/1849	N/A	SER	
CALEDONIAN ROAD	26 / 3B		15/12/1906	N/A	UERL (GNPBR)	Closed 20/03/2020 – 08/06/2020 (COVID-19).
CALEDONIAN ROAD & BARNSBURY Barnsbury Caledonian Road	26 / 3C		10/06/1852	N/A	EWIDBJR	Opened as 'Caledonian Road', renamed 'Barnsbury' 01/07/1870, Re-sited to east as 'Barnsbury' 21/11/1870. Prefix 'Caledonian Road' added 22/05/1893. Closed 20/02/2010 - 01/06/2010, upon reopening, platforms reconfigured with new island platform 2 & 3 in between two pairs of tracks, and platform 1 to south abandoned.
CALEDONIAN ROAD GOODS (GNR)	26 / 3B 75		*1878*	*30/10/1967*	GNR	Adjacent to North London Railway but no physical connection to it.
CALEDONIAN ROAD GOODS (EWIDBJR)	26 / 3B 75		*c.1851*	*06/09/1969*	EWIDBJR	Originally on north side of line, relocated to south side 1869, transferred to LNWR 01/09/1871.
CAMBERWELL Camberwell New Road Camberwell	39 / 4D	P	06/10/1862	03/04/1916	LCDR	Opened as 'Camberwell', 'New Road' suffix added 01/05/1863, dropped 01/10/1908. Passenger station closed 03/04/1916, goods & coal yard closed 18/04/1964. Has been proposed for reopening, but the bid for funding was unsuccessful in the June 2022 'Restoring your railway' update.
		G	*06/10/1862*	*18/04/1964*		
Cambria Junction	39 / 5D		01/07/1872	N/A	LCDR / LBSCR	Junction at southern end of Cambria Spur. Sometimes referred to 'Cambria Road Junction'.
Cambria Spur	39 / 5C	P	01/07/1872	N/A	LCDR	Also referred to as 'East Curve'.
		G	*01/07/1872*	N/A		
CAMBRIDGE HEATH	27 / 4B		27/05/1872	N/A	GER	Closed 22/05/1916 - 05/05/1919, 27/07/1984 - September 1984 (fire), 17/02/1986 - 16/03/1986 (rebuilding).

Name	Page / grid		Date opened	Date closed	Opened by	Notes
CAMDEN CARRIAGE SIDINGS	25 / 4D 58		*c.1960's*	N/A	LNWR	Formerly Camden Engine shed.
CAMDEN 'PASSENGER' ENGINE SHED	25 / 4D 58		*c.1847*	*03/01/1966*	LNWR	Built at same time as Camden Roundhouse, both replacing earlier LBIR structure on Roundhouse site. Extended 1932, closed to steam 09/09/1963 then diesel 03/01/1966. Demolished, became Camden carriage sidings.
Camden Junctions	25 / 3D		09/06/1851	N/A	LNWR / EWIDBJR	Extensively remodelled with the addition of 'flying' junctions to the 'DC' lines 10/07/1922.
CAMDEN 'LUGGAGE' ENGINE SHED	58		*1847*	*c.1857*	LNWR	Replaced earlier LBIR engine shed on same site, became obsolete within 10 years (too small for engines). Utilised as warehouse for approx. 100 years, became cultural / music venue 1964 (Camden Roundhouse).
CAMDEN ROAD (MID)	26 / 3B		13/07/1868	01/01/1916	MID	
CAMDEN ROAD (NLR) Camden Town	26 / 3A		05/12/1870	N/A	NLR	Replaced first Camden Town station to east. Renamed 'Camden Road' 25/09/1950. Reduced from four tracks to two 05/10/1981 when 'No.1' (northern) lines were 'temporarily' taken out of use (last use of associated platforms unknown). Closed 20/02/2010 - 01/06/2010 (LO upgrade works).
Camden Road Central Junction	26 / 3A 76		1853	N/A	NLR / GNR	Junction between GNR North London Incline and North London Line.
Camden Road East Junction	26 / 3A 76		11/11/1987	N/A	BR	Junction formed when former 'No.1' (northern) lines were reinstated between here and Canonbury to ease congestion (taken out of use 05/10/1981). 11/11/1987 is inaugural use of reinstated lines, regular use from 07/12/1987.
Camden Road Incline Junction	76		14/11/2007	N/A	LCOR / NR	
Camden Road Tunnels	26 / 3B		07/09/1867	N/A	MID	Midland Main line first goods train ran 07/09/1867, first passenger 13/07/1868 (to King's Cross MET).
Camden Road West Junction Kentish Town Junction	26 / 3A		03/01/1860	N/A	HJR / NLR	Junction renamed 26/03/1955. The 'No.1' (northern) lines between here and Canonbury were 'temporarily' taken out of use 05/10/1981 due to the condition of a bridge east of Camden Road, and were never reinstated to this point (later reinstated to Camden Road East Junction 11/11/1987).
CAMDEN TOWN (CCEHR)	26 / 4A		22/06/1907	N/A	UERL (CCEHR)	
CAMDEN TOWN (EWIDBJR) Camden Road Camden Town	26 / 3A		07/12/1850	05/12/1870	EWIDBJR	Original station on St Pancras Way, opened as 'Camden Town'. Renamed 'Camden Road' 1853, reverted to 'Camden Town' 01/07/1870. Replaced by Camden Town (NLR) Station to West 05/12/1870.
Camden Town Junctions	26 / 4A		22/06/1907	N/A	UERL (CCEHR)	Extensively remodelled 20/04/1924 due to extension of Bank Branch from Euston.
Campbell Road Junction	27 / 5D 88		02/06/1902	13/09/1959	LTSR / MDR	Junction between LTSR and MDR, physical connection removed 13/09/1959 (although name still in use).
Campden Hill Tunnel	38 / 1B 84		01/10/1868	N/A	MET	
CANADA CREEK RAILWAY	48 / 5A		23/03/1989	07/11/2011	PRIV	2ft gauge, within Thorpe Park, last ran 06/11/2011. Originally a 2km route connecting Thorpe Park with Thorpe Farm, truncated to a 350m loop at the east end of original route after end of 2006 season (last train ran 05/11/2006).
CANADA WATER	40 / 2B		19/08/1999	N/A	LUL (ELL)	Jubilee Line platforms opened 17/09/1999. East London Line platforms closed 22/12/2007, reopened 27/04/2010 as TfL (LO).
Canal Junction	40 / 3C 79 / 80		01/04/1880	N/A	ELR	Junction formed when spur from ELR to New Cross (SER) opened.
Canal Tunnel	76	P	26/02/2018	N/A	NR	Route commissioned at 01:45 on 11/09/2016. Passenger services commenced 26/02/2018.
		G	*11/09/2016*	N/A		
Canal Tunnel Junction	76		11/09/2016	N/A	NR	See 'Canal Tunnel'
CANARY WHARF (DLR)	40 / 1D 31 / 6A		12/08/1991	N/A	DLR	Opened to construction workers 02/04/1991, date given is public opening. Closed 09/02/1996 - 09/03/1996 (bomb).
CANARY WHARF (LUL)	40 / 1D		17/09/1999	N/A	LUL (JUB)	
CANARY WHARF (TFL)	40 / 1D 31 / 6B		24/05/2022	N/A	TFL (EL)	
CANNING TOWN Barking Road	28 / 6A		14/06/1847	N/A	ECTJR	Renamed 01/07/1873, originally on south side of Barking Road, relocated to north side 1888 in connection with quadrupling works. Closed 29/05/1994 in connection with Jubilee Line extension works, reopened 29/10/1995 on a new site again south of Barking Road and to south of original 1847 site. DLR platforms opened 05/03/1998, LUL Jubilee Line platforms opened 14/05/1999. NR platforms closed 09/12/2006, reopened as DLR 31/08/2011.
CANNING TOWN NORTH GOODS	28 / 6A		22/08/1881	06/03/1967	LNWR	Renamed 'North' by BR 01/07/1950 to distinguish from 'South'.
CANNING TOWN SOUTH GOODS	28 / 6A		14/06/1847	01/07/1968	GER	Renamed 'South' by BR 01/07/1950 to distinguish from 'North'.
CANNON STREET	26 / 6D 87		01/09/1866	N/A	SER	Metropolitan & District Railways joint station opened 06/10/1884. Closed 25/12/2010 – 10/01/2011, 24/12/2011 – 09/01/2012 (NR engineering works).
CANNON STREET ROAD	27 / 6A 74 / 2D		21/08/1842	??/12/1848	LBLR	
Cannon Street South Junction	39 / 1D 87		01/09/1866	N/A	SER	
CANONBURY Newington Road & Balls Pond	26 / 3D		01/09/1858	N/A	NLR	Opened as 'Newington Road & Balls Pond' 01/09/1858, re-sited west and renamed 'Canonbury' 01/12/1870. Closed 20/02/2010 - 01/06/2010 (LO upgrade works), upon reopening trains called at northern platforms 3 & 4 (previously southern 1 & 2 used), all four platforms restored from 06/01/2011.
Canonbury Tunnel	26 / 3C	P	18/01/1875	08/11/1976	GNR	Line through tunnel singled July 1987 due to electrification (clearance for overhead wires).
		G	*14/12/1874*	N/A		
Canonbury West Junction	26 / 3D		14/12/1874	N/A	NLR / GNR	
CANONS PARK Canons Park (Edgware)	12 / 3A		10/12/1932	N/A	MET	Opened by Metropolitan Railway. 'Edgware' Suffix dropped ??/09/1933. Transferred to Bakerloo Line 20/11/1939, Jubilee Line 01/05/1979. Due to embankment stabilisation and platform resurfacing works, northbound platform closed 17/02/1993 – 15/05/1993, southbound closed 17/05/1993, followed by the northbound again 09/08/1993 (so station closed completely from this date). Station reopened 13/09/1993.
Canterbury Road Junction	39 / 5C		01/08/1865	N/A	LCDR	Junction between 01/05/1863 LCDR line Brixton to Loughborough Junction and 01/08/1865 line to Crystal Palace (High Level).
Carlton Road Junction	26 / 2A 9		02/04/1883	N/A	MID	
CARPENDERS PARK	10 / 1D		01/04/1914	N/A	LNWR	Closed 01/01/1917 – 05/05/1919. Re-sited south 17/11/1952. Served by London Underground Bakerloo Line Trains 16/04/1917 - 24/09/1982.
Carpenters Road Curve	27 / 4D 77 / 78	P	N/A	N/A	GER	No regular passenger traffic carried.
		G	*1892*	N/A		
CARPENTERS ROAD GOODS	27 / 4D 77		1892	02/11/1964	GER	

Name	Page / grid		Date opened	Date closed	Opened by	Notes
Carpenters Road North Junction	27 / 3D 77 / 78		1892	N/A	GER	Junction at north end of Carpenters Road Curve.
Carpenters Road South Junction	27 / 4D 77 / 78		1892	N/A	GER	Junction at south end of Carpenters Road Curve.
CARSHALTON	65 / 2D		01/10/1868	N/A	LBSCR	
CARSHALTON BEECHES Beeches Halt	65 / 4D		01/10/1906	N/A	LBSCR	Renamed 01/04/1925.
CARTERHATCH LANE	7 / 3B		12/06/1916	01/07/1919	GER	Single platform on current 'down' side only due to line being subject to single line working at this time.
CASSIOBRIDGE	2 / 4A		On hold	N/A	TFL (MET)	Proposed station on Metropolitan Line Watford Junction extension, on hold due to funding issues.
CASTLE BAR PARK Castle Bar Park Halt	23 / 5C		01/05/1904	N/A	GWR	Original wooden platforms replaced by concrete structures to north ??/11/1960. 'Halt' suffix dropped 05/05/1969.
CASTLE GREEN	29 / 5C		N/A	N/A	NR	Proposed station on Barking Riverside branch.
CATERHAM	74 / 5A	P	05/08/1856	N/A	CR	Rebuilt slightly to the west 01/01/1900. Goods yard closed 28/09/1964.
		G	*05/08/1856*	*28/09/1964*		
CATFORD	54 / C1		01/07/1892	N/A	LCDR	
CATFORD BRIDGE	54 / D1	P	01/01/1857	N/A	MKR	Goods yard closed 23/03/1968.
		G	*01/01/1857*	*23/03/1968*		
Cedar Junction	76		14/11/2007	N/A	LCOR / NR	
CENTRAL	41 / 1D 62 / 3C		03/08/1880	09/09/1940	LSKD	Initially temporary terminus per Quick, Connor and Jackson ('for first few weeks' in latter), precise date of services to Gallions commencing unknown, but had appeared in Bradshaw by November 1880. Gallions branch single until 14/11/1881. Operated by GER after 1896, ownership later transferred to PLA. Branch closed from 09/09/1940 due to 'Black Saturday' air raid 07/09/1940 (no Sunday service after 27/06/1915). Listed as 'Royal Albert Dock Central' in Borley, also referred to as such in 1914 GER timetable per Quick, although this prefix was only used in early timetables rather than for the station itself. Became a 'halt' 01/11/1933.
CENTRAL CROYDON	66 / 2C		01/01/1868	01/09/1890	LBSCR	Closed 01/12/1871 - 01/06/1886. Between 1886 reopening and 1890 final closure often also 'Croydon Central'.
CENTRALE	66 / 2C		10/12/2005	N/A	CTL	

CHADWELL HEATH
  Chadwell Heath for Becontree
  Chadwell Heath
	29 / 1D	P	11/01/1864	N/A	GER	Suffix 'for Becontree' used between 1927 and 1955. Goods yard opened 1876, closed 07/12/1970.

		G	*1876*	*07/12/1970*		
CHAFFORD HUNDRED	45 / 3A		30/05/1995	N/A	RT	Ceremonial opening 29/05/1995. C2C timetable carries suffix '(Intu Lakeside)' and name boards carry various references to the shopping centre, including 'Chafford Hundred for Lakeside Shopping Centre'.
CHALFONT & LATIMER Chalfont Road	1 / 3C	P	08/07/1889	N/A	MET	Renamed 01/11/1915. Goods yard closed 14/11/1966.
		G	*08/07/1889*	*14/11/1966*		
CHALK FARM (UERL)	25 / 3D		22/06/1907	N/A	UERL (CCEHR)	Named 'Adelaide Road' until opening. Closed 21/03/2020 – 14/09/2020 (COVID-19).

CHALK FARM (LNWR)
  Camden (Chalk Farm)
  Camden
	25 / 3D 58	P	01/11/1851	10/05/1915	LNWR	Open as a ticket platform (up line only) 1837-46, until July 1844 this marked the point where locomotive traction was detached from 'up' trains (which continued to Euston by gravity), or where 'down' carriages were attached to locomotives after being hauled up Camden Incline by rope / static engines. In 1846, by which time trains were locomotive hauled in / out of Euston, the platform was re-sited to the south side of Regent's Canal. Darley states that this platform was also a short-lived passenger station. Camden station opened to NLR exchange passengers 09/06/1851 (up only) using the original 1837 'up' ticket platform. Opened as a normal advertised public station 01/11/1851 with a new 'down' platform (either opposite the original 'up' platform, or on the site of the 01/05/1852 station?). Replaced by station of same name to west 01/05/1852; Quick states: "*Replaced 1 May 1852 by a station more convenient for locals (first site determined by operational needs)*". The main line was moved to the south in 1854/5 and the platforms moved with it, being connected to NLR station by footbridge at same time (see 'Primrose Hill'). Suffix '(Chalk Farm)' added 1866. Rebuilt 01/04/1872 on an overlapping site, essentially with the 1854/5 platforms extending westwards towards Chalk Farm Bridge. Renamed 'Chalk Farm' 1876. Borley states goods opened 'probably' 1839, Camden Yard disused by 1982 (BLN).

		G	*c.1839*	*c.1982*		
CHALVEY HALT	33 / 2C		06/05/1929	07/07/1930	GWR	

CHANCERY LANE
  Chancery Lane (Gray's Inn)
  Chancery Lane
	26 / 6C		30/07/1900	N/A	CLR	'Gray's Inn' suffix introduced 25/06/1934, gradually dropped. Closed 01/09/1939 – 15/12/1939 (installation of flood protection). Closed 20/03/2020 – 15/06/2020 (COVID-19).

Channelsea Curve	77	P	15/08/1854	N/A	GER	No regular passenger traffic 1881 - 30/05/2000, then 11/09/2002 - 14/04/2009. Quadrupled 14/04/2009.
		G	*15/08/1854*	N/A		
Channelsea North Junction	27 / 3D 77 / 78		1881	N/A	GER	Junction at south end of High Meads Loop.
Channelsea South Junction	27 / 3D 77 / 78		1881	N/A	GER	Re-arranged due to new Stratford platforms 1 & 2 opening from the evening of 14/04/2009.
CHARING CROSS (SER)	39 / 1B		11/01/1864	N/A	SER	Closed 05/12/1905 - 19/03/1906 (roof collapse) & 24/07/1993 - 16/08/1993 (track remodelling).

CHARING CROSS (UERL)
  Strand (*Northern Line*)
  Charing Cross (Strand) (*Northern Line*)
  Charing Cross (*Northern Line*)
  Trafalgar Square (*Bakerloo Line*)
	39 / 1B 19		10/06/1906	N/A	UERL (BSWR)	Bakerloo Line platforms opened 10/06/1906 as 'Trafalgar Square', retaining this name until 01/05/1979. 'Trafalgar Square' closed 01/09/1939 – 17/12/1939. Northern Line platforms opened as separate station 'Charing Cross' 22/06/1907, renamed 'Charing Cross (Strand)' 06/04/1914, then 'Strand' 01/05/1915. Northern Line platforms closed 17/06/1973 - 01/05/1979 in connection with Jubilee Line construction. A temporary pair of narrow gauge tracks transported spoil from the station worksite to a road transfer point on the west side of Trafalgar Square. Jubilee Line platforms opened, Northern Line platforms reopened, and station combined as 'Charing Cross' 01/05/1979. Bakerloo Line platforms closed 11/11/1996 – 14/07/1997 (tunnel strengthening). Jubilee Line platforms closed when line diverted at Green Park to Westminster 20/11/1999, retained for turnback (out of service from Green Park) and filming work. Closed 20/03/2020 – 10/08/2020 (COVID-19).

CHARLTON
  Charlton Junction
  Charlton
	41 / 3B	P	30/07/1849	N/A	SER	Goods yard does not appear to have opened with passenger station: Borley gives goods opening date of c.1904, but a coal yard is depicted on 1895 OS map (none apparent on the 1882 survey), so opening date c.1890 assumed. Suffix 'Junction' often added between 1877/8 and 1928/9, with this name appearing on station nameboards and OS maps. Bay platform on 'down' side added when branch to Greenwich (Maze Hill) opened 01/01/1873. At some point the bay road was incorporated into the goods yard and fenced off. Goods yard closed 20/05/1963.

		G	*c.1890*	*20/05/1963*		

Name	Page / grid		Date opened	Date closed	Opened by	Notes
Charlton Junction	41 / 3B		01/01/1873	N/A	SER	Junction between SER North Kent Line and branch to Greenwich (Maze Hill).
Charlton Tunnel	41 / 2C		30/07/1849	N/A	SER	
Chatham Loops	55 / 5D	P	19/06/1904	N/A	SECR	Originally 'up' and 'down', but former 'down' loop resignalled for bidirectional working 1983 (= 'Reversible'). Referred to as 'Chislehurst Loops' until 1959.
	56 / 6A	G	19/06/1904	N/A		
CHEAM	65 / 4A	P	10/05/1847	N/A	LBSCR	Line through station quadrupled 01/10/1911, central island platform allowed for but never built. Through roads removed 1977-8 (signal box closed 28/05/1978). Goods yard closed 28/09/1964.
		G	10/05/1847	28/09/1964		
CHELSEA & FULHAM Chelsea	38 / 3C 84		02/03/1863	14/09/1940	WLER	'& Fulham' after 01/01/1902. Passenger service withdrawn Willesden Junction to Clapham Junction 14/09/1940.
CHELSEA BASIN GOODS	38 / 4C		1863	11/09/1981	LNWR / GWR	
CHERTSEY	61 / 1A	P	14/02/1848	N/A	LSWR	Re-sited north 01/10/1866 to opposite side of level crossing when line extended to Virginia Water. Goods yard closed 05/10/1964
		G	14/02/1848	05/10/1964		
CHESHAM	1 / 1A	P	08/07/1889	N/A	MET	Served by GCR trains (later LNER, later BR) 01/03/1906 - 16/10/1967. Goods yard closed 04/07/1966.
		G	08/07/1889	04/07/1966		
CHESHUNT Cadmores Lane, Cheshunt	7 / 1B	P	22/11/1841	N/A	NER	Original station 150m north of present site. Opened as 'Cadmores Lane Cheshunt' by NER 22/11/1841, closed 1842. Reopened 31/05/1846 as 'Cheshunt', Re-sited to present site 01/10/1891, goods yard closed 01/06/1966.
		G	22/11/1841	01/06/1966		
Cheshunt Junction	7 / 2B		01/10/1891	N/A	GER	
CHESSINGTON NORTH	63 / 3D		28/05/1939	N/A	SR	
CHESSINGTON SOUTH	63 / 4D	P	28/05/1939	N/A	SR	Intended to be a through station on route to Leatherhead, but line never completed beyond goods yard and 'up' platform never used (footbridge not completed). Goods yard opened 01/07/1939 (per Jackson, Borley states goods yard opened with passenger station), closed 18/03/1963 (see Chessington South Sidings).
		G	01/07/1939	18/03/1963		
CHESSINGTON SOUTH SIDINGS (Cemex)	63 / 4D		01/07/1939	N/A	SR	Was Chessington South goods yard, closed to general goods 18/03/1963. Reopened as coal concentration depot May 1963, last inbound train 04/11/1988, empty wagons removed 08/11/1988. Reopened by Cemex as aggregates terminal 10/12/2021 (test train), first inbound train 01/02/2022.
CHESSINGTON ZOO RAILWAY	63 / 5C		1937	1997	PRIV	Opened 1937 with a 12in gauge, rebuilt 1970 to a 2ft gauge, closed 1985. Redeveloped as 'Chessington Railroad' (also 2ft gauge) and reopened 1986, closed for good 1997.
CHIGWELL	17 / 2A		01/05/1903	N/A	GER	Fairlop Loop closed by LNER 30/11/1947 for electrification and transfer to LTE Central Line, reopened 21/11/1948.
Chiltern Tunnel	1 / 4A		2029-33	N/A	NR	HS2 tunnel under construction, expected opening 2029-33.
CHINGFORD (1st)	16 / 1A	P	17/11/1873	02/09/1878	GER	Original terminus of extension from Walthamstow. Closed to passengers 02/09/1878, goods 04/10/1965. Often referred to as 'Bull Lane'.
		G	17/11/1873	04/10/1965		
CHINGFORD (2nd)	8 / 6B		02/09/1878	N/A	GER	New passenger terminus opened to north of original, which closed the same day. Arranged for through running on an aborted extension to High Beech; stub of extension blocked and platforms connected beyond buffers c.1962. Carriage sidings added 1920, and subsequently expanded. Loco release crossover between platform 2 and 3 out of use for some years and to be removed (BLN1419 04/03/2023).
CHIPSTEAD Chipstead & Banstead Downs	72 / 2D	P	02/11/1897	N/A	CVR	02/11/1897 is given as opening date for Chipstead Valley Railway (Purley to Kingswood) in Borley, but it also states regular passenger service 'probably' commenced 09/11/1897, Quick states first train 09/11/1897, so 02/11/1897 may have been official / ceremonial opening. Suffix dropped 09/07/1923. Goods yard closed 07/05/1962.
		G	02/11/1897	07/05/1962		
CHISLEHURST Chislehurst & Bickley Park	55 / 5D	P	01/07/1865	N/A	SER	Renamed 01/09/1866. Passenger station re-sited to the south 02/03/1868. Goods yard closed 18/11/1968. ARC Stone Terminal later used goods yard site, noted in BLN as being in use in December 1977 and disused in late February 1995 (still connected to main line, but rail removed from siding).
		G	01/07/1865	18/11/1968		
Chislehurst Junction	55 / 5D		19/06/1904	N/A	SECR	Junctions at north end of Chatham Loops.
Chislehurst Tunnels	55 / 3C		01/07/1865	N/A	SER	Fast tunnel opened 01/07/1865, Slow tunnel added by SECR 18/06/1905 (St Johns to Elmstead Woods quadrupling).
CHISWICK Chiswick for Grove Park Chiswick & Grove Park Chiswick	37 / 3B	P	22/08/1849	N/A	LSWR	Suffix in use 01/11/1872 - 1955 ('for Grove Park' after c.1920). Goods yard closed 14/06/1958.
		G	22/08/1849	14/06/1958		
Chiswick Curve	37 / 3B 51 / 3A	P	01/06/1870	22/02/1915	LSWR	Opened at same time as Kensington (Addison Road) to Richmond, passenger service 01/06/1870 - 22/02/1915.
		G	01/01/1869	24/07/1932		
Chiswick Junction (1st)	37 / 4C		01/02/1862	01/01/1869	LSWR	Junction at north end of Barnes Curve. Barnes Curve disused since 01/01/1869 but not dismantled until 1881.
Chiswick Junction (2nd)	37 / 3A 51 / 3A		01/01/1869	24/07/1932	LSWR	Junction at south end of Chiswick Curve.
CHISWICK PARK Chiswick Park & Acton Green Acton Green	37 / 2B 51 / 2B		01/07/1879	N/A	MDR	Opened as 'Acton Green', renamed 'Chiswick Park & Acton Green' ??/03/1887, renamed 'Chiswick Park' 01/03/1910. Completely rebuilt 1932-33 due to quadrupling works. Westbound platform closed 15/10/2006 – 15/11/2006, eastbound platform closed 15/11/2006 – 13/12/2006. Served by Piccadilly Line 26/12/2013 – 30/12/2013 (District Line engineering works).
CHISWICK PARK SIDINGS	37 / 2B 51 / 2C		N/A	N/A	TFL (DIS)	Proposed set of three double-length stabling sidings for District Line S7 stock, accessed from the western end, to be built on former LSWR track-bed parallel to the westbound Richmond branch.
Chobham Farm Junction	28 / 3A 77		29/04/1846	01/06/1969	ECTJR / NER	
CHORLEYWOOD Chorley Wood Chorley Wood & Chenies Chorley Wood	1 / 4A	P	08/07/1889	N/A	MET	Opened as 'Chorley Wood', '& Chenies' suffix in use 01/11/1915 - c.1934 (LPTB) and c.1950 (BR). Became 'Chorleywood' c.1964 (LTB) and 1987 (BR). Goods yard closed 14/11/1966.
		G	08/07/1889	14/11/1966		
Christian Street Junction	27 / 6A 74 / 2D		17/04/1886	N/A	LTSR	Originally Junction for Commercial Road Goods, now point where four tracks become two.
CHURCH MANOR WAY HALT	42 / 2C		01/01/1917	01/01/1920	SECR	Provided for munitions workers.
CHURCH PATH SIDINGS	59 / 1D		14/11/2007	N/A	LCOR	Stabling / turnback sidings built in connection with HS1.
CHURCH STREET	66 / 2C		10/05/2000	N/A	CTL	
CHURCHYARD SIDINGS	76		1868	N/A	MID	Now Castle Cement terminal.
CITY GOODS	74 / 2C		01/10/1862	01/07/1949	MID	Site subsequently used for DLR Bank extension tunnel portals. Hydraulic accumulator tower remains in situ (listed).
CITY ROAD	26 / 5C		17/11/1901	09/08/1922	CSLR	
CITY THAMESLINK St Paul's Thameslink	26 / 6C 32 / 4C		29/05/1990	N/A	BR	Renamed 30/09/1991.
CLAPHAM COMMON (LSWR) Wandsworth	38 / 5C		21/05/1838	02/03/1863	LSWR	Renamed ??/07/1846. Replaced by Clapham Junction Station to north.

Name	Page / grid		Date opened	Date closed	Opened by	Notes
CLAPHAM COMMON (CSLR)	39 / 5A		03/06/1900	N/A	CSLR	Terminus of City & South London Railway 03/06/1900 - 13/09/1926. Closed 29/11/1923 - 01/12/1924 and 01/09/1939 – 24/11/1939 (flood protection).
CLAPHAM HIGH STREET Clapham Clapham & North Stockwell Clapham	39 / 5B	P	25/08/1862	N/A	LCDR	Suffix '& North Stockwell' in use between 01/05/1863 and 27/09/1937. Northern platforms opened 01/01/1867, closed 03/04/1916. Station also referred to as 'Clapham Road' or 'Clapham Road & North Stockwell'. LSWR timetable for trains serving here to / from Ludgate Hill referred to 'Clapham Town' (distinct from 'Junction'). Goods yard closed 10/06/1963. Renamed 'Clapham High Street' 15/05/1989.
		G	25/08/1862	10/06/1963		
CLAPHAM JUNCTION	38 / 5D 89		02/03/1863	N/A	LSWR / LBSCR	Replaced Clapham Common (LSWR) station to south.
Clapham Junction Battersea Junction	38 / 5D 89		27/07/1846	N/A	LSWR	Junction between original LSWR line to Southampton and branch to Richmond.
CLAPHAM NORTH Clapham Road	39 / 5B		03/06/1900	N/A	CSLR	Closed 29/11/1923 - 01/12/1924, Renamed 13/09/1926.
CLAPHAM SOUTH	39 / 6A		13/09/1926	N/A	UERL (NOR)	Closed 21/03/2020 – 13/07/2020 (COVID-19).
CLAPHAM YARD	38 / 5C 89		*c.1850's*	N/A	LSWR	Sidings had appeared in angle between lines between 1850 and 1863. Sidings 1-5 had been disconnected by 14/06/2021.
CLAPTON	27 / 1B		01/07/1872	N/A	GER	Goods yard remote to north (see separate entry).
Clapton Curve	15 / 6B	P	01/07/1872	N/A	GER	
		G	01/07/1872	N/A		
CLAPTON GOODS	27 / 1B		1898	07/12/1964	GER	Yard enlarged 02/07/1900.
Clapton Junction	27 / 1B		01/08/1872	N/A	GER	Facing / trailing crossovers plain-lined during July 2020.
Clapton Tunnel	27 / 1B		01/07/1872	N/A	GER	
CLARENCE YARD GOODS	26 / 2C 81		*c.1874*	13/06/1960	GNR	Yard enlarged 1881, upon closure replaced by Finsbury Park Diesel Depot.
Clarence Yard Junction	81		c.1874	N/A	GNR	Formerly divergence of Clarence Yard goods, currently junction between down goods and down line ex-Canonbury.
CLAYGATE Claygate for Claremont Claygate & Claremont	63 / 3B	P	02/02/1885	N/A	LSWR	Named 'Claygate & Claremont' until 1913, then '- for Claremont' until 1955, when suffix dropped. Goods yard closed 06/05/1963
		G	02/02/1885	06/05/1963		
Clerkenwell Tunnels	26 / 5C 32 / 2B		10/01/1863	N/A	MET	Quadrupled 17/02/1868.
CLOCK HOUSE	54 / 5C	P	01/05/1890	N/A	SER	Named 'Penge Road' until opening. Goods yard closed 19/04/1965.
		G	01/05/1890	19/04/1965		
COBHAM & STOKE D'ABERNON Cobham for Stoke D'Abernon Cobham & Stoke D'Abernon	69 / 1D	P	02/02/1885	N/A	LSWR	Opening notice referred to 'Stoke D'Abernon & Cobham', but never appeared as such in Bradshaw. 'for' was substituted for '&' 1913 - 09/09/1953. Goods yard closed 03/05/1965.
		G	02/02/1885	03/05/1965		
COBORN ROAD Coborn Road (Old Ford) Old Ford	27 / 5C		01/02/1865	08/12/1946	GER	Opened as 'Old Ford', renamed 'Coborn Road (Old Ford)' 01/03/1879, but suffix usually omitted. Re-sited west 02/12/1883. Closed 22/05/1916 - 05/05/1919, then for good 08/12/1946.
COCKFOSTERS	6 / 4A		31/07/1933	N/A	LPTB (PIC)	
COCKFOSTERS DEPOT	6 / 5A		31/07/1933	N/A	LPTB (PIC)	Complete redevelopment commenced early 2022, expected to last for around 28 months in readiness for new trains in 2025.
Coleman Street Tunnel	41 / 2D		30/07/1849	N/A	SER	
COLINDALE	12 / 4C		18/08/1924	N/A	UERL (CCEHR)	
COLLIERS WOOD	52 / 4C		13/08/1926	N/A	UERL (NOR)	
COLNBROOK	34 / 3A	P	09/08/1884	29/03/1965	GWR	Terminus of branch from West Drayton 09/08/1884 - 02/11/1885. Passing loop and 'up' platform opened 02/05/1904. Passenger service withdrawn between West Drayton and Staines West 29/03/1965 and Colnbrook station closed; goods yard remained open until 03/01/1966, oil (Gulf) and steel (Pike Bros, later GKN) traffic commenced thereafter (latter siding opened late 1967 / early 1968). Oil traffic had ceased by the end of 1979, traffic to GKN Steel terminal had ceased by January 1981. By mid-1984 M25 construction works had temporarily blocked the line south of Thorney Mill. Current aviation fuel terminal opened on site 01/03/1990.
		G	09/08/1884	03/01/1966		
COLNBROOK – AGGREGATE INDUSTRIES London Concrete and Aggregate Industries asphalt	34 / 3A		*??/05/2014*	N/A	PRIV	Opened May 2014 adjacent to Colnbrook Logistics Centre (see entry below)
COLNBROOK ESTATE HALT	34 / 3A		01/05/1961	29/03/1965	BR	
COLNBROOK LOGISTICS CENTRE	34 / 3A		*??/09/2003*	*c.2011*	PRIV	Terminal for Heathrow Airport construction materials built for Terminal 5 construction. Inward steel traffic commenced September 2003. Terminal 5 completed 2011 and logistics terminal became disused, aggregate traffic continues (see entry above).
COLNBROOK OIL TERMINAL (TOTAL)	34 / 3A		01/03/1990	N/A	PRIV	Aviation Fuel terminal for Heathrow Airport.
Colne Junction	2 / 5C		10/02/1913	19/09/1966	LNWR	Last train on Colne Junction to Croxley Green Junction spur 06/06/1966, date is that of official closure / removal.
Colne Valley Viaduct	9 / 5A		2029-33	N/A	NR	HS2 viaduct currently under construction.
COLNE VALLEY WATERWORKS RAILWAY	2 / 6B		1931/1932	1967	PRIV	2ft gauge light railway conveying coal, salt, and chlorine. Coal to Eastbury Pumping Station ceased 1956.
COLNEY HATCH CEMETERY	14 / 1A		10/07/1861	03/04/1863	GNR	Funeral traffic only (see King's Cross Funeral Station). May have reopened 1866-7 during a cholera epidemic. 'Private and Untimetabled Railway Stations' (Croughton / Kidner / Young) gives a c.1871 closure date.
COMMERCIAL DOCK	40 / 2B 79		01/05/1856	01/01/1867	SER	OS evidence (1875-6 1:1,056) strongly suggests that the platforms for this station were on the same site as the later Southwark Park Station, albeit with the station entrance and ticket hall further south than those of the later station. Commercial Dock does not appear on any OS, but the aforementioned survey c.8 years after closure clearly shows the northernmost pair of tracks splaying apart adjacent to Corbett's Lane Junction signal box as if to accommodate an island platform. Southwark Park was a much larger station, its platforms completely overlapping the presumed location of Commercial Dock's platforms. Reference to 'Commercial Docks' (plural) now believed to be erroneous.
COMMERCIAL ROAD GOODS	27 / 6A 74 / 1C		17/04/1886	03/07/1967	LTSR	
Connaught Bridge	41 / 1C 62 / 3B	P	26/11/1855	??/06/1976	ECR	Crossing of channel between Victoria and Albert Docks, passenger traffic diverted via Connaught Tunnel from June 1876 but route retained for heavier goods trains (1/50 gradients associated with Connaught Tunnel). Passenger services restored 30/09/1935 - 28/03/1936 due to temporary Connaught Tunnel closure. Last goods movement October 1967, line dismantled soon afterwards.
		G	26/11/1855	??/10/1967		

Name	Page / grid		Date opened	Date closed	Opened by	Notes
CONNAUGHT ROAD	41 / 1C 62 / 3B		03/08/1880	08/09/1940	LSKD	Gallions branch single until 14/11/1881. Operated by GER after 1896, ownership later transferred to PLA. Branch closed from 09/09/1940 due to 'Black Saturday' air raid 07/09/1940 (no trains on Sundays since 27/06/1915). Listed as 'Royal Albert Dock, Connaught Road' in Borley.
Connaught Tunnel	41 / 1C 62	P	??/06/1876	N/A	GER	North Woolwich Branch diverted underground due to construction of Royal Albert Dock. No service 30/09/1935 -28/03/1936, 08/09/1940 - 01/01/1941 and 29/05/1994 - 29/10/1995. Passenger route singled 25/08/1969, the original 'up' road then becoming bi-directional and the original 'down' becoming a siding accessing the 'Silvertown Tramway' (taken out of use 29/03/1993). Stratford to North Woolwich closed by Network Rail 10/12/2006. Refurbished for Elizabeth Line Abbey Wood branch, reopening 24/05/2022.
		G	??/06/1876	29/03/1993		
COOMBE LANE	67 / 3B		10/05/2000	N/A	CTL	
COOMBE ROAD Coombe Lane	66 / 3D		10/08/1885	16/05/1983	LBSCR / SER	Closed 01/01/1917 - 30/09/1935, Renamed upon reopening, closed again 16/05/1983.
Coopersale	8 / 1B		28/11/2004	N/A	EOR	Current limit of Epping Ongar Railway operation, no platform. Service from North Weald commenced Easter 2005. Service suspended 31/12/2007 - 25/05/2012 (engineering works).
Copenhagen Junction	75 / 76		1853	N/A	GNR / NLR	Also referred to as 'Belle Isle Junction'.
Copenhagen Tunnels	26 / 3B 75 / 76		07/08/1850	N/A	GNR	Middle bore first, West bore opened 1877, East bore 1886. East bore abandoned c.1977.
Coppermill Curve	15 / 6B	P	01/08/1885	06/09/1926	GER	Originally 'Copper Mills'. Regular year-round passenger service ceased 12/07/1920, then LNER commenced a summer-only Gospel Oak to Chingford service 01/06/1923, ceasing 06/09/1926. Freight use ceased and curve abandoned 11/06/1960.
		G	01/08/1885	11/06/1960		
Coppermill North Junction	15 / 6B		01/07/1872	N/A	GER	Originally 'Copper Mills'. Junction of Lea Valley Line and Clapton Curve.
Coppermill South Junction	15 / 6B		01/08/1885	11/06/1960	GER	Originally 'Copper Mills'. Junction between Lea Valley Line and Coppermill Curve (see notes for latter).
CORBETT'S LANE	79		08/06/1835	12/11/1835	LGR	Temporary station for LGR preopening trials between Blue Anchor Lane and Grand Surrey Canal, Commercial Dock and then Southwark Park stations both subsequently opened on same site.
Corbett's Lane Junction	40 / 3B 79 / 80		05/06/1839	N/A	LGR / LCRR	Junction between LGR and LCRR.
CORY OIL (SELSDON)	66 / 3D		c.1968	18/03/1993	PRIV	On site of Selsdon goods yard (closed 07/10/1968). Closed March 1993, track remains in situ.
Cottage Junction	66 / 1D 86		03/10/1983	N/A	BR	Created through remodelling of Gloucester Road Triangle 1983.
COULSDON NORTH Coulsdon West Coulsdon & Smitham Downs Stoat's Nest & Cane Hill	73 / 1B	P	05/11/1899	03/10/1983	LBSCR	Renamed 'Coulsdon & Smitham Downs' 01/06/1911, renamed 'Coulsdon West' 09/07/1923 for 3 weeks, then finally renamed 'Coulsdon North' 01/08/1923. Goods yard closed 07/10/1968. Opened as two through and two terminal platforms (with goods yard beyond terminal platforms), weekend services ceased September 1965, then peak hours only from May 1970. Closed altogether 03/10/1983. At point of closure, trains did not call at 'though' platforms, only terminal platforms served.
		G	05/11/1899	07/10/1968		
COULSDON NORTH ENGINE SHED	73 / 1B		1900	??.06.1929	LBSCR	
COULSDON SOUTH Coulsdon East Coulsdon & Cane Hill Coulsdon	73 / 2A	P	01/10/1889	N/A	SER	Suffix '& Cane Hill' added 1896. Renamed 'Coulsdon East' 09/07/1923 for 3 weeks then 'Coulsdon South' 01/08/1923. Goods yard closed 01/10/1931.
		G	01/10/1889	01/10/1931		
COULSDON TOWN Coulsdon Town (Smitham) Smitham	73 / 1A	P	01/01/1904	N/A	SECR	Closed 01/01/1917 - 01/01/1919. Goods yard closed 07/05/1962. Renamed 22/05/2011, initially 'Coulsdon Town (Smitham)' on TfL map and Southern timetable, while station nameboards displayed both 'Coulsdon Town' and 'Coulsdon Town (formerly Smitham)' after renaming. Winter timetable 11/12/2011 became 'Coulsdon Town'.
		G	01/01/1904	07/05/1962		
Courthill Loop	40 / 5D	P	07/07/1929	N/A	SR	
		G	07/07/1929	N/A		
Courthill Loop North Junction	40 / 5D		07/07/1929	N/A	SR	Junction at north end of Courthill Loop.
Courthill Loop South Junction	40 / 6D		07/07/1929	N/A	SR	Junction at south end of Courthill Loop.
COVENT GARDEN	26 / 6B		11/04/1907	N/A	UERL (GNPBR)	Closed 19/03/2020 – 24/08/2020 (COVID-19).
Cow Lane Junction	40 / 4A		01/08/1865	N/A	LCDR / LBSCR	Boundary between LCDR & LBSCR ('End-on' Junction). Was intended to be the junction for a more direct LCDR route running across Peckham and Camberwell to Walworth Road station (roughly parallel to Southampton Way). Although a short section of viaduct was built crossing the LBSCR below and the viaduct widened to four tracks to Nunhead, no other works completed.
COWLEY	21 / 5C		01/10/1904	10/09/1962	GWR	Passenger services withdrawn from Uxbridge Vine Street Branch 10/09/1962.
COX & DANKS SCRAPYARD (Park Royal)	24 / 5B		1961	15/04/1988	PRIV	On site of GWR Park Royal Power Station.
COXES LOCK MILL (FLOUR)	61 / 3C		c.1901	c.1980	PRIV	Mill rebuilt 1901, siding assumed to have been laid then (appeared between 1896 and 1914 OS). Traffic ceased c.1980; present in 1980 Baker 3rd Edition, absent from 1984 4th Edition.
CRANLEY GARDENS	14 / 5A	P	02/08/1902	05/07/1954	GNR	Opened to goods first, passenger station opened 02/08/1902. Closed to passengers when Alexandra Palace to Finsbury Park service withdrawn 05/07/1954 after a previous closure period 29/10/1951 - 07/01/1952. Branch had been intended for electrification and transfer to Northern Line, but works abandoned post-WW2. Goods yard closed 08/05/1957 and route to Park Junction abandoned.
		G	29/06/1897	08/05/1957		
CRAYFORD	57 / 1C	P	01/09/1866	N/A	SER	Goods yard closed 04/01/1965.
		G	01/09/1866	04/01/1965		
Crayford Creek Junction	43 / 5D		01/05/1895	N/A	BHR / SER	
Crayford Spur	43 / 6D	P	25/05/1998	N/A	SR	Borley refers to spur opening in 1918 and closing to regular traffic c.1920, before reopening 11/10/1942, however contemporary OS maps show no evidence of the line before WW2. Regular advertised passenger services did not commence until 25/05/1998; per BLN there was an unadvertised service from 10/07/1967 which remained in timetables until May 1976.
		G	11/10/1942	N/A		
Crayford Spur 'A' Junction	43 / 6D		11/10/1942	N/A	SR	Junction at north end of Crayford Spur.
Crayford Spur 'B' Junction	43 / 6D		11/10/1942	N/A	SR	Junction at south end of Crayford Spur.
Cremorne Bridge	38 / 4C		02/03/1863	N/A	WLER	
Crescent Wood Tunnel	54 / 2A		01/08/1865	20/09/1954	LCDR	Nunhead to Crystal Palace (High Level) closed 20/09/1954 (to both passengers and Goods).
CREWS HILL	6 / 1C	P	04/04/1910	N/A	GNR	Goods yard closed 01/10/1962.
		G	04/04/1910	01/10/1962		
CRICKLEWOOD Childs Hill & Cricklewood	25 / 2A 85	P	02/05/1870	N/A	MID	Renamed 01/05/1903. Goods yard closed 06/10/1969.
		G	02/05/1870	06/10/1969		

Name	Page / grid		Date opened	Date closed	Opened by	Notes
Cricklewood Curve	25 / 1A 85	P	03/08/1875	01/10/1902	MID	Opened to passenger and goods traffic 03/08/1875. No passenger traffic between 01/07/1888 - 01/03/1893. Passenger traffic withdrawn for good 01/10/1902, freight traffic remains. Passenger traffic proposed for re-introduction (West London Orbital).
		G	03/08/1875	N/A		
Cricklewood Curve Junction	25 / 1A 85		03/08/1875	N/A	MID	
CRICKLEWOOD DEPOT	25 / 1A 85		04/11/1979	N/A	BR	Built for Midland main line electrification, completed Bedford - Moorgate May 1982 and into St Pancras Summer 1982. Depot and associated signal box commissioned 04/11/1979 but only used for storage of class 317 EMUs between delivery and their entry into passenger service October 1983 (delayed by trade union dispute). Following introduction of 'Thameslink' service 16/05/1988, maintenance moved to Selhurst Depot and Cricklewood Depot became largely disused and the EMU shed rented out (Jerich's Warehouse – now demolished). Some Thameslink EMU and East Midland Railway HST/DMU stabling remains on site.
CRICKLEWOOD DOWN SIDINGS	25 / 2A 85		c.1870's	c.1960's	MID	Had appeared by late 19th century, possibly laid in association with Cricklewood Curve. Lifted by 1970's.
CRICKLEWOOD ENGINE SHED	25 / 1A 85		1882	14/12/1964	MID	First shed 1882, second added 1893. After steam stabling ceased, sheds used for diesel stabling for a short while.
CRICKLEWOOD FREIGHT SIDINGS Cricklewood Brent Sidings	25 / 1A 85		c.1870	28/08/2021	MID	First sidings on 'up' side had appeared by early 1870's, greatly expanded in late 19th and early 20th centuries. Most of goods sidings removed to allow construction of the TMD then EMU depot, but spoil traffic remained up until closure (access removed 28/08/2021).
CRICKLEWOOD RECESS SIDINGS	25 / 1A 85		c.1870's	N/A	MID	Had appeared by late 19th century, possibly laid in association with Cricklewood Curve. Hosted Redland (now Lafarge) aggregate terminal until early 2000's, now DB Cargo aggregates terminal (opened 25/11/2019, light engine test run 15/11/2019).
Cricklewood South Junction Watling Street Junction	25 / 2A		25/06/1899	N/A	MID	
CRICKLEWOOD TMD	25 / 1A 85		c.1965	??/07/1983	BR	Replaced Cricklewood Engine Shed, maintained diesel locos and DMUs for Midland main line.
CROFTON PARK	40 / 6C		01/07/1892	N/A	LCDR	
Crofton Road Junction	40 / 4A		Pre 1992	N/A	LCDR / LBSCR	Not present on 1950 OS, first BLN mention in 1992. Possibly installed through Victoria area resignalling c.1980?
Cromwell Curve	38 / 2C 84	P	03/07/1871	12/02/1956	MDR	Opening coincided with MDR's platforms opening at High Street Kensington.
		G	03/07/1871	12/02/1956		
Cromwell Curve North Junction	38 / 2C 84		03/07/1871	12/02/1956	MDR	Junction at north end of Cromwell Curve.
Cromwell Curve South Junction	38 / 2C 84		03/07/1871	12/02/1956	MDR	Junction at south end of Cromwell Curve.
Cromwell Road Junction	38 / 2B 84		03/07/1871	N/A	MDR	Remodelled as grade separated junction 01/02/1878.
CROSSHARBOUR Crossharbour & London Arena Crossharbour	40 / 2D		31/08/1987	N/A	DLR	On site of former Millwall Docks station. '& London Arena' suffix added 14/08/1995, not dropped until 2007 despite The London Arena having been demolished in June 2006. Closed by IRA bomb at South Quay 09/02/1996 - 15/04/1996. Southern terminus of DLR during Lewisham extension works 11/01/1999 - 20/11/1999.
Cross Street Tunnel	42 / 2A		30/07/1849	N/A	SER	
CROUCH END	14 / 6B		22/08/1867	05/07/1954	GNR	Closed when Alexandra Palace to Finsbury Park service withdrawn 05/07/1954 after a previous closure period 29/10/1951 - 07/01/1952. Branch had been intended for electrification and transfer to Northern Line, but works abandoned post-WW2.
CROUCH HILL	14 / 6C		21/07/1868	N/A	THJR	Closed 31/01/1870 - 01/10/1870. Gospel Oak to South Tottenham (formerly Barking) trains suspended at weekends 04/06/2016 to 25/09/2016, and then entire Overground service suspended and station closed 26/09/2016 to 27/02/2017 due to electrification works on Gospel Oak to Barking Line.
CROWLANDS	18 / 6B		N/A	N/A	GER	Platform foundations built west of Jutsums Lane 1901, but station never completed.
CROXLEY Croxley Green	2 / 5A	P	02/11/1925	N/A	MET / LNER	LNER services ceased 04/05/1926. 'Green' suffix dropped 23/05/1949. Goods yard closed 14/11/1966.
		G	02/11/1925	14/11/1966		
CROXLEY DEPOT	2 / 5C		16/04/1917	02/11/1985	LNWR	Facilities shared by Bakerloo Line and mainline until 24/09/1982. Final Class 501 EMU departed 01/11/1985 (BLN)
CROXLEY GREEN	2 / 5A	P	15/06/1912	25/03/1996	LNWR	Goods yard opened 01/10/1912 (per disused-stations.org.uk; Borley states goods & passenger opened on same date), closed 14/11/1966. Platform relocated south of track 1989 (temporary structure due to subsidence beneath original platform). Last train ran on Croxley Green Branch 22/03/1996 (no weekend service so Monday 25/03/1996 is given as closure date), initially closed 'temporarily' for bridge work, replaced by bus service which ran until 26/09/2003.
		G	01/10/1912	14/11/1966		
Croxley Green Junction	2 / 5C		10/02/1913	19/09/1966	LNWR	Last train on Colne Junction to Croxley Green Junction spur 06/06/1966, date is that of official closure / removal.
CROXLEY PAPER MILLS	2 / 5A		c.1900	19/12/1980	PRIV	Mills in operation on site since 1830. Expanded c.1886, when an internal railway system was laid. Connection to Rickmansworth Branch appeared between 1899 and 1914 OS. Mills closed 19/12/1980, although Cobb gives branch closure date as 1983.
CROXLEY TIP	1 / 6D		1902	1980's	MET	London Transport refuse tip, former gravel pit. Regular use into 1980's per Horne 'Metropolitan Line - an illustrated history'.
CROYDON 'A' POWER STATION	66 / 2C		1896	1973	PRIV	
CROYDON 'B' POWER STATION	66 / 1B		1950	??/11/1981	PRIV	
CRYSTAL PALACE Crystal Palace Low Level Crystal Palace	54 / 4A	P	10/06/1854	N/A	LBCSR	Suffix 'Low Level' 01/11/1898 - 13/06/1955 to distinguish from LCDR station. Goods yard closed 06/12/1965. Original (eastern) section of station remodelled to accommodate LO services which commenced 23/05/2010.
		G	10/06/1854	06/12/1965		
CRYSTAL PALACE HIGH LEVEL Crystal Palace & Upper Norwood Crystal Palace High Level & Upper Norwood Crystal Palace High Level	54 / 3A	P	01/08/1865	20/09/1954	LCDR	Suffix '& Upper Norwood' added 01/11/1898 after which time 'High Level' was sometimes omitted. Renamed 'Crystal Palace High Level' 09/07/1923. Closed 01/01/1917 - 01/03/1919 and 22/05/1944 - 04/03/1946. Nunhead to Crystal Palace (High Level) closed 20/09/1954 (Passengers and Goods).
		G	01/08/1865	20/09/1954		
Crystal Palace Tunnel	54 / 3A		01/12/1856	N/A	WELCPR	
Crystal Palace Tunnel Junction	54 / 4A		01/10/1857	N/A	LBSCR / WELCPR	

Name	Page / grid		Date opened	Date closed	Opened by	Notes
CUSTOM HOUSE (suffix 'for ExCeL' DLR only) Custom House Victoria Dock Victoria Dock, Custom House Custom House	41 / 1B 62		26/11/1855	N/A	ECR	Bay platform provided on 'down' side for terminating trains ex-Gallions. Station became temporary terminus from 08/09/1940 due to 'Black Saturday' air raid the previous day, North Woolwich service not restored until 01/01/1941 and Gallions service was never restored. Also referred to as 'Victoria Dock, Custom House' and 'Custom House Victoria Dock', the prefix being consistently used in Bradshaw. DLR Platforms opened 28/03/1994. NR platforms closed 10/12/2006, reopened 24/05/2022 (Elizabeth Line). Station closed entirely 03/02/2017 – 07/01/2018 (reopened at 16:00 that afternoon) (Elizabeth Line works). Carries suffix 'for ExCeL' on TfL map and DLR station name boards, and on-train DLR recorded announcements also have 'west' added after ExCeL, but no suffix on Elizabeth Line platform roundels.
Custom House Junction	62 / 3B		??/06/1876	??/10/1967	GER	Junction between routes via Connaught Bridge and Connaught Tunnel.
CUTTY SARK (for Maritime Greenwich)	40 / 3D		03/12/1999	N/A	DLR	Suffix 'for Maritime Greenwich' appears on TfL map, station name boards and on-train recorded announcements.
CYPRUS	41 / 1D 62 / 5C		28/03/1994	N/A	DLR	Platform nameboards have suffix 'for University of East London' but this does not appear on TfL map or on-board recorded announcements.

D

Name	Page / grid		Date opened	Date closed	Opened by	Notes
DAGENHAM DOCK	30 / 5A	P	01/07/1908	N/A	LTSR	Goods yard closed 02/11/1964; site became East London Waste Terminal.
		G	01/07/1908	02/11/1964		
DAGENHAM DOCK	30 / 6A		1887	c.1980's	PRIV	Rail-served dock, sidings still apparent on OS maps until mid-1980's.
Dagenham Dock East Junction (Down)	30 / 5A		14/11/2007	N/A	LCOR / NR	
Dagenham Dock East Junction (Up)	30 / 5B		14/11/2007	N/A	LCOR / NR	
DAGENHAM EAST Dagenham	30 / 3B	P	01/05/1885	N/A	LTSR	Served by District Railway trains 02/06/1902 - 01/10/1905, then by excursion trains to Southend (later Shoeburyness) from 01/06/1910. Regular District Line service reintroduced 12/09/1932 when route quadrupled, District Line trains utilising the new 'local' platforms. 'East' suffix added 01/05/1949. British Rail services withdrawn by 15/06/1962 and 'fast' platforms abandoned. Goods yard closed 06/05/1968. Ownership of 'local' platforms transferred to LTB 01/01/1969. Active proposal to reopen NR platforms.
		G	01/05/1885	06/05/1968		
DAGENHAM HEATHWAY Heathway	30 / 3A		12/09/1932	N/A	LMS	Barking to Upminster quadrupled and two new stations opened by LMS 12/09/1932, but an LMS service was never provided, served solely by District Line from opening. Renamed 01/05/1949, ownership transferred to LTB 01/01/1969.
Dalston Eastern Curve	27 / 3A 6	P	01/11/1865	15/05/1944	NLR	Opened to passengers 01/11/1865, goods May 1868. Passenger service suspended 15/05/1944 (enemy action) and was never reinstated. Regular goods traffic ceased 01/03/1965, points removed 02/01/1966. Route safeguarded for possible future reopening for LO services.
		G	??/05/1868	02/01/1966		
Dalston Eastern Junction	27 / 3A 6		01/11/1865	02/01/1966	NLR	Junction at north end of Dalston Eastern Curve.
DALSTON JUNCTION	27 / 3A 6		01/11/1865	N/A	NLR	Original platforms 5 & 6 closed 15/05/1944, 3 & 4 closed 08/11/1976. Closed completely 30/06/1986 - 27/04/2010.
Dalston Junction	27 / 3A 6		01/11/1865	02/01/1966	NLR	Junction at south end of Dalston Western and Eastern Curves.
DALSTON KINGSLAND Kingsland	27 / 3A 6		09/11/1850	N/A	BR	Opened as 'Kingsland' 09/11/1850, closed 01/11/1865 when Broad Street extension opened by NLR and platforms subsequently demolished. Goods yard to east (see 'Kingsland Goods'). Reopened as 'Dalston Kingsland' 16/05/1983. Closed 20/02/2010 - 01/06/2010 (LO upgrade works).
Dalston Western Curve	27 / 3A 6	P	01/11/1865	N/A	NLR	Carried goods traffic from May 1868 to 11/04/1969. Closed with Broad Street and Dalston Junction Stations 30/06/1986 and dismantled, but subsequently reinstated (06/01/2011 test train, 28/02/2011 passenger service).
		G	??/05/1868	11/04/1969		
Dalston Western Junction	27 / 3A 6		01/11/1865	20/04/2009	NLR	Broad Street route eliminated 30/06/1986, but this remained convergence of 'No.1' freight lines and 'No.2' DC electrified passenger lines until 'No.1' lines temporarily taken out of use 20/04/2009 for works associated with East London Line extension. Although this restored trains on Dalston Western Curve 06/01/2011 (date of first test train), there is now no physical junction.
DARTFORD Dartford Junction for Farningham Dartford Junction Dartford	58 / 1A	P	30/07/1849	N/A	SER	Suffix 'Junction' added 1870, 'for Farningham' added 1871, reverted to 'Dartford' 1879/80. Remodelled 1895 to three through lines with the third road extending to Dartford Junction, carriage sidings expanded to current five at this time (previously two). Goods yard closed 01/05/1972. Remodelled to four bidirectional through lines / four platform faces 05/08/1973.
		G	30/07/1849	01/05/1972		
Dartford Junction	43 / 6D		01/09/1866	N/A	SER	
DATCHET	33 / 4D	P	22/08/1848	N/A	LSWR	Terminus of extension from Richmond until 01/12/1849. Goods yard closed 17/01/1965.
		G	22/08/1848	17/01/1965		
DAY & SONS GRAVEL (PURLEY)	66 / 5C		Late 1970's	N/A	PRIV	Established on site of Purley goods yard, closed 06/01/1969 (see 'Purley' entry). Initially Brett Marine, appeared between 1977 and 1980 Baker.
DEBDEN Chigwell Lane Chigwell Road	8 / 4A	P	24/04/1865	N/A	GER	Opened as 'Chigwell Road', renamed 'Lane' 01/12/1865. Closed 22/05/1916 - 03/02/1919. Ownership and majority of passenger services transferred to LTE and station renamed 'Debden' 25/09/1949. First trains in the morning remained BR services until 01/06/1970. Goods yard closed 18/04/1966.
		G	24/04/1865	18/04/1966		
DENHAM Denham for Harefield Denham	9 / 6B	P	02/04/1906	N/A	GCR / GWR	Suffix 'for Harefield' 01/10/1907 - 1955. Projected terminus of Central Line extension from West Ruislip, but works cancelled during WW2. Goods yard closed 06/01/1964. Through roads removed 12/12/1965 (up) & 19/12/1965 (down). Down platform relocated to north of track 27/07/2008 due to subsidence under original, using the vacant through roads' track bed.
		G	02/04/1906	06/01/1964		
Denham East Curve	9 / 6C	P	N/A	N/A	GWR	Only saw occasional goods traffic and was lifted during WW1.
		G	01/05/1907	??/??/1917		
Denham East Junction	9 / 6C		01/05/1907	??/??/1917	GWR	Junction between Denham East Curve and GWR / GCR main line.
Denham South Junction	9 / 6C		01/05/1907	30/04/1965	GWR	Junction eliminated when East curve lifted c.1917, but reinstated 14/05/1942 - 30/04/1965 for access to oil depot.
Denham West Curve	9 / 6C	P	01/05/1907	01/09/1939	GWR	Uxbridge High Street branch closed 01/09/1939 (passengers) & 24/02/1964 (goods), northern portion remained open to serve an oil depot until 30/04/1965.
		G	01/05/1907	30/04/1965		
Denham West Junction	9 / 6B		01/05/1907	30/04/1965	GWR	Junction between Uxbridge High Street branch and GWR / GCR main line.
DENMARK HILL	39 / 5D		01/12/1865	N/A	LBSCR	Entire station owned by LBSCR, but the northern platforms which were used exclusively by LCDR opened first on 01/12/1865, line through station having opened four months earlier on 01/08/1865. Southern (LBSCR) platforms added 13/08/1866.
Denmark Hill Tunnels	39 / 5D		01/08/1865	N/A	LBSCR	North bore opened 01/08/1865, south bore 13/08/1866.

Name	Page / grid		Date opened	Date closed	Opened by	Notes

DENTON HALT
    Denton Road
    Denton Halt
	60 / 1C		01/07/1906	04/12/1961	SECR	Named 'Denton Road' 1914 - 1919, otherwise 'Denton Halt'.

DEPTFORD	40 / 3C		08/02/1836	N/A	LGR	Country terminus of LGR 08/02/1836 - 24/12/1838. 3-road engine shed provided on 'up' side, with an incline down to carriage storage under the viaduct arches (incline still in situ, and 'listed'). Shed closed 1904. Station closed 15/03/1915 as a WW1 economy, did not reopen until 19/07/1926.
DEPTFORD BRIDGE	40 / 4D		20/11/1999	N/A	DLR	Suffix 'for Lewisham College' appears on station name boards (but not on TfL map or on-train recorded announcements).
Deptford Lift Bridge Junction	40 / 3B 79		15/05/1869	01/01/1964	LBSCR	Junction where Deptford Wharf branch split into lines to Old Kent Road (added 05/05/1869) and separate 'up' and 'down' lines to New Cross (Gate). Separate 'up' line added 01/10/1884 (until this date Deptford Wharf branch joined LBSCR main line on 'down' side only). Entire branch and connection effectively closed 14/10/1963, officially closed 01/01/1964.
DEPTFORD WHARF	40 / 2C 79		02/07/1849	01/01/1964	LBSCR	Effectively closed by 14/10/1963, 01/01/1964 is official date of closure.
DEVONSHIRE STREET, MILE END	27 / 5C		20/06/1839	c.1841	ECR	London Terminus of ECR 20/06/1839 - 01/07/1840. Definitely remained open after line extended to Bishopsgate, but exact closure date unknown; late 1840 or early 1841 coinciding roughly with Mile End (ECR) opening to west.
DEVONS ROAD	27 / 5D 88		31/08/1987	N/A	DLR	
DEVONS ROAD DEPOT	27 / 5D 88		1882	10/02/1964	NLR	Locomotive Depot, upon losing last steam allocation 25/08/1958, became Britain's first diesel-only depot. An unadvertised staff return journey between here and Broad Street appeared in the 1953 timetable early mornings.
DEVONS ROAD GOODS	27 / 5D 88		??/07/1874	02/11/1964	LNWR	Originally coal only, opened to general goods February 1891.
District Junction (South Acton)	37 / 1B 51 / 1B		15/05/1899	1915	MDR / NSWJR	Points 'clipped' out of use since 1915 (last traffic the year before), but not physically removed until c.1930.
Dock Junction North	75 / 76		01/10/1868	N/A	MID	Junction between MID routes to St Pancras terminus and MET 'Widened Lines'.
Dock Junction South	75 / 76		01/11/1887	N/A	MID	Formerly divergence of line to Somers Town goods, currently crossovers on Midland main line.
Dockyard Tunnel	41 / 2D		30/07/1849	N/A	SER	

DOLLIS HILL
    Dollis Hill & Gladstone Park
    Dollis Hill
	24 / 2D		01/10/1909	N/A	MET	Suffix '& Gladstone Park' in use 1931-1933. First served Bakerloo Line 20/11/1939. Last served Metropolitan Line 07/11/1940. Bakerloo Line service replaced by Jubilee Line 01/05/1979.

Dolphin Junction	33 / 1B		01/06/1879	N/A	GWR	Junctions between 'fast' and 'slow' lines between Langley and Slough.
DOWN EMPTY CARRIAGE SHED (EUSTON)	26 / 4A		c.1900	Early 2007	LNWR	Appeared between 1896 and 1916 OS. Last train movements thought to be early 2007 to remove stored vans, demolished 2018. Site used for covered way at 'throat' of Euston HS2 station.
Down Riverside Junction	29 / 4C		18/07/2022	N/A	NR	
DOWN SIDINGS (PLUMSTEAD)	42 / 2B		c.1900	N/A	SER	No sidings apparent on 1896 OS, but had appeared by 1914.
DOWN SIDINGS (SHENFIELD)	20 / 1C		01/01/1934	c.2016	LNER	Had not been in regular use, removed in connection with provision of new platform 6 at Shenfield.
DOWN SIDINGS (WIMBLEDON)	52 / 3B		c.1895	N/A	LSWR	Berthing sidings, apparent on 1895 OS, one greatly extended 1898 to access Wimbledon Borough Council siding. Electrified c.1935, shortened 1984.
DOWN STREET Down Street, Mayfair	39 / 1A		15/03/1907	22/05/1932	UERL (GNPBR)	Opened with 'Mayfair' suffix, subsequently dropped. During WW2 the site was used for underground Government Cabinet Offices and trains made stops during this time for Cabinet Ministers (who rode with the motormen).
DOWN YARD (REDHILL)	73 / 6C		c.1900	N/A	SECR	Not depicted on 1896 OS, but appeared on 1913 survey.
DOWN YARD (SOUTHALL)	35 / 1D		01/05/1839	N/A	GWR	On site of first goods yard at Southall.
DOWNHAM ESTATE RAILWAY	55 / 2A		1927	1929	LCC	Sidings, engine shed, and trailing junction with up main line. Route and full extent of standard gauge railway unknown as no OS evidence found, but surmised from photographic evidence to have been a loop along the southern boundary of Hither Green Cemetery, then along the middle of Whitefoot Lane, curve across Whitefoot Lane Playing Fields, then along Shroffold Road and onto Glenbow Road, Rangefield Road, Southover, then returning back towards the connection with the main line via Downham Way, with several branches following other existing roads. Railway in use 1927 – 1929 (estate complete Summer 1930).
DRAYTON GREEN Drayton Green Ealing Halt	23 / 6C		01/03/1905	N/A	GWR	Renamed 'Drayton Green' 05/05/1969.
Drayton Green Junction	23 / 6C		03/06/1903	N/A	GWR	
Drayton Green Tunnel	23 / 6C		??/04/1974	N/A	BR	Covered Way erected over line in connection with housing development above, completed April 1974.
DRAYTON PARK	26 / 2C 81		14/02/1904	N/A	GNCR	Opened by GNCR, absorbed by Metropolitan Railway 01/07/1913, transferred to LPTB Edgware - Morden Line (later Northern Line) 01/07/1933. Became northern terminus of line from Moorgate 04/10/1964 (Victoria Line works). Closed by LTE 05/10/1975, reopened by British Rail 16/08/1976.
DRAYTON PARK DEPOT	26 / 2C 81		14/02/1904	05/10/1975	GNCR	GNCR depot, closed when Northern City Line closed by LTE prior to transfer to BR. Was connected to GNR.

DUDDING HILL FOR WILLESDEN & NEASDEN
    Dudding Hill
    Dudding Hill for Church End Willesden
    Willesden & Dudden Hill
	24 / 2D	P
		G
			03/08/1875
			01/01/1872
				01/10/1902
				06/07/1964
					MID	Opened to goods traffic 01/01/1872, passenger station opened 03/08/1875 as 'Willesden & Dudden Hill'. Renamed 'Dudding Hill for Church End Willesden' 01/02/1876, then 'Dudding Hill' 01/05/1878, then 'Dudding Hill for Willesden & Neasden' 01/06/1880. Closed to passengers 02/07/1888 - 01/03/1893, then for good 01/10/1902. Goods yard closed 06/07/1964.

Dudding Hill Junction	24 / 2D		02/05/1870	N/A	MID	
DUNDONALD ROAD	52 / 4A		30/05/2000	N/A	CTL	
DURNSFORD ROAD POWER STATION	52 / 2B		25/10/1915	1965	LSWR	LSWR power station, opening date denotes first section of route to be supplied (Wimbledon - East Putney). After closure and demolition, Wimbledon Traincare Depot inspection shed erected on site 1976.
DURNSFORD ROAD SIDINGS	52 / 2B		1914	N/A	LSWR	Originally 15-road shed built to stable LSWR's first fleet of electric multiple units, which entered service 25/10/1915. 1914 shed demolished c.1974 and replaced by Wimbledon Traincare Depot inspection shed to the south.

Name	Page / grid	Date opened	Date closed	Opened by	Notes

E

Name	Page / grid	Date opened	Date closed	Opened by	Notes
EAGLE LANE GOODS	16 / 5B	*15/05/1899*	*18/04/1966*	GER	
EALING BROADWAY Ealing	23 / 6D	01/12/1838	N/A	GWR	Suffix 'Broadway' added 1875. Served by District Railway since 01/07/1879. Served by Central London Railway since 03/08/1920. Connection between LTE and BR east of station removed 17/09/1972 (disused since ??/05/1945). Connection between District / Central Lines last used 02/05/2010, removed by start of traffic 31/05/2010. Served by Piccadilly Line 26/12/2013 – 30/12/2013 (Engineering works). District Line sidings east of station decommissioned October 2014, removed for start of traffic 02/11/2015.
EALING COMMON Ealing Common & West Acton Ealing Common	37 / 1A	01/07/1879	N/A	MDR	Suffix '& West Acton' 1886 - 01/03/1910. Served by Piccadilly Line since 04/07/1932.
EALING COMMON DEPOT *Mill Hill Park Depot*	37 / 1A	*13/06/1905*	N/A	MDR	District Line Depot built 1904-1905 for stabling electric trains; date quoted is that of the first section electrified. Used also for Piccadilly Line stabling 04/07/1932 - 10/10/1964, but had carried out overhaul work for GNPBR trains since that line's opening (15/12/1906).
EARDLEY CARRIAGE SIDINGS	53 / 4A	*c.1900*	*post-1960*	LBSCR	Exact opening date unknown; do not appear on 1898 OS, but had appeared by 1909. Never electrified. Regular use ceased c.1960, sidings remained in situ, used occasionally for several more years.
EARL'S COURT	38 / 2B 84	30/10/1871	N/A	MDR	Re-sited to west side of Earl's Court Road 01/02/1878 after first structure destroyed by fire 30/12/1875. GNPBR platforms opened 15/12/1906. Closed 23/11/1997 - 06/04/1998 and 24/11/2001 - 05/03/2002 (both Piccadilly Line only, escalator works).
Earl's Court Junction	38 / 2B 84	01/02/1872	03/03/1958	MDR / WLER	Junction between MDR and WLER, removed when segregated District Line track provided to Kensington Olympia.
EARLSFIELD Earlsfield & Summerstown Earlsfield	52 / 1C	01/04/1884	N/A	LSWR	Suffix '& Summerstown' 1884 - 01/06/1902. Originally two platforms, one on each side of four-track formation (before up slow flyover opened at Wimbledon 17/05/1936, slow lines were outside fast). Island platform constructed between former 'fast' lines for 17/05/1936 reconfiguration ('slow' south of 'fast'), original 'up' platform on 'up fast' line subsequently abandoned and further demolished. 'Down fast' platform remains, but not regularly used.
Earlswood North Junction	73 / 6C	05/11/1899	N/A	LBSCR / SER	
EAST ACTON	24 / 6C	03/08/1920	N/A	CLR	Viaduct Junction to North Acton opened by GWR 16/04/1917, but no passenger service until CLR opened. Eastbound platform closed for reconstruction 02/08/2021, reopened 19/09/2022.
EAST BRIXTON Loughborough Park & Brixton Loughborough Park	39 / 5C	13/08/1866	05/01/1976	LBSCR	Terminus of LBSCR extension from Corbett's Lane Junction until 01/05/1867 high level route to Shepherd's Lane Junction opened. Renamed 'Loughborough Park & Brixton' ??/01/1870, then 'East Brixton' 01/01/1894. Closed 19/05/1926 - 20/09/1926, then for good 05/01/1976 (lack of patronage).
EAST CROYDON East Croydon Local / East Croydon Main New Croydon / East Croydon Croydon East Croydon	66 / 2D	P 12/07/1841 G 12/07/1841	N/A 07/05/1973	LBRR	Opened as 'Croydon', 'East' suffix added ??/02/1850, reversed to 'East Croydon' 01/05/1862. Adjoining station for local traffic named 'New Croydon' opened 01/05/1862, renamed 'East Croydon Local' 01/06/1909, on which date the adjoining original station was renamed 'East Croydon Main'. Two stations combined as 'East Croydon' ??/07/1924. Goods yard closed 07/05/1973. Croydon Tramlink opened 10/05/2000 at street level outside station entrance.
EAST DULWICH Champion Hill	39 / 5D	P 01/10/1868 G *01/10/1868*	N/A *10/09/1962*	LBSCR	Renamed 01/06/1888. Goods yard closed 10/09/1962.
EAST FINCHLEY East End Finchley	13 / 5D	P 22/08/1867 G *22/08/1867*	N/A *01/10/1962*	GNR	Renamed 01/02/1887. First served by, and ownership transferred to, LPTB Northern Line 03/07/1939 (terminus of LPTB Northern Line extension from Archway 03/07/1939 - 14/04/1940). Became terminus of LNER service from Finsbury Park 14/04/1940 when LPTB took over High Barnet service. LNER passenger trains withdrawn 02/03/1941, goods yard closed 01/10/1962.
East Finchley Junction	13 / 5D	03/07/1939	N/A	LPTB / LNER	Junction of Northern Line with former LNER route to Finsbury Park (now depot access).
EAST GOODS YARD (FINSBURY PARK)	81	*1877*	*13/06/1960*	GNR	
EAST GREENWICH GAS WORKS	41 / 2A	*1886*	*1976*	PRIV	Constructed 1881-1886, initially internal railway network only but connection to SER Angerstein Wharf branch added early 20th Century (between 1899 and 1916 per OS maps). Narrow gauge 2ft 5½in system present at northern end of site, closed 1933. Production at works ceased 1976.
EAST HAM	28 / 4D	P 31/03/1858 G *31/03/1858*	N/A *??/04/1962*	LTSR	First served by District Railway 02/06/1902, line quadrupled 1905, District trains then using 'slow' platforms to north. Served by Metropolitan Line since 30/03/1936 ('Hammersmith & City Line' since 30/07/1990). Bay platform ex-Kentish Town via TFGR and THJR abandoned 26/10/1958 (last train 15/09/1958). Main line services non-stopped since 15/06/1962 and 'Fast' platforms abandoned. Goods yard closed ??/04/1962. Westbound platform closed 28/08/2000 – 23/09/2000, eastbound closed 01/11/2002 – 01/12/2002.
EAST HAM DEPOT	28 / 3D	*06/11/1961*	N/A	BR	Built for LTSR electrification on Site of former District Line Little Ilford Depot, date is that of first AC electric service.
East Ham Loop	28 / 3D	P 09/07/1894 G *01/09/1894*	15/09/1958 *30/11/1958*	LTSR	First goods use 01/09/1894, last passenger use 15/09/1958 (TFGR trains diverted to Barking).
East Ham Loop North Junction	28 / 3D	09/07/1894	30/11/1958	LTSR	Junction at north end of East Ham Loop.
East Ham Loop South Junction	28 / 3D	09/07/1894	30/11/1958	LTSR	Junction at south end of East Ham Loop.
EAST INDIA	41 / 1A 31 / 5D	28/03/1994	N/A	DLR	Station name boards carry suffix 'for Tower Hamlets Town Hall', but this does not appear on TfL map or on-train recorded announcements.
EAST INDIA DOCKS GOODS	41 / 1A 31 / 4D	*1859*	*1961*	GER	
East London Down Junction	40 / 4C 79	01/04/1880	16/04/1966	SER / ELR	SER service to Liverpool Street via ELR commenced 01/04/1880. Rolt Street Junction to New Cross (SER) became bi-directional (former 'down' only spur) 01/10/1884 when ELR bay platform opened at New Cross. 'Up' spur remained in use for goods / through traffic until 16/04/1966 when this and the connection on the 'down' side were both taken out of use (removed 1968).
East London Up Junction	40 / 3C 79	01/04/1880	16/04/1966	SER / ELR	See notes for 'East London Down Junction' above.
EAST PUTNEY	38 / 5A	03/06/1889	N/A	LSWR	Platforms to / from Putney Bridge opened first (built by LSWR but operated by MDR from outset). Platforms on curve to Wandsworth Town opened 01/07/1889, regular service withdrawn 05/05/1941, although some services called on occasions until 1969. Point Pleasant Junction to Wimbledon still used for empty stock working / diversions; some late night and/or early morning services have remained routed this way in most working timetables.
East Putney Junction	38 / 6A	01/07/1889	N/A	LSWR	First use East Putney Junction to Point Pleasant Junction 01/07/1889.

Name	Page / grid		Date opened	Date closed	Opened by	Notes
East Putney Tunnel	38 / 6A		03/06/1889	N/A	LSWR	Built by LSWR, but first use by MDR 03/06/1889. Ownership transferred to LU 01/04/1994.
EAST SIDINGS (ACTON TOWN)	37 / 1B 51 / 1A		*04/07/1932*	N/A	UERL	Current layout since 1932 quadrupling Turnham Green to Acton Town.
EAST SMITHFIELD / LONDON DOCKS GOODS	40 / 1A 74 / 2C		*17/06/1864*	*01/09/1966*	GER	
EAST TILBURY East Tilbury Halt	46 / 3D		07/09/1936	N/A	LMS	Suffix 'Halt' dropped February 1949.
EASTCOTE Eastcote Halt	10 / 6C	P	26/05/1906	N/A	MET	Served by District Line Trains 01/03/1910 - 23/10/1933, Piccadilly Line thereafter. Suffix 'Halt' until 1934/5. Goods yard closed 10/08/1964
		G	26/05/1906	10/08/1964		
EASTERN DISTRICT OFFICE	27 / 6B 90		02/01/1928	31/05/2003	POR	POR mothballed 31/05/2003.
EBBSFLEET INTERNATIONAL	59 / 1B		19/11/2007	N/A	LCOR	Opened five days after line. Two International and two Domestic platforms at low level, two Domestic platforms at high level. Latter did not receive regular train service until 13/12/2009 (Faversham to St Pancras). International traffic ceased 'temporarily' 18/03/2020 due to COVID-19 pandemic and remains so.
EDDIE STOBART LOGISTICS (Dagenham)	30 / 5A		?	N/A	PRIV	Formerly 'Kuehne + Nagel' and 'Hays Distribution'. Possibly disused?
EDEN PARK	54 / 6D		29/05/1882	N/A	SER	
EDGWARE (GNR)	12 / 2B	P	22/08/1867	11/09/1939	GNR	Originally two platforms; the northern 'up' platform was taken out of use 1872. A small engine shed and turntable north of the station were taken out of use in 1878. Closed to passengers 11/09/1939, goods 01/06/1964 (official date – last train was 04/05/1964).
		G	22/08/1867	01/06/1964		
EDGWARE (UERL)	12 / 2B		18/08/1924	N/A	UERL (CCEHR)	Built for through running to Bushey Heath, but extension abandoned c.1940 along with construction of additional terminating platforms to west.
EDGWARE ROAD (MET)	25 / 6D		10/01/1863	N/A	MET	Rebuilt 01/11/1926.
EDGWARE ROAD (UERL)	25 / 6D		15/06/1907	N/A	UERL (BSWR)	Northern terminus of Bakerloo Line 15/06/1907 – 01/12/1913. Closed for lift replacement 25/06/1990 – 28/01/1992 and 25/05/2013 – 21/12/2013. Unplanned closure due to lift repairs 29/01/2001 – 17/02/2001.
EDGWARE SIDINGS	12 / 2B		18/08/1924	N/A	UERL (CCEHR)	Northern Line stabling sidings. Southern fan on site of aborted curve to GNR Edgware branch.
EDMONTON GREEN Lower Edmonton Lower Edmonton (High Level) Edmonton (High Level)	15 / 1B		22/07/1872	N/A	GER	Opened as 'Edmonton (High Level)' as distinct from the existing 01/03/1849 station (which became 'Low Level'). Both stations renamed 'Lower Edmonton' ('High Level' and 'Low Level' respectively) 01/07/1883. Suffix 'High Level' dropped when 'Low Level' station closed to passengers 11/09/1939 (remained open for goods). Renamed 'Edmonton Green' 28/09/1992.
Edward Street Junction	80		?	N/A	BR	
EFFINGHAM JUNCTION	69 / 4B		02/07/1888	N/A	LSWR	
Effingham Junction	69 / 4B		02/02/1885	N/A	LSWR	
EFFINGHAM JUNCTION MPV DEPOT	69 / 4B		*c.1926*	N/A	SR	Originally EMU stabling shed commissioned for electrification of route (1926), became disused c.mid-1990's. Used by AMEC as a base for MPVs since late 2003, fully commissioned as an MPV maintenance depot 2005.
EGHAM Egham for Englefield Green Egham	47 / 2C	P	04/06/1856	N/A	LSWR	Suffix 'for Englefield Green' 17/07/1902 - 1955. Goods yard closed 04/01/1965.
		G	04/06/1856	04/01/1965		
ELEPHANT & CASTLE	39 / 2D		06/10/1862	N/A	LCDR	Initially temporary, replaced by permanent structure ??/02/1863. Terminus until 01/06/1864. CSLR station opened 18/12/1890 (closed 29/11/1923 - 01/12/1924), BSWR station opened 05/08/1906 (closed 11/11/1996 - 14/07/1997). Original BSWR 'over-run' tunnels headed due east under New Kent Road, diverted to head due south under Newington Butts in 1940 as the aborted Camberwell extension. Southbound Northern Line closed Moorgate to Kennington 01/07/1996 – 21/10/1996 (tunnel realignment at London Bridge). Northern Line closed 15/01/2022 to allow completion of works to re-align southbound tunnel through Bank, reopened 15/05/2022. Proposed Bakerloo Line Extension would result in the current terminal platforms being closed and new platforms aligned west to east replacing them.
ELEPHANT & CASTLE COAL	39 / 2D		*1871*	*01/07/1963*	GNR	GNR coal depot accessed via LCDR.
ELM PARK	30 / 2D		13/05/1935	N/A	LMS	Barking to Upminster quadrupled by LMS 12/09/1932, new station opened at Elm Park 13/05/1935, served by District Line exclusively from opening. Ownership transferred to LTB 01/01/1969.
ELMERS END	54 / 6B	P	01/04/1864	N/A	MKR	Goods yard closed 06/05/1963. 'Down' bay secured out of use 1985. Branch to Addiscombe closed 02/06/1997. Croydon Tramlink opened 30/05/2000 using former bay platform on 'up' side.
		G	01/04/1864	06/05/1963		
Elmers End Junction	54 / 6B		29/05/1882	02/06/1997	SER	Re-sited 50m south 1956 (platform extensions). Elmers End to Addiscombe closed by RT 02/06/1997.
ELMSTEAD WOODS Elmstead	55 / 4C		01/07/1904	N/A	SECR	Renamed 01/10/1908.
ELSTREE & BOREHAMWOOD Elstree Elstree & Borehamwood Elstree Elstree & Boreham Wood Elstree	4 / 4B	P	13/07/1868	N/A	MID	Opened as 'Elstree'. Suffix '& Boreham Wood' added 01/06/1869, dropped 01/04/1904, added again as '& Borehamwood' 21/09/1953, dropped again 06/05/1974, restored again by mid-1988. Goods yard closed 19/06/1967.
		G	13/07/1868	19/06/1967		
ELSTREE BRICK WORKS	4 / 4B		*Post 1896*	*1915*	PRIV	Works originally opened 1865 to provide bricks for adjacent Elstree Tunnels, no rail connection evident on 1896 OS but present on 1913 survey. An online source refers to a 1915 closure.
ELSTREE SOUTH	3 / 6D		N/A	N/A	LPTB (NOR)	On Northern Line extension to Bushey Heath from Edgware, construction abandoned 1940.
Elstree Tunnels	4 / 5B		09/09/1867	N/A	MID	
ELTHAM Eltham Well Hall Well Hall & North Eltham Well Hall	41 / 6D	P	01/05/1895	N/A	BHR	Opened as 'Well Hall', suffix '& North Eltham' added 01/10/1916. Renamed 'Eltham Well Hall' 26/09/1927. Goods yard expanded 1915, closed 07/10/1968. Relocated east and renamed 'Eltham' 17/03/1985 due to construction of A2 Rochester Way Relief Road through original station site, adjacent Eltham Park station closed on same date due to proximity of re-sited station.
		G	01/05/1895	07/10/1968		
ELTHAM PARK Shooters Hill & Eltham Park	41 / 6D		01/07/1908	17/03/1985	SECR	Renamed 26/09/1927. Replaced by Eltham Station 17/03/1985 (see note above).
ELVERSON ROAD	40 / 5D		20/11/1999	N/A	DLR	
EMBANKMENT Charing Cross Embankment Charing Cross	39 / 1B 19		30/05/1870	N/A	MDR	BSWR platforms added 10/03/1906. CCEHR Loop platform added 06/04/1914, southbound platform on Kennington extension opened 13/09/1926. Renamed 'Charing Cross Embankment' 04/08/1974, shortened to 'Embankment' 12/09/1976. Bakerloo Line platforms closed 11/11/1996 – 14/07/1997 (tunnel strengthening), and both Bakerloo and Northern platforms closed 08/01/2014 – 01/11/2014 (escalator replacement).

Name	Page / grid		Date opened	Date closed	Opened by	Notes
EMERSON PARK Emerson Park & Great Nelmes	31 / 1A		01/10/1909	N/A	LTSR	Suffix '& Great Nelmes' only appeared on one station nameboard and was not published elsewhere. Loco run-around loop installed for terminating trains 14/10/1909, subsequently removed.
EMPIRE PAPER MILLS	45 / 6A		1908	c.1980's	PRIV	Connection to North Kent line appears to have been removed with 08/11/1970 resignalling of Greenhithe area, but internal railway network within works remained active for at least a decade longer.
EMR (European Metal Recycling) BRENTFORD	36 / 3C		?	?	PRIV	Formerly Perry Metals, sidings shown in situ in Quail, but have been removed.
EMR (European Metal Recycling) WILLESDEN	24 / 5D 91 & 92		c.1960's	Disused	PRIV	Opened in 1960's on site of former LNWR electric carriage sidings; formerly Mayer-Parry, rail connection in situ but appears disused.
Engine Shed Junction	26 / 2A 9		16/12/1900	05/01/1981	MID	Junction at south end of Low Level Curve, abandoned after diversion of Barking Trains to Gospel Oak.
ENFIELD	6 / 4D	P	01/04/1871	04/04/1910	GNR	Original terminus of branch from Wood Green (Alexandra Palace). Passenger station closed 04/04/1910 when extension from Grange Park to Cuffley opened (replaced by present day Enfield Chase). Goods yard closed 01/07/1974, carriage sidings remained in use on west side of former station until 10/12/1978.
		G	01/04/1871	01/07/1974		
ENFIELD CHASE Enfield	6 / 4D		04/04/1910	N/A	GNR	Replaced original Enfield (GNR) station when line extended from Grange Park to Cuffley. Suffix 'Chase' added 01/07/1923.
Enfield Goods Junction	6 / 5D		04/04/1910	1979	GNR	Formed when route opened from Grange Park to Cuffley, eliminated when carriage sidings at first Enfield (GNR) station abandoned 1979.
ENFIELD LOCK Enfield Lock for Enfield Wash Enfield Lock for Enfield Highway Ordnance Factory	7 / 3C	P	??/04/1855	N/A	ECR	Exact opening date unknown. First reference to 'Ordnance Factory' in timetable April 1855. Renamed 'Enfield Lock for Enfield Highway' 01/04/1886. Suffix altered to 'for Enfield Wash' 01/11/1910, dropped 1955. 'Down' platform originally sited north of level crossing, rebuilt to south c.1890/91. Goods yard closed 07/12/1964.
		G	??/04/1855	07/12/1964		
ENFIELD TOWN Enfield	7 / 4A	P	01/03/1849	N/A	ECR	Suffix 'Town' added 01/04/1886. Goods yard closed 14/09/1959. Engine shed opened 1869, closed November 1960. Platform 2 withdrawn from use for several months following buffer stop collision 12/10/2021.
		G	01/03/1849	14/09/1959		
EPPING	8 / 2B	P	24/04/1865	N/A	GER	Ownership and majority of passenger services transferred to LTE 25/09/1949. First Trains in the morning remained British Rail services until 01/06/1970 (last train 31/05/1970). Goods yard closed 18/04/1966.
		G	24/04/1865	18/04/1966		
EPPING GLADE	8 / 2B		N/A	N/A	EOR	Proposed western terminus of Epping-Ongar Railway.
EPSOM Epsom High Street Epsom	64 / 6B	P	01/02/1859	N/A	LSWR / LBSCR	Opened as temporary terminus of LSWR / LBSCR Epsom & Leatherhead Railway to Leatherhead, became a through station when line to LSWR main line at future site of Raynes Park opened 04/04/1859. When connection to LBSCR Epsom (Town) station opened 08/08/1859, LBSCR trains continued to call at Epsom (Town) and passed LSWR station without stopping. Sometimes referred to as 'Epsom High Street' 1874-1884 to distinguish from LBSCR's 'Town' and 'Downs' stations. Platforms opened on LBSCR line 03/03/1929, allowing Epsom Town station to close. Goods yard closed 02/01/1928, with goods traffic being transferred to Epson (Town).
		G	01/02/1859	02/01/1928		
EPSOM DOWNS	71 / 1D		22/05/1865	N/A	LBSCR	Station had nine platforms at its peak, from 01/05/1972 all but platforms 4 & 5 (re-numbered 1 & 2) were abandoned. Re-sited 300 metres east as a single platform, first trains called late evening 13/02/1989; site of original station sold for housing development.
EPSOM TOWN Epsom	64 / 6C	P	10/05/1847	03/03/1929	LBSCR	Terminus 10/05/1847 - 01/02/1859. Suffix 'Town' used at times c.1870-1900 and again permanently after 09/07/1923. Closed to passengers 03/03/1929 when platforms opened at Epsom (former LSWR). Goods yard closed 03/05/1965.
		G	10/05/1847	03/05/1965		
ERITH	43 / 3C	P	30/07/1849	N/A	SER	Original layout was of platforms staggered either side of a foot crossing; subsequent platform lengthening has resulted in slight overlap of facing platforms. Goods yard closed 07/10/1968.
		G	30/07/1849	07/10/1968		
Erith Loop	43 / 5C	P	01/05/1895	N/A	BHR	Opened with rest of BHR.
		G	01/05/1895	N/A		
ERITH WHARF	43 / 3C		c.1880	c.1970	SER	Not on 1872 OS map, but had appeared by 1895. Depicted on OS into the 1970's, but date of abandonment unknown.
ESHER Esher for Sandown Park Esher for Claremont Esher & Claremont Ditton Marsh	63 / 1A	P	21/05/1838	N/A	LSWR	Opened as 'Ditton Marsh' (per opening notice; also referred to as 'Esher & Hampton Court' in some timetables). Renamed 'Esher & Claremont' 1844, 'Esher for Claremont' 1912/3, then 'Esher for Sandown Park' 1934, suffix dropped 13/06/1955. Additional pair of platforms on 'up' side added for returning race traffic from Sandown Park racecourse 20/04/1882, closed 18/10/1965. Goods yard closed 03/12/1962.
		G	21/05/1838	03/12/1962		
Essex Portals	44 / 5D		14/11/2007	N/A	LCOR	
ESSEX ROAD Canonbury & Essex Road Essex Road	26 / 3D		14/02/1904	N/A	GNCR	Opened by GNCR, absorbed by Metropolitan Railway 01/07/1913, transferred to LPTB Edgware - Morden Line (later Northern Line) 01/07/1933. Closed by LTE 05/10/1975, reopened by British Rail 16/08/1976. 'Canonbury &' prefix applied 20/07/1922 - 11/07/1948.
EUSTON	26 / 5A		20/07/1837	N/A	LBIR	London & Birmingham Railway terminus, referred to as 'Euston Square' (e.g. February 1863 Bradshaw) or simply 'London' at times in early history. Until July 1844, trains arrived by gravity and departed by rope haulage (see 'Camden'). CSLR platforms opened 12/05/1907 (closed 09/08/1922 - 20/04/1924), terminus until 20/04/1924. CCEHR platforms opened 22/06/1907. The northbound Northern Line Bank branch was diverted through a new tunnel opening June 1967, the new platform opening 15/10/1967, and the previous northbound Line was infilled to widen the Southbound platform for Victoria line use. Victoria Line opened 01/12/1968. HS2 platforms had commenced construction but works currently paused (predicted opening 2041-43), to have direct connection to Euston Square station.
EUSTON SQUARE Gower Street	26 / 5B		10/01/1863	N/A	MET	Renamed 01/11/1909. To have a direct connection to Euston HS2 station.
Euston Square Junction	76		15/03/1926	27/04/1935	MET	Link between Metropolitan and City Widened Lines using aborted 'Widened Lines' tunnel to Euston (eastbound only). Name given as 'Euston Square Junction' in Borley; Clives Underground Line Guides gives 'Chalton Street Junction'.
EWELL EAST Ewell for Worcester Park Ewell	64 / 5D	P	10/05/1847	N/A	LBSCR	Suffix 'for Worcester Park' in use after 1871. Renamed 'Ewell East' 09/07/1923. Goods yard closed 04/04/1960.
		G	10/05/1847	04/04/1960		
EWELL WEST Ewell	64 / 4C	P	04/04/1859	N/A	LSWR	Renamed 'Ewell West' 09/07/1923. Goods yard closed 01/05/1961.
		G	04/04/1859	01/05/1961		
EWER STREET DEPOT (LOCOMOTIVES)	39 / 1D 87		1901	1961	SECR	Adjacent to Southwark Depot (goods). No engine shed provided, but turntable, coaling stage, water tower present. Closed 1961, in advance of 18/06/1962 introduction of full electric timetable.
EXPRESS DAIRY (MORDEN)	52 / 6B		1954	16/12/1978	PRIV	Milk bottling plant. Rail traffic ceased 16/12/1978, sidings decommissioned 02/02/1979.

F

Name	Page / grid		Date opened	Date closed	Opened by	Notes
Factory Junctions	39 / 4A 82		01/07/1863	N/A	LCDR	
FAIRFIELD YARD	66 / 2D		*01/09/1890*	*??/02/1933*	*LBSCR*	Permanent Way yard on truncated Central Croydon branch.
FAIRLOP	17 / 4B	P	01/05/1903	N/A	GER	Fairlop Loop closed to LNER passenger services 30/11/1947 to allow electrification and transfer to LTE Central Line. First served by LTE Central Line Trains 31/05/1948. Goods yard closed 24/03/1958.
		G	01/05/1903	24/03/1958		
Falcon Junction	38 / 6D 89		02/03/1863	N/A	LBSCR / WLER	
FALCON LANE GOODS	38 / 5D 89		*01/06/1869*	*03/06/1968*	*LNWR*	
FALCONWOOD	42 / 5A		01/01/1936	N/A	SR	
FAR TOTTERING & OYSTERCREEK RAILWAY (later *LAKESIDE MINIATURE RAILWAY*)	38 / 3D		*1951*	*1975*	*PRIV*	15in gauge railway open 1951-1953, opened for Festival of Britain in Battersea Park. Relocated within park, reopening 1954 as Lakeside Miniature Railway, closed 1975.
FARNINGHAM ROAD Farningham & Sutton-at-Hone Farningham Farningham & Sutton-at-Hone Farningham	58 / 5B	P	03/12/1860	N/A	LCDR	Opened as 'Farningham', suffix '& Sutton-at-Hone' added 01/04/1861, dropped 01/08/1861, renamed 'Farningham Road' 1869. Became 'Farningham & Sutton-at-Hone' again 1872, renamed 'Farningham Road' again 05/05/1975. Goods yard closed May 1968, siding serving adjacent British Steel works in use until 1980.
		G	03/12/1860	20/05/1968		
FARRINGDON Farringdon & High Holborn Farringdon Street	26 / 5C 32 / 2C		23/12/1865	N/A	MET	Replaced original Farringdon Street station. City Widened Lines platforms added 01/03/1866 (now 'Thameslink'). Suffix '& High Holborn' replaced 'Street' 26/01/1922, dropped 21/04/1936. NR platforms extended to 12 cars and new entrance hall opened 12/12/2011. Elizabeth Line platforms opened 24/05/2022.
FARRINGDON CITY SIDINGS	32 / 3D		*c.2030*	*N/A*	*TFL*	S Stock stabling sidings utilising the former NR 'City Widened Lines' route between Farringdon and Moorgate (closed 23/03/2009). Had been intended for commissioning late 2019, but now deferred until c.2030.
FARRINGDON GOODS	26 / 5C 32 / 2B		*01/11/1909*	*01/07/1936*	*MET*	Also referred to as 'Vine Street' Goods.
Farringdon Junction	32 / 3C		01/01/1866	23/03/2009	LCDR / MET	Junction first eliminated 24/03/1969 (date of closure, last train 23/03/1969 but junction not disconnected until 03/05/1971). Reinstated 16/05/1988 (introduction of 'Thameslink'), disconnected again following Farringdon to Moorgate service withdrawal 23/03/2009 (last train 20/03/2009).
FARRINGDON STREET	26 / 6C 32 / 3C		*10/01/1863*	*01/03/1866*	*MET*	Original City terminus of Metropolitan Railway, partially abandoned when new station opened 23/12/1865, but not closed to passengers until 'Widened Lines' platforms opened at new station 01/03/1866. Became GNR goods station (see entry below).
FARRINGDON STREET GOODS	26 / 6C 32 / 3C		*02/11/1874*	*16/01/1956*	*GNR*	On site of original Metropolitan Railway passenger terminus (see entry above).
Fawkham Junction	59 / 5A		10/05/1886	N/A	LCDR	Originally junction for Gravesend West Branch, disused 24/03/1968 – 1972 and 1976 – 28/09/2003.
FELTHAM	49 / 1B	P	22/08/1848	N/A	LSWR	Goods yard closed 09/09/1968.
		G	22/08/1848	09/09/1968		
FELTHAM DEPOT	35 / 6C		*02/11/2020*	*N/A*	*NR*	On western end of Feltham marshalling yard; connections to main line commissioned 02/11/2020. A photo entitled 'first train in new Feltham marshalling yard' posted on 'Disused Railways' Facebook 25/04/2021.
Feltham Junction	35 / 6D		01/02/1850	N/A	LSWR	
FELTHAM LOCO SHED	35 / 6D		*1922*	*09/07/1967*	*LSWR*	Steam shed closed 09/07/1967. Diesel shed built on site of former coal stacking ground, closed 06/01/1969.
FELTHAM MARSHALLING YARD	35 / 6C		*1921-1922*	*06/01/1969*	*LSWR*	First eight sidings opened on site 1917. Marshalling yard opened in stages 1921-1922. Western end of site reopened as Feltham Depot.
FENCHURCH STREET	27 / 6A 74 / 2B		29/07/1841	N/A	LBLR	Advertised opening 02/08/1841, but services actually commenced 29/07/1841. Redeveloped into current layout April 1935.
FERME PARK DOWN SIDINGS	14 / 5C 3 / 4A		*??/01/1888*	*N/A*	*GNR*	Formerly Ferme Park goods, opened ??/01/1888, effectively closed by 1973.
Ferme Park Flyover	14 / 6C 3 / 5B		pre-1895	N/A	GNR	Appeared between 1876 and 1895 OS, originally 'Harringay Engine Viaduct', and double track (now single).
Ferme Park North Junction	3 / 6A		??/01/1888	N/A	GNR	
Ferme Park South Junction	3 / 2A		??/01/1888	N/A	GNR	
FIELDWAY	67 / 4D		10/05/2000	N/A	CTL	
FINCHLEY CENTRAL Finchley (Church End) Finchley Finchley & Hendon	13 / 4B	P	22/08/1867	N/A	GNR	Opened as 'Finchley & Hendon', '& Hendon' suffix dropped 01/02/1872, 'Church End' suffix added 01/02/1894. Renamed 'Finchley Central' 01/04/1940, first served by and transferred to LPTB Northern Line 14/04/1940, closed to LNER passenger services on same date. Goods yard closed 01/10/1962.
		G	22/08/1867	01/10/1962		
Finchley Central Junction	13 / 3B		01/04/1872	N/A	GNR	Divergence of High Barnet Branch from original Edgware Line (now Mill Hill East Branch).
FINCHLEY ROAD (MID) Finchley Road & St John's Wood	25 / 3C	P	13/07/1868	11/07/1927	MID	Renamed 01/09/1868. Re-sited 03/02/1884 per Borley and Quick, but OS evidence shows this was simply the opening of platforms on the new lines through the north bore of Belsize Tunnel, opened on this date. Goods yard provided a connection to the Metropolitan Line (removed between 1955 and 1960 OS), remained in use for coal traffic until 16/05/1983.
		G	13/07/1868	16/05/1983		
FINCHLEY ROAD (MSJWR) Finchley Road (South Hampstead) Finchley Road	25 / 3C	P	30/06/1879	N/A	MSJWR	Suffix 'South Hampstead' 11/09/1885 - c.1914. Served by Bakerloo Line 20/11/1939 - 01/05/1979, Jubilee Line replacing Bakerloo Line from 01/05/1979. Goods yard opened 01/01/1894, closed 01/08/1941. Separate from MID goods yard, situated immediately north of station.
		G	01/01/1894	01/08/1941		
FINCHLEY ROAD & FROGNAL Finchley Road St John's Wood	25 / 2C	P	02/01/1860	N/A	HJR	Renamed 01/10/1880. Goods yard open c.1870 - 02/01/1967. Closed 29/10/1995 - 29/09/1996.
		G	c.1870	02/01/1967		
FINSBURY PARK Seven Sisters Road	26 / 1C 81	P	01/07/1861	N/A	GNR	Renamed 15/11/1869, also referred to as 'Seven Sisters Road, Holloway' before renaming. GNCR opened 14/02/1904, closed 04/10/1964. GNPBR opened 15/12/1906, southbound tunnel diverted through abandoned northbound GNCR tunnel 03/10/1965. LTB Victoria Line opened 01/09/1968 using former southbound GNCR & GNPBR platforms. Goods yard opened 1865, closed 01/04/1968.
		G	1865	01/04/1968		
FINSBURY PARK DIESEL DEPOT	26 / 2C		*1960*	*??/10/1983*	*BR*	On site of Clarence Yard. First purpose-built diesel Traction Maintenance Depot in UK, downgraded to a stabling point ??/06/1981.
Finsbury Park North Junctions	26 / 1C 81		22/08/1867	N/A	GNR	Originally junction between GNR main line and branch to Edgware, now a series of crossovers.
Finsbury Park South Junctions	26 / 1C 81		14/12/1874	N/A	GNR	Junction of Great Northern main Line with routes ex-Canonbury & Moorgate.

Name	Page / grid		Date opened	Date closed	Opened by	Notes
FIRESTONE TYRES (BRENTFORD)	36 / 3C		*1928*	*31/05/1964*	PRIV	
Fisher Street Crossover	26 / 6B		24/05/2022	N/A	TFL (EL)	Date is start of public operation, date of commissioning / first use unknown.
FORD FREIGHTLINER TERMINAL (DAGENHAM)	30 / 5B		*c.1967*	N/A	PRIV	
FORD MOTOR WORKS (DAGENHAM)	30 / 6A		*??/10/1932*	N/A	PRIV	Production commenced October 1932, continues to manufacture engines.
FOREIGN CATTLE MARKET	40 / 3C 79		*15/12/1900*	*1914*	PRIV	Accessed via tramway along Grove Street. Market purchased by War Office 1914 and became an army depot remaining in use until at least WW2, Ordnance Survey maps depict tramway in situ up until 1960's. A railtour traversing the tramway in 1958 may have been the final train movement.
FOREST GATE	28 / 3B		20/06/1839?	N/A	ECR	Opening date unknown, however an advertisement in the 'Morning Advertiser' 13/07/1839 seems to suggest the station was open (Quick), and so it possibly opened with the line (20/06/1839). Borley states 1840 opening (no day/month). Not featured in Bradshaw until about March 1841. Closed 01/06/1843 - 31/05/1846. Goods yard was east of station (see entry below).
FOREST GATE GOODS	28 / 2C		*c.1890's*	*07/12/1970*	GER	Site closer to Manor Park station than Forest Gate, adjacent to LTSR route to Barking. Although Borley states Forest Gate opened to 'all' traffic 1840 (i.e. including goods), the yard does not appear on OS maps before 1895, so may have been opened at approximately same time as GER quadrupling work (c.1894).
Forest Gate Junction	28 / 2C		13/04/1854	N/A	ECR / LTSR	

FOREST HILL
   Forest Hill for Lordship Lane
   Forest Hill
   Dartmouth Arms
	54 / 1B	P
		 G
			05/06/1839
			 05/06/1839
				N/A
				 04/05/1964
					LCRR	Named 'Dartmouth Arms' until 03/07/1845, when renamed 'Forest Hill'. Suffix 'for Lordship Lane' in use c.1877 to c.1943. Goods yard closed 04/05/1964. Island platform serving the middle 'fast' roads was present, partially staggered to the south of the 'slow' side platforms, but since demolished. Present on 1970 OS, but had been removed by 1983.

Fork Junction	28 / 3A 77		15/08/1854	01/06/1969	ECR	
Fulham Bridge	38 / 5A		03/06/1899	N/A	LSWR	Built by LSWR but only ever used by District Railway trains. Purchased by LUL 01/04/1994.
FULHAM BROADWAY Walham Green	38 / 3B 84		01/03/1880	N/A	MDR	Renamed 01/03/1952. Rebuilt 1905 & 2003 (latter rebuilding almost entirely covered over platforms).

FULWELL
   Fulwell & Hampton Hill
   Fulwell (New Hampton)
   Fulwell
	50 / 2B		01/11/1864	N/A	TVR	Suffix '(New Hampton)' added 1874, changed to '& Hampton Hill' 1887, dropped 01/06/1913.

Fulwell Junction	50 / 2B		01/07/1894	N/A	LSWR	Junction at west end of Shepperton Spur (Fulwell Curve).
Fulwell Tunnel	50 / 2B		01/11/1864	N/A	TVR	

G

Name	Page / grid		Date opened	Date closed	Opened by	Notes
GALLIONS	42 / 1A 62 / 3D	P G	*late 1880* *late 1880*	09/09/1940 17/04/1966	LSKD	Initially 'Central' (opened 03/08/1880) was the branch terminus per Quick, Connor and Jackson ('for first few weeks' in latter), so precise date of services to Gallions commencing unknown, had appeared in Bradshaw by November 1880. Gallions branch single until 14/11/1881. Re-sited east 12/12/1886, then again 1924/5 (per Quick). Operated by GER after 1896, ownership later transferred to PLA. Branch closed from 09/09/1940 due to 'Black Saturday' air raid 07/09/1940 (no Sunday service after 27/06/1915). Listed as 'Royal Albert Dock, Gallions' in Borley. Branch continued to be used to access coal wharf at Gallions (Cory Brothers) until 17/04/1966.
GALLIONS REACH	42 / 1A 62 / 4D		28/03/1994	N/A	DLR	
GANTS HILL	17 / 6A		14/12/1947	N/A	LPTB (CEN)	
GARDNER'S PLEASURE RESORT RAILWAY	66 / 6C		*1893*	*By 1934*	PRIV	Circular miniature railway in Gardner's Pleasure Resort, Riddlesdown. Gauge unknown.
GARSTON	2 / 1D		07/02/1966	N/A	BR	St Albans Abbey branch service suspended 19/12/2021 – 21/02/2022 (COVID-19 related).
Gas Factory Junction Bow Common Junction	27 / 5D 88		26/09/1850	N/A	LBLR / NLR	Junction with curve to Bow (NLR) established 26/09/1850, eliminated 29/12/1967. Junction with LTSR added 31/03/1858 (only extant junction). Junction with access to Bow Road Goods added 1885, eliminated 07/12/1964.
Gasworks Tunnels	26 / 4B 75 / 76		14/10/1852	N/A	GNR	Tunnels under Regent's Canal approaching King's Cross. Middle bore opened first, Eastern bore added 1878, Western bore 1892. Eastern bore abandoned Spring 1977, reopened 26/04/2021.
George IV Tunnel	41 / 2D		30/07/1849	N/A	SER	
GEORGE STREET	66 / 2C		10/05/2000	N/A	CTL	
GIBBS CEMENT WORKS (WEST THURROCK)	45 / 4A		*c.1880*	*c.1965*	PRIV	Formerly Thames Cement works. Not on 1873 OS map, but present in 1897. Removed from OS between 1961 and 1966.

GIDEA PARK
   Gidea Park & Squirrels Heath
   Squirrels Heath & Gidea Park
	18 / 5D	P
		 G
			01/12/1910
			 06/02/1911
				N/A
				 07/12/1970
					GER	Opened as 'Squirrels Heath & Gidea Park', renamed 'Gidea Park & Squirrels Heath' 01/12/1913, '& Squirrels Heath' suffix dropped 20/02/1969. Goods yard in use 06/02/1911 - 07/12/1970 (sited to east of station, page 19 / 5A).

GIDEA PARK CARRIAGE SIDINGS	19 / 5A		*c.1930*	N/A	LNER	
Gidea Park Country End Junction	19 / 5A		01/01/1934	N/A	LNER	Dates from Romford to Brentwood quadrupling.
Gifford Street Portals	76		14/11/2007	N/A	LCOR	

GIPSY HILL
   Gipsy Hill for Upper Norwood
   Gypsy Hill
	53 / 3D	P
		 G
			01/12/1856
			 01/12/1856
				N/A
				 07/12/1968
					WELCPR	Sometimes referred to as 'Gypsy Hill' in early years (current spelling by February 1863 Bradshaw). Suffix 'for Upper Norwood' in use c.1911 - c.1955. Goods yard closed 07/12/1968.

GLOBE ROAD & DEVONSHIRE STREET	27 / 5B		01/07/1884	22/05/1916		
GLOBE WORKS	45 / 4D		*c.1870's*	*??/??/1940*	PRIV	Chalk pit, established in 1870's, railway system not used after 1940.
GLOUCESTER ROAD Brompton (Gloucester Road)	38 / 2C 84 & 45		01/10/1868	N/A	MET	Initially terminus of MET extension from Praed Street Junction, extended east to Westminster (Bridge) 24/12/1868. MDR platforms opened 12/04/1869 (initially terminus, extended east 01/08/1870). UERL (GNPBR) platforms opened 15/12/1906 as 'Gloucester Road', this name applying to entire station from 1907. Platforms re-arranged 28/07/1957 such that former MET platforms both became eastbound, and former MDR both became westbound. Middle eastbound track removed 01/03/1970 and eastbound former platform 2 (now 3) widened into vacated space and former platform 1 abandoned. Piccadilly Line closed 31/08/1987 – 21/05/1989 and 24/05/2014 – 10/12/2014 (both lift replacement works). District / Circle platforms rafted over due to development above, completed June 1993. Closed 21/03/2020 – 06/07/2020 (COVID-19)
Gloucester Road Junction	66 / 1D 86		c.1865	N/A	LBSCR	Originally junction at north end of 'New Croydon Line', now junction at south end of Selhurst Spur.

Name	Page / grid		Date opened	Date closed	Opened by	Notes
GOLDERS GREEN	13 / 6B		22/06/1907	N/A	UERL (CCEHR)	Northern terminus of CCEHR from opening to 19/11/1923.
GOLDERS GREEN DEPOT	*13 / 6B*		*22/06/1907*	*N/A*	*UERL (CCEHR)*	Northern Line depot.
GOLDHAWK ROAD	37 / 1D 83		01/04/1914	N/A	MET / GWR	Replaced first Shepherd's Bush MET / GWR station to north.
GOODGE STREET Tottenham Court Road	26 / 5B		22/06/1907	N/A	UERL (CCEHR)	Renamed 09/03/1908. Closed 19/03/2020 – 31/08/2020 (COVID-19).
GOODMANS YARD GOODS	*27 / 6A 74 / 2B*		*01/02/1861*	*01/04/1951*	*LBLR*	Sometimes referred to as 'Minories Goods'.
GOODMAYES	29 / 1C	P	08/02/1901	N/A	GER	Goods yard opened 03/06/1901, closed 31/07/1962.
		G	*03/06/1901*	*31/07/1962*		
GOODMAYES MARSHALLING YARD	*29 / 1C*		*1899*	*31/07/1962*	*GER*	Enlarged 1911.
Goods & Mineral Junction	75		14/10/1852	05/03/1973	GNR	Divergence of route into King's Cross terminus from original route to Maiden Lane station / King's Cross Goods.
GORDON HILL	6 / 3D		04/04/1910	N/A	GNR	
GOSPEL OAK Kentish Town	26 / 2A 9	P	02/01/1860	N/A	HJR	Renamed 01/02/1867. Platform for THJR opened 04/06/1888, closed to regular traffic 06/09/1926, some excursion traffic remained until 07/08/1939 and platform subsequently demolished. Platform reopened 05/01/1981 when Barking trains diverted from Kentish Town. Goods yard in use 1862 - 07/08/1972. Became temporary terminus of Richmond trains 20/02/2010 - 01/06/2010 due to engineering works. Gospel Oak to South Tottenham (formerly Barking) trains suspended at weekends 04/06/2016 to 25/09/2016, and then entire South Tottenham service suspended and bay platform closed 26/09/2016 to 27/02/2017 due to electrification works on Gospel Oak to Barking Line.
		G	*1862*	*07/08/1972*		
Gospel Oak Junction	26 / 2A 9		30/01/1916	N/A	HJR / THJR	Junction established 30/01/1916, eliminated 03/09/1922, reinstated 11/03/1940.
GRAHAME-WHITE AVIATION CO. WORKS	*12 / 4B*		*15/06/1918*	*28/01/1921*	*PRIV*	Dates of first and last trains on branch unknown, dates quoted are for the opening / closing of Hendon Factory signal box, which controlled the junction between the branch and Midland main line. Branch lifted c.1930, but engine shed in Montrose Park and tunnel under Northern Line still remain.
Graham Road Curve	27 / 3B	P	30/06/1986	28/09/1992	BR	Opened for diverted trains ex-Watford Junction upon closure of Broad Street station. Regular passenger services withdrawn 28/09/1992, but curve retained for empty stock workings.
		G	*30/06/1986*	*N/A*		
GRAHAM ROAD GOODS	*27 / 3B*		*??/05/1894*	*04/10/1965*	*GER*	

GRANGE HILL
   Grange Hill for Chigwell Row
   Grange Hill
	17 / 2B	P	01/05/1903	N/A	GER	Suffix 'for Chigwell Row' added July 1912, probably used until closure by LNER. Fairlop Loop closed to LNER passenger services 30/11/1947 to allow electrification and transfer to LTE Central Line, reopening 21/11/1948. Goods yard closed 04/10/1965.

		G	*01/05/1903*	*04/10/1965*		
GRAND SURREY CANAL	*40 / 3C 79*		*08/06/1835*	*12/11/1835*	*LGR*	Temporary country terminus of LGR during preopening trials between here and Blue Anchor Lane.
Grange Hill Tunnel	17 / 2B		20/04/1903	N/A	GER	
GRANGE PARK	6 / 5D		04/04/1910	N/A	GNR	
GRAVEL HILL	67 / 4C		10/05/2000	N/A	CTL	
GRAVESEND (GRR)	*60 / 1B*	P	10/02/1845	30/07/1849	GRR	Terminus of Gravesend & Rochester Railway, situated on south side of Thames & Medway canal basin. Closed 13/12/1846 – 23/08/1847 by SER due to line improvement works. Closed for good 30/07/1849, replaced by Gravesend (SER) station on its North Kent line, opened the same day.
		G	*10/02/1845*	*30/07/1849*		

GRAVESEND (SER)
   Gravesend Central
   Gravesend
	60 / 1A	P	30/07/1849	N/A	SER	Replaced Gravesend (GRR) station. Carried suffix 'Central' 01/06/1899 – 14/06/1965. Goods yard closed 03/12/1961. Originally laid out with two platform roads either side of a pair of central reversing sidings (one west-facing, one east facing) altered to two 'through' roads c.1899. Bay was present on 'up' side (abolished by 14/03/1971 resignalling?). Further remodelled Christmas 2013 when the up through road was removed and replaced by a new up platform, with the former down through road becoming the new up road. The former up platform road became a London-facing bay.

		G	*30/07/1849*	*03/12/1961*		

GRAVESEND WEST
   Gravesend West Street
   Gravesend
	60 / 1A	P	10/05/1886	03/08/1953	LCDR	Suffix 'West Street' added 01/06/1899, 'Street' dropped 26/09/1949. Closed to passengers with entire branch 03/08/1953, goods withdrawn and branch abandoned 24/03/1968.

		G	*10/05/1886*	*24/03/1968*		
GRAYS	45 / 4C	P	13/04/1854	N/A	LTSR	Sometimes referred to as 'Grays Thurrock' in early years. Bay on down side opened 05/11/1900. Closure date of goods yard unknown. Not noted in Borley which suggests it was open in some capacity after 1977, goods shed still depicted on 1974-7 OS, removed by 1984-7.
		G	*13/04/1854*	*Post 1977?*		
GRAYS CEMENT WORKS	*45 / 4B*		*c.1880*	*1920*	*PRIV*	Not on 1873 OS map, but present in 1897. Closed 1920 (Middleton Press 'Tilbury Loop').
Grays East Junction	45 / 4C		c.1960	N/A	BR	Junction providing access to Tilbury Docks via Seabrook Sidings, replaced former Tilbury North Junction.

GREAT PORTLAND STREET
   Great Portland Street & Regent's Park
   Great Portland Street
   Portland Road
	26 / 5A		10/01/1863	N/A	MET	Opened as 'Portland Road', renamed 'Great Portland Street' 01/03/1917, '& Regent's Park' suffix added 1923, dropped 1933. Eastbound platform closed 12/05/2001 – 28/05/2001. Closed 20/03/2020 – 06/07/2020 (COVID-19).

GREAT WESTERN JUNCTION *a.k.a. WEST LONDON JUNCTION*	*24 / 5D 91*		*27/05/1844*	*01/12/1844*	*GWR / WLR*	Exchange platforms built for traffic between WLR / GWR, abandoned when WLR passenger services ceased. Borley and Quick both refer to this and the WLR/LBIR exchange station as 'West London Junction'. To avoid confusion, and as this station did not appear in any GWR timetables, its name in WLR timetables is used. Per Atkinson, location of GWR platforms was east of the pre-1860 level crossing between the WLR and GWR.
GREEN PARK Dover Street	39 / 1A		15/12/1906	N/A	UERL (GNPBR)	Renamed 18/09/1933. Closed 01/09/1939 – 01/12/1939. Victoria Line platforms opened 07/03/1969, Jubilee Line platforms opened 01/05/1979.
GREENFORD (GWR)	*23 / 3B*	P	01/10/1904	17/06/1963	GWR	Platforms on loops off GWR Birmingham Main line, closed 17/06/1963 although used for excursion traffic until August 1971. Timetables referred to 'Greenford (Main Line)' after LPTB station opened, also service drastically reduced from then until closure (e.g. one weekday 'up' train only by February 1951). Goods yard closed 23/05/1980, subsequently becoming a Rugby Cement terminal in the early 1980's (first appears in 1984 Baker), believed disused by May 1992; BLN at this time refers to all sidings on 'up' side at Greenford being clipped out of use due to poor track condition.
		G	*01/10/1904*	*23/05/1980*		
GREENFORD (LPTB)	23 / 3B		30/06/1947	N/A	LPTB (CEN)	Terminus of Central Line extension from North Acton from opening until 21/11/1948, incorporating central bay for BR Greenford Loop trains (first served 21/11/1948).
Greenford Bay Junction	23 / 3B		21/11/1948	N/A	BR	Greenford Loop passenger services diverted into bay platform 21/11/1948.

Name	Page / grid		Date opened	Date closed	Opened by	Notes
Greenford East Curve	23 / 4B	P	15/06/1903	10/10/1905	GWR	Initially used by temporary goods (03/06/1903) and passenger (15/06/1903) services serving the Park Royal Royal Agricultural showground, disused 04/07/1903 (passenger) 10/08/1903 (goods) - 01/05/1904. Regular passenger services ceased 10/10/1905. Singled ??/06/1970.
		G	03/06/1903	N/A		
Greenford East Junction	23 / 4C		01/10/1904	N/A	GWR	
GREENFORD S & T	23 / 3B		*1989*	*By 2005*	BR	Sidings formerly served Rockware Glass works, shown as disused in 2005 Quail Trackmaps.
Greenford South Junction	23 / 4B		01/10/1904	N/A	GWR	
Greenford West Curve	23 / 4B	P	01/10/1904	N/A	GWR	Passenger service north of Greenford Bay Junction ceased 21/11/1948. Partially singled 29/05/1990. Passenger service north of Greenford Bay Junction reintroduced 10/12/2018 ('Parliamentary' Chiltern service South Ruislip to Paddington diverted via Greenford Loop). This service was amended to one weekly West Ealing to West Ruislip train which last ran 07/12/2022 so Greenford Bay Junction to South Ruislip was closed to passengers 14/12/2022 (i.e. one week after the last train).
		G	01/10/1904	N/A		
Greenford West Junction	23 / 3B		01/10/1904	N/A	GWR	
GREENHITHE FOR BLUEWATER Greenhithe	44 / 6D		30/07/1849	N/A	SER	Renamed c.1999 (Bluewater shopping centre opened 16/03/1999). Rebuilt 14/03/2008.
Greenhithe Tunnel	45 / 6A		30/07/1849	N/A	SER	
GREENWICH	40 / 4D 41		24/12/1838	N/A	LGR	Originally temporary station to west of current, sometimes referred to as 'Church Row', replaced by second station to east 12/04/1840, which originally had two central engine release roads and a traverser at the country end. Rebuilt slightly to the north on an overlapping, and lower, site 01/02/1878 when extension to Maze Hill opened. Third (current) station had platforms on loops with two central through roads until first half of 20th century, when through roads removed. DLR platforms opened 20/11/1999, the space was created by using the former through roads' track beds to realign 'up' main line road northwards and reposition platform.
Greenwich College Tunnel	41 / 3A		01/02/1878	N/A	SER	
GREENWICH PARK *Greenwich*	40 / 4D		01/10/1888	01/01/1917	LCDR	Renamed 01/07/1900. Nunhead to Greenwich Park closed 01/01/1917.
GREYSTONE LIME WORKS	73 / 6A		*24/07/1805*	*28/09/1838*	CMGR	Terminus of CMGR, last day of operation 27/09/1838.
Grosvenor Bridge	39 / 3A 82		01/10/1860	N/A	VSPR	
GROSVENOR ROAD	39 / 3A		01/11/1867	01/10/1911	LCDR / LBSCR	Open from January 1867 as ticket platforms, full opening 01/11/1867. LBSCR platforms closed before LCDR, on 01/04/1907. LBSCR platforms sometimes referred to as 'Grosvenor Road & Battersea Pier'.
Grove Junction (LSWR)	37 / 2D		01/06/1870	01/01/1911	LSWR	Junction at south end of link between MET / GWR Hammersmith & City Railway and LSWR Kensington & Richmond Railway.
Grove Junction (MET / GWR)	37 / 2D		01/06/1870	01/01/1911	LSWR	Junction at north end of link between MET / GWR Hammersmith & City Railway and LSWR Kensington & Richmond Railway. Junction severed November 1914, track lifted along link May 1916.
GROVE PARK	55 / 2B	P	01/11/1871	N/A	SER	Became a junction station with opening of Bromley (North) branch 01/01/1878, at which point the station was two through platforms with an 'up' side bay. Rebuilt with three island platforms (six faces) for quadrupling of main line (complete 18/06/1905). Goods yard on 'up' side (closed 04/12/1961), carriage sidings on down (closed 06/11/1976).
		G	*01/11/1871*	*04/12/1961*		
GROVE PARK CARRIAGE SERVICE SHED	55 / 2B		*1959*	N/A	BR	Commissioned coinciding with Kent Coast electrification scheme.
GROVE PARK DOWN (BRAMDEAN) SIDINGS	55 / 1B		*c.1900*	N/A	SECR	Eight EMU stabling sidings and five unelectrified freight sidings. On site of SECR Hither Green marshalling yard, established c.1900.
Grove Park Junction	55 / 2B		01/01/1878	N/A	SER	
GROVE PARK UP (ST MILDRED'S) SIDINGS	55 / 2A		*c.1900*	N/A	SECR	EMU stabling sidings. On site of SECR Hither Green marshalling yard, established c.1900.
Grove Tunnels	39 / 4D		01/08/1865	N/A	LBSCR	North bore opened 01/08/1865, south bore 13/08/1866.
Guildford Line Junction	73 / 5C		04/07/1849	N/A	SER	
GUINNESS (PARK ROYAL)	24 / 4A		*1936*	*06/07/1995*	PRIV	Brewing occurred 1936 to Summer 2005. Last rail traffic left 06/07/1995.
GUNNERSBURY Brentford Road	37 / 2B 51 / 2A		01/01/1869	N/A	LSWR	Renamed 01/11/1871. First served District & Metropolitan Railways 01/06/1877 & 01/10/1877 respectively. Last served Metropolitan Railway 01/01/1907. Last served LSWR 05/06/1916. Originally had five platforms, three of which were abandoned in 1930. Remodelled 1932 (SR).
Gunnersbury Junction *Gunnersbury East Junction*	37 / 2B 51 / 2A		01/01/1869	N/A	LSWR	Renamed 24/07/1932 when 'West' junction eliminated.
Gunnersbury West Junction	37 / 2B 51 / 3A		01/01/1869	24/07/1932	LSWR	Chiswick Curve last use 24/07/1932.
GWR CREOSOTING WORKS (HAYES)	35 / 1C		*06/06/1877*	*1965*	GWR	GWR works for creosoting wooden sleepers, creosote being a by-product from nearby Southall Gas works.
GWR POWER STATION (PARK ROYAL)	24 / 5B		*1907*	*1936*	GWR	Site later became Cox & Danks scrapyard.

H

Name	Page / grid		Date opened	Date closed	Opened by	Notes
HACKBRIDGE	65 / 2D	P	01/10/1868	N/A	LBSCR	Goods yard closed 04/01/1965.
		G	*01/10/1868*	*04/01/1965*		
HACKNEY CENTRAL Hackney	27 / 3B	P	26/09/1850	N/A	EWIDBJR	First station opened to east of current site 26/09/1850 as 'Hackney', with goods yard opening 20/10/1850. Re-sited west 01/12/1870, train service suspended 15/05/1944 (enemy action) but station building remained open to sell tickets, full closure 23/04/1945. Goods yard closed 04/10/1965. Reopened to passengers 12/05/1980 as 'Hackney Central'. Closed 20/02/2010 – 01/06/2010 (LO upgrade works). Interchange walkway to Hackney Downs in use 01/12/1885 - 15/05/1944, reopened 23/07/2015.
		G	*20/10/1850*	*04/10/1965*		
HACKNEY DOWNS Hackney Downs Junction	27 / 3B		27/05/1872	N/A	GER	Suffix 'Junction' usually added until 1897/8. Rebuilt with two central through roads 01/06/1876, further rebuilt with 4 platforms 1894. Interchange walkway to Hackney Central in use 01/12/1885 - 15/05/1944, reopened 23/07/2015.
Hackney Downs North Junction	27 / 2B		01/07/1872	N/A	GER	
Hackney Downs South Junction	27 / 3B		01/06/1876	N/A	GER	Date given is that of quadrupling through Hackney Downs station.
Hackney Downs Tunnel	27 / 2B		01/07/1872	N/A	GER	
HACKNEY WICK	27 / 3D		12/05/1980	N/A	BR	Closed 20/02/2010 – 01/06/2010 (LO upgrade works).
HACKNEY WICK GOODS	27 / 3C		*25/03/1877*	*06/11/1967*	GNR	Closed ??/06/1877 – 01/03/1878.
HADLEY WOOD Beech Hill Park (goods yard only)	5 / 3C	P	01/05/1885	N/A	GNR	Goods yard opened at some point in 1884 as 'Beech Hill Park', passenger station opened 01/05/1885. Goods yard closed 01/03/1950. East Coast main line quadrupling through Hadley Wood station / tunnels complete 03/05/1959
		G	*1884*	*01/03/1950*		
Hadley Wood North Tunnels	5 / 2C		07/08/1850	N/A	GNR	Original bore is today's 'Up' tunnel, 'Down' bore added 03/05/1959.
Hadley Wood South Tunnels	5 / 3C		07/08/1850	N/A	GNR	Original bore is today's 'Up' tunnel, 'Down' bore added 03/05/1959.

Name	Page / grid		Date opened	Date closed	Opened by	Notes
HAGGERSTON (NLR)	27 / 4A		02/09/1867	06/05/1940	NLR	Closed 06/05/1940, current Haggerston (TFL) is slightly to the north.
HAGGERSTON (TFL)	27 / 4A		27/04/2010	N/A	TFL (LO)	Built by TFL for LO services.
HAINAULT	17 / 3B	P	01/05/1903	N/A	GER	Closed to passengers & goods 01/10/1908, reopened to passengers 03/03/1930 (goods yard remained closed). Fairlop Loop closed to LNER passenger services 30/11/1947 to allow electrification and transfer to LTE Central Line. First served by LT Central Line Trains 31/05/1948 (terminus until 21/11/1948). Until 08/04/1991 the station was a double terminus with Woodford to Hainault operating as a shuttle; from that date trains began to work around the Hainault Loop.
		G	01/05/1903	01/10/1908		
HAINAULT DEPOT	17 / 3B		14/12/1947	N/A	LPTB (CEN)	Ostensibly complete by 1939, used ??/06/1943 – ??/01/1945 for temporary wartime use (rolling stock assembly for US Army Transportation Corps) – a large area of lifted sidings west of the Central Line depot was present on aerial photographs dated 1947 and 1950, so perhaps the Central Line depot was never used for this purpose? The Limes Farm housing estate now occupies this site. Central Line depot since 14/12/1947 (partial opening), 31/05/1948 (full opening).
Halfpence Lane Tunnel	60 / 5D		28/09/2003	N/A	LCOR	
Hall Farm Curve	15 / 6B	P	26/04/1870	04/10/1914	GER	Part of original GER branch from Lea Valley Line to Shern Hall Street Walthamstow. Passenger service withdrawn 04/10/1914, closed to freight and abandoned 06/11/1967.
		G	26/04/1870	06/11/1967		
Hall Farm North Junction	15 / 6B		01/08/1872	06/11/1967	GER	Junction between original Shern Hall Street Walthamstow branch and 01/08/1872 line to Hackney Downs, eliminated when Hall Farm Curve abandoned 06/11/1967.
Hall Farm South Junction	15 / 6B		01/08/1885	11/06/1960	GER	Junction at north end of Coppermill Curve (refer to Coppermill Curve notes).
HALLILOO PLATFORM	74 / 4A		c.1856	c.1897	CR	Non-timetable; served Halliloo farm which was some distance to the east of the Caterham Railway. Presumed to have been in the vicinity of Burntwood Lane (OS evidence suggests possibly to the north, on the west side of the then single track). Sources state use had ceased 'by 1899', logically the platform was demolished to make way for the 1897 doubling of the line as the newer track was to the west of the original at this point.
HAM RIVER GRIT Co.	50 / 2C		1904	1952	PRIV	2ft narrow gauge network within gravel pits, also serving a riverside wharf.
HAMMERSMITH (MDR)	38 / 2A 72		09/09/1874	N/A	MDR	MDR terminus 09/09/1874 - 01/06/1877. GNPBR terminus opened to north 15/12/1906, entire station rebuilt with Piccadilly Line platforms between District Line platforms for Piccadilly Line westward extension 04/07/1932.
HAMMERSMITH (MET / GWR)	38 / 2A 72	P	13/06/1864	N/A	MET / GWR	Relocated slightly south 01/12/1868. Goods yard closed 01/02/1960.
		G	13/06/1864	01/02/1960		
HAMMERSMITH & CHISWICK / Hammersmith	37 / 2C 51 / 2D	P	08/04/1858	01/01/1917	NSWJR	Opened to goods traffic 01/05/1857, passenger traffic 08/04/1858. '& Chiswick' suffix added 01/07/1880. Passenger traffic withdrawn 01/01/1917, goods remaining until 03/05/1965, branch formally abandoned 01/01/1966.
		G	01/05/1857	03/05/1965		
HAMMERSMITH DEPOT	38 / 2A		05/11/1906	N/A	GWR	Hammersmith & City Line depot, built by GWR but used exclusively for Metropolitan Railway electric trains.
HAMMERSMITH (GROVE ROAD)	37 / 2D 72		01/01/1869	05/06/1916	LSWR	Served by GWR 01/06/1870 - 01/11/1870, MET 01/10/1877 - 01/01/1911. Addison Road to Studland Road Junction closed 05/06/1916.
HAMPSTEAD	25 / 2C		22/06/1907	N/A	UERL (CCEHR)	Was named 'Heath Street' up until point of opening, when renamed 'Hampstead'. Former name still appears on tiles at platform level. Closed 19/03/2020 – 13/07/2020 (COVID-19).
HAMPSTEAD HEATH	25 / 2D	P	02/01/1860	N/A	HJR	Closed 04/12/1984 – 15/04/1985 (cutting wall collapse) & 29/10/1995 – 29/09/1996 (engineering works). Goods yard opened 01/03/1863, closed 30/09/1972.
		G	01/03/1863	30/09/1972		
Hampstead Heath Tunnel	25 / 2D		02/01/1860	N/A	HJR	Closed 29/10/1995 – 29/09/1996 (engineering works).
Hampstead Tunnel	25 / 3C		15/03/1899	N/A	GCR	
HAMPTON	49 / 4D	P	01/11/1864	N/A	TVR	Originally passing point on single line until 17/07/1878 doubling. Goods yard initially on 'down' side only, additional sidings on 'up' side added 1899, closed 03/05/1965.
		G	01/11/1864	03/05/1965		
HAMPTON & KEMPTON WATERWORKS RAILWAY	49 / 3B		17/05/2013	N/A	PRIV	Currently a 2ft gauge loop with a single platform, with future plans to reopen the original Metropolitan Water Board Railway route between Bunny Lane and the Upper Sunbury Road (Hydes Field) – permission granted by Thames Water 19/03/2018. Branch also proposed to Kempton Park NR station.
HAMPTON COURT / Hampton Court for East & West Molesey / Hampton Court for East Molesey / Hampton Court for East Moulsey / Hampton Court & East Moulsey / Hampton Court	50 / 5B	P	01/02/1849	N/A	LSWR	Suffix '& East Moulsey' added 1869, became 'for East Moulsey' 1897/8, spelling changed to 'for East Molesey' 1903/4 (suffix also '& East Molesey' at this time). Suffix then changed to 'for East & West Molesey' at some point until 1955, when it was dropped and the station became simply 'Hampton Court' again. A ticket platform existed on approach to the station until 1899 (location unknown). Quick refers to an excursion / race platform also; dates / location also unknown. Goods yard closed 03/05/1965.
		G	01/02/1849	03/05/1965		
HAMPTON COURT GAS WORKS	50 / 4C		c.1895	1961	PRIV	Hampton Court Gas Co. Works founded in mid-19th century, but no rail connection apparent on OS before 1896.
Hampton Court Junction	63 / 1C		01/02/1849	N/A	LSWR	Line to Guildford added 02/02/1885. Remodelled with an 'up' diveunder on Guildford line 1908, further 'down' flyover to eliminate 'flat' junction for Hampton Court branch added 04/07/1915.
HAMPTON WATERWORKS	49 / 3B		1897	??/07/1964	PRIV	Waterworks at riverside site established c.1855, receiving coal by river. In 1897 a pumping station was built at Kempton Park, with a standard gauge rail connection. In 1915 a 2ft narrow gauge railway system approx. 5km in length was constructed connecting the three pumping station complexes and riverside wharves. The narrow gauge system was dismantled in 1947 due to a switch from coal to oil, with the standard gauge sidings ceasing to be used after July 1964.
HAMPTON WICK	50 / 4D		01/07/1863	N/A	LSWR	
HANDLEY'S BRICKWORKS	54 / 6A		c.1930	c.1970	PRIV	1ft gauge internal railway installed in existing brick works c.1930, still in situ on 1968 OS but had disappeared by 1974/5 (works closed 1976).
HANGER LANE	24 / 4A		30/07/1947	N/A	LPTB (CEN)	
Hanger Lane Junction	24 / 6A		23/06/1903	N/A	MDR	Divergence of MDR South Harrow branch from line to Ealing Broadway.
HANSON AGGREGATES (DAGENHAM DOCK)	30 / 6A		?	N/A	PRIV	
HANSON AGGREGATES (WEST DRAYTON)	34 / 1D		?	N/A	PRIV	
HANWELL / Hanwell & Elthorne / Hanwell	23 / 6B		01/12/1838	N/A	GWR	Served by District Railway trains 01/03/1883 - 01/10/1885. Suffix '& Elthorne' 01/04/1896 - 06/05/1974. Southern entrance and platform 1 demolished 1977.
HANWELL BRIDGE SIDINGS	36 / 1A		?	N/A	GWR	Currently used by DBS.
Hanwell Junction	23 / 6B		03/06/1903	N/A	GWR	Converted to 'single lead' junction 1974.
HAREFIELD ROAD	9 / 6C		N/A	N/A	LTE (CEN)	Station to have been built on aborted Central Line extension to Denham, adjacent to former South Harefield Halt.
HARLESDEN	24 / 4C 68 / 6D		15/06/1912	N/A	LNWR	Adjacent to site of LBIR 'Willesden' station open 1842 - 01/09/1866. Served by Bakerloo Line trains since 16/04/1917. Proposed to have platforms on Dudding Hill Loop (West London Orbital).

Name	Page / grid		Date opened	Date closed	Opened by	Notes
HARLESDEN FOR WEST WILLESDEN & STONEBRIDGE PARK Stonebridge Park for West Willesden & Harlesden Harrow Road for Stonebridge & Harlesden Harrow Road Harrow Road for Stonebridge Park & Harlesden Harrow Road for Stonebridge Park & West Willesden	24 / 3C	P	03/08/1875	01/10/1902	MID	Opened as 'Harrow Road for Stonebridge Park & West Willesden', 'Harlesden' substituted for 'West Willesden' ??/02/1876. Renamed 'Harrow Road' 01/05/1878, suffix 'for Stonebridge & Harlesden' added 01/11/1880. Renamed 'Stonebridge Park for West Willesden & Harlesden' 01/07/1884. Closed to passengers 02/07/1888, reopened 01/03/1893. Renamed 'Harlesden for West Willesden & Stonebridge Park' 01/02/1901. Closed to passengers for good 01/10/1902, then to goods 06/07/1964.
		G	03/08/1875	06/07/1964		
Harlesden Junction	24 / 4C 91 & 92		02/01/1860	N/A	LNWR / HJR	
HAROLD WOOD	19 / 4B	P	01/02/1868	N/A	GER	Was named 'Heril Wood' until point of opening. Rebuilt due to quadrupling 01/01/1934, platforms were staggered previously ('up' west of 'down'). Goods yard closed 04/10/1965, track removed c.1968.
		G	01/02/1868	04/10/1965		
HARRINGAY Harringay West Harringay	14 / 6C 3 / 6A	P	01/05/1885	N/A	GNR	Suffix 'West' in use 18/06/1951 - 27/05/1971. Goods yard closed 01/01/1968.
		G	01/05/1885	01/01/1968		
Harringay Curve	14 / 6C	P	N/A	N/A	GNR / THJR	Harringay Curve possibly laid April 1864 (junction recorded as having been established, but eliminated five months later, according to GNR records) then lifted by 1881 perhaps without being used. As the THJR did not open until 21/07/1868, if it were used, it could have been in connection with the THJR's construction. Laid again 15/05/1916 then lifted ??/04/1920, again possibly without having been used. Laid for a third time 08/01/1940.
		G	??/04/1864	N/A		
HARRINGAY GREEN LANES Harringay East Harringay Stadium Harringay Park Harringay Park, Green Lanes Green Lanes	14 / 6D	P	01/06/1880	N/A	THJR	Opened as 'Green Lanes' 01/06/1880, Goods yard probably opened 1882. 'Harringay Park' prefix added 30/08/1884. 'Green Lanes' suffix dropped 09/06/1951, renamed 'Harringay Stadium' 27/10/1958. Goods yard closed 03/02/1964. Renamed 'Harringay East' 14/05/1990, then 'Harringay Green Lanes' 08/07/1991. Gospel Oak to South Tottenham (formerly Barking) trains suspended at weekends 04/06/2016 to 25/09/2016, and then entire Overground service suspended and station closed 26/09/2016 to 27/02/2017 due to electrification works on Gospel Oak to Barking Line.
		G	c.1882	03/02/1964		
Harringay Junction	14 / 6C		??/04/1864	N/A	GNR / THJR	See notes re: Harringay Curve (junction at north end of curve).
Harringay Park Junction	14 / 6C		21/07/1868	N/A	THJR	See notes re: Harringay Curve (junction at south end of curve).
HARRINGTON ROAD	54 / 5B		23/05/2000	N/A	CTL	
HARROW LANE SIDINGS	31 / 4B		1866	30/08/1981	NLR	Scrap metal from Harrow Lane represented the last traffic on the Victoria Park to Poplar route.
Harrow North Junction	11 / 6B		04/07/1904	N/A	MET	Divergence of Uxbridge Branch, became a 'flying' junction with opening of Uxbridge Branch diveunder 14/10/1925.
HARROW-ON-THE-HILL Harrow	11 / 6B	P	02/08/1880	N/A	MET	Country terminus of Metropolitan Railway 02/08/1880 - 02/05/1885. Renamed 01/06/1894. Served by GCR since 15/03/1899. Goods yard closed 03/04/1967.
		G	02/08/1880	03/04/1967		
HARROW & WEALDSTONE Harrow	11 / 4B	P	20/07/1837	N/A	LBIR	Renamed 01/05/1897. First served by Bakerloo Line trains 16/04/1917, service withdrawn after 24/09/1982, reinstated 04/06/1984 as terminus. Goods yard closed 03/04/1967.
		G	20/07/1837	03/04/1967		
HATCH END Hatch End (For Pinner) Pinner & Hatch End Pinner	11 / 3A		08/08/1842	N/A	LBIR	Opened as 'Pinner', suffix '& Hatch End' added 01/02/1897. Renamed 'Hatch End (for Pinner)' 01/02/1920, suffix dropped 11/06/1956. Served by London Underground Bakerloo Line trains 16/05/1917 – 24/09/1982. Platforms 3-6 abandoned 07/01/1963. Goods yard to the south, adjacent to future Headstone Lane station (see entry below).
HATCH END GOODS	11 / 3A		08/08/1842	14/11/1966	LBIR	Adjacent to Headstone Lane station.
HATTON CROSS	35 / 5B		19/07/1975	N/A	LTE (PIC)	Terminus 19/07/1975 - 16/12/1977 (empty trains ex-Hounslow West commenced reversing here from 14/07/1975).
HAVERSTOCK HILL	25 / 2D		13/07/1868	01/01/1916	MID	Platforms repositioned from original (now 'fast') to new (now 'slow') lines when these opened 03/02/1884.
Hawkswood Junctions	55 / 5D 56 / 5A		1992	N/A	BR	Physical junctions formed 1992 when Tonbridge Slow Loop doubled, leading to short section of bidirectional track.
HAYDON SQUARE GOODS	27 / 6A 74 / 1B		??/02/1853	02/07/1962	LNWR	Temporary opening February 1853, full opening 12/03/1853.
Haydon Square Junction	74 / 2C		??/02/1853	02/07/1962	LNWR / LBLR	
HAYDONS ROAD Haydens Lane	52 / 3C	P	01/10/1868	N/A	LBSCR / LSWR	Renamed 01/10/1889. Closed to passengers 01/01/1917 - 27/08/1923. Goods yard closed 05/12/1966.
		G	01/10/1868	05/12/1966		
HAYES	68 / 2B	P	29/05/1882	N/A	SER	Initially single platform (current platform 2). Station rebuilt 1933, turntable removed at this time and built over. Goods yard closed 19/04/1965, but sidings retained until January 1971 for engineering purposes.
		G	29/05/1882	19/04/1965		
HAYES & HARLINGTON Hayes	35 / 1D	P	01/05/1864	N/A	GWR	Served by District Railway trains 01/03/1883 - 01/10/1885. Renamed 22/11/1897. Goods yard closed to general goods traffic 02/01/1967, but parcels traffic and a 'Silcock Express' terminal remained until 15/04/1978. Bay platform 5 extended during Christmas 2015, commissioned May 2016.
		G	01/05/1864	02/01/1967		
HEADSTONE LANE	11 / 3A		10/02/1913	N/A	LNWR	Served by London Underground Bakerloo Line trains 16/05/1917 – 24/09/1982. Hatch End goods yard was adjacent.
Heathrow Airport Junction	35 / 1A		19/01/1998	N/A	RT	Remodelled with new 'up' flyovers 30/12/2016
HEATHROW EXPRESS / CONNECT DEPOT	24 / 5C 91		19/01/1998	16/02/2021	BAA	Last train left depot 16/02/2021 to enable demolition (HS2 works / Old Oak Common Station). See also 'Old Oak Common Depot' entry.
HEATHROW JUNCTION	34 / 1D		19/01/1998	25/05/1998	BAA	Temporary terminus due to delayed opening of HEX tunnel (collapse during construction 21/10/1994). Closed 31/01/1998 - 03/02/1998 (operational problems), closed for good 25/05/1998 when HEX opened fully.
HEATHROW TERMINALS 2 & 3 Heathrow Terminals 1, 2 & 3 Heathrow Central Terminals 1, 2 & 3 Heathrow Central	34 / 4D		16/12/1977	N/A	LTE (PIC)	Terminus 16/12/1977 – 12/04/1986. Suffix 'Terminals 1, 2 & 3' added 03/09/1983, 'Central' dropped 12/04/1986. Heathrow Express platforms opened 25/05/1998. Renamed 'Heathrow Terminals 2 & 3' 20/05/2018 to reflect the closure of Terminal 1 29/06/2015.
HEATHROW TERMINAL 4	34 / 5D		12/04/1986	N/A	LUL (PIC)	LUL platform closed 21/10/1994 – 04/12/1994, then again 07/01/2005 – 17/09/2006 (Terminal 5 Extension). Heathrow Express platforms opened 25/05/1998. Closed 09/05/2020 – 14/06/2022 due to airport terminal closure (reduced demand due to COVID-19 pandemic).
HEATHROW TERMINAL 5	34 / 4B		27/03/2008	N/A	BAA	Entire station owned & operated by BAA. Platforms for 'Airtrack' (branch from Windsor & Eton Riverside branch) built, but project cancelled 11/04/2011.
Heathrow Tunnel Junction	34 / 1D		25/05/1998	N/A	RT / BAA	Crossover at mouth of tunnel to Heathrow Airport, HAH / NR boundary.
HENDON	12 / 5D	P	13/07/1868	N/A	MID	Goods yard opened 09/03/1868, passenger station opened 13/07/1868. Goods yard closed 01/01/1968.
		G	09/03/1868	01/01/1968		
HENDON CENTRAL	12 / 5D		19/11/1923	N/A	UERL (CCEHR)	Terminus of extension from Golders Green 19/11/1923 – 18/08/1924.
Hendon Chord	12 / 5D		17/04/1977	N/A	BR	
HENDON FACTORY PLATFORM	12 / 4D		19/05/1918	??/??/1919	PRIV	For workers of the Grahame-White aircraft factory. Possibly never used.

Name	Page / grid		Date opened	Date closed	Opened by	Notes
HENDON RAIL TRANSFER STATION *Brent Waste Terminal*	25 / 1A 85		*c.1979*	N/A	PRIV	Originally GLC facility (30 year lease signed March 1979), subsequently operated by Shanks & McEwan Ltd until expiry of lease. Now operated by Waste Recycling Group, closed on original site 31/03/2021 and is currently being relocated to west side of Midland mainline, to reopen during 2023.
HERNE HILL	39 / 6C	P	25/08/1862	N/A	LCDR	Terminus of line from Elephant & Castle until 01/07/1863. Goods yard closed 01/08/1966.
		G	*25/08/1862*	*01/08/1966*		
Herne Hill North Junction	39 / 6C		25/08/1862	N/A	LCDR	
Herne Hill South Junction	39 / 6C		01/01/1869	N/A	LCDR	
HERNE HILL SORTING SIDINGS	39 / 5C		*c.1860s*	*01/08/1966*	LCDR	Didn't open with line in 1862, but sidings appeared by 1870.
HERON QUAYS	40 / 1D		31/08/1987	N/A	DLR	Closed 09/02/1996 – 22/04/1996 (IRA bomb) and 01/10/2001 – 18/12/2002 (reconstruction).
HERSHAM	62 / 2D		28/09/1936	N/A	SR	
HIGH BARNET	5 / 4B	P	01/04/1872	N/A	GNR	First served by and transferred to LPTB Northern Line 14/04/1940, closed to LNER passenger services on same date. Goods yard closed 01/10/1962.
		G	*01/04/1872*	*01/10/1962*		
HIGH BARNET SIDINGS	5 / 4B		01/04/1872	N/A	GNR	Originally GNR carriage sidings, became stabling sidings for Northern Line.
High Level (or Tottenham South) Curve	26 / 2A 9	P	01/07/1870	19/01/1964	MID	Connection between THJR and MID goods lines. First passenger use 01/07/1870, closed 19/01/1964.
		G	*03/01/1870*	*19/01/1964*		
High Meads Curve	27 / 3D 77 / 78	P	?	20/10/2008	GER	Used by passenger trains ex-Lea valley Line terminating at Stratford in combination with High Meads Loop as an anticlockwise reversing loop. No regular passenger use since 20/10/2008 (see 'High Meads Loop' entry).
		G	*1881*	N/A		
High Meads Junction	27 / 3D 77 / 78		??/07/1891	N/A	GER	Junction at north end of Lea & High Meads Curves.
High Meads Loop	27 / 3D 77 / 78	P	?	20/10/2008	GER	Used by passenger trains ex-Lea valley Line terminating at Stratford in combination with High Meads Curve as an anticlockwise reversing loop. Closure commenced 20/10/2008 during which time route was enclosed under covered way, upon reopening 14/04/2009 Driver Only Operation (DOO) trains restricted from using route due to lack of radio coverage arising from enclosure, no regular passenger use since.
		G	*1881*	N/A		
HIGH STREET KENSINGTON Kensington (High Street)	38 / 1B 84	P	01/10/1868	N/A	MET	Metropolitan District Railway platforms opened 03/07/1871. Renamed gradually by 1880. Adjacent goods yard opened by Midland Railway 04/03/1878, closed 25/11/1963. Terminus from the south 23/07/2011 – 23/08/2011 (engineering work).
		G	*04/03/1878*	*25/11/1963*	MID	
HIGHAMS PARK Highams Park & Hale End Highams Park (Hale End) Hale End	16 / 3A	P	17/11/1873	N/A	GER	Renamed 'Highams Park (Hale End)' 10/10/1894, then became '& Hale End' 01/05/1899. Suffix dropped 20/02/1969. Goods yard closed 04/10/1965.
		G	*17/11/1873*	*04/10/1965*		
HIGHBURY & ISLINGTON Highbury *(GNCR)* Highbury or Islington *(NLR)* Islington *(EWIDBJR)*	26 / 3C	P	26/09/1850	N/A	EWIDBJR	Opened as 'Islington', renamed 'Highbury or Islington' 01/06/1864, then 'Highbury & Islington' 01/07/1872. GNCR station (separate from NLR premises) opened 28/06/1904 as 'Highbury', '& Islington' suffix added 20/07/1922. LTB Victoria Line platforms opened 01/09/1968, with the southbound using the former northbound GNCR platform, and a new northbound GNCR platform built alongside the northbound Victoria Line. Interchange provided with BR at this time and original GNCR entrance closed. GNCR platforms closed by LTE 05/10/1975, reopened by BR 16/08/1976. Goods yard opened for coal only 20/10/1851, transferred to LNWR and opened to general goods traffic 22/12/1872, closed 04/08/1969. LO platforms closed 20/02/2010 – 01/06/2010, upon reopening formerly abandoned northern platforms used (now numbered 7 & 8), with southern platforms 1 & 2 reopening 06/01/2011 as terminus.
		G	*20/10/1851*	*04/08/1969*		
Highbury Vale Junction	26 / 2C 81		??/07/1987	N/A	BR	Junction formed when line through Canonbury Tunnel singled due to electrification works.
HIGHBURY VALE GOODS	26 / 2C 81		1876	05/04/1971	GNR	
HIGHGATE (GNR)	14 / 6A		22/08/1867	05/07/1954	GNR	Nominally opened by Edgware, Highgate & London Railway, which was absorbed by GNR a month before opening. Original layout of central siding and side platforms replaced by island platform c.1883. Closed when Alexandra Palace to Finsbury Park service withdrawn 05/07/1954. Had been intended for electrification and transfer to Northern Line, but works abandoned post-WW2.
HIGHGATE (LPTB)	14 / 6A		19/01/1941	N/A	LPTB (NOR)	Line through station opened 03/07/1939, trains stopped from September 1940 onwards for people sheltering from air raids, public opening 19/01/1941.
Highgate East Tunnel	14 / 6A		22/08/1867	05/10/1970	GNR	Last passenger use 05/07/1954, remained in use for Northern Line stock transfer until 05/10/1970.
HIGHGATE ROAD HIGH LEVEL Highgate Road for Parliament Hill Highgate Road	26 / 2A 9		21/07/1868	01/03/1918	THJR	Closed 31/01/1870 – 01/10/1870. Carried suffix 'for Parliament Hill' ??/11/1894 – 01/07/1903, after which suffix 'High Level' added to distinguish from Low Level station. Most use ceased 01/10/1915, although some MID trains originated from here until complete closure 01/03/1918.
Highgate Road Junction	26 / 2A 9		03/01/1870	19/01/1964	THJR / MID	Junction at north end of High Level Curve, although route toward Gospel Oak saw no traffic before 04/06/1888.
HIGHGATE ROAD LOW LEVEL	26 / 2A 9		17/12/1900	01/03/1918	MID	
Highgate West Tunnel	14 / 6A		22/08/1867	05/10/1970	GNR	Last passenger use 05/07/1954, remained in use for Northern Line stock transfer until 05/10/1970.
HIGHGATE DEPOT	13 / 5D		01/10/1962	N/A	LTE (NOR)	On site of GNR Wellington Sidings, nominal opening date is that of withdrawal of BR usage of sidings, as Northern Line trains had stabled there since 1940. Remodelled 1969 – 1970, closed 25/03/1984 – 23/01/1989.
HILLINGDON Hillingdon (Swakeleys) Hillingdon	21 / 2D	P	10/12/1923	N/A	MET	Served by District Line from opening until 23/10/1933, Piccadilly Line thereafter. 'Swakeleys' suffix added ??/04/1934, gradually dropped. Goods yard closed 10/08/1964. Re-sited west 28/06/1992 (road scheme). Closed 18/07/2014 – 11/08/2014 (track renewal).
		G	*10/12/1923*	*10/08/1964*		
HINCHLEY WOOD	63 / 2B		20/10/1930	N/A	SR	
HITHER GREEN	41 / 6A		01/06/1895	N/A	SER	Rebuilt for St Johns to Elmstead Woods quadrupling (completed 18/06/1905) with six platforms. Dartford Line platform roads had a central through road between them, removed 1937. Parcels traffic withdrawn 14/05/1983.
HITHER GREEN DEPOT	41 / 6A		10/09/1933	N/A	SR	Opened by SR 10/09/1933 as a TMD with a six-road engine shed. BR Engineering depot established on part of site 1991. Half of original shed demolished 1993 (reduced from six roads to three). TMD transferred to EWS (now DBS) and engineering depot transferred to Balfour Beatty 24/02/1996.
Hither Green Junction	41 / 6A		01/09/1866	N/A	SER	
HOGSMILL CORN MILLS	64 / 4C		*c.1890*	1955	PRIV	Siding serving corn mills on Hogsmill River.
HOLBORN Holborn (Kingsway) Holborn	26 / 6B		15/12/1906	N/A	UERL (GNPBR)	Suffix 'Kingsway' added 22/05/1933, then Central Line platforms opened 25/09/1933. Suffix gradually dropped. Platform for Aldwych service in use 30/11/1907 – 21/09/1940, then 01/07/1946 – 03/10/1994 (last train 30/09/1994, no weekend service at point of closure). Piccadilly Line non-stopped 02/06/1997 – 30/06/1997 (defective escalators).

Name	Page / grid		Date opened	Date closed	Opened by	Notes
HOLBORN VIADUCT Holborn Viaduct (High Level) Holborn Viaduct	26 / 6C 32 / 4C		02/03/1874	29/01/1990	LCDR	Suffix 'High Level' 01/05/1912 - 01/06/1916. Some platforms closed and track removed 1967.
HOLBORN VIADUCT (LOW LEVEL) Snow Hill	26 / 6C 32 / 4C		01/08/1874	01/06/1916	LCDR	Renamed 01/05/1912.
HOLLAND PARK	38 / 1B		30/07/1900	N/A	CLR	Closed 02/01/2016 – 31/07/2016 (lift works) and 20/03/2020 – 08/06/2020 (COVID-19).
HOLLOWAY & CALEDONIAN ROAD Holloway	26 / 2C		1852	01/10/1915	GNR	Originally open for alighting 'up' passengers only, opened fully 01/08/1856. Renamed 06/05/1901.
HOLLOWAY CATTLE	26 / 2C		1854	c.1930's	GNR	Platforms later used by Holloway Motorail Terminal.
HOLLOWAY MOTORAIL TERMINAL	26 / 2C		30/05/1960	15/09/1968	BR	Used platforms of former Holloway Cattle Station (see above), road access from Caledonian Road.
Holloway North Junctions	26 / 2C 81		14/12/1874	N/A	GNR	
HOLLOWAY ROAD	26 / 2C		15/12/1906	N/A	UERL (GNPBR)	
HOMERTON	27 / 3C		01/10/1868	N/A	NLR	Train service suspended 15/05/1944 (enemy action), station fully closed 23/04/1945, subsequently demolished. Station rebuilt and reopened 13/05/1985 on same site as original (coinciding with electrification of route). Closed 20/02/2010 – 01/06/2010 (LO upgrade works).
HONOR OAK	40 / 6B 54 / 1B	P G	01/12/1865 01/12/1865	20/09/1954 20/09/1954	LCDR	Closed 01/01/1917 – 01/03/1919 and 22/05/1944 – 04/03/1946. Nunhead to Crystal Palace (High Level) closed to 20/09/1954 (goods yard depicted on page 54 / 1B).
HONOR OAK PARK	40 / 6B		01/04/1886	N/A	LBSCR	
Hoo Junction	60 / 3C		01/04/1882	N/A	SER / HHR	Junction between SER and HHR branch to Sharnal Street.
HOO JUNCTION SIDINGS	60 / 3C		20/02/1926	N/A	SR	Laid out as a marshalling yard by SR, opening 20/02/1926, although some sidings were present on site before this.
Hoppity Tunnel	71 / 4D		01/07/1900	N/A	SECR	
HORNCHURCH	31 / 2A	P G	01/05/1885 01/05/1885	N/A 05/08/1981	LTSR	Served by District Railway trains 02/06/1902 – 01/10/1905, then by excursion trains to Southend (later Shoeburyness) from 01/06/1910. Regular District Line service reintroduced 12/09/1932 when route quadrupled, District Line trains utilising the new 'local' platforms. British Rail services withdrawn by 15/06/1962 and 'fast' platforms abandoned. Ownership of 'local' platforms transferred to LTB 01/01/1969. Traffic to goods yard ceased 05/08/1981 (poor track condition), formal closure followed 08/02/1982. Crossover west of station removed 10/01/2016.
HORNSEY	14 / 5C 3 / 1A	P G	07/08/1850 07/08/1850	N/A 07/04/1975	GNR	Goods yard enlarged 01/05/1885, closed 07/04/1975.
HORNSEY ROAD	26 / 1B		01/01/1872	03/05/1943	THJR	Suffix 'for Hornsey Rise' added in MID timetable 01/02/1880 - 01/07/1903.
HORNSEY STEAM SHED	14 / 5C 3 / 1B		??/11/1899	??/07/1961	GNR	Shed remains as an overhead line store building within Hornsey TMD.
HORNSEY TMD	14 / 5C 3 / 2B		16/08/1976	N/A	BR	Built for electrification of King's Cross suburban routes, first electric service Drayton Park-Old Street 16/08/1976 followed by remainder of suburban lines 08/11/1976. On site of Ferme Park 'Up' Yard and Hornsey steam shed.
HORNSEY TRAINCARE FACILITY Siemens Hornsey Up Carriage Sidings	14 / 4C		13/12/2016	N/A	GNR	Former carriage sidings developed into a Thameslink Maintenance Depot by Siemens, official opening 13/12/2016.
HORSLEY Horsley & Ockham & Ripley Horsley & Ockham	69 / 5A	P G	02/02/1885 02/02/1885	N/A 01/06/1964	LSWR	Originally listed in Bradshaw as 'Horsley & Ockham', then became 'Horsley & Ockham & Ripley', sometimes 'for' substituted for '&'. Settled on 'Horsley' 1955. Goods yard closed 01/06/1964.
HORTON KIRBY BOYS HOME or HORTON KIRBY HOME FOR LITTLE BOYS	58 / 5C		11/10/1870	c.1939	LCDR	Unadvertised station, served home for destitute boys, opened 15/06/1867 (station first used 11/10/1870). Home closed 1961, but station had been demolished in 1939 although date of last use unknown. Down platform only. Listed in Quick as 'Farningham – Home for Little Boys'; 'Private and Untimetabled Railway Stations' by Croughton, Kidner & Young have a photograph confirming 'Horton Kirby' name and single down platform.
Hotel Curve	26 / 4B 75	P G	01/10/1863 01/10/1863	08/11/1976 24/03/1969	GNR	Curve in 'down' direction connecting MET with GNR, originally to 10/01/1863 MET lines but later to 'Widened Lines'. Carried goods traffic 20/02/1866 - 24/03/1969. Rebuilt with an easier radius 1892. Closed 10/09/1939 – 01/01/1940 and 06/01/1941 – 01/10/1945 as a consequence of WW2. Closed when Moorgate trains diverted via GNCR 08/11/1976 (official closure date 07/03/1977).
HOUNSLOW Hounslow & Whitton Hounslow	36 / 5A	P G	01/02/1850 01/02/1850	N/A 06/05/1968	LSWR	Suffix '& Whitton' 1852 – 06/07/1930 (date that Whitton station opened). Original goods yard closed 06/05/1968. Second goods yard north of the original (also on 'up' side) opened by SR 1931, closed 06/02/1967.
HOUNSLOW CENTRAL Heston-Hounslow	36 / 4A		01/04/1886	N/A	MDR	Originally single platform, line doubled 01/11/1912 (station rebuilding completed 19/10/1912). Renamed 01/12/1925. First served by Piccadilly Line 13/03/1933. District Line service ceased 10/10/1964.
HOUNSLOW EAST Hounslow Town	36 / 4A		02/05/1909	N/A	MDR	Opened to replace original Hounslow Town terminal station (closed on same day). Renamed 01/12/1925. First served by Piccadilly Line 13/03/1933. District Line service ceased 10/10/1964.
Hounslow Junction	35 / 6D		01/01/1883	N/A	LSWR	Junction at north end of Hounslow Spur.
Hounslow Spur	35 / 6D	P G	01/01/1883 01/01/1883	N/A N/A	LSWR	Service reduced significantly May 1987 ('Roundabout' service around Hounslow Loop ceased).
HOUNSLOW TOWN Hounslow	36 / 4A		01/05/1883	02/05/1909	MDR	Original country terminus of MDR branch from Mill Hill Park (Acton Town). Arranged for through running for never- realised extension to junctions with LSWR on Hounslow Loop and at Strawberry Hill. Suffix 'Town' added 1884. Closed 01/04/1886 – 01/03/1903, then for good 02/05/1909.
HOUNSLOW WEST Hounslow Barracks	35 / 4D		21/07/1884	N/A	MDR	Opened by District Railway, renamed 'Hounslow West' 01/12/1925. First served by Piccadilly Line 13/03/1933, District Line service ceased 10/10/1964. Closed 12/07/1975 and replaced by new station at lower level to north which opened 14/07/1975. New station terminus until 19/05/1975 when Hatton Cross extension opened (between 14/07/1975 and 19/05/1975 trains detrained at Hounslow West and ran empty to Hatton Cross to reverse).
HOXTON	27 / 4A		27/04/2010	N/A	TFL (LO)	Built by TfL for LO services.
Hungerford Bridge	19 / 3C		11/01/1864	N/A	SER	
HYDE PARK CORNER	39 / 1A		15/12/1906	N/A	UERL (GNPBR)	Closed 01/09/1939 – 08/12/1939 and 20/03/2020 – 13/07/2020 (latter closure COVID-19).
HYTHE ROAD	24 / 5D 92		2029-2033	N/A	NR	Proposed station on West London Line, providing interchange with Old Oak Common HS2 / Elizabeth Line stations

I J K

Name	Page / grid		Date opened	Date closed	Opened by	Notes
ICKENHAM	22 / 1A		25/09/1905	N/A	MET	Served by District Line 01/03/1910 – 23/10/1933, Piccadilly Line thereafter. Closed 18/07/2014 – 11/08/2014 (track renewal).
ILFORD	29 / 2A	P	20/06/1839	N/A	ECR	Goods yard to east of station, closed to general goods traffic 06/05/1968 but milk dock remained open until c.1980 and parcels traffic until 28/03/1983.
		G	20/06/1839	06/05/1968		
ILFORD DEPOT	29 / 1A		*c.1900*	N/A	GER	First carriage sidings on site c.1900, car sheds added for EMUs March 1949, 'New Shed' opened 1959.
Ilford Carriage Sidings Junction	29 / 1B		20/04/1903	30/11/1947	GER	West-facing junction between GER main line and Fairlop Loop.
Ilford Depot Country End Junction Seven Kings West Junction	29 / 1B		20/04/1903	19/03/1906	GER	Junction at south end of Seven Kings curve.
Ilford Depot London End Junction	29 / 2A		1949	N/A	BR	
IMPERIAL PAPER MILLS (GRAVESEND)	60 / 1A		*c.1912*	*c.1968*	PRIV	Mills founded 1912, closed 1981. Connected to Gravesend West branch, so external traffic must have ceased by 24/03/1968, although OS maps depict internal railway network in situ until closure of mills.
INGRESS ABBEY PLATFORM	45 / 6A		July 1917?	31/01/1919?	PRIV	Unadvertised platform on Empire Paper Mills Branch, serving a WW1 military hospital at Ingress Abbey. Records show Ingress Abbey came into use as an annexe for Rosherville Hospital July 1917, the latter closing 31/01/1919
IMPERIAL WHARF	38 / 4C		27/09/2009	N/A	NR (LO)	
International Junction	39 / 2C		14/11/1994	N/A	RT	Divergence of lines into platforms 20-24 Waterloo. Disused after 14/11/2007, reinstated when platform 20 reopened 23/10/2013.
Intersection Tunnel	24 / 3A 68 / 2A		15/06/1912	N/A	LNWR	
ISLAND GARDENS	40 / 3D		31/08/1987	N/A	DLR	One terminus of original DLR system. First station partially built on MER North Greenwich branch viaduct, two platforms present but platform one seldom used after train sets lengthened to two units. Closed on the night of 09/02/1996 by IRA bomb at South Quay, did not reopen until 15/04/1996. Closed 11/01/1999 due to works on the Lewisham extension, new subterranean station opened with extension 20/11/1999, original abandoned.
ISLEWORTH Spring Grove & Isleworth Isleworth	36 / 4B		01/02/1850	N/A	LSWR	Replaced Smallberry Green to east (closed same day). Named 'Spring Grove & Isleworth' 01/10/1855 - ??/08/1911(Borley). Quick refers to station opening as 'Isleworth', having '& Spring Grove' suffix added 1854/5, name then reversed 1874/5 (Spring Grove & Isleworth), reversed back 1895/6, then 'Isleworth for Spring Grove' 1912/3, before becoming 'Isleworth' again 1955.
IVER	34 / 1A	P	01/12/1924	N/A	GWR	Goods yard closed 06/01/1964; sidings remained on site until c.1989.
		G	01/12/1924	06/01/1964		
J PARISH & Co. LOAM & BALLAST PITS	43 / 4B		*c.1850*	1957	PRIV	4ft gauge system connecting loam & ballast pits with a riverside wharf.
JOHNSONS PORTLAND CEMENT WORKS	44 / 6D		1877	*c.1970*	PRIV	Originally 3ft 9½in narrow gauge internal system, converted to standard gauge 1928 and connected to main line.
JUNCTION ROAD Junction Road for Tufnell Park	26 / 2A & 9		01/01/1872	03/05/1943	THJR	Suffix 'for Tufnell Park' dropped 01/07/1903. Has been proposed to be reopened as 'Tufnell Park'.
Junction Road Junction	26 / 2A & 9		02/04/1883	N/A	THJR / MID	Junction between THJR and MID line to Carlton Road Junction.
KEMPTON PARK Sunbury Racecourse	49 / 3B		18/07/1878	N/A	LSWR	At first platform on 'down' side only, 'up' platform added 1879. Initially members only and named 'Sunbury Racecourse'. Opened to public 1890, renamed 1891. Bay platform on 'up' side removed 1964. Race Days only until 06/03/2006, when full passenger service commenced (unadvertised service started from 05/03/2006).
KENLEY Coulsdon	73 / 1C	P	05/08/1856	N/A	CR	Renamed December 1856. Goods yard closed 03/04/1961.
		G	05/08/1856	03/04/1961		
KENNINGTON	39 / 3C		18/12/1890	N/A	CSLR	Sometimes had suffix 'New Street' added 1890-1894. Closed 01/06/1923 - 06/07/1925 (tunnel widening). Charing Cross Branch platforms opened 13/09/1926. Closed 19/05/2008 – 12/01/2009. Bank Branch platforms closed 26/05/2018 – 16/09/2018 to allow additional cross passages to be built.
KENSAL GREEN	25 / 4A		01/10/1916	N/A	LNWR / UERL	Served by Bakerloo Line from opening.
KENSAL GREEN & HARLESDEN	24 / 4D 91		01/11/1861	01/07/1873	HJR	Platforms were staggered on either side of present Wrottesley Road bridge (down on west, up on east). Replaced by Kensal Green (later Kensal Rise) station to east, opened on same date as closure.
Kensal Green Junctions	24 / 4D 91 & 92		02/01/1860	N/A	HJR	
Kensal Green Tunnels	24 / 4D 91 & 92		20/07/1837	N/A	LBIR	Quadrupled by LNWR 1879. DC lines (two single bores) added 10/05/1915.
KENSAL RISE Kensal Green	25 / 4A		01/07/1873	N/A	LNWR	Renamed 24/05/1890. Closed 29/10/1995 – 29/09/1996 (engineering works).
KENSINGTON & CHELSEA DISTRICT SCHOOL	65 / 6A		1880	*c.1930*	PRIV	School near Banstead for poor children of Kensington & Chelsea, served by siding from Epsom Downs branch. Established 1880, siding apparent on 1913 OS but had been removed by 1934-5.
KENSINGTON (OLYMPIA) Kensington (Addison Road) Kensington	38 / 2A 84		27/05/1844	N/A	WLR	Opened by WLR as passenger terminus, but passenger services withdrawn and station closed 01/12/1844. Note that prior to the WLR opening, a platform was built on Kensington Canal basin itself, but this was never served by trains. Reopened by WLR slightly to north 02/06/1862, again as terminus (extended to Clapham Junction 02/03/1863). First served MET 01/07/1864, renamed 'Kensington (Addison Road)' 01/10/1868. LNWR trains to Earl's Court started 01/02/1872. Station closed to all services 21/10/1940 (enemy action). Reopened after WW2 for workers' shuttle service to Clapham Junction (in operation by summer 1946), also to exhibition traffic via District Line starting 19/12/1946, on which date station renamed Kensington (Olympia). District Line bay platform and segregated track towards Earl's Court opened 03/03/1958. Mainline platforms regularly served 01/04/1963 - 15/06/1965 (diversions due to WCML electrification), then again 15/10/1967 - 20/12/1967 (diversions due to Paddington rebuilding). Workers' shuttle to Clapham Junction advertised between 18/06/1951 – 11/06/1956, between 01/04/1963 – 15/06/1965, and then since 05/05/1969. Regular District Line service started 07/04/1986. Mainline station fully reopened 12/05/1986 (long distance trains), local service Clapham Junction to Willesden Junction restored 31/05/1994. Regular weekday District Line service withdrawn 12/12/2011 (weekend and exhibition traffic remain, as well as reversal of trains at other times for service recovery).
KENSINGTON OLYMPIA MOTORAIL TERMINAL	38 / 2A 84		24/05/1966	late 1982	BR	Service withdrawn at end of summer timetable 1982.
KENSINGTON SIDINGS	38 / 5C 89		*02/03/1863*	N/A	WLER	Formerly seven sidings used primarily for goods traffic, currently a solitary siding used by LO.

Name	Page / grid		Date opened	Date closed	Opened by	Notes
KENT HOUSE	54 / 4B		01/10/1884	N/A	LCDR	Line through station quadrupled 10/05/1886.
KENT PORTLAND CEMENT WORKS	44 / 6D		1922	c.1970	PRIV	
KENTISH TOWN	26 / 2A & 9		13/07/1868	N/A	MID	UERL (CCEHR) station opened 22/06/1907. Northern Line platforms closed 26/06/2023 (escalator replacement), remaining closed at point of publication.
KENTISH TOWN ENGINE SHEDS	26 / 2A & 9		08/09/1867	1963	MID	No.2 and No.3 sheds added 1899.
Kentish Town Junction	26 / 2A & 9		03/01/1870	N/A	MID	High Level Curve to Highgate Road Junction closed 19/01/1964. Remains as divergence of lines to St Pancras International Low Level.
KENTISH TOWN WEST Kentish Town	26 / 3A		01/04/1867	N/A	HJR	Suffix 'West' added 02/06/1924. Closed 18/04/1971 – 05/10/1981 (arson), again 29/10/1995 – 29/09/1996 (engineering works), and again 20/02/2010 – 01/06/2010 (LO upgrade works).
KENTON Kenton (for Northwick Park) Kenton	11 / 5D	P	15/06/1912	N/A	LNWR	Goods yard opened 13/03/1911, passenger station opened later; 15/06/1912. Goods closed 03/05/1965. Suffix 'for Northwick Park' in use 01/10/1927 - 07/05/1973. Served by London Underground Bakerloo Line trains since 16/04/1917, but no service 27/09/1982 (last train 24/09/1982) to 04/06/1984.
		G	13/03/1911	03/05/1965		
KEW	37 / 2A 19	P	01/08/1853	01/02/1862	NSWJR	Initially terminus, through services onto Hounslow Loop commenced 01/06/1854. Passenger service effectively ceased when NSWJR trains to Richmond diverted via Kew and Barnes Curves 01/02/1862, but a weekly service between Windsor and the Metropolitan Cattle Market at Caledonian Road continued to call until October 1866. Coal yard south of down platform opened July 1856, later incorporated into Kew Bridge North Goods. Proposed to reopen as 'Lionel Road' (West London Orbital).
		G	??/07/1856	?		
KEW BRIDGE Kew	37 / 2A 19	P	22/08/1849	N/A	LSWR	Platforms on Kew Curve opened 01/02/1862 (initially had separate NSWJR entrance, which closed 12/09/1918), closed 12/09/1940. Entire station renamed 'Kew Bridge' December 1868. Adjacent goods yard renamed 'Kew Bridge South' 1948 (as distinct from the former MID yard in the Kew Bridge triangle, which became 'North', and the 1929 SR 'New' yard adjacent to Old Kew Junction), goods yard closed 03/04/1967. Per Borley goods facilities opened with passenger station, but none evident on OS before 1895 when a single siding had appeared behind down platform. Platform on Kew Curve proposed to reopen (West London Orbital).
		G	c.1890	03/04/1967		
KEW BRIDGE NEW GOODS	37 / 2A 19		1929	1977	SR	Expanded 1930.
KEW BRIDGE NORTH GOODS	37 / 2A 19		1863	c.1980's	NSWJR	NSWJR, later MID, goods yard situated in Kew Bridge triangle. Named 'Kew Bridge North' 1948. Closure date not known, possibly c.1980's (still extant in Borley). Note 1863 opening date is sourced from Borley; no evidence is seen of yard until 1895 OS (not present on 1870 1:1,056 or 1882-94 1:2,500 surveys).
Kew Curve (LSWR)	37 / 2A 19	P	01/02/1862	12/09/1940	LSWR	Regular passenger service (Kew Bridge to Willesden Junction) withdrawn 12/09/1940.
		G	01/02/1862	N/A		
Kew Curve (LNWR)	24 / 5C 91 & 92	P	20/07/1885	N/A	LNWR	Link built to connect NSWJR and HJR, allowing closure of original HJR high level route / platforms to passengers.
		G	20/07/1885	N/A		
Kew East Junction	37 / 2A 19		01/02/1862	N/A	NSWJR / LSWR	Junction at north end of Kew Curve.
KEW GARDENS	37 / 4A		01/01/1869	N/A	LSWR	Served by GWR 01/06/1870 – 01/11/1870, first served MDR 01/06/1877, served by MET 01/10/1877 – 01/01/1911. Sidings and Bay platform in use until 04/07/1931, crossover north of platforms until 31/01/1954.
KEW GARDENS RAILWAY	37 / 4A		c.10/1848	1961	PRIV	A single-track underground railway conveying coal between Kew Gardens' main entrance and boilers beneath The Palm House (completed October 1848). Wagons hand-hauled, then converted to electric traction 1950. Fuel switched to oil 1961 and the railway closed, tunnel remains in situ carrying heating pipes for The Palm House (its course evident after snowfall).
Kew Railway Bridge	37 / 3A		01/01/1869	N/A	LSWR	Also known as Strand-on-the Green Bridge.
KIDBROOKE	41 / 5C	P	01/05/1895	N/A	BHR	Goods yard a single siding on 'down' side, west of station. In 1917 a large military depot was established to the south of the station, remaining in situ until at least the early 1960's (subsequently redeveloped as the Ferrier Estate). Goods yard closed 07/10/1968.
		G	01/05/1895	07/10/1968		
Kidbrooke Tunnel	41 / 5B		01/05/1895	N/A	BHR	
KILBURN Kilburn & Brondesbury	25 / 3B		24/11/1879	N/A	MSJWR	First served Bakerloo Line 20/11/1939, last served Metropolitan Line 07/12/1940. Suffix '& Brondesbury' until 25/09/1950. Transferred from Bakerloo Line to Jubilee Line 01/05/1979.
KILBURN HIGH ROAD Kilburn & Maida Vale Kilburn	25 / 4B	P	c.1851/1852	N/A	LNWR	Opening date unknown, late 1851 or early 1852. Renamed 'Kilburn & Maida Vale' 01/06/1879. Closed 01/01/1917, reopened 10/07/1922, then renamed 'Kilburn High Road' 01/08/1923. Closed 17/09/2004 – 22/08/2005 (fire). Goods facilities opened with passenger, closed 05/11/1962.
		G	c.1851/1852	05/11/1962		
KILBURN PARK	25 / 4B		31/01/1915	N/A	UERL (BAK)	Terminus from opening until 11/02/1915. Closed 21/03/2020 – 13/07/2020 (COVID-19).
KING EDWARD BUILDING	26 / 6D 32		19/12/1927	c.1996	POR	King Edward Building ceased operation 1996, so POR station below presumed to have closed at same time.
KING GEORGE V	41 / 1D 62 / 5C		02/12/2005	N/A	DLR	Terminus until 10/01/2009 extension to Woolwich Arsenal.
KING HENRY'S DRIVE	67 / 5D		10/05/2000	N/A	CTL	
KING WILLIAM STREET	26 / 6D 87		18/12/1890	25/02/1900	CSLR	Original terminus of CSLR from Stockwell. Abandoned when line extended from Borough to Moorgate.
KING'S CROSS	26 / 4B 75 / 76		14/10/1852	N/A	GNR	Replaced original terminus to north (see Maiden Lane GNR). 'Suburban' portion of station to west of main station was separate from opening on 18/12/1874 until being incorporated into main station 05/03/1977. Platform 16 of the Suburban station on gradient ascending from the 'Hotel Curve' in use 01/02/1878 – 08/11/1976.
KING'S CROSS FUNERAL STATION	75		10/07/1861	03/04/1863	GNR	Funeral traffic to Colney Hatch Cemetery only, last recorded departure 03/04/1863. 'Private and Untimetabled Railway Stations' (Croughton / Kidner / Young) gives a c.1873 closure date.
KING'S CROSS GOODS	26 / 4B 75		18/11/1850	05/03/1973	GNR	Amalgamation of various facilities, including Potato Market, Granary, Eastern & Western Coal Drops, and MID goods shed.
King's Cross Junction	75		01/10/1863	08/11/1976	GNR / MET	
King's Cross Loop	76	P	N/A	N/A	UERL	Connection between Northern and Piccadilly Lines for stock transfer / engineering use. No passenger service ever provided.
		G	27/03/1927	N/A		

Name	Page / grid		Date opened	Date closed	Opened by	Notes
KING'S CROSS ST PANCRAS King's Cross for St Pancras King's Cross	26 / 5B 75 / 76		15/12/1906	N/A	UERL (GNPBR)	UERL GNPBR (Piccadilly Line) platforms opened 15/12/1906 as 'King's Cross', 'for St Pancras' added 1927, became 'King's Cross St Pancras' 1933. Closed 01/09/1939 – 17/11/1939 (flood protection), 19/09/2000 – 10/10/2000 (escalator defect) and 08/07/2005 – 04/08/2005 (7/7 terrorist attacks). CSLR (Northern Line) platforms opened 12/05/1907 as 'King's Cross for St Pancras', became 'King's Cross St Pancras' 1933, closed 09/08/1922 - 20/04/1924 (tunnel widening), 01/09/1939 – 17/11/1939 (flood protection), 19/11/1987 - 05/03/1989 (fire), 15/10/1995 – 17/06/1996 (escalator works) and 08/07/2005 – 15/07/2005 (7/7 terrorist attacks). Relocated Metropolitan Line platforms opened 14/03/1941 (see entry for 'King's Cross Thameslink'), initially had a central 'bay' platform that was subsequently lifted late 1940's and later filled in. Closed 08/07/2005 – 25/07/2005 (7/7 terrorist attacks). Victoria Line platforms opened 01/12/1968, closed 08/07/2005 – 15/07/2005 (7/7 terrorist attacks).
KING'S CROSS THAMESLINK King's Cross Midland City King's Cross Midland King's Cross St Pancras King's Cross & St Pancras King's Cross	26 / 4C 75		10/01/1863	09/12/2007	MET	Original MET station at King's Cross, platforms on 'Widened Lines' added 17/02/1868. '& St Pancras' after 1925, '&' dropped 1933. Original MET platforms replaced by current station to the west 14/03/1941 (last train 09/03/1941), but platforms on 'Widened Lines' remained open after this date. BR trains ceased to call 03/10/1977 (down) and 14/05/1979 (up), with the station closed from this date. Platforms on 'Widened Lines' reopened 11/07/1983 as 'King's Cross Midland', also referred to as 'King's Cross Midland City'. Renamed 'King's Cross Thameslink' 16/05/1988, closed again 09/12/2007 (last train 08/12/2007), replaced by platforms under St Pancras.
KING'S CROSS 'TOP SHED'	26 / 4B		1851	17/06/1963	GNR	One of three engine sheds at King's Cross, the others being the Midland roundhouse (opened February 1859) and the 'Main Line Running shed' (opened 1862).
King's Cross Tunnel	75 / 76		13/07/1868	N/A	MID	Connection between MID and MET 'Widened Lines', currently used by 'Thameslink' services. Closed 12/05/1979 – 11/07/1983 (electrification).
KING'S CROSS YORK ROAD	26 / 4B 75		01/01/1866	05/03/1977	GNR	Up (southbound) only, at north end of York Road Curve towards the Metropolitan Railway. Rebuilt slightly to east 04/03/1878 (due to new bore of Gasworks Tunnel opening). Closed 08/11/1976 when Moorgate trains diverted along GNCR at Finsbury Park, but briefly reopened 31/01/1977 - 05/03/1977 for use by terminating trains.
KINGSBURY	12 / 5B		10/12/1932	N/A	MET	Opened by Metropolitan Railway. Transferred to Bakerloo Line 20/11/1939, Jubilee Line 01/05/1979.
KINGSLAND GOODS	27 / 3A 6		20/10/1851	07/08/1972	EWIDBJR	
Kingsley Road Junction	36 / 4A		13/06/1905	02/05/1909	MDR	Junction at north end of curve linking Hounslow Town and Heston-Hounslow.
KINGSTON (1st)	51 / 6A		21/05/1838	??/??/1845	LSWR	Situated east of King Charles Road. Replaced by Kingston (second station, later Surbiton) to west in 1845.
KINGSTON (2nd)	50 / 4D	P	01/07/1863	N/A	LSWR	Opened as terminus of branch from Twickenham (Low Level station). High level platforms opened on extension to New Malden 01/01/1869, although low level platforms remained open. Station rebuilt 1935 with a new bay platform at the high level, allowing the original low level platforms to close (track retained for a period as carriage sidings). Engine shed became goods shed 1898, goods yard closed 05/09/1966.
		G	01/07/1863	05/09/1966		
Kingston Bridge	50 / 4D		01/07/1863	N/A	LSWR	
KINGSWOOD Kingswood & Burgh Heath	72 / 4A	P	02/11/1897	N/A	CVR	02/11/1897 is given as opening date for Chipstead Valley Railway (Purley to Kingswood) in Borley, but it also states regular passenger service 'probably' commenced 09/11/1897, Quick states first train 09/11/1897, so 02/11/1897 may have been official / ceremonial opening. Country end terminus until 01/07/1900 SECR extension to Tadworth. Goods yard closed 07/05/1962. Suffix dropped 01/12/1968.
		G	02/11/1897	07/05/1962		
Kingswood Tunnel	72 / 4A		01/07/1900	N/A	SECR	
KNIGHT'S HILL GOODS	53 / 1D		16/05/1892	07/10/1968	LNWR	
Knight's Hill Tunnel	53 / 1C		01/10/1868	N/A	LBSCR	
KNIGHTSBRIDGE	38 / 1D		15/12/1906	N/A	UERL (GNPBR)	Reconstructed, with new Sloane Street entrance, 18/02/1934. Closed 01/09/1939 – 01/12/1939 and 16/09/2000 – 11/10/2000 (escalator defect).

L

Name	Page / grid		Date opened	Date closed	Opened by	Notes
LADBROKE GROVE Ladbroke Grove (North Kensington) Notting Hill & Ladbroke Grove Road Notting Hill (Ladbroke Road) Notting Hill	25 / 6A		13/06/1864	N/A	MET / GWR	Opened as 'Notting Hill', sometimes had '(Ladbroke Road)' suffix added 1869 – 1880. '& Ladbroke Grove Road' suffix added 1880, renamed 'Ladbroke Grove (North Kensington)' 01/06/1919, suffix dropped 1938. Eastbound platform closed 06/03/1999 – 28/03/1999, westbound platform closed 10/04/1999 – 01/05/1999.
LADYWELL Lady Well	40 / 6D		01/01/1857	N/A	MKR	Built by the Mid Kent Railway, but operated by SER from opening. 'Lady Well' used at times as late as 1960.
Ladywell Junction	40 / 6D		01/09/1866	N/A	SER	Junction at south end of Ladywell Loop.
Ladywell Loop	40 / 5D	P	01/09/1866	N/A	SER	
		G	01/09/1866	N/A		
LAFARGE AGGREGATES (WEST DRAYTON)	21 / 6B		post-1999	N/A	PRIV	On site of former coal yard.
LAMBETH NORTH Lambeth (North) Westminster Bridge Road Kennington Road	39 / 2C 89		10/03/1906	N/A	UERL (BSWR)	Opened as 'Kennington Road', renamed 'Westminster Bridge Road' 05/08/1906, renamed 'Lambeth (North)' 15/04/1917, then 'Lambeth North' c.1928. Closed 11/11/1996 – 14/07/1997 (Bakerloo Line tunnel strengthening) then again 13/07/2016 – 13/02/2017 (lift replacement).
Lampton Junction	36 / 4A		21/07/1884	02/05/1909	MDR	Junction between original MDR Hounslow Town route and subsequent Hounslow Barracks extension.
LANCASTER GATE	25 / 5C		30/07/1900	N/A	CLR	Closed 03/07/2006 – 13/11/2006 and 04/01/2017 – 26/06/2017 (lift works). Closed 21/03/2020 – 10/08/2020 (COVID-19).
LANGDON PARK	27 / 6D		10/12/2007	N/A	DLR	Slightly to south of site of South Bromley station (NLR).
LANGLEY Langley Marsh	33 / 1C	P	01/12/1845	N/A	GWR	Served by MDR trains 01/03/1883 – 01/10/1885. Suffix 'Marsh' dropped 1849. Goods yard closed 06/01/1964, became oil terminal (see entry below).
		G	01/12/1845	06/01/1964		
LANGLEY ELECTRIFICATION DEPOT formerly LANGLEY OIL TERMINAL	33 / 1C		15/06/1969	2017	GWR	Originally oil terminal operated by Total opened 15/06/1969, lease expired December 2002 but usage ceased c.2000, purchased by EWS but subsequently abandoned. Reopened as an electrification depot by Balfour Beatty c.01/06/2014 in connection with GWR mainline electrification, disused once works completed to Maidenhead early 2017.
Latchmere Curve	38 / 5D 89	P	02/03/1863	N/A	WLER	Singled at time of electrification July 1993, restored to double track 26/04/2011.
		G	02/03/1863	N/A		
Latchmere No.1 Junction	38 / 4D		02/03/1863	N/A	WLER	
Latchmere No.2 Junction	38 / 4D		02/03/1863	N/A	WLER	

Name	Page / grid		Date opened	Date closed	Opened by	Notes
Latchmere No.3 Junction	38 / 4D		06/07/1865	N/A	WLER	Junction eliminated 21/01/1936 – 17/08/1994.
LATIMER ROAD	25 / 6A 83		16/12/1868	N/A	MET / GWR	Due to platform lengthening works westbound platform closed 03/07/2010 (entire station then closed due to line closure 24/07/2010 – 16/08/2010, see footnotes). Due to structural issues discovered during the westbound platform works, the entire station closed 17/01/2011 – 24/04/2011, with only the westbound reopening initially. The eastbound platform then reopened on 01/08/2011. Eastbound platform closed again 06/10/2014 – 03/11/2014 (staircase refurbishment).
Latimer Road Junction Kensington Junction	25 / 6A 83		01/07/1864	01/03/1954	MET / GWR	Originally 'Kensington Junction' before Latimer Road station was opened.
LCC CENTRAL TRAM REPAIR WORKS	41 / 3B		1909	05/07/1952	LCC	
LEA BRIDGE Lea Bridge Road	27 / 1C	P	15/09/1840	N/A	NER	Suffix 'Road' dropped 1841. Goods yard closed 07/12/1970. Closed with Tottenham Hale to North Woolwich service 08/07/1985. Reopened evening of 15/05/2016.
		G	15/09/1840	07/12/1970		
Lea Bridge Junction	27 / 1C		26/04/1870	N/A	GER	Originally southern junction of Hall Farm Curve (closed 06/11/1967). Junction re-established 16/04/2018 for third track to Meridian Water, passenger service commenced 03/06/2019.
LEA BRIDGE WATERWORKS	27 / 1C		1892	Pre 1969	PRIV	Branch partially dismantled by locals protesting about blockage of a bridleway soon after being laid. Date traffic ceased unknown; present on OS until 1969.
Lea Curve	27 / 3D 77 & 78	P	N/A	N/A	GER	No regular passenger service.
		G	??/07/1891	N/A		
Lea Junction	27 / 3D 77 & 78		??/07/1891	N/A	GER	Junction at south end of Lea Curve.
LEATHERHEAD (LBSCR)	70 / 3C	P	04/03/1867	N/A	LBSCR	Replaced joint station to north. Combined with former LSWR station by SR 10/07/1927. Goods yard closed 02/08/1965.
		G	04/03/1867	02/08/1965		
LEATHERHEAD (LBSCR & LSWR)	70 / 3C	P	01/02/1859	04/03/1867	LBSCR / LSWR	First station in Leatherhead, at country end of LBSCR / LSWR joint line. Replaced by two separate LBSCR and LSWR termini to south, opened on same day as closure.
		G	01/02/1859	04/03/1867		
LEATHERHEAD (LSWR)	70 / 3B	P	04/03/1867	10/07/1927	LSWR	Replaced joint station to north. Closed (passenger & goods) when new connection made between former LSWR and LBSCR by SR 10/07/1927. Track through station remained in situ until at least 1970's (rolling stock storage), with northern portion of former LSWR route remaining until c.1985.
		G	04/03/1867	10/07/1927		
Leatherhead Joint Line Junction	70 / 3C		04/03/1867	10/07/1927	LBSCR / LSWR	Junction between branches to separate LBSCR / LSWR termini. LSWR ceased to be through route 10/02/1927, but sidings on former route diverged at this location until c.1985.
Leatherhead Junction	70 / 4C		10/07/1927	N/A	SR	Connection installed between former LSWR and LBSCR by SR, allowing LSWR station at Leatherhead to close.
LEATHERHEAD NORTH	70 / 2C		N/A	N/A	SR	One of two intermediate stations on Chessington South to Leatherhead route, works abandoned at outset of WW2.
LEBANON ROAD	66 / 2D		10/05/2000	N/A	CTL	
LEE	41 / 6B	P	01/09/1866	N/A	SER	Goods yard closed 07/10/1968.
		G	01/09/1866	07/10/1968		
Lee Loop Junction	41 / 6A		c.1900	N/A	SECR (?)	Junction at north end of Lee Spur.
Lee Spur	41 / 6A	P	N/A	N/A	N/A	Opened c.1900, coinciding approximately with opening of Hither Green marshalling yards.
		G	c.1900	N/A	SECR (?)	
Lee Spur Junction	55 / 1A		c.1900	N/A	SECR (?)	Junction at south end of Lee Spur.
LEICESTER SQUARE	26 / 6B		15/12/1906	N/A	UERL (GNPBR)	(UERL) CCEHR platforms opened 22/06/1907.
Leigham Court Tunnel	53 / 2B		01/12/1856	N/A	WELCPR	
Leigham Junction	53 / 2C		01/08/1871	N/A	LBSCR	
Leigham Spur	53 / 2C	P	01/08/1871	N/A	LBSCR	Passenger service very limited since 1969 and then temporarily suspended 30/03/2020 (COVID-19) before being restored 22/05/2023.
		G	01/08/1871	N/A		
Leigham Tunnel	53 / 2B		01/10/1868	N/A	LBSCR	
LEMAN STREET	27 / 6A 74 / 2C		01/06/1877	07/07/1941	LBLR	Originally built 1872 but Board of Trade refused to sanction opening, so reconstructed and opened 01/06/1877, closed 22/05/1916 - 01/07/1919.
Leman Street Junction	74 / 2C		17/06/1864	01/09/1966	LBLR / GER	Divergence of East Smithfield / London Docks branch from LBLR line.
LEWISHAM Lewisham Junction Lewisham	40 / 5D	P	30/07/1849	N/A	SER	Although no re-siting is explicitly mentioned in Borley or Quick, 1850 OS evidence shows the first station was east of Lewisham Road, which remained the site of the goods yard until its closure 06/05/1963. The report into a fatal collision at Lewisham 28/06/1857 refers to it occurring at Lewisham 'Old' Station, as opposed to Lewisham 'Junction'. It is presumed that the first station was replaced by the current one and had the suffix 'Junction' added 01/01/1857, when the MKR opened from here to Beckenham Junction. Suffix 'Junction' dropped 07/07/1929. DLR platforms opened 20/11/1999. Proposed to become terminus of Bakerloo Line Extension.
		G	30/07/1849	06/05/1963		
Lewisham Crossover Junctions Lewisham Junction	40 / 5D		01/01/1857	N/A	MKR / SER	Originally simple junction between SER and MKR routes, developed into crossovers following 30/06/1929 opening of SR connection from former LCDR Greenwich Park branch to Lewisham.
LEWISHAM ROAD	40 / 5D		18/09/1871	01/01/1917	LCDR	Passenger service withdrawn Nunhead to Greenwich Park 01/01/1917.
Lewisham Vale Junction	40 / 5D		29/03/1976	N/A	BR	Junction at south end of Tanners Hill Flydown.
LEY STREET YARD SIDINGS	29 / 1A		c.1900	N/A	GER	Part of Ilford Depot complex.
LEYTON Low Leyton	28 / 2A	P	22/08/1856	N/A	ECR	Prefix 'Low' dropped 27/11/1867. First served by LPTB Central Line trains 05/05/1947, first trains in the morning remained British Rail services until 01/06/1970 (last train 31/05/1970). Goods yard (P27 / 2D) closed 06/05/1968.
		G	22/08/1856	06/05/1968		
Leyton Junction	28 / 2A		05/05/1947	03/05/1971	LPTB / LNER	Junction of ECR Loughton Branch and LPTB Central Line ex-Stratford. Closed 03/05/1971, dismantled 29/10/1972.
LEYTON MIDLAND ROAD Leyton	27 / 1D	P	09/07/1894	N/A	TFGR	Renamed 01/05/1949. Goods yard (P28 / 1A) open 01/09/1894 – 06/05/1968. Station closed 04/06/2016 to 27/02/2017 due to electrification works on Gospel Oak to Barking Line.
		G	01/09/1894	06/05/1968		
LEYTONSTONE	28 / 1A	P	22/08/1856	N/A	ECR	Original layout with 'down' platform south of 'up' and a small goods yard on 'up' side. 'Down' platform relocated north 1891 and new goods yard opened partially on site of original 'down' platform. First served by LPTB Central Line trains 05/05/1947 (terminus until 14/12/1947). Goods yard closed 02/09/1955. First trains in morning remained British Rail services until 01/06/1970 (last train 31/05/1970).
		G	22/08/1856	02/09/1955		
LEYTONSTONE HIGH ROAD Leytonstone	28 / 1A	P	09/07/1894	N/A	TFGR	Renamed 01/05/1949. Goods yard opened 01/09/1894, closed 06/05/1968. Station closed 04/06/2016 to 27/02/2017 due to electrification works on Gospel Oak to Barking Line.
		G	01/09/1894	06/05/1968		
Leytonstone Junction	28 / 1B		14/12/1947	N/A	LPTB / LNER	Divergence of 1947 route to Newbury Park from Epping Line.

Name	Page / grid		Date opened	Date closed	Opened by	Notes
LILLIE BRIDGE DEPOT	38 / 3B 84		*Mid-1872*	N/A	MDR	Originally built by MDR to house their first fleet of locos / coaches (delivered mid-1871), depot complete by mid-1872. Became UERL GNPBR (Piccadilly Line) depot between 15/12/1906 - 04/07/1932. Subsequently used for engineering purposes, but again became a District Line stabling point after 11/12/2010 (S7 Stock upgrade works). Proposed to close c.2024 for housing development, replaced by additional stabling at Parsons Green and new stabling at Chiswick Park Sidings.
LIMEHOUSE (1st)	27 / 6C		06/07/1840	04/05/1926	LBLR	Passenger service to Blackwall and North Greenwich withdrawn 04/05/1926.
LIMEHOUSE (2nd) Stepney East Stepney	27 / 6C		03/08/1840	N/A	LBLR	Opened as 'Stepney', renamed 'Stepney East' 01/07/1923, platforms to/from Blackwall closed 04/05/1926. Renamed 'Limehouse' 11/05/1987. Former Blackwall platforms reopened by DLR 31/08/1987, RT platforms closed 22/07/1994 – 12/09/1994 (engineering works).
Limehouse Curve	27 / 6C	P G	01/09/1880 *05/04/1880*	01/03/1881 *05/11/1962*	LBLR	Saw passenger use 01/09/1880 – 01/03/1881, not officially closed until 10/05/1963 (date given is last use).
Limehouse Junction	27 / 6C		05/04/1880	05/11/1962	LBLR	Junction at south end of Limehouse Curve.
Linford Street Junction	39 / 4A 82		17/08/1994	N/A	RT	Date quoted is start of trial Eurostar service, advertised service commenced 14/11/1994. Largely disused since 14/11/2007 (diversion of Eurostar to St Pancras), but chord still in situ and traversed by test trains.
LION CEMENT WORKS (WEST THURROCK)	45 / 4B		*c.1880*	*1976*	PRIV	Originally Wouldham works. Not on 1873 OS map, but had appeared by 1897. Closed 1976.
LIONEL ROAD	37 / 2A		N/A	N/A	NR	Proposed station to open as part of 'West London Orbital', on same site as 'Kew'.
Lismore Circus Tunnel	9		09/09/1867	N/A	MID	
LITTLE ILFORD DEPOT	28 / 3D		20/08/1905	01/12/1959	UERL (MDR)	District Railway depot. Closed when Upminster Depot opened, replaced by East Ham BR Depot on same site.
LITTLEBROOK POWER STATIONS	44 / 5C		*1939*	*Pre 1977*	PRIV	'A' station was commissioned 1939 and initially received coal by rail before switching to river traffic, and later was converted to being oil-fired. 'B' and 'C' station were commissioned 1949 and 1952 respectively and similarly were initially coal-fired. 'A', 'B' and 'C' stations closed in 1973, 1975 and 1981 respectively, date rail traffic ceased is unknown: not marked on the 1977 'Baker' so before then.
LIVERPOOL STREET Bishopsgate *(Metropolitan Railway only)*	26 / 6D 90		02/02/1874	N/A	GER	First served by Metropolitan Railway 01/02/1875 (direct into GER station, platforms 1 & 2). Separate MET platforms opened as 'Bishopsgate' 12/07/1875, terminus until 18/11/1876 (became 'Liverpool Street' 01/11/1909). CLR platforms opened 28/07/1912 (terminus until 04/12/1946). POR station opened 19/12/1927, trains had ceased calling before POR was mothballed 31/05/2003, but subsequent to 1987 re-branding to 'Mail Rail'. Elizabeth Line platforms opened 24/05/2022, linked to Moorgate station at western end. Platforms 16 & 17 extended, and platform 18 closed in consequence, during works between Christmas 2020 and Easter 2021.
Liverpool Street Junction	90		12/07/1875	1907	MET / GER	Junction between MET and connection to GER at Liverpool Street platforms 1 and 2. Last through train 1904, junction severed 1907.
LLOYD PARK	67 / 3A		10/05/2000	N/A	CTL	
LODGE FARM PARK MINIATURE RAILWAY	18 / 5C		17/04/2017	N/A	PRIV	7¼in gauge miniature railway, first section (northern loop) opened 17/04/2017, southern loop opened 12/08/2018.
LONDON & BIRMINGHAM JUNCTION a.k.a. WEST LONDON JUNCTION	24 / 4D 91		27/05/1844	01/12/1844	WLR / LBIR	Exchange platforms built for traffic between WLR / LBIR, abandoned when WLR passenger services ceased. Appeared as 'London & Birmingham Junction' in WLR timetable and reciprocally 'West London Junction' in LBIR timetable. Former preferred to avoid confusion with GWR exchange station.
LONDON BRIDGE Tooley Street London	39 / 1D 87		14/12/1836	N/A	LGR	Replaced Bermondsey Street temporary terminus to east. Separate terminus opened by LCRR to north of the LGR one 05/06/1839. Initially referred to as simply 'London', or also as 'Tooley Street', in timetables before 1844. Station rebuilt as joint terminus July 1844 (opened while incomplete), and rearranged with LGR / SER trains using the northern (ex LCRR) portion and LCRR / LBRR the southern (ex LGR) portion to eliminate conflicting train movements at Corbett's Lane Junction. Joint station divided into SER and LBSCR portions 02/08/1850 (during this rebuilding period, temporary stations were provided), enlarged 1854. Original LCRR station demolished 1863 to make way for line to Charing Cross (through platforms opened 11/01/1864). Goods traffic handled between 1864 – 1901 (when transferred to Ewer Street). Station combined by SR 1928, rebuilt 1971 – 1977, again 2010 – 2018. CSLR Platforms opened 25/02/1900. Closed 16/07/1922 - 23/02/1925, 01/07/1996 – 21/10/1996 (southbound line diverted via new tunnel), 02/07/1999 - 05/09/1999 (further tunnel works), and 15/01/2022 – 15/05/2022 (realignment of southbound tunnel at Bank). Jubilee Line platforms opened 07/10/1999.
LONDON CITY AIRPORT	41 / 1D 62 / 5C		02/12/2005	N/A	DLR	
LONDON CONCRETE (Hornsey Depot)	14 / 6C 3 / 4A		*2011*	N/A	PRIV	
LONDON FIELDS	27 / 3B		27/05/1872	N/A	GER	Closed 22/05/1916 – 01/07/1919 and 13/11/1981 – 29/09/1986* (fire) *per Quick, Connor states 25/09/1986.
LONDON MUSEUM OF STEAM & WATER	37 / 3A		*1986*	N/A	PRIV	2ft gauge demonstration railway (formerly Kew Bridge Steam Museum).
LONDON ROAD DEPOT	39 / 2C		*10/03/1906*	N/A	UERL (BSWR)	Bakerloo Line depot.
LONG GROVE HOSPITAL	64 / 4A		*20/05/1905*	*1950*	PRIV	Horton Estate Light Railway opened to supply building materials, later fuel, to hospitals.
LONGFIELD Longfield for Fawkham and Hartley Longfield Fawkham for Hartley and Longfield Fawkham Fawkham Road	59 / 6A	P G	12/06/1872 *12/06/1872*	N/A *07/05/1962*	LCDR	Opened as 'Fawkham Road', 'Road' dropped by 1875. Became 'Fawkham for Hartley and Longfield' 1895/6. Renamed 'Longfield for Fawkham and Hartley' 12/06/1961, then 'Longfield' 1968/72. Single carriage siding present on 'up' side, two-road goods yard on 'down', all closed 07/05/1962.
LONGFIELD HALT	59 / 5A		01/07/1913	03/08/1953	SECR	Opened by SECR on existing LCDR Gravesend West branch, closed with entire branch 03/08/1953.
Longhedge Junctions	39 / 4A 82		02/03/1863	N/A	WLER / LBSCR	
LORD'S St John's Wood St John's Wood Road	25 / 5D		13/04/1868	20/11/1939	MSJWR	Opened as 'St John's Wood Road', 'Road' suffix dropped 01/04/1925, renamed 'Lord's' 11/06/1939, closed 20/11/1939 and replaced by St John's Wood Station (Bakerloo Line) to north. 'Private and Untimetabled Railway Stations' (Croughton / Kidner / Young) suggests cricket traffic continued after closure (no end date given).
LORDSHIP LANE	54 / 1A		01/09/1865	20/09/1954	LCDR	Closed 01/01/1917 – 01/03/1919 and 22/05/1944 – 04/03/1946. Closed for good 20/09/1954.

Name	Page / grid		Date opened	Date closed	Opened by	Notes
LOUGHBOROUGH JUNCTION Loughborough Road	39 / 5C		??/10/1864	N/A	LCDR	First platforms opened on Brixton Spur October 1864 as 'Loughborough Road'. Platforms on lines to Herne Hill and Cambria Spur added 01/12/1872 and station renamed 'Loughborough Junction'. Line to Herne Hill originally quadruple track, one 'up' track removed to make room for island platform while two 'down' roads retained. Post-1925 middle 'down' road removed, side 'down' platform closed, and island platform widened into space vacated by middle 'down' road. Brixton Spur platforms closed 03/04/1916, Cambria Spur platforms closed 12/07/1925. *Note: The above dates are per Borley and Quick; Mitchell & Smith in 'Holborn Viaduct to Lewisham' state that the Brixton Spur platforms were named 'Brixton Junction' upon opening, and the platforms on the Herne Hill route and Cambria Spur opened 01/07/1872 as 'Loughborough Road', before the entire station complex was renamed as 'Loughborough Junction' 01/12/1872.*
Loughborough Junction	39 / 5C		01/05/1863	N/A	LCDR	North end of Brixton and Cambria Spurs (latter added 01/07/1872).
LOUGHTON (ECR)	8 / 5D	P	22/08/1856	24/04/1865	ECR	Original terminus of ECR branch from Stratford, sited just south of the High Road. Closed to passengers when line extended to Ongar 24/04/1865. Line lifted beyond a relocated goods station c.1866, second goods yard remaining open until 18/04/1966.
		G	22/08/1856	18/04/1966		
LOUGHTON (GER)	8 / 6D		24/04/1865	N/A	GER	Station built to replace original ECR terminus on extension to Ongar, re-sited to east 28/04/1940 by LNER in readiness for LTE services. Majority of passenger services transferred to LTE 21/11/1948 when LTE service commenced (terminus until 25/09/1949), but first trains in the morning remained British Rail services until 01/06/1970.
Loughton Junction	27 / 2D		22/08/1856	03/05/1971	ECR	Divergence of ECR Loughton Branch from NER Lea Valley Line. Closed 03/05/1971, dismantled 29/10/1972.
LOUGHTON SIDINGS	8 / 6D		21/11/1948	N/A	LTE (CEN)	Stabling Sidings for Central Line.
Low Level Curve	26 / 2A 9	P	17/12/1900	05/01/1981	MID	Curve between THJR and MID 'slow' passenger lines at Kentish Town, abandoned when Barking trains diverted from Kentish Town to Gospel Oak.
		G	17/12/1900	05/01/1981		
LOW STREET	46 / 4C	P	c.01/07/1861	05/06/1967	LTSR	Exact opening date unknown; first appeared in Bradshaw July 1861. Goods yard closed 28/09/1964, passenger station followed 05/06/1967.
		G	c.01/07/1861	28/09/1964		
LOWER EDMONTON (LOW LEVEL) Edmonton (Low Level) Edmonton	15 / 1B	P	01/03/1849	11/09/1939	ECR	Opened as 'Edmonton' on original ECR Enfield Branch from Angel Road. 'Low Level' suffix added 22/07/1872 with opening of 'High Level' station. Renamed 'Lower Edmonton (Low Level)' 01/07/1883. Became passenger terminus 01/08/1872 when High Level platforms commenced Enfield (Town) service, closed to passengers 11/09/1939, goods yard closed 07/12/1964 along with entire Angel Road to Lower Edmonton Junction route.
		G	01/03/1849	07/12/1964		
Lower Edmonton Junction	15 / 1B		01/08/1872	07/12/1964	GER	Angel Road Junction to Lower Edmonton Junction closed to goods 07/12/1964.
LOWER SYDENHAM	54 / 3C	P	01/01/1857	N/A	MKR	Station re-sited south 1906 (no more precise date known). Goods yard opened 'probably' 1857 per Borley, but is not apparent on 1863 OS map, and cannot be discerned before 1895 survey. Originally short siding north of 'down' platform, much extended through site of original 'down' platform after 1906. Yard closed 20/06/1966.
		G	c.1857	20/06/1966		
LOWER SYDENHAM GASWORKS	54 / 2C		1878	22/04/1969	PRIV	Works established 1854, rail connected since 1878. Closed 22/04/1969, rail connection severed 1971.
Lucas Street Tunnel	40 / 4C		30/07/1849	N/A	SER	
LUDGATE HILL	26 / 6C 32 / 5B		21/12/1864	02/03/1929	LCDR	Terminus until extension to Farringdon opened 01/01/1866. Two island platforms until 1910, when eastern island removed and western island widened.
Ludgate Hill Junction	32 / 4B		02/03/1874	29/01/1990	LCDR	Divergence of Holborn Viaduct Branch.
Ludgate Junction	38 / 5D 89		02/03/1863	N/A	LSWR / WLER	
LYONS WORKS (GREENFORD)	23 / 3B		1920	1970	PRIV	

M

Name	Page / grid		Date opened	Date closed	Opened by	Notes
MAIDA VALE	25 / 5C		06/06/1915	N/A	UERL (BSWR)	Closed 01/09/1939 – 09/01/1940.
MAIDEN LANE (GNR)	26 / 4B 75		07/08/1850	14/10/1852	GNR	London terminus of GNR until King's Cross opened. Also referred to as 'King's Cross'. Trainshed roof retained after closure to passengers as the Potato Market.
MAIDEN LANE (NLR)	26 / 3B 75		01/07/1887	01/01/1917	NLR	Platforms only ever provided on unelectrified northern 'No.1' NLR lines (original southern lines were 'No.2'). Proposed for reopening.
Maiden Lane Curve	75	P	10/01/1863	10/01/1863	GNR	West-facing curve between MET and GNR York Road Curve. Crossed Hotel Curve on level. Possibly never used.
		G	10/01/1863	10/01/1863		
Maiden Lane Junction	75		24/06/1867	??/05/1968	NLR	Junction accessing Maiden Lane goods (later York Way Freightliner terminal).
MAIDEN LANE GOODS	26 / 3B 75		24/06/1867	??/??/1965	NLR	Initially cattle only, general goods from 07/01/1868. Site subsequently occupied by York Way Freightliner terminal.
MALDEN MANOR	64 / 1C		29/05/1938	N/A	SR	
MANOR HOUSE	14 / 6D		19/09/1932	N/A	UERL (GNPBR)	Closed 19/03/2020 – 16/08/2020 (COVID-19).
MANOR PARK Manor Park & Little Ilford Manor Park for Little Ilford	28 / 2C	P	06/01/1873	N/A	GER	Suffixes 'for Little Ilford' or '& Little Ilford' sometimes used 1895 – 1940. Goods yard opened 1882, closed 01/01/1968.
		G	1882	01/01/1968		
MANOR ROAD GOODS	27 / 1A		??/12/1872	07/12/1964	GER	
MANOR SIDINGS	44 / 4D		c.1960's	by 2022	BR	Access now removed (points plain lined), had been disused for several years.
MANOR WAY Manor Road	42 / 1A 62 / 3D		??//07/1881	09/09/1940	LSKD	Opened July 1881 as 'Manor Road', renamed 'Manor Way' June 1882. Initially single track, doubled 01/04/1882. Original station west of road bridge demolished and replaced by new station east of bridge c.1887. Operated by GER after 1896, ownership later transferred to PLA. Branch closed from 09/09/1940 due to 'Black Saturday' air raid 07/09/1940 (no trains on Sundays since 27/06/1915). Listed as 'Royal Albert Dock, Manor Way' in Borley, although this prefix was only used in early timetables rather than for the station itself.
MANSION HOUSE	26 / 6D 32 / 5D		03/07/1871	N/A	MDR	Terminus until 06/10/1884. Former southern bay road (Platform 4) became main westbound road and Platform 3 westbound road became a central bay platform with stops at east end 15/01/1911. Northern bay (former Platform 1) abolished 04/02/1968. Closed 30/10/1989 - 11/02/1991 (rebuilding). Central bay platform abolished weekend of 08-09/10/2016 (last train 07/10/2016). Closed 20/03/2020 – 18/05/2020 (COVID-19).
MARBLE ARCH	25 / 6D		30/07/1900	N/A	CLR	Closed 01/09/1939 – 15/11/1939 (installation of flood protection).
MARLBOROUGH ROAD	25 / 4C		13/04/1868	20/11/1939	MSJWR	Replaced by St John's Wood (then Bakerloo Line) to south.

Name	Page / grid		Date opened	Date closed	Opened by	Notes
MARSH FARM SEWAGE WORKS	46 / 6B		c.1940	by 1979	PRIV	First appeared on 1940 OS, railway had ceased operating by 1979.
MARYLAND Maryland Point	28 / 3A		06/01/1873	N/A	GER	Renamed 28/10/1940.
Maryland East Crossovers	28 / 3A		?	N/A	BR	
MARYLEBONE Great Central (UERL only)	25 / 5D		15/03/1899	N/A	GCR	Terminus of Great Central Railway. UERL BSWR platforms opened as 'Great Central' 27/03/1907, were terminus until 15/06/1907, renamed to 'Marylebone' 15/04/1917 ('Great Central' tiling remains at platform level). NR station closed 15/08/2011 – 22/08/2011 (engineering work at Neasden South Junction).
MARYLEBONE GOODS & COAL	25 / 5C		11/04/1899	28/03/1966	GCR	Coal & minerals traffic commenced 11/04/1899, general goods commenced 27/04/1899.

MAZE HILL
   Maze Hill (for National Maritime Museum)
   Maze Hill & East Greenwich
   Maze Hill & Greenwich Park
   Maze Hill & East Greenwich
   Greenwich (Maze Hill)
	41 / 3A		01/01/1873	N/A	SER	Opened as terminus of short branch from Charlton 01/01/1873 as 'Greenwich (Maze Hill)'. Through line to original Greenwich station opened and station renamed 'Maze Hill & East Greenwich' 01/02/1878. Became 'Maze Hill & Greenwich Park' 01/07/1878, reverted to 'Maze Hill & East Greenwich' (or 'Maze Hill [East Greenwich]') 01/01/1899. Suffix dropped and became 'Maze Hill' ??/04/1937 (Borley), although alternative suffix 'for National Maritime Museum' referred to in Quick, with this being dropped in 1955. Two 'down' roads flanked an island platform, with five carriage sidings on the 'down' side and six on the 'up' (including a two-road carriage shed). Carriage sidings were never electrified and had ceased to be used by North Kent Line full electrification (1962). Signal box abolished 29/11/1969.

MCVITIE & PRICE'S SIDING	24 / 4B		1902	?	PRIV	Later United Biscuits.
MERIDIAN WATER	15 / 3B		03/06/2019	N/A	NR	Replaced Angel Road to north. Fourth platform planned.
MERSTHAM	73 / 3D	P	01/12/1841	N/A	LBRR	Quick states opened with line 12/07/1841, but LBRR Board minute of 01/07/1841 refers to tender for construction being delayed. J.T. Howard-Turner quotes an opening date of Wednesday 01/12/1841 in 'LB&SCR – Origins & Formation' which is consistent with this delayed opening. The same source states that the station platforms were on loops off the main line. Closed by SER 02/10/1843, reopened 04/10/1844 pending completion of new (current) station to north, re-sited c.1845.
		G	01/12/1841	06/01/1969		
Merstham Tunnel	73 / 5A		12/07/1841	N/A	LBRR	
MERTON ABBEY	52 / 4C	P	01/10/1868	03/03/1929	LBSCR / LSWR	Closed to passengers 01/01/1917 – 27/08/1923, then again for good 03/03/1929 (passenger service Tooting Junction to Merton Park withdrawn). Goods yard remained open to general goods traffic until 01/05/1972, coal traffic continued until 05/05/1975.
		G	01/10/1868	05/05/1975		
MERTON PARK Lower Merton	52 / 4B		01/10/1868	N/A	LBSCR / LSWR	Opened by LBSCR & LSWR on their joint loop line from Streatham to Wimbledon as 'Lower Merton', initially platforms on this route only (none on WCRR route), single platform on WCRR route added 01/11/1870. Renamed 'Merton Park' 01/09/1887. Platforms on route to Tooting Junction closed 01/01/1917 – 27/08/1923, then again for good 03/03/1929. Platform on Wimbledon to Croydon route sometimes had 'Halt' added on timetables / tickets 1918 – 1923/4. Closed 02/06/1997 (last train 31/05/1997, no Sunday service), reopened by Croydon Tramlink 30/05/2000.
Merton Park Junction	52 / 4B		01/10/1868	05/05/1975	LBSCR / LSWR	
MERTON SEWAGE WORKS	52 / 3C		c.1915	1963	PRIV	Opened by Wandle Valley Joint Sewerage Board, 2ft gauge internal railway in operation c.1915 – 1963.
Metropolitan Junctions	39 / 1D 87		01/09/1866	N/A	SER	Junction with curve to Blackfriars opened 01/06/1878. Borough Market Viaduct opened 04/01/2016.
Mickleham Tunnel	70 / 6C		11/03/1867	N/A	LBSCR	
MILDMAY PARK	26 / 3D		01/01/1880	01/10/1934	NLR	
MILE END (ECR)	27 / 5B		c.1841	24/05/1872	ECR	Replaced Devonshire Street, Mile End station to east, later replaced by Bethnal Green Junction station to west.
MILE END (MDR)	27 / 5C		02/06/1902	N/A	MDR / LTSR	Served by Metropolitan Line since 30/03/1936 ('Hammersmith & City Line' since 30/07/1990). Central Line platforms opened 04/12/1946.

MILE END GOODS
   Mile End & Devonshire Street Goods
   Devonshire Street Goods
	27 / 5C		1850	06/11/1967	ECR	Opened as 'Devonshire Street Goods', prefix 'Mile End &' added 01/09/1922, suffix '& Devonshire Street' dropped 01/01/1939.

MILEAGE YARD Crimea Yard	25 / 6B 67 / 5A		c.1850's	17/07/1967	GWR	Yard was in situ by 1863, originally referred to as 'Crimea Yard' which may suggest opening date between October 1853 and February 1856 (Crimean War). Closed 17/07/1967.
MILL HILL BROADWAY Mill Hill	12 / 2C	P	13/07/1868	N/A	MID	Goods yard opened first; 09/03/1868, passenger station opened 13/07/1868. Suffix 'Broadway' added 25/09/1950, although goods yard was renamed previously (01/07/1950). Goods yard closed 03/08/1964.
		G	09/03/1868	03/08/1964		

MILL HILL EAST
   Mill Hill East for Mill Hill Barracks
   Mill Hill for Mill Hill Barracks
   Mill Hill
	13 / 3A	P	22/08/1867	N/A	GNR	Opened as 'Mill Hill', suffix 'for Mill Hill Barracks' added 17/04/1916, renamed 'Mill Hill East for Mill Hill Barracks' 01/02/1928. Closed by LNER 11/09/1939 to allow transfer to LPTB, doubling, and electrification (reopened by LPTB 18/05/1941 as terminus), but electrification only reached Mill Hill East and second track to Mill Hill (The Hale) dismantled without being used. Goods yard closed 01/10/1962.

		G	22/08/1867	01/10/1962		
MILL HILL (THE HALE) The Hale Halt	12 / 2C	P	11/06/1906	11/09/1939	GNR	Goods yard opened 18/07/1910. Originally opened as 'The Hale Halt', renamed 'Mill Hill (The Hale)' 01/03/1928. Closed to passengers 11/09/1939 to enable doubling and electrification of Finchley Central to Edgware prior to transfer to LPTB Northern Line. Works abandoned and station did not reopen. Goods yard closed 29/02/1964.
		G	18/07/1910	29/02/1964		
MILLWALL DOCKS	40 / 2D		18/12/1871	04/05/1926	MER	Terminus until 29/07/1872, before this date a temporary station served by horse-drawn trains, after this date reconstructed as a permanent station south of Glengall Road. Often also referred to as 'Millwall Dock'. Passenger service to Blackwall and North Greenwich withdrawn 04/05/1926. Crossharbour DLR on same site.
MILLWALL GOODS	40 / 2D		18/12/1871	01/06/1925	MER	Goods station closed 01/06/1925, but goods trains continued to serve the adjacent dock.
MILLWALL JUNCTION	40 / 1D 31 / 4B	P	18/12/1871	04/05/1926	LBLR / MER	Opening coincided with that of Millwall Extension Railway to Millwall Docks. Rebuilt & re-sited 1888, two platform faces on Blackwall route, one on route to North Greenwich. Passenger services withdrawn from both 04/05/1926.
		G	18/12/1871	14/11/1927		
MILTON RANGE HALT	60 / 2D		01/07/1906	17/07/1932 (see notes)	SECR	Removed from timetables 17/07/1932, only served 'as required' for adjacent rifle ranges thereafter. Rebuilt in concrete 1954 (previously wood), continued to be served until at least 1956, local services ceased on route 04/12/1961, even then station did not 'officially' close and platforms remained standing until 2008 (up) / 2009 (down).
MILTON ROAD HALT	60 / 1B		01/07/1906	01/05/1915	SECR	Closed as a WW1 economy, did not reopen.
MINORIES	27 / 6A 74 / 6A		06/07/1840	24/10/1853	LBLR	Original LBLR London terminus. Replaced by Fenchurch Street, although both open until 15/02/1849 (Minories closed) then again 09/09/1849 - 24/10/1853 (Minories reopened, then closed again for good).
Minories Junction	27 / 6A 74 / 1B		06/10/1884	N/A	MDR / MET	

Name	Page / grid		Date opened	Date closed	Opened by	Notes
MITCHAM	52 / 6D	P	22/10/1855	N/A	WCRR	Station opened by WCRR as only intermediate station between Wimbledon and Croydon, two platforms from outset (passing loop on single line), following a landslip in 1971 'up' (northern) abandoned. Goods yard closed 01/05/1967, passenger station closed 02/06/1997 (last train 31/05/1997, no Sunday service), reopened on a new site slightly to east by Croydon Tramlink 30/05/2000.
		G	22/10/1855	01/05/1967		
MITCHAM EASTFIELDS	52 / 5D		02/06/2008	N/A	NR	Opened during afternoon of 02/06/2008, platforms staggered either side of level crossing.
MITCHAM JUNCTION	52 / 6D		01/10/1868	N/A	LBSCR	Station opened with Streatham - Sutton line (no station on WCRR line prior to this). Separate Croydon Tramlink platforms opened 30/05/2000 following withdrawal of Wimbledon - West Croydon NR trains 02/06/1997.
Mitre Bridge Curve	24 / 5D 91 & 92	P	02/09/1867	N/A	LNWR	Loop built to connect WLR with HJR.
		G	02/09/1867	N/A		
MITRE BRIDGE GOODS	24 / 5D 91		*c.1870*	*02/01/1967*	LNWR	Sidings had appeared by 1870 OS. Closed 02/01/1967.
Mitre Bridge Junction	24 / 5D 91 & 92		02/09/1867	N/A	LNWR	
MONUMENT The Monument Eastcheap	26 / 6D 87		06/10/1884	N/A	MDR / MET	Opened as 'Eastcheap', renamed 'The Monument' 01/11/1884, 'The' prefix gradually dropped.
MOOR PARK Moor Park & Sandy Lodge Sandy Lodge	10 / 1A	P	09/05/1910	N/A	MET / GCR	Opened as 'Sandy Lodge', 'Moor Park' prefix after 18/10/1923, 'Sandy Lodge' suffix dropped 25/09/1950. Goods yard closed ??/06/1938. Rebuilt with two new island platforms for quadrupling 23/04/1961.
		G	*09/05/1910*	*??/06/1938*		
MOORGATE Moorgate Street	26 / 6D		23/12/1865	N/A	MET	City Widened Lines platforms opened 01/07/1866, closed 12/09/2004 – 16/05/2005 (building work at St Pancras), and then closed for good 23/03/2009 (last train 20/03/2009). CSLR platforms opened 25/02/1900. GNCR (later Northern Line, then British Rail) platforms opened 14/02/1904. Station renamed 24/10/1924. Interchange provided with Liverpool Street via Elizabeth Line platforms 24/05/2022.
MORDEN	52 / 5B		13/09/1926	N/A	UERL (NOR)	Southern terminus of Northern Line.
MORDEN DEPOT	52 / 6B		*13/09/1926*	N/A	UERL (NOR)	
MORDEN ROAD Morden Road Halt Morden Halt Morden	52 / 4B		c.01/03/1857	N/A	WCRR	Did not open with WCRR, first appeared in timetables March 1857 as 'Morden'. Removed from timetables October & November 1918, upon re-appearing in December 1918, became 'Morden Halt'. Further renamed 'Morden Road Halt' 02/07/1951. 'Halt' dropped 1968. Closed 02/06/1997 (last train 31/05/1997, no Sunday service), reopened by Croydon Tramlink 30/05/2000. In its mainline guise, was always a single platform on north side of single track.
MORDEN SOUTH	52 / 6B		05/01/1930	N/A	SR	
MORNINGTON CRESCENT	26 / 4A		22/06/1907	N/A	UERL (CCEHR)	Closed due to wildcat strikes 06/06/1924 – 02/07/1924. Closed 24/10/1992 – 27/04/1998 (lift replacement works) and 21/03/2020 – 08/06/2020 (COVID-19).
Mortimer Street Junction	26 / 2A 9		17/12/1900	05/01/1981	MID	Junction at north end of Low Level Curve, abandoned after diversion of Barking Trains to Gospel Oak.
MORTLAKE Mortlake & East Sheen Mortlake	37 / 5B		27/07/1846	N/A	LSWR	Carried '& East Sheen' suffix 01/04/1886 – 30/01/1916.
MORTLAKE BREWERY	37 / 5B		*Pre-1910*	*Post-1913*	PRIV	Small system of standard gauge tramways within the brewery and accessing a riverside wharf. Some track remains in situ embedded in Thames Path. Brewery dates back to late 18th Century, tho tramways possibly laid as part of 1869 expansion under auspices of Phillips & Wigan. In situ on 1913 OS, but had been removed by 1930 revision.
Mortlake Junction	37 / 5C		01/02/1862	01/01/1869	LSWR	Junction at south end of Barnes Curve; disused since 01/01/1869 but not dismantled until 1881.
MOTSPUR PARK	51 / 6D		12/07/1925	N/A	SR	
Motspur Park Junction	64 / 1D		29/05/1938	N/A	SR	
MOTTINGHAM Eltham & Mottingham Eltham for Mottingham Eltham & Mottingham Eltham	55 / 1D	P	01/09/1866	N/A	SER	Opened as 'Eltham', suffix '& Mottingham' added 01/01/1892. '&' became 'for' 1914, reverted to '&' 1922. 'Eltham' dropped and station became 'Mottingham' 26/09/1927. Six carriage sidings were laid west of the station c.1900, all but one was decommissioned along with the goods yard 07/10/1968. The remaining siding was usually left 'clipped' out of use and eventually lifted.
		G	*01/09/1866*	*07/10/1968*		
MOUNT PLEASANT	26 / 5C		*05/12/1927*	*31/05/2003*	POR	POR mothballed 31/05/2003, a portion of the route centred upon Mount Pleasant and the depot reopened for visitors as part of The Postal Museum 28/07/2017. Trains run on a loop to/from the former depot and pass non-stop both platforms of the former station (see 'The Postal Museum' entry).
Mount Street Tunnel	41 / 2C		30/07/1849	N/A	SER	
Mountnessing Junction	20 / 4C		01/01/1934	N/A	LNER	Dive-under for Southend Victoria Branch built by LNER 01/01/1934.
MUDCHUTE	40 / 2D		31/08/1987	N/A	DLR	Closed on part of 09/02/1996 by IRA bomb at South Quay, did not reopen until 15/04/1996. Closed 11/01/1999 due to works on the Lewisham extension, new station at a lower level opened with the extension 20/11/1999.
MUSEUM DEPOT	37 / 1A		*??/10/1999*	N/A	LUL	Opened on part of Ealing Common Depot site (and accessible by rail from there) to house London Transport Museum exhibits.
MUSWELL HILL	14 / 4A	P	*24/05/1873*	*05/07/1954*	GNR	Nominally opened by Edgware, Highgate & London Railway, which was absorbed by GNR a month before opening. Closed to passengers 01/08/1873 – 01/05/1875 and again 29/10/1951 – 07/01/1952 along with entire branch. Had been intended for electrification and transfer to the Northern Line, but works abandoned post-WW2. Finally closed to passengers when Alexandra Palace to Finsbury Park service permanently withdrawn 05/07/1954. Goods yard remained in use until 14/06/1956 after which time branch abandoned beyond Cranley Gardens.
		G	*24/05/1873*	*14/06/1956*		

N

Name	Page / grid		Date opened	Date closed	Opened by	Notes
Navarino Road Junction	27 / 3A		30/06/1986	N/A	BR	Junction at north end of Graham Road Curve.
NEASDEN Neasden & Kingsbury Kingsbury & Neasden	24 / 2C 22	P	02/08/1880	N/A	MET	Opened as 'Kingsbury & Neasden', renamed 'Neasden & Kingsbury' 01/01/1910, suffix dropped 01/01/1932. Goods yard opened 01/01/1894, closed April 1958. Served by Bakerloo Line 20/11/1939 – 01/05/1979, Jubilee Line thereafter. Last served regularly by Metropolitan Line 07/12/1940. Proposed to have platforms on Dudding Hill Loop (West London Orbital).
		G	*01/01/1894*	*??/04/1958*		
NEASDEN COAL	24 / 2C 22		*25/07/1898*	*04/03/1968*	GCR	

Name	Page / grid		Date opened	Date closed	Opened by	Notes
Neasden Curve	24 / 2C 22	P	N/A	N/A	GCR	Curve only regularly used for freight services, originally double track but subsequently singled.
		G	01/08/1899	N/A		
NEASDEN DEPOT	24 / 2C 22		1882	N/A	MET	Originally Metropolitan Railway Works & Power Station. Substantially rebuilt in 1930s. Stabled Bakerloo Line Trains 20/11/1939 - 01/05/1979, Jubilee Line trains thereafter.
NEASDEN ENGINE SHED	24 / 3C 22		15/03/1899	18/06/1961	GCR	
NEASDEN FREIGHT TERMINAL	24 / 2B 22		05/04/2002	24/03/2007	PRIV	Tibbett & Britten, terminal for imported mineral water. Dates quoted are for beginning of / break in lease of building. Sidings remain in situ and connected to main line despite 2011 junction remodelling, but are obstructed. Current owner Seneca Resource Recovery has never generated rail traffic.
Neasden Junction	24 / 2C 22		01/08/1899	N/A	GCR	Junction at southern end of Neasden Curve.
Neasden North Junction	24 / 2B 22		28/04/1923	18/05/1968	LNER	Junctions between Wembley Stadium Loop and former GCR main line.
NEASDEN POWER STATION	24 / 1B 22		??/12/1904	21/07/1968	MET	Metropolitan Railway Power Station, commissioned December 1904, electric services commenced 01/01/1905.
Neasden South Junction	24 / 2C 22		20/11/1905	N/A	GCR	Junction between GCR lines to Aylesbury and 1905 High Wycombe route (first passenger use 01/03/1906). Extensively remodelled 15/08/2011 – 22/08/2011.
NEASDEN SOUTH SIDINGS	24 / 2B 22		?	N/A	GCR	
NECROPOLIS	39 / 2C 89		13/11/1854	11/05/1941	LSWR	Station for funeral traffic to Brookwood Cemetery. Re-sited south 16/02/1902 (Waterloo station expansion). Last recorded funeral departure 11/04/1941. Partially destroyed by air raid night of 16-17/04/1941, officially declared closed 11/05/1941.
NEVER STOP RAILWAY	24 / 1B 22		23/04/1924	??/10/1925	PRIV	The system had four stations; North End, Tree Top, Mid Way and South End.
NEW ADDINGTON	67 / 5D		10/05/2000	N/A	CTL	
NEW BARNET Barnet	5 / 5D	P	07/08/1850	N/A	GNR	Prefix 'New' added 01/05/1884. Goods yard closed 22/08/1966.
		G	07/08/1850	22/08/1966		
NEW BECKENHAM	54 / 4C		01/04/1864	N/A	MKR	Opening coincided with MKR route from here to Addiscombe. Original site south of current station and junction, it is thought that there were four platform faces serving the Addiscombe and Beckenham Junction routes. Replaced by current two-platform station to north c.1868 (Borley) / 1866-8 (Quick) / 1866 (Mitchell & Smith). Jackson provides the most detail; with the original station closing 'autumn 1866' and the replacement opening 'from October 1866, if not a little earlier'. There was a central through road in use 1904 - 1926* to facilitate joining / dividing of trains. *Jackson states track removed 1926, Mitchell & Smith states road eliminated 1929*
New Beckenham Junction	54 / 4C		01/04/1864	N/A	MKR	
NEW CROSS (SER)	40 / 4C 79 / 80		??/10/1850	N/A	SER	Precise opening date unknown; October 1850. SER began running own trains over ELR 01/04/1880, separate bay platform for ELR added on 'down' side 01/10/1884. Served by MDR 01/10/1884 – 06/10/1884 only. Served by MET 06/10/1884 – 03/12/1906, then again 31/03/1913 onwards, gaining separate 'East London Line' identity during 1980's. No LUL service 26/03/1995 – 25/03/1998 (engineering work), withdrawn for good 23/12/2007. Former LUL bay reopened by TfL (LO) 27/04/2010.
NEW CROSS (ELR)	40 / 4C 79		07/12/1869	01/09/1886	ELR	Original ELR southern terminus. Closed 01/11/1876 - 01/10/1884, MDR service commenced 06/10/1884, station closed entirely 01/09/1886 and all services diverted to adjacent New Cross (Gate). Sometimes differentiated from New Cross (Gate) by use of 'Low Level' suffix. At times ELR used both this and New Cross (Gate) station for terminating services.
NEW CROSS DEPOT	40 / 3C 79		31/03/1913	23/12/2007	MET	Carriage shed built for ELR electrification, MET EMU stabling. Closed with ELL prior to transfer to TfL (LO). Was served by a staff halt on the west side of the adjacent ELL, at the southern end of the shed. Proposed to be reinstated as LO stabling sidings.
NEW CROSS GATE New Cross	40 / 4C 79 / 80		05/06/1839	N/A	LCRR	Served by ELR 01/11/1876 – 01/10/1884. Served by MDR 01/09/1886 – 01/08/1905. Served by MET 31/03/1913 onwards, gaining separate 'East London Line' identity during 1980's. 'Gate' suffix added 09/07/1923. No LUL service 26/03/1995 – 25/03/1998 (engineering work), withdrawn for good 23/12/2007. Served by TfL (LO) services since 27/04/2010 (terminus until 23/05/2010).
NEW CROSS GATE DEPOT	40 / 3C 80		27/04/2010	N/A	TFL (LO)	LO depot opened coinciding with reopening / transfer of ELL 27/04/2010, replaced former New Cross Depot.
New Cross Gate Down Junction	40 / 4C 79 / 80		01/11/1876	N/A	NR	Re-established 23/05/2012 due to LO extension to West Croydon / Crystal Palace. Connection between ELR and LBSCR first formed 01/11/1876 to north of New Cross (Gate) station, junction for 'down' trains relocated to present site in late 19th century. Direct connection between LTE and BR removed 17/09/1972. Indirect connection between LTE and BR carriage / permanent way sidings removed 12/01/1975. Access to sidings remained from south until their abandonment c.1990, current junction established on same site.
New Cross Gate Up Junction	40 / 4C 79 / 80		23/05/2010	N/A	NR	Junction eliminated after 27/04/1966, re-established 23/05/2010 for new flyover (LO).
NEW CROSS GOODS	40 / 4C 79		05/06/1839	06/11/1967	LCRR	Goods yard opened with New Cross (Gate) passenger station, expanded over the years and became GER owned, occupying site of New Cross (ELR) station and area to immediate east. Closed 06/11/1967, carriage sidings then occupying part of site until c.1990.
NEW CROSS LOCO WORKS & ENGINE SHEDS	40 / 4C 79		05/06/1839	14/06/1947	LCRR	LCRR's original loco works / shed, first shed being an octagonal 'roundhouse'. Loco works subsequently transferred to Brighton by LBSCR. Additional engine sheds added ('Middle' and 'New'), as well as carriage works and sidings. Depot officially closed 14/06/1947, but locos continued to stable until 1951. Sheds demolished 1957, replaced by carriage sidings which remained until c.1990, removed for supermarket development (opened 1996).
New Croydon Line	66 / 1D 86	P	c.1865	??/10/1983	LBSCR	In situ by 1870 OS, eliminated during 1983 remodelling of Gloucester Road Triangle.
		G	c.1865	??/10/1983		

NEW ELTHAM
  New Eltham & Pope Street
  Pope Street
	56 / 2A	P	01/04/1878	N/A	SER	Opened as 'Pope Street', prefix 'New Eltham &' added 01/01/1886, suffix 'Pope Street' dropped 26/09/1927. Goods yard closed 13/05/1963 (Borley), Jackson states November 1965.

		G	01/04/1878	13/05/1963		
New Guildford Line Junction	63 / 1B		02/02/1885	N/A	LSWR	
New Kew Junction	37 / 3A 19		01/02/1862	N/A	LSWR	Junction at south end of Kew Curve. 'Up' road extended 220 metres west 1932.
NEW MALDEN	51 / 5C		c.01/12/1846	N/A	LSWR	Opened as 'Malden', exact opening date uncertain, first in timetable December 1846. Renamed 'New Malden & Coombe' May 1859, then

Name	Page / grid		Date opened	Date closed	Opened by	Notes
Malden Malden for Coombe Coombe & Malden New Malden & Coombe Malden						'Coombe & Malden' March 1862, 'Malden for Coombe' November 1912, 'Malden' 1955, then finally 'New Malden' 16/09/1957. Goods yard was remote from station (see separate entry).
NEW MALDEN GOODS	51 / 5B		c.1869	03/08/1964	LSWR	Borley states goods opened with passenger station, but no facilities are evident on contemporary OS maps. Remote from passenger station, accessed from Kingston Loop, which precludes an opening date before 01/01/1869. Single siding evident on 1868 OS (Kingston loop depicted although not opened until 01/01/1869). Closed 03/08/1964.
New Malden Junction	51 / 5C		??/??/1883	N/A	LSWR	Junction between LSWR main line and Kingston Loop. No physical connection until 1883.
NEW SOUTHGATE New Southgate & Friern Barnet New Southgate for Colney Hatch New Southgate & Colney Hatch Southgate & Colney Hatch Colney Hatch & Southgate	14 / 2A	P G	07/08/1850 07/08/1850	N/A 07/12/1970	GNR	Opened as 'Colney Hatch & Southgate', reversed to 'Southgate & Colney Hatch' 01/02/1855. Prefix 'New' added 01/10/1876, became 'New Southgate for Colney Hatch' 01/03/1883. Platforms originally staggered with 'up' south of 'down', rearranged April 1890. Renamed 'New Southgate & Friern Barnet' 01/05/1923, suffix dropped 18/03/1971. Closed 25/12/1976 – 14/02/1977 (fire), goods yard closed 07/12/1970.
NEW WANDSWORTH	38 / 6C	P G	29/03/1858 29/03/1858	01/11/1869 07/10/1968	WELCPR	Passenger station closed 01/11/1869, goods yard 07/10/1968.
NEWBURY PARK	17 / 6B	P G	01/05/1903 01/05/1903	N/A 04/10/1965	GER	LNER Fairlop Loop closed to passengers 30/11/1947 to allow electrification and transfer to Central Line. Station reopened by LPTB Central Line as terminus from Leytonstone 14/12/1947 (until Hainault extension opened 31/05/1948). Goods yard closed 04/10/1965.
Newbury Park Junction	29 / 1B		20/04/1903	30/11/1947	GER	Junction at north end of Newbury Park Junction to Ilford Carriage Sidings Junction curve.
NEWBURY PARK SIDINGS	17 / 6B		14/12/1947	12/10/1969	GER	Opened for Central Line extension from Leytonstone, but lightly used after Hainault Depot's full opening 31/05/1948. Sidings 23-29 abolished 30/01/1955, removed 11/02/1955, with associated signalling alterations effective 17/03/1956. Sidings 21 & 22 (the two nearest the running line) were retained until 12/10/1969.
NEWINGTON VESTRY DEPOT	39 / 3D		?	?	LCDR	
NINE ELMS (LSWR)	39 / 3B 57	P G	21/05/1838 21/05/1838	11/07/1848 29/07/1968	LSWR	LSWR London terminus until Waterloo opened. Remained in use for goods traffic until 29/07/1968 ('North' goods).
NINE ELMS (TFL)	39 / 3B		20/09/2021	N/A	TFL (NOR)	Intermediate station on Northern Line extension from Kennington to Battersea Power Station.
NINE ELMS DEPOT	39 / 4A 57		1885	1967	LSWR	Locomotive sheds.
NINE ELMS GAS WORKS	57		c.1879	1970	PRIV	Works opened 1853 but had no standard gauge railway connection until c.1880 (not present on 1874 OS, had appeared by 1895). Narrow gauge internal system opened c.1879, initially 3ft gauge but then some 2ft gauge lines laid. Narrow gauge system function replaced by conveyors 1926-7 and probably disused thereafter. Works closed 1970.
Nine Elms Junction	39 / 3A 82		17/08/1994	N/A	RT	Date quoted is start of trial Eurostar service, advertised service commenced 14/11/1994. Little used since 14/11/2007 (diversion of Eurostar to St Pancras), but chord still in situ and traversed by test trains.
NINE ELMS ROYAL STATION	39 / 3B 57		1854	1876	LSWR	Station provided for the use of Queen Victoria and the Royal family, also used by visiting foreign dignitaries.
NINE ELMS SOUTH GOODS (formerly locomotive works)	39 / 4B 57		1843	29/07/1968	LSWR	Opened as LSWR's loco works, which transferred to Eastleigh in 1909. Site then became 'South' goods yard.
NINE ELMS, SOUTH LAMBETH GOODS South Lambeth Goods	39 / 4A 82		25/03/1910	03/10/1977	GWR	Opened for milk traffic 25/03/1910, then to general goods 01/01/1911. Renamed 29/07/1968, but closed 03/10/1977, but retained for a while thereafter for stabling engineers trains during Victoria resignalling works.
NOEL PARK & WOOD GREEN Green Lanes & Noel Park Green Lanes	14 / 4C	P G	01/01/1878 01/01/1878	07/01/1963 07/12/1964	GER	Initially terminus of branch from Seven Sisters, until Palace Gates extension opened 07/10/1878. Opened as 'Green Lanes', Suffix '& Noel Park' added 01/05/1884, renamed 'Noel Park & Wood Green' 01/01/1902. Station and entire Palace Gates Branch closed to passengers 07/01/1963, goods yard closed 07/12/1964.
NORBITON Norbiton for Kingston Hill Norbiton for Kingston Hill and Richmond Park Norbiton Norbiton and Kingston Hill	51 / 4A	P G	01/01/1869 01/01/1869	N/A 03/05/1965	LSWR	Various suffixes used from opening; 'and Kingston Hill' initially, dropped 1890. 'for Kingston Hill and Richmond Park' 1894, 'for Kingston Hill' 1914, dropped again and became 'Norbiton' 1955. Goods closed 03/05/1965.
NORBURY	53 / 4B		01/01/1878	N/A	LBSCR	
NORLAND	38 / 1A 83		N/A	N/A	MET / GWR	Construction sanctioned by HCR board 27/06/1864 and station reported as complete in August 1864. GWR inspection in September deemed the station incomplete and incorrectly sited so it did not open. Uxbridge Road Station opened slightly to the south 01/11/1869.
NORTH ACTON	24 / 5C 91 & 92		05/11/1923	N/A	UERL / GWR	Platforms built on GWR Birmingham main line and electrified lines used by UERL Central Line. Central pair of GWR goods lines did not have platform faces provided. GWR Birmingham main line platforms closed 30/06/1947, after this date station served by Central Line only. Central pair of goods-only lines abandoned 09/03/1964, the 'down' line subsequently being re-used as the LU Central Line eastbound road, allowing the original eastbound to become a central reversible road after 22/03/1993.
NORTH ACTON HALT	24 / 5B		01/05/1904	01/02/1913	GWR	
North Acton Junction (1)	24 / 5B		30/06/1947	N/A	LPTB (CEN)	Junction between Central Line and extension to Greenford (later West Ruislip).
North Acton Junction (2)	24 / 5B		16/04/1917	09/03/1964	GWR	Junction between GWR Birmingham Direct Line and route ex-Viaduct Jcn.
NORTH DULWICH	39 / 6D		01/10/1868	N/A	LBSCR	
NORTH EALING	24 / 6A		23/06/1903	N/A	MDR	First served Piccadilly Line 04/07/1932, last served District Line 22/10/1933.
NORTH END (or BULL & BUSH)	25 / 1C		N/A	N/A	UERL (CCEHR)	Platforms built but station buildings and platform access never completed. Access stairway sunk c.1950's.
NORTH GREENWICH (LUL)	41 / 1A		14/05/1999	N/A	LUL (JUB)	Three platform faces from outset, layout to facilitate possible future branch towards Royal Docks.
NORTH GREENWICH (MER)	40 / 3D		29/07/1872	04/05/1926	MER	Suffix '(Cubitt Town)' or '& Cubitt Town' sometimes used. Services to North Greenwich and Blackwall ceased 04/05/1926, subsequent DLR station at Island Gardens to north (north side of Manchester Road).
NORTH HARROW	11 / 5A		22/03/1915	N/A	MET / GCR	
North Junction (Mitcham)	52 / 6D		01/10/1868	02/06/1997	LBSCR	Junction eliminated when Wimbledon to West Croydon line closed 02/06/1997 prior to conversion to Tramlink.
North Kent East Junction	40 / 3C 79 / 80		30/07/1849	N/A	LGR / SER	Junction between SER and LGR

Name	Page / grid		Date opened	Date closed	Opened by	Notes
North Kent Line Connection	45 / 6B		14/11/2007	N/A	LCOR / NR	Junction between HS1 and North Kent Line.
NORTH KENT JUNCTION	40 / 3C 79		01/09/1849	21/08/1850?	SER / LGR	Exchange traffic only, not listed in Bradshaw. Possibly point where London Bridge and Bricklayers Arms portions of SER trains were divided / coupled. An accident / partial collapse of Bricklayers Arms 21/08/1850 led to a suspension of services to there and probably the end of North Kent Junction. However, 'Private and Untimetabled Railway Stations' (Croughton / Kidner / Young) gives a 01/10/1850 closure date.
North Kent West Junction Bricklayers Arms Junction	40 / 3B		01/05/1844	21/06/1981	LCRR / SER	Spur to North Kent East Junction disused after 21/06/1981 (closure of parcels depot at Bricklayers Arms), remaining Bricklayers Arms traffic then worked via New Cross Gate.
North London Incline (GNR)	75 / 76	P	N/A	N/A	GNR	No regular passenger service. Originally double track. Re-aligned during HS1 works to take a more southerly route.
		G	1853	N/A		
North London Incline (MID)	75	P	N/A	N/A	MID	No regular passenger service.
		G	1867	31/12/1975		
North London Incline Junction	75		1867	31/12/1975	MID	
NORTH MIDDLESEX GASWORKS	13 / 3A		1869	01/10/1962	PRIV	Jackson gives dates as 1886-1956 (Borley dates quoted).
NORTH POLE HITACHI IEP DEPOT North Pole Eurostar Depot	24 / 5D 91 & 92		11/11/1992	N/A	ES	Official opening 11/11/1992 although revenue earning Eurostar operations did not begin until 14/11/1994. Closed when Temple Mills Depot opened 14/11/2007. Converted for use by Great Western Railway's fleet of Hitachi IEP trains, signalling commissioned 04/07/2015, first IEP train visited depot 24/10/2015, public service commenced 16/10/2017.
North Pole Junction	24 / 5D & 91 & 92		??/10/1860	N/A	WLR / GWR	Formerly provided connection to GWR Main Line, now only North Pole Depot.
North Quay Junction Delta Junction	31		31/08/1987	N/A	DLR	Northern side of original triangular 'flat' junction eliminated at time of Beckton extension and renamed at that time. Eastbound trains ex-Bank diverted via new diveunder 24/08/2009.
NORTH SHED (QUEENS PARK)	25 / 4A		11/02/1915	N/A	UERL (BAK)	Stabling Shed for Bakerloo Line also traversing running lines.
NORTH SHEEN	37 / 5A		06/07/1930	N/A	SR	
NORTH SURREY SEWAGE BOARD RAILWAYS	51 / 5A		1939	post-1965	PRIV	Three separate systems opened 1939 (Malden & Berrylands) and 1953 (Hogsmill). Amalgamated 1961.
NORTH SURREY WATER (Walton on Thames)	62 / 1A		c.1970	N/A	PRIV	3ft 6in gauge line alongside semi-treated reservoirs, still sees occasional use.
NORTH WEALD	8 / 1C	P	24/04/1865	N/A	GER	Epping to Ongar transferred to LTE 25/09/1949, Electrified 18/11/1957. Between these dates passenger services provided by BR (steam). Line closed by LUL 03/10/1994 (last train 30/09/1994, no weekend service at point of closure), reopened by Epping-Ongar Railway between Ongar and North Weald 10/10/2004, closed 31/12/2007 for engineering works, reopened 25/05/2012. Goods yard closed 06/01/1964.
		G	24/04/1865	06/01/1964		
NORTH WEMBLEY	23 / 1D	P	15/06/1912	N/A	LNWR	Referred to as 'East Lane' before opening. Goods yard opened before passenger station 31/10/1910, passenger station opened 15/06/1912, goods yard closed 05/05/1965. Served by Bakerloo Line since 16/04/1917, no service 27/09/1982 (last train 24/09/1982) to 04/06/1984.
		G	31/10/1910	05/07/1965		
NORTH WOOLWICH	41 / 2D 62 / 4D	P	14/06/1847	10/12/2006	ECR	Closed 08/09/1940 – 01/01/1941 (air raid damage), 29/05/1994 – 29/10/1995 (Jubilee Line extension works), then permanently 10/12/2006 (closure of North Woolwich branch for partial conversion to DLR). Formerly three platform faces with a central run-around siding and turntable. Reduced to one platform after 25/08/1969 singling east of Custom House, platform switched from 'down' to 'up' side with 1979 rebuilding. Goods yard closed 07/12/1970.
		G	14/06/1847	07/12/1970		

NORTHFIELDS
   Northfields & Little Ealing
   Northfield (Ealing)
	36 / 1D		16/04/1908	N/A	UERL (MDR)	Opened as 'Northfield (Ealing)', renamed 'Northfields & Little Ealing' 11/12/1911. Relocated east and renamed 'Northfields' 18/12/1932 due to opening of Northfields Depot. First served by Piccadilly Line 09/01/1933 (terminus), District Line service ceased 10/10/1964.

NORTHFIELDS DEPOT	36 / 2C		early 1932	N/A	UERL (MDR)	Opened first half of 1932 (before July). Used by Piccadilly Line since 09/01/1933. Ceased to be regularly used by District Line Trains from 10/10/1964.
NORTHFLEET	59 / 1C	P	01/11/1849	N/A	SER	According to Quick does not appear to have opened with line (30/07/1849), first recorded in timetable alteration 01/11/1849 (kentrail.org.uk states opened with line 30/07/1849). Goods yard closed 09/09/1968.
		G	01/11/1849	09/09/1968		
NORTHFLEET CEMENT WORKS	59 / 1C		14/12/1970	13/03/1993	PRIV	APCM (later Blue Circle) works, rail consignments 14/12/1970 - 13/03/1993, Elizabeth Line logistics centre later used site (see below).
NORTHFLEET ELIZABETH LINE LOGISTICS CENTRE	59 / 1C		27/04/2012	23/04/2015	PRIV	Elizabeth Line spoil terminal, reconnected to mainline 10-11/09/2011, commissioned 01/02/2012, first test train 27/04/2012, first spoil train 18/05/2012, last spoil train c.23/04/2015 (per Elizabeth Line website article of this date). Became Lafarge aggregates terminal (see entry below).
NORTHFLEET HOPE CONTAINER TERMINAL	45 / 6C		1978	N/A	BR	Upgraded to accommodate relocated Tilbury International Freight Terminal (Maritime Transport) c.13/06/2019.
NORTHFLEET LAFARGE AGGREGATES TERMINAL (disused)	59 / 1C		29/06/2016	N/A	PRIV	Opened on site of Elizabeth Line logistics centre, first arrival of empty wagons 29/06/2016, first cement train departed 01/07/2016 for Weaste. Flow ceased after just four departures, last being 21/07/2016. One-off movement 18/11/2016 to remove empty wagons.
NORTHFLEET PAPER MILLS	45 / 6B		c.1886	c.1970	PRIV	Mills erected 1884-1886, appeared to retain rail connection into 1970's.
NORTHOLT (GWR) Northolt Halt	23 / 3A	P	01/05/1907	21/11/1948	GWR	Suffix 'Halt' until 23/09/1929. Closed to passengers 21/11/1948 (replaced by LTE station), goods 01/09/1952. Suffix 'for West End Halt' referred to in Dewick, but no reference in Borley or Quick.
		G	01/05/1907	01/09/1952		
NORTHOLT (LTE)	23 / 3A		21/11/1948	N/A	LTE (CEN)	Replaced BR (former GWR) station closed on same day.
Northolt Junction	22 / 2C		02/04/1906	N/A	GCR / GWR	New 'down fast' road commissioned alongside original 'up' 30/08/2011.

NORTHOLT PARK
   Northolt Park for Northolt Village
   South Harrow & Roxeth
	23 / 2A		19/07/1926	N/A	LNER	Opened as 'South Harrow & Roxeth', renamed 'Northolt Park for Northolt Village' 13/05/1929 suffix 'for Northolt Village' dropped 13/06/1955.

Northolt Park Junction	22 / 2D		30/08/2011	N/A	NR	Junction between original 'down' line (now slow) and new down fast (parallel to 'up'), commissioned 30/08/2011.

NORTHUMBERLAND PARK
   Park
   Marsh Lane
	15 / 3B		01/04/1842	N/A	NER	Opening date given as 01/04/1842 in Borley, April / October 1841 in Quick. Probably closed for a period late 1842 / early 1843. Opened as 'Marsh Lane', renamed 'Park' 01/06/1852, 'Northumberland Park' 01/07/1923. Third platform opened for Stratford to Meridian Water service 03/06/2019, fourth proposed.

NORTHUMBERLAND PARK DEPOT	15 / 4B		01/09/1968	N/A	LTB (VIC)	Sole Depot for Victoria Line. Formerly BR sidings on part of site, laid c.1900's. Four staff platforms within depot; two on 19 Road and two on 60 Road. The depot initially had a connection to the adjacent BR route, used for delivery of the original 1967 Tube Stock.
NORTHWICK PARK Northwick Park & Kenton	11 / 6C		28/06/1923	N/A	MET	Suffix '& Kenton' dropped 15/03/1937.

Name	Page / grid		Date opened	Date closed	Opened by	Notes
NORTHWOOD	10 / 3B	P	01/09/1887	N/A	MET	Goods yard closed 14/11/1966.
		G	01/09/1887	14/11/1966		
NORTHWOOD HILLS	10 / 4B		13/11/1933	N/A	MET / GCR	
Norwood Fork Junctions	54 / 6A 86		01/12/1862	N/A	LBSCR	
Norwood Fork Spurs	86	P	01/12/1862	?	LBSCR	Originally both single-directional, single-track routes forming a 'flying' junction at the Norwood Junction end. Southerly spur was doubled during pre-WW1 remodelling and northerly spur became depot access. Southerly spur abandoned 14/02/1983. Passenger traffic was carried from outset, last services were a return football special 29/01/1983.
		G	01/12/1862	N/A		
NORWOOD JUNCTION Norwood Jcn & South Norwood for Woodside Norwood Junction Norwood Jolly Sailor	54 / 6A 86	P	05/06/1839	N/A	LCRR	Opened with line as 'Jolly Sailor', renamed 'Norwood' October 1846. Re-sited south 01/06/1859 and 'Junction' suffix added. Further suffix '& South Norwood for Woodside' added 01/10/1910, dropped 13/06/1955. Goods yard closed 01/01/1982.
		G	05/06/1839	01/01/1982		
NORWOOD JUNCTION LOCO SHED	54 / 5A		1935	??/01/1964	SR	
Norwood North Junctions	54 / 5A		01/10/1857	N/A	WELCPR / LBSCR	
Norwood Spur	54 / 5A	P	18/06/1862	01/01/1917	LBSCR	Passenger services ceased 01/01/1917. Singled 1928. All use ended 30/10/1966, but not dismantled until 1972.
		G	18/06/1862	30/10/1966		
NORWOOD YARD	86		c.1870's	c.1980's	LBSCR	Extensive freight sidings; traffic continued into 1980's but date of last use unknown.
NOTTING HILL GATE	38 / 1B		01/10/1868	N/A	MET	CLR station opened 30/07/1900 (no interchange provided). Served by District Line since 01/11/1926. Interchange facilities between Central and Circle / District Lines completed 31/07/1960. Circle / District lines platforms closed 23/07/2011 – 23/08/2011 (engineering work).
No.1 NATIONAL AIRCRAFT FACTORY	66 / 3B		1917	1924	PRIV	Factory completed 1917, first aircraft completed June 1918. Became National Aircraft Depot 1919, branch lifted 1924.
NUNHEAD	40 / 5B	P	18/09/1871	N/A	LCDR	Opened as junction station for Blackheath Hill branch, original advertised opening date 01/09/1871, hence Borley gives this as opening date. Quick states that station opening coincided with the delayed opening of the branch, on 18/09/1871. Originally three through tracks / five platform faces with reversing siding to west of station. Relocated West 03/05/1925 by SR, as a new single island platform on the site of former reversing siding. Goods yard closed 02/04/1962.
		G	18/09/1871	02/04/1962		
Nunhead Down Freight Loop	40 / 5B		N/A	N/A	NR	Proposed down freight loop utilising the never-used additional width of the viaduct between Cow Lane Junction and Nunhead. This section was planned by LCDR to be quadruple, with a line diverging at Cow Lane Junction to Walworth Road Station, but all that was built was the extra width of viaduct and a very short section of viaduct crossing the LBSCR (since demolished).
Nunhead Junction	40 / 5B		18/09/1871	N/A	LCDR	Crystal Palace (High Level) branch junction eliminated 20/09/1954.

O

Name	Page / grid		Date opened	Date closed	Opened by	Notes
OAKLEIGH PARK	5 / 6D		01/12/1873	N/A	GNR	
OAKWOOD Enfield West (Oakwood) Enfield West	8 / 5B		13/03/1933	N/A	UERL (GNPBR)	Opened as 'Enfield West', 'Oakwood' suffix added 03/05/1934, renamed 'Oakwood' 01/09/1946.
OCKENDON	32 / 5A	P	01/07/1892	N/A	LTSR	Goods yard closed 06/05/1968. Passing loop out of use 24/12/1977 – November 1978 (signal box fire).
		G	01/07/1892	06/05/1968		
OLD FORD	27 / 4C	P	01/07/1867	N/A	NLR	Goods yard opened 1868, transferred to LNWR 01/11/1870. Passenger service Dalston Junction to Poplar withdrawn 15/05/1944, 'officially' closed 23/04/1945. Goods yard closed 06/11/1967.
		G	1868	06/11/1967		
OLD KENT ROAD	40 / 3B		N/A	N/A	TFL	Proposed station on Bakerloo Line extension, safeguarded but on hold.
OLD KENT ROAD & HATCHAM Old Kent Road	40 / 4B 79		13/08/1866	01/01/1917	LBSCR	Renamed 01/02/1870.
OLD KENT ROAD GAS WORKS	40 / 3A		1892	??/05/1953	PRIV	South Metropolitan Gas Company, 3ft gauge internal railway system.
Old Kent Road Junction	40 / 4B 79 / 80		13/03/1871	N/A	LBSCR / ELR	Junction formed 13/03/1871, ELR route abandoned 30/06/1911, Old Kent Road Spur abandoned 02/11/1964 and junction eliminated. Re-established 24/06/2012 (date of line being energised to allow testing to begin).
Old Kent Road Spur	40 / 3B 79	P	N/A	N/A	LBSCR	Opened at some point in 1871, never saw regular passenger traffic (if any). Although engineered for double track, continuous double track never appears to have been present. Closed 02/11/1964.
		G	1871	02/11/1964		
Old Kew Junction	37 / 2A 19		15/02/1853	N/A	NSWJR / LSWR	Remodelled 08/11/1981 to a single-lead junction.
OLD OAK COMMON	24 / 6C 92		??/05/2030?	N/A	NR	HS2 / Elizabeth Line / Great Western Railway interchange, currently under construction on site of former HST stabling & maintenance sheds and Heathrow Express / Connect Traincare Depot. Elizabeth Line / GWR portion expected to open May 2030, HS2 2029-33 (would be terminus initially).
OLD OAK COMMON DEPOT	24 / 5D 91		c.1880	16/02/2021	GWR	First sidings appeared on site c.1880 (between 1871 and 1896 OS), initially named 'West London Sidings' adjacent to GWR main line. Old Oak Common steam shed established 17/03/1906 on area now occupied by Elizabeth Line Depot; steam allocation ceased March 1964 and shed demolished with one turntable retained for the diesel depot that was then established on that site. An HST stabling and maintenance shed was established on part of the carriage sidings September 1976 (formerly carriage shed). A depot for Heathrow Express (HEX) and later Heathrow Connect EMUs was opened at the south end of the site 19/01/1998. The diesel depot closed April 2009 and that site was used as an Elizabeth Line tunnel ring manufacturing facility (subsequently Elizabeth Line Depot, see separate entry below). The HST shed closed 09/12/2018 with the site becoming the HS2 Old Oak Common station, followed by the Heathrow Express depot 16/02/2021 with that site becoming the GWR Old Oak Common station (to open May 2030).
Old Oak Common East Junction	91 & 92		??/11/1912	N/A	GWR	
OLD OAK COMMON ELIZABETH LINE DEPOT	24 / 5C 92		01/03/2018	N/A	TFL (EL)	On site of Old Oak Common Diesel Depot; operations commenced 01/03/2018 due to Class 345 testing on GWR main line to Maidenhead (first Class 345 test run through EL Central London tunnel was 25/02/2018).
Old Oak Common Flyover	24 / 5D 91		??/11/1912	N/A	GWR	Built for light engine / empty carriage access to Old Oak Common Depot, singled 04/09/1967.
OLD OAK COMMON LANE	24 / 5C 92		2029-33	N/A	NR	Proposed station on North London Line and 'West London Orbital', providing interchange with Old Oak Common HS2 / Elizabeth Line stations

Name	Page / grid		Date opened	Date closed	Opened by	Notes
OLD OAK COMMON STEAM SHED	24 / 5C 91		*17/03/1906*	*??/03/1964*	GWR	After shed's demolition one turntable retained as part of diesel depot.
Old Oak Common West Junction	91 & 92		03/06/1903	01/01/2019	GWR	Line between here and Park Royal Tarmac terminal closed to passengers 10/12/2018 in readiness for HS2 / Old Oak Common Station construction works (last passenger train 07/12/2018). Junction severed 01/01/2019.
Old Oak Junction	24 / 5C 91		20/07/1885	1977	NSWJR / LNWR	Junction abolished 1977 (effectively moved south to Acton Wells Junctions).
OLD OAK LANE HALT	24 / 5C 91		01/10/1906	30/06/1947	GWR	Closed 01/02/1915 – 29/03/1920. 'Bay' platform on down side in use 20/10/1932 – 02/06/1940.
OLD OAK SIDINGS	24 / 4C 91 & 92		*c.1890*	Disused	NSWJR	Sidings had appeared on site by 1893 OS. Disused since at least 2013 (Quail).
OLD STREET	26 / 5D		17/11/1901	N/A	CSLR	GNCR (later Metropolitan Railway, then Northern Line, then British Rail) platforms opened 14/02/1904. CSLR platforms closed 09/08/1922 – 20/04/1924 (tunnel widening) and 01/09/1939 – 08/12/1939 (flood protection). GNCR platforms became southern terminus 06/09/1975, closed 04/10/1975, reopened by British Rail 16/08/1976 (terminus until 08/11/1976).
Olympic Park Junction	78		c.2010	N/A	NR	Appeared between 3rd and 4th edition of TrackMaps Eastern region (referred to as 'Olympia Park Junction' herein – typo?).
ONGAR	8 / 1D	P	24/04/1865	N/A	GER	Epping to Ongar transferred to LTE 25/09/1949, Electrified 18/11/1957. Between these dates passenger services provided by BR (steam). Line closed by LUL 03/10/1994 (last train 30/09/1994, no weekend service at point of closure), reopened by Epping-Ongar Railway between Ongar and North Weald 10/10/2004, closed 31/12/2007 for engineering works, reopened 25/05/2012. Goods yard closed 18/04/1966.
		G	24/04/1865	18/04/1966		
ORIENT WAY SIDINGS	27 / 1C		*30/05/2008*	N/A	NR	On site of Stratford Traction Maintenance Depot. Replaced Thornton Fields Sidings. First test train 19/05/2008, was to open 29/05/2008, but no trains stabled until 30/05/2008.
ORPINGTON	56 / 4C	P	02/03/1868	N/A	SER	Initially two platform faces on double track, although Borley states goods facilities opened with passenger station, kentrail.org.uk website states goods facilities not provided until c.1890, corroborated by contemporary OS maps. Extensively remodelled 1904 for quadrupling; engine shed and four carriage sidings provided on 'down' side and passenger facilities expanded to four through platforms and London-facing bays on the 'up' and 'down' sides. At time of electrification (c.1925), 'down' carriage sidings covered by shed and engine shed abandoned (becoming permanent way depot). Goods yard closed 07/10/1968, site then occupied by 'up' carriage sidings. Additional 'down' bay platforms 7 and 8 opened and 'down' carriage shed demolished 1992, 'up' carriage sidings lifted weekend of 13-14/03/1993.
		G	c.1890	07/10/1968		
Orpington North Junction	56 / 3C		06/06/1904	N/A	SECR	Junction formed through Chislehurst to Orpington quadrupling.
Orpington South Junction	56 / 4C		06/06/1904	N/A	SECR	Junction formed through Chislehurst to Orpington quadrupling.
OSTERLEY Osterley & Spring Grove	36 / 3B		01/05/1883	N/A	MDR	First served by Piccadilly Line 13/03/1933. Re-sited west and renamed 'Osterley' 25/03/1934. District Line service ceased 10/10/1964.
OVAL The Oval	39 / 3C		18/12/1890	N/A	CSLR	Opened as 'The Oval', prefix dropped c.1894. Also known as 'Kennington Oval' between 1890-1894. Closed 29/11/1923 - 01/12/1924 (tunnel widening) and 01/09/1939 – 24/11/1939 (flood protection).
OXFORD CIRCUS	26 / 6A		30/07/1900	N/A	CLR	UERL (BSWR) station opened 10/03/1906 (combined with original CLR station 16/08/1925). Closed to entries/exits 01/09/1939 – 20/11/1939 (installation of flood protection), but interchange remained available between Bakerloo and Central Lines. New concourse opened 1967/1968 in advance of Victoria Line opening. Victoria Line platforms opened 07/03/1969.
OXSHOTT Oxshott & Fair Mile	63 / 6A	P	02/02/1885	N/A	LSWR	Variously '- & Fair Mile', '- & Fairmile', '- for Fair Mile' and 'for Fairmilc' until becoming 'Oxshott' 13/06/1955. Goods yard closed 14/09/1959.
		G	02/02/1885	14/09/1959		
OXSHOTT BRICK WORKS	62 / 6D		*c.1885*	1958	PRIV	Works established 1866 but could not have been rail served before 02/02/1885 opening of adjacent line. Sidings present on 1895 OS, the previous 1884 OS pre-dated line opening. Production ceased 1958.
OXTED LIME WORKS	74 / 6D		*c.1890*	1971	PRIV	Standard gauge branch from the main line appeared between 1883 and 1896 OS, had disappeared by 1961 OS. Internal 2ft narrow gauge system appeared between 1896 and 1912 OS, much truncated then closed in 1971 (per Middleton Press 'Industrial Railways of the South-East').
Oxted Tunnel	74 / 6C		10/03/1884	N/A	SER / LBSCR	

P Q

Name	Page / grid		Date opened	Date closed	Opened by	Notes
PADDINGTON (GWR 1st)	25 / 6C 67 / 5C	P	04/06/1838	29/05/1854	GWR	Original GWR terminus. Replaced by Paddington (2nd) 29/05/1854 (passenger traffic), closed to goods traffic 29/12/1975.
		G	04/06/1838	29/12/1975		
PADDINGTON (GWR 2nd)	25 / 6C 67 / 6C		16/01/1854	N/A	GWR	Replaced first station (passengers only), opened to departures 16/01/1854, arrivals 29/05/1854. Post Office Railway station opened 05/12/1927, mothballed 31/05/2003. Elizabeth Line platforms opened 24/05/2022.
PADDINGTON (MET 1st) Paddington (Bishop's Road)	25 / 6C 67 / 5C		10/01/1863	N/A	MET / GWR	Suffix 'Bishop's Road' dropped, station designated 'Paddington Suburban', and rebuilt as four through roads / two island platforms 10/091933. Two middle roads became terminal 1966. Northernmost platforms 15 & 16 became LTB only and southernmost platforms 13 & 14 became BR only, and terminal, 12/11/1967. Connections between LTB and BR removed and subsequently connecting footway built between platform 12 and 13 across old trackbed. Crossover to west commissioned 02/09/2019 (replaced that at Royal Oak).
PADDINGTON (MET 2nd) Paddington (Praed Street)	25 / 6C 67 / 6C		01/10/1868	N/A	MET	Platforms on District / Circle Lines, subway to GWR station built 22/10/1887. UERL BSWR platforms added 01/12/1913 (terminus until 31/01/1915). Suffix 'Praed Street' dropped 11/07/1948 (never applied to Bakerloo Line). Circle / District lines platforms closed 23/07/2011 – 23/08/2011 (engineering work). Bakerloo Line platforms closed 02/04/2016 – 01/08/2016 (Elizabeth Line works).
PADDINGTON NEW YARD	25 / 5B 67 / 4A		13/04/1908	29/12/1972	GWR	Goods yard opened on site of former engine shed (open 02/03/1852 - 18/03/1906). Replaced by stone terminal 1974.
PALACE GATES WOOD GREEN	14 / 4C	P	07/10/1878	07/01/1963	GER	Entire Palace Gates Branch closed to passengers 07/01/1963. Goods yard opened 14/10/1878, closed 05/10/1964.
		G	14/10/1878	05/10/1964		
PALACE GATES COAL CONCENTRATION DEPOT	14 / 4C		??/07/1958	1984	PRIV	Charringtons Ltd.
PALACE OF ENGINEERING	24 / 2B 22		23/04/1924	03/12/1962	PRIV	Originally rail-served exhibition hall, later goods station
PALMERS GREEN Palmers Green & Southgate Palmer's Green	14 / 2C	P	01/04/1871	N/A	GNR	Suffix added 01/10/1876, dropped 18/03/1971. Goods yard closed 01/10/1962.
		G	01/04/1871	01/10/1962		

Name	Page / grid		Date opened	Date closed	Opened by	Notes
Park Junction	13 / 5D		24/05/1873	18/05/1957	GNR	Junction between Alexandra Palace Branch and original line to Edgware. Goods traffic ceased to Cranley Gardens 18/05/1957, after which time junction eliminated.
PARK ROYAL (GWR)	24 / 5B		15/06/1903	27/09/1937	GWR	Opened to special traffic 25/05/1903, public traffic commenced 15/06/1903. Closed 05/07/1903 – 01/05/1904 then again 01/02/1915 – 29/03/1920. Large goods yard to north (see separate entry below).
PARK ROYAL (UERL) Park Royal (Hanger Hill) Park Royal	24 / 5A		06/07/1931	N/A	UERL (DIS)	Replaced original station to north. Served by Piccadilly Line since 04/07/1932, last served District Line 22/10/1933. Suffix 'Hanger Hill' in use 01/03/1936 – 1947.
PARK ROYAL GOODS	24 / 5B		*03/06/1903*	*1982*	GWR	
PARK ROYAL & TWYFORD ABBEY Park Royal	24 / 4A		23/06/1903	06/07/1931	MDR	Briefly terminus (for five days). Suffix '& Twyford Abbey' added 01/05/1904. Replaced by current Park Royal station to south.
PARK ROYAL WEST HALT	24 / 5A		20/06/1932	15/06/1947	GWR	
Park Street Tunnels	26 / 4A		20/07/1837	N/A	LBIR	
Parks Bridge Junction	40 / 5D		01/09/1866	N/A	SER	Junction at north end of Ladywell Loop.
PARSONS GREEN	38 / 4B		01/03/1880	N/A	MDR	
PARSONS GREEN SIDINGS	38 / 4B		01/03/1880	N/A	MDR	District Line stabling sidings. 29 road adjacent to westbound platform disused since withdrawal of C Stock June 2014. Three new sidings plus an extension of the existing 28 road proposed, accommodating five more trains.
Paxton Tunnel	54 / 3A		01/08/1865	20/09/1954	LCDR	Nunhead to Crystal Palace (High Level) closed 20/09/1954.
PECKHAM COAL	40 / 4A		*23/03/1891*	*??/08/1961*	LNWR / MID	High and low level sidings connected by a wagon hoist. Traffic ceased in 1958, officially closed August 1961.
PECKHAM RYE	40 / 4A		01/12/1865	N/A	LBSCR	Entire station built by LBSCR, but LCDR-served platforms (to / from Crystal Palace H.L.) opened first 01/12/1865. LBSCR-served platforms (to / from London Bridge) opened 13/08/1866, originally 3 platforms (two up, one down), additional 'up main' platform and track removed 1933, new island platform constructed in vacant space and original side 'up local' and 'down' platforms abandoned 1961.
PECKHAM RYE DEPOT	40 / 5A		*01/02/1909*	*c.1961*	LBSCR	Originally built to accommodate stock for LBSCR South London Line overhead electrification. Site previously occupied by berthing sidings for East London Railway trains. Overhaul work transferred to Selhurst 31/12/1958, Lighter repairs continued for a further two years.
Peckham Rye Junction	40 / 5A		01/10/1868	N/A	LBSCR	
PENGE	54 / 4C		03/05/1858?	c.1860	WELCPR	Probably opened with WELCPR Bromley Junction to Shortlands line 03/05/1858. Closure date unknown, 'by end of 1860' per Quick, c.1861 per Cobb. Also referred to as 'Beckham Road', Tramlink station of that name on site today.
PENGE EAST Penge Lane Penge	54 / 3B	P	01/07/1863	N/A	LCDR	Opened as 'Penge', but listed as 'Penge Lane' in Bradshaw 1864-79 (Borley), Quick states 1864-9 & 1867. Renamed 'Penge East' 09/07/1923. Goods yard closed 07/11/1966.
		G	*01/07/1863*	*07/11/1966*		
Penge Junction	54 / 4C		01/07/1863	N/A	LCDR / WELCPR	
Penge Tunnel	54 / 3A		01/07/1863	N/A	LCDR	
PENGE WEST Penge Bridges Penge	54 / 4B	P	05/06/1839	N/A	LCRR	Opened as 'Penge' with line 05/06/1839, closed c.1841 (Borley), or 'probably by mid-1840' (Quick). Reopened 01/07/1863, listed as 'Penge Bridges' in Bradshaw 1864 - 1879. Suffix 'West' added 09/07/1923. Goods yard closed 04/05/1964.
		G	*01/07/1863*	*04/05/1964*		
Pepper Hill Tunnel	59 / 3C		14/11/2007	N/A	LCOR	
PERIVALE (GWR) Perivale Halt	23 / 4C		01/05/1904	15/06/1947	GWR	Closed 01/02/1915 – 29/03/1920 and again for good 15/06/1947 (replaced by Perivale [LPTB] to the east). Carried 'Halt' suffix until 1927.
PERIVALE (LPTB)	23 / 4C		30/06/1947	N/A	LPTB (CEN)	
Perry Street Fork Junction	43 / 5C		01/05/1895	N/A	BHR	Junction at south end of Erith Loop.
PETTS WOOD	56 / 6A	P	09/07/1928	N/A	SR	Goods yard closed 07/10/1968.
		G	*09/07/1928*	*07/10/1968*		
Petts Wood Junctions Orpington Junction	56 / 6A		08/09/1902	N/A	SECR	Junctions at southern ends of Tonbridge Loops, originally 'Orpington Junction', renamed 'Petts Wood' upon opening of latter station (09/07/1928). 'Slow' junction made 08/09/1902, 'Fast' 14/09/1902.
Petts Wood South Junction	56 / 2B		?	N/A	BR?	
PHIPPS BRIDGE	52 / 5C		30/05/2000	N/A	CTL	
PICCADILLY CIRCUS	26 / 6A		10/03/1906	N/A	UERL (BSWR)	UERL (GNPBR) platforms opened 15/12/1906, extensively rebuilt 10/12/1928 (original buildings closed 21/07/1929). Became temporary terminus of Bakerloo Line 11/11/1996 – 14/07/1997 (closure south of here due to tunnel strengthening works).
PIG HILL SIDINGS	89		*c.1868*	N/A	WLER	Laid at approximately same time as Falcon Lane Goods' opening.
PIMLICO (LTE)	39 / 3B		14/09/1972	N/A	LTE (VIC)	Closed 20/03/2020 – 18/05/2020 (COVID-19).
PIMLICO (WELCPR)	39 / 3A 82		29/03/1858	01/10/1860	WELCPR	Original terminus of WELCPR (later LBSCR). Closed when VSPR route to Victoria station opened.
PINNER	10 / 4D	P	25/05/1885	N/A	MET	Country terminus of Metropolitan Railway until 01/09/1887. Goods yard closed 03/04/1967.
		G	*25/05/1885*	*03/04/1967*		
PITLAKE	66 / 2C		*26/07/1803*	*31/08/1846*	SIR	Croydon terminus of SIR and junction with CMGR.
PLAISTOW	28 / 4B	P	31/03/1858	N/A	LTSR	First served by District Railway 02/06/1902, line quadrupled 1905, District trains then using 'slow' platforms to north. Served by Metropolitan Line since 30/03/1936 ('Hammersmith & City Line' since 30/07/1990). Main line services non-stopped since 15/06/1962, and 'Fast' platforms abandoned. Goods yard closed 01/05/1953.
		G	*31/03/1858*	*01/05/1953*		
PLAISTOW MOTIVE POWER DEPOT	28 / 5B		*30/09/1911*	*??/06/1962*	LTSR	Steam shed replacing original 1899 shed adjacent to Plaistow Works, closed when steam traction withdrawn.
PLAISTOW WORKS	28 / 4B		*1880*	*1932*	LTSR	LTSR locomotive works, ceased servicing locos 1925, remained as servicing point for wagons until 1932. Buildings remained in use as rail-served works thereafter ('Toy works' and 'Pressed hinge works' on 1939 OS).
PLAISTOW & WEST HAM GOODS	28 / 6A		*01/10/1906*	*06/08/1984*	GER	Connection to main line taken out of use 13/06/1984, 'official' closure date 06/08/1984. Date of last train unknown.
PLASSER WORKS (WEST EALING)	23 / 6C		*1969*	N/A	PRIV	Assembly of railway equipment, manufacture since 1977. Formerly GWR signal engineers works (c.1900's); latter had a staff halt in use post-1905 until pre-11/1915.
PLUMSTEAD	42 / 2B	P	16/07/1859	N/A	SER	Goods yard closed 04/12/1967. Reopened 08/12/1971, mainly for paper and coal traffic and subsequently became a S&T depot. The last traffic is believed to have been MoD traffic operated by EWS in 1998 (BLN1421). The goods yard site was then developed as part of the Elizabeth Line Plumstead Railhead, accessed via Plumstead Depot head shunt. Access was removed circa Elizabeth Line opening to revenue traffic 24/05/2022. By April 2023 the sidings had been lifted; to be replaced by a DCRail aggregates terminal with two long sidings and a cripple siding (BLN1421).
		G	*16/07/1859*	*04/12/1967*		

Name	Page / grid		Date opened	Date closed	Opened by	Notes
PLUMSTEAD DEPOT and INFRASTUCTURE MAINTENANCE FACILITY *PLUMSTEAD RAILHEAD*	42 / 2C		*2015*	N/A	TFL (EL)	Initially part of railhead for Elizabeth Line construction traffic, concreting train arrived on site 2015. Closed 28/09/2017 for conversion to maintenance facility and stabling point (revenue service commenced 24/05/2022).
Plumstead East Junction	42 / 2C		*2015*	N/A	NR	Junction established for Elizabeth Line construction traffic, then became junction providing access to Plumstead Depot.
Point Pleasant Junction	38 / 5B		01/07/1889	N/A	LSWR	'Up' line abandoned 04/04/1987, bridge demolished 1990 (poor condition). 'Down' line bi-directional since 11/02/1991.
PONDERS END	7 / 5C	P	15/09/1840	N/A	NER	Goods yard closed 02/11/1964. Current 'up' platform to become a bidirectional loop line, with a new 'up' line and platform being opened to the east of the existing platform (expected 12/05/2024).
		G	*15/09/1840*	*02/11/1964*		
PONTOON DOCK	41 / 1C 62 / 5B		02/12/2005	N/A	DLR	
POPLAR (LBLR)	41 / 1A 31 / 4C		06/07/1840	04/05/1926	LBLR	Passenger service to Blackwall withdrawn 04/05/1926.
POPLAR (EWIDBJR - Did Not Open)	40 / 1D 31 / 4B		N/A	N/A	EWIDBJR	Platforms constructed 1851 but station did not open.
POPLAR (NLR) Poplar (East India Road)	27 / 6D 31 / 4B		01/08/1866	15/05/1944	NLR	Station initially carried suffix '(East India Road)' to distinguish from the first, unopened, EWIDBJR station to the south. Operated as terminus for service ex-Broad Street except between 01/09/1870 - 01/07/1890 when some trains continued to Blackwall. Passenger service Dalston Junction to Poplar withdrawn 15/05/1944, 'official' closure did not occur until 23/04/1945. Present-day DLR 'All Saints' station built on same site.
POPLAR (DLR)	40 / 1D 31 / 6B		31/08/1987	N/A	DLR	Reconstructed with four platforms 28/03/1994 (Beckton extension). Name boards carry suffix 'for Tower Hamlets College' (suffix not on TfL map).
POPLAR DEPOT	40 / 1D 31 / 6B		31/08/1987	N/A	DLR	Original DLR Depot.
POPLAR DOCK GOODS (GNR)	40 / 1D 31 / 5C		*01/09/1878*	*1968*	GNR	
POPLAR DOCK GOODS (GWR)	40 / 1D 31 / 4C		*01/04/1878*	*1940*	GWR	
POPLAR DOCK GOODS (MID)	41 / 1A 31 / 5C		*01/12/1882*	*04/05/1956*	MID	Suffix 'Riverside' added by BR January 1951.
Poplar Junction	31 / 4C		01/12/1882	c.1961	LBLR	East India / Blackwall (GNR) Goods closed c.1961.
Portland Place	39 / 4C		22/10/1923	29/11/1923	UERL (CSLR)	During the widening of the CSLR tunnels, waterlogged gravel leakage between Oval and Stockwell resulted in single line working being introduced to allow compressed air working in one tunnel at a time. Temporary crossovers were installed at South Island Place (Jul/Aug 1923) and Portland Place (Sep 1923), and single line working commenced 22/10/1923. On 27/11/1923 a partial tunnel collapse and resulting gas explosion north of Elephant & Castle resulted in the CSLR being operated as two shuttles, before the entire line was suspended 29/11/1923 until 01/12/1924. As both crossovers were built for smaller CSLR loading gauge, they did not reopen.
Portobello Junction	25 / 5B		16/01/1854	N/A	GWR	Originally divergence of routes into original and current Paddington termini.
Potters Bar Tunnels	5 / 1C		07/08/1850	N/A	GNR	Original bore is today's 'Up' tunnel, 'Down' bore added 03/05/1959.
Pouparts Junction	38 / 4D 82		01/12/1867	N/A	LBSCR	Junction between original WELCPR route to Pimlico and subsequent route to Victoria.
POYLE ESTATE HALT	34 / 4A		04/01/1954	29/03/1965	BR	
POYLE FOR STANWELL MOOR HALT Stanwell Moor & Poyle Halt	34 / 5A		01/06/1927	29/03/1965	GWR	Renamed 26/09/1927.
Praed Street Junction	25 / 6C		01/10/1868	N/A	MET	No service towards High Street Kensington 23/07/2011 - 23/08/2011 (engineering works).

PRESTON ROAD
   Preston Road for Uxendon
   Preston Road for Uxendon and Kenton
	12 / 6A		21/05/1908	N/A	MET	Opened with 'for Uxendon and Kenton' suffix, 'and Kenton' dropped 01/07/1923, 'for Uxendon' dropped c.1924. Southbound / Up platform re-sited north 22/11/1931, Northbound re-sited north 03/01/1932.

PRIMROSE HILL
   Chalk Farm
   Hampstead Road
	25 / 3D
	58
			09/06/1851	23/09/1992	EWIDBJR	The three incarnations of this station have all been on the same site. The first 'Hampstead Road' station was on the original EWIDBJR single track route through Camden Goods Station and consisted of a single platform with run-around loop. The EWIDBJR (by then NLR) was re-routed slightly to the north and doubled, necessitating a new station being built on the realigned route 05/05/1855 (connected to 'Camden' station by footbridge at this time). This new station was the same distance east of the Junction with the LBIR. Renamed 'Chalk Farm' 01/12/1862. Rebuilt 1871-1872 (works complete 24/05/1872); although the new station extended further west than its predecessor, the third site almost completely overlapped the second. Closed 01/01/1917 - 10/07/1922, southern island platform closed 1922 per Borley (presumably it simply did not reopen?). Renamed 'Primrose Hill' 25/09/1950. Station was due to close when Watford Junction to Liverpool Street service withdrawn, but trains ceased calling prematurely due to flooding (last eastbound 18/09/1992, last westbound 22/09/1992).

Primrose Hill Junction	58		10/07/1922	N/A	LNWR	
Primrose Hill Tunnels	25 / 3D 58		20/07/1837	N/A	LBIR	Second tunnel added 02/06/1879, third tunnel added 10/07/1922.
PRINCE REGENT	41 / 1C 62 / 5B		28/03/1994	N/A	DLR	Platform name boards carry suffix 'for ExCeL East' and on-train recorded announcements state 'for ExCeL East and ICC London', but no suffix appears on TfL map. Closed 30/03/2020 – 11/05/2020 (COVID-19 – ExCeL converted to a 'Nightingale' Hospital).
PRINCESS ROYAL DISTRIBUTION CENTRE	24 / 3B 68 / 3D		*30/09/1996*	N/A	PRIV	Royal Mail depot.
PUDDING MILL LANE	27 / 4D 88		15/01/1996	N/A	DLR	Planned opening 02/01/1996, but delayed. Closed 14/07/2012 – 13/09/2012 (Olympic & Paralympic games) and again 18/04/2014, reopening 28/04/2014 on a new site to the south on a new alignment (this resulted in a line closure north of Bow Church for this period).
Pudding Mill Lane Junction	27 / 4D		06/11/2022	N/A	NR	Whitechapel to Stratford opened to passengers 06/11/2022, although the junction was installed since 25/09/2017 (up) / 12/11/2017 (down), signalling commissioned 07/03/2018, and the junction commissioned 25/04/2021.
PURFLEET	44 / 3B	P	13/04/1854	N/A	LTSR	Goods yard closed 02/11/1964 (although adjacent oil terminal remained open significantly longer). Proposed to be moved slightly to the north in connection with adjacent redevelopment and replacement of existing level crossing by a bridge. Associated name change to 'Purfleet-on-Thames' also possible.
		G	*13/04/1854*	*02/11/1964*		
PURFLEET STONE TERMINAL (FOSTER YEOMAN)	44 / 4C		?	N/A	PRIV	Deep Water Wharf.
PURFLEET RIFLE RANGE HALT	44 / 2B		??/10/1921	31/05/1941	LTSR	Opened to public October 1921, but had been served as required since July 1910 for military traffic.
PURFLEET THAMES TERMINAL	44 / 4C		c.1960's	N/A	PRIV	Deep Water Wharf (containers).

Name	Page / grid		Date opened	Date closed	Opened by	Notes

PURLEY
  Caterham Junction
  Godstone Road, Caterham Junction
  Godstone Road
	66 / 5C	P
		G
			12/07/1841
			12/07/1841
				N/A
				06/01/1969
					LBRR	Opened as 'Godstone Road', closed to passengers 01/10/1847 - 05/08/1856. Reopened 05/08/1856 as 'Godstone Road, Caterham Junction'. Renamed 'Caterham Junction' October 1856, then 'Purley' 01/10/1888. Goods yard closed to general traffic 06/01/1969, coal continued (Charringtons), ceased 22/06/1991. Brett Marine stone terminal established in late 1970's (between 1977 & 1980 Baker). Day & Sons aggregate terminal remains.

Purley Chipstead Line Junction	66 / 6C		21/11/1897	N/A	SER	
PURLEY DOWNS GOLF CLUB HALT	66 / 5D		1914	c.1926	LBSCR / SECR	No OS evidence, but believed to have been sited on Purley Downs Road. Golfers only; request stop. Golf club's website states: '…for a dozen or so years after 1914, the club had its own request stop on the line.'
Purley North Junction	66 / 5C		?	N/A	LBSCR	
PURLEY OAKS	66 / 5D		05/11/1899	N/A	LBSCR	
Purley South Junction	66 / 5C		05/08/1856	N/A	CR / LBSCR	
PUTNEY	38 / 5A		27/07/1846	N/A	LSWR	Expanded to four platforms 1886 (quadrupling).

PUTNEY BRIDGE
  Putney Bridge & Hurlingham
  Putney Bridge & Fulham
	38 / 5A		01/03/1880	N/A	MDR	Opened as 'Putney Bridge & Fulham' as terminus of MDR extension from West Brompton. Extension to Wimbledon opened 03/06/1889 by LSWR, although no LSWR trains used route north of East Putney. Suffix '& Fulham' replaced by '& Hurlingham' 01/09/1902, station re-arranged 1910. Suffix '& Hurlingham' dropped 1932. Bay platform 2 last used 02/06/2014 (withdrawal of shorter C Stock trains), lifted and points removed over weekend of 13-14/06/2015. Westbound road then re-routed via former bay, and original westbound route abandoned from 31/05/2016, to lift speed restriction.

QUAKER OATS (SOUTHALL)	36 / 1A		?	?	PRIV	
Quarry Tunnel	73 / 5A		05/11/1899	N/A	LBSCR	
QUEENS PARK Queens Park (West Kilburn)	25 / 4B	P G	02/06/1879 02/06/1879	N/A 06/07/1964	LNWR	Served by Bakerloo Line since 11/02/1915 (terminus until 10/05/1915). LNWR mainline platforms closed 01/01/1917 but retained for occasional use. Suffix 'West Kilburn' dropped by 1954 (never applied to Bakerloo Line). Goods yard (to west of station between DC lines and LNWR main lines) opened with passenger station, closed 06/07/1964.
QUEEN'S ROAD	27 / 2B		N/A	N/A	GER	Platforms built 1875 but station did not open, formally abandoned 1895. Also referred to as 'Queen's Down Road' and 'Down Road, Clapton'. Platforms demolished c.1965.
QUEENS ROAD GOODS Boundary Road Goods	15 / 6D		01/09/1894	06/05/1960	MID	Opened as 'Boundary Road Goods', but renamed 'Queen's Road Goods' late in 1894.
QUEENS ROAD PECKHAM Peckham	40 / 4B		13/08/1866	N/A	LBSCR	Renamed 01/12/1866. Opened with three platform faces / tracks, middle track / platform taken out of use 1933. Rebuilt with island platform on space vacated by middle track 1977, side platforms demolished.
QUEENSTOWN ROAD BATTERSEA Queens Road Battersea	39 / 4A 82		01/11/1877	N/A	LSWR	Renamed 12/05/1980.
QUEENSBURY	12 / 4A		16/12/1934	N/A	LPTB (MET)	Opened by LPTB Metropolitan Line. Transferred to Bakerloo Line 20/11/1939, Jubilee Line 01/05/1979.
QUEENSWAY Queens Road	25 / 5C		30/07/1900	N/A	CLR	Renamed 01/09/1946. Following complete closure of Central Line 26/01/2003 due to Chancery Lane derailment the day before (see footnote), station reopened four days after the line (28/03/2003). Closed 11/10/2003 – 29/10/2003 (lift repairs), 08/05/2005 – 14/06/2006 (lift replacement), and 20/03/2020 – 06/07/2020 (COVID-19).

R

Name	Page / grid		Date opened	Date closed	Opened by	Notes
RADLETT	3 / 1C	P G	13/07/1868 Post 09/09/1867	N/A 25/03/1968	MID	Goods yard opened before passenger station (date unknown but line opened to goods 09/09/1867 so no earlier than this date), and was initially named 'Aldenham' prior to passenger opening. Goods yard closed 25/03/1968.
Radlett Junction	3 / 2D		?	N/A	?	
RAINHAM	30 / 6C	P G	13/04/1854 13/04/1854	N/A 04/10/1965	LTSR	Station re-sited south 1962, new platforms on original goods yard site. Replacement goods yard closed 04/10/1965.
RANELAGH BRIDGE DEPOT	25 / 6C 67 / 5B		1907	1980	GWR	Depot for stabling locomotives, converted from steam to diesel April 1964.
RAVENSBOURNE	55 / 4A	P G	01/07/1892 01/07/1892	N/A 04/09/1961	LCDR	Goods yard closed 04/09/1961.
RAVENSCOURT PARK Shaftesbury Road	37 / 2D		01/04/1873	N/A	LSWR	Opened by LSWR. First served MDR 01/06/1877. Served by MET 01/10/1877 – 01/01/1911 (MET / GWR joint after 01/01/1894). Renamed 01/03/1888. Rebuilt from two side platforms to two island platforms when route quadrupled 03/12/1911 (LSWR northern island, MDR southern island). LSWR service ceased and northern island abandoned 05/06/1916. Eastbound District Line started using north face of north island from 05/06/1932. Piccadilly Line started running non-stop through middle platforms 04/07/1932. Served by Piccadilly Line 26/12/2013 – 30/12/2013 (District Line engineering works).
Ray Street Gridiron	32 / 2B		17/02/1868	N/A	MET	Widened Lines dive-under, replaced by a concrete raft 1960.
RAYNERS LANE Rayners Lane Halt	10 / 6D	P G	26/05/1906 26/05/1906	N/A 10/08/1964	MET	Served by District Line Trains 01/03/1910 – 23/10/1933, Piccadilly Line thereafter. 'Halt' suffix dropped 1934/5. Goods yard closed 10/08/1964.
Rayners Lane Junction	11 / 6A		01/03/1910	N/A	MET / MDR	Rayners Lane to South Harrow built by Metropolitan Railway 1904, but no regular trains until MDR service commenced in 01/03/1910.
RAYNES PARK	51 / 4D	P G	30/10/1871 c.1900	N/A 04/12/1967	LSWR	From the 04/04/1859 opening of the LSWR Epsom route there was a junction at this location with no station (initially 'Wimbledon Junction'). Subsequent to station opening 30/10/1871, new 'up' platforms constructed due to diveunder for up Epsom line (opened 16/03/1884). Date of goods yard opening uncertain: Borley states open with passenger station, but no yard is apparent on 1897-8 OS (had appeared on 1913 OS). Yard closed 04/12/1967, but sidings retained for use as a permanent way depot until late 1983.
Raynes Park Junction Wimbledon Junction	51 / 4D		04/04/1859	N/A	LSWR	Junction between LSWR main line and Epsom line. Initially named 'Wimbledon Junction'.
Reading Lane Junction	27 / 3B		30/06/1986	N/A	BR	Junction at south end of Graham Road Curve.
RECTORY ROAD	27 / 2A		27/05/1872	N/A	GER	Closed 09/12/1972 – 17/01/1973 (fire).
REDBRIDGE	16 / 6D		14/12/1947	N/A	LPTB (CEN)	Closed 21/03/2020 – 06/07/2020 (COVID-19).

Name	Page / grid		Date opened	Date closed	Opened by	Notes

REDHILL
  Red Hill Junction
  Reigate
	73 / 5C		29/01/1844	N/A	SER	First served by SER trains 29/01/1844 as 'Reigate', allowing original SER Reigate station south of the SER / LBRR junction to close. Building from original station moved to this location during February 1844, fully opened 05/03/1844. LBRR trains began calling here 15/04/1844, allowing their original station to south to close. Rebuilt 1858 and renamed 'Red Hill Junction'. Became 'Redhill' 07/07/1929 (before this date variously 'Red Hill' / 'Redhill' / 'Reigate' with 'Junction' sometimes added per Quick). Separate goods yards associated with original LBRR and SER stations (see entries for 'Reigate'), supplemented by larger yard in vee between Tonbridge and Brighton Lines, appeared on OS between 1896 and 1913 surveys so presumably opened c. time of Quarry Line opening 1899. Post Office and Down sidings on down side (adjacent to Platform 3) removed 27/02/2017. Extensively remodelled and new through Platform 0 opened 02/01/2018, Platform 1 becoming a bay at this time.

Redhill Tunnel	73 / 5C		05/11/1899	N/A	LBSCR	
REEDHAM Reedham Halt	66 / 6B		01/03/1911	N/A	SECR	Closed 01/01/1917 – 01/01/1919. 'Halt' dropped 05/07/1936.
REEDHAM SIDINGS	73 / 1B		c.1899	N/A	LBSCR	Appear to have been laid c. time of Quarry Line opening.
REEVES CORNER	66 / 2C		10/05/2000	N/A	CTL	
Regent's Canal Junction	76		14/11/2007	N/A	LCOR / NR	
REGENT'S PARK	26 / 5A		10/03/1906	N/A	UERL (BSWR)	Closed 11/07/2006 – 13/06/2007 (lift replacement), and 21/03/2020 – 27/07/2020 (COVID-19).

REIGATE (LBRR)
  Red Hill
  Red-Hill & Reigate Road
	73 / 6C	P	12/07/1841	15/04/1844	LBRR	First station in Reigate area, opened with LBRR route Croydon Junction to Haywards Heath, situated on Hooley Lane. Platforms were situated on loops off the main line. Closed when LBRR trains began serving present-day Redhill station north of junction with SER 15/04/1844. Opened as 'Red-Hill & Reigate Road', before being shortened to 'Red Hill', named 'Reigate' at point of closure. Goods yard depicted on OS until 1963-8, unknown when public goods traffic ceased.

		G	12/07/1841	c.1965		
REIGATE (SER)	73 / 6C	P	26/05/1842	29/01/1844	SER	Second station in Reigate area, situated immediately south of SER / LBRR junction. Closed when SER trains first began to serve present-day Redhill station, allowing first station building to be dismantled and rebuilt at new site. Goods yard closed 28/09/1964.
		G	26/05/1842	28/09/1964		
REMENHAM SIDING	33 / 5B		c.1920's	c.1930's	PRIV	Served a gravel pit. Does not appear on OS maps before 1926 or after 1938.
Renwick Road Junction	29 / 5C		Pre 2004	N/A	LCOR / NR?	Had been installed by 2004 Baker (absent from 2001) in anticipation of opening of HS1 Section 2.
RICHMOND	36 / 5D	P	27/07/1846	N/A	LSWR	Opened as country terminus of branch from Battersea Junction (east of current Clapham Junction station), goods facilities assumed to have opened at same time as passenger station. Original terminus given over wholly to goods traffic and new through platforms built to north on extension to Datchet 22/08/1848. New five-platform terminus opened to north of 22/08/1848 station 01/01/1869 to coincide with opening of line from Kensington (Addison Road). First served MDR 01/06/1877, then MET 01/10/1877. MET service ceased from 01/01/1907. Original 1846 terminus closed to goods traffic 1936 and demolished, new goods station opening north-east of 1869 passenger station November 1936. 1848 and 1869 portions of station rebuilt and combined 01/08/1937. November 1936 goods station (on page 37 / 5A) closed 06/05/1968. Centre road between platforms 3 and 4 taken out of use 1970.
		G	27/07/1846	06/05/1968		
Richmond Bridge	36 / 5D		22/08/1848	N/A	LSWR	
RICHMOND GASWORKS	37 / 5A		1882	1933	PRIV	
Richmond Junction (Kensington)	38 / 1A 83		01/01/1869	05/06/1916	LSWR / WLR	Junction between WLR and LSWR Richmond branch.
Richmond Junction (Richmond)	37 / 5A		01/01/1869	28/12/1972	LSWR	Direct connection between lines ex-Kew Gardens and ex-North Sheen eliminated 28/12/1972. Indirect link via Richmond station platform 3 established 1985 for stock transfer between North London Line and Selhurst Depot, but eliminated 07/12/2015.
RICHMOND MAIN SEWERAGE BOARD RWY.	37 / 4A		1887	c.1950	PRIV	Tramway between pumping house and dock accessing The Thames (dock since filled in), 2ft 9in gauge. Works opened 1891, but tramway recorded as being in operation 1887 – c.1950 (source = The British Internal Combustion Locomotive 1894-1940 – Webb, Brian 1973).
RICKMANSWORTH	1 / 6C	P	01/09/1887	N/A	MET	Country terminus of MET until 08/07/1889. Goods yard closed 14/11/1966.
		G	01/09/1887	14/11/1966		
RICKMANSWORTH (CHURCH STREET) Rickmansworth	1 / 6C	P	01/10/1862	03/03/1952	WRR	Branch from Watford Junction; closed to passengers 03/03/1952, goods 02/01/1967. Suffix 'Church Street' in use from 25/09/1950 until closure.
		G	01/10/1862	02/01/1967		
RICKMANSWORTH NORTH SIDINGS	1 / 5C		c.1890	N/A	MET	Stabling Sidings for Metropolitan Line, first siding on site by 1896 OS.
RICKMANSWORTH SOUTH SIDINGS	1 / 5C		c.1960	N/A	LTE (MET)?	Not present on 1938 OS, but had appeared by 1961/2 (possibly commissioned for 1960 Amersham electrification?).
RIDDLESDOWN	66 / 6D		05/06/1927	N/A	SR	
Riddlesdown Tunnel	66 / 6D		10/03/1884	N/A	LBSCR / SER	
RIPPLE LANE EXCHANGE SIDINGS	29 / 5C		Pre 2004	N/A	LCOR / NR?	Had been installed by 2004 Baker (absent from 2001) in anticipation of opening of HS1 Section 2.
RIPPLE LANE TMD	29 / 5D		c.1960	1993	BR	Four-road diesel shed. Site obliterated by Barking Riverside viaduct.
Ripple Lane West Yard Junction	29 / 4C		c.1940?	N/A	LMS?	Presumably installed in conjunction with Ripple Lane Yard opening.
RIPPLE LANE YARD	29 / 5D		c.1940	N/A	LMS	Opened c.1940, main line tracks diverted around site 27/05/1960, reconstructed as 'Hump' marshalling yard 1961, closed 1968 and replaced by Freightliner Terminal (opened 1972).
RODING VALLEY	16 / 2C		03/02/1936	N/A	LNER	Fairlop (later Hainault) Loop closed by LNER 30/11/1947 to allow electrification and transfer to LTE Central Line. Station reopened 21/11/1948 by LTE following electrification.
Rolt Street Junction	40 / 3C 79 / 80		01/04/1880	N/A	ELR	SER service to Liverpool Street via ELR commenced 01/04/1880. Rolt Street Junction to New Cross (SER) became bi-directional (former 'down' only spur) 01/10/1884 when ELR bay platform opened at New Cross. 'Up' spur remained in use for goods / through traffic until 16/04/1966. After this date junction became the point where double track ex-Canal Junction becomes single bi-directional track to New Cross.
ROMFORD	18 / 6C	P	20/06/1839	N/A	ECR	Carried the suffix 'for Hornchurch, Upminster & Corbet's Tey' according to Dewick, but no other reference found. Platform for Upminster originally a separate LTSR station, opening 07/06/1893, combined 01/04/1934. Goods yard currently engineer's depot, closure date to goods traffic unknown.
		G	20/06/1839	?		
ROMFORD FACTORY (latterly 'Railstore')	19 / 5A		1843	c.2003	ECR	ECR's locomotive works until 1847 (when relocated to Stratford) then wagon cover factory after 1854. Buildings became 'Railstore' and the sidings were resignalled with the adjacent route in 1992. Railstore continued in operation until c.2003 and the sidings were disconnected c.2005.

Name	Page / grid		Date opened	Date closed	Opened by	Notes
Romford Junction	18 / 6C		07/06/1893	N/A	LTSR / GER	Removed 1930's, reinstated 21/07/1940.
ROSHERVILLE HALT Rosherville	60 / 1A		10/05/1886	16/07/1933	LCDR	Suffix 'Halt' added 17/06/1928.
ROTHERHITHE	40 / 1B		07/12/1869	N/A	ELR	First served MET & MDR 01/10/1884, last served MDR 01/08/1905, no service MET 03/12/1906 – 31/03/1913. Separate 'East London Line' identity introduced during 1980's. Closed 26/03/1995 – 25/03/1998 and 23/12/2007 – 27/04/2010 (engineering work), upon latter reopening became TfL (LO)
ROYAL ALBERT	41 / 1C 62 / 5B		28/03/1994	N/A	DLR	Station name boards have suffix 'for West Beckton' which is also added to on-train recorded announcements, but it does not appear on TfL map.
ROYAL ARMY SERVICE CORPS DEPOT (FELTHAM)	49 / 1B		c.1930	1958	PRIV	Absent on 1920 OS, but present on 1932. Branch partly tramway, passing west side of 'The Green' and along Browells Lane. Disused after 1958.
Royal Arsenal Narrow Gauge Railway (RANG)	29 / 6D		23/06/2019	N/A	PRIV	An 18in gauge railway constructed for the preservation of loco 'Woolwich', which formerly worked in the Woolwich Arsenal railway complex (see below). Opening date of 23/06/2019 given in BLN1334.
ROYAL ARSENAL RAILWAY (WOOLWICH)	42 / 2C		1859	1967	SER	A network of Standard, 18in, and Mixed gauge lines covering the Plumstead and Erith Marshes. First Standard gauge lines laid by SER 1859, followed by 18in Narrow gauge from 1871 onwards. After a zenith during WW1, operations were wound down until eventual closure in 1967. Passenger trains ran within the system for workmen
ROYAL BETHLEM HOSPITAL	67 / 1C		1928	1930	PRIV	1.2km siding from Eden Park in use during construction of the Hospital, abandoned when construction completed.
Royal Curve	33 / 1C	P	Late 1890's	??.01.1917	GWR	Predominantly Royal and excursion trains; advertised passenger services were carried from the late 1890's until January 1917.
		G	08/10/1849	26/07/1970		
ROYAL DOCKYARD (WOOLWICH)	41 / 2D		c.1880	c.1962	PRIV	Branch to dockyard not apparent on 1873 OS, but had appeared by 1896, so approximate 1880 opening assumed. Still in use 11/07/1961 (Middleton Press album 'Charing Cross to Dartford'), but abandoned by 1962 and the tunnel under Woolwich Church Street blocked.
ROYAL MINT STREET GOODS	74 / 2B		01/08/1858	01/04/1951	LBLR	Tower Gateway DLR station occupies much of site.
Royal Mint Street Junction	27 / 6A 74 / 2C		29/07/1991	N/A	DLR	Divergence of DLR Bank extension from original route to Tower Gateway.
ROYAL OAK	25 / 6C 67 / 5B		30/10/1871	N/A	MET / GWR	Last GWR service called 01/10/1934. Ownership transferred to LTE 01/01/1970. Closed 11/04/2015 – 11/05/2015 (staircase replacement). Crossover west of station decommissioned 02/09/2019.
ROYAL SHOWGROUND	24 / 4B		13/06/1903	05/07/1903	LNWR	Only open for duration of Royal Agricultural Society show 1903.
ROYAL VICTORIA	41 / 1B 62 / 5A		28/03/1994	N/A	DLR	
RUGBY ROAD	37 / 1C		08/04/1909	01/01/1917	NSWJR	
RUISLIP	10 / 6B	P	04/07/1904	N/A	MET	Served by District Line Trains 01/03/1910 – 23/10/1933, Piccadilly Line thereafter. Goods yard closed 10/08/1964.
		G	04/07/1904	10/08/1964		
RUISLIP DEPOT	22 / 1B		21/11/1948	N/A	LTE (CEN)	Depot for Central Line and Transplant (Engineering). A connection to the Metropolitan Line via Ruislip reversing siding was opened 24/07/1973.
RUISLIP GARDENS	22 / 1B		09/07/1934	N/A	GWR / LNER	Platforms on 'slow' GWR / LNER lines only (South Ruislip to West Ruislip formerly quadruple). LTE Central Line platforms added 21/11/1948, BR platforms closed 21/07/1959.
RUISLIP LIDO RAILWAY	10 / 4A		1946	N/A	PRIV	1ft gauge miniature railway, first section (Woody Bay to a point halfway to Eleanor's Loop) opened 1946. Closed 1978-1980 following an accident, upon reopening extended to Eleanor's Loop (1986), then Haste Hill (21/07/1990), and finally Willow Lawn (originally Ruislip Lido) in 1997.
RUISLIP MANOR Ruislip Manor Halt	10 / 6B		05/08/1912	N/A	MET	Served by District Line trains from opening to 23/10/1933, Piccadilly Line thereafter. Closed 12/02/1917 – 01/04/1919. Suffix 'Halt' until 1934/5. Southbound platform closed 03/01/2005 – 09/07/2005, northbound closed 10/07/2005 – 22/12/2005.
RUSHETT	63 / 5D		N/A	N/A	SR	One of two intermediate stations on Chessington South to Leatherhead route, works abandoned at outset of WW2.
RUSSELL SQUARE	26 / 5B		15/12/1906	N/A	UERL (GNPBR)	

S

Name	Page / grid		Date opened	Date closed	Opened by	Notes
ST ANN'S ROAD	14 / 6D		02/10/1882	09/08/1942	THJR	
ST HELIER	52 / 6B	P	05/01/1930	N/A	SR	Goods yard closed 06/05/1963.
		G	05/01/1930	06/05/1963		
ST HELIER ESTATE RAILWAY	65 / 1C		1928	1936	LCC	Railway system built by the LCC to convey building materials to the then under construction St Helier Estate.
St James Road Junction	66 / 1D 86		22/05/1865	16/05/1983	LBSCR	Junction at southern end of West Croydon Spur.
ST JAMES'S PARK	39 / 1B		24/12/1868	N/A	MDR	Also spelt 'St James' Park'. Rebuilt 1927-1929 (construction of 55 Broadway). Closed 21/03/2020 – 16/08/2020 (COVID-19).
ST JAMES STREET WALTHAMSTOW	15 / 5C		26/04/1870	N/A	GER	Originally single platform on 'up' side, Shern Hall Street to Clapton Junction doubled 1873 and 'down' platform built.
ST JOHNS	40 / 4D		01/06/1873	N/A	SER	Originally had three island platforms with six faces onto five tracks, southernmost island abandoned 1926, then middle ('fast') island demolished 1973 and 'fast' roads straightened. Now only 'slow' island remains, with two faces.
ST JOHN'S WOOD	25 / 4C		20/11/1939	N/A	LPTB (BAK)	Replaced Marlborough Road Station to north. Named 'Acacia Road' until opening. Opened by Bakerloo Line, transferred to Jubilee Line 01/05/1979. Closed March to May 1989 due to escalator replacement.
St John's Wood Tunnel	25 / 4C		15/03/1899	N/A	GCR	
ST MARGARETS	36 / 6C		02/10/1876	N/A	LSWR	Additional 'up' platform added 26/11/1899.
ST MARY CRAY	56 / 6C	P	03/12/1860	N/A	LCDR	Rebuilt with four platforms due to quadrupling 31/05/1959. Goods yard closed 07/10/1968.
		G	03/12/1860	07/10/1968		
St Mary Cray Junctions	56 / 5A 56 / 6A		19/06/1904	N/A	SECR	Junctions at southern end of Chatham Loops.
ST MARY'S (WHITECHAPEL ROAD) St Mary's	27 / 6B 90		03/03/1884	01/05/1938	SER	First served by SER trains ex-ELR (terminus), withdrawn 01/10/1884. MET trains ex-ELR commenced 01/10/1884. Remained a terminus until MDR / MET joint line from Aldgate/Minories Junctions to Whitechapel opened 06/10/1884. Renamed 26/01/1923. Closed when Aldgate East station was relocated eastwards.

Name	Page / grid		Date opened	Date closed	Opened by	Notes
St Mary's Curve	27 / 6B 90	P	03/03/1884	06/10/1941	MDR / MET	Built as part of MDR / MET Whitechapel extension, but first used by SER between 03/03/1884 - 01/10/1884. MET use commenced 01/10/1884, MDR 06/10/1884. Closed to passenger services 01/08/1905 (MDR) and 06/10/1941 (MET), retained for stock transfer thereafter until 23/12/2007 when ELL closed for extension. Football specials used the curve until 1990 when Millwall were relegated from the First Division.
		G	03/03/1884	23/12/2007		
St Mary's Junction	27 / 6B 90		01/10/1884	23/12/2007	MDR / MET	Junction at north end of St Mary's Curve, MDR service to Whitechapel commenced 06/10/1884 although empty stock workings to Whitechapel commenced five days before this with the MET service to New Cross.
ST PANCRAS INTERNATIONAL St Pancras	26 / 4B 75 / 76		01/10/1868	N/A	MID	Extensively rebuilt for Eurostar services; last Midland mainline train left trainshed 09/04/2004, temporary station to northeast opened 12/04/2004. Main trainshed reopened for international trains and suffix 'International' added 14/11/2007. Platforms below original station opened for 'Thameslink' 09/12/2007 (see 'King's Cross Thameslink', which they replaced).
ST PANCRAS GOODS	26 / 4B 75 / 76		??/07/1862	29/04/1968	MID	Initial access via GNR, then also NLR (GNR connection subsequently severed) full opening 09/09/1867.
St Pancras Junction (MID)	75		1867	31/12/1975	MID/NLR	
St Pancras Junction (GNR)	75		1853	14/11/2007	GNR/NLR	
ST PAUL'S Post Office	26 / 6D		30/07/1900	N/A	CLR	Renamed 01/02/1937.
St Paul's Bridge	32 / 6C		10/05/1886	N/A	LCDR	Built alongside original Blackfriars Bridge.
St Paul's Road Junction	26 / 3B 75 / 76		13/07/1868	N/A	MID	Junction providing access to St Pancras Goods (MID route to MET 'Widened Lines' opened 13/07/1868.) Access to St Pancras goods removed 29/04/1968, Churchyard sidings remain as truncated route.
ST QUINTIN PARK & WORMWOOD SCRUBS Wormwood Scrubs	24 / 5D 91		01/08/1871	03/10/1940	LNWR / GWR	Opened as 'Wormwood Scrubs', renamed 'St Quintin Park & Wormwood Scrubs' 01/08/1892. 'Scrubs' sometimes spelt 'Scrubbs' in both titles. Platforms relocated north 01/11/1893. Destroyed by fire 03/10/1940 and so ceased to be served by trains, not officially closed until 01/12/1940.
Salmons Lane Junction	27 / 6C		05/04/1880	05/11/1962	LBLR	Junction at north end of Limehouse Curve.
SANDERSTEAD	66 / 4D	P	10/03/1884	N/A	LBSCR / SER	Goods yard closed 20/03/1961.
		G	10/03/1884	20/03/1961		
SANDILANDS	67 / 2A		10/05/2000	N/A	CTL	
Sandilands Tunnels (Woodside, Park Hill & Coombe Road)	67 / 2A		10/08/1885	N/A	LBSCR / SER	Line through tunnels closed by BR 16/05/1983, reopened by CTL 10/05/2000.
SCRATCHWOOD SIDINGS	4 / 6B		c.1890	Post 1935	MID	Single siding appeared c.1890 (present on 1895 OS), but absent from 1911 OS. Reappeared on 1935 OS, by which time they had significantly expanded. Remained in situ into the 1950's but site then became Scratchwood (London Gateway) M1 Services so had become disused by its opening in 1969.
SEABROOK SIDINGS	45 / 4C		1884	N/A	PRIV	Sidings provided access to Seabrookes Brewery (see below). Now provide access to Tilbury Docks following abolition of Tilbury North Junction c.1960.
SEABROOKES BREWERY	45 / 4C		1884	1940	PRIV	Established 1799, siding added 1884, sold to Charringtons 1929, lifted 1940.
SELHURST	53 / 6D 86		01/05/1865	N/A	LBSCR	
SELHURST DEPOT	53 / 6D 86		1911	N/A	LBSCR	Sidings first laid on site c.1890 (not on 1879-1887 OS but had appeared by 1896). Became a depot 1911.
Selhurst Junctions	53 / 6D 86		01/12/1862	N/A	LBSCR	
Selhurst Spur	86	P	c.1910	N/A	LBSCR	
		G	c.1910	N/A		
SELSDON Selsdon Road Selsdon Road Junction	66 / 3D	P	10/08/1885	16/05/1983	LBSCR / SER	For first month 'Selsdon Road Junction', then 'Selsdon Road'. Woodside platforms closed 01/01/1917 – 01/05/1919. Renamed 'Selsdon' 30/09/1935. Oxted Line platforms closed 14/06/1959, Woodside platforms 16/05/1983. Goods yard closed 07/10/1968, but oil depot established on site (latterly Cory), remaining open until March 1993.
		G	10/08/1885	07/10/1968		
Selsdon Road Junction	66 / 4D		10/03/1884	??/03/1993	LBSCR / SER	Last traffic to Selsdon oil depot March 1993, but junction remains in situ.
SEVEN KINGS	29 / 1B		01/03/1899	N/A	GER	
Seven Kings Curve	29 / 1B	P	N/A	N/A	GER	Never used for regular passenger traffic, route obliterated by Ilford Depot 'New Shed' 1959.
		G	20/04/1903	19/03/1956		
SEVEN SISTERS	15 / 5A		22/07/1872	N/A	GER	Platforms for Palace Gates Branch open 01/01/1878 – 07/01/1963. Victoria Line station opened 01/09/1968. Borley refers to goods yard opening c.1878 (no closure date), may refer to cold store to north.
Seven Sisters Chord	15 / 5A	P	01/01/1880	N/A	GER	Open to goods 1879, passengers 01/01/1880. Closed to passengers 07/01/1963 – 1989 (when electrified), singled ??/05/1977.
		G	1879	N/A		
Seven Sisters Junction Seven Sisters South Junction	15 / 5A		1879	N/A	GER	Junction at north end of Seven Sisters Chord (see entry above).
Seven Sisters North Junction	15 / 5A		01/01/1878	07/02/1965	GER	Junction of Palace Gates branch.
Shacklegate Junction	50 / 2B		01/07/1894	N/A	LSWR	Junction at east end of Shepperton Spur (Fulwell Curve).
SHADWELL Shadwell & St George's East *(LBLR)* Shadwell & St George-in-the-East *(ELR)* Shadwell	27 / 6B		01/10/1840	N/A	LBLR	LBLR station opened 01/10/1840 as 'Shadwell', suffix '& St George's East' added 01/07/1900. Closed 22/05/1916 – 05/05/1919, and again 07/07/1941. Rebuilt as an island platform and reopened by DLR 31/08/1987 as 'Shadwell'. ELR station opened 10/04/1876 as 'Shadwell', first served MET & MDR 01/10/1884. Suffix '& St George-in-the-East' added 01/07/1900, last served MDR 01/08/1905, suffix dropped 1918. No service MET 03/12/1906 – 31/03/1913. ELL platforms closed 26/03/1995 – 25/03/1998 and 23/12/2007 – 27/04/2010 (engineering work).
Sheet Factory Junction	28 / 4A 77		29/04/1846	12/03/1973	ECTJR	Junction at south end of Stratford Eastern Curve.
Sheepcote Lane Curve	38 / 4D	P	06/07/1865	25/05/2004	WLER	Opened 06/07/1865 (all traffic), passenger services ceased 13/03/1912, goods 21/01/1936, track lifted 1937. Re-laid for Eurostar access to North Pole Depot (commissioned in advance of 17/08/1994 commencement of 'demonstration' service), Eurostar connecting service to Cardiff commenced 24/10/1994, regular passenger services ceased with effect from 25/05/2004 (last train 21/05/2004), shadowed by token bus service until 'official' closure 14/12/2004 (last bus 07/12/2004). Curve effectively redundant since 14/11/2007 opening of St Pancras International and closure of North Pole Depot, but remains in situ.
		G	06/07/1865	14/11/2007		
SHENFIELD Shenfield & Hutton Shenfield & Hutton Junction Shenfield	20 / 5B	P	29/03/1843	N/A	ECR	Opened as 'Shenfield', but closed to passengers ??/03/1850 due to lack of patronage. Reopened by GER 01/01/1887 as 'Shenfield & Hutton Junction', with the suffix 'Junction' being dropped later that year. Rebuilt 01/01/1934 due to quadrupling work. Goods yard closed 04/05/1964. Suffix '& Hutton' dropped 20/02/1969. New bay platform 6 first used 02/05/2017 (empty stock working) and 03/05/2017 (passenger use); for terminating Elizabeth Line trains.
		G	29/03/1843	04/05/1964		
Shenfield Country End Junction	20 / 4C		01/01/1934	N/A	LNER	

Name	Page / grid		Date opened	Date closed	Opened by	Notes
Shenfield London End Junction	20 / 1C		01/01/1934	N/A	LNER	
Shenfield Southend Line Junction	20 / 5C		01/10/1889	N/A	GER	
SHENFIELD STABLING SIDINGS *Middle Sidings*	20 / 5B		01/01/1934	N/A	LNER	Originally between the 'down' Southend and Colchester roads, the former was realigned.
SHEPHERD'S BUSH (CLR)	38 / 1A 83		30/07/1900	N/A	CLR	Terminus until 14/05/1908, originally crossovers both west and east of the station. West of the station, the current westbound continued towards Wood Lane Depot while the current eastbound was a reversing siding. Sometimes had suffix 'Green' added. Closed 02/02/2008 – 05/10/2008 (reconstruction).
SHEPHERD'S BUSH (MET / GWR)	37 / 1D 83		13/06/1864	01/04/1914	MET / GWR	Replaced by Shepherd's Bush (now Shepherd's Bush Market) to north and Goldhawk Road to south.
SHEPHERD'S BUSH (LSWR)	38 / 1A 83		01/05/1874	05/06/1916	LSWR	Addison Road to Studland Road Junction abandoned 05/06/1916.
SHEPHERD'S BUSH (WLR)	38 / 1A 83		27/05/1844	N/A	WLR	Inaugural WLR passenger service withdrawn 01/12/1844 and station closed, when services to Kensington recommenced 02/06/1862, station did not reopen but was subsequently replaced by Uxbridge Road to south 01/11/1869 (later closing 21/10/1940). New NR station named Shepherd's Bush built on original 1844 station site, opening 28/09/2008. Present 'down' platform occupies approximate site of 27/05/1844 platform. Present 'up' platform built upon site of southern end of MET / GWR spur to Latimer Road.
SHEPHERD'S BUSH MARKET *Shepherd's Bush*	37 / 1D 83		01/04/1914	N/A	MET / GWR	Replaced Shepherd's Bush (MET / GWR) to south. Renamed 12/10/2008.
Shepherd's Lane Junction	39 / 5B		01/01/1867	N/A	LCDR	Initially junction between 25/08/1862 LCDR Herne Hill to Stewarts Lane route and new line to Factory Junction (quadrupling), but the junction was eliminated when 01/05/1867 high level route to Denmark Hill via East Brixton was opened. Connection reinstated through Victoria resignalling c.1980.
SHEPPERTON *Shepperton for Halliford*	48 / 6D	P G	01/11/1864 *01/11/1864*	N/A 01/08/1960	TVR	Suffix 'for Halliford' sometimes used 1914 - 1955. 'Up' platform road designated a siding after 05/02/1915 and all passenger traffic reversed via 'down' platform. Turntable removed August 1942, goods yard closed 01/08/1960 (Borley), Jackson states 07/10/1960.
Shepperton Spur *Fulwell Curve*	50 / 2B	P G	01/07/1894 *01/07/1894*	N/A N/A	LSWR	Curve opened 01/07/1894, but possibly saw no regular traffic until 01/02/1895 (Borley). Utilised for race specials to Kempton Park from opening (as well as goods), but no ordinary passenger services used curve before 01/06/1901.
SHERN HALL STREET, WALTHAMSTOW	15 / 5D		26/04/1870	17/11/1873	GER	Terminus of single-track branch from Lea Bridge Junction, replaced by Wood Street when the line extended to Chingford.
SHERWOOD HOSPITAL & POWER STATION	64 / 5A		1918	1950	PRIV	Horton Estate Light Railway supplied building materials then fuel to hospitals.
SHOREDITCH (NLR)	27 / 5A 90		01/11/1865	04/10/1940	NLR	Closed by enemy action, booking office remained open until 17/11/1941.
SHOREDITCH (ELR)	27 / 5A 90		10/04/1876	11/06/2006	ELR	Became northern passenger terminus of ELR upon electrification 31/03/1913 (through goods traffic remained). 'Down' platform abandoned 1928 and all services reversed off 'up'. Through goods traffic, connection to GER main line, and down through road abandoned 17/04/1966. Closed 26/03/1995 – 27/09/1998 (engineering works). Closed for good 11/06/2006 (last train 09/06/2006) to allow East London Line Extension works to commence.
SHOREDITCH (DUNLOE STREET) GOODS DEPOT	27 / 4A		??/03/1893	03/06/1968	LNWR	
SHOREDITCH HIGH STREET	27 / 5A 90		27/04/2010	N/A	TFL (LO)	On site of northern portion of Bishopsgate Goods yard (formerly Bishopsgate High Level station), under covered way to allow for development above.
SHORTLANDS *Bromley*	55 / 5A		03/05/1858	N/A	WELCPR	Opened as 'Bromley' at terminus of WELCPR extension from Bromley Junction. Renamed 'Shortlands' 01/07/1858, line then extended to Southborough Road (now Bickley) four days later 05/07/1858.
Shortlands Junction	55 / 5A		01/07/1892	N/A	LCDR	Remodelled 1958-9, then again as a 'flying' junction June 2003.
SIDCUP	56 / 2C	P G	01/09/1866 *01/09/1866*	N/A 15/08/1966	SER	Opened with line 01/09/1866 according to Borley, Quick & Jackson, but kentrail.org.uk website states station did not open until the following month (i.e. October 1866). Goods yard closed 15/08/1966, partially replaced by new siding 1967 to facilitate reversal of trains. According to Quick carried suffix 'for Halfway Street' in Bradshaw 1867 – 1893.
Silk Stream Junction	12 / 4D		14/09/1890	N/A	MID	Junction between Midland Main Line and freight flyover.
Silo Curve	76	P G	N/A *14/11/2007*	N/A N/A	LCOR / NR	No regular passenger service.
Silo Curve Junction	76		14/11/2007	N/A	LCOR / NR	
SILVER STREET *Silver Street for Upper Edmonton* *Silver Street*	15 / 2A		22/07/1872	N/A	GER	Suffix 'for Upper Edmonton' in use c.1883 – 1933.
SILVERTOWN *Silvertown & London City Airport* *Silvertown*	41 / 1C 62 / 4B	P G	19/06/1863 *19/06/1863*	10/12/2006 early 1993	ECR	Closed 08/09/1940 – 01/01/1941 (air raid damage), 29/05/1994 – 29/10/1995 (Jubilee Line extension works), then permanently 10/12/2006 (closure of North Woolwich branch for partial conversion to DLR). Former 'up' platform closed 25/08/1969 when passenger route singled (former 'up' line became bidirectional goods line, taken out of use 29/03/1993). Goods yard to west of station accessed via Silvertown Tramway, scrap metal traffic remained until early 1993 (formally abandoned 29/03/1993). '& London City Airport' suffix added 04/10/1987, removed 24/09/2000. Line through station site reopened 24/05/2022 (Elizabeth Line Abbey Wood branch), a new Silvertown station has been proposed, but would be sited to the east of the original.
Silvertown Tramway *Woolwich Abandoned Line*	41 / 1B 62 / 4B	P G	14/06/1847 *14/06/1847*	26/11/1855 29/03/1993	ECR	Part of original ECR extension from Thames Wharf to North Woolwich. After opening of diversionary route via Custom House 26/11/1855, line became goods only but remained a through route. Swing Bridge across entrance to Royal Victoria Dock removed c.1950 and line became accessible from Silvertown end only. Last goods movement took place in early 1993 and line abandoned 29/03/1993. Route now partially followed by DLR Woolwich Arsenal line. Officially became 'Woolwich Abandoned Line' in 1855, but more commonly referred to as 'Silvertown Tramway'.
Silwood Junction *Deptford Road Junction*	40 / 2B 79 / 80		13/03/1871	N/A	ELR	Junction established 13/03/1871, further junction for 'up' road to New Cross Gate added 01/07/1876. Old Kent Road route closed 30/06/1911, lifted 1913. Junction eliminated 01/11/1964 with 'up' road to New Cross Gate closing. Remodelled to a 'flying' layout and re-established 24/06/2012 as 'Silwood Junction' (date line energised to allow testing to begin).
SILWOOD SIDINGS	80		19/08/2014	N/A	TFL (LO)	First test train used sidings 19/08/2014.
SINGLEWELL MAINTENANCE DEPOT	60 / 4B		??/04/2007	N/A	LCOR	
SLADE GREEN *Slades Green*	43 / 5C		01/07/1900	N/A	SECR	Renamed 01/08/1953.
SLADE GREEN DEPOT	43 / 5D		27/10/1899	N/A	SECR	Current EMU berthing shed is original 27/10/1899 steam shed (extended June 1954). Maintenance shed added 1925, demolished and completely rebuilt on same site 08/04/1991.
Slade Green Junction	43 / 5C		01/05/1895	N/A	BHR / SER	Junction at north end of Erith Loop.

Name	Page / grid		Date opened	Date closed	Opened by	Notes
SLOANE SQUARE	38 / 2D		24/12/1868	N/A	MDR	
SLOUGH	33 / 1C	P	01/06/1840	N/A	GWR	Trains began calling at Slough 01/05/1839, although objections from Eton College initially prevented the construction of a station. Station opened 01/06/1840, initially with a single platform to the south of the main line. Served by MDR trains 01/03/1883 – 01/10/1885. Station rebuilt and relocated west 08/09/1884. Goods yard closed 27/07/1975.
		G	01/06/1840	27/07/1975		
Slough West Junction	33 / 1C		08/10/1849	N/A	GWR	Originally junction at northern end of Royal Curve (closed 26/07/1970), today set of junctions between the 'fast' and 'slow' roads west of Slough.
SMALLBERRY GREEN Hounslow	36 / 4C		22/08/1849	01/02/1850	LSWR	Temporary country terminus of LSWR Hounslow Loop until 01/12/1850 completion, situated at Wood Lane level crossing. Officially named 'Hounslow' (timetable, and almost certainly tickets and station nameboards), but was so remote from Hounslow that 'Smallberry Green' was more commonly used. Replaced by Isleworth to west when line extended.
Smithfield Curve	32 / 3C	P	01/09/1871	01/04/1916	LCDR	
		G	01/09/1871	01/04/1916		
SMITHFIELD GOODS	26 / 6C 32 / 3C		03/05/1869	30/07/1962	GWR	
Smithfield Junction	32 / 3C		01/09/1871	01/04/1916	LCDR	Junction at northern end of Smithfield Curve.
Smithfield Sidings	32 / 3C		c.1885	N/A	LCDR	Laid originally c.1885 (portion of Smithfield market above built 1886-8). Abandoned with Snow Hill Tunnel but two sidings (originally four) re-laid as part of 'Thameslink' project, used by services terminating at City Thameslink.
Smithfield Tunnel	32 / 3C		01/07/1866	22/03/2009	MET	Farringdon to Moorgate (NR) closed 22/03/2009 due to platform lengthening at Farringdon. To reopen as 'Farringdon City Sidings' (S Stock stabling).
SNARESBROOK Snaresbrook for Wanstead Snaresbrook & Wanstead Snaresbrook	16 / 5B	P	22/08/1856	N/A	ECR	Opened as 'Snaresbrook', suffix '& Wanstead' added ??/11/1898, became 'for Wanstead' 1929, dropped 14/12/1947. Bay platform on 'down' side added 1893. Majority of passenger services transferred to LPTB 14/12/1947. Goods yard closed 01/08/1949. Bay platform abandoned 1950. First trains in the morning remained BR services until 01/06/1970 (last train 31/05/1970).
		G	22/08/1856	01/08/1949		
Snow Hill Junction	32 / 3C		01/09/1871	01/04/1916	LCDR	Junction at southern end of Smithfield Curve.
Snow Hill Tunnel	32 / 3C		01/01/1866	N/A	LCDR	Line closed through tunnel 24/03/1969 - 16/05/1988.
SOMERS TOWN GOODS St Pancras New Goods	26 / 4B 75		01/11/1887	23/04/1968	MID	Renamed 01/08/1892. British Library now occupies site.
SOUTH ACTON	37 / 2B 51 / 1B		01/01/1880	N/A	NSWJR	UERL (MDR) platform opened 13/06/1905, closed 02/03/1959 (last train 28/02/1959). Bay on 'down' side for Hammersmith & Chiswick Branch.
South Acton Junction	37 / 2B 51 / 1B		01/01/1869	N/A	NSWJR / LSWR	
SOUTH BERMONDSEY Rotherhithe	40 / 3B 79 / 80		13/08/1866	N/A	LBSCR	Renamed 01/12/1869. Closed 01/01/1917 – 01/05/1919. Relocated south by SR 17/06/1928.
South Bermondsey Junction	40 / 3B 79 / 80		01/01/1871	N/A	LBSCR	Spur to Bricklayers Arms Junction opened 01/01/1871.
SOUTH BROMLEY	27 / 6D		01/09/1884	15/05/1944	NLR	Passenger service Dalston Junction to Poplar withdrawn 15/05/1944, 'official' closure 23/04/1945.
SOUTH CROYDON	66 / 3D		01/09/1865	N/A	LBSCR	
South Croydon Junction	66 / 3D		10/03/1884	N/A	LBSCR / SER	
SOUTH DOCK South West India Dock South Dock	40 / 1D		18/12/1871	04/05/1926	MER	Island platform between single passenger line and passing loop. Due to locomotives not being permitted to work through West India Docks initially, trains were horse-hauled through station until August 1880. Traction was switched to steam at boundary of Millwall Dock Company until this date for final stretch to North Greenwich. Sometimes known as 'South West India Dock' 1881 - 1895. Passenger service withdrawn 04/05/1926.
SOUTH EALING	36 / 1D		01/05/1883	N/A	MDR	First served by Piccadilly Line 09/01/1933. District Line ceased from 10/10/1964. Rebuilt with four platforms 1932.
SOUTH GREENFORD South Greenford Halt	23 / 4B		20/09/1926	N/A	GWR	Suffix 'Halt' dropped 05/05/1969. 'Up' platform removed mid-September 1993 due to embankment instability, not reinstated until 26/10/1999.
SOUTH HAMPSTEAD Loudoun Road	25 / 3C		02/06/1879	N/A	LNWR	Closed 01/01/1917, reopened and renamed 10/07/1922.
SOUTH HAREFIELD HALT Harefield Halt	9 / 6C	P	24/09/1928	01/10/1931	GCR / GWR	Renamed 29/05/1929. Goods yard opened 27/06/1929. Closed to passengers and general goods 01/10/1931. Goods siding served Peerless wire fence co. between 1933 and 01/01/1953.
		G	27/06/1929	01/01/1953		
SOUTH HARROW	23 / 1B		28/06/1903	N/A	MDR	Terminus 28/06/1903 – 01/03/1910. First served Piccadilly Line 04/07/1932. Last served District Line 23/10/1933. Re-sited to north 05/07/1935.
SOUTH HARROW GASWORKS	23 / 1B		1910	04/04/1954	PRIV	
SOUTH HARROW SIDINGS	23 / 1B		28/06/1903	N/A	MDR	Stabling sidings (formerly depot) for Piccadilly Line (previously District Railway). Temporarily taken out of use 12/07/2021 for expansion works, sidings 1, 3, 4 and 5 were recommissioned 17/07/2022. Sidings 2 and 6-12 commissioned May 2023. There is a possibility to extend all sidings to double length (stabling 24 trains).
South Harrow Tunnel	23 / 2B		02/04/1906	N/A	GCR	
South Island Place	39 / 4C		22/10/1923	29/11/1923	UERL (CSLR)	During the widening of the CSLR tunnels, waterlogged gravel leakage between Oval and Stockwell resulted in single line working being introduced to allow compressed air working in one tunnel at a time. Temporary crossovers were installed at South Island Place (Jul/Aug 1923) and Portland Place (Sep 1923), and single line working commenced 22/10/1923. On 27/11/1923 a partial tunnel collapse and resulting gas explosion north of Elephant & Castle resulted in the CSLR being operated as two shuttles, before the entire line was suspended 29/11/1923 until 01/12/1924. As both crossovers were built for smaller CSLR loading gauge, they did not reopen.
South Junction (Mitcham)	52 / 6D		01/10/1868	02/06/1997	LBSCR	Junction eliminated when Wimbledon to West Croydon line closed 02/06/1997 prior to conversion to Tramlink.
SOUTH KENSINGTON	38 / 2C 45		24/12/1868	N/A	MET	Opened by MET as part of 24/12/1868 MET / MDR extension to Westminster (Bridge) - boundary between two companies was east of station (South Kensington East Junction). MDR opened its own platforms to south of MET 10/07/1871. UERL (GNPBR) platforms opened 08/01/1907. Middle bay road removed & filled in 28/07/1957, tracks reconfigured at same time such that former MET = eastbound and former MDR = westbound. Northernmost platform road (eastbound Circle) removed 08/01/1967, southernmost (westbound District) removed 30/03/1969, station reconstruction completed 21/10/1973. Piccadilly Line platforms closed 27/02/2021 – 01/06/2022 (escalator refurbishment).
South Kensington East Junction	38 / 2D 45		10/07/1871	28/07/1957	MDR / MET	Initially site of 'end on' junction between MET and MDR, became traditional junction when MDR opened its own lines through South Kensington 10/07/1871. Junction eliminated when tracks reconfigured 28/07/1957.
SOUTH KENTISH TOWN	26 / 3A		22/06/1907	06/06/1924	UERL (CCEHR)	'Castle Road' prior to opening. Initially closed as the result of the 1924 wildcat strikes affecting power supply, and never reopened.

Name	Page / grid		Date opened	Date closed	Opened by	Notes
SOUTH KENTON	23 / 1D		03/07/1933	N/A	LMS	Served by Bakerloo Line since opening, except between 27/09/1982 (last served 24/09/1982) and 04/06/1984.
SOUTH MERTON	52 / 5B		07/07/1929	N/A	SR	Temporary country terminus of Wimbledon - Sutton line until 05/01/1930.
SOUTH QUAY	40 / 1D		31/08/1987	N/A	DLR	Closed 09/02/1996 – 15/04/1996 (IRA bomb adjacent to station). Closed again 23/10/2009, reopening 125m east 26/10/2009 to facilitate longer platforms (original site constrained by adjacent curves).
SOUTH RUISLIP South Ruislip & Northolt Junction Northolt Junction	22 / 2C	P	01/05/1908	N/A	GCR / GWR	Opened as 'Northolt Junction', renamed 'South Ruislip & Northolt Junction' 12/09/1932, suffix dropped 30/06/1947. Served by Central Line since 21/11/1948. Goods closed 27/01/1964, milk traffic remained until 1972. Up slow track removed / up platform widened to abut former up fast track 1973.
		G	01/05/1908	27/01/1964		
SOUTH SHED (QUEENS PARK)	25 / 4B		11/02/1915	N/A	UERL (BAK)	Stabling Shed for Bakerloo Line.
SOUTH TOTTENHAM South Tottenham & Stamford Hill	15 / 6A	P	01/05/1871	N/A	THJR	Goods yard opened by MID on same date as passenger station. Suffix '& Stamford Hill' dropped 01/07/1903. Goods yard closed 04/07/1966 (usually referred to as 'Tottenham Goods'). Became weekday terminus of Gospel Oak trains 04/06/2016 to 25/09/2016 (no service weekends), and then entire Overground service suspended 26/09/2016 to 27/02/2017 due to electrification works on Gospel Oak to Barking Line.
		G	01/05/1871	04/07/1966	MID	
South Tottenham East Junction	15 / 5A		09/07/1894	N/A	TFGR / THJR	Junction between THJR and TFGR.
South Tottenham West Junction	15 / 5A		1879	N/A	GER	Junction between THJR and Seven Sisters Chord (refer to notes for latter).
SOUTH WEST SIDINGS	24 / 5C 91 & 92		c.1870	N/A	NSWJR	Sidings had appeared on site by 1871 OS.
SOUTH WIMBLEDON South Wimbledon (Merton) South Wimbledon	52 / 4B		13/09/1926	N/A	UERL (NOR)	(Merton) suffix added c.1928, but gradually dropped. Still appears on some station signage at platform level. Closed 31/01/2000 – 13/03/2000 (escalator repairs) and 21/03/2020 – 17/08/2020 (COVID-19).
SOUTH WOODFORD South Woodford (George Lane) George Lane	16 / 4B	P	22/08/1856	N/A	ECR	Opened as 'George Lane', Renamed 'South Woodford (George Lane)' 05/07/1937. Ownership and majority of passenger services transferred to LPTB 14/12/1947, when 'George Lane' suffix dropped. Goods yard closed 06/01/1964. First Trains in the morning remained British Rail services until 01/06/1970.
		G	22/08/1856	06/01/1964		
SOUTHFLEET	59 / 3C	P	10/05/1886	03/08/1953	LCDR	Opened as an island platform with Gravesend West branch. Closed to passengers 03/08/1953, to goods 11/06/1962. Line through station site closed 24/03/1968, but was reopened due to establishment of APCM (later Blue Circle) coal terminal on station site 1972 – 26/01/1976.
		G	10/05/1886	11/06/1962		
Southfleet Junction	59 / 3D		14/11/2007	N/A	LCOR	Route to Fawkham Junction rarely used after 14/11/2007.
SOUTHALL	35 / 1D	P	01/05/1839	N/A	GWR	Sometimes had suffix 'Brentford Junction' added. Served by District Railway 01/03/1883 – 01/10/1885. Goods yard closed 02/01/1967.
		G	01/05/1839	02/01/1967		
SOUTHALL EAST SIDINGS	36 / 1A		??/07/1859	N/A	GWR	First engine shed on site ??/07/1859 (single road). Rebuilt 1884 & 1954, steam allocation withdrawn 31/12/1965. Became DMU depot 03/01/1966, until November 1986. Taken over by GWR Preservation Group 1988 (became 'Southall Railway Centre'), further taken over by Flying Scotsman Railways 19/04/1991.
SOUTHALL GAS WORKS	35 / 1C		1869	1961	PRIV	Opened by Brentford Gas Company.
Southall West Junction	35 / 1D		18/07/1859	N/A	GWR	Junction between GWR main line and Brentford Branch. Direct access from branch to main line restored March 1995 (shunt move via Down Yard had been necessary previously).
SOUTHBURY Churchbury	7 / 5B	P	01/10/1891	N/A	GER	Opened as 'Churchbury', closed 01/10/1909 – 01/03/1915 then again 01/07/1919. Reopened as 'Southbury' 21/11/1960, goods closed 07/12/1970.
		G	01/10/1891	07/12/1970		
SOUTHFIELDS	52 / 1A		03/06/1889	N/A	LSWR	Putney Bridge to Wimbledon built by LSWR, initially operated by MDR only, LSWR services commenced 01/07/1889. Last regular main line passenger service withdrawn 05/05/1941, although services called on occasions until 1969. Station ownership transferred to LUL 01/04/1994 along with entire Putney Bridge to Wimbledon route.
SOUTHGATE	6 / 6B		13/03/1933	N/A	UERL (GNPBR)	Renamed 'Gareth Southgate' start of traffic 16/07/2018 to close of traffic 17/07/2018 in honour of the England manager following 2018 World Cup.
SOUTHWARK	39 / 1C		20/11/1999	N/A	LUL (JUB)	Line through station opened 24/09/1999, but station itself did not open until the Jubilee Line Extension was connected to the original line 20/11/1999. Closed 21/03/2020 – 13/07/2020 (COVID-19).
SOUTHWARK DEPOT (GOODS)	39 / 1D 87		1901	03/10/1960	SECR	Provided goods facilities transferred from London bridge, adjacent to Ewer Street locomotive depot. General goods ceased 03/10/1960 (replaced by British Rail Continental Freight Depot at Hither Green), parcels ceased 1969. Became EMU stabling sidings after 1969, decommissioned May 1983.
SOUTHWARK PARK	40 / 2B 79		01/10/1902	15/03/1915	SECR	OS evidence (1875-6 1:1,056 compared with 1916 1:2,500) strongly suggests that the platforms for this station were on the same site as the earlier Commercial Dock, albeit with the station entrance and ticket hall further north than those of the earlier station. After public closure, continued in use for railwaymen until 21/09/1925.
SPA ROAD, BERMONDSEY Spa Road & Bermondsey	40 / 2A		08/02/1836	15/03/1915	LGR	Temporary London terminus of LGR until 10/10/1836 extension to Bermondsey Street. Closed 14/12/1836 (Quick), 'end of 1838' (Mitchell & Smith) or 'probably' February 1843 (Borley). Reopened as permanent structure 'probably' 30/10/1842 (Quick - also Mitchell & Smith), or 'probably' February 1843 (Borley). Re-sited east 01/09/1872. Usually 'Spa Road & Bermondsey' until 1877, after 1877 usually 'Spa Road, Bermondsey'. After public closure, continued in use for railwaymen until 21/09/1925.
SPENCER ROAD HALT	66 / 3D		01/09/1906	15/03/1915	LBSCR / SER	
SPITALFIELDS GOODS Whitechapel Coal Brick Lane Goods	27 / 5B 90		c.1840	06/11/1967	ECR	Brick Lane Goods (opened ECR c.1840) amalgamated with Whitechapel Coal (which had been opened by GER 01/11/1866) 01/01/1881 to form Spitalfields Goods. Closed 06/11/1967.
Springhead Junctions	59 / 1C		13/12/2009	N/A	NR	Regular services Faversham to St Pancras commenced 13/12/2009.
Spur Junction	54 / 5A		18/06/1862	30/10/1966	LBSCR	Junction at north end of Norwood Spur.
STAINES Staines Central Staines Junction Staines Old Staines	48 / 2A	P	22/08/1848	N/A	LSWR	Opened as 'Staines', suffix 'Old' added 1885, changed to 'Junction' 1889, suffix dropped 1920/1. Suffix 'Central' added 26/09/1949, dropped 18/04/1966. Two goods yards (west and east) closed 31/08/1971.
		G	22/08/1848	31/08/1971		
Staines Bridge	48 / 2A		04/06/1856	N/A	LSWR	
STAINES CARRIAGE SIDINGS	48 / 2B		Pre 1913	N/A	LSWR	Evident on 1913 revision of the OS, current layout dates from 1974.
Staines Curve	48 / 2A	P	01/07/1884	30/01/1916	LSWR	Utilised by a Windsor to Weybridge (via Staines High Street) passenger service.
		G	07/04/1877	18/03/1965		
Staines East Junction	48 / 2A		04/06/1856	N/A	LSWR	
STAINES HIGH STREET	48 / 2A		01/07/1884	30/01/1916	LSWR	Served by Windsor to Weybridge services only (Waterloo to Windsor services did not call).
Staines High Street Junction	48 / 2A		07/04/1877	18/03/1965	LSWR	Junction at north end of Staines Curve.

Name	Page / grid		Date opened	Date closed	Opened by	Notes
STAINES LINOLEUM WORKS	48 / 2A		1887	1957	PRIV	Extensive internal network of narrow gauge lines as well as standard gauge lines connected to GWR and LSWR.
Staines Moor Junction	47 / 1D		23/06/1940	16/12/1947	SR	Curve between GWR and SR established as a diversionary route during WW2, little used.
STAINES WEST Staines	48 / 2A	P	02/11/1885	29/03/1965	GWR	Suffix 'West' added 26/09/1949. Passenger service West Drayton to Staines West withdrawn 29/03/1965, but traffic to Staines West oil terminal remained. Goods yard closed 02/11/1953, but reopened as oil terminal 24/06/1964.
		G	02/11/1885	02/11/1953		
Staines West Junction (1st)	48 / 2A		07/04/1877	18/03/1965	LSWR	Junction at south end of Staines Curve.
Staines West Junction (2nd)	47 / 1D		24/01/1981	24/06/1991	BR	Established for access to Staines West oil terminal after M25 severed GWR route to West Drayton. First train special passenger service 24/01/1981, last use 24/06/1991. Despite this, junction remained in situ until 11/01/2016 when the points were finally removed.
STAINES WEST OIL TERMINAL (SHELL / BP)	48 / 2A		24/06/1964	24/06/1991	PRIV	On site of former Staines West goods yard (closed 02/11/1953). Accessed by GWR Staines West branch from West Drayton until 16/01/1981. New connection to Windsor & Eton Riverside branch commissioned 24/01/1981, when a special passenger train became last train to traverse length of GWR Staines West branch. Oil trains ran via Southern Region after this date, GWR branch was subsequently severed by M25 motorway south of Colnbrook.
STAMFORD BROOK	37 / 2C 51 / 2D		01/02/1912	N/A	UERL (MDR)	Island platform built only for District Line (LSWR trains non-stopped). Due to forthcoming Piccadilly Line extension, eastbound District Line diverted via former 'up' LSWR road so new platform opened on that line 05/06/1932. Served by Piccadilly Line 26/12/2013 – 30/12/2013 due to District Line engineering works.
STAMFORD HILL	15 / 6A		22/07/1872	N/A	GER	
STANMORE	11 / 2D	P	10/12/1932	N/A	MET	Opened by Metropolitan Railway. Transferred to Bakerloo Line 20/11/1939, Jubilee Line 01/05/1979. Goods yard closed 31/03/1936 (now stabling sidings). Third platform opened 26/06/2011.
		G	10/12/1932	31/03/1936		
STANMORE VILLAGE Stanmore	11 / 2D	P	18/12/1890	15/09/1952	LNWR	'Village' suffix added 25/09/1950. Stanmore Village to Belmont closed to passengers 15/09/1952, to goods 06/07/1964.
		G	18/12/1890	06/07/1964		
Stanmore Branch Junction	11 / 4C		18/12/1890	05/10/1964	LNWR	Southern quarter mile of branch retained as head shunt for Harrow & Wealdstone goods until 03/04/1967.
Star Bridge	73 / 3A		05/11/1899	N/A	LBSCR	Point where LBSCR 'Quarry Line' crosses original LBRR.
STAR LANE	28 / 6A		31/08/2011	N/A	DLR	
STEPNEY GREEN	27 / 5B		23/06/1902	N/A	MDR / LTSR	Served by Metropolitan Line since 30/03/1936 ('Hammersmith & City Line' since 30/07/1990). Closed 21/03/2020 – 01/09/2020 (COVID-19).
Stepney Green Junction	27 / 6C		06/11/2022	N/A	TFL (EL)	Opening date of Whitechapel to Stratford section to revenue service.
Stepney East Junction Stepney Junction	27 / 6C		02/04/1849	1951	LBLR	Junction points removed 1951, although original LBLR route along north side of Limehouse Basin remained accessible from east end (Limehouse Junction) as a siding until 1962.
STEWARTS LANE (LCDR)	39 / 4A 82		01/05/1863	01/01/1867	LCDR	
STEWARTS LANE (WELCPR)	39 / 4A 82		29/03/1858	01/12/1858	WELCPR	Opened by WELCPR, but operated by LBSCR from outset.
STEWARTS LANE DEPOT Longhedge Locomotive Works	39 / 4A 82		??/02/1862	N/A	LCDR	Land purchased by LCDR 1861. Roundhouse opened February 1862, erecting shop in operation 1869 – 1904 (work then transferred to Ashford, Kent). Renamed 'Stewarts Lane' after 1933-4 rebuilding. Steam ceased 1963.
STEWARTS LANE GOODS	39 / 4A 82		15/01/1862	02/11/1970	LCDR	
Stewarts Lane Junction	39 / 4A 82		25/08/1862	N/A	LCDR	
STEWARTS LANE STONE TERMINAL	82		?	N/A	PRIV	
STOKE NEWINGTON	27 / 1A		27/05/1872	N/A	GER	Terminus from opening until 22/07/1872. Goods yard to north of Stoke Newington Tunnel (see 'Manor Road Goods').
Stoke Newington Tunnel	27 / 1A		22/07/1872	N/A	GER	
STOAT'S NEST	73 / 1B		12/07/1841	01/12/1856	LBRR	Opened with LBRR Croydon Junction to Haywards Heath route as request stop, permanent premises opened 1842.
Stoat's Nest Junction	73 / 1B		05/11/1899	N/A	LBSCR / SER	Junction formed by opening of LBSCR 'Quarry Line'.
STOAT'S NEST QUARRY	73 / 2B		pre-1868	c.1970	PRIV	Quarry began to be worked c.1805, rail connection depicted on 1868 OS, last shown 1965-7, absent 1975.
Stockley Park Flyover	34 / 1D		19/01/1998	N/A	RT	Flyover carrying 'up' line ex-Heathrow Airport branch.
STOCKWELL	39 / 4B		18/12/1890	N/A	CSLR	Terminus of CSLR 18/12/1890 – 03/061900. Line closed for tunnel widening 29/11/1923, station reopened to south 01/12/1924. Victoria Line platforms opened 23/07/1971.
STOCKWELL DEPOT	39 / 4B		18/12/1890	29/11/1923	CSLR	Original CSLR Depot, accessed by a steep incline (cable haulage), later replaced by hydraulic lift (one car capacity). Closed with rest of CSLR 29/11/1923 for tunnel widening works, remained closed when CSLR reopened 1924 due to access having become available to Golders Green Depot via 20/04/1924 Euston to Camden Town link.
STONE CROSSING Stone Crossing Halt	44 / 6D		02/11/1908	N/A	SECR	Suffix 'Halt' dropped 05/05/1969.
STONEBRIDGE PARK	24 / 3B 68 / 6B		15/06/1912	N/A	LNWR	Closed 10/01/1917 (fire), reopened 01/08/1917 and served by Bakerloo Line from this date. Terminus of Bakerloo Line services 24/09/1982 – 04/06/1984. Goods station site remote (to north west), see separate entry below.
STONEBRIDGE PARK DEPOT	24 / 3A 68 / 3B		09/04/1979	N/A	LTE (BAK)	Bakerloo Line Depot, on site of former LNWR power station.
STONEBRIDGE PARK GOODS	24 / 3A 68 / 4B		19/08/1912	??/06/1951	LNWR	Heavy Repair shop later built on same site.
STONEBRIDGE PARK POWER STATION	24 / 3A 68 / 3B		24/02/1916	30/07/1967	LNWR	LNWR power station, Stonebridge Park Depot later built on same site.
STONELEIGH	64 / 3C		17/07/1932	N/A	SR	
STRATFORD Stratford (West Ham) Stratford	28 / 3A 77 / 78	P	20/06/1839	N/A	ECR	NER platforms opened 22/11/1841 (initially separate station, combined with ECR station 01/04/1847). 'Low Level' ECR platforms opened 16/10/1854. Sometimes had suffix '(West Ham)' appended 1898 - 1923. LPTB Central Line platforms opened 04/12/1946 (terminus until 05/05/1947). First DLR platform 4 opened 31/08/1987 (until then a never utilised BR bay platform), closed and replaced by platforms 4a & 4b 18/06/2007 & 09/12/2007 respectively. LUL Jubilee Line platforms opened 14/05/1999. 'Low Level' NR platforms closed and replaced by new platforms 1 & 2 14/04/2009 before being converted for DLR use (opened 31/08/2011 as platforms 16 & 17). Central Line westbound platform 3a opened 05/09/2010. Goods yard to east of station ('Angel Lane'), closed 04/10/1965.
		G	20/06/1839	04/10/1965		
Stratford Central Junction East	28 / 3A 77 / 78		15/09/1840	N/A	ECR / NER	

Name	Page / grid		Date opened	Date closed	Opened by	Notes
Stratford Central Junction West	28 / 3A 77 / 78		15/08/1854	N/A	ECR	
Stratford Country End Crossovers	28 / 3A 78		?	N/A	BR	
Stratford Eastern Curve	28 / 3A 77	P	Post-1914	Pre-1920	ECTJR	1918 Bradshaw shows an Ilford to North Woolwich passenger service which was not present in the 1914 or 1920 editions, presumably associated with WW1 munitions production in the Royal Docks.
		G	29/04/1846	12/03/1973		
Stratford Eastern Junction	28 / 3A 77		29/04/1846	12/03/1973	ECTJR / ECR	Junction at north end of Stratford Eastern Curve.
STRATFORD FREIGHTLINER TERMINAL	27 / 3D		04/07/1967	Pre 01/02/1998	BR	Observed abandoned and cranes removed 01/02/1998 (BLN828).
STRATFORD HIGH STREET	28 / 4A 78		31/08/2011	N/A	DLR	On site of former Stratford Market station.
STRATFORD INTERNATIONAL	27 / 3D 78		30/11/2009	N/A	LCOR	Intended as the London calling point for international trains by-passing St Pancras to/from other UK destinations, but they have never operated. Opened with advent of Southeastern domestic services into St Pancras International. DLR platforms opened 31/08/2011.
STRATFORD MARKET Stratford Market (West Ham) Stratford Market Stratford Bridge	28 / 4A 77		14/06/1847	06/05/1957	ECR	'Stratford Bridge' until 01/11/1880 when renamed 'Stratford Market'. Relocated slightly to east 1892 (quadrupling). Carried suffix '(West Ham)' 1898 - 1923. Current Stratford High Street DLR station occupies same site. Large goods yard to south of station (see separate entry below).
STRATFORD MARKET DEPOT	28 / 4A		14/05/1999	N/A	LUL (JUB)	Jubilee Line Depot, on site of former Stratford Market Goods. Served by a Staff Halt on the Jubilee Line eastbound road, adjacent to Abbey Road DLR.
STRATFORD MARKET GOODS	28 / 4A		01/10/1879	05/11/1984	GER	Fruit & Vegetable Market, with adjacent goods depot. Sidings retained for engineering use until 1988 (North London Line electrification), then lifted.
Stratford Southern Curve	28 / 4A 77	P	14/06/1847	28/10/1940	ECR	Closed to passenger services 28/10/1940, fell into disuse by early 1980's, junctions eliminated 03/11/1984.
		G	14/06/1847	03/11/1984		
Stratford Southern Junction	28 / 4A 77		14/06/1847	03/11/1984	ECR	Junction at east end of Stratford Southern Curve.
STRATFORD TMD (1st) Stratford Works	77		c.1847	2001	ECR	ECR locomotive works. Overhaul work continued until 31/03/1991 (closure of diesel repair shop), loco stabling continued. Relocated to Temple Mills 2001 due to Channel Tunnel Rail Link works at Stratford (see Stratford TMD [2nd]). The area of the works east of the Cambridge main line was later occupied by Chobham Farm Container Terminal, with two roads connected at Temple Mills East Junction and opened by 1972 but little used. East of High Meads Loop, the London International Freight Terminal (LIFT) opened in 1966/67, last train departed 22/06/2001.
STRATFORD TMD (2nd)	27 / 1C		2001	2007	EWS	Relocated depot closed and subsequently replaced by Orient Way Sidings.
Stratford Western Junction	28 / 4A 77		14/06/1847	03/11/1984	ECR	Junction at west end of Stratford Southern Curve.
STRAWBERRY HILL	50 / 1B		01/12/1873	N/A	LSWR	
STRAWBERRY HILL DEPOT Fulwell Depot	50 / 2B		01/05/1897	N/A	LSWR	Fulwell Depot opened 01/05/1897 with a six-road engine shed (current 'A' shed). In 1908 the shed was extended by three roads with the addition of the 'B' shed. The shed roads were electrified 30/01/1916, the steam allocation subsequently being transferred to the new Feltham shed in 1923. EMU depot always referred to as 'Strawberry Hill Depot'. Site of former coal dump sidings became additional stabling sidings ('Field Sidings') in 1936.
Strawberry Hill Junction Thames Valley Junction	50 / 2B		01/11/1864	N/A	LSWR / TVR	Junction between LSWR Kingston Branch (now Loop) and Thames Valley Railway (Shepperton Branch).
STREATHAM	53 / 3B	P	01/10/1868	N/A	LBSCR	
		G	01/10/1868	07/10/1968		
STREATHAM COMMON Streatham Common (Greyhound Lane) Streatham Common	53 / 4B	P	01/12/1862	N/A	LBSCR	Suffix 'Greyhound Lane' in use 01/09/1868 - 01/01/1870.
		G	01/12/1862	07/10/1968		
Streatham Common Junction	53 / 3A		01/10/1868	N/A	LBSCR	Spurs at Streatham thought to have opened at same time as Peckham - Sutton line (01/10/1868) (Borley).
STREATHAM HILL Streatham & Brixton Hill Streatham	53 / 2B	P	01/12/1856	N/A	WELCPR	Opened as 'Streatham', became either 'Streatham & Brixton Hill' or simply 'Brixton Hill' 01/09/1868, further renamed 'Streatham Hill' 01/01/1869. Coal yard was present on 'down' side west of station as early as 1869 OS, possibly opened with passenger station, closed and converted to EMU stabling sidings 1938 (no mention in Borley).
		G	c.1856	1938		
STREATHAM HILL DEPOT	53 / 2B		c.1890	N/A	LBSCR	Carriage sidings had appeared by 1895 OS on 'up' side (not present on 1874-5 OS). Shed added in mid-20th century (not apparent before 1951-2 OS). Sidings on down side originally coal yard, converted for stabling 1938.
Streatham Junction	53 / 3B		01/10/1868	N/A	LBSCR	Spurs at Streatham thought to have opened at same time as Peckham - Sutton line (01/10/1868) (Borley).
Streatham North Junction	53 / 3A		01/10/1868	N/A	LBSCR	Spurs at Streatham thought to have opened at same time as Peckham - Sutton line (01/10/1868) (Borley).
Streatham South Junctions A & B	53 / 3A		01/10/1868	N/A	LBSCR	Spurs at Streatham thought to have opened at same time as Peckham - Sutton line (01/10/1868) (Borley).
Streatham South Junction C	53 / 3A		01/10/1868	N/A	LSWR / LBSCR	Spurs at Streatham thought to have opened at same time as Peckham - Sutton line (01/10/1868) (Borley).
Streatham Tunnel	53 / 2B		01/10/1868	N/A	LBSCR	
STROUD GREEN	14 / 6C		11/04/1881	05/07/1954	GNR	Closed when Alexandra Palace to Finsbury Park service withdrawn 05/07/1954 after a previous closure period 29/10/1951 – 07/01/1952. Branch had been intended for electrification and transfer to Northern Line, but works abandoned post-WW2.
Studland Road Junction	37 / 2D		01/06/1877	03/12/1911	LSWR / MDR	Junction eliminated through 03/12/1911 quadrupling between there and Turnham Green.
Subway Tunnel	25 / 6B 67 / 5A		12/05/1878	N/A	MET / GWR	Diveunder provided to eliminate the Hammersmith & City Railway's original level crossing of the GWR main line.
SUDBURY & HARROW ROAD	23 / 2C	P	01/03/1906	N/A	GCR	Goods yard closed 03/05/1965. Platforms originally provided on loops off two central 'fast' roads, which were subsequently removed. Original platforms then abandoned and replaced by current island platform on site of 'fast' roads.
		G	01/03/1906	03/05/1965		
SUDBURY HILL Sudbury Hill for Greenford Green	23 / 2B		28/06/1903	N/A	MDR	Suffix 'for Greenford Green' 1904 - 1938. First served Piccadilly Line 04/07/1932, last served District Line 23/10/1933.
SUDBURY HILL HARROW South Harrow	23 / 2B	P	01/03/1906	N/A	GCR	Terminus from opening until 02/04/1906. Renamed 19/07/1926. Goods yard closed 03/05/1965. Platforms originally provided on loops off two central 'fast' roads. Loops and platforms later removed with new platforms being constructed alongside original 'fast' roads. Closed 22/09/1990 - 07/10/1990.
		G	01/03/1906	03/05/1965		
Sudbury Junction Brent Junction	24 / 3B 68 / 2C		c.1890	N/A	LNWR	Willesden Relief lines and diveunder added c.1890.

Name	Page / grid		Date opened	Date closed	Opened by	Notes

SUDBURY TOWN
   Sudbury Town for Horsenden
   Sudbury Town
	23 / 3D		28/06/1903	N/A	MDR	Suffix 'for Horsenden' 1904 - 1938. First served Piccadilly Line 04/07/1932, last served District Line 23/10/1933.

SUNBURY	49 / 4B	P	01/11/1864	N/A	TVR	Originally passing point on single line until 17/07/1878 doubling. Goods yard closed 01/08/1960 (Borley), Jackson states 07/10/1960.
		G	*01/11/1864*	*01/08/1960*		
SUNDRIDGE PARK Plaistow	55 / 4B		01/01/1878	N/A	SER	Initially private, became a public station and renamed 01/07/1894.
SUNNYMEADS	33 / 4B		10/07/1927	N/A	SR	

SURBITON
   Surbiton & Kingston
   Kingston Junction
   Kingston
	50 / 6D	P	1845	N/A	LSWR	Replaced Kingston (1st) station ½ mile to east at some point in 1845. Also initially named 'Kingston', suffix 'Junction' added December 1852. Renamed 'Surbiton & Kingston' 01/07/1863 (on same day that current 'Kingston' station opened). Renamed 'Surbiton' 01/10/1867. Goods yard closed 01/11/1971.

		G	*1845*	*01/11/1971*		
SURREY CANAL	40 / 3B 80		Early 2025?	N/A	TFL (LO)	Proposed station on LO East London Line extension phase 2. Did not open with line 09/12/2012, due to insufficient funds, but foundations for station building / platforms were constructed. Originally 'Surrey Canal Road', then 'New Bermondsey'. Planning application approved December 2021, predicted opening early 2025.
Surrey Canal Junction	40 / 3C 79 / 80		01/09/1849	N/A	SER / LGR	Initially junction between SER route towards Bricklayers Arms and the LGR, also site of 'North Kent Junction' exchange platforms. Spur to North Kent West Junction disused after 21/06/1981. Current junction established 30/12/2016 between 'Southwark Reversible' and LGR route; somewhat to the west of the original junction.

SURREY QUAYS
   Surrey Docks
   Deptford Road
	40 / 2B
	79 / 80
			07/12/1869	N/A	ELR	First served MET & MDR 01/10/1884, last served MDR 01/08/1905, no service MET 03/12/1906 – 31/03/1913. Renamed 'Surrey Docks' 17/07/1911, then 'Surrey Quays' 24/10/1989. Closed 26/03/1995 – 25/03/1998 and 23/12/2007 – 27/04/2010 (engineering work), upon latter reopening became TfL (LO) station.

SUTTON	65 / 3B	P	10/05/1847	N/A	LBSCR	Originally two-platform through station, additional platforms on Epsom Downs branch added 22/05/1865. Goods yard closed 07/10/1968.
		G	*10/05/1847*	*07/10/1968*		
SUTTON COMMON	65 / 2B		05/01/1930	N/A	SR	
Sutton East Junction	65 / 3C		22/05/1865	N/A	LBSCR	Route to Mitcham Junction opened 01/10/1868.
Sutton West Junction	65 / 3B		05/01/1930	N/A	SR	

SWANLEY
   Swanley Junction
   Sevenoaks Junction
	57 / 6B	P	01/07/1862	N/A	LCDR	Opened by LCDR at divergence of Sevenoaks Railway (nominally independent but operated by LCDR) branch to Bat & Ball station from LCDR main line. Four platform faces, opened a month after branch line. Initially 'Sevenoaks Junction', renamed 'Swanley Junction' 01/01/1871, then 'Swanley' 16/04/1939. Rebuilt on a site west of the junction with two island platforms 02/07/1939. Goods yard closed 16/05/1964, but two sidings were retained as part of Westinghouse training compound (lifted c.2015).

		G	*01/07/1862*	*16/05/1964*		
Swanley Junction Sevenoaks Junction	57 / 6B		02/06/1862	N/A	SOR / LCDR	Initially 'Sevenoaks Junction', presumably renamed in conjunction with Swanley (Junction) station 01/01/1871.
SWANSCOMBE Swanscombe Halt	45 / 6B		02/11/1908	N/A	SECR	Re-sited 770 metres east 06/07/1930. Suffix 'Halt' dropped 05/05/1969.
SWANSCOMBE PORTLAND CEMENT WORKS	45 / 6B		*1929*	*1982*	PRIV	Britain's first cement works, opened 1825 with internal narrow gauge rail network. Connected to North Kent line and converted to Standard gauge 1929. Closed when chalk pits exhausted 1982.
SWISS COTTAGE (LPTB)	25 / 3C		20/11/1939	N/A	LPTB (BAK)	Opened by Bakerloo Line, transferred to Jubilee Line 01/05/1979. Closed March to May 1989 due to escalator replacement. Closed 21/03/2020 – 13/07/2020 (COVID-19).
SWISS COTTAGE (MSJWR)	25 / 3C		13/04/1868	18/08/1940	MSJWR	Terminus of MSJWR from Baker Street until 30/06/1879.
SYDENHAM	54 / 3B		05/06/1839	N/A	LCRR	Rebuilt 1853-4 (quadrupling).
Sydenham Down Junction	54 / 3B		10/06/1854	N/A	LBSCR	
SYDENHAM HILL	54 / 2A		01/08/1863	N/A	LCDR	
Sydenham Up Junction	54 / 3B		10/06/1854	N/A	LBSCR	
SYON LANE	36 / 3C		05/07/1931	N/A	SR	

T

Name	Page / grid		Date opened	Date closed	Opened by	Notes
TADWORTH Tadworth & Walton on the Hill	71 / 4D	P	01/07/1900	N/A	SECR	Terminus until extension to Tattenham Corner opened 04/06/1901 (please see Tattenham Corner entry for pre-25/03/1928 service patterns beyond Tadworth). Goods yard closed 07/05/1962. Suffix dropped 01/12/1968.
		G	*01/07/1900*	*07/05/1962*		
Tanners Hill Flydown	40 / 5D	P	29/03/1976	N/A	BR	Doubled for Thameslink upgrade, works completed 02/04/2013.
		G	*29/03/1976*	*N/A*		
Tanners Hill Junction	40 / 5D		29/03/1976	N/A	BR	Junction at north end of Tanners Hill Flydown.
Tanners Hill Tunnel	40 / 4C		30/07/1849	N/A	SER	
TARMAC STONE TERMINAL (HAYES)	35 / 1B		*1968*	N/A	PRIV	
TARMAC CONCRETE TERMINAL (PADDINGTON)	25 / 5B 67 / 5A		*1975*	*N/A*	PRIV	Opened 1975 on site of Paddington New Yard, closed 2010 to allow site to become railhead for construction of 'Elizabeth Line'. Reopened on same site upon completion of Elizabeth Line works (first train 08/10/2020).
TARMAC READYMIX & AGGREGATE TERMINAL (PARK ROYAL)	24 / 5B		*Pre-1990*	N/A	PRIV	Originally Marcon. First appeared in 6th edition of Baker (1990), referenced in BLN December 1990 as receiving traffic.
TATTENHAM CORNER	71 / 2D	P	04/06/1901	N/A	SECR	First use for a race meeting 04/06/1901, initially appears to have been race / excursion specials only. All day service commenced June 1902 (Bradshaw), albeit Summer only until end Summer 1914. Army camp use September 1914 to 1919. Race specials recommenced 29/04/1919, full public reopening 25/03/1928 (electrification). Goods yard closed 02/04/1962. Reduced from original six platforms to three 29/11/1970. Original station building demolished by a train over-running buffers 01/12/1993, replacement opened March 1994.
		G	*04/06/1901*	*02/04/1962*		
TAYLOR'S LANE POWER STATION	24 / 3C		*1903*	*Post-1990*	PRIV	Originally built by Willesden Urban District Council. Decommissioned 1972 and replaced by current power station 1979, oil delivered by rail until at least January 1990. Sidings still remain in situ at power station end.

TEDDINGTON
   Teddington for Bushey Park
   Teddington & Bushey Park
   Teddington (Bushey Park)
	50 / 3C	P	01/07/1863	N/A	LSWR	Suffix variously '(Bushey Park)', '& Bushey Park' or 'for Bushey Park' until August 1911 when station became simply 'Teddington' (Borley). Suffix carried until 1955 in Bradshaw (per Quick). 'Bushey' also spelt 'Bushy' at times. Goods yard closed 03/05/1965.

		G	*01/07/1863*	*03/05/1965*		
TEMPLE The Temple	26 / 6C		30/05/1870	N/A	MDR	Prefix 'The' dropped gradually by c.1883. Closed 21/03/2020 – 24/08/2020 (COVID-19).
Temple Mills East Junction	28 / 2A 77 / 78		1881	N/A	GER	High Meads Loop opened 1881.
TEMPLE MILLS EUROSTAR DEPOT	27 / 1D		*07/10/2007*	*N/A*	LCOR	Partly on site of Temple Mills Marshalling Yard. Formal opening 02/10/2007, came into use 07/10/2007.

Name	Page / grid		Date opened	Date closed	Opened by	Notes
TEMPLE MILLS LOCO & WAGON WORKS	27 / 2D 27		1850	1963	ECR	
TEMPLE MILLS YARD	27 / 1D 27		1871	N/A	GER	First goods sidings opened 1871. Expanded 1877, 1893 & 1930, reconstructed as a 'hump' yard December 1958. Use as a Marshalling yard ceased 1992; reopened for engineering use 03/09/1994. Much of original site occupied by Eurostar Depot and Orient Way Sidings (see respective entries).
THAMES AMMUNITION WORKS	44 / 3A		1890	c.1962	PRIV	Connected to external rail network during latter stages of WW1, via 1½ mile light railway from Slade Green. 'Private and Untimetabled Railway Stations' (Croughton / Kidner / Young) gives a 06/06/1916 opening date for the munitions workers' halt in the works (see 'Trench Warfare Halt'), so rail connection to works presumed to be from same date. Same publication gives a 'by 07/1925' closure date and 'in use 06/1920' in the comments, but the branch does not appear on the 1920 OS (this may be solely due to its military nature, although the internal tramway system and buildings are marked).
Thames Bridge (Windsor)	33 / 4B		08/10/1849	N/A	GWR	Track singled 09/09/1963.
THAMES DITTON	50 / 6B		??/11/1851	N/A	LSWR	Opened November 1851 (Jackson), Quick states first in timetable December 1851.
Thames Tunnel (ELR)	40 / 1B		07/12/1869	N/A	ELR	Opened to pedestrian traffic 25/03/1843, first trains ran through tunnel 07/12/1869.
Thames Tunnel (LCOR)	44 / 5D 45 / 5A		14/11/2007	N/A	LCOR	
THAMES WHARF	41 / 1B 62 / 4A		29/04/1846	04/10/1965	ECTJR	Midland Railway goods yard opened 1870 adjacent to existing GER (former ECTJR / ECR).
THAMES WHARF	41 / 1B 62 / 5A		N/A	N/A	TFL (DLR)	Proposed station on DLR Woolwich Arsenal line, dependant on adjacent housing development.
Thames Wharf Junction	41 / 1B 62 / 3A		26/11/1855	04/10/1965	ECR	Junction between original line to North Woolwich and 1855 route via Custom House. Eliminated when Thames Wharf Goods closed (original North Woolwich route 'Silvertown Tramway' had been severed by then).
THAMESMEAD CENTRAL	42 / 1C		N/A	N/A	TFL (DLR)	Proposed terminus of branch from existing Beckton branch.
THE POSTAL MUSEUM Formerly POR DEPOT	26 / 5C		05/12/1927	N/A	POR	POR mothballed 31/05/2003, a portion of the route centred upon Mount Pleasant and the depot reopened for visitors as part of The Postal Museum 28/07/2017. Trains run on a loop to/from the former depot and past both platforms of the former station. Closed 18/03/2020 – 29/10/2020 and then for three further temporary spells until reopening 20/05/2021 (COVID-19).
THEOBALDS GROVE	7 / 2A	P	01/10/1891	N/A	GER	Closed 01/10/1909 – 01/03/1915 and 01/07/1919 – 21/11/1960. Goods yard opened 02/04/1900, closed 03/01/1966.
		G	02/04/1900	03/01/1966		
THERAPIA LANE	66 / 1B		30/05/2000	N/A	CTL	
THERAPIA LANE DEPOT	66 / 1B		10/05/2000	N/A	CTL	Sole depot for London Trams (first section opened 10/05/2000), on site of former permanent way sidings. Was served by a staff halt on both main roads connected by a foot crossing; currently disused.
THEYDON BOIS Theydon	8 / 3A	P	24/04/1865	N/A	GER	Suffix 'Bois' added 01/12/1865. Goods yard opened 1886. Majority of Passenger services transferred to LTE 25/09/1949, first trains in the morning remained BR until 01/06/1970. Goods closed 18/04/1966.
		G	1886	18/04/1966		
THORNEY MILL SIDINGS	34 / 1B		11/07/1943	N/A	GWR	Formerly used for coal, oil, scrap metal and stone traffic, latterly only stone traffic (Bardon, opened 1986) and spoil traffic remained until this ceased 2013/2014. Inward aggregate traffic recommenced 21/06/2019 ('Link Park Heathrow' / Ashville Aggregates) to re-laid and remodelled sidings.
THORNTON FIELDS CARRIAGE SIDINGS	27 / 4D 77		1928	16/06/2008	GER	Points 'clipped' out of use and overhead wires de-energised 16/06/2008, 'officially' closed 30/06/2008, site then cleared for 2012 Olympic Park. Replaced by Orient Way Sidings (opened 30/05/2008).
THORNTON HEATH	53 / 5C	P	01/12/1862	N/A	LBSCR	Goods yard on 'up' side, coal yard on 'down' side, all closed 07/10/1968.
		G	01/12/1862	07/10/1968		
Three Bridges	36 / 1A		15/07/1859	N/A	GWR	Unusual feature where rail, canal, and road intersect (rail below canal, road above canal). Date stated is that of special passenger train run on Brentford Dock branch, regular goods trains followed three days later.
THURROCK AGGREGATES CENTRE (LAFARGE)	44 / 5C		??/12/2007	N/A	PRIV	
THURROCK CHALK & WHITING Co. WORKS	44 / 3C		?	c.1980	PRIV	
TIDAL BASIN	41 / 1B 62 / 3A		??/02/1858	15/08/1943	ECR	Borley gives name as 'Victoria Docks, Tidal Basin', this name also given in Quick in use 1882-1914 (GER timetables), the prefix also being consistently used in Bradshaw.
TILBURY EAST CONTAINER TERMINAL	45 / 5D		1970	N/A	BR	
Tilbury East Curve	46 / 6A	P	14/08/1854	1985	LTSR	Opened as part of LTSR extension from Tilbury to Stanford-Le-Hope. Regular passenger trains ceased 1985 when trains from London to / from Southend ceased reversing at Tilbury Riverside.
		G	14/08/1854	30/11/1992		
Tilbury East Junction	46 / 6A		c.1855	30/11/1992	LTSR	Junction at east ends of Tilbury North / East curves.
TILBURY GRAIN TERMINAL	45 / 5C		1969	N/A	BR	
TILBURY INTERNATIONAL RAIL FREIGHT TERMINAL	46 / 6A		c.2004	13/06/2019	BR	Opened on site of former carriage sidings subsequent to closure of Tilbury Riverside station. Closed and relocated to Northfleet Hope Container Terminal c.13/06/2019 (date of online article) – BLN confirms June 2019.
Tilbury Junction	27 / 5D 88		17/05/1869	13/09/1959	NLR	Junction at north end of curve between NLR at Bow and LTSR at Bromley.
TILBURY MARINE	46 / 6A		15/05/1927	01/05/1932	PLA	Adjacent to tidal basin in Tilbury Docks, opened by PLA to serve boat trains.
TILBURY MPD	46 / 6A		13/04/1854	18/06/1962	LTSR	Original two road engine shed adjacent to Tilbury South Junction, replaced by four road shed adjacent to Tilbury North Junction 1912 (original closed 1908). Rebuilt 1956, closed 18/06/1962 (LTSR electrification).
Tilbury North Curve	46 / 6A	P	c.1855	N/A	LTSR	Opened c.1855. Few passenger trains until 1985 when London to Southend services ceased reversing at Tilbury Riverside station and began to run direct from Tilbury Town to East Tilbury. Until 1985, typically two peak services in each direction per day omitted Tilbury Riverside since at least November 1960 timetable. Such passenger use may have commenced from opening of the curve (shown in August 1887 timetable, just before direct route via Laindon opened), but not consistently as absent from August 1951 timetable.
		G	c.1855	N/A		
Tilbury North Junction	45 / 4D		17/04/1886	c.1960	LTSR	Primary junction giving access to Tilbury Docks (opened 17/04/1886), eliminated during resignalling c.1960 when access provided via Grays East Junction instead.
TILBURY POWER STATIONS	46 / 6B		1956	?	PRIV	Tilbury 'A' (oil fired) commissioned 1956, mothballed 1981, demolished 1999. Tilbury 'B' (coal & biomass fired) commissioned 1968, still in operation but rail connection severed (date unknown).
Tilbury Railport Junction Tilbury West Junction	46 / 5A		c.1855	N/A	LTSR	Junction at west end of Tilbury West / North Curves. Eliminated when Tilbury Riverside closed 30/11/1992, but re-established to provide access to Tilbury International Rail Freight Terminal. When the latter closed, junction retained to provide access to 'Tilbury2'.

Name	Page / grid		Date opened	Date closed	Opened by	Notes
TILBURY RIVERSIDE Tilbury Tilbury Fort	46 / 6A	P	13/04/1854	30/11/1992	LTSR	Terminus of original LTSR line from Forest Gate Junction. Branch to Stanford-Le-Hope (and subsequently towards Southend) added 14/08/1854. 'Fort' suffix applied from opening until 1866 (although not always), 'Riverside' suffix added 1935 (in timetable with effect from 06/07/1936). Until 1985 almost all services reversed at station (typically two peak services in each direction per day used the North Curve), after 1985 trains between London and Southend ran direct, with the only trains remaining being Upminster via Ockendon service. Upminster via Ockendon service truncated at Grays and station closed 30/11/1992. Goods yard closed 06/05/1968. Site was partially occupied by Tilbury International Rail Freight Terminal (closed c.13.06.2019).
		G	13/04/1854	06/05/1968		
Tilbury South Junction	46 / 6A		14/08/1854	30/11/1992	LTSR	Junction at south end of Tilbury West and East curves.
TILBURY TOWN Tilbury Town for Tilbury Docks Tilbury Docks	45 / 5D		17/04/1886	N/A	LTSR	Opened to public on same date as adjacent Tilbury Docks (17/04/1886) according to Quick (who also states had been open to dock construction workers from c. May 1884). Borley gives opening date of 15/06/1885. Renamed 'Tilbury Town for Tilbury Docks' 03/08/1934, suffix dropped 1958.
Tilbury West Curve		P	13/04/1854	30/11/1992	LTSR	Part of original LTSR route from Forest Gate to Tilbury (Riverside). After 1985 London to Southend trains ceased reversing via Tilbury Riverside, only Upminster via Ockendon trains remained, these withdrawn 30/11/1992. Curve remained as access to Tilbury International Rail Freight Terminal until that closed c.13.06.2019.
		G	13/04/1854	13/06/2019		
TILBURY2	46 / 4B		23/11/2021	N/A	PRIV	Container and construction materials/aggregates terminal (Forth Ports) on site of former Tilbury Power Stations. Route learning trips commenced 15/11/2021, commercial traffic commenced 23/11/2021. 'Official' opening 31/01/2022. Tarmac Construction Materials & Aggregates Terminal (CMAT) traffic commenced 08/03/2022.
TOLWORTH	64 / 2A	P	29/05/1938	N/A	SR	Initially temporary terminus with 'down' platform only in use; extended to Chessington South and 'up' platform opened 28/05/1939. Goods yard expanded 1940, ceased handling general goods traffic 03/05/1965 but dedicated coal terminal had opened 04/01/1965. Aggregates traffic commenced c.1981, then coal traffic ceased Summer 1988 (per BLN 608 of 20/04/1989). Aggregates traffic then ceased July 1993 before re-starting c.1998 (Day Group).
		G	29/05/1938	N/A		
Tonbridge Fast Loop	55 / 5D	P	14/09/1902	N/A	SECR	Referred to as 'Bickley Loop' until 1959. Originally single track, doubled in readiness for Eurostar services 1992.
	56 / 6A	G	14/09/1902	N/A		
Tonbridge Line Junction	73 / 6C		26/05/1842	N/A	SER / LBRR	
Tonbridge Slow Loop	55 / 5D	P	08/09/1902	N/A	SECR	Referred to as 'Bickley Loop' until 1959. Originally single track, doubled in readiness for Eurostar services 1992.
	56 / 6A	G	08/09/1902	N/A		
TOOTING Tooting Junction	52 / 3D	P	01/10/1868	N/A	LBSCR / LSWR	Opened as a four-platform station at divergence of LBSCR / LSWR joint loop line from Streatham to Wimbledon. Named 'Tooting Junction' initially, original closed and replaced by two-platform station east of junction 12/08/1894. Closed to passengers 01/01/1917 – 27/08/1923. Suffix 'Junction' dropped 01/03/1938 (physical junction had been severed 10/03/1934), after 10/03/1934 goods yard accessed via Merton Park, closed 05/08/1968.
		G	01/10/1868	05/08/1968		
TOOTING BEC Trinity Road (Tooting Bec)	52 / 2D		13/09/1926	N/A	UERL (NOR)	Closed 01/09/1939 – 22/12/1939 (flood protection). Renamed 10/10/1950.
TOOTING BROADWAY	52 / 3D		13/09/1926	N/A	UERL (NOR)	
Tooting Junction	52 / 3D		01/10/1868	10/03/1934	LBSCR / LSWR	Junction eliminated 10/03/1934 and Tooting (Junction) to Merton Park route became a siding accessed from latter.
TOTTENHAM COURT ROAD Oxford Street (CCEHR only)	26 / 6B		30/07/1900	N/A	CLR	UERL (CCEHR) platforms opened 22/06/1907 as 'Oxford Street', renamed 09/03/1908. Closed to entries/exits 01/09/1939 – 15/11/1939 (installation of flood protection), but interchange between the Central and Northern Lines remained available. Northern Line platforms closed 02/04/2011 – 28/11/2011 (Elizabeth Line work). Central Line platforms closed 05/01/2015 – 06/12/2015 (station rebuilding). Elizabeth Line platforms opened 24/05/2022.
TOTTENHAM HALE Tottenham Tottenham Hale Tottenham	15 / 5B	P	15/09/1840	N/A	NER	Opened as 'Tottenham', suffix 'Hale' added ??/06/1875, dropped ??/11/1938, reinstated 1968. LTB Victoria Line station opened 01/09/1968. Goods yard closed 1968. Third NR platform opened 03/06/2019 for Stratford to Meridian Water service, fourth platform proposed.
		G	15/09/1840	1968		
Tottenham North Curve (MID)	9	P	17/12/1900	05/01/1981	MID	While Borley gives no indication of a regular passenger service ever having operated between Carlton Road and Mortimer Street Junctions, the August 1951 timetable shows two daily trains from the Southend area to / from the MID mainline, and per Middleton Press 'St Pancras to Barking' a Luton to Southend summer Sundays only return journey continued until 1963, so regular (albeit infrequent) passenger traffic operated until the end of Summer 1963. Section north of Mortimer Street Junction saw regular passenger trains until 05/01/1981 diversion of Barking trains to Gospel Oak. Route used for passenger diversions as recently as August 2014 (First Hull Trains, due to Kings Cross closure - Flickr).
		G	02/04/1883	N/A		
Tottenham North Curve (THJR)	15 / 5B	P	21/07/1868	01/11/1925	THJR	Opened with rest of THJR 21/07/1868 (passenger service), no regular freight until 1886. Closed to passengers 01/11/1925, closed to freight and abandoned 11/06/1961.
		G	1886	11/06/1961		
Tottenham North Curve Tunnels Nos. 1, 2 & 3	9		02/04/1883	N/A	MID	
Tottenham North Junction	15 / 5B		21/07/1868	11/06/1961	THJR / GER	Northern end of Tottenham North Curve (THJR) (see notes above).
Tottenham South Curve	15 / 5B	P	01/01/1880	N/A	THJR	First trains 1868 (goods), passenger services commenced 01/01/1880, ceased 07/01/1963, reintroduced 1989.
		G	1868	N/A		
Tottenham South Junction	15 / 5B		1868	N/A	THJR / GER	Junction between Tottenham South Curve and GER (see notes above).
Tottenham West Junction	15 / 5B		1868	11/06/1961	THJR	Southern end of Tottenham North Curve (THJR) (see notes regarding Tottenham North Curve THJR).
TOTTERIDGE & WHETSTONE Totteridge	5 / 6C	P	01/04/1872	N/A	GNR	Suffix '& Whetstone' added 01/04/1874. First served by and transferred to LPTB Northern Line 14/04/1940, closed to LNER passenger services on same date. Goods yard closed 01/10/1962. Crossover south of station removed over weekend of 24-25/03/2012.
		G	01/04/1872	01/10/1962		
TOWER GATEWAY	27 / 6A 74 / 2B		31/08/1987	N/A	DLR	Closed 28/06/2008 – 02/03/2009 (rebuilding from two tracks to one track to accommodate longer trains).
TOWER HILL (MDR / MET) Mark Lane	27 / 6A 74 / 2B 87		06/10/1884	05/02/1967	MDR / MET	Replaced former 'Tower of London' Station to East. Renamed 'Tower Hill' 01/09/1946, closed and replaced on original 'Tower of London' site to east by 'Tower Hill' (MET) 05/02/1967.

Name	Page / grid		Date opened	Date closed	Opened by	Notes
TOWER HILL (MET) *Tower of London*	27 / 6A 74 / 2B		25/09/1882	N/A	MET	Terminus of MET extension from Aldgate 25/09/1882 - 06/10/1884, replaced by Mark Lane station to west 06/10/1884 when MET / MDR route from Mansion House to Aldgate East opened, although 'Tower of London' did not close until 13/10/1884. Reopened as 'Tower Hill' 05/02/1967, replacing 'Tower Hill' (MDR / MET) station (former 'Mark Lane'). Westbound trains used central platform 2 as a through route until 03/09/1967, then diverted and platform 2 commissioned as a bay accessed from the west end 21/01/1968. Platform 2 connected at eastern end to eastbound road over weekend of 01-02/07/2017 but not commissioned. Eastbound points temporarily plain-lined April 2021 due to track defect. Reinstated 16-17/07/2022 and then commissioned 23/10/2022.
Tower Subway	40 / 1A 87		02/08/1870	07/12/1870	PRIV	A single-bore tunnel pioneering the use of a circular cast iron 'shield'. A 2ft 6in railway was laid with a single cable-hauled car powered by static steam engines at each end, this was unprofitable and the tunnel was converted for pedestrians after just four months, reopening 24/12/1870.
TREASURE ISLAND RAILWAY	48 / 5A		??/04/1984	1993	PRIV	2ft gauge railway within Thorpe Park.
TRENCH WARFARE HALT	44 / 3A		06/06/1916	Post-06/1920	PRIV	Halt for munitions workers within Thames Ammunition Works (see relevant entry). Location of platform unknown. 'Private and Untimetabled Railway Stations' (Croughton / Kidner / Young) gives a 'by 07/1925' closure date and 'in use 06/1920' in the comments, but the branch does not appear on the 1920 OS (this may be solely due to its military nature, although the internal tramway system and buildings are marked). The other end of the branch was an unnamed halt adjacent to current Slade Green Depot EMU maintenance shed (see 43 / 5D).
TRIANGLE SIDINGS	38 / 2C 84		c.1915	N/A	UERL (MDR)	Sidings laid between 1914 and 1916 Ordnance surveys. Closed for S Stock upgrade work 11/12/2010, trains stabled at Lillie Bridge instead. Reopened with three longer roads 22/05/2011 (previously five).
TRUMPER'S CROSSING HALTE *Trumper's Crossing (for Osterley Park) Halte*	36 / 1B		01/07/1904	01/02/1926	GWR	Closed 22/03/1915 – 12/04/1920. The full-length former name stated is that which appeared on nameboards.
TUFNELL PARK	26 / 2A 9		22/06/1907	N/A	UERL (CCEHR)	Closed 08/06/2015 – 04/03/2016 (lift replacement) and 21/03/2020 – 31/08/2020 (COVID-19).
TUFNELL PARK GOODS	26 / 1B		*15/02/1886*	*06/05/1968*	GER	After closure, BP oil terminal established on down side of THJR.
TULSE HILL	53 / 1C	P	01/10/1868	N/A	LBSCR	Goods yard to south of station in triangle beyond Tulse Hill South Junction, closed 07/09/1964. Pair of sidings provided on 'down' side. Station had an overall roof spanning its four platforms until c.1900.
		G	*01/10/1868*	*07/09/1964*		
Tulse Hill North Junction	53 / 1C		01/01/1869	N/A	LBSCR / LCDR	
Tulse Hill South Junction	53 / 2C		01/11/1870	N/A	LBSCR	Junction at north end of Leigham and West Norwood Spurs.
TUNNEL CEMENT WORKS (THURROCK)	44 / 4D		?	?	PRIV	
TURKEY STREET *Forty Hill*	7 / 2B	P	01/10/1891	N/A	GER	Opened 01/10/1891 as 'Forty Hill', closed 01/10/1909 – 01/03/1915 and again 01/07/1919. Reopened 21/11/1960 as 'Turkey Street'. Goods yard closed 01/06/1966.
		G	*01/10/1891*	*01/06/1966*		
TURNHAM GREEN	37 / 2C 51 / 2C		01/01/1869	N/A	LSWR	Opened by LSWR. Served by GWR 01/06/1870 – 01/11/1870. First served MDR 01/06/1877. Served by MET 01/10/1877 – 01/01/1911 (MET / GWR joint after 01/01/1894). Rebuilt from two side platforms to two island platforms when route quadrupled 03/12/1911 (LSWR northern island, MDR southern island). LSWR service ceased and northern island abandoned 05/06/1916. Eastbound District Line started using north face of north island from 05/06/1932. Piccadilly Line started running non-stop through middle platforms 04/07/1932 (but started calling at these platforms at extremes of traffic day from 23/06/1963, apart from a break between 29/09/1996 – 26/01/1997).
Turnham Green Junction	51 / 2C		01/07/1879	N/A	LSWR / MDR	Junction between LSWR route to Richmond and MDR branch to Ealing Broadway.
TURNPIKE LANE	14 / 5C		19/09/1932	N/A	UERL (GNPBR)	
TWICKENHAM	36 / 6C	P	22/08/1848	N/A	LSWR	Original station west of London Road. Engine shed added June 1850, rebuilt 01/07/1863, closed 1897. Additional 'up' platform added when junction to west of station became 'flying' 22/10/1883. New station to east of London Road with two bay platforms for rugby traffic opened 28/03/1954 (original station closed same day). Goods yard closed 02/01/1967. By 2015 bay platforms 1 & 2 had been disused for some time. Platform 1 had track removed while platform 2 had track re-laid, but it is yet to be recommissioned.
		G	*22/08/1848*	*02/01/1967*		
Twickenham Junction	50 / 1B		01/07/1863	N/A	LSWR	Junction between LSWR Windsor Line and branch to Kingston. Was a 'flat' junction until flyover opened 22/10/1883.
TWYFORD ABBEY HALT	24 / 4A		01/05/1904	01/05/1911	GWR	Replaced by Brentham station to west. Slightly east of present Hanger Lane station.
TWYFORD ABBEY SIDINGS	24 / 4B		26/03/1903	c.1955	LNWR	Built to serve Royal Agricultural Showground, remained in situ until lifted by 1955.

U V

Name	Page / grid	Date opened	Date closed	Opened by	Notes
UP CARRIAGE SIDINGS (VICTORIA)	39 / 3A	c.1880's	N/A	LBSCR	Not present on 1875 OS map, but had appeared by 1896.
Up Empty Carriage Tunnel	26 / 4A 58	10/07/1922	c.2000	LNWR	Colloquially known as the 'Rat Hole', abandoned circa resignalling in Euston area 1999 – 2000.
UP SIDINGS (EUSTON)	26 / 4A	?	N/A	LNWR	
UP SIDINGS (WEST RUISLIP)	10 / 6A	*1942*	N/A	LNER	Currently in use for HS2 works, reinstated for this purpose 26/01/2023.
Up Slow Flyover (Wimbledon)	52 / 2B	17/05/1936	N/A	SR	Allowed reconfiguration of LSWR main line between Wimbledon and Clapham Junction.
UP YARD (REDHILL)	73 / 5C	*post 1849*	*pre 23/12/2017*	SER	Sidings on site on 1871 OS, possibly laid at same time as Guildford Line c.1849. Sidings removed due to works associated with Redhill Platform 0 construction, closure commenced 23/12/2017, although sidings had been abandoned some time prior to this to allow the new platform to commence construction (at same time as Post Office & Down Sidings; 27/02/2017?).
UPMINSTER	31 / 2C	P 01/05/1885	N/A	LTSR	Served by District Railway trains 02/06/1902 - 01/10/1905, then by excursion trains to Southend (later Shoeburyness) from 01/06/1910. Regular District Line service reintroduced 12/09/1932 when route quadrupled, which also resulted in station rebuilding and relocation of original 1893 engine shed (demolished 1931, rebuilt 1935). District Line excursion trains beyond Upminster withdrawn 30/09/1939. Separate platform for Romford service opened 20/05/1957. Goods yard closed 07/12/1964.
		G *01/05/1885*	*07/12/1964*		
UPMINSTER or POT KILNS BRICK WORKS	19 / 6C	*Post 1885*	*By 1933*	PRIV	Connected via exchange sidings at Upminster via a horse-drawn tramway (gauge unknown but appears narrower than standard gauge on OS).
UPMINSTER BRIDGE	31 / 2B	17/12/1934	N/A	LMS	Opened by LMS on the 1932 'local' lines only, served exclusively by District Line trains from outset.

Name	Page / grid		Date opened	Date closed	Opened by	Notes
UPMINSTER DEPOT	31 / 1C		*01/12/1959*	N/A	LTE (DIS)	South of site accommodated five stabling sidings for District Line trains since 12/09/1932. Depot construction commenced 01/12/1958, completed 29/06/1959, full opening 01/12/1959.
Upminster East Junction	31 / 2C		01/07/1892	N/A	LTSR	Junction between LTSR main line and Ockendon Loop.
Upminster West Junction	31 / 2C		07/06/1893	20/05/1957	LTSR	Junction between LTSR main line and Romford Branch, eliminated when LTE and BR segregated at Upminster.
UPNEY	29 / 4B		12/09/1932	N/A	LMS	Barking to Upminster quadrupled by the LMS 12/09/1932 and Upney station opened, served by UERL District Line from opening. Ownership transferred to LTB 1970.
Upper Abbey Mills Junction	28 / 5A		31/03/1858	27/07/1958	LTSR	Junction at north end of Abbey Mills Curve.
UPPER HALLIFORD Upper Halliford Halt Halliford Halt	49 / 4A		01/05/1944	N/A	SR	Opened as 'Halliford Halt', prefix 'Upper' added 22/05/1944. 'Halt' dropped 05/05/1969. Initially opened with only a 'down' platform (single line working), 'up' platform opened 06/05/1946. 'Down' platform closed 17/05/2022 – 06/11/2022 (reconstruction work).
UPPER HOLLOWAY Upper Holloway for St John's Park U.H. for St John's Park and Highgate Hill Upper Holloway	26 / 1B	P G	21/07/1868 *c.1870*	N/A 06/05/1968	THJR	Closed 31/01/1870 – 01/10/1870. Opened as 'Upper Holloway', suffix 'for St John's Park and Highgate Hill' added 01/03/1871, '- and Highgate Hill' dropped 01/04/1875, then '- for St John's Park' added 01/07/1903 (i.e. returned to 'Upper Holloway' from this date). Goods yard opened c.1870, closed 06/05/1968. Gospel Oak to South Tottenham (formerly Barking) trains suspended at weekends 04/06/2016 to 25/09/2016, and then entire Overground service suspended and station closed 26/09/2016 to 27/02/2017 due to electrification works on Gospel Oak to Barking Line.
UPPER SYDENHAM	54 / 2A		01/08/1884	20/09/1954	LCDR	Closed 01/01/1917 – 01/03/1919 and 22/05/1944 – 04/03/1946. Closed for good 20/09/1954.
UPPER WARLINGHAM Upper Warlingham for Riddlesdown Upper Warlingham Upper Warlingham & Whyteleafe Upper Warlingham	74 / 2A	P G	10/03/1884 *10/03/1884*	N/A 04/05/1964	LBSCR / SER	Opened as 'Upper Warlingham', '& Whyteleafe' suffix added 01/01/1894, dropped 01/10/1900. 'for Riddlesdown' suffix added 1912 (LBSCR timetable), until 1926/7. Goods yard closed 04/05/1964.
UPTON PARK	28 / 4C		17/09/1877	N/A	LTSR	First served by District Railway 02/06/1902, line quadrupled 1905, District trains then using 'slow' platforms to north. Served by Metropolitan Line since 30/03/1936 ('Hammersmith & City Line' since 30/07/1990). Main line services non-stopped since 15/06/1962, and 'fast' platforms abandoned. Goods yard situated to east of passenger station on a short branch line (see separate entry below). Westbound platform closed 20/05/2001 – 11/06/2001, eastbound platform closed 17/06/2001 – 09/07/2001.
UPTON PARK GOODS	28 / 4C		*01/04/1895*	??/07/1989	LNWR	
URALITE HALT	60 / 3C		01/07/1906	04/12/1961	SECR	Built to serve adjacent British Uralite plc. works; opened for workers only early 1901, to public 01/07/1906.
Uttley Junction	40 / 3B 80		25/02/2013	N/A	NR	Crossover south of South Bermondsey station; installed over weekend of 23-24/02/2013.
UXBRIDGE (1st)	21 / 2C	P G	04/07/1904 04/07/1904	04/12/1938 01/05/1939	MET	Served by District Line 01/03/1910 - 23/10/1933, Piccadilly Line thereafter until closure. Closed to passengers 04/12/1938 and replaced by Uxbridge (2nd) to west, goods yard remained open until 01/05/1939 (became sidings).
UXBRIDGE (2nd)	21 / 3C		04/12/1938	N/A	LPTB (MET / PIC)	Replaced 1st station, closed on same date. Closed 18/07/2014 – 11/08/2014 (track renewal).
UXBRIDGE HIGH STREET	21 / 2B	P G	01/05/1907 11/05/1914	01/09/1939 24/02/1964	GWR	Goods yard open 11/05/1914. No passenger service 01/01/1917 – 03/05/1920, withdrawn for good 01/09/1939 although 'official' closure not until 25/09/1939. Goods yard closed 24/02/1964 and most of branch abandoned.
UXBRIDGE ROAD	38 / 1A 83		01/11/1869	21/10/1940	WLR	Located to south of 1844 WLR Shepherd's Bush station, Shepherd's Bush (NR) station in turn opened partially on the 1844 site 28/09/2008.
UXBRIDGE ROAD GOODS Shepherd's Bush Goods	38 / 1A 83		1844	01/11/1967	WLR	Goods yard to north of Shepherd's Bush (WLR) station, probably not open continuously in early years. Subsequently renamed after Uxbridge Road passenger station (opened 01/11/1869).
Uxbridge Road Junction	38 / 1A 83		01/07/1864	01/03/1954	WLR / MET/GWR	Junction at southern end of spur to Latimer Road, 'up' platform of present-day Shepherd's Bush NR station occupies site of junction.
UXBRIDGE SIDINGS	21 / 3C		1942	N/A	LPTB (MET)	Metropolitan Line stabling sidings. On site of former Goods yard, closed 01/05/1939 (see Uxbridge [1st]). Remodelled with effect from 09/04/2018 (no access at east end from westbound road).
UXBRIDGE VINE STREET Uxbridge	21 / 3C	P G	08/09/1856 *08/09/1856*	10/09/1962 13/07/1964	GWR	'Vine Street' suffix added 01/05/1907. Passenger station closed with withdrawal of passenger services on branch 10/09/1962, goods yard closed and branch abandoned 13/07/1964.
VAN DEN BURGHS & JURGENS (PURFLEET)	44 / 4C		?	?	PRIV	Stork margarine manufacturers
VAUXHALL Vauxhall Bridge	39 / 3B		11/07/1848	N/A	LSWR	Victoria Line station opened 23/07/1971. No dedicated goods yard, but milk traffic was handled on platform 1.
VAUXHALL GAS WORKS	39 / 3B		*c.1890*	1958	PRIV	South Metropolitan Gas Company, 3ft gauge internal railway system.
Ventnor Road	65 / 4B		03/10/1982	N/A	BR	Point where single track commences on Epsom Downs Branch (singled 03/10/1982).
Viaduct Junction	25 / 6A 83		16/04/1917	09/03/1964	GWR	Through goods route closed on quoted date, but access to Wood Lane milk depot remained until 1966.
VICTORIA	39 / 2A		01/10/1860	N/A	VSPR	Opened by Victoria Station & Pimlico Railway, a joint venture between the LBSCR, LCDR, GWR & LNWR. LBSCR portion opened first, served by LCDR trains from 03/12/1860. Separate LCDR station opened 25/08/1862. LBSCR and LCDR stations reconstructed 1908 and 1907-9 respectively, entire station combined by SR 1924 and platforms numbered consecutively 21/09/1925. MDR station opened 24/12/1868, connected to mainline termini via a subway 12/08/1878. Victoria Line platforms opened 07/03/1969 (terminus until 23/07/1971), these closed 22/12/2007 – 07/01/2008 (refurbishment works).
VICTORIA & ALBERT GOODS	41 /1C 62 / 3B		1902	?	GWR	GWR goods depot accessed via Gallions Branch, opened 1902, closure date unknown.
VICTORIA (GROSVENOR) CARRIAGE SHED	39 / 3A		*c.1860's*	N/A	LCDR	Was in situ by early 1870's.
VICTORIA PARK Victoria Park, Hackney Wick	27 / 3C		14/06/1856	08/11/1943	NLR	Opened for a single day 29/05/1856 (celebrations for end of Crimean War), date quoted is date of full opening. Sometimes referred to as 'Victoria Park, Hackney Wick' until c.1859. Re-sited South 01/03/1866 with four platforms. Stratford-bound 'down' platform little used and removed 1895, with all GER trains reversing via the 'up' platform ex-Stratford. Former GER platform abandoned 01/11/1942 followed by former NLR platforms 08/11/1943.
VICTORIA PARK & BOW	27 / 4D 88		02/04/1849	06/01/1851	LBLR / ECR	Exchange platforms between ECR and LBLR (Blackwall Extension Railway), opened with latter route from Stepney (East) Junction. LBLR platforms closed 26/09/1850, ECR platforms closed 06/01/1851. Also referred to as 'Old Ford'.
Victoria Park Junction	27 / 3C		15/08/1854	03/10/1983	NLR / ECR	Poplar Branch singled 19/08/1979, officially closed 03/10/1983 (little or no traffic subsequent to Harrow Lane Sidings closure 30/08/1981). Junction points eliminated and remainder of branch dismantled 05/05/1984.
Victoria Road Crossover	92		2029-2033	N/A	NR	
VICTORIA ROAD GOODS (ROMFORD)	18 / 6D		*??/07/1896*	04/05/1970	LTSR	

Name	Page / grid		Date opened	Date closed	Opened by	Notes
VICTORIA ROAD WASTE TRANSFER STATION	22 / 2D		1980	N/A	PRIV	SUEZ UK Ltd
VIRGINIA WATER Virginia Water for Wentworth Virginia Water	47 / 5B		09/07/1856	N/A	LSWR	Suffix 'for Wentworth' January 1929 – 1955.
Virginia Water East Junction	47 / 5B		01/10/1866	??/06/1966	LSWR	Junction at east end of Virginia Water West Curve.
Virginia Water Junction Virginia Water North Junction	47 / 5B		01/10/1866	N/A	LSWR	
Virginia Water South Junction	47 / 5B		01/10/1866	??/06/1966	LSWR	Junction at west end of Virginia Water West Curve.
Virginia Water West Curve	47 / 5B	P	N/A	N/A	LSWR	Opened 1866 as single track (at same time as line to Chertsey, 01/10/1866?). No regular passenger service, doubled by 1914 per OS, closed June 1966.
		G	01/10/1866	??/06/1966		
Voltaire Road Junction	39 / 5A		early 1980's	N/A	BR	Junction installed during Victoria resignalling c.1980.
VOPAK (PURFLEET)	44 / 5D		?	Summer 2005	PRIV	Formerly Van Ommeren. Petrochemical / liquid gas storage and distribution, still active but rail connection removed. Last traffic Summer 2005 (BLN1374).

W Y

Name	Page / grid		Date opened	Date closed	Opened by	Notes
WADDON	66 / 2B	P	c.01/02/1863	N/A	LBSCR	Exact opening date unknown, first appeared in timetables February 1863. Goods yard closed 07/10/1968.
		G	c.01/02/1863	07/10/1968		
WADDON MARSH Waddon Marsh Halt	66 / 2B		06/07/1930	N/A	SR	Opened by SR at time of electrification with an island platform and passing loop on otherwise single passenger line. Suffix 'Halt' dropped 05/05/1969. Passing loop decommissioned 13/05/1984. Wimbledon to West Croydon closed by Railtrack 31/05/1997 (date of last train; official date of closure 02/06/1997). Reopened by Croydon Tramlink on new site to the south 30/05/2000.
WALLINGTON Carshalton	66 / 3A	P	10/05/1847	N/A	LBSCR	Renamed 01/09/1868. Goods yard closed 06/05/1963. Reversing siding west of station installed c.1916, present on 1956-7 OS, possibly decommissioned with signal box 26/11/1972. Station extensively rebuilt 13/09/1983.
		G	10/05/1847	06/05/1963		
WALTHAM CROSS Waltham Cross (& Abbey) Waltham Cross Waltham	7 / 1C	P	15/09/1840	N/A	NER	Opened as 'Waltham', suffix 'Cross' added 01/12/1882. Passenger station closed and relocated South 1885 (exact date unknown). Suffix '& Abbey' in use 01/05/1894 – 20/02/1969. Goods yard closed 04/07/1966.
		G	15/09/1840	04/07/1966		
WALTHAMSTOW CENTRAL Hoe Street, Walthamstow Hoe Street	15 / 5D	P	26/04/1870	N/A	GER	Originally single platform on 'up' side, Shern Hall Street to Clapton Junction doubled 1873 and 'down' platform built. Opened as 'Hoe Street'; suffix 'Walthamstow' added 1886, although this was often omitted. Goods yard closed 02/11/1964. Renamed 'Walthamstow Central' 06/05/1968. LTB Victoria Line terminus opened 01/09/1968.
		G	26/04/1870	02/11/1964		
WALTHAMSTOW QUEEN'S ROAD Walthamstow	15 / 5D		09/07/1894	N/A	TFGR	Suffix 'Queen's Road' added 06/05/1968, see 'Queen's Road Goods' entry for goods yard (remote from station). Station closed 04/06/2016 to 27/02/2017 due to electrification works on Gospel Oak to Barking Line.
WALTON-ON-THAMES Walton for Hersham Walton & Hersham Walton	62 / 2B	P	21/05/1838	N/A	LSWR	Opened as 'Walton', suffix '& Hersham' added 1849, became 'Walton for Hersham' 1913, then 'Walton-on-Thames' 30/09/1935. Goods yard closed 01/11/1966.
		G	21/05/1838	01/11/1966		
WALWORTH ROAD Camberwell Gate	39 / 3D		01/05/1863	03/04/1916	LCDR	Renamed January 1865.
WALWORTH ROAD COAL	39 / 2D		16/11/1871	30/04/1973	MID	
WANDLE PARK	66 / 2C		30/05/2000	N/A	CTL	
WANDSWORTH BASIN	38 / 5B		01/06/1804	31/08/1846	SIR	Wandsworth terminus of SIR. Railway operational as far south as Summerstown by October 1802, but per Jackson the basin at Wandsworth was not in use until 01/06/1804.
WANDSWORTH COMMON Wandsworth	52 / 1D	P	01/12/1856	N/A	WELCPR	Opened as 'Wandsworth', suffix 'Common' added January 1858. WELCPR's temporary London terminus until 29/03/1858 extension to Pimlico (WELCPR). After this date both Wandsworth Common and New Wandsworth to north were open concurrently, until Wandsworth Common's closure 01/06/1858. When New Wandsworth closed 01/11/1869, it was replaced by the second 'Wandsworth Common' slightly to the south of the 01/12/1856 station. Goods yard given as opening c.1869 in Borley (at same time as 2nd passenger station?), closed 28/09/1964.
		G	c.1869	28/09/1964		
WANDSWORTH ROAD	39 / 4A 82		01/03/1863	N/A	LCDR	Original (western) platforms opened by LCDR 01/03/1863 on 25/08/1862 route, closed 01/01/1867, reopened by LBSCR 01/05/1867. Eastern platforms opened by LCDR with its 01/01/1867 route, closed 03/04/1916.
WANDSWORTH ROAD GOODS	39 / 4A 82		1874	30/04/1973	MID	
WANDSWORTH TOWN Wandsworth	38 / 5C		27/07/1846	N/A	LSWR	Original site slightly to west of present (on current Smugglers Way, formerly North Street). Relocated to current site on Old York Road c.1860. Line quadrupled 1886. Suffix 'Town' added 07/10/1903.
WANSTEAD	16 / 6C		14/12/1947	N/A	LPTB (CEN)	Closed March to May 1989 (escalator replacement). Closed 22/06/2009 – 31/08/2009 (reconstruction).
WANSTEAD PARK	28 / 2B		09/07/1894	N/A	TFGR	Station closed 04/06/2016 – 27/02/2017 due to electrification works on Gospel Oak to Barking Line.
WAPPING Wapping & Shadwell	40 / 1B		07/12/1869	N/A	ELR	Northern terminus of ELR until 10/04/1876, suffix '& Shadwell' also dropped on same date. First served MET & MDR 01/10/1884, last served MDR 01/08/1905, no service MET 03/12/1906 – 31/03/1913. Separate 'East London Line' identity introduced during 1980's. Closed 26/03/1995 – 25/03/1998 and 23/12/2007 – 27/04/2010 (engineering work), upon latter reopening became TfL (LO) station.
WARREN STREET Euston Road	26 / 5A		22/06/1907	N/A	UERL (CCEHR)	Renamed 07/06/1908. Victoria Line platforms opened 01/12/1968 (terminus until 07/03/1969).
WARWICK AVENUE	25 / 5C		31/01/1915	N/A	UERL (BSWR)	Closed 21/03/2020 – 18/05/2020 (COVID-19).
WARWICK ROAD GOODS Kensington Canal Basin	38 / 2B 84		27/05/1844	17/07/1967	WLR	Southern end of WLR (Kensington Canal Basin). In c.1865 basin filled in and site developed as Warwick Road goods yard accessed from south ex-WLER.
Warwick Road Junction	38 / 3B 84		01/02/1872	N/A	MDR	Curve towards Kensington (Addison Road) built 1869-1870, but no regular use until 01/02/1872. Remodelled as a 'flying' junction 05/01/1913.

Name	Page / grid		Date opened	Date closed	Opened by	Notes
WATERLOO	39 / 1C 89		11/07/1848	N/A	LSWR	LSWR terminus, replacing Nine Elms station. Known alternatively as 'Waterloo Bridge' until 1882. Expanded 03/08/1860 (Windsor or 'North' station), link to SER opened 11/01/1864 (only used July 1865 - December 1867). Through platforms to SER referred to as 'New Waterloo' in contemporary timetables. Expanded again 16/12/1878 ('South' station), further platforms added November 1885, 1909, 06/03/1910. Connection to SER removed 26/03/1911. Designations of 'North', 'Central' and 'South' stations removed and platforms renumbered 01/10/1912. Station rebuilt to pre-Eurostar form, official opening 21/03/1922. WCIR platforms opened 08/08/1898, UERL (BSWR) 10/03/1906, UERL (CCEHR) 13/09/1926, LUL (JUB) 24/09/1999 (terminus until 20/11/1999). Waterloo & City Line platforms closed 08/08/1992 – 06/09/1992 and 28/05/1995 – 19/07/1993, transferred to LUL 01/04/1994. Bakerloo Line platforms closed 11/11/1996 – 14/07/1997. Eurostar services terminated here 14/11/1994 – 14/11/2007 (unadvertised trial services commenced 17/08/1994), dedicated platforms 20-24 then abandoned until 23/10/2013, when platform 20 reopened for domestic services (as a contingency), followed by timetabled services from 18/05/2014. Platforms 21-24 recommissioned 03/07/2017, passenger test runs during week commencing Sunday 30/07/2017 then full use from 05/08/2017.
Waterloo Curve	82	P	17/08/1994	14/11/2007	RT	Date quoted is start of trial Eurostar service, advertised service commenced 14/11/1994. Regular traffic ceased 14/11/2007 (diversion of Eurostar to St Pancras), but chord still in situ and traversed by test trains / railtours. Briefly blocked late 2011 but reinstated. Used for Southeastern passenger diversions to Waterloo during Christmas 2017 engineering works 23/12/2017 – 01/01/2018.
		G	17/08/1994	N/A		
WATERLOO DEPOT	39 / 1C 89		*08/08/1898*	N/A	WCIR	Waterloo & City Line depot.

WATERLOO EAST
  Waterloo
  Waterloo Junction
	39 / 1C 89		01/01/1869	N/A	SER	Replaced Blackfriars (SER) station to the east. Opened as 'Waterloo Junction', connection to Waterloo LSWR opened 11/01/1864, but only used July 1865 - December 1867 (i.e. before station opened), and taken out of use 26/03/1911. Suffix 'Junction' dropped 07/07/1935, renamed 'Waterloo East' 02/05/1977. Closed 24/07/1993 – 16/08/1993.

WATFORD	2 / 4B	P	02/11/1925	N/A	MET / LNER	Not intended to be terminus (see Watford Central below). Goods yard closed 14/11/1966. Proposed to close to passengers if 'Croxley Link' built (but to remain as stabling sidings), although project is currently on hold.
		G	*02/11/1925*	*14/11/1966*		
WATFORD CENTRAL	2 / 4C		N/A	N/A	MET / LNER	Envisaged as terminus of MET / LNER Watford branch, station building remains ('Moon Under Water' pub).
WATFORD ENGINE SHED	2 / 3C		*1872*	*??/03/1965*	LNWR	
WATFORD HIGH STREET	2 / 4C		01/10/1862	N/A	WRR	Served by Bakerloo Line trains 16/04/1917 – 27/09/1982. Proposed to be served by Metropolitan Line if 'Croxley Link' built.
Watford High Street Junction	5 / 5C		10/02/1913	25/03/1996	LNWR	Last train ran ex-Croxley Green 22/03/1996 (no weekend service), but junction not severed until 2005. Proposed to be re-established (on hold).
Watford East Junction	1 / 5D		02/11/1925	N/A	MET / LNER	
WATFORD JUNCTION Watford	2 / 3C	P	20/07/1837	N/A	LBIR	Opened as 'Watford', re-sited south and suffix 'Junction' added 05/05/1858 coinciding with opening of the St Albans (Abbey) branch. Served by Bakerloo Line 06/04/1917 – 27/09/1982. Former goods yard (closed to public goods traffic 1965) now used as Civil Engineers' sidings and aggregates terminal. Proposed to become terminus of Metropolitan Line (diversion from Watford station via 'Croxley Link'), but project on hold. St Albans Abbey branch service suspended 19/12/2021 – 21/02/2022 (COVID-19 related).
		G	*20/07/1837*	*1965*		
WATFORD NORTH Callowland	2 / 2C	P	01/10/1910	N/A	LNWR	Renamed 01/03/1927. Goods yard situated to north, opened with passenger station. General goods traffic ceased 01/04/1970, but remained open for heating oil, later M25 construction materials, finally dog food, until 1988 closure. St Albans Abbey branch service suspended 19/12/2021 – 21/02/2022 (COVID-19 related).
		G	*01/10/1910*	*1988*		
Watford North Curve	1 / 5D	P	02/11/1925	N/A	MET / LNER	Used by early morning and late night passenger services only. More frequent daytime passenger service in operation 02/11/1925 - 31/12/1933 and 06/10/1941 - 03/01/1960, proposed to be reinstated for an Aylesbury to Watford Junction service operated by Chiltern if 'Croxley Link' is built.
		G	*02/11/1925*	N/A		
Watford North Junction (1)	1 / 6D		02/11/1925	N/A	MET / LNER	
Watford North Junction (2)	2 / 3B		1874	2015	LNWR	Temporarily plain-lined 2015, restored Easter 2022, as of May 2023 'points out if use until further notice' remains in Sectional Appendix.
Watford South Curve	1 / 6D	P	02/11/1925	N/A	MET / LNER	
		G	*02/11/1925*	N/A		
Watford South Junction (1)	1 / 6D		02/11/1925	N/A	MET / LNER	
Watford South Junction (2)	2 / 3C		01/10/1862	N/A	WRR / LNWR	
WATFORD STADIUM	2 / 5B		04/12/1982	14/05/1993	BR	Opened using funds from Watford FC. Only served on Match days, last recorded train 14/05/1993. Not proposed to reopen if 'Croxley Link' built (would be replaced by Watford Vicarage Road immediately to west).
Watford Tunnels	2 / 1B		20/07/1837	N/A	LBIR	Original tunnel used by 'fast' roads, second bore used by 'slow' roads added by LNWR 1874.
WATFORD VICARAGE ROAD	2 / 5B		On hold	N/A	TFL (MET)	Proposed new station on reopened Croxley Green branch (funding announcement 14/12/2011, expected opening was 2017 but on hold due to funding issues). Immediately to west of former Watford Stadium station, to replace this and former Watford West stations.
WATFORD WEST	2 / 5B		15/06/1912	25/03/1996	LNWR	Last train ran on Croxley Green Branch 22/03/1996 (no weekend service), initially closed 'temporarily' for bridge work, replaced by bus service which ran until 26/09/2003. Not proposed to reopen if 'Croxley Link' built (would be replaced by Watford Vicarage Road).
Watford West Junction	2 / 5C		15/06/1912	02/01/1967	LNWR	
WELLESLEY ROAD	66 / 2D		10/05/2000	N/A	CTL	
WELLING	42 / 5C	P	01/05/1895	N/A	BHR	Goods yard closed 03/12/1962.
		G	*01/05/1895*	*03/12/1962*		
WELLINGTON SIDINGS	13 / 5D		*1867*	*01/10/1962*	GNR	Goods sidings in use in 1867, Carriage sheds opened 1881. Latter used by Northern Line Trains after 1940, BR use ceased 01/10/1962. Now Highgate Depot (Northern Line).
WELSH HARP	12 / 6D		02/05/1870	01/07/1903	MID	Primarily for excursion traffic to Brent Reservoir (Welsh Harp), although a reasonably regular daily service was provided (c.12 trains each way).

WEMBLEY CENTRAL
  Wembley (for Sudbury)
  Sudbury & Wembley
  Sudbury
	24 / 2A	P	08/08/1842	N/A	LBIR	Opened as 'Sudbury', '& Wembley' suffix added 01/05/1882. Became 'Wembley for Sudbury' 01/11/1910, renamed 'Wembley Central' 05/07/1948. Served by Bakerloo Line Trains 16/04/1917 – 24/09/1982, then 04/06/1984 – present. Goods yard closed 04/01/1965.

		G	*08/08/1842*	*04/01/1965*		

Name	Page / grid		Date opened	Date closed	Opened by	Notes
Wembley Central Junction	24 / 3A		15/06/1912	N/A	LNWR	
WEMBLEY DEPOT	24 / 2B 22		30/06/2005	N/A	NR	Chiltern Railways light maintenance depot.
WEMBLEY PARK	24 / 1B	P	12/05/1894	N/A	MET	Opening date is for regular public service; first served by football special 14/10/1893 and again 21/10/1893. Additional pair of terminal platforms south of road bridge built for British Empire Exhibition 1924 ('Exhibition Station', subsequently used for football traffic), reduced to a single platform 1931, demolished 1937. Served by Bakerloo Line 20/11/1939 – 01/05/1979, Jubilee Line thereafter. Goods yard transferred to LNER 01/12/1937, closed 05/07/1965. Southbound Jubilee Line non-stopped 26/09/2004 – 14/02/2005, northbound non-stopped 14/02/2005 – 29/05/2005 (station reconstruction).
		G	12/05/1894	05/07/1965		
WEMBLEY PARK SIDINGS	24 / 1A		c.1894	30/05/2022	MET	First two sidings laid to facilitate construction of adjacent station, so slightly predate 12/05/1894. Much expanded with nine-road carriage shed 1926, demolished 2005 and replaced by five open air sidings. Used to stable S7 stock trains after withdrawal of A60 (too short for S8), became disused May 2017, then points giving access plain lined after close of traffic 29/05/2022.
WEMBLEY STADIUM (LNER) *Wembley Exhibition* *Exhibition Station, Wembley*	24 / 2B 22	P	28/04/1923	18/05/1968	LNER	Renamed 'Wembley Stadium' 15/09/1927, name varied before this date. Loop last used 18/05/1968, officially closed 01/09/1969, dismantled 19/10/1969. Goods yard in use 1921 – 03/12/1962.
		G	1921	03/12/1962		
WEMBLEY STADIUM (GCR) *Wembley Complex* *Wembley Hill*	24 / 2A		01/03/1906	N/A	GCR	Opened as 'Wembley Hill', renamed 'Wembley Complex' 08/05/1978, renamed 'Wembley Stadium' 11/05/1987.
WEMBLEY YARD	24 / 3A 68 / 5A		c.1912	N/A	LNWR	First sidings appeared on site by 1912, subsequently expanded. New freight distribution centre opened 06/09/1993.
Wembley Yard South Junction	68 / 3C		c.1912	N/A	LNWR	
Wennington Crossovers	43 / 1D		14/11/2007	N/A	LCOR	
WEST ACTON	24 / 6B		05/11/1923	N/A	UERL (CEN)	Line through station opened by GWR 16/04/1917 (goods only) with UERL passenger trains commencing 03/08/1920. Station built by UERL, opening 05/11/1923. Following complete closure of Central Line 26/01/2003 due to Chancery Lane derailment the day before (see footnote), station reopened a day after the line to Ealing Broadway (25/03/2003).
WEST BROMPTON	38 / 3B 84		01/09/1866	N/A	WLER	MDR platforms opened 12/04/1869 as terminus from Gloucester Road, line extended to Putney Bridge 01/03/1880. Main line platforms closed 21/10/1940 and subsequently demolished, but rebuilt and reopened 30/05/1999.
WEST BYLFEET *Byfleet for Woodham & Pyrford* *Byfleet & Woodham*	61 / 5A	P	01/12/1887	N/A	LSWR	Opened as 'Byfleet & Woodham', renamed 'Byfleet for Woodham & Pyrford' 1913, then 'West Byfleet' 05/06/1950. Goods yard closed 09/09/1963.
		G	01/12/1887	09/09/1963		
WEST CENTRAL DISTRICT OFFICE	26 / 6B		13/02/1928	c.2000	POR	Had become disused prior to mothballing of POR on 31/05/2003.
WEST CROYDON *Croydon*	66 / 1C		05/06/1839	N/A	LCRR	Country terminus of LCRR until 10/05/1847, original terminus was 'up' bay, current through platforms added on Epsom extension on this date. Gained prefix 'West' 1850 (sometimes reversed to 'Croydon West') per Borley, Mitchell & Smith refer to opening as 'Croydon', becoming 'Croydon Town' May 1847, then 'West Croydon' April 1851. Bradshaw February 1863 listed as 'Croydon (West)'. Engine shed closed 1935. No record of goods facilities. Bay platform for Wimbledon services closed 02/06/1997. Croydon Tramlink platform opened at street level 10/05/2000.
West Croydon Junction (1st) *Croydon Junction*	86		12/07/1841	N/A	LBRR / LCRR	Divergence of original LBRR and LCRR routes, current junction location just south of Norwood Junction station, but original junction (Croydon Junction) was further south near present Norwood Fork Junction.
West Croydon Junction (2nd)	66 / 2C		22/10/1855	02/06/1997	LBSCR / WCRR	
West Croydon Spur	66 / 1D 86	P	22/05/1865	16/05/1983	LBSCR	Opened on same day as Epsom Downs Branch. Closed due to Gloucester Road Triangle remodelling 1983.
		G	22/05/1865	16/05/1983		
WEST DRAYTON *West Drayton & Yiewsley* *West Drayton*	34 / 1C		04/06/1838	N/A	GWR	Served by MDR trains 01/03/1883 – 01/10/1885. Re-sited east 09/08/1884. Suffix '& Yiewsley' added 1895.
WEST DRAYTON COAL	21 / 6B		18/12/1963	07/04/1999	PRIV	Lafarge stone terminal now on site.
WEST DULWICH *Dulwich*	53 / 1D		c.01/10/1863	N/A	LCDR	Opened as 'Dulwich', first in Bradshaw October 1863. 'West' prefix added 20/09/1926.
WEST EALING *Castle Hill, Ealing Dean* *Castle Hill*	23 / 6C	P	01/03/1871	N/A	GWR	Opened as 'Castle Hill', suffix 'Ealing Dean' added ??/06/1875. Served by District Railway 01/03/1883 – 01/10/1885. Renamed 'West Ealing' 01/07/1899. 'New' goods yard opened 03/02/1908, 'Old' goods yard closed ??/11/1968. Platform 1 removed ??/11/1973. Milk dock closed c.1978, 'New' goods yard closed 23/05/1980. Platform 4 (up slow) originally east of bridge, re-sited to west 1991. Bay platform commissioned for terminating trains ex-Greenford 12/06/2016, timetabled use not planned until 01/08/2016, but came into use almost immediately due to a derailment at Paddington 16/06/2016.
		G	01/03/1871	23/05/1980		
West Ealing Junction	23 / 6C		03/06/1903	N/A	GWR	
WEST EALING LMD (Light Maintenance Depot)	23 / 6C		26/01/2017	N/A	NR	On site of former Up Goods Loops, EMU stabling / light maintenance. First EMUs delivered night of 26-27/01/2017
West Ealing West Loop *Hanwell Loop*	23 / 6C	P	15/06/1903	10/10/1905	GWR	Initially used by temporary goods (03/06/1903) and passenger (15/06/1903) services serving the Park Royal Royal Agricultural showground, disused 04/07/1903 (passenger) 10/08/1903 (goods) – 01/05/1904. Regular passenger services ceased 10/10/1905. Originally 'Hanwell Loop', became 'West Ealing West Loop' in the 1950's. Singled at southern end 1974.
		G	03/06/1903	N/A		
WEST END SIDINGS	25 / 3B		1868	1968	MID	
WEST FINCHLEY	13 / 3C		01/03/1933	N/A	LNER	First served by and transferred to LPTB Northern Line 14/04/1940, closed to LNER passenger services on same date.
WEST GREEN	14 / 5D	P	01/01/1878	N/A	GER	Station and entire Palace Gates Branch closed to passengers 07/01/1963. Goods yard closed 05/10/1964.
		G	01/01/1878	05/10/1964		
WEST HAM *West Ham Manor Road* *West Ham*	28 / 5A		01/02/1901	N/A	LTSR	First served by District Railway 02/06/1902, line quadrupled 1905, District trains then using 'slow' platforms to north. Served by Metropolitan Line since 30/03/1936 ('Hammersmith & City Line' since 30/07/1990). Carried suffix 'Manor Road' between 11/02/1924 - ??/01/1969. 'Fast' platforms taken out of use 1940, then demolished 1956. Low Level (BR) Platforms opened 14/05/1979, closed 29/05/1994 – 29/10/1995, then again 10/12/2006 for conversion to DLR, reopening 31/08/2011. District / Hammersmith & City eastbound platform closed 14/03/1999 – 07/11/1999, westbound platform closed 07/11/1999 – 30/06/2000 (rebuilding works). Jubilee Line Platforms opened 14/05/1999. 'Fast' (former LTSR) platforms re-built and reopened 30/05/1999.
WEST HAM SOUTH GOODS	28 / 6C 62 / 3B		c.1892	07/12/1964	GER	

Name	Page / grid		Date opened	Date closed	Opened by	Notes
WEST HAMPSTEAD (LNWR) West End Lane	25 / 3B		01/03/1888	N/A	LNWR	Renamed 05/05/1975. Closed 29/10/1995 – 29/09/1996 (engineering works).
WEST HAMPSTEAD (MSJWR)	25 / 3B		30/06/1879	N/A	MSJWR	Country terminus of MSJWR until 24/11/1879. Last served Metropolitan Line 07/12/1940. Served by Bakerloo Line 20/11/1939 – 01/05/1979, Jubilee thereafter.
WEST HAMPSTEAD THAMESLINK West Hampstead Midland West Hampstead West End & Brondesbury* West End West End (For Kilburn & Hampstead)	25 / 3B	P G	01/03/1871 *01/03/1871*	N/A 03/08/1970	MID	Opened as 'West End (for Kilburn & Hampstead)', suffix dropped 01/07/1903. Renamed 'West End & Brondesbury' 01/04/1904*, then 'West Hampstead' 01/09/1905. Renamed 'West Hampstead Midland' 25/09/1950, 'Thameslink' substituted for 'Midland' 16/05/1988. Goods yard closed 03/08/1970. Rebuilt with a new entrance on Iverson Road, opening 14/12/2011. *Discrepancy between Borley and Quick; Quick states 'West Hampstead & Brondesbury' 01/04/1904 - 01/09/1905*
WEST HARROW	11 / 6A		17/11/1913	N/A	MET	
WEST HORNDON East Horndon	32 / 1D	P G	01/05/1886 01/05/1886	N/A 07/09/1964	LTSR	Country terminus of LTSR from opening until 01/06/1888. Served by District Line excursion trains 01/06/1910 – 30/09/1939. Renamed 01/05/1949. Goods yard closed 07/09/1964.
WEST INDIA DOCKS	40 / 1D 31 / 4A	P G	06/07/1840 c.1892	04/05/1926 06/11/1967	LBLR	Goods yard to north east of passenger station on a lower level, Midland Railway coal yard adjacent.
West India Down Viaduct	31 / 6A		24/08/2009	N/A	DLR	
WEST INDIA QUAY	40 / 1D 31 / 6A		31/08/1987	N/A	DLR	Closed 14/10/1991 (last train 11/10/1991) to 28/06/1993 due to reconstruction. Original platform 1 closed 2008 and demolished to make way for new diveunder, eastbound trains ex-Bank ceased serving after 24/08/2009.
WEST KENSINGTON North End (Fulham)	38 / 2B 84		09/09/1874	N/A	MDR	Renamed 01/03/1877. Adjacent goods yard opened by Midland Railway (see entry below).
WEST KENSINGTON GOODS & COAL	38 / 3B 84		25/03/1878	14/07/1965	MID	
West Kensington East Junction	38 / 2B 84		09/09/1874	N/A	MDR	Junction between 1872 route to WLER and 1874 extension to Hammersmith.
West Kensington West Junction	38 / 2A 84		25/03/1878	14/07/1965	MDR / MID	Junction allowing access to West Kensington Goods.
West London Extension Junction	84		02/03/1863	01/01/1923	WLR / WLER	'End on' junction between WLR and WLER, elimination given here nominally as date of Grouping.
West London Junction (1st)	91		27/05/1844	N/A	WLR / LBIR	
West London Junction (2nd)	24 / 5D 91		??/10/1860	29/10/1990	GWR	Junction between 'West London Loop' (linking WLR and GWR) and GWR main line.
West London Junction (3rd)	38 / 4D		06/07/1865	N/A	WLER / LSWR	Junction eliminated 21/01/1936 - 17/08/1994.
West London Loop	91	P G	01/04/1863 ??/10/1860	29/10/1990 29/10/1990	GWR	Country-facing connection between GWR and WLR. Regular local passenger services ceased 22/03/1915, although long distance services traversed loop until the last train 27/10/1990. 29/10/1990 is official closure date (BLN).
WEST NORWOOD Lower Norwood	53 / 2C		01/12/1856	N/A	WELCPR	Opened as 'Lower Norwood', renamed 01/01/1886.
West Norwood Junction	53 / 2C		01/11/1870	N/A	LBSCR	Junction at south end of West Norwood Spur.
West Norwood Spur	53 / 2C	P G	01/11/1870 01/11/1870	N/A N/A	LBSCR	
WEST PARK HOSPITAL	64 / 5A		1918	1950	PRIV	Horton Estate Light Railway opened to supply building materials, later fuel, to hospitals.
WEST RUISLIP West Ruislip (For Ickenham) Ruislip & Ickenham	22 / 1A	P G	02/04/1906 02/04/1906	N/A 06/10/1975	GCR / GWR	Opened as 'Ruislip & Ickenham', renamed 'West Ruislip for Ickenham' 30/06/1947. First served by LTE Central Line 21/11/1948 as terminus, suffix 'for Ickenham' gradually dropped thereafter. Goods yard closed 06/10/1975. Down slow line removed and down platform widened to abut former down fast line ??/05/1990. No Central Line service 24/08/1991 – 10/12/1991 (engineering works – service terminated at Ruislip Gardens).
WEST SIDINGS (SOUTHALL)	35 / 1D		c.1860	N/A	GWR	First sidings on site by late 1860's, expanded to current layout in early 20th Century. Southernmost three sidings referred to as 'Down Yard'.
WEST SILVERTOWN	41 / 1B 62 / 5A		02/12/2005	N/A	DLR	
WEST SUTTON	65 / 3B		05/01/1930	N/A	SR	
West Thurrock Junction	45 / 4A		01/07/1892	N/A	LTSR	Third road added between here and Grays for Upminster trains early 1960.
WEST THURROCK POWER STATION	45 / 4A		1962	1993	PRIV	
WEST THURROCK SIDINGS	45 / 4A		c.1940	pre-2022	LMS	Not present on 1920 OS map, but had appeared by 1947. Officially 'disused' for some years and connections to 'up' mainline remain in situ.
WEST WICKHAM	67 / 1D	P G	29/05/1882 29/05/1882	N/A 02/09/1963	SER	Goods yard closed 02/09/1963.
WEST YARD (RIPPLE LANE)	29 / 5C		c.1940	N/A	LMS	See entry for 'Ripple Lane Yard'.
WESTBOURNE PARK Westbourne Park & Kensal Green	25 / 5B 67 / 5A		01/02/1866	N/A	MET / GWR	GWR ticket platform nearby since at least 09/10/1857. HCR board sanctioned construction of a station on this site 27/06/1864 named 'Green Lane', which was reported as complete in August 1864. GWR inspection in September deemed the station incomplete and incorrectly sited so it did not open. Opened eighteen months later as 'Westbourne Park & Kensal Green' (HCR only), re-sited west and suffix dropped 30/10/1871. GWR main line services not thought to call until 01/11/1871. BR platforms closed 16/03/1992, remaining platforms had previously transferred to LTE ownership 01/01/1970.
Westbourne Road Junction	26 / 3C		04/01/2011	N/A	NR	Convergence of quadruple track to double on North London Line, with connection to LO East London Line (currently not in use). Created as part of remodelling in preparation for East London Line opening to Highbury & Islington 28/02/2011. Under covered way.
WESTCOMBE PARK Coombe Farm Lane	41 / 3B		01/05/1879	N/A	SER	Opened as 'Coombe Farm Lane', renamed later in 1879.
WESTERN DISTRICT OFFICE (1st)	26 / 6A		*05/12/1927*	*03/08/1965*	POR	Replaced by Western District Office (2nd) to east.
WESTERN DISTRICT OFFICE (2nd)	26 / 6A		*03/08/1965*	*31/05/2003*	POR	Replaced by Western District Office (1st) and Western Parcels Office, construction involved diverting POR route with original tunnels becoming abandoned. Open until POR mothballing 31/05/2003.
WESTERN PARCELS OFFICE	25 / 6D		*05/12/1927*	*03/08/1965*	POR	Replaced by Western District Office (2nd) to east.
WESTFERRY	40 / 1D		31/08/1987	N/A	DLR	
WESTMINSTER Westminster Bridge	39 / 1B		24/12/1868	N/A	MDR	Terminus until 30/05/1870. Renamed 1907. Jubilee Line platforms opened and station rebuilt 22/12/1999. The westbound Jubilee Line platform is directly beneath the eastbound platform.
WEYBRIDGE Weybridge Junction Weybridge	61 / 3D	P G	21/05/1838 21/05/1838	N/A 03/08/1964	LSWR	Carried suffix 'Junction' 1848 - 1858/9. Goods yard closed 03/08/1964.
Weybridge Junction	61 / 3D		14/02/1848	N/A	LSWR	Junction with branch to Chertsey (later Virginia Water).

Name	Page / grid		Date opened	Date closed	Opened by	Notes
Wharncliffe Viaduct	23 / 6B		04/06/1838	N/A	GWR	GWR main line crossing of the Brent Valley.
Wheeler Street (or Bishopsgate) Junction	27 / 5A 90		10/04/1876	N/A	GER / ELR	Originally junction between ELR and GER (severed 17/04/1966), crossovers remain on GER main line.
Whipps Cross Tunnel	16 / 6B		22/08/1856	N/A	ECR	
WHITE CITY (LPTB)	25 / 6A 83		23/11/1947	N/A	LPTB (CEN)	Replaced Wood Lane (CLR) Station.
WHITE CITY (MET / GWR) Wood Lane (White City) Wood Lane (Exhibition)	38 / 1A 83		01/05/1908	25/10/1959	MET	Opened as 'Wood Lane (Exhibition)', closed to regular traffic 01/11/1914, opened on special occasions thereafter including 12/12/1914 – 29/04/1915 (weekday evenings and weekends for servicemen). Renamed 'Wood Lane (White City)' 07/10/1920, renamed 'White City' 23/11/1947, closed for good 25/10/1959. TfL opened new station 12/10/2008 on opposite side of Wood Lane ('Wood Lane').
WHITE CITY SIDINGS White City Depot Wood Lane Depot	38 / 1A 83		30/07/1900	N/A	CLR	Opened as Wood Lane Depot, the CLR's sole depot. Rebuilt as White City Depot 1949 on the eastern half of the site, replaced by new facility to west 15/01/2007 which was subsequently rafted over and covered by Westfield shopping centre. Referred to as 'White City Sidings' at current location.
WHITE HART LANE	15 / 3A	P	22/07/1872	N/A	GER	Goods yard closed to public traffic ??/01/1968, saw some private traffic until 02/07/1977.
		G	22/07/1872	02/07/1977		
WHITECHAPEL Whitechapel (Mile End)	27 / 6B 90		10/04/1876	N/A	ELR	MDR platforms opened 06/10/1884 (terminus until 02/06/1902). 'Whitechapel (Mile End)' until 13/11/1901, suffix then dropped. MDR platforms served by MET 03/12/1906 – 31/03/1913 then again 30/03/1936 – present ('Hammersmith & City Line' since 30/07/1990). ELR platforms first served by MET 31/03/1913, later became 'East London Line', closed 26/03/1995 – 25/03/1998 and 22/12/2007 – 27/04/2010 (engineering works). London Underground platforms reduced from four to two 31/01/2011. Elizabeth Line platforms opened 24/05/2022.
Whitechapel Junction	27 / 6B 90		01/10/1884	23/12/2007	SER / ELR	Junction at southern end of St Mary's Curve.
WHITECROSS STREET GOODS	32 / 3D		c.1880	pre-1965	MID	Appeared between 1875 and 1896 OS. Present on 1954 OS, but site cleared for 1965 re-alignment of railway.
WHITTON	36 / 6A		06/07/1930	N/A	SR	
Whitton Junction	36 / 6A		01/01/1883	N/A	LSWR	Junction at southern end of Hounslow Spur.
WHYTELEAFE	73 / 2D	P	01/01/1900	N/A	SECR	
		G	01/01/1900	28/09/1964		
WHYTELEAFE SOUTH Warlingham	74 / 3A		05/08/1856	N/A	CR	Opened as 'Warlingham', renamed 'Whyteleafe South' 11/06/1956.
WILLESDEN	24 / 4C 68 / 6C		early 1841	01/09/1866	LBIR	Exact opening date unknown; thought to be 1841 and before 10/06/1841. On Acton Lane Adjacent to current Harlesden station, replaced by Willesden Junction to east 01/09/1866.
WILLESDEN BRENT SIDINGS	24 / 4B 68 / 5C		c.1890	N/A	LNWR	First sidings appeared on site c.1890.
WILLESDEN EURO TERMINAL	24 / 4C 91 & 92		1967	N/A	BR	On site of Willesden North Carriage Sidings. Originally a Freightliner terminal, it was redeveloped into an Intermodal 'Euro terminal' for Channel Tunnel traffic (first departure 27/06/1994). Container traffic ceased by 2005, some engineering traffic remained thereafter. Now terminal for tunnelling spoil removal / materials delivery re: HS2 (first loaded train departed 29/06/2021). 'Official' reopening 14/09/2021.
WILLESDEN 'F' SIDINGS	24 / 3B 68 / 2C		c.1940	N/A	LMS	Sidings appeared between the late 1930's and mid-1950's. After a prolonged period of disuse, DC Rail (Cappagh) inert spoil traffic commenced 20/03/2018 (displaced from Willesden Euro Terminal – see above).
WILLESDEN GREEN Willesden Green & Cricklewood Willesden Green	25 / 3A		24/11/1879	N/A	MSJWR	Country terminus of MSJWR until 02/08/1880 (by which time it had been absorbed by MET). Suffix '& Cricklewood' 01/06/1894 – 1938. Last served by Metropolitan Line 07/12/1940 (although services have continued to call as required due to engineering works and service disruption). First served by Bakerloo Line 20/11/1939, transferred to Jubilee Line 01/05/1979. Goods yard remote from station (see separate entry below).
WILLESDEN GREEN GOODS	24 / 2D		1899	03/01/1966	MET	
Willesden High Level Junction	24 / 5C 91 & 92		20/07/1885	N/A	LNWR	
WILLESDEN JUNCTION	24 / 4D 91 & 92	P	01/09/1866	N/A	LNWR / HJR	Replaced 'Willesden' station to west (closed on same date). Initially platforms on LNWR main line (low level) and original 1860 HJR route (high level). Further high level platforms added 02/09/1867 with opening of LNWR Mitre Bridge Curve linking HJR and WLR. Original high level platforms closed 20/07/1885 with opening of Kew Curve, which allowed all high level passenger traffic to pass through 02/09/1867 platforms, although the original high level line remained in use until 01/05/1892. Third high level platform (no.11) added 1894 for reversing trains ex-WLR. New low level platforms (two 'through' and two 'bay') added for DC electric trains 15/06/1912, served by Bakerloo Line trains since 10/05/1915. Platform 11 abandoned 20/10/1940. All low level platforms except the 'DC line' platforms closed 03/12/1962. One of the low level bays taken out of use c.1964. Goods yard north of station off HJR route, after closure to general goods traffic, sidings remained open to serve works (MG gas products) until c.2000.
		G	01/09/1866	c.2000		
Willesden Junction (Acton Branch)	24 / 4C		21/07/1963	N/A	BR	
WILLESDEN SHED	24 / 4C 18 & 91		1873	27/09/1965	LNWR	Upon closure loco allocation transferred to Willesden TMD, Willesden Euro terminal built on site 1967.
Willesden Suburban Junction	91 & 92		15/06/1912	N/A	LNWR	
WILLESDEN TRAINCARE CENTRE	24 / 4D 91 & 92		c.1965	N/A	BR	Built to replace Willesden Shed, opened on site of former South Carriage Shed.
WILLOW WALK GOODS	40 / 2A 4		1847	07/03/1932	LBSCR	Amalgamated with Bricklayers Arms by SR 07/03/1932, but fabric of depot remained in use until 01/08/1977 closure.
WIMBLEDON Wimbledon & Merton	52 / 3A	P	21/05/1838	N/A	LSWR	Opened as 'Wimbledon & Merton' south of Wimbledon Bridge. Upon its opening on 22/10/1855, the WCRR had a separate terminus, which was incorporated into main station during 1869 rebuilding. Entire station re-sited to north side of bridge 21/11/1881. Current District Line platforms opened 03/06/1889 as a separate station, referred to as 'Wimbledon North' until amalgamated with rest of station 1929. Suffix '& Merton' dropped 01/06/1909. A platform remained in vicinity of original station, south of the bridge, on the north side of the formation, referred to as 'Volunteer Platform' due to military use pre-WW1, subsequently became a milk dock in 1926. There were 3 other goods facilities: Wimbledon West yard (see separate entry), a small yard on the east side of the station, and a larger yard adjacent to Wimbledon North station. All public goods traffic ceased 05/01/1970. Former island platforms 9 & 10 used by trains between Tooting and Sutton reduced to a single through platform 9 to allow formation of a terminal bay for Tramlink, opening 30/05/2000. Further terminal London Trams bay platform opened 02/11/2015.
		G	c.1838	05/01/1970		

Name	Page / grid		Date opened	Date closed	Opened by	Notes
WIMBLEDON BOROUGH COUNCIL SIDING	52 / 2B		*1898*	1965	PRIV	Power station and refuse destructor.
WIMBLEDON CHASE	52 / 4A		07/07/1929	N/A	SR	
Wimbledon East 'A' Junctions	52 / 3B		01/10/1868	N/A	LSWR / LBSCR	
Wimbledon North Junction	52 / 3A		03/06/1889	N/A	LSWR	
WIMBLEDON PARK	52 / 2B		03/06/1889	N/A	LSWR	Putney Bridge to Wimbledon built by LSWR, initially operated by MDR only, LSWR services commenced 01/07/1889. Last regular main line passenger service withdrawn 05/05/1941, although services called on occasions until 1969. Station ownership transferred to LUL 01/04/1994 along with entire Putney Bridge to Wimbledon route.
WIMBLEDON PARK SIDINGS	52 / 2B		*c.1910*	N/A	LSWR	Part of Wimbledon Traincare Depot (SWR). Not present on 1899 OS but had appeared by 1913. Shed erected over six roads nearest the main line c. time of electrification (25/10/1915), now carriage cleaning shed.
Wimbledon South 'B' Junction	52 / 3A		22/10/1855	02/06/1997	LSWR / WCRR	Junction eliminated when Wimbledon to West Croydon line closed prior to conversion to Tramlink.
WIMBLEDON TRAINCARE DEPOT	52 / 2B		*c.1910*	N/A	LSWR	First carriage sidings appeared c.1910 (see 'Wimbledon Park Sidings'). Site expanded to north with Durnsford Road sidings & power station 1915 (see separate entries). Served by Staff Halt on adjacent 'up fast' road.
Wimbledon West 'C' Junctions	52 / 4A		07/07/1929	N/A	SR	
WIMBLEDON WEST YARD	52 / 4A		*c.1880*	*c.2000*	LSWR	Sidings on site appeared between 1869-77 and 1895 OS. S&T works and coal yard also on site. Some track remains in situ, but disconnected from running line.
WINCHMORE HILL	6 / 6C	P	01/04/1871	N/A	GNR	Goods yard closed 01/10/1962.
		G	*01/04/1871*	*01/10/1962*		
Windmill Bridge Junctions	66 / 1D 86		01/12/1862	N/A	LBSCR	
WINDSOR & ETON CENTRAL	33 / 4B	P	08/10/1849	N/A	GWR	Opened as 'Windsor', suffix '& Eton' added 01/06/1904, further suffix 'Central' added 26/09/1949. Served by MDR trains 01/03/1883 – 01/10/1885. Goods yard closed 06/01/1964. Platforms 3 & 4 decommissioned 17/11/1968, followed by platform 2 on 05/09/1969. Platform 1 subsequently truncated twice (station rebuilding).
Windsor & Eton Windsor		G	*08/10/1849*	*06/01/1964*		
WINDSOR & ETON RIVERSIDE	33 / 4C	P	01/12/1849	N/A	LSWR	Original station temporary, a permanent station opened 01/05/1851. Opened as 'Windsor', suffix '& Eton' added 10/12/1903, further suffix 'Riverside' added 26/09/1949. Engine shed probably opened with station and remained in use for a while after electrification (1930). Goods yard closed 05/04/1965.
Windsor & Eton Windsor		G	*01/12/1849*	*05/04/1965*		
Windsor Branch Junction Slough East Junction	33 / 1C		08/10/1849	N/A	GWR	
WOLDINGHAM Marden Park	74 / 4B	P	01/07/1885	N/A	LBSCR / SER	Renamed 01/01/1894. Goods yard closed 04/05/1959.
		G	*01/07/1885*	*04/05/1959*		
WOOD GREEN	14 / 4C		19/09/1932	N/A	UERL (GNPBR)	
Wood Green North Junction	14 / 4B		01/04/1871	N/A	GNR	Divergence of GNR Enfield Branch (now Hertford Loop) from main Line.
Wood Green Tunnels	14 / 3B		07/08/1850	N/A	GNR	
WOOD LANE (CLR)	38 / 1A 83		14/05/1908	23/11/1947	CLR	Terminus of CLR until 03/08/1920 (on terminal loop). After 03/08/1920 through platforms to Ealing Broadway opened resulting in triangular formation. Replaced by White City (LPTB) to north 23/11/1947.
WOOD LANE (TFL)	25 / 6A 83		12/10/2008	N/A	TFL (HCL)	
Wood Lane Junction	24 / 6D		03/08/1920	19/06/1938	GWR	Eliminated when parallel freight lines opened to North Acton 19/06/1938.
WOOD LANE MILK DEPOT	83		*c.1935*	Post-1980	PRIV	Present until 1980 Baker.
WOOD STREET Wood Street, Walthamstow	16 / 5A	P	17/11/1873	N/A	GER	Goods yard in use 20/04/1893 – 06/05/1968. Also referred to as 'Walthamstow Wood Street'. Became 'Wood Street' 18/03/1971. Loco shed and carriage sidings opened ??/03/1897. Loco shed closed 1960 and Carriage Sidings abandoned 1986.
		G	*20/04/1893*	*06/05/1968*		
WOODFORD	16 / 3C	P	22/08/1856	N/A	ECR	Platforms originally 'staggered' (up south of down). Majority of passenger services transferred to LPTB 14/12/1947, terminus for Central Line from that date until 21/11/1948. Goods yard closed 18/04/1966. First trains in the morning remained British Rail services until 01/06/1970 (last train 31/05/1970).
		G	*22/08/1856*	*18/04/1966*		
Woodford Junction	16 / 2C		20/04/1903	N/A	GER	Divergence of Fairlop Loop (= Hainault Loop) from Epping Line.
WOODFORD SIDINGS	16 / 3C		*Pre 1920*	N/A	GER	Central Line stabling sidings, laid by the GER by 1920 (appear on 1920 Ordnance Survey map, but not on 1898).
WOODGRANGE PARK	28 / 3C	P	09/07/1894	N/A	LTSR	Goods yard opened 01/01/1895, closed 07/12/1964. Station closed 04/06/2016 – 27/02/2017 due to electrification works on Gospel Oak to Barking Line.
		G	*01/01/1895*	*07/12/1964*		
Woodgrange Park Junction	28 / 3C		09/07/1894	N/A	LTSR / TFGR	
WOODMANSTERNE	72 / 1D		17/07/1932	N/A	SR	
WOODSIDE Woodside & South Norwood Woodside	67 / 1A	P	c.01/07/1871	N/A	LBSCR / SER	Exact opening date unknown, first appeared in Bradshaw July 1871. Carried suffix '& South Norwood' 01/10/1908 – 02/10/1944. Goods yard closed 30/09/1963. Closed by RT 02/06/1997 (last train 31/05/1997, no Sunday service), reopened by Croydon Tramlink 23/05/2000.
		G	*c.01/07/1871*	*30/09/1963*		
Woodside Junction	67 / 1A		10/08/1885	16/05/1983	LBSCR / SER	
WOODSIDE PARK Woodside Park for North Finchley Woodside Park Torrington Park, Woodside Torrington Park	13 / 2C	P	01/04/1872	N/A	GNR	Opened as 'Torrington Park', suffix 'Woodside' added 01/05/1872. Renamed 'Woodside Park' 01/05/1882. Suffix 'for North Finchley' added 01/02/1894, dropped by 1927. First served by and transferred to LPTB Northern Line 14/04/1940, closed to LNER passenger services on same date. Goods yard closed 01/10/1962.
		G	*01/04/1872*	*01/10/1962*		
WOODSTOCK ROAD	37 / 1C		08/04/1909	01/01/1917	NSWJR	
WOOLWICH	42 / 2A		24/05/2022	N/A	TFL (EL)	
WOOLWICH ARSENAL	42 / 2A	P	01/11/1849	N/A	SER	Goods yard closed 17/05/1965. DLR platforms opened 10/01/2009 (official opening 12/01/2009).
		G	*01/11/1849*	*17/05/1965*		
WOOLWICH DOCKYARD Woolwich	41 / 2D		30/07/1849	N/A	SER	Initially simply 'Woolwich', suffix 'Dockyard' added when Woolwich Arsenal station opened 01/11/1849.
WORCESTER PARK Old Malden & Worcester Park	64 / 1C	P	04/04/1859	N/A	LSWR	Renamed February 1862. Goods yard closed 06/05/1963.
		G	*04/04/1859*	*06/05/1963*		
WORCESTER PARK BRICKWORKS	64 / 2C		*1898*	*c.1950s*	PRIV	
WRAYSBURY	33 / 6C	P	22/08/1848	N/A	LSWR	Village name formerly spelt 'Wyrardisbury', but station always appears to have used modern spelling. Re-sited south 01/04/1861. Goods yard closed 13/08/1962.
		G	*22/08/1848*	*13/08/1962*		

Name	Page / grid		Date opened	Date closed	Opened by	Notes

YEOVENEY
    Runemede
    Runemede Range
	33 / 6D		c.01/04/1887	14/05/1962	GWR	Initially a private halt serving a rifle range, opening c.01/04/1887, became a public station 01/03/1892. Opened as 'Runemede Range', suffix dropped 09/07/1934. Renamed 'Yeoveney' 04/11/1935. Suffix 'Halt' sometimes appended to all three names. Request stop in daylight hours only, closed prior to withdrawal of passenger services from branch.

YORK ROAD	26 / 4B 75		15/12/1906	17/09/1932	UERL (GNPBR)	Proposed for reopening.
York Road Curve	75	P	01/10/1863	08/11/1976	GNR	Curve in 'up' direction connecting GNR with MET, originally to 10/01/1863 MET lines but later to 'Widened Lines'. Carried goods traffic 20/02/1866 - 24/03/1969. Closed 10/09/1939 – 01/01/1940 and 06/01/1941 – 01/10/1945 as a consequence of WW2. Closed when Moorgate trains diverted via GNCR 08/11/1976 (official closure date 07/03/1977).
		G	20/02/1866	24/03/1969		
YORK WAY FREIGHTLINER TERMINAL	26 / 3B		*15/11/1965*	*??/05/1968*	BR	On site for former Maiden Lane goods yard.
York Way North Junction	76		14/11/2007	N/A	LCOR / NR	
York Way South Junction	76		14/11/2007	N/A	LCOR / NR	

Footnotes

Significant TfL temporary route closures* (not necessarily recorded against individual stations):

*'Significant' is subjective, to be included below, closures were for a period of at least two weeks, or if less than two weeks were of particular historical interest. World War One resulted in multiple station closures and service reduction due to staff shortages. World War Two witnessed frequent unplanned line closures associated with installation of flood defences and then bomb damage. Firefighter's industrial action has resulted in subsurface station and line closures of several days at a time.
COVID-19 resulted in significant service reduction, subsurface station closures, and some line closures.

Closures associated with reconstruction of City & South London Railway / creation of Northern Line:

09/08/1922: Euston to Moorgate, reopened 20/04/1924 (tunnel widening).

25/04/1923: Oval to Clapham Common, reopened 17/05/1923 (tunnel collapse).

29/11/1923: Moorgate to Clapham Common, reopened 01/12/1924 (tunnel widening).
London Bridge to Elephant & Castle section had already closed 28/11/1923 (tunnel collapse).

Closures associated with World War Two:

01/09/1939: Northern Line closed Charing Cross to Kennington, reopened 17/12/1939 (flood protection).

07/09/1939: Northern Line closed Moorgate to London Bridge, reopened 19/05/1940 (flood protection).

11/09/1940: Entire East London Line closed due to bombs in the Surrey Docks area, reopened 30/10/1940.
Closed again 11/05/1941 due to further bomb damage, reopening later that year.

22/09/1940: Piccadilly Line closed Holborn to Aldwych, reopened 01/07/1946.

14/10/1940: Piccadilly Line closed Wood Green to Cockfosters, reopened Cockfosters to Arnos Grove 09/12/1940 and Arnos Grove to Wood Green 16/12/1940 (bomb at Bounds Green).

15/10/1940: Piccadilly Line closed Kings Cross St Pancras to Wood Green, reopened 05/12/1940 (bomb at Holloway Road).

15/10/1940: Bomb damage near Kings Cross caused Baker Street to Farringdon to close at first intermittently and then completely 10/05/1941 (Metropolitan and Circle Lines). Reopened Baker Street to Euston Square 21/07/1941, Euston Square to Farringdon 04/10/1941.

15/10/1940: Northern Line closed Clapham South to Tooting Bec (flooding following bomb at Balham), reopened 08/01/1941.

10/12/1940: Entire Waterloo & City Line (then SR owned), reopened 03/03/1941 (bomb damage).

17/01/1941: Bomb damage at Lambeth North (16/01/1941) closed the Bakerloo Line south of Waterloo, reopened April 1941.

Post-war closures:

24/11/1975: Entire Waterloo & City Line (then BR owned), reopened 12/01/1976 (flooding due to burst water main).

24/11/1984: Victoria Line closed Warren Street to Victoria, reopened 18/12/1984 (fire damage at Oxford Circus).

24/08/1991: Central Line closed Ruislip Gardens to West Ruislip, reopened 10/12/1991.

09/08/1992: Entire Waterloo & City Line (then BR owned), reopened 07/09/1992 (resignalling and installation of 4th rail).

29/05/1993: Entire Waterloo & City Line (then BR owned), reopened 19/07/1993 (conversion to 4th rail electrification, delivery of new rolling stock).

26/03/1995: Entire East London Line due to Jubilee Line Extension works, reopened 25/03/1998 (to Whitechapel), Shoreditch remained closed until 27/09/1998.

10/02/1996: DLR closed Canary Wharf to Island Gardens (bomb adjacent to South Quay station), reopened Canary Wharf to Heron Quays 16/03/1996, Heron Quays to Island Gardens 15/04/1996.

11/05/1996: DLR closed East India to Beckton (Jubilee Line extension works), reopened 10/06/1996.

02/07/1996: Northern Line closed Moorgate to Kennington (southbound only), reopened 21/10/1996 (London Bridge station rebuilding).

11/11/1996: Bakerloo Line closed Piccadilly Circus to Elephant & Castle (tunnel strengthening), reopened 14/07/1997.

11/01/1999: DLR closed Crossharbour to Island Gardens (Lewisham extension works), reopened with extension 20/11/1999 (albeit largely new route).

03/07/1999: Northern Line closed Moorgate to Kennington, reopened 05/09/1999 (tunnel maintenance).

12/06/1999: Circle Line closed due to strengthening of the covered way High Street Kensington to Gloucester Road, reopened 23/08/1999.
(In consequence, no service High Street Kensington to Gloucester Road and Aldgate to Tower Hill)

05/08/2000: Victoria Line closed Victoria to Brixton, reopened 26/08/2000 (crossover replacement at Brixton).

03/02/2001: District Line closed between Earl's Court and Edgware Road and Kensington Olympia and Earl's Court due to strengthening of the covered way High Street Kensington to Earl's Court, reopened 13/05/2001.

26/01/2003: Entire Central and Waterloo & City Lines closed following Chancery Lane derailment (occurred 25/01/2003) for rolling stock safety checks / modifications. Waterloo & City Line reopened 18/02/2003. Central Line reopened in stages; Bethnal Green to Leytonstone 14/03/2003, Leytonstone to Woodford 16/03/2003, Ealing Broadway to Marble Arch 24/03/2003 (West Acton and Queensway reopened later), Marble Arch to Bethnal Green and Woodford to Loughton 03/04/2003, West Ruislip to North Acton, and Loughton to Epping plus the Hainault Loop 12/04/2003.

20/10/2003: Northern Line closed 20/10/2003 between Hampstead and Charing Cross and East Finchley and Euston (Bank Branch) due to a derailment at Camden Town (occurred 19/10/2003). Reopened Hampstead to Charing Cross 29/10/2003, East Finchley to Euston 30/10/2003.

31/07/2004: Croydon Tramlink closed Arena to Beckenham Junction, reopened 28/08/2004 (engineering work).

07/01/2005: Piccadilly Line Heathrow Terminal 4 Loop closed, reopened 17/09/2006 (construction of Terminal 5 extension).

19/03/2005: Croydon Tramlink closed Sandilands to New Addington, reopened Sandilands to Lloyd Park 04/04/2005, then Lloyd Park to New Addington 11/04/2005 (engineering work).

08/07/2005: Bombs on Circle Line trains at Edgware Road and Aldgate, and a Piccadilly Line train at Russell Square on 07/07/2005, resulted in the following:
Circle Line closed 08/07/2005 – 04/08/2005
Hammersmith & City Line closed Paddington to Barking 08/07/2005 – 25/07/2005
Metropolitan Line closed Moorgate to Aldgate 08/07/2005 – 25/07/2005
District Line closed High Street Kensington to Edgware Road 08/07/2005 – 29/07/2005
(In consequence, no service High Street Kensington to Baker Street, High Street Kensington to Gloucester Road, and Moorgate to Aldgate East / Tower Hill)
Piccadilly Line closed Hyde Park Corner to Arnos Grove and Rayners Lane to Uxbridge 08/07/2005 – 04/08/2005

23/07/2005: Croydon Tramlink closed Addington Village to New Addington, reopened 05/09/2005 (engineering work).

01/04/2006: Entire Waterloo & City Line, reopened 11/09/2006 (track replacement and other works)

28/06/2008: Tower Gateway to Royal Mint Street Junction closed (rebuilding at Tower Gateway), reopened 02/03/2009.

11/08/2009: London Trams closed East Croydon to Sandilands, reopened 01/09/2009 (engineering work).
Temporary terminus at Dingwall Road in use 11/08/2009 - 07/09/2009 for trams arriving from the west.

24/07/2010: Elizabeth Line works resulted in closure of Hammersmith & City and Circle Lines Edgware Road to Hammersmith until 16/08/2010.

23/07/2011: No Circle and District Line services High Street Kensington to Edgware Road, reopened 24/08/2011.

19/07/2014: No Metropolitan and Piccadilly Line services Ruislip to Uxbridge, reopened 11/08/2014 (track replacement).

13/07/2015: London Trams closed Dundonald Road to Wimbledon, reopened 02/11/2015 (construction of second platform at Wimbledon).

08/08/2015: Victoria Line closed Seven Sisters to Walthamstow Central, reopened 29/08/2015 (crossover replacement at Walthamstow Central).

10/11/2016: Derailment at Sandilands on 09/11/2016 resulted in closure of entire London Trams system east of East Croydon until 18/11/2016.

18/06/2017: Hammersmith & City and Circle Lines closed Wood Lane to Edgware Road part way through 17/06/2017 due to safety concerns following Grenfell Tower fire (occurred 14/06/2017), reopened 25/06/2017.

20/03/2020: Entire Waterloo & City Line closed due to the COVID-19 pandemic, restored 04/06/2021 (weekdays only, it remains closed at weekends).
There was a second much shorter COVID-19 related closure 23/12/2021 – 04/01/2022.

21/03/2020: Circle Line closed due to the COVID-19 pandemic, restored 18/05/2020 (in consequence, no service High Street Kensington to Gloucester Road and Aldgate to Tower Hill).

30/03/2020: Piccadilly Line suspended Rayners Lane to Uxbridge due to the COVID-19 pandemic, reopened 18/05/2020.

09/05/2020: Piccadilly Line Heathrow Terminal 4 Loop closed due to the COVID-19 pandemic, reopened 14/06/2022.

15/01/2022: Northern Line closed Moorgate to Kennington, reopened 15/05/2022 (realignment of southbound tunnel at Bank)

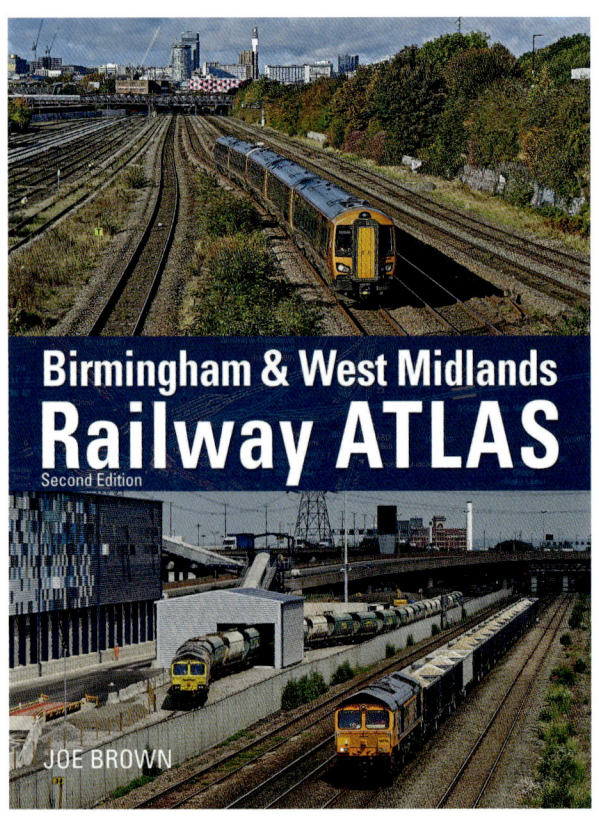

Birmingham & West Midlands Railway Atlas

Second Edition

Joe Brown

Much has changed in this region since the previous edition of this Atlas was published in 2016, notably the confirmation of the route of HS2 and extensions to the West Midlands Metro. As a consequence, a completely revised edition of this masterly cartographic portrayal of the railways and tramways of the West Midlands by leading railway cartographer, Joe Brown, was long overdue.

The Atlas covers the entire West Midlands continuous urban area of Birmingham, Walsall, Wolverhampton, West Bromwich, Stourbridge and Dudley. It also features the towns and cities surrounding this core area. This includes Stafford, Lichfield, Tamworth, Nuneaton, Coventry, Rugby, Leamington Spa, Stratford-upon-Avon, Bromsgrove and Kidderminster. As well as dealing with the complex railway system that served the area, the entire historic passenger tramway network of the region is mapped with opening and closing details provided in an Appendix. This is brought up to date with the current West Midlands Metro system and future extensions to it which have been announced as well as the planned Coventry 'Very Light Rail' system.

Intricate and finely drawn mapping shows individual track and platforms for all lines whether open and closed, as well as stations, changes of station name and opening and closing dates, and much, much more. Many of those both interested in both transport and local history will already be aware of the superb quality of Joe Brown's cartography and will wish to add this new and much enhanced edition of the Birmingham and West Midlands Railway Atlas to their libraries.

ISBN: 9781800351462
128 pages, Hardback
£25.00

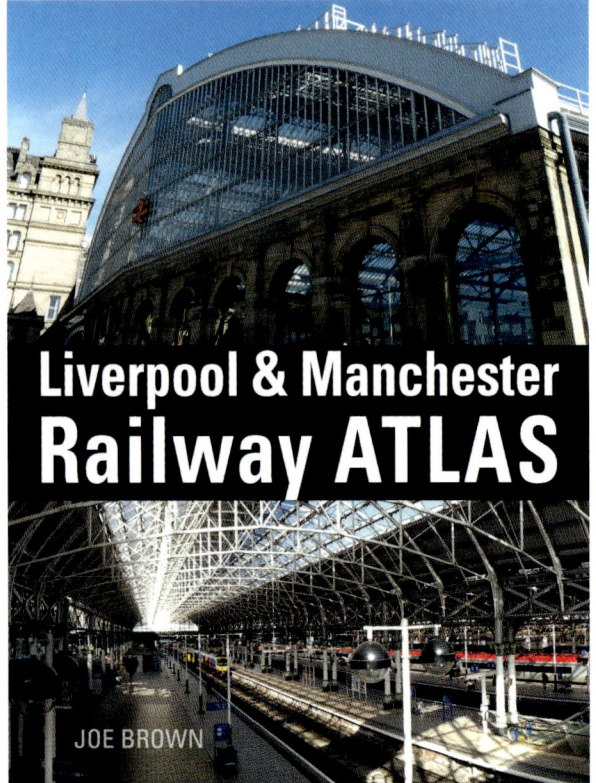

Liverpool & Manchester Railway Atlas

Joe Brown

In 2021, Joe Brown turned his attention to one of the most interesting and complex railway landscapes outside the capital, that around the Liverpool to Manchester axis. The content embraces much more than the railways of the two cities in the title; it covers most of the historic county of Lancashire and other areas outside of this. In addition to lines and locations within the current boundaries of Merseyside and Greater Manchester, the book extends to include places such as Blackpool, Fleetwood, Preston, Blackburn, Burnley, Colne, Chorley, Warrington, Chester, Northwich and Buxton. As well as the railway network to the railways, the atlas will also map the many tramway systems which once flourished in the area. The index to the maps alone will be in excess of 70 pages in extent.

This will be a splendid addition to our growing and popular range of railway atlases, the publication of the first edition of the *Liverpool & Manchester Atlas* will be eagerly anticipated by many railway enthusiasts.

ISBN: 9780860936879
256 pages, Hardback
£30.00